W9-CAB-177

MAGILL'S LITERARY ANNUAL 2001

Essay-Reviews of 200 Outstanding Books
Published in the United States during 2000

With an Annotated Categories List

Volume Two
M-Z

Edited by
JOHN D. WILSON
STEVEN G. KELLMAN

SALEM PRESS
Pasadena, California   Hackensack, New Jersey

LIBRARY OF CONGRESS CATALOG CARD NO. 77-99209
ISBN 0-89356-275-0

FIRST PRINTING

PRINTED IN THE UNITED STATES OF AMERICA

MAGILL'S
LITERARY ANNUAL
2001

M
The Man Who Became Caravaggio

Author: Peter Robb (1946-   )
First published: 1998, in Australia
Publisher: Henry Holt (New York). Illustrated. 570 pp.
   $30.00
Type of work: Biography and fine arts
Time: 1571-1610
Locale: Italy and Malta

≈

Drawing on earlier studies and recent discoveries, Robb presents a fascinating, though at times speculative, biography of the leading artist of the first decade of the seventeenth century

≈

Principal personages:
    MICHELANGELO MERISI, the man who became Caravaggio
    GIOVANNI BAGLIONE, a rival painter to Merisi in Rome
    GIUSEPPE CESARI, painter and early employer of Caravaggio
    FRANCESCO MARIA BOURBON DEL MONTE, cardinal and longtime patron
      of Caravaggio
    VINCENZO GIUSTINIANI, rich banker; owner of fifteen Caravaggio paint-
      ings
    FILLIDE MELANDRONI, courtesan and Caravaggio model
    CONSTANZA COLONNA SFORZA, marchesa of Caravaggio

Because of his short and violent life as much as because of his artistic innovations, Caravaggio has become a cultural icon at the turn of the millennium. Although many details of his life, and indeed death, remain shrouded, and questions of attribution similarly remain unresolved, biographies and other studies of the artist continue to issue from what has become a Caravaggio industry. One is reminded of the similar situation in the case of Caravaggio's contemporary William Shakespeare, where lacunae in fact have encouraged speculation. Robb tells a fascinating story about his subject, and if some of what Robb recounts is not true, perhaps it should be.

Caravaggio's resemblance to Shakespeare begins with his birth: In both cases the precise date is unknown, though the name Michelangelo suggests September 19, the feast day of St. Michael. The year is 1571, but the location again is lost. The Milanese records for the period are missing, and the birth is not noted among those in the town of Caravaggio, some twenty miles east of Milan, where the future painter spent his childhood. In 1584 he began a four-year apprenticeship with Simone Peterzano, who in turn had studied under Titian, though apparently with little effect. Also like Shake-

549

shadows, showing more flesh. Imitation was not, however, always intended as flattery. One of Caravaggio's most exquisite canvases is *Love the Winner* (c. 1601), acquired by Vincenzo Giustiniani, who regarded it as the greatest of his three hundred paintings. He kept it covered with a green cloth, lest it overshadow all the other works in the collection. Vincenzo's older brother, Cardinal Benedetto Giustiniani, wanted a comparable piece, and Caravaggio's rival Giovanni Baglione responded with *Divine Love Conquering Earthly Love* (1602-1603). In one version a dismayed devil stares at the spectator. The face is that of Caravaggio. Baglione had the further audacity to secure a commission that Caravaggio had hoped to get. Caravaggio and his friends began circulating poems mocking Baglione, who sued them for libel in August of 1603. The offense was capital in the Rome of 1600, but the French ambassador, Philippe de Béthune, intervened to arrange a minimal sentence for the artist.

In July, 1605, Caravaggio assaulted the young lawyer Mariano Pasqualone for insulting Maddalena Antognetti, a courtesan and model for Caravaggio. Caravaggio fled Rome for Genoa, but influential friends patched over the fracas. They were unable to do the same a year later when Caravaggio killed Ranuncio Tomassoni in a brawl and again fled Rome, this time never to return. In Naples, on Malta, in Sicily, and once more in Naples, Caravaggio continued to create masterpieces, but death was closing in. On Malta, where Caravaggio was made a knight of the order of St. John, the artist offended a powerful person. Robb believes that the offense was sexual. Desmond Seward, in his 1998 *Caravaggio: A Passionate Life*, argues that the low-born painter insulted a member of the nobility.

Whatever occurred, Caravaggio fled Malta and never felt safe again. In 1609 he was nearly killed in an attack in Naples, and he died the next year. Robb believes that Caravaggio was murdered and officials constructed a tale of death by fever. Seward accepts the official version. Even without speculative embellishment, Caravaggio had led a life crowded with violent incident: Between 1598, when he was charged with illegally wearing a sword, and 1606 he was brought before a Roman magistrate nearly a dozen times, and his sojourn on Malta ended in flight from prison.

Robb's account is richly detailed. In an effort to capture the flavor of Caravaggio, he lapses into Australian slang that mars an otherwise pleasant style. Robb's book would benefit from more reproductions—it offers only eight color pictures and eight pages of black-and-white close-ups. He does, however, offer good descriptions of some eighty paintings, and the text highlights significant details. One wishes that Robb were more willing to note differences of opinion about events, dating, and attribution of works and to identify speculation as such. The Caravaggio who emerges from Robb's pages cannot fail to engage the reader's interest, but the real Caravaggio remains half-hidden in the shadows of the silent past.

Joseph Rosenblum

Sources for Further Study

The Atlantic Monthly 285 (March, 2000): 116.
Booklist 96 (January 1, 2000): 855.
The Boston Globe, February 22, 2000, p. F2.
Library Journal 124 (December, 1999): 127.
The New York Review of Books 46 (October 7, 1999): 11.
The New York Times Book Review 105 (March 5, 2000): 6.
Time 155 (February 28, 2000): 100.
The Times Literary Supplement, April 9, 1999, p. 14.

MAO
A Life

Author: Philip Short (1945-   )
First published: 1999, in Great Britain
Publisher: Henry Holt (New York). Illustrated. 782 pp.
$37.50
Type of work: Biography and history
Time: 1893-1976
Locale: China

≈

An extensive discussion and analysis of the life and times of Mao Zedong, the communist revolutionary and ruler of modern China

≈

Principal personages:
MAO ZEDONG, leader of the People's Republic of China
CHIANG KAI-SHEK, leader of the Guomintang party
ZHOU ENLAI, premier of the People's Republic of China
JIANG QING, Mao's third wife
RICHARD NIXON, U.S. president

Philip Short has been a journalist for the United Kingdom's British Broadcasting Corporation (BBC), the Associated Press, *The Economist, Time* magazine, and the London *Times.* The author of *The Dragon and the Bear: Inside China and Russia Today* (1982), a comparison of the Soviet Union after Joseph Stalin with China after Mao Zedong, Short is eminently qualified to write the life of Mao, one of the twentieth century's most controversial figures.

Mao, born in 1893 to a prosperous peasant family in Hunan province, never entirely transcended his rural roots. After years of striving, he emerged as the leader of the Chinese Communist Party during the Long March of the 1930's, and after World War II he led the party and its armies to victory over Chiang Kai-Shek's Nationalists. From that time until his death almost thirty years later he was the undisputed ruler of the world's most populous state, dragging the overwhelmingly rural and backward China into the atomic age. In the process millions of Chinese died, either through the many political and social purges that characterized Mao's reign or through ideologically misguided and disastrous policies and programs.

His youth was spent in an era of upheaval. The ruling Qing dynasty collapsed in the early twentieth century, in part because of its own corrupt incompetence, in part because China, in the distant past one of the world's leading states, had fallen far behind the West and westernized Japan. New influences brought into doubt the traditional Confucian ideology that had long been the paradigm for Chinese society. The

creation of the Chinese Republic in 1911 resulted in no immediate solution to China's difficulties. As a result of World War I the Japanese
increased their influence in China and regional
warlords became the de facto rulers. Various
possibilities were advanced to rectify China's
circumstances, including Marxism, established
in Russia in the 1917 Bolshevik Revolution.

The Marxist road was not immediately obvious to Mao. His earliest education was Confucian, and he retained a fascination with Chinese

*Philip Short has been a foreign
correspondent for* The London
Times, The Economist, *and the*
BBC *in Uganda, Moscow, China,
and Washington. He is the author of*
The Dragon and the Bear, *which
examines relations between China
and Russia in the 1980's.*

history. His adoption of Marxism crystallized slowly, but by 1923 he was a member
of the Chinese Communist Party (CCP). Mao did not idealize his fellow citizens. In a
revealing passage, he described the Chinese as "slavish in character and narrow-
minded," and he admired the first Chinese emperor of the third century B.C.E., who
unified China through violent means, including the burning of books and manuscripts.

A countryman, Mao was initially intimidated by the urbanites of Beijing, and
throughout his long life he distrusted intellectuals, perhaps a reflection of his own
haphazard education. An additional complication was the Soviet Union's long domination of the fledgling CCP. Initially most Chinese communists lacked a comprehensive knowledge of Marxism. The orthodox Marxist interpretation was that the urban
working classes were to be the revolutionary vanguard, but China's limited urban
proletariat paled in comparison to its vast rural population. Mao argued that China's
communist revolution must be a peasant revolution and that the landlords were the
class enemies, and as early as 1927 he claimed that at least some should be executed.
His advocacy of a peasant revolution caused difficulties for Mao, resulting in his exclusion from the CCP leadership on occasion.

One of the strengths of Short's *Mao* is the clear description it brings of the many
convolutions that occurred within the CCP, its relations with the Soviet Union, and
Mao's own changing circumstances during the 1920's and early 1930's. One issue
was the CCP's relationship to the Guomindang, the party of Sun Yat-sen, which came
under the control of Chiang Kai-Shek after Sun's death in 1925. Under Soviet orders,
the CCP and the Guomindang were to cooperate. Mao was a member of both, but it
was an uneasy relationship that became violent in 1927 when Chiang attempted to
crush the CCP. The CCP's response was to establish its own military wing, famously
captured in Mao's comment that "political power is obtained out of the barrel of a
gun," although these were guns held by a trained army using guerrilla tactics, not by
the masses of workers in spontaneous uprising. Mao's position estranged him from
party policy.

By the early 1930's Mao's advocacy of violence against landlords and other class
enemies broadened to include violence against supposed enemies within the CCP.
The "AB-*tuan*" purge resulted in "confessions" induced by torture and the subsequent
suicides and executions of thousands of seemingly loyal communists, a phenomenon

that would continue as long as Mao lived. The "Long March," one of the central events of Chinese communist history, occurred in 1934-1935. Portrayed as an almost religious event, the march took place when the CCP deserted its bases in the south, escaped the Guomindang's net, and established itself in the northern province of Shanxi. Out of the original eighty-six thousand, fewer than five thousand survived the march. The city of Ya'nan became Mao's redoubt for the next twelve years while he solidified his power and rebuilt the Red Army, initially to resist the Japanese and eventually to fight the Guomindang.

In Ya'nan, Mao, a master of public relations, first achieved worldwide attention thanks to Western journalists. However, behind the favorable public image he was ruthlessly solidifying his power. He eliminated Soviet-trained rivals by positing an indigenous Chinese-style communism. One of the questions raised by Short is Mao's understanding of Marxism. For Mao, human will was more important than economic or material circumstances, and Short suggests that he was never at ease with Marxist theory. He added to his power through a series of "rectification" campaigns, and only those who were submissive, sometimes after being tortured, survived by publicly confessing their errors. The biography portrays the respected Zhou Enlai as constantly groveling and bowing to Mao's words and whims. By 1944 Mao, like V. I. Lenin, Stalin, and Adolf Hitler, had a personality cult, and Mao's "thought" was its ideology.

The end of World War II again forced Mao and Chiang Kai-Shek together, the result of pressure by the United States and the Soviet Union, but with the emergence of the Cold War, in 1947 China slid into civil war. Short's discussion of the civil war is relatively brief, and he implies that Mao's victory was nearly inevitable, even though Chiang had the advantage of more men and material, supplied by the United States. However, the Guomindang's initial victories were soon followed by defeats, and Mao announced the formal founding of the People's Republic of China in Beijing's Tiananmen Square on October 1, 1949.

In the twenty-seven years until his death in 1976, Mao governed the world's most populous country in the manner of both a twentieth century totalitarian dictator and a traditional Chinese emperor. Unfortunately, Short devotes two-thirds of his biography to recounting Mao's rise to that pinnacle of power, leaving only two hundred pages to discuss Chairman Mao's rule, and because the events of those later years are better known, Short's account breaks little new ground. In 1950 Mao was lukewarm to North Korea's invasion of the South, believing China needed time to develop economically, but he felt he had no choice but to support the North in spite of only limited support from the Soviet Union. The war resulted in 400,000 Chinese casualties, including the death of Mao's son, Anying. Propaganda and political campaigns engendered by the war led to the execution or suicide of over 700,000 Chinese in just six months, and, as Short notes, one and one-half million more disappeared into "reform through labor" camps. From the beginning of the People's Republic, the road to socialism was paved with Mao's victims.

In pursuit of the socialist society, material obstacles were to be overcome by human will, a will inspired by Mao's thoughts. He had frequently been critical of the Soviet Union, and he distrusted Stalin, but he criticized Nikita Khrushchev's 1956 denunciation of Stalin and his excessive cult of personality—no surprise given Mao's own cult. With his 1957 pronouncement "Let a hundred flowers bloom, a hundred schools of thought contend," there appeared to be some chance of liberalization. His motives were perhaps mixed. Always attracted to the concept of contradictions, or opposites, and with his understanding of Marxist dialectics, Mao supported a public campaign of criticism of the party; but his ultimate response was to cut down the subsequent flowers of criticism, suggesting a calculated attempt to identify those whose revolutionary commitment was meager. In the aftermath, over 500,000 Chinese were sentenced to labor reform. Inspired in part by the successful launch of the Soviet satellite Sputnik and his own superficial understanding of science, in 1958 Mao launched the Great Leap Forward. Agricultural communes were created and backyard steel furnaces established; however, the crops failed and the steel produced was worthless. Few were willing to criticize the chairman and his misguided policies, and it is estimated that twenty million starved to death in 1959 and 1960.

The giant agricultural communes were abandoned and farmers given a personal incentive to produce. Mao temporarily retreated to the "second front," but his power remained undiminished. Short claims that Mao was sulking in the early 1960's, opposing the necessary retreat from the failures of the Great Leap, still confident that radical advance would come again. The eventual result was the Great Proletarian Cultural Revolution. Short is excellent in establishing that it was Mao alone who was responsible, becoming in the process an infernal deity to whose portrait the populace bowed and prayed and whose words in the "Little Red Book" became divine law. As Zhou Enlai claimed, "Whatever accords with Mao Zedong Thought is right, while whatever does not accord with Mao Zedong Thought is wrong." However, Short argues, it was more about power than ideology, and when the violence threatened to get out of hand, Mao turned to the army to restore order after millions had had their lives destroyed. Nevertheless, the CCP claimed that the Cultural Revolution was a great success.

The major accomplishment of Mao's last years was China's new relationship with the West, epitomized by President Richard Nixon's visit in 1972. Much of the initiative came from the United States, and because of Mao's failing health, it was Zhou Enlai who was China's public face during the negotiations, although it was Mao who sanctioned the change. Without his approval, China's policy of isolation from the West would have continued, perhaps making a reversal of that policy more difficult for Mao's successors.

Mao's physical health remained good until his last decade in spite of heavy smoking and accompanying respiratory problems. His emotional and psychological state is more difficult to determine. By the 1960's the all-powerful Mao was largely isolated from the realities of life, at least the life of ordinary Chinese. His most recent marriage to the onetime actress Jiang Qing had become superficial. Most of his children were dead, his second wife had died during the struggles of the 1920's, and his third wife had left him while he was in Ya'nan. His sexual demands were met by the many much younger women who were brought to his bed. His associates had been transformed into courtiers, and, according to Short, paranoia was rife around Mao; Zhou Enlai would betray anyone to stay in his good graces. If power tends to corrupt, Mao had truly been corrupted.

What of his legacy? Instead of socialism, within a decade of Mao's death in 1976 capitalism was transforming China, even though the CCP retained dictatorial power. In 1981 the CCP concluded that Mao's accomplishments surpassed his errors by a ratio of seven to three. However, his errors, if that is what they should be called, led to the demise of millions. In a century of death-dealing despots, Mao was responsible for more deaths than Hitler or Stalin or any other single individual in history. Short makes note of his victims, but claims that Mao's tragedy—a word the author uses—is that he remained a slave to his ideology of class struggle and revolution. He destroyed much of the old, and Short implies that its destruction was necessary in order to usher in the new; but even if that is true, and it could be debated, can anything justify the devastation that Mao caused?

Eugene Larson

Sources for Further Study

Booklist 96 (December 15, 1999): 755.
Library Journal 124 (November 15, 1999): 78.
The New York Review of Books 47 (February 24, 2000): 20.
The New York Times Book Review 105 (February 6, 2000): 6.
Publishers Weekly 246 (November 15, 2000): 49.

MARCEL PROUST
A Life

Author: William C. Carter (1941-   )
Publisher: Yale University Press (New Haven, Conn.).
  Illustrated. 960 pp. $35.00
Type of work: Literary biography
Time: 1870-1922
Locale: France, Italy, Belgium, and Holland

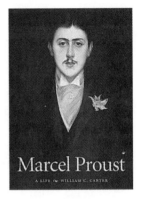

∼

A meticulous portrait of one of the twentieth century's most original and complex writers, one who made a remarkable and permanent contribution to the novel through his depiction of a unique and poetic Parisian belle époque through the lens of evolving time

∼

Principal personages:

MARCEL PROUST, author of *À la recherche du temps perdu* (1913-1927; *Remembrance of Things Past*, 1922-1931, 1981) and recipient in 1969 of the Nobel Prize in Literature

ALFRED AGOSTINELLI, his chauffeur and secretary, with whom Proust was deeply in love

ADRIEN PROUST, his father, an epidemiologist of international reputation, elected to the Académie de médicine in 1879

JEANNE PROUST, his mother, a shy and strict parent who possessed a profound appreciation of literature and music

ANDRÉ GIDE, cofounder of the *Nouvelle Revue Française* and recipient in 1947 of the Nobel Prize in Literature

MADELEINE LEMAIRE, renowned watercolorist and music lover whose Parisian salon was frequented by Proust as well as by other writers and composers

COMTE ROBERT DE MONTESQUIOU-FEZENSAC, one of the most eccentric and extravagant figures of early twentieth century Parisian society; poet, artist, critic, and patron of the arts with whom Proust developed a long-lasting friendship

One of the most imposing figures in twentieth century French literature, Marcel Proust is the author of the vast seven-part *À la recherche du temps perdu* (1913-1927; *Remembrance of Things Past*, 1922-1931, 1981). In this work, he depicts French society before and after World War I through sensitive and in-depth portrayals of the human psyche, the vicissitudes engendered by the passage of time, and the human struggle to achieve love and an understanding of human existence. In this monumental tableau, Proust intermingles autobiographical details, compelling reflections on the

∼

*William C. Carter is a professor of
French at the University of
Alabama at Birmingham. He is the
author of* The Proustian Quest *and
the coproducer of the documentary*
Marcel Proust: A Writer's Life.

∼

nature of time, and the complexities of a writer's
vocation. An interior monologue narrated in the
first person, *Remembrance of Things Past* is
unique in the psychological evolution of characters and in the narrator's reflections upon the nature and effects of the passing of time.

William C. Carter is eminently qualified to
undertake a daunting project such as the biography of one of the twentieth century's most com-
plex and intriguing writers. Carter is the coproducer of the documentary film *Marcel
Proust: A Writer's Life* (1992) and the author of *The Proustian Quest* (1992). The
abundance of detail woven into the fabric of biography attests to his dedication and
seriousness in composing a multifaceted portrait of Proust's social, creative, and inner beings; homosexual liaisons; fascination with Parisian high society; and, above
all, vocation as a writer. In addition to this central focus, Carter composes an intricate
mosaic of the Parisian literary world in which Proust existed, including the fierce and
sustained competition that prevailed between such publishing houses as les Éditions
Grasset and les Éditions Gallimard, the latter the publisher of Proust's award-winning
À l'ombre des jeunes filles en fleurs (1919; *Within a Budding Grove*, 1924). The richness of documentation supporting Carter's re-creation of Proust's life was made possible through correspondence, memoirs, and manuscripts that became available for
consultation. Carter's work is commensurate with the intricacies and compelling portrayals found in Proust's own work and underlines, in the case of Proust, that an author's life could indeed be translated through metaphor and invention into a literary
work. Ultimately, it becomes clear that the composition of *Remembrance of Things
Past* is built upon Proust's intense self-reflection, and that to fully comprehend and
appreciate his work, it is indeed of interest and benefit to explore the author's existence.

Proust was born on St. Felicity's Day, July 10, 1871, near Paris, in Auteuil, a country village that was, at the time, considered a safe haven from the fighting between
monarchists and republicans that gripped Paris. This civil strife followed the defeat of
France and the signing of the Treaty of Frankfurt that had ended the Franco-Prussian
War (1870-1871). The boy's father, Dr. Adrien Proust, was an acclaimed epidemiologist who, in 1869, undertook a successful and daring mission to Russia, Persia, Turkey, and Egypt in order to learn the routes by which cholera had traveled from Russia
to Europe. The Proust family, one of the oldest in the small town of Illiers, near
Chartres, can be traced as far back as the sixteenth century. Dr. Proust's ancestors belonged, for the most part, to the middle class and held administrative posts—they
were lawyers, bailiffs, and elected representatives. Proust's mother, born Jeanne
Weil, studied Greek and Latin in addition to English and German, and as was the cus-
tom at the time, did not attend the *lycées* that functioned as preparatory schools for
men but studied at home. An accomplished pianist, she was descended from wealthy
families who were members of the Jewish haute bourgeoisie of Paris. Jeanne agreed

to raise her children as Catholics, but out of respect for her parents refused to convert to Catholicism herself.

The baby's precarious health was attributed to the privations, anxiety, and lack of proper nourishment caused by the siege and bombardment of Paris during the Prussian assault. During these difficult times in Paris, firewood was scarce; zoo animals, pigeons, and rats were consumed, and bread was rationed. It was in Paris that the young family resided. At the age of twenty-two months, Marcel saw the birth of his brother, Robert. Robert was robust and athletic like his father while Marcel, frail, was subject to fits of hysteria and tantrums. The influence of Jeanne Proust on her elder son was particularly pronounced. They not only were physically similar—each having an oval face with large, dark eyes—but shared a curiosity for literature, music, and cultural activities as well. Both parents would worry about their son's weak physical condition, pronounced asthma, and nervous state, as well as about his peculiar habits, as a young adult, of sleeping during the day, writing for hours during the night, and overlooking the necessity of proper nourishment.

In the fall of 1882, at the age of eleven, Proust entered the Lycée Condorcet. It was at this school that Proust completed his secondary education, met many of his lifelong friends, and discovered his homosexual nature. Life for him during this time was indeed difficult because of ill health and constant respiratory problems. Proust's illness, extreme sensitivity, insomnia that would plague him his entire life, and severe asthma attacks are said by Carter to have increased his nervous condition and his extreme dependency on his mother. When Dr. Proust died of a massive stroke in 1903, and Jeanne of uremia in 1905, Proust and his brother became very wealthy young men. This financial security allowed Proust to indulge his already excessive spending habits, and, perhaps more important, permitted the continuation of his daily routine, criticized by his parents, consisting of sleeping during the day, writing at night, frequenting dinner salons, and gradually destroying his health.

In the early 1890's, Proust began frequenting the salon of Madeleine Lemaire, where the Parisian *beau monde*—aristocrats, artists, writers, musicians, singers, actors, political figures, foreign ambassadors, and army generals—assembled to listen to concerts and encourage the development of the arts. Such high-society gatherings were infinitely intriguing to Proust, who observed and recorded character traits and bits of conversation that would be reinvented in *Remembrance of Things Past*. One such luminary was Comte Robert de Montesquiou-Fezensac, the epitome of aristocratic hauteur—artist, poet, patron of the arts, and a figure who had served as the decadent aesthete in Joris-Karl Huysmans's *À rebours* (1884; *Against the Grain*, 1922). Montesquiou introduced Proust to his own circle of family and friends, including Parisian homosexual groups—fascinating worlds that Proust would never leave.

Proust received his law degree in 1893 and undertook a two-week internship in a Parisian law office. This would constitute the entirety of Proust's work in the legal profession, for he was overpowered by his desire to write but also limited in his physical existence by his poor health. His health was adequate to allow a short trip to Belgium and Holland in 1902, during which he saw the beauty of Flemish and Dutch painting and architecture. It was at the Hague that Proust was to be astounded by Jan

THE MARRIED MAN

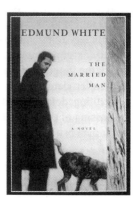

Author: Edmund White (1940-   )
Publisher: Alfred A. Knopf (New York). 321 pp. $25.00
Type of work: Novel
Time: The early 1990's
Locale: Paris, central France, Nice, Italy, Rhode Island,
  Vermont, Florida, Mexico, and North Africa

∼

*An aging American homosexual who is HIV-positive
has his wildest dreams come true when he wins the heart of
a handsome young Frenchman with whom he shares the
same cultural aspirations and discriminating tastes*

∼

Principal characters:
> AUSTIN SMITH, a gay American expatriate in his early fifties who earns
>   his living writing about eighteenth century French furniture
> JULIEN, Austin's lover, a handsome young French bisexual architect
>   with aristocratic pretensions but little money
> CHRISTINE, Julien's eccentric, promiscuous young wife
> PETER, Austin's former lover who is dying of AIDS

Edmund White's new novel, like much of his former fiction, is thinly disguised autobiography. In *The Married Man*, White, who is sixty, goes back to the year 1990 when his hero was turning fifty. Austin Smith, like White himself, is a likeable, intelligent, cultivated, amusing, friendly, generous homosexual who writes for a living. Like White, Austin does not take his writing seriously. He is not ambitious or competitive. Just as Austin is restricted to a limited audience because of his specialized subject matter, White is similarly restricted because he writes mainly about homosexuality for a predominantly homosexual audience. Austin, like White, is a hedonist. He wants to enjoy gourmet food, fine wine, witty conversation, aesthetic experiences of all kinds—but, most of all, he wants love. Love for Austin, as for most aging queens, is so hard to find that his meeting with Julien, a "gerontophile" (a young man who likes older men), seems a miraculous last chance for happiness.

Julien is "the married man" referred to in the title, but his wife Christine is not what Austin expected. She appears at their first meeting in a leather motorcycle jacket, her hair dyed a bright magenta and her lips painted fire-engine red. She is surprisingly tolerant of her husband's bisexuality (they are getting a divorce, anyway). Her function as a character seems to be to make Julien more romantic to an effeminate male because the Frenchman is at least partly heterosexual and not just another of the passive homosexuals forced to pair up by default.

Austin lives on the prestigious Île Saint Louis in the heart of Paris. He has the advantage of being bilingual in English and French, and the reader is to understand that much of the dialogue is in French and translated into English. Austin is called upon to appraise antiques and has gotten a big advance on a definitive encyclopedia of eighteenth century French furniture. His work brings him into contact with wealthy and socially prominent people, enabling him to see a side of Paris unknown to tourists. Although born in the United States, he has become more French than American. He resembles Henry James, who

Edmund White teaches at Princeton University and is an officer of the Ordre des Arts et des Lettres. He is the author of A Boy's Own Story, The Beautiful Room Is Empty, *and* The Farewell Symphony, *as well as a biography of Jean Genet, a study of Proust, and* States of Desire, *a travel book about gay America.*

became so thoroughly Europeanized that his native United States seemed like a foreign land when he was forced to revisit it. White himself lived in Paris from 1983 until 1998. He then moved to New York City to begin a teaching assignment at Princeton University.

One of the most interesting parts of *The Married Man* describes Austin's impressions of the United States when he makes the mistake of accepting a professorship in cold, gloomy Providence, Rhode Island, and bringing his exotic lover with him. He is appalled by the laziness and rudeness of American students and "the dumbing down of America." He is attacked by three militant feminists for making statements about eighteenth century women that they consider politically incorrect. He does not like Rhode Island, and Rhode Island does not like him. Like Humbert Humbert and his nymphet in Vladimir Nabokov's *Lolita* (1955), Austin and Julien are soon off to a succession of temporary destinations chosen at random.

In fact, the novel relies heavily on travel description, as if to create the illusion of movement and to compensate for the fact that the plot is an old one and not very dramatic. An aging queen meets a younger man, falls in love, then has to nurse him through the physical and psychological horrors experienced by a person dying of AIDS. Austin (like White himself) is HIV-positive and finds it ironic that his beautiful French paramour, about half his age, should be the one destined to die first. Both Austin and Julien are determined to remain "gay" for whatever years or months are left ahead of them. Their travels are financed by the generous and wildly improvident Austin, who is using up his savings and not earning much from writing because of his personal problems. His main purpose is to enable Julien to experience as much aesthetic enrichment as possible before he dies. This attitude, according to White, is common in the gay subculture among those who have contracted AIDS. Do not talk about "the plague": Eat, drink, and be merry, for tomorrow, or the next day, who knows?

After Austin loses his job in Rhode Island, he and Julien travel to Miami, Cancún, Italy, and other parts of Europe. They end their rather desperate odyssey in North Africa, a part of the world White knows well. They display the peculiar kind of courage of effeminate men who know they are doomed and really do not much care whether death claims them a little sooner or a little later. They entrust themselves to Arab guides who take them into bleak desert villages where they could easily be robbed and murdered.

During their African travels, Julien enters the last stages of his debilitating disease. He looks like a skeleton. He and Austin have given up intimate relations because Julien can hardly bear to be touched. He has to be lifted in and out of the bathtub. He becomes incontinent. He has no appetite and cannot hold anything down. His beauty has disappeared in a few short years; he looks so wasted that people cannot conceal their horrified reactions. Austin finds it more and more difficult to get them checked into hotel rooms because the desk clerks, quite understandably, are afraid of what might be a contagious disease; they are also worried that Julien might drive away some of their more squeamish guests.

White was part of the gay liberation movement that exploded in New York City in the 1970's, and his experiences with AIDS are many. In his interesting collection of short stories, *Skinned Alive* (1995), and in his earlier novel, *The Farewell Symphony* (1997), he describes the deaths of many of his friends and lovers who experienced the joy of liberation and the excitement of wild promiscuity only to have to face the grim aftermath of the previously unknown scourge of AIDS.

White, like many another gay writer, was strongly influenced by the great French novelist and aesthete Marcel Proust. White even published an excellent short biography titled *Marcel Proust* (1999). The influence of the French master is unmistakable on every page of White's fiction. Like Proust, he writes novels that are thinly disguised autobiography dealing with his own mental and emotional development. In *Marcel Proust* he writes, "This idea, that life presents us with but one book to write, the story of our own existence which we must merely 'translate,' was one to which Proust would remain faithful." White himself remains faithful to that idea. The story of the star-crossed lovers, Austin and Julien, was based on White's own relationship with Hubert Sorin, who contributed the sketches to their book *Our Paris: Sketches from Memory* (1995) shortly before the young French artist's tragic death. The relationship between Austin and Julien resembles the tempestuous one between the twenty-three-year-old Proust and the composer Reynaldo Hahn, who was only eighteen when they met.

> [T]heir affair displayed the chief characteristics of love in a Proust story or novel: wild attacks of jealousy, recriminations and disputes, brooding and hurt feelings, and ecstatic reconciliations, all endured under the sign of love-as-war and courtship-as-strategy.

To this description can be added the specter of AIDS. Perhaps such ambivalent feelings are common to homosexual relationships. White makes it clear that AIDS imposes monogamy on homosexuals for safety's sake.

Proust's masterpiece, *À la recherche du temps perdu* (1913-1927; *Remembrance of Things Past*, 1922-1931, 1981), was published in seven separate volumes between 1913 and 1927. (Proust died in 1922.) White is following in his master's footsteps by publishing a series of related autobiographical novels, beginning with *A Boy's Own Story* (1982), followed by *The Beautiful Room Is Empty* (1988), *The*

Farewell Symphony (1997), and *The Married Man*. One difference between Proust's rambling autobiographical *Bildungsroman* and White's is that Proust, who wasted a fortune on young male lovers, never came out of the closet. In fact, the narrator of *Remembrance of Things Past* turns out to be just about the only "straight" character in the novel.

The most striking feature of White's fiction is his constant use of Proustian metaphors and similes, which make both writers' novels seem like poems in prose. White quotes Proust as saying: "Truth—and life too—can be attained by us only when, by comparing a quality common to two sensations, we succeed in extracting their common essence and in reuniting them to each other within a metaphor." It is difficult to discuss White's fiction without offering a few examples of Proust's indelible influence.

The following is part of a description of Austin's anxiety as he tries to get Julien admitted to the United States: "As Austin waited for Henry to call him back, his mind raced like hands playing scales—methodical and irritating." Here is White's description of autumn leaves in Vermont: "They went walking down country roads; Austin felt they were inside a badly bombed Gothic cathedral, half of the stained glass shattered and on the ground, the rest still clinging to the leadings." He offers this image during the good times when Austin and Julien are living in central France: "Around noon the heat became more intense and the world seemed to hold its breath like a child hiding in a dusty closet." The following passage is from their time in Venice: "A standing gondolier glided past, but neither the canal nor his barque were visible and he looked as though he were a moving target in a shooting gallery."

The story is not sufficiently dramatic to make the book a page-turner. There is little suspense; the reader knows early on that Julien is going to die. The petty conflicts White introduces are never sustained. Austin has problems dealing with both his present lover, Julien, and his former lover, Peter, both of whom are younger and crave attention and pity because of their illness. Austin has problems getting Julien into the United States, but he knows so many important people that such problems are taken care of offstage without his intervention. He has problems with spoiled, hostile, lazy American students when he returns to the United States to teach a course about eighteenth century French furniture, but he is not dependent on teaching for a living and actually seems relieved when he gets fired.

What White has to offer is not drama but a graceful and interesting style as well as an insider's view of gay society. One does not have to be gay in order to find White engaging and instructive. The thoughts, feelings, and problems of homosexuals are of importance to everybody because homosexuals are out of the closet with a vengeance, including White himself. One of his most admirable traits is his candor. There is no shortage of controversies concerning gays: gays in the military, gay marriages, gay troop leaders in the Boy Scouts, gay-bashing, gays in the clergy, and many other conflicts. The heterosexual majority is being called upon not only for tolerance, but also for understanding, compassion, and justice. White is not writing a mere fantasy or romance in *The Married Man* but an exploration of the international gay subculture. He is well qualified to do so because of his maturity, intelligence, education, and talent.

Yet while he is generally regarded as the leading gay writer in the English language, he is also one of the best writers in the English language, without any qualifying adjectives.

Bill Delaney

Sources for Further Study

The Advocate, June 20, 2000, p. 138.
Booklist 96 (May 1, 2000): 1654.
Library Journal 125 (May 15, 2000): 123.
New York 33 (June 26, 2000):142.
The New York Review of Books 47 (August 10, 2000): 42.
Publishers Weekly 247 (April 17, 2000): 48.
The Times Literary Supplement, March 17, 2000, p. 21.

MARY WOLLSTONECRAFT
A Revolutionary Life

Author: Janet Todd (1942-   )
Publisher: Columbia University Press (New York). 544
   pp. $29.95
Type of work: Literary biography
Time: 1759-1797
Locale: England, Ireland, France, Portugal, and Scandi-
   navia

≈

*A close examination of the life and work of the radical
eighteenth century author and the mother of modern feminism*

≈

Principal personages:
   MARY WOLLSTONECRAFT, writer and feminist
   FANNY BLOOD, her closest friend
   WILLIAM GODWIN, her husband and also a writer
   JOSEPH JOHNSON, her friend and publisher
   GILBERT IMLAY, her lover and also a writer and businessman
   EDWARD JOHN WOLLSTONECRAFT, her father
   ELIZA WOLLSTONECRAFT, her sister
   EVERINA WOLLSTONECRAFT, her sister

Mary Wollstonecraft (1759-1797) is one of those rare commodities to the would-
be biographer—an author whose writings are inextricably linked with her life. To the
general reader, she is probably most closely associated with Mary Wollstonecraft
Shelley, her daughter and the author of the most famous tale of horror ever written—
Frankenstein (1818). To her contemporaries, however, she was the scandalous hack
writer who flouted the conventions of society and bore her first child out of wedlock.
She also established her literary reputation as the author of the radical feminist manifesto *A Vindication of the Rights of Woman, with Strictures on Political and Moral
Subjects* (1792). One of the vexing problems in crafting a biography of Wollstonecraft is whether to emphasize the work, which anticipated modern feminism in its stri-
dent call for a new social order, or the life, which challenged contemporary mores and
touched on many of the leading thinkers of the day. Happily for her readers, Janet
Todd focuses far less on her subject's theories of living than on her life as she lived it.
As Todd declares in the excellent preface, "Wollstonecraft insists we attend to her
life." Readers of this substantial volume will soon note Wollstonecraft's truly colos-
sal ego: With her self-absorbed stance of an all-encompassing "I," Wollstonecraft
projects a subjectivity in the modern sense of the word. For this very reason, Todd de-

Janet Todd is a professor of English literature at East Anglia University. She is the author of The Sign of Angelica: Women, Writing and Fiction, 1600-1800 *and the editor of* A Wollestonecraft Anthology *and the Everyman edition of Jane Austen's* Sense and Sensibility.

scribes the importance of the works and their place in the history of letters: "In Wollstonecraft's writings a new female consciousness comes into being, one that valued and reflected endlessly on its own workings, refusing to acknowledge anything absurd in the stance." Appropriately, it is the intersection of the writings with the life that forms the basis of Todd's book.

Ironically, the structure of this biography is solid and workmanlike—quite unlike the revolutionary nature of its subject. In addition to the aforementioned preface, Todd precedes the body of the book with a quite useful list of "principal characters"—rather in the manner of a *dramatis personae*. More than a simple alphabetical listing of important personages, these are truncated biographies. They provide not only the dates of birth and death but also the accomplishments of the person being described and his or her relationship to the subject of Todd's book. Given the large number of people who figured in Wollstonecraft's brief life, Todd does her readers a real service by including this listing. (One small but annoying error in this section is the entry for Edmund Burke, whose dates are given as 1729-1850—which would make it a very long life indeed. Burke's actual year of death was 1797.)

The biography proper is logically divided into four sections: Part 1 follows Wollstonecraft from her birth until her decision to move to London, part 2 shows her living a life of independence as a freelance writer, part 3 describes her sojourn in revolutionary France, and part 4 recounts her last two years as her relationship with William Godwin intensified. One could hardly find fault with the organization, but one can take Todd to task for her stinginess with dates. Unlike many biographies that include the dates covered at the beginning of each chapter or large section, Todd's book forces the reader to hunt through the text to locate this information. Given the fact that this study will probably achieve wide currency in academe, this paucity of dates will impede its usefulness as a research tool.

It is the content of the biography, however, that is paramount, and Todd properly begins her book by demonstrating how Wollstonecraft experienced the wrongs against women in her early life. When her prosperous grandfather, Edward Wollstonecraft, died, five-year-old Mary received nothing from the substantial estate—apparently because the master weaver attached little value to women. A more significant figure in Mary's life, though, was her father, Edward John Wollstonecraft, a physically abusive alcoholic who squandered his share of the legacy on a series of failed farming ventures. Clearly, Wollstonecraft sprang from a deeply dysfunctional family, and the young woman had as much contempt for the brutal father as she did for the mother who often became his victim. Todd correctly hones in on her parents' marriage as a crucial factor in Wollstonecraft's development: "Marriage and tyranny were joined, as were love and power." Her lifelong revulsion toward conventional marriage sprang from the glaring example of her own parents.

Unlike many of her own sex, Wollstonecraft did have some training at a country day school, but Todd deserves praise for paying less attention to her subject's education than to the significant personality that emerged from this troubled childhood. Wollstonecraft is tangible proof that revolutionaries do not merely arise from the clash of ideas. Todd notes that even as a teenager, Wollstonecraft exhibited the personality traits that she would carry through life—emotional instability and a supreme belief in the importance of her sensitive nature. As Todd's narrative eloquently reveals, Wollstonecraft's personality was one that needed to make its influence felt on others, and despite the impoverished nature of her formal education, writing early on became the means by which she did this. Her real education came from the school of life, and in the middle class of the late eighteenth century, those women who eschewed marriage had the unappealing options of servitude or forming their own schools. Wollstonecraft did both. As a governess to the children of Lord and Lady Kingsborough, Wollstonecraft was in a position that many middle-class women would have relished. Though Lady Kingsborough was under no obligation to do so, she made conciliatory moves toward her prickly governess, even taking her to social functions normally beyond Wollstonecraft's middle-class status. Todd's narrative, however, describes a woman who was a social irritant to the very core of her being. Uncomfortable with herself as well as with others, Wollstonecraft became a critical observer, the outsider who viewed upper-class women as little more than social ornaments. Her work as a governess did not prove to be very remunerative, but it did provide the raw material that would later find its way into *A Vindication of the Rights of Woman*.

Todd has the one fundamental skill that is essential to the biographer—the ability to sift through massive amounts of data from myriad sources and locate the repeated patterns in her subject's life. One scenario that played itself out at pivotal moments in her life was Wollstonecraft's belief that, when faced with a desperate situation, action—almost any action—was preferable to passivity. This was the case when her sister Eliza fell victim to what is now known as postpartum depression. Rather than allowing time to determine whether her sister's condition would improve, Mary spirited Eliza away from her husband and kept her location secret. While the future writer's devotion was laudable, the act of "saving" Eliza had far-reaching consequences. Since divorce was out of the question—it would have taken an act of Parliament—both Eliza and her husband were barred from marrying again. Moreover, Eliza would risk severe censure if she did not remain celibate. In this as in so many instances in her life, Wollstonecraft indulged her zeal for action rather than face what she regarded as an intolerable situation. It was this very impetuousness that prompted her to set herself up as a freelance writer in London, to flee to France and bear a child out of wedlock during the bloodiest years of the French Revolution, and to travel to Scandinavia without the benefit of a male chaperone. Such actions were anathema to the middle class of the eighteenth century; Wollstonecraft risked much in assuming such novel roles because, like all women of her class, her social survival rested upon her reputation.

One of the reasons Todd's book succeeds so well is the skill with which she traces her subject's evolution as both a thinker and a writer. It is astonishing to think that only five years separated the publication of *A Vindication of the Rights of Woman* and Wollstonecraft's tragic early death from the complications of childbirth in 1797. Yet there was a significant growth of character in these final years. While many contemporaries ostracized her as a fallen woman, Wollstonecraft the writer had a strong puritanical strain. Indeed, one of the chief arguments of her manifesto was that in order for women to raise their status in society, they had to employ reason to attenuate sexual passion. However, *A Vindication of the Rights of Woman* was a work of anger; it was written just after Wollstonecraft's bitter experience as a governess and before she had sexual intercourse. As Todd astutely notes, this work is distinguished from modern feminism in that it did not advocate sexual liberation. Wollstonecraft did not find that freedom until her affair with American businessman Gilbert Imlay in revolutionary France. It was only in France that she came to realize the dilemma faced by every writer of advice books—the hazards of trying to apply one's own advice to oneself.

After having achieved fame and notoriety through her pronouncements on women in society and the dangers of passion, Wollstonecraft's affair with Imlay caused her to become the very embodiment of what she criticized in her feminist manifesto—an insecure, desperately clinging woman who was terrified of losing her lover. As Todd's book makes evident, this was no mere passing phase in Wollstonecraft's life. Mary was obsessed with writing, and when Imlay's questionable business ventures and love affairs kept him away on trips, she responded with a daily torrent of script. In letter after letter, she lectured Imlay, begged for his return, and then threatened the very separation she so desperately feared. These letters do not make for easy reading, and they will come as quite a shock to anyone who is familiar with the author's fierce feminism. Unabashedly manipulative and endlessly self-pitying, her letters presage the two abortive suicide attempts that marked the nadir of her life. Todd deserves much credit in her fair-minded approach to this dark underside of her subject's character. On one hand, Todd could have written a hagiography, an act of obeisance that would have minimized this less savory aspect of her subject. On the other hand, Todd could just as easily have labeled Wollstonecraft a hypocrite, one who played out the very feminine stereotype she had so recently railed against. Todd steers a middle course between these two extremes, and while she acknowledges Wollstonecraft's flaws, she is also quick to underscore the fact that Wollstonecraft's actions reflected in part a tendency toward depression and the effects of her grim childhood.

In this sense, Todd's most significant achievement is the fact that the reader is allowed to witness a truly original thinker as she attempts to redefine the meaning of womanhood. While it would be easy to condemn her self-pity, one can also admire her as she acted the role of the surrogate mother to her younger siblings while simultaneously achieving fame as an author. Though Wollstonecraft is best known for her famous manifesto, Todd's superb biography demonstrates that it was indeed

Wollstonecraft's life that was truly revolutionary as she negotiated the conflicting demands of a career, motherhood, and a marriage that honored the independence of both parties. Sadly, it was the book she never lived to write.

Cliff Prewencki

Sources for Further Study

Booklist 97 (September 15, 2000): 204.
Lambda Book Report 9 (Otcober, 2000): 45.
Library Journal 125 (August, 2000): 120.
New Statesman 129 (May, 2000): 55.
The New Yorker 76 (September 11, 2000): 97.
Spectator 284 (April 29, 2000): 35.
The Times Literary Supplement, April 21, 2000, p. 36.
The Women's Review of Books 18 (November, 2000): 17.

A MAYAN ASTRONOMER IN HELL'S KITCHEN
Poems

Author: Martín Espada (1957-   )
Publisher: W. W. Norton (New York). 84 pp. $21.00
Type of work: Poetry

∽

A bold and haunting collection of poems that speaks to the hardships and injustices that both Hispanics and other minorities have had to endure for centuries

∽

Born in Brooklyn, New York, Martín Espada is of Puerto Rican ancestry. Before his English professorship at the University of Massachusetts at Amherst, Espada worked as a salesman, a clerk, a bouncer, and a tenant lawyer. He is the author of several poetry collections, including *The Immigrant Iceboy's Bolero* (1982), *Trumpets from the Islands of Their Eviction* (1987), *Rebellion Is the Circle of a Lover's Hands* (1990), *City of Coughing and Dead Radiators* (1993), and *Imagine the Angels of Bread* (1996). Espada is also the author of an acclaimed collection of essays: *Zapata's Disciple* (1998). *Rebellion Is the Circle of a Lover's Hands* won both the PEN/Revson Fellowship and the Paterson Poetry Prize. *Imagine the Angels of Bread* won an American Book Award for poetry. Whether as attorney, poet, or English professor, he again and again proves vocal about Latino social issues and injustices wherever they may appear. Through his poetry, Espada exposes the dark side of the immigrant experience in the United States. He details the plight of those who must adjust to a new world—an Anglo-American world. Having to overcome bigotry, poverty, and violence, the characters that populate his poems show great courage in their attempts to persevere against the brutality done to them. In addition to speaking up for an entire minority community, Espada also touches on the more personal tragedies that can beat down an individual in his or her daily life. While there are pitfalls for the poet who takes it upon himself to bear witness to injustice in his poetry, for Espada there is no other choice but to give names to the victims of the United States. As a poet, he does not fall into the trap of being bombastic and self-righteous to the detriment of his art. He wants both justice and art to inhabit his poems. The real tragedy, as Espada sees it, would be for him to remain silent—to not tell the truth as completely as he can.

In *A Mayan Astronomer in Hell's Kitchen*, Espada continues to speak with urgency concerning the lives of those who are less fortunate. The collection is divided into three sections: "A Tarantula in the Bananas," "A Mayan Astronomer in Hell's Kitchen," and "A Library of Lions." The collection is dedicated to Abe Osheroff, a veteran of the Spanish Civil War. Never one to shy away from sensitive political issues, the poet clearly views life itself as a political statement. As Espada witnesses too frequently, the working-class individual, the minority person, or the recent immigrant always seems to be shortchanged or worse. Having felt the cold hand of Anglo-American contempt himself, Espada resolved never to be less than an advocate for the cause of freedom and human dignity.

The first section includes ten poems that speak to the plight of Puerto Ricans and focus especially on the Espada family. The opening poem, "My Name Is Espada," boldly states that the name Espada is "the word for sword in Spain." In the fourth stanza, the reference becomes personal:

> Espada: sword in Puerto Rico, family name of bricklayers
> who swore their towels fell as leaves from iron trees;
> teachers who wrote poems in galloping calligraphy;
> saintcarvers who whittled a slave's gaze and a conqueror's beard;
> shoemaker spitting tuberculosis, madwoman
> dangling a lantern to listen for a cough;
> gambler in a straw hat inhabited by mathematical angels;
> preacher who first heard the savior's voice
> bleeding through the plaster of the jailhouse;
> dreadlocked sculptor stunned by visions of birds,
> sprouting wings from his forehead, earthen wings in the fire.

The poem details the history of a name, the poet's name, a name that has survived for decades against all odds. In times of doubt or in times when it looks like the whole world is standing on the neck of the neglected—a Latino, an Espada—it is incumbent on the poet and other family members of conscience to find strength, resolve, and a weapon of justice in the family name, the name Espada.

The poet proves passionate about the unique position that Puerto Ricans find themselves in an Anglo-American world. From his perspective, Puerto Ricans are "the Palestinians of Latin America." The migrant story always remains fresh for Espada, whether it is his own family's story or that of the many millions of other Puerto Ricans, Latinos, or faceless immigrants. In the second poem of the collection, "Preciosa Like a Last Cup of Coffee," Espada pays tribute to his grandmother Luisa Roig. The Spanish word *preciosa* can mean beautiful, precious, or valuable. There is real value and beauty in a person's life, in that person's memories, and in what gives comfort to that person when he or she is dying. In "For Jim Crow Mexican Restaurant in Cambridge, Massachusetts Where My Cousin Esteban Was Forbidden to Wait Tables Because He Wears Dreadlocks," the poet lashes out at the injustice done to his cousin. He ends the poem with the lines:

> may you hallucinate dreadlocks
> braided in thick vines around your ankles;
> and may the Aztec gods pinned like butterflies
> to the menu wait for you in the parking lot
> at midnight, demanding that you spell their names.

Espada is not without a sense of humor. It can be, though, a very biting humor. The first section ends with the short poem "What Francisco Luis Espada Learned at

Martín Espada teaches at the University of Massachusetts, Amherst. He is the author of six books of poetry, including The City of Coughing and Dead Radiators *and* Imagine the Angels of Bread, *as well as* Zapata's Disciple: Essays.

Age Five, Standing on the Dock." What Francisco learned at the age of five was that "Sometimes/ there's a/ tarantula/ in the/ bananas." It is imperative for an Espada to always stay alert, never let down his guard, and be wary of things that seem too good to be true. This is a hard lesson that not everyone comes to learn, but not learning this lesson for the Puerto Rican, the Hispanic, the new immigrant, or any other person of color could become a matter of life or death.

The second section includes thirteen wonderfully heartbreaking and haunting poems. While there is less in-your-face rage in this section, the poet's more subtle approach to telling his human stories is nonetheless as blistering as any of the poems in the entire collection. The title poem introduces the reader to a man who leans "on the third-floor fire escape" and smokes a cigarette while down below a fire rages. He is "a Mayan astronomer in Hell's Kitchen/ watching galaxies spiral in the fingerprints of smoke." For "Pitching the Potatoes," Espada remembers how his father was a pitcher for a semiprofessional baseball team. When Espada's younger brother declares that he does not want to eat the mashed potatoes served to him, this father who had been a semiprofessional pitcher throws the plate of mashed potatoes "over my brother's bristling crewcut head." While famous for his curveball, he did not employ it to throw this plate. Espada's mother prays and, eventually, sponges off the wall. The last stanza of the poem brings the reader into the present. While his mother still prays and is "patient with God," his brother has become a vegetarian and his father believes that "the Giants have no pitching." Espada confesses that when he sleeps he ducks "beneath a plate of mashed potatoes" that orbits his head "like a fake flying saucer/ suspended by wire," and this whole scene is a "snapshot from thirty years ago."

This section also includes two poems dedicated to his wife, Katherine. In "Ode to Your Earrings," the poet describes a rich imaginary world that grows out of the significance of the earrings. The poem opens with the exotic line: "There are parrots of the Amazon peeking from your hair." This line stands on its own. The first full stanza of the poem boldly states: "On your earlobes twin Taíno goddesses of the river/ squat, their eyes in slits, and dream/ the cloud of underwater birth." In the next stanza, Katherine's ears are described as being the "shoreline/ of an ocean after the hurricane"— the "seahorses of Thailand curl their tails,/ brushing your neck." The stanza continues with the introduction of "purple wooden fish," "fish of clay," and "silver dolphins." All these creatures have taken refuge in Katherine. In the fifth stanza, there is a list of sounds that are heard in Katherine's ears, including a "Zuni flute," "dolphin chatter," "a prayer," and the chant of "goddesses and birds." The chant is no less than the "recipe for the creation of planets." The poem ends with Katherine waking the poet in order to tell him what she hears.

As tender and exotic as this poem for Katherine is, the other poem dedicated to her, "I Apologize for Giving You Poison Ivy by Smacking You in the Eye with the Crayfish at the End of My Fishing Line," is amusing almost to point of being silly and yet extremely poignant. Espada is sorry for such things as not being able to fish and not understanding what poison ivy can do to someone's skin. He does not know about these things because of where he was born. Because he was a Puerto Rican born in the Bronx, Espada is clueless about fishing, poison ivy, and crayfish. He apologizes for everything, especially for "tangling my fishing line in the poison ivy" and for the "hooked crayfish, oiled with poison ivy,/ that flew over my shoulder like a cockroach with wings/ and smacked you in the eye." Katherine's eye swells and Espada knows that he must do penance. He resolves to "return to the lake at midnight" and "shout this poem repeatedly/ til sunrise, or until the police/ club me with their flashlights." This six-stanza poem adeptly uses humor to draw in the reader on one level and also open up the poem to be a powerful description of a clash of cultural experiences.

The nine poems that make up the third section are the most directly political of the collection. The most controversial poem of the group, "Another Nameless Prostitute Says the Man Is Innocent," concerns Mumia Abu-Jamal, a journalist and former member of the Black Panthers who is on death row for the murder of a Philadelphia police officer that he says he did not commit. Thousands of concerned citizens, including Espada, questioned whether Abu-Jamal should be in prison. Espada was commissioned by National Public Radio's (NPR) program *All Things Considered* to write a poem concerning a current topical issue. NPR decided against airing this particular poem because, as Espada sees the situation, it spoke out in support of Abu-Jamal. The poet's hard political edge is more evident in this section. The plight of American political prisoners takes center stage. Without a touch of sentiment, Espada expresses his disapproval of the execution of Julius and Ethel Rosenberg in "The Eleventh Reason." The poet wishes to make the reader uncomfortable, to make the United States take a second look at itself.

These poems are more than mere harangues, more than mere posturing. Espada never loses sight of the fact that a serious subject does not make a poem. A successful poem is made by the strength of its words, its images, and its form. Espada clearly understands the need to wed the subject with these essential poetic requirements. This is nowhere more evident than in the last poem of the collection, "The River Will Not Testify." The poem speaks about human dignity and how hard it is to hold as it describes the slaughter of Native Americans by Puritans in the seventeenth century.

There is a helpful glossary of Spanish words and expressions used by Espada at the end of the collection. While some readers of *A Mayan Astronomer in Hell's Kitchen* may prefer the more personal poems found in the first two sections, Espada, overall, exhibits a powerful range of poems in the collection. He is the Mayan astronomer. He is the gifted individual who takes on the responsibility of shedding light on those who are less fortunate and of letting the attentive reader view this largely obscured part of the American landscape. As with other poets of conscience such as Amiri Baraka,

Adrienne Rich, Philip Levine, Ai, Garrett Kaoru Hongo, and Jimmy Santiago Baca, Martín Espada tells the all-too-human stories of the downtrodden with boldness and strength of conviction.

Jeffry Jensen

Sources for Further Study

Booklist 96 (February 15, 2000): 1074.
Library Journal 125 (March 1, 2000): 96.
Publishers Weekly 247 (February 7, 2000): 69.

MAYFLIES
New Poems and Translations

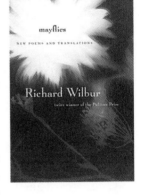

Author: Richard Wilbur (1921-   )
Publisher: Harcourt (New York). 80 pp. $20.00
Type of work: Poetry

Wilbur focuses on nature as a subject with which to meditate upon humankind, the civilized and the wild

~

Mayflies is a brief book of new poems and translations by the distinguished American poet Richard Wilbur. Though nearing eighty at the time *Mayflies* was published, Wilbur demonstrates in this volume that his poetic skills and very perceptive eye are still sharp. Wilbur also retains his ear for the absolutely appropriate word and the precise rhyme. The poems are, for the most part, short lyrics that meditate upon a scene in nature or comment wittily on the glories of the natural world and humanity's incomplete perception of it. The poems are beautifully structured, full of surprising words and images, and are a delight to read.

The first section is called "Changes" and consists of a number of brief lyric poems. The first poem in the sequence, "A Barred Owl," is a meditative-descriptive poem on the theme of the wild and the domestic. In the first stanza, "warping" night brings, with its strange changes, the discordant "boom" of an owl into a child's room. The child is now "awakened" and apparently receptive to that dark world. However, the parents comfort her by claiming that the disturbing sound was only "an odd question from a forest bird," meaning "Who cooks for you?"

The second stanza comments on the implications of this parental reassurance in the face of the wild. First of all, "Words . . . Can also thus domesticate a fear." This essential element of the civilized abates the natural fear of the wild, so that the child does not return to that night world in a dream. Without the word, she would be initiated into a world where "some small thing in a claw" is "Borne up to some dark branch and eaten raw."

The poem cleverly contrasts the two worlds of Claude Levi-Strauss's "the raw and the cooked." Wilbur is usually classified as a "cooked poet," but he acknowledges the "raw" and brilliantly describes it. However, there is in this poem a time for that acknowledgment. To make a young child aware of the "raw" too early would warp her view of the world and unbalance the relationship between the wild and the civilized.

"For C." is a poem of contrasts, as are many of the poems in this collection. Wilbur first describes romantic love and then opposes it to a domestic and constant love. The romantic lovers, predictably, part with showy gestures and clashing sounds. They even disturb nature, and it takes "three thousand miles of knitting seas" to undo "The

Richard Wilbur won the Pulitzer Prize for his New and Collected Poems *in 1989. He is a member of the American Academy of Arts and Letters and the Academy of American Poets. In addition to his poetry, his translations of the works of Molière and Racine are now the standard theatrical versions in English.*

amorous rough and tumble of their wake." Wilbur then contrasts "that long love/ Which constant spirits are the keepers of" to the brief and disturbing love of the romantics. This love may seem "tame and staid," but it reconciles the opposites as "A passion joined to courtesy and art." This love is finally depicted in four brilliant similes. It is "Like a good fiddle, like the rose's scent,/ Like a rose window or the firmament." The similes expand from the evanescent sound of a "fiddle" to the smell of a "rose" to the rose window of the Gothic cathedral, such as that at Chartres, and finally to the stars and the immensity of the "firmament." The poem once more contrasts the wild and the untamed to the made and civilized, and Wilbur exposes the brevity in the gaudy romantic love and redeems and glorifies the ordinary.

In "Zea," Wilbur describes some stalks of corn in their changing states. After the corn has been picked, the stalks "lighten" in color, although they keep to "their strict rows." Later, they will become sound images ("whistling") and change color to the "lightest brown." They transform themselves later into an up-and-down movement like "goose-wings beating southward." The last stage is in days of "utter calm," when they are "Oddly aflutter" and "The sole thing breathing."

Wilbur sees nature as a living thing, as "Zea" makes clear; the stalks of corn may even have a soul. However, he does not romanticize it, but views it with a precision of observation and image that renews the most common scenes and objects. His use of the simile is especially noteworthy in this and many other poems in *Mayflies*. This figure seems to fit his sensibility and vision; he consistently prefers it to metaphor, since metaphor insists on identity, not likeness.

The title poem of the collection sees nature in religious terms after the usual precise description. The mayflies arise in "quadrillions," with a glittering that is compared to "a crowd/ Of stars." They then become dancers, rising and falling. That dance is seen not as "a muddled swarm," but as a "figured scene." Nature and art are reconciled here and not distinct as they are in some of Wilbur's poems. The poem then takes a Wordsworthian turn, and it is no accident that Wilbur's mayflies dance as Wordsworth's daffodils did. The speaker of the poem feels suddenly alone, "In a life too much my own." However, this moment of melancholy is overcome, as it is in Wordsworth's "I Wandered Lonely as a Cloud," by the speaker's seeing himself not as one whose task is a thing of nature, but as one who is there "joyfully to see/ How fair the fiats of the caller are." There is an acknowledgment of the speaker as being called to be a witness to the beauty and order in the commands of the sole caller, God. The poem seems to use the theological argument from design at the end, although it is also a moment of personal illumination.

The theme of there being a design in the universe is continued in "Fabrications." Wilbur's speaker begins by describing a spider web that has been repaired. One can see through the web and perceive "steeples" and "One loitering star, and off there to the south/ Slow vultures kettling in the lofts of air." This world is, once more, made up of the civilized "steeple" and the wild "vultures." Wilbur then connects the web of the spider metaphorically with man: "Each day men frame and weave/ In their own way whatever looms in sight." That construction, like that of the spider, is only partial, and much must remain "unseen." The theme of the incomplete in the world is then developed with a parable from the Talmud about a "bottomless" river. The world too is "bottomless," although "it is not true/ That we grasp nothing till we grasp it all." The metaphor of an ancient map is then used to show the limits of man's view of an uncertain world. It has blanks and "namelessness," but there are towers from which one can "infer civility." In that civilized place, people see "those loves which hint of love itself" and the "spider's web" that now upholds the universe, metaphorically seen as an "architrave." The spider image appears early in the poem, and it is now used as a resolving metaphor. The poem uses the theme of the civilized and the wild once more, and both are included, although the civilized triumphs at the end.

The first section of "Personae" is a witty commentary on the role of the poet today. In the past, he "dwelt in garrets, dined in dives," and lived the life of the "laboring poor." Today he reads his verse dressed "like a sandhog, stevedore, or worse." Even though he may now be very well off, he "wears a collar of memorial blue/ To give the grave Bohemian past its due." The tone of the poem is more amused at than mocking the pretensions and adopted roles of poets who are very far from the proletarian 1930's.

The first section of "A Wall in the Woods: Cummington" is one of the best poems in the collection. It is another meditative-descriptive poem as the speaker comes upon a decayed wall in the woods and comments on its significance. He asks, "What is it for" now that what the wall was intended for has collapsed with the years. The answer is that "It is for grief at what has come to nothing." He then imaginatively re-creates the sounds and sights of that vanished world: "Whipcrack, the ox's lunge, the stoneboat's grating." All that was dreamed by those who built the wall is now gone, except the remains of the wall itself. It now exists to "prompt a fit of elegy" over the loss of those hopes. However, something of it does remain: "It is a sort of music for the eye,/ A rugged ground bass like the bagpipe's drone/ On which the leaf-light like a chanter plays."

The poem is similar to Robert Frost's "Directive" in its recovery of a lost world and in its evocation of a beneficent place, and the connected images of light and sound at the end of the poem are very powerful in finding something beautiful and of value in this lost world.

The third section of "The Pleasing Anxious Being" is a beautiful evocation of a childhood ride through the snow in the 1920's. The snow is "Wild, lashing," but Father is in control, driving while Mother lights the way. The children in the back seat are soothed by the "jingling chains/ And by their parents' pluck and gaiety." The one child who is awake imagines the experience metaphorically as a plane landing at a "bombarded shore" and a ship that "dances through the rocks" to arrive at a safe harbor. The final metaphor and place of arrival is the "bedstead at whose foot/ The world will swim and flicker and be gone." The threats of a wild nature are overcome by the imaginative dreaming, so that the threatening world is finally eclipsed and undone.

In the second half of the book, there are translations of poems by Stéphane Mallarmé and Valeri Petrov, and of Charles Baudelaire's "Albatross" and "Correspondences." The Baudelaire translations are especially impressive. Wilbur follows the French of Baudelaire closely, and his alternating rhymes and diction are perfectly done. "Albatross" is an interesting poem that first describes the large bird and then compares it metaphorically to the poet. The poet, like the albatross, is a "monarch of the clouds." However, when he returns to earth, he is an exile who is hooted at by the jeering crowds. Like the albatross, "He cannot walk, borne down by giant wings."

The last section in the book is called "Transformations," and it consists of a translation of the "Prologue" to Molière's *Amphitryon* (pr., pb. 1668; trans. 1755) and canto 25 of the "Inferno" of Dante's *La divina commedia* (c. 1320; *The Divine Comedy*, 1802). The "Prologue" is a debate between Mercury, the messenger of the gods, and Night. Mercury announces that Jove commands Night to cover the presence of Jove as he makes love to the wife of Amphitryon. Heracles will be born out of this union of a mortal and a god, so the poem embodies the theme of transformation, as does the Dante canto. In that canto, thieves are transformed into snakes that attack other thieves; they join together, so they are neither snake nor human. The theme is that since the thieves have taken others' goods, their own identity is taken away from them in an eternal transformation from snake to human and back.

The Molière "Prologue" is done in the witty alternating rhymes at which Wilbur is so proficient. Wilbur is acknowledged as the best translator of Molière in English, and the "Prologue" demonstrates that mastery once more. The Dante canto is done in the alternating rhymes of the terza rima stanza. The harsh, judgmental vision of Dante, however, seems alien to Wilbur. He does skillfully use the terza rima stanza, but the imagery and diction do not seem to fit Wilbur's poetic technique very well.

James Sullivan

Sources for Further Study

Booklist 96 (March 1, 2000): 1190.
The Christian Century 117 (May 24, 2000): 607.
The New York Review of Books 47 (June 29, 2000): 59.
Publishers Weekly 247 (February 7, 2000): 69.

MEN IN THE OFF HOURS

Author: Anne Carson (1950-   )
Publisher: Alfred A. Knopf (New York). 168 pp. $24.00
Type of work: Poetry and essays

~

Carson continues to dazzle readers with her strange conjunctions of opposites in this new collection of poetry and prose

~

Anne Carson's *Men in the Off Hours* is challenging and exciting, and if it does not have quite the emotional pull of her last book, *Autobiography of Red* (1998), it teases and invigorates. Carson's work invariably pushes the envelope; there are no boundaries she respects, and a part of the appeal of her work is in the odd juxtapositions and minglings that combine prose and poetry, ancient and modern, exalted and trivial, abstract and concrete. She is a true practitioner of bricolage, building surprising structures from the most unlikely materials.

The poetry books of Anne Carson, a teacher of classics at McGill University in Montreal, include *Plainwater* (1995), *Glass, Irony, and God* (1995), and *Autobiography of Red*. She has received a Lannan Literary Award as well as other awards and fellowships, including a Guggenheim fellowship, and has written in other genres besides poetry—indeed, *Men in the Off Hours* is not all poetry.

Carson's previous book, *Autobiography of Red*, tells the story of the minor character Geryon from fragments of Stesichorus's work that she herself had translated. She gives Geryon center stage and makes him a troubled youth whose sexual coming of age is strange and poignant. The reader finds in Geryon's freakishness and self-consciousness a painful reminder of acute adolescence. The "novel in verse" has the excitement and suspense of a novel—knowing what happened to Geryon in the Greek myth does not mean one knows what this Geryon's fate is—and it also has the linguistic richness and precision characteristic of good poetry.

Men in the Off Hours is more a treat for the mind; its mingling of poetry and prose essay challenges the reader's expectations and provides intriguing insights. Carson wrenches characters out of history and places them in other contexts. In a very basic way this can be seen as a book about time—how time is experienced and what history means. The odd pairings force a reconsideration of time and the implications of historicizing. The book examines the questions of how different eras might hold dialogue and what such dialogue might re-

~

Anne Carson is the author of two other collections of poems, Autobiography of Red *and* Plainwater. *In July, 2000, she was named a MacArthur Fellow.*

~

veal. Together with the sense of time's irrevocable passing, there is also the presence of elegy—for historical periods, persons, and places that are either gone or vanishing.

What Carson does with elegy is astounding. For instance, the very brief poem "Epitaph: Europe" has an uncanny sense of rightness as well as a nod to Paul Celan in the language:

> Once live X-rays stalked the hills as if they were
> Trees. Bones stay now
> And their Lent stays with them, black on the nail.
> Tattering on the daywall.

The poem seems in four lines to encapsulate an elegy for the war dead, for the Christianity of the past, perhaps even for Celan himself. Other moving elegies are a strong presence in the collection.

This book is even more of a mixture than Carson's other work, and the disparity of its contents is more evident. There are brief elegiac poems, sequences of poems on a figure, essays, and reflections. The collection is longer than most single collections, and the essay that provides much of the extra length may hold less appeal than the poems for some readers.

This long essay is a lot like the criticism of some of the French essentialists, particularly perhaps Hélène Cixous, and, although it is quite interesting and the writer often hides successfully behind her words, it takes a different kind of attention from the poetry. It may be a requirement of the postmodern sensibility to have no expectations, to be ready to be led at any time in a new direction, but for many readers this essay is something very different and possibly distracting. Called "Dirt and Desire: Essay on the Phenomenology of Female Pollution in Antiquity," it appears to provide a theory of male/female wet/dry, overflowing of female boundaries, and so forth, and as such to be in line with work of other theorists, but questions of possible irony and multiple meaning arise as the reader attempts to look at the essay in the same light as the poetry. The essay is somewhat frustrating, and many will return happily to the translucent layers of the poems, which are rewarding at whatever depth the reader enters.

An intellectually intriguing sequence is "TV Men," in which the characters Sappho, Antonin Artaud, Leo Tolstoy, Lazarus, Antigone, Anna Akhmatova, and Thucydides—the last in conversation with Virginia Woolf—are represented in quick little glimpses as though for a television spot. Apparently Carson herself put together a series for public television about the history of Nobel Prize winners. "I was supposed to attack science from the view of a humanist in these little 30-second sound bites," she said. "It was just ridiculous." Clearly, though, the difficulty and potential of such a task intrigued her, as she created her own series of snapshots, actually very complex reinventions of some well-known figures. "Tolstoy" begins thus:

I. CHAMBRE

A curiously tender man and yet
even after their marriage he

called his desire to kiss her
"the appearance of Satan."

*Her in right profile against the light, all the music in the room streams
toward the blue frosty window.*

Desire, the trees are rags. Desire, streaks of it
scalding the fog. This is not what I meant (Lev thinks wildly)—
words from a bad play, embraces that knock the lamp,
you are so young! And this fog.

*His bedroom on a March morning as cool as pearls, close-up on rustling,
coats or shawls.*

A new Tolstoy emerges from the imaginary film, a man sensuous as well as uncompromising, who lives in a lovely broken world that cries out for a forbidden touch. The sequence demonstrates intertextuality in practice. The figures and eras play off one another, redefining both. These are indeed strange but telling brief appearances, with interpretations/interpolations of other times and sensibilities popping up in the middles of scenes. The reader does not know where to step in these poems, where their firm ground is, but the flux and the betrayals are part of their power.

Another quirky but profound pairing that serves as the basis of a sequence is "Hopper: Confessions," which plays Edward Hopper's paintings off against Saint Augustine's *Confessiones* (397-400; *Confessions*, 1620). A sample from the series is "Evening Wind":

> What dog or horse will wish to be remembered
> after passing away from this world
> where it moved
> as a frailty.
> You on the other hand creature whitely Septembered
> can you pause in the thought
> that links origin
> and tendency?
>
> *Shut it not up I beseech thee, do not shut up these
> usual yet hidden things
> from my desire.*
>
> (Augustine, *Confessions XI*)

The sequence allows the saint and the painter to trade their images, the spiritual for the sensual, the interior for the exterior. Thus the poem brings out the shadow side of each. Does Augustine reject the world and Hopper accept it, or vice versa? Or does each man do both? In the case of Hopper's paintings, is not the surface also the substance? Is it also true in Augustine's work? In this poem, as in most in the collection, the possibilities multiply.

Not all the work is so difficult; the concluding "Appendix to Ordinary Time" is a brief, touching tribute to Carson's mother, which also serves as a recapitulation of the thematic content of the book as it relates to time and death. "Father's Old Blue Cardigan," a poem earlier in the book, also is simple and direct, although there are some vibrations beneath the surface. The speaker tells of putting on the cardigan—in a sense, in the same way she has put on all the other identities in the collection. Wearing someone else, she is transformed, and this transformation brings understanding.

> Now it hangs on the back of the kitchen chair
> where I always sit, as it did
> on the back of the kitchen chair where he always sat.
>
> I put it on whenever I come in,
> as he did, stamping
> the snow from his boots.
>
> I put it on and sit in the dark.
> He would not have done this.
> Coldness comes paring down from the moonbone in the sky.

The speaker remembers "the moment at which I knew/ he was going mad inside his laws"; this was the moment when she found him dressed in the buttoned-up cardigan on a "hot July afternoon," the look on his face reminding her of "a small child who has been dressed by some aunt early in the morning/ for a long trip" and who sits

> . . . very straight at the edge of his seat
> while the shadows like long fingers
>
> over the haystacks that sweep past
> keep shocking him
> because he is riding backwards.

It would be too simple for Carson to include only complicated, intellectually dense work; readers are led to expect this, and therefore it does not occur. However, most of the poems are rich and layered, and certainly some of the pleasure of Carson's work is in the game itself, in unraveling the skeins that are woven together in the poem. This is especially true in poems such as "Sumptuous Destitution," which runs a directive to Emily Dickinson made by a contemporary speaker through a sequence of sentences from Dickinson's letters to and from her mentor, Thomas Higginson. The result is a comment on Emily Dickinson, feminist theory, and the meaning of historical time.

Typically—if one can generalize at all—Carson's work is postmodern in technique, usually without the flatness of affect that characterizes the work of many postmodern poets. It does have the randomness, mingling of discourses, odd yet strangely apposite connections, and appropriation of literature and history that characterize postmodern work. It also demonstrates some very contemporary playful techniques such as the interruption of one discourse by another and the inclusion of "drafts" that are actually different poems. She sets up expectations that are not met, plays with the boundaries of genres, and uses the notion of "drafts" to suggest that nothing is "fixed," not time, not history, and certainly not poetry. However, the poems are emotionally convincing; the use of experimental techniques and the embedded chunks of classicism do add up in ways even a casual reader can see. Carson's history is twisted and fictionalized, but in her reinventions there is an exhilaratingly fresh perspective.

One never knows what to expect from Carson; there is not an easily identifiable "Anne Carson poem" as there is an identifiable style of poem for many other contemporary writers. Her contribution is that she is always searching for the new but without discarding the old. The poems are demanding, but one might say that they plead for in-depth reading rather than simply requiring attention as a right. Carson is one of the rare contemporary poets who bridge the gap between the usual readership of other poets and the wider audience of those who love literature, and does so without compromise. Often poem sequences picked up by the reading public have been of questionable literary value, desirable for their sensationalism or suspense, but Carson's appeal is subtle and complex. No confessionalist, she hides behind her literary and historical figures, and only in the space between her conflated images do readers catch a brief glimpse of her.

Janet McCann

Sources for Further Study

Booklist 96 (March 1, 2000): 1190.
Library Journal 125 (February 15, 2000): 168.
The New Leader 83 (March/April, 2000): 34.
The New York Times Book Review 105 (May 14, 2000): 44.
Publishers Weekly 247 (February 7, 2000): 70.

THE MONK IN THE GARDEN
The Lost and Found Genius of Gregor Mendel, the Father of Genetics

Author: Robin Marantz Henig (1953-   )
Publisher: Houghton Mifflin (Boston). 192 pp. $24.00
Type of work: Biography, history of science, natural history, and science
Time: 1822-1989
Locale: Eastern Europe

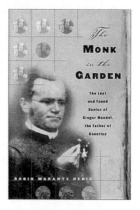

≈

An accessible retelling of Mendel's life, work, and influence

≈

Principal personages:
GREGOR JOHANN MENDEL (1822-1884),
    Austrian botanist, Augustinian monk, and father of modern genetics
HUGO MARIE DE VRIES (1848-1935), Dutch botanist whose studies on
    discontinuous variations led him to rediscover Mendel's work
WILLIAM BATESON (1861-1926), English biologist who coined the term
    "genetics" and based this new science on Mendel's ideas

In 1854 Gregor Mendel began the pea-plant experiments that would originate a new biological science in the twentieth century. In 2000, with the mapping of the human genome (the genetic instructions for making a human being), his work seemed destined to grow in importance in the twenty-first century. Ironically, Mendel's accomplishments, whose significance became obvious to twentieth century scientists, were largely neglected in the nineteenth century, and this neglect and rediscovery have raised questions that biographers and historians of science have been wrestling with ever since: What did Mendel do? Why did he do it? Did he really understand what he had done? Why were his results so poorly received?

Robin Marantz Henig, a freelance writer specializing in science and medicine, thinks she has the answers to these questions. As a science journalist, she has worked for the magazines *BioScience* and *Human Behavior* and has written six books, including *A Dancing Matrix: How Science Confronts Emerging Viruses* (1994), which won an award from the American Society of Journalists and Authors. Though not a trained historian of science, Henig claims that she can use the work of these scholars to solve the "enigma" of Mendel and tell his story in a way that scholars never have. She agrees with those scholars who feel that the myth of Mendel as a misunderstood genius needs to be debunked, but she also disagrees with those revisionists who reduce Mendel to a dabbler who stumbled into discoveries whose real meaning he failed to grasp. For Henig, the truth lies between these extremes. She sees Mendel as a creative gardener with a deep faith in science's power to reveal the secrets of how plants propagate their traits. All her chapters have epigraphs from writers on gardening, and she believes that Mendel's life is

> primarily the story of a gardener, patiently tending his plants, collecting them, counting them, working out his ratios, and calmly, clearly explaining an amazing finding— then waiting for someone to understand what he was talking about.

To help her understand Mendel, Henig revisited the sites of his life and read all the primary and many of the secondary sources. Because the majority of Mendel's papers have been lost or destroyed, she has been forced to speculate about what he was thinking and feeling at pivotal moments in his career. Such speculations are problematic, however, since what appear to her to be reasonable reconstructions of Mendel's interior life may be unreasonable or even absurd to others, and indeed scholars as well as popularizers have come up with conflicting interpretations of his aims and analyses.

Henig structures her book in two "acts" separated by a sixteen-year interlude. Act One is her account of Mendel's life and a contextualized explanation of his work. In Act Two, "Mendel Redux," she shows how, in the twentieth century, Mendel's accomplishments were rediscovered, reformulated, mythologized, revised, condemned, rehabilitated, and refurbished. Previous biographers have also dealt with Mendel's "resurrection," but generally as a modest epilogue to their treatment of his life, whereas Henig's analysis of a rejuvenated Mendelism constitutes a substantial part of her book.

Act One begins not with Mendel's birth and childhood but in the "glasshouse" of St. Thomas Monastery in Brünn, Austria (now Brno, Czech Republic), where he conducted his extensive experiments on the common garden pea. What is not widely known is that he actually began his scientific investigations of inheritance by breeding wild mice with albinos to see what color fur the hybrids would have, but the local bishop thought it inappropriate for a monk with a vow of chastity to be studying copulating rodents, so Mendel was required to shift from animal to plant breeding (the bishop apparently was ignorant of the sexuality of plants).

It is surprising that Henig, who speculates so freely about Mendel's personality, says so little about her subject's early years, because the time, place, culture, and conditions of his upbringing did much to shape his identity. An only son between an older and younger sister, Johann (his birth name) Mendel was born in Silesia, then part of the Habsburg Empire, in a region where German, not Czech, was the predominant language. His father was a peasant farmer and his mother was the daughter of a gardener, and they taught their son how to care for animals and graft fruit trees. Silesian culture was Roman Catholic, and priests played a significant role in Johann's education. For example, the village priest, impressed by Johann's intellectual abilities, advised his parents to send their son to an advanced school some sixteen miles away. Johann later traveled to a gymnasium (roughly equivalent to an American high school) in Troppau (Opava to the Czechs). After graduating, he moved to a philosophical institute at Olmütz (Olomouc in Czech) to complete his preparation for university studies. Courses were taught in Czech, a language that Johann had not yet mastered, and he was lonely and unhappy. According to his own account, anxieties over his future

Robin Marantz Henig is a freelance science and medical writer. She was named Author of the Year by the American Society of Journalist and Authors for her book A Dancing Matrix: How Science Confronts Emerging Viruses. *She regularly contributes to* USA Today, *The* New York Times, *and* The Washington Post.

affected him so intensely that he became ill and had to return home to recover.

Following the advice of one of his Olomouc professors who had spent twenty years at St. Thomas Monastery, Mendel decided to become an Augustinian monk to liberate himself from a struggle for existence that he was finding increasingly unendurable. Though the culture of the monastery was predominantly Czech, several monks were, like Mendel, of German background. Besides, the monastery was economically prosperous because of its estates and it was therefore able to support its members, including the novice Gregor (Johann's name in religion), in their various pursuits, both sacred and secular.

Because of her interest in Mendel's scientific achievements, Henig says little about his religious life, but it is important to realize that Gregor loved his order, which traced its spiritual lineage back to Saint Augustine. The Augustinians pursued both the contemplative and the active life. With his fellow friars, Mendel engaged in penance, prayer, and good works. Indeed, after he completed his theological studies and was ordained a priest in 1847, his first position was chaplain to a parish served by the monastery. Unfortunately, his shy and sensitive disposition made it difficult for him to minister to the impoverished, sick, and dying. Consequently, his abbot, Cyrill Napp, thought that he should pursue a teaching rather than a pastoral career.

Though Mendel's students and colleagues later testified to his pedagogical gifts, he performed poorly in the formal examinations that would have allowed him to be better paid and to advance academically. To correct his deficiencies, the abbot sent Mendel in 1851 to the University of Vienna, where he received an excellent education in the sciences and learned about the hybridization studies of such botanists as Josef Kölreuter and Karl Friedrich von Gärtner. After two years in Vienna Mendel returned to the monastery, where he resumed teaching and began his pea-plant experiments.

Like many scientists and biographers before her, Henig tries to reconstruct Mendel's famous researches. Because records of when, how, and why Mendel performed particular botanical experiments no longer exist, her reconstructions have to be treated with caution. Nevertheless, it is clear that for the first few years Mendel tested numerous varieties of peas to make sure that the traits he was interested in were constant. Previous botanists had not carefully distinguished between constant hybrids, whose traits persisted unchanged for generations, and variable hybrids, whose traits might change in some generations. For example, he developed plants that constantly gave round peas and plants that constantly gave angular peas. Then, when he crossed these round and angular varieties, he discovered that all the hybrids were alike in giving round peas. Angular-shaped peas did not appear until the next generation, when they constituted twenty-five percent of the population. Mendel called the round trait "dominant" and the angular trait "recessive," because the angular shape remained latent in the first generation.

In one series of experiments on seed color, Mendel counted 6,022 yellow peas and 2,001 green peas in the second generation. He had an explanation for this three-to-one ratio. Each plant had two elements (or factors) that determined seed color, one from each parent. Any plant possessing either one of two elements for the dominant trait displayed that trait, but to display the recessive trait, a plant had to have two recessive elements. Mendel represented the dominant factor with a capital letter and the recessive factor with a lowercase letter. With four kinds of germ cells available—pollen A, pollen a, egg A, and egg a—he was able to explain his experimental results in both the first and second generations. The first generation was all hybrids (Aa), whereas the second generation included one true-breeding dominant (AA), two hybrids (Aa), and one recessive (aa). His results were thus in direct contradiction to the blending theory of inheritance, since that theory proposed that offspring were intermediate forms between their parents. The English naturalist Charles Darwin believed in this theory, even though the idea caused problems for his views on natural selection.

Because the modern theory of evolution and heredity has twin founders, Darwin and Mendel, Henig is very interested in the relationship between them. Mendel's annotated copy of the German translation of Darwin's *On the Origin of Species by Means of Natural Selection* (1859; German edition, 1862) has survived, and it thus is known that he appreciated and admired many of Darwin's ideas, though he was critical of Darwin's defective understanding of plant fertilization. Furthermore, it is known that Mendel sent Darwin a copy of his paper describing his experiments on plant hybridization, but the paper was found after Darwin's death in his library with its pages uncut.

Darwin was not the only person to neglect Mendel's paper. After its publication by the Brünn Society for the Study of Natural Science in 1866, Mendel commissioned forty reprints, many of which he sent to prominent scientists all over the world. The society's journal was also distributed to 124 scientific institutions in various countries. These facts counter the common misconception that Mendel's discoveries were never made public in the nineteenth century. Despite this dissemination of Mendel's discoveries, only one scientist, Karl von Nägeli, a professor of botany at the University of Munich, responded, but he failed to understand what Mendel was saying. As a proponent of the blending theory of plant inheritance, Nägeli distrusted Mendel's disproof of blending.

Despite this disheartening response, Mendel continued to do research on plants, and he also extended his scientific work to include the crossbreeding of bees and the statistical study of the weather. However, his life was dramatically changed in 1868 when he was elected abbot of the monastery. Napp had died, and now Mendel had to take on his administrative duties. These duties became onerous when a new government in Vienna passed a law in 1875 requiring all monasteries to pay taxes on their property. Mendel, who felt that the law was unconstitutional and unjust, was the only abbot who refused to accept the law, which, ironically, had been passed by the liberal party he supported. Despite pleas by his relatives, friends, and colleagues to compromise, he persisted in his opposition, creating tensions that had deleterious effects on his health. He stoically endured a protracted illness, and he insisted on a postmortem exam to determine the nature of the kidney disease that would cause his death. In his obituaries he was lauded as an exemplary priest, a champion of the poor, an opponent of injustice, and a promoter of the natural sciences.

Act Two of Henig's book focuses on the fate of Mendel's work in the twentieth century, beginning with the rediscovery of his studies on plant hybridization by three scientists in three different countries. In Holland, Hugo de Vries claimed to have discovered Mendel's results independently, before learning of the monk's publications, but scholars have questioned this claim since de Vries's use of the terms "dominant" and "recessive" suggests that Mendel influenced his studies before they were done. In Germany, Karl Correns stated that he had discovered Mendel's three-to-one ratio before hearing of his work, and Correns went on to cast his understanding of Mendel's discoveries in the form of scientific laws. In Austria, Erich von Tschermak's experiments with pea plants mentioned Mendel when they were published, but several scholars think he stole rather than rediscovered Mendel's findings.

For Henig, the real founder of Mendelism was William Bateson, who made the Austrian monk the hero of the new science he called genetics. Bateson's apotheosization of Mendel was soon challenged when Ronald Fisher, a British statistician, concluded that the odds were thirty thousand to one that Mendel had arrived at his published ratios by chance. In other words, Fisher was charging Mendel with "cooking" his data to make his published numbers fit his theory. Some geneticists agreed with Fisher that Mendel's results were too good to be true, but others defended the founder of their science by claiming that Fisher had used faulty mathematical methods in his study. The scholarly consensus that has built up after Fisher's work is that Mendel was not deliberately fraudulent in his work, though he may not have dealt with ambiguous experimental results in the way that contemporary biologists have been trained to do.

In general, Henig exhibits an astute understanding of the power of Mendel's ideas, and her account of the man responsible for these ideas captures his warmth, humor, and humanity. Her book does not supplant Vítězslav Orel's *Gregor Mendel: The First Geneticist* (1996), the standard source for the orthodox interpretation of Mendel's life and work. In fact, she draws heavily from this book as well as from Hugo Iltis's *Life of Mendel* (1932; German ed., 1924) for many of her details and interpretations. Her book is similar in approach and intended audience to Edward Edelson's *Gregor Mendel and the Roots of Genetics* (1999), written for the series Oxford Portraits in Science. Her account is more extensive than Edelson's, but it also contains inaccuracies. For example, in her treatment of Darwin's voyage on the *Beagle*, she correctly understands that Robert McCormick, not Darwin, was the ship's official naturalist, but she has McCormick leaving the ship in 1862, after just six months at sea, whereas he in fact left in 1832 after four months on the job. Her treatment of Mendel's religious life is also weak and not without errors. For example, she thinks the Greek letters alpha and omega on Mendel's shield stand for scientific inquiry, while Mendel intended these letters in their traditional symbolism for God the Father and Jesus Christ.

Despite these and other limitations, Henig's treatment of Mendel's life and the fate of his work makes available to a wide readership the insights of several Mendelian scholars. Her account deftly wends a path between the extremes of hagiography and hero-bashing. While dismissing the myth of Mendel created by the founders of genetics (Mendel was not a modern Mendelian), she nevertheless realizes the originality of his methods, experiments, and interpretations. She also believes that Mendel himself recognized that he had done something important. He once told a plant breeder, "My time will come." Some scientists consider the completion of the Human Genome Project as the ultimate fulfillment of Mendel's work, but this completion does not really end the work that Mendel started; instead, it represents a new beginning.

Robert J. Paradowski

Sources for Further Study

Booklist 96 (June 1, 2000): 1822.
Kirkus Reviews 68 (May 1, 2000): 611.
Library Journal 125 (June 1, 2000): 185.
New Statesman 129 (July 3, 2000): 53.
The New York Times Book Review 105 (August 27, 2000): 16.
Publishers Weekly 247 (May 22, 2000): 83.

MR. PHILLIPS

Author: John Lanchester (1962-   )
Publisher: G. P. Putnam's Sons (New York). 291 pp.
    $24.95
Type of work: Novel
Time: 1995
Locale: London

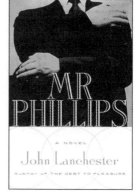

≈

A fifty-year-old accountant who has just lost his job spends a day drifting about London

≈

Principal characters:
  VICTOR PHILLIPS, the protagonist, a former
   accountant
  MRS. PHILLIPS, his wife, a piano teacher
  MARTIN PHILLIPS, their older son, a music producer
  THOMAS PHILLIPS, their younger son, a student
  MARTHA ERITH, a neighbor, the widow of one of Phillips's teachers
  CLARISSA COLINFORD, a television personality
  FORTESCUE, a pornographer

John Lanchester made an auspicious debut with his widely praised novel *The Debt to Pleasure* (1996). This sardonic satire featuring a witty serial killer was translated into twenty-two languages and left Lanchester's readers looking forward to his second novel. *Mr. Phillips* has few characteristics in common with its predecessor, however, focusing on a considerably less flamboyant protagonist. Victor Phillips is a fifty-year-old accountant who has just lost his job after twenty-six years with Wilkins and Co. Unable to tell his wife and two sons about this disruption in his placid life, Phillips leaves his suburban home in South London as usual on a Monday morning, taking the train to the city and spending the day wandering about, looking for ways to fill the time. The complete opposite of Lanchester's previous protagonist, Phillips is an unremarkable man who has never thought much about the quality of his life. Being suddenly unemployed forces him to do so, but he fights the urge to be too reflective, trying to think about anything else but his frightening future, not even acknowledging his new status until one-third of the way into the novel.

Even though his hero is reluctant to reflect on work, Lanchester explores its nature, observing how people's identities shift when they are at work:

> Most men are at their most attractive when at work, their attention directed outside themselves, with chores to perform and decisions to exercise, all unlike the sulking, shifty tyrants of the domestic stage, wanting everything their own way and locked in a battle to the death to get it.

For Phillips, work is an escape from thinking about his passionless marriage, his inability to communicate with his sons, the general meaninglessness of his life.

One of the least subtle ironies in *Mr. Phillips* is that one of Victor's duties, as deputy chief of accounts, is determining the costs of making his fellow employees redundant. (The British term is clearer and blunter than the American jargon "downsized.") Phillips spends an uncomfortable ninety minutes stuck in an elevator with someone about to be fired. Wondering who prepared the report about dismissing him, Phillips realizes that because he is not entitled to any bonuses, unlike Mr. Mill, his immediate boss at the catering-services supply company, dismissing him is relatively straightforward. Lanchester's hero is never self-pitying or angry, always able to see his redundancy objectively. Phillips's passivity is not presented as a character flaw but merely as a defining characteristic. Phillips gets some satisfaction out of knowing that Wilkins and Co. will never learn of his plan to save several thousand pounds a year by preventing employees from stealing office supplies such as Post-it Notes, an item he has been stealing for years.

If Phillips tries not to think too much about work, what does he think about? One of his two favorite concerns is sex. *Mr. Phillips* opens with his dreaming about other women while lying next to his sleeping wife. (One of the many well-known literary characters Victor Phillips resembles is James Thurber's Walter Mitty, because when he is not dreaming about sex, he dreams about performing heroic deeds such as rescuing a group of women from a runaway train.) He is obsessed by sex because he feels he has discovered sex's biggest secret, "the truth no one wants to tell you and which even adults don't discuss or admit, and which, like all important secrets, is surprising and radical and obvious." This secret is that no one ever actually has sexual relations. Well, not never but rarely, and much less than the culture would have people believe. Phillips's evidence is the year-by-year dwindling of sexual intimacy in his marriage and what seems self-evident about his neighbors and coworkers. (Phillips has no friends, no one in whom he can confide.) He finds it hard to believe that he and Mrs. Phillips—her first name is never given—are usually too tired for sex.

In Battersea Park, Phillips encounters a stranger who observes him watching some tennis players and recognizes him as the type who, having reached fifty, begins paying more attention to younger women, even girls. The stranger, Fortescue, understands such impulses because he publishes adult magazines. He tries to share with his new friend his hard-earned insight into the opposite sex:

> Speaking as a pornographer, I can tell you that the important thing is never to try and work out what a woman is thinking. It only confuses you, and they change their minds so much anyway the main thing is just to steam ahead with your plan intact.

John Lanchester is the former deputy editor of The London Review of Books *and restaurant critic for* The London Observer. *His book* The Debt to Pleasure *was a finalist for the* Los Angeles Times Book Award, *winner of the* Whitbred Best First Novel Award, *and a* New York Times *Notable Book.*

Sex is such a mystery to Phillips because he has, like most men, Lanchester suggests, no understanding of women at all. He is thus a devotee of masturbation because actual women do not get in the way of his enjoyment. Phillips blunders into an adult film theater to witness something entitled *Jim MacTool and the Salmon of Wisdom*, during which he is constantly surprised by the unreality of what he is seeing. (Lanchester's pornographic parody is a comic highlight of the novel.) Finding himself excited despite himself, Phillips flees the theater in embarrassment.

Phillips's second obsession is appropriate given his work and his tendency to lose himself in accounting. On his day out in London, whenever he begins feeling oppressed by the reality of his insecure position in society, Phillips retreats into numbers. He begins counting the number of people he sees picking their noses so that he can become lost in contemplating "how much nose-picking goes on in normal circumstances." Thinking about jumping off a bridge, he calculates how fast his body would be traveling upon impact. He figures that he has spent 16.375 percent of his waking life doing nothing, realizing this number will rise given his redundant status: "The thought of this is an immense strain. It must be why so many men die after their retirement."

Reflecting on how relatively uneventful his life has been, Phillips decides that 33.6 of his fellow bus travelers have never been on the Thames, seen a dead body, or engaged in anal intercourse. Thanks to his late father and a former girlfriend, he "is in the relatively suave and experienced subset who have only not been on the Thames. He has lived." Such observations are typical of Lanchester's low-key irony.

Phillips combines his two main concerns by creating statistical analyses of sexual matters. Contemplating the general lack of sexual activity in his milieu, he derives "an average daily probability of 96.7 percent against having sex." Thinking about how many tabloid newspapers publish photographs of nude women, he adds to the total those who appear in adult magazines and concludes that 16,744 of his fellow female citizens thus expose themselves annually: "That's a whole small townful of naked British women among us disguised as normal people." Anything for which he can find a statistical equivalent can be understood. The staleness of his marriage does not fall under this numerical umbrella. Neither does what he will do with the rest of his life.

Sex and numbers offer escapes from the daily worries and guilt that wear Phillips down. He feels guilty over fantasizing about women other than his wife, about not being someone his sons can admire. He worries about the effects of aging, especially being overweight, and the inevitability of death. He prefers to read autobiographies and memoirs "on the grounds that there is something comforting about them, perhaps to do with the fact that the hero never dies at the end." Phillips finds himself overwhelmed by "sheer accumulated livedness, the sense that nothing again would ever be new or surprising, that vital reserves of energy and luck had been critically and irreversibly depleted."

To live without sex or love or obligations would be ideal—but impossible. Phillips realizes that one of his virtues has been doing what he is told. Redundant, he must decide about things for himself and does not know how to begin. Not that he is incapable of action. Many of his recent sexual fantasies have centered on television personality Clarissa Colingford. Seeing her enter a branch of his bank, he follows, only to find himself in the midst of a robbery. Tired of lying on the floor while waiting for the robbers to finish their tasks, Phillips rises and proclaims, like Herman Melville's Bartleby, "I'm not doing that anymore." Standing up for himself in the face of armed criminals makes him feel weightless, as if he could float free of the planet. Just as a thug aims his shotgun at Phillips's head, the police arrive. Phillips finds his modest, Mittyesque heroism tempered somewhat, however, by having to explain why he is in the bank in the middle of the day.

Many reviewers of *Mr. Phillips* have pointed out the similarity to James Joyce's *Ulysses* (1922). Both novels center on one day in the life of a disillusioned, sex-obsessed, middle-aged man, but Phillips, a rather mundane everyman, is considerably less universal and compelling than Leopold Bloom. Joyce's hero is exploring life; Lanchester's is just passing through. While Phillips has some similarities to the Thurber and Melville characters mentioned previously, he more closely resembles the protagonist of John Cheever's "The Swimmer," about another middle-aged suburban man whose once secure life has fallen apart. However, Victor Phillips has an even closer literary progenitor. He resembles Gregor Samsa in Franz Kafka's *Die Verwandlung* (1915; *The Metamorphosis*, 1936) because he has suddenly awakened into a changed world that views him entirely differently from how it did before. Lanchester makes this comparison overt by having a minor character observe about reincarnation, "Finally you end up as a cockroach." This metaphor perfectly captures Phillips's transformation into a highly vulnerable creature.

It would be stretching matters to claim that Lanchester is using Phillips to say something about the state of contemporary England, where redundancy has become a way of life. While Lanchester includes a passage about the pomposity and ineffectuality of government, he does not seem to be interested in social or political commentary. His approach to fiction here is understated, almost genteel, more like Penelope Fitzgerald than such contemporaries as Martin Amis or Ian McEwen, who delineate their culture's darker sides.

Lanchester seems much more interested in his hero's digressions for their own sake than in any thematic concerns beyond his hero's using his banal existence as a weapon against the complexities of life. *Mr. Phillips* is one of those writerly works admired by literary critics and its creator's fellow writers for its economic style and its acerbic wit, but it may be too minimal, having no lasting impact beyond the acknowledgment that it is well written. Lanchester, to his credit, does not attempt to replicate the success of *The Debt to Pleasure*, but he might be faulted for not aiming a bit higher. Even though the protagonist is a rather static character, the reader is kept interested by Phillips's often insightful observations about a wide variety of subjects and by a wish to see how his melancholy saga ends. The conclusion can be seen as the novel in miniature: clever in one sense, insufficient in another. If Lanchester's first novel is a tour de force, his second is merely a tour.

Michael Adams

Sources for Further Study

Booklist 96 (February 15, 2000): 1052.
The Economist 355 (June 17, 2000): 14.
Library Journal 125 (March 15, 2000): 127.
Los Angeles Times Book Review, April 9, 2000, p. 7.
New Statesman 129 (January 31, 2000): 56.
The New York Review of Books 47 (June 29, 2000): 18.
The New York Times, April 12, 2000, p. E8.
Publishers Weekly 247 (January 31, 2000): 77.
The Times Literary Supplement, January 21, 2000, p. 21.
USA Today, April 13, 2000, p. D4.
The Washington Post Book World, April 9, 2000, p. 15.

MUSIC AND SILENCE

Author: Rose Tremain (1943-   )
First published: 1999, in Great Britain
Publisher: Farrar, Straus and Giroux (New York). 485
  pp. $25.00
Type of work: Novel
Time: 1629
Locale: Denmark

∽

Tremain's eighth novel is a multilayered historical narrative that interconnects the lives of out-of-the-ordinary characters during the reign of King Christian IV of Denmark

∽

Principal characters:

> KING CHRISTIAN IV OF DENMARK, melancholy ruler deeply concerned over the financial welfare of his nation and his wife's adultery
> KIRSTEN MUNK, royal consort of King Christian, who despises her fawning husband and plots against him
> PETER CLAIRE, King Christian's new British lutenist whose musical ability, good looks, and gentle demeanor prompt his role as the king's angel
> EMILIA TILSEN, lady-in-waiting to Kirsten
> JOHANN TILSEN, Emilia's father
> MAGDALENA, Johann's maidservant who sexually preys upon him and his sons after his wife's death
> QUEEN SOFIE, King Christian's unsupportive mother
> ELLEN MARSVEN, Kirsten's mother, who exploits her servant to keep her position in the king's court
> VIBEKE KRUSE, Ellen's servant, who falls in love with the king

In Rose Tremain's hypnotic portrayal of seventeenth century Denmark, the royal orchestra is obliged to perform in a freezing wine cellar. In 1629, as his political and personal life move inextricably toward disaster, the corpulent King Christian IV, with "a face like a loaf" and "who compulsively weighs the same pieces of silver over and over," employs music to bring order to his tumultuous court, financially in ruin after the Thirty Years' War. In his attempt to gain financial footing, King Christian, contemporaneous with Elizabeth I and James I and a relative of Charles I of England, jumps from one flawed scheme to another: a silver mine, a whale fleet, and even a bargain to pawn Iceland. Music soothes his soul and musical perfection becomes his obsession. In this effort, his multinational musicians play in a cold dark cellar directly underneath his cozy *vinterstue*, where he takes his meals, for the inimitable effect with which the sound rises into the music room through specially designed ducts. The

∼

*Rose Tremain is the author of eight
novels. Her previous work has been
short-listed for the Booker Prize
and has won the Prix Femina
Etranger and the Sunday Express
Book of the Year Award.*

∼

king's mad obsession with his much younger wife, Kirsten, continues unabated despite her flagrant adulterous affairs. Indeed, he will overlook her behavior even after she becomes pregnant with her lover's child, if only she will once again give herself to him. The king also finds himself at odds with his own mother, Queen Sofie, who hoards gold in her wine casks in Elsinore behind her son's back instead of bailing him out financially. In addition, King Christian finds himself obsessively tormented by memories of boyhood and his sudden ascension to the throne and, in particular, the memory of his Frederiksborg boyhood friend Bror Brorson. Full of rage, and in fear for his life, the king finds himself in dire need of a friendly companion.

Meanwhile, the defiant, self-indulgent royal consort, Kirsten, who detests music, experiences strikingly similar manic emotions. In her "private papers," she records her sexual exploits with Count Otto Ludwig of Satin in deviant detail. Sadomasochistic sexual behavior colors this lustful, all-consuming relationship, and Kirsten weaves "Beautiful Plans" to rid herself of her husband and dominate her lover. In addition, she plots to seduce a pair of teenage African slave boys presented to her as a gift. A cold, self-centered woman, she completely disregards her children. A strong believer in "absence of luxury" for anyone but herself, she keeps her ladies-in-waiting in icy, dark rooms. At odds with her husband, and not sure of Count Otto's intentions, she, like the King, requires a confidant.

Within a short time of each other, two personages arrive at this wildly dysfunctional Danish court: Peter Claire, the sublimely handsome blue-eyed British lutenist in the king's underground orchestra, and the unassuming, gentle Emilia Tilsen, the newest lady-in-waiting to Kirsten.

As the newest member of the royal orchestra, Peter finds his way to the Danish court after a disappointing love affair with the Countess Francesca O'Fingal of Cloyne, Ireland. Employed by the countess to aid her deeply distressed husband in his obsession to recover an imagined heavenly piece of music, Peter finds himself deeply in love. At first, the lovers remain chaste, but eventually come to express their love physically. In light of the circumstances, Peter and the countess part. Peter also leaves behind his British family. His father, the Reverend James Wittaker Claire, dreadfully misses his son and wants once more to look upon his face to gladden his heart before he dies. He writes to his son with a job offer as choirmaster. Also, Peter's sister Charlotte, who seems almost preternaturally attached to her brother, yearns for his return for her wedding to Sir George Middleton, an English squire.

Although initially appalled by his "imprisonment" in the dark, icy wine cellar, Peter adjusts in the company of his fellow musicians who fight against numb fingers by imagining their musical efforts as rehearsals for an ultimate grand performance in magnificent surroundings. Before long, the king senses something special in Peter's musical ability to play the lute and summons him to play privately for his entertainment and comfort during the long, dark, Scandinavian winter evenings. After Peter manages to intelligently answer the king's inquiries, the king comes to trust his English lutenist, and persuades him to never leave and to watch over him while he sleeps. Peter continues in his guardian angel role but finds life very lonely. His mind wanders at times to his Irish countess but only until the time he sees the royal consort's newest lady-in-waiting picking flowers in the Rosenberg Castle's royal gardens.

Like Peter, Emilia seeks out the Danish court to escape mental turmoil. However, it is hardly a failed romance that propels her. Emilia takes on a position as lady-in-waiting to the king's royal consort after her father, Johann Tilsen, remarries a servant woman shortly upon the death of Karen, her much-beloved mother. Actually, by the time Emilia arrives at her new post, she has become entirely disenchanted with the idea of marriage after observing her father in the sexual act with the family's former serving woman. Shortly after the death of his children's mother in childbirth with his youngest son Marcus, Johann develops a sexual obsession for Magdalena (appropriately named), who sees her mistress's death as a financial opportunity. She caters to his every sexual fantasy and soon has him and his older sons enthralled. After her father's marriage, predictably, the two women do not see eye to eye and, despite serious misgivings about leaving her young brother, Emilia escapes to the Danish court. In time, Magdalena casts her rapacious eye upon her husband's teenage sons, and the family continues to decay. The four-year-old boy Marcus remains the only one impervious to Magdalena's ploys but suffers severe physical and mental abuse under her hand. Shared loneliness is the bond that unites Emilia and Kirsten, her new mistress. Emilia cares gently for Kirsten in the manner she did her late mother, and Kirsten takes Emilia completely into her confidences and reacts jealously when her new lady-in-waiting considers the advances of the king's lutenist. At first, the inexperienced Emilia cannot imagine what Peter sees in her and heeds Kirsten's warnings that he merely wants to seduce her, but in time she comes to trust his love. The couple seeks and finds solace in each other and considers a happy future together; however, they find it impossible to nurture their love within the deceitful Danish court.

Because of their inferior social positions, Peter and Emilia find themselves powerless against the whims and wiles of their betters. After her continual rejection of his sexual advances, King Christian eventually spurns his consort, Kirsten, and orders her to return home to her mother. Her lover, Count Otto, is dismissed from the country. While Kirsten plans to bargain court documents to King Christian's enemies for the return of her lover to Denmark, her scheming mother similarly plots to regain her own influential position in the court. She carefully grooms her servant, Vibeke Kruse, to please the king. Vibeke must diet to fit into richly embroidered gowns, learn proper speech, and even wear painful false teeth. What Ellen Marsvin, the king's mother-in-law, fails to take into account, however, is the fact that Vibeke and the king could actually fall in love. In this common woman, King Christian finally finds the female kindness and acceptance he craved but never received from his aristocratic mother and wife. Ultimately, he divorces Kirsten, marries Vibeke, overcomes his depression, and regains control of his kingdom.

After Kirsten's fall from grace and subsequent dismissal, she insists that Emilia accompany her to Boller, her mother's home in Jutland. Since her father's lands border those of Kirsten's mother, Emilia unhappily finds herself back where she started, but the opportunity presents itself whereby she can rescue her younger brother Marcus. Kirsten intercepts Peter's letters to Emilia and writes to him threatening that if he does not provide her with the king's private court documents, he will never see Emilia again. In time, Kirsten's sexual obsessions get the better of her. After Kirsten makes sexual advances toward her, Emilia flees to her father's house in horror. Shortly after, Emilia's father comes to his senses, and Magdalena, pregnant by either her husband or his son, dies a violent death. The family works toward unification, with Johann planning to marry off his daughter to a local minister. The despairing Emilia contemplates suicide just before the happy arrival of Peter. It seems that King Christian, in dire need of funds, has sold his musical services to the British king.

A decade after the appearance of *Restoration* (1989), with its splendid evocation of the seventeenth century British court of Charles II, Tremain returns to this era, this time to the Danish court of King Christian IV. *Music and Silence* is a luminously inventive, intricately composed historical novel, replete with rich historical and imagined characters, intrigue, passion, and betrayals. Tremain's fertile imagination this time concerns itself with power (class power, male/female power, intergenerational power), and consuming obsessions revolving around sex, money, and music. Unlike many historical novelists who treat servants as part of the furniture, Tremain skillfully imbues them with all the distinctiveness of their betters. Magdalena gains social power by sexually corrupting the Tilsen family. In opposition, Vibeke moves up the social ladder to the first lady's position through love and devotion. In a patriarchal society, females vie for power throughout. The disenfranchised but shrewd dowager-queen Sofie, Christian's mother, who, unlike some widows, neither takes lovers nor surrenders herself to God, obsessively hides gold instead, wherein lies her only power. Kirsten, Christian's wife, resents being called the diminutive "mousie" and feels she has no power of her own except what she can exercise through her body. She obsessively utilizes sexual domination in her effort to gain power. In addition, Kirsten's mother Ellen takes on the role of pimp in her attempt to regain her foothold in the palace after her daughter is expelled. Interestingly, when one considers the powerlessness of women, their deceitful, obsessive methodology becomes somewhat more benign. Even the sexually voracious, evil stepmother Magdalena becomes an object of sympathy when Tremain vividly paints her background of ongoing childhood sexual abuse. Similarly, readers cheer on Sofie, who, set aside alone in a dark castle after her days in the sun, hides her money from her ineffective son.

Within a fairy-tale atmosphere complete with castles, kings, lonely princes, evil stepmothers, and Cinderella transformations, the author ultimately finds harmony in opposition by intricately balancing the high notes of human loyalty and love with the low notes of human deceit and betrayal. Evil stepmothers such as Magdalena are counterbalanced by Emilia's devoted mother, Karen. Ineffective fathers such as Johann, who fall under the sway of sexual obsession, are neutralized by Peter's father, who loves unconditionally. In addition, the dysfunctional, obsessive marriage of King Christian and Kirsten is counterbalanced by the inspirational relationship of Peter's sister, Charlotte, and her squire, George, and by the absolute and transcendent love of Peter and Emilia. However, *Music and Silence* is not perfect. Too many characters and side plots at times keep the plot from coalescing.

M. Casey Diana

Sources for Further Study

Booklist 96 (April 1, 2000): 1441.
New York Review of Books 47 (June 29, 2000): 53.
The New Yorker 76 (June 5, 2000): 92.
Publishers Weekly 247 (February 28, 2000): 60.

MY WAR GONE BY, I MISS IT SO

Author: Anthony Loyd (1967-   )
Publisher: Atlantic Monthly Press (New York). 321 pp.
  $25.00
Type of work: Memoirs
Time: 1993-1996
Locale: Bosnia, Chechnya, and London

∾

*A powerful account of the author's experiences as a war
correspondent covering the wars in Bosnia and Chechnya*

∾

Anthony Loyd's *My War Gone By, I Miss It So* is a searing account of the author's experiences as a war correspondent in Bosnia and Chechnya. He writes with a savage passion of conflicts that seemed far away and alien to most Europeans and Americans. Loyd reminds his readers that their governments, actively or passively, were deeply implicated in the way that these struggles played themselves out. He also brilliantly evokes the human drama of what he witnessed. Readers will not soon forget Loyd's descriptions of atrocities and carnage, cynicism and suffering, idealism and courage.

As such, Loyd's book is a compelling contribution to the growing body of war correspondents' memoirs, a distinguished genre of twentieth century literature. That distracted century offered writers ample opportunity to practice this branch of letters. In war after war reporters were confronted with the results of official and individual belligerence. World War I, the Spanish Civil War, World War II, Korea, Vietnam—all these conflicts, and others besides, bred their own distinctive literatures. Now, with Loyd, it is the time of the dirty little wars of the 1990's.

Newspaper correspondents first began sending home dispatches from a military front during the Crimean War of 1853-1856. Rapid technological change in the late nineteenth century revolutionized communications and helped create the mass media—newspapers and periodicals hungry for stories. During these years journalism began actively to interest itself in war. A press baron such as William Randolph Hearst could boast of fomenting the Spanish-American War, while reporters such as Richard Harding Davis crafted the enduring image of the dashing war correspondent. Thus, from the turn of the century, the war correspondent became a fixture of modern military life. These reporters might have varying degrees of access to the battlefield, and their reports might be subject to a range of censorship, but their presence somewhere in the area of military operations was no longer questioned. Indeed, over time, the great militaries of the world grew adept at using, and sometimes managing, the press. The hard and dangerous profession of war correspondent attracted many literary luminaries to its ranks. Among others, Winston Churchill, Stephen Crane, Ernest

Hemingway, George Orwell, and John Steinbeck found themselves drawn to covering contemporary struggles for the press. During great
wars, some correspondents become popular legends, such as Ernie Pyle during World War II.
Classic war reporting is the raw material of history. Exciting and often moving, it captures the
immediacy of men and women's lives at the ex-
tremities of human existence.

It is this latter dimension of the war correspondent's experience, the intense encounter
with death at its most abrupt and violent, that
fostered a genre within a genre. Some of the
most enduring writing about war by foreign
correspondents has intentionally gone beyond
straightforward narrative. In these cases, the
book instead becomes an exploration of the
evolving consciousness of the author. Here war
reportage becomes an existential journey, and
the correspondent becomes as much the subject
of the work as the war being covered. A classic
forerunner of this style of journalistic memoir

*Anthony Loyd served as a platoon
commander in the British army in
Northern Ireland and the Persian
Gulf. He now lives in Bosnia and
has covered conflicts in Chechnya,
Afghanistan, Sierra Leone, and
Kosovo as a special correspondent
for* The London Times.

was Vincent Sheean's *Personal History* (1935). This book recounted Sheean's adventures as a correspondent in a succession of capitals and wars in the 1920's and
early 1930's. In addition to providing insight into current events, the author described
the impact of these events upon his own life, leading to his gradual embrace of revolutionary politics (hence the title). Sheean was recording the stuff of history, but his perspective was determinedly individual, subordinating objective observation to the im-
peratives of his subjective spiritual progress. This made for engrossing reading, and
Sheean's book inspired a host of imitators as the coming of World War II provided
correspondents with the greatest moral drama of the century.

Anthony Loyd has written his own "personal history," and, just as Sheean captured
something essential about his day, Loyd's book casts a mordant light upon contemporary times. Sheean in the 1930's was caught up in a great clash of ideologies. Communism, fascism, and democracy were words of genuine substance then, connected as
they were to vigorous political experiments around the world. Idealism, strictly con-
strued, seemed natural in a poisoned international landscape, with the great powers
girding themselves for war. Loyd inhabits a far different world. Instead of a depres-
sion-wracked Europe, on the brink of a major cataclysm, he writes against the backdrop of the prosperity of the 1990's and a West largely untouched by conflict. If political commitment seemed a burning and obvious necessity to Sheean, Loyd wrestles
with the absence of ideological passion in his own life. Sheean wrote about events that
he believed were of profound significance to his country and readership. Loyd knows
that he is describing tragedies largely peripheral to the concerns of the people in his

homeland. At its heart, Loyd's book is an essay on the ways in which plenty and security have spiritually diminished the West.

Anger suffuses Loyd's book. In part, this anger is fed by the gulf between the suffering of the people whose lives he has recorded and the cool complacency of his compatriots in the West, who looked on uncomprehending and unconcerned. The wars in Bosnia, Chechnya, and elsewhere vaguely haunted the consciences of the Western peoples. They challenged the optimistic hopes born of 1989 and the collapse of communism. They made a mockery of the notion of a benign new world order. For too long, though, the West, acting under the aegis of the United Nations, did little to stop the slaughter in Bosnia and Herzegovina. The efforts of United Nations "peace-keepers" were risibly inadequate at best, and tragically so at worst, such as when a U.N. detachment looked on helplessly as Serb forces launched the bloody ethnic cleansing of the Muslim enclave of Srebrenica. Loyd reserves his deepest scorn for the Western diplomats who responded to mass killing with pious utterances and smug remonstrances, and who were willing to accept a wilderness in Bosnia and call it peace. Moreover, if the West did too little, too late in Bosnia, it did next to nothing at all in Chechnya, as the Russians attempted to crush Chechen aspirations with callous brutality.

However, Loyd also directs his anger against himself in this book. Though in time he came to espouse fiercely the cause of the Muslim Bosnians, Loyd did not initially travel to Bosnia out of sympathy and concern for their plight. He was answering the siren call of personal demons. In fact, Loyd was slumming, in search of the kicks only combat could provide. Loyd had grown up the scion of a family with a strong military tradition. From his earliest days, he had been conscious of the heroics of his great-grandfather in the trenches of the Great War and his grandfather who flew with the British Bomber Command in World War II. As a boy and beyond, Loyd wanted to experience war. Though he always chafed at authority in school, Loyd swallowed his doubts about military discipline and joined the British army. He served in Northern Ireland and the Gulf War. While he enjoyed military camaraderie, however, his thirst for battle went unsatisfied. The Gulf proved a disappointing anticlimax to his military career. During the great Allied advance into Kuwait, he spent his time collecting dispirited prisoners. Victory brought only personal crisis.

Loyd left the army and sought new employment. He took a course in photojournalism. When the Bosnian War broke out in 1992, opportunity seemed to beckon. By 1993, Loyd was in Sarajevo as a freelance journalist. He soon was seeing enough action to satisfy most men for life. Indeed, Loyd writes frankly of the overpowering fear that frequently possessed him in the field. However, he kept going back, and in the course of his book Loyd reveals some of the inner springs of his craving for the stimulus of war. The product of a broken marriage, and rejected by his father, Loyd grew up a prodigal who could never return home. Intermittently he entertained the thought of suicide, and over time he became increasingly dependent on drugs. Home in London after tours in Bosnia or Chechnya, he would party with hedonistic West End friends, experimenting with a variety of substances until he ended up addicted to heroin. Smack became his refuge when away from combat zones, providing for him the same sort of bleak existential clarity about the hopelessness and meaninglessness of life as his war experiences. Increasingly caught up in the impetus of his own death wish, Loyd came to see himself as a messenger bringing journalistic doses of reality to comfortable Westerners trapped like himself in a corrupt pleasure dome sustained by empty materialism and spiritual aridity. A sort of nihilistic knight, Loyd recognized his kinship with the people he loathed, both the coddled bohemians of London and the murderers he shared drinks and cigarettes with in Bosnia. His rage at himself and the world is etched on every page of his book.

Loyd's anger against the West for its self-satisfied indifference to Bosnian and Chechen misery did not blind him to the tribal hatreds that drove these wars. His book catalogs many of the atrocities that characterized the struggles in the Balkans and the Caucasus. He describes the capture of a Croat soldier, with the ear of a young woman carefully wrapped up in his pouch. He writes of Muslim prisoners wired to claymore mines and forced to run toward their friends, only to be exploded by remote control. Loyd was in the first party of Western reporters to enter the little hamlet of Stupni Do, where all the Muslim inhabitants—men, women, and children—had been massacred. Loyd vividly evokes the terrifying aura of a place where so many innocent people had been suddenly, pitilessly butchered. What was left of the houses still burned. Inside them, the bodies of their inhabitants still sputtered and sizzled. The evil of what had been done there still hung heavy over the village's remains, as real a presence as the more tangible contributions to the oppressive atmosphere. Loyd followed a colleague into a stone shed, the sole structure not consumed by the flames. Inside, still clutching each other in death, were the bodies of three women. They had been shot and slashed to death, but their faces were untouched. Still frozen on their faces were their last expressions of terror. This flesh-and-blood memorial to contemporary barbarism was the most bloodcurdling sight Loyd experienced in Bosnia. It opened a window to dizzying vistas of human depravity and savagery, only pallidly captured by philosophers such as Thomas Hobbes and horror writers such as Clive Barker. The lone survivor of the village was a cow with a plastic bucket pulled over its head so that it could neither see nor eat. As the day's light failed, all that Loyd and his colleagues could do for the ghosts of the village was clumsily struggle to pull and cut the bucket from the cow's head, so that it, at least, might live.

Anthony Loyd's *My War Gone By, I Miss It So* demonstrates that even in the age of instant televised images, more traditional dispatches from the front lines of war retain their power. Loyd's book is worthy of comparison with the best journalistic memoirs of the century. Loyd's reporting makes it impossible for Westerners simply to dismiss the "little" wars of the 1990's as inevitable eruptions in backward regions. Uncompromising in its honesty, his book compels one to examine more closely the market-driven society that was triumphantly celebrated in the decade following 1989. The greatest strength of Loyd's book is that it demands that readers think more seriously about life and death, about what is important and what is not.

Daniel P. Murphy

Sources for Further Study

Booklist 96 (November 1, 1999): 506.
The Christian Science Monitor, January 27, 2000, p. 18.
Library Journal 124 (October 1, 1999): 114
The New York Times Book Review 105 (March 26, 2000): 34.
Publishers Weekly 246 (November 8, 1999): 52.
The Village Voice 45 (April 11, 2000): 93.
The Wall Street Journal, January 21, 2000, p. W8

THE MYSTERIES WITHIN
A Surgeon Reflects on Medical Myths

Author: Sherwin B. Nuland (1930-   )
Publisher: Simon & Schuster (New York). 286 pp.
  $24.00
Type of work: Medicine
Time: Ancient Greece to the present

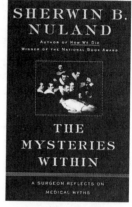

＜

Nuland discusses both contemporary and historical in-
formation and misinformation about major body organs,
providing a history of the growth of medical knowledge

＜

    Dr. Sherwin B. Nuland, a clinical professor of surgery at the Yale School of Medicine, is the author of several books designed to make current medical information accessible to a general readership. Among them are *The Wisdom of the Body* (1997) and *How We Die* (1994), the latter a national best seller that has been translated into sixteen languages. *The Mysteries Within* considers specifically five of the major organs of the central part of the body: stomach, liver, spleen, heart, and uterus. Nuland discusses the current state of information about these organs in the historical context of the development of that information in the Western world over the past 2,500 years. As he looks at the myths and misunderstandings surrounding these organs in the past, he effectively presents a history of Western medicine.

    Nuland sometimes presents cases from his own experience, starting with an operation on a baby's stomach that he performed forty years earlier at the beginning of his career. The baby boy was six weeks old and had been born prematurely. Now he had a badly distended stomach with a large, firm mass just below the rib cage. This bezoar, a clump of foreign material in the stomach that cannot be passed along to the intestines, did not respond to other treatment and needed surgical intervention. By the end of the chapter the reader learns that the operation successfully removed a lump of wax from the baby's stomach. The baby's young and inexperienced mother had regularly been heating waxed cardboard cartons of milk in a pan of hot water, then pouring the milk into the baby's bottle. Tiny bits of wax lining the inside of the container were being melted and passed directly into the milk. Once the collection of wax in the infant's little stomach started blocking passage out of the stomach, buildup became rapid. Apparently the mother was remembering her own mother saying she had heated milk that way, but in her mother's time milk was packaged in glass bottles.

    Nuland uses this example and others to illustrate the varying levels of knowledge in a culture at any one time and to discuss prevailing attitudes throughout written history. In the Middle Ages, for example, a bezoar, an unexpected object found in an animal's stomach, was thought to have magical powers, especially against poisons.

Sherwin B. Nuland, M.D., has taught at the Yale School of Medicine since 1962. He is the author of several books, including The Wisdom of the Body *(published in paperback as* How We Live*) and* How We Die, *which won the National Book Award and was a finalist for the Pulitzer Prize and the National Book Critics Circle Award.*

Nuland notes that this notion lives on in the form of some people's belief in amulets and lucky stones and even rabbits' feet.

Nuland's examples from his own practice serve also as a starting point for thinking about entire systems of belief that have shaped attitudes toward medicine. One of the main points he makes throughout the work is that societies have traditionally started with some inclusive system that they claim explains everything, including the built-in notion that whatever is not actually known is part of the system too, attributed to God or the gods or the supernatural in general. Thus, any particular observation about the way the body works must be made to fit into the overall belief system or religion. In fact, since the premise is that there is some overall truth or known system, there is really no point in looking further.

The medical thinkers of ancient Greece, for example, considered sickness the result of disequilibrium in the balance of the "four humors"— blood, yellow bile, black bile, and phlegm. Hippocrates, often called "the father of medicine," spread this theory. Aristotle, who was a young man when Hippocrates died in approximately 370 B.C.E., is the first known person to have used animal dissection to study the body, but that analytical practice did not spread because it was assumed the fluids theory of the four humors explained everything anyway.

The belief in the four humors, inaccurate as it was, continued well into the Renaissance, in effect limiting inquiry into other possibilities. As Nuland says, "The loud, clear voice with which authority so often proclaims itself has ever been a danger to the pursuit of truth." This was particularly the case throughout the centuries in which religion dominated all attitudes toward life in Western Europe. Early scientists designed their theories to conform to the divine plan as taught by the Church. This practice thus limited their objectivity and even the questions they thought needed to be asked. While it is easy to laugh at some of the absurd notions from the past, it is amazing that the early pioneers in medicine achieved so much given the constraints of their time and the effort to make their discoveries fit pervasive religious beliefs. It should be remembered too that not until relatively recently did physicians and scientists have the benefit of even such now-basic tools as the stethoscope (invented in 1816) or the microscope (invented in the 1600's but of very different quality from current microscopes).

Nuland repeatedly makes the point that interpretations of nature and observed phenomena are inevitably determined by the zeitgeist, the spirit of the time. This applies also to the dominant current acceptance of science. Even science is limited in terms of "objectivity," not only by personal limitations, but also by political, theological, philosophical, and social influences. An example of such a limitation can be seen by considering what kinds of medical research contemporary society chooses to fund, and why. The great switch from the past, however, is that science has at its core the idea of critical inquiry separated from preconceived notions. Observations of natural phenomena need not be fit into some all-inclusive system. Modern science is willing to admit ignorance and therefore to pursue answers. Theoretically, the scientist observes and researches to learn what something is, how it works, quite apart from how it may or may not fit in with some other bit of information or overall system; the connections come later, through further scientific investigation. Once this basic principle of critical inquiry was accepted, advances in knowledge about the body and all natural phenomena were and continue to be rapid.

What Nuland does about the continued acceptance of nonscientific systems such as religion or holistic medicine is precisely to separate them from scientific evidence. Science and religion, he says, explain two separate realms of human experience. The faithful need no justification for their faith; it is enough that they believe. He is particularly annoyed, however, with the tradition of calling on the supernatural as the basis for information still unexplained by science, or the idea that there are things humans should not know. Nuland comments: "Remaining gaps in current knowledge are not evidence for the existence of God. . . . God should not be invoked in place of knowledge not yet discovered."

In addition to Nuland's attitudes about the importance of science, his history of medicine and citation of famous physicians and innovators of the past, and his anecdotes about his own experience as a surgeon, there is other interesting information in *The Mysteries Within*. There are little details about the body that emerge as Nuland discusses the internal organs. To cite two examples: "The life of each of our seventy-five trillion cells depends on the uninterrupted beat of the heart"; most bezoars or concretions found in human stomachs are "composed of hair that a troubled young person has pulled from his own head and then ingested."

The discussions of the organs themselves are also interesting, though perhaps less technical and informative about the actual function of the organ than one might expect. Nuland's commentaries about the organs often serve as reminders of things most readers have forgotten or refer to subjects they have never studied. Take, for example, the discussion of that large organ, the liver. Fortunately, there is a clear line drawing to illustrate the location and relative sizes of the organs of the abdomen that shows the liver at the top, just under the diaphragm, and another drawing of the liver itself. The larger section of the liver is on the right side of the body, but a smaller lobe, separated from it by the falciform ligament, extends to the left. The liver is a difficult organ for a surgeon to work with because its spongy consistency makes it slippery to stitch, and it holds stitches poorly. The liver is the only organ, really the only part of the body, capable of regenerating a lost part of itself. This ability of the liver to regrow seems to have been known in ancient times, for legends abound. Probably the best known is the Greek myth of Prometheus. Prometheus, whose name means "forethought," is credited with being the inventor of medicine, astronomy, architecture, and civilization itself, along with stealing fire from the gods for humans to use. In punishment for the latter offense, the god Zeus chained Prometheus to a huge rock and had a ravenous vulture peck out his liver. The liver kept regenerating, which in effect kept Prometheus alive for more torture until, finally, he was rescued by Hercules.

In addition to the myths and legends of the past, the evolution of language itself often provides a key to the early history of Western culture. "Liver" derives from the Indo-European root *leip*, associated with life, based on the ancient assumption that the liver was the seat of life because, it was thought, it was the liver that manufactured blood. The Middle English word was *lifer*, and in German it is *die Leber*, from *leben*, the verb meaning "to live." With all this background, Nuland notes, it seems hardly a coincidence that the mythological Prometheus who gave life and fire to humankind should be punished by having his liver chewed. The notion that the liver is the seat of life and perhaps the center of the soul is at least as old as the Mesopotamian culture of twenty centuries B.C.E. In that culture, an animal—usually a sheep—was slaughtered and its liver ritually examined to see what it might portend for a sick patient. The priest's divination led to a prediction about the person's health and was also used to predict a wide range of future events. This practice of hepatoscopy, divination by examination of the hepatic (liver) surface, is mentioned in the Book of Ezekiel (21:21) and is well documented in the archaeological evidence of later cultures such as the Etruscans. All this was based on the assumption that the liver was the prime organ of life because it was thought to be the producer of blood.

The Mysteries Within successfully continues the discussion of aspects of medicine and medical practice that Nuland has presented in previous works. There is a helpful index for easy reference to his topics. On a stylistic note, it is odd that the author insists on using "man," "he," and "his" in the generic sense to refer to both men and women. That he is aware of this, providing a comment on his usage as a footnote on the first page of the introduction, only makes it more untenable. It seems odder still since the final two chapters of the book are "The Uterus" and "Reproduction." At least Dr. Nuland does not refer to the possessor of a uterus as "he," though in fact he manages to discuss the uterus with scarcely the use of the word "she," either.

Lois A. Marchino

Sources for Further Study

Booklist 96 (December 15, 1999): 738.
Discover 21 (March, 2000): 110.
Library Journal 125 (January, 2000): 146.
The New York Times Book Review 105 (February 13, 2000): 11.
Publishers Weekly 246 (December 13, 1999): 71.
The Wall Street Journal, February 14, 2000, p. A40.
The Washington Post Book World, February 13, 2000, p. 3.

THE NATURE OF ECONOMIES

Author: Jane Jacobs (1916-   )
Publisher: The Modern Library (New York). 194 pp.
$21.95
Type of work: Economics and philosophy
Time: 1990's
Locale: Worldwide

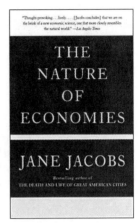

∼

A series of conversations among five New York friends reveals that human economies work much like the systems of nature and that human actions fit into the patterns of nature, rather than being separate from the natural world

∼

Over four decades, Jane Jacobs produced several book-length analytical essays examining human systems, particularly cities, and their operation. *The Nature of Economies* continues in this tradition, offering comparisons of human economies to the systems of the natural world.

The Nature of Economies is, in a sense, a continuation and extension of Jacobs's *Systems of Survival* (1993), which focused on the moralities of commerce and politics. Jacobs brings back several characters from the earlier book and employs a similar format—that of narrating and transcribing a series of conversations among friends in New York. Armbruster, a retired publisher, organizes meetings among the friends. He is joined by his niece, Hortense, an environmental lawyer; Kate, a science writer and former research scientist specializing in bioneurology; and Hiram Murray IV, a new character, an ecologist Hortense is dating. Later conversations bring in another new character, Hiram's father, an economist. Missing from the circle is Ben, Hortense's former boyfriend, who used to gloat over industrial disasters as evidence backing up his opinion that anything industrial or technological is inherently bad. His voice would have added more depth to the conversations; only rarely are objections raised to the points being made even when such objections are valid.

Jacobs herself states in the foreword that she uses didactic dialogue, a better description than "Platonic dialogue," which appears on the flyleaf. Most of the conversations consist primarily of monologues by Hiram expounding on his theories. Hiram is a fund raiser and assists in finding grants for people to develop products and production methods based on nature—activities that he refers to as "biomimicry." This work has led him to contemplate how human systems fit into what traditionally has been called the "natural" world. Throughout, he stresses that humans are a part of nature and that principles that apply to "nature" should apply equally well to human activities.

Armbruster is at first skeptical of Hiram's program of biomimicry, and Hortense ac-

Jane Jacobs first came to notice with speeches and articles that eventually became The Death and Life of American Cities. *She is also the author of* The Economy of Cities, Cities and the Wealth of Nations, *and* Systems of Survival. *She lives in Toronto, where she is a noted activist for mixed-use urban planning.*

cuses him of sounding like her former boyfriend, Ben. When Armbruster states that biomimicry seems to be an exploitation of nature, Hiram responds that biomimicry is a form of development and states his belief in connections between economies and ecosystems. He also announces his personal project of learning economics through a study of nature (he had studied economics in college but switched to environmental science). This idea interests Armbruster, who wants to find out what Hiram has learned and asks permission to tape-record later conversations.

The initial conversation introduces four of the five characters and sets the groundwork for later discussion. Hiram points out that the word "ecology" was coined to refer to the economy of nature. He believes that human economies, like nature, are ruled by processes and principles that people did not invent and that they cannot transcend. Furthermore, knowledge of these principles can promote development and make development more harmonious with nature. Kate notes that Hiram's theoretical framework implies that humans are a part of nature, an implication with which she agrees.

At the beginning of the first tape-recorded conversation, Armbruster admits that he does not know where to begin in questioning Hiram and requests that Hiram start his discussion wherever appropriate. This request sets the tone for the remainder of the book: Throughout, Hiram explains his theories, with the others listening and, occasionally, elaborating with examples from their own experience.

Chapter 2 is Hiram's explanation of development, which he defines as significant qualitative change—that is, for development to occur, a system must change rather than simply grow. This differs from some economic definitions that measure development as an increase in economic capacity gauged by gross national product or income per capita. Hiram believes that all development is similar, consisting of differentiation resulting from generality; the differentiations then become new generalities.

Invention is an important aspect of development but is not synonymous with it. Some inventions are ahead of their time; they cannot be exploited fully because other conditions do not adequately support them. Kate mentions that the engineering of the *Titanic*, for example, was advanced for its time but that the best steel then available could not withstand the stresses created by the engineering design. Knowledge is thus part of the development process, and knowledge in one area often will have effects that reach many other areas. In addition, "lost" knowledge—that associated with obsolete techniques and technologies—may later resurface as important in new contexts. This idea ties into the importance of retaining biodiversity—certain species may serve purposes not yet realized.

Hiram notes that many governmental attempts to promote economic development have been based on what he calls the "Thing Theory of Economic Development," which states that development results from possession of such things as factories, schools, and farming machinery. Such programs usually fail, he says, because possession of any of these "things" is meaningless unless people have the knowledge of how to use them and unless people themselves are allowed to and are able to provide input into what they do and how they do it. Thus, caste systems or economic systems involving serfdom, slavery, or male domination are hindered in development: The people doing the actual work of the system are not given an opportunity to express how they could do their jobs better or more easily, and decision makers often have neither a good idea of how work is done nor any incentive to have that work done more efficiently.

Chapter 3 introduces Hiram Murray III, who calls himself Murray to avoid confusion with his son. Murray shares his insight that an explanation of growth requires a look at energy infusion and discharge, along with an examination of how energy is used within a system. Systems, whether natural or economic, have varying degrees of sophistication. A desert, for example, is very simple compared to a forest, which converts the energy of sunlight and transmits it to various organisms, recycling it numerous times. Expansion depends on capturing and using energy. This, Hiram elaborates, is why government programs to create jobs often fail: They do not capture any economic energy and offer only the illusion of productivity. Idleness and need can coexist, and the solutions are not obvious.

One way to bring economic energy into a system is through export markets—an economy can produce goods to sell abroad. Murray states that he used to believe that exports drive growth through the "multiplier" effect that has been part of standard economic theory at least since the 1930's. He then realized that when an economy sends one of its products outside its borders, it loses the energy that went into that product; exports are thus discharged energy and cannot simultaneously be the energy that drives expansion. Imports are the energy entering the system, and exports are the result.

Armbruster suggests that the analogy of sunlight to economic energy breaks down because sunlight is free. Exports must be the driving force, he says, because exports are needed to buy imports. Hiram responds that the first inputs into an economic system are natural resources, which are free. Hiram and Murray then continue the argument that the most interesting processes of an economy are those that occur between the import and export stages, and Murray suggests that some measure of "import stretching" would be valuable as an indicator of economic development and dynamism, showing how many times economic inputs are "recycled" within the system before being sent back out as exports. He concludes that no matter how diverse or extensive their exports, rural economies are poor by their very nature because they lack complex systems for recycling economic energy.

Chapter 4 continues the same conversation and takes place after the participants have eaten dinner. Appropriately, the new topic is refueling. Armbruster continues to insist that exports are the fuel of an economy and provide the money needed to expand

and run it. Hiram points out that economies have also grown and developed by bringing ideas from the outside rather than importing physical goods, and that they sometimes self-refuel, creating new jobs and new markets from within. He describes how cities expand and discusses economies of location that can make an area prosper once it reaches a critical mass. Murray points out that economies of scale (large firms being able to produce at a lower cost than small firms) often are overridden by economies of location (costs are lower if customers or suppliers are nearer to the point of production). He mistakenly says that this concept is not taught in college; it is commonly presented in upper-level economics courses. This is the most glaring example of Jacobs's characters believing an idea to be novel when in fact it is well established in either economics or ecology. Uninformed readers will be led to believe that the characters (and perhaps the author) are much more clever and innovative than they really are.

The discussion of importing leads to Murray dismissing, as a failed experiment, attempts during the 1970's to encourage development through import substitution. Developing countries were urged to manufacture products rather than buy them from abroad, thus serving the dual ends of reducing spending on imports and of creating a manufacturing base that would provide jobs. The experiment failed, in Murray's opinion, because manufacturing facilities were located where jobs were needed, not where they made economic sense.

In chapter 5, it is the next day, and the group has reconvened to discuss issues of dynamic stability, or how an economy can continue to change without collapsing. Hiram describes change as consisting of bifurcations, positive or negative feedback loops, and emergency adaptations. He notes the contribution of Adam Smith, an eighteenth century Scottish philosopher often credited with being the father of modern economics, in seeing how prices act as regulators of production and sales. He sees prices as a very good feedback mechanism unless governments or other agencies interfere through taxes or subsidies. Murray suggests that economics accepted the principle of prices as regulating mechanisms but then tried to use it to explain too much, and that Smith led economics astray by asserting that specialization, rather than diversity, is the key to economic growth.

While Hiram summarizes his previous points, Murray falls asleep. Kate, the neurobiological scientist, takes the opportunity to discuss fitness for survival, noting that some animals have the ability to destroy their environment (by overhunting, for example) but somehow restrain themselves, thus avoiding disaster. To survive, she says, organisms must be successful at feeding, breeding, and maintaining their habitats. Humans have survived because they developed aesthetic appreciation of nature and have a fear of divine retribution for destroying nature; more recently, science has provided rational reasons to protect the environment. Armbruster mentions tendencies toward crime and exploitation; Hiram answers that intelligence and morality protect the human race.

In the penultimate chapter, Hiram expounds on an economy's ability to adapt to unpredictability. Society, like nature, develops unpredictably, so humans, like nature, must experiment with solutions and let them evolve. Prematurely promoting one solution over others—as was done, Hiram argues, with nuclear power—starves research into other avenues that might prove more fruitful.

When asked what economies are for, Hiram answers that the question is much like asking what nature is for. He says they exist simply to partake in a universal flow. Kate says the purpose of economies is to teach people responsibility toward the planet and the rest of nature. Armbruster suggests that economies fill material needs and develop cultures. This conclusion is striking in that after all their agreement on earlier issues, the group members come up with different answers to the same question.

In the closing chapter, Murray asks Armbruster to promise that Hiram's ideas get into print. In the epilogue, Hiram and Hortense marry. Armbruster looks younger and has stopped hanging out at his favorite unpopular coffee shop. This offers a subtle, sly answer to the question of what economies are for—they give people something to do.

The Nature of Economies will be of most value to those with a passing interest in ecology or economics. Serious students of either subject will find some interesting examples of principles at work but few or no new ideas. The book does serve the purpose of reminding readers that economic development takes place within the natural world and that repercussions of human actions should be considered in development plans.

A. J. Sobczak

Sources for Further Study

Booklist 96 (April 1, 2000): 1419.
The New Republic 222 (May 15, 2000): 34.
The New York Review of Books 47 (June 15, 2000): 4.
The New York Times Book Review 105 (March 12, 2000): 8.
Publishers Weekly 247 (March 6, 2000): 94.

NAZI TERROR
The Gestapo, Jews, and Ordinary Germans

Author: Eric A. Johnson (1948-   )
Publisher: Basic Books (New York). 636 pp. $35.00
Type of work: History
Time: 1933-1945
Locale: Germany

~

A well-researched case study of how German civilians cooperated with the Gestapo in three German cities to make possible the murder of Jews in concentration camps

~

Principal personages:
THE REVEREND DIETRICH BONHOEFFER, victim of Nazi persecution
ALFRED EFFENBERG, Gestapo officer in Krefeld
LUDWIG JUNG, Krefeld Gestapo head
JOSEF MAHLER, victim of Nazi persecution
EMANUEL SCHAFER, Cologne Gestapo head
RICHARD SCHULENBERG, Gestapo officer in Krefeld
FATHER JOSEF SPIEKER, S.J., victim of Nazi persecution

Eric Johnson is a professor of history at Central Michigan University. He is a specialist in criminology and modern German history. His previous books on the Holocaust include *Urbanization and Crime: Germany 1871-1914* (1995) and *The Civilization of Crime: Violence in Town and Country Since the Middle Ages* (1996), coedited with Eric H. Monkkonen.

Many recent scholars have argued persuasively that ordinary Germans and not just Nazis and members of the Gestapo and the SS should be held responsible for the crimes against humanity committed during the Nazi reign of terror from 1933 to 1945. In his 1996 book, *Hitler's Willing Executioners: Ordinary Germans and the Holocaust* (1996), Daniel Goldhagen argued that the Holocaust would not have taken place without the full cooperation of the German public. Goldhagen's book provoked a lively controversy in Germany because he questioned the revisionist claims that most Germans did not know about the "final solution" until the liberation of the concentration camps in 1945 and would have opposed the Holocaust had they known of the enormity of the crimes committed by the Nazis against the Jews and all who opposed their policies. The title of Johnson's book on the Gestapo contains a clear reference to Goldhagen's analysis of the role of "ordinary Germans" in the implementation of the Nazis' program of exterminating the Jews.

Some German reviewers criticized Goldhagen's book, claiming that his accusations were too general. This argument can certainly not be made about Johnson's

book, which he based on rigorous research conducted on Gestapo and court archives in three
German cities. He selected a very large city (Cologne), a medium-sized city (Krefeld), and a
small city (Bergheim). In his introductory chapter, he persuasively justifies his choice of these
three cities. First of all, Gestapo and court records have been very well preserved in all three
cities, and they are accessible to scholars. Second, the diversity in size of these three cities can
serve as a model for the operation of the Nazi
reign of terror throughout Germany and other

∽

*Eric A. Johnson is a professor of
history at Central Michigan
University and a fellow of the
Netherlands Institute for Advanced
Study. His previous books include*
Urbanization and Crime: Germany
1871-1914 *and* The Civilization of
Crime: Violence in Town and
Country Since the Middle Ages.

∽

occupied countries. Finally, in the 1933 election, the number of votes for Adolf Hitler
by citizens of these cities was somewhat lower than the national average. Johnson argues that this fact is important because it suggests that the residents of Cologne,
Krefeld, and Bergheim were not at first rabid supporters of National Socialism.

Johnson's research is very impressive. He thoroughly went through all the relative
documents in the archives of these three cities, and he reveals a solid knowledge of
historical studies on the Gestapo and the Holocaust. He also supplemented his research by sending questionnaires to Jewish and non-Jewish people who had been at
least of adolescent age in Cologne, Krefeld, and Bergheim during the Nazis' reign of
terror.

In the years immediately after World War II, many people had the mistaken belief
that the Gestapo was an extremely large and efficient agency that did not need to rely
on informants or ordinary Germans to arrest Jews and others whom the Nazis viewed
as enemies. Approximately 170,000 people lived in Krefeld during the Nazi years,
and there were never more than fourteen Gestapo officers and two secretaries for this
entire town—that is, there was less than one Gestapo employee for ten thousand residents. Gestapo records in the Krefeld archives clearly reveal that many Jews and other
Nazi enemies had been arrested not as a result of investigations started by Gestapo officers and their paid spies but because of denunciations made by ordinary Germans
against their neighbors and coworkers. The motivation for such unsolicited collaboration with the Gestapo varied. Sometimes denunciations were made after a dispute
with a neighbor or the ending of a love affair and not for ideological reasons. Both
Jews and Gentiles were denounced by their neighbors, but Johnson demonstrates that
the Gestapo systematically treated Jews much more harshly than non-Jews for violation of Nazi laws.

Johnson explains very well that the first targets of the Nazis from 1933 to approximately 1935 were Communists, whom the Nazis viewed as a threat to their power.
Some prisoners were brought to trial, but many were either sent directly to concentration camps or assigned "special treatment," a euphemism for immediate execution by
Gestapo officers. On their own authority, Gestapo officers could order the torture or
execution of any prisoner they had interrogated.

These executions were carried out either in local Gestapo headquarters or in local prisons. Prisoners were referred to local tribunals only if the Gestapo officer was unsure how to treat criminals. At first, judges in Cologne conducted trials fairly, and several defendants were actually acquitted, but the Nazis quickly put an end to judicial independence. Judges soon did as they were told and returned the guilty verdicts and death sentences requested by the prosecutors. Johnson argues that those who denounced neighbors to the Gestapo must have understood the consequences of their actions because so many of those brought to Gestapo headquarters never returned home alive.

Johnson explains that until the systematic destruction of synagogues and Jewish businesses known as *Kristallnacht*, which took place on the evening of November 9, 1938, throughout Germany, Nazi policy had been to dismiss Jews from almost all jobs, seize their businesses, and make their lives so miserable that they would willingly leave Germany. This situation changed drastically on November 10, 1938, when Hermann Göring and the SS head Heinrich Himmler decreed that Jews would henceforth be targeted for systematic and organized elimination.

On the afternoon of November 10, 1938, Krefeld Gestapo officers set fire to the Krefeld synagogue and made sure that firemen were not called to extinguish the blaze. That same day, sixty-three Jews in Krefeld were arrested and soon thereafter sent to the Dachau concentration camp. Gestapo officers used information supplied by cooperative informants to locate and arrest Jews. Once again these innocent people would not have been sent to their deaths without the active collaboration of "ordinary Germans."

In a thoughtful chapter entitled "The Cross and the Swastika: Quieting Religious Opposition," Johnson examines specific cases of Christians who resisted the Nazis and who were severely punished by the Gestapo. He examines the case of a Jesuit priest named Josef Spieker. In October, 1934, Father Spieker began giving sermons in which he explained very calmly and eloquently that German Catholics owed their allegiance to God and not to Hitler. He later wrote essays in Catholic newspapers in which he argued that National Socialism was incompatible with Catholicism. For these remarks, Father Spieker was sent to a concentration camp. Since he was such a well-known Catholic priest, the Nazis decided for public relations reasons to send him into exile in 1937 instead of killing him. Father Spieker was a priest in Chile from 1937 until 1950. He returned to Germany in 1950 and died in Düsseldorf eighteen years later. In 1937, the local Catholic bishop in Cologne criticized Spieker for his anti-Nazi comments, but by the 1960's German Catholics came to view him as a courageous Christian.

Although many other Catholics and Protestants collaborated with the Nazis, there were many Christians such as the Lutheran pastor Dietrich Bonhoeffer who sacrificed their lives to remind others that one could not be a Nazi and a Christian.

Johnson also points out that Jehovah's Witnesses were especially targeted for extermination because they continued to argue in public that Christianity was incompatible with National Socialism. They were right, but speaking the truth cost them their lives.

Johnson explains very thoroughly that the "final solution" would never have killed so many Jews had "ordinary Germans" not willingly cooperated with the Gestapo so that so many Jews could be killed by "special treatment" or in concentration camps. His very accurate analysis of the functioning of the Gestapo and Nazi terror in three representative German cities indicates how the Gestapo operated throughout Germany and other countries occupied by the Nazis.

Johnson does not limit his fascinating historical study solely to the twelve years of the Third Reich. He also examines postwar trials of Gestapo officers from Cologne, Krefeld, and Bergheim. It is well known that leading Nazis were sentenced either to death or to long prison terms at the end of the Nuremberg Trials for their crimes against humanity. However, what happened to other Gestapo officers who also had blood on their hands?

Johnson examines two specific trials of former Gestapo officers. Emanuel Schafer served for years as the Gestapo head in Cologne. During his 1954 trial, a Holocaust survivor named Moritz Goldschmidt testified that only 600 of the 13,500 Cologne Jews whom the local Gestapo under the command of Schafer had sent to various concentration camps had survived World War II. Despite Schafer's obvious guilt, the judges accepted his claim that he was innocent because he did not know what happened in concentration camps and because he had simply obeyed the orders of his superiors. This was, in fact, the same claim that the judges had rejected at the famous Nuremberg Trials. The Cologne judges at Schafer's 1954 trial accepted this specious claim even though several witnesses testified that Schafer had played an active role in arresting Jews and sending them to their deaths. He was acquitted on the capital charge of mass murder. The judges convicted him of the charge of "aggravated deprivation of liberty." For causing the deaths of almost thirteen thousand Cologne Jews, Schafer spent only six years in jail.

Other Gestapo officers were treated even more leniently. Alfred Effenberg was tried in 1949 before a Krefeld court for crimes against humanity. The indictment accused him of having caused the deaths of several Krefeld Jews. The surviving spouses of a Jewish man named Toni M. and a Jewish woman named Sibylla C. had been denounced to the Krefeld Gestapo by neighbors. Both spouses had spoken personally with Effenberg and both the widow of Toni M. and the widower of Sibylla C. testified under oath that Effenberg had signed the papers that sent their spouses to their deaths in concentration camps. Both witnesses indicated that he was alone responsible for their deaths. The Krefeld Gestapo chief, Ludwig Jung, stated that it was his policy to simply sign recommendations from Gestapo officers that Jews be sent to concentration camps. He indicated that his officers had complete authority to assign people to concentration camps. Despite this clear indication of Effenberg's guilt, the judges accepted his assertion that he had simply been following orders. The court acquitted him on the capital charge but found him guilty on the minor charge of acting as an accomplice in an aggravated case of deprivation of liberty. He was sentenced to three months in prison. Johnson describes many other trials of Gestapo officers from Krefeld and Cologne that resulted in acquittals or very light sentences. Prosecutors and judges did not seriously punish local residents who had clearly committed crimes against humanity by causing the deaths of Jewish people from Krefeld, Cologne, and Bergheim.

Nazi Terror: The Gestapo, Jews, and Ordinary Germans is an extremely well-researched historical study that enriches a reader's understanding of how the active collaboration of ordinary Germans and the Gestapo made possible the extermination of millions of ordinary Germans' fellow citizens.

Edmund J. Campion

Sources for Further Study

Library Journal 125 (February 1, 2000): 100.
New Statesman 129 (April 10, 2000): 62.
The New York Times Book Review 105 (February 20, 2000): 14.
Publishers Weekly 247 (January 3, 2000): 64.
Sunday Telegraph, March 19, 2000, p. 13.
The Washington Post, March 26, 2000, p. X03.

A NEW WORLD

Author: Amit Chaudhuri (1962-   )
Publisher: Alfred A. Knopf (New York). 192 pp. $24.95
Type of work: Novel
Time: April through August, 1994
Locale: Calcutta, India

~

*During a visit to his parents in India, a recently di-
vorced American professor realizes that nothing in life is
certain except change*

~

Principal characters:
> DR. JAYOJIT "JOY" CHATTERJEE, a thirty-seven-year-old economist and
> writer
> VIKRAM "BONNY" CHATTERJEE, his seven-year-old son
> ANANDA CHATTERJEE, his father, a retired admiral
> RUBY CHATTERJEE, his mother

Since Amit Chaudhuri himself was born in Calcutta and raised in Bombay, then sent to England for his university and postgraduate education, it is hardly surprising that so many of the characters in his fiction feel like outsiders in the place where they happen to reside. During his summer visits to relatives in Calcutta, Chaudhuri became aware of the subtle cultural differences even between two cities in the same country. His own experience became the basis of the critically acclaimed novella *A Strange and Sublime Address* (1991). When the ten-year-old protagonist of that work visits relatives in Calcutta, he finds himself among people who are poorer and less well educated than his family in Bombay. However, it is not just the difference in social class that makes him ill at ease; even more important are the unfamiliar customs and the daily rituals that are so much a part of life in Calcutta as to make it seem like a foreign country. In *An Afternoon Raag* (1993), Chaudhuri again describes how even the most minor details remind him that he is far from home. The central character in this novel is a man from Bombay who is completing his education at Oxford University. Unsuccessful in his attempts to reach out to English students, he turns for solace to two Indian women. However, much of the time he simply retreats into memory, imagining himself in his own familiar room in Bombay.

A *Strange and Sublime Address* and *An Afternoon Raag* are both about temporary displacement; there is no suggestion that Bombay will seem different to the protagonists when they return to the city. In *A New World*, however, when Dr. Jayojit Chatterjee goes back to Calcutta to spend a summer with his parents, he finds that he feels just as much an outsider there as he does in the American Midwest, where he now lives.

~

Amit Chaudhuri has won several awards for his writing. He is a contributor to The London Review of Books, *the* Times Literary Supplement, *and* The New Yorker, *and is the author of three novellas published under the title* Freedom Song.

~

Admittedly, Jayojit has every reason to feel unsettled. After falling in love with her gynecologist, Jayojit's Bengali wife, Amala, put her husband through a nasty divorce, gained custody of their young son, Vikram, or "Bonny," and took him with her to San Diego. Now Jayojit can have Bonny with him only during his school vacation, which begins in April and ends in August. Since his father, Admiral Chatterjee, and his mother Ruby have not seen their grandson for some time—when they cancelled a trip to the United States when they heard about the divorce—Jayojit felt obligated to take Bonny to Calcutta as soon as he could. *A New World* begins with the arrival of Jayojit and Bonny at his parents' apartment and ends with them on the plane from Dhaka to New York.

Although the first few chapters of *A New World* are uneventful, there are hints that the summer will not pass without incident. Any family get-together can produce a quarrel, and Jayojit knows that his parents are troubled about the divorce, which has limited their access to their grandchild, and also about their son's failure to marry again, which would at least give them the hope of other grandchildren. Moreover, as Ruby keeps reminding Jayojit, Bonny may become ill either from too much exposure to the sun or from something he eats, not to mention his being exposed to germs for which his American immune system is unprepared. Jayojit is also well aware that his father might have another stroke, perhaps this time a fatal one.

However, the months pass by without a crisis. Every day is much like another. Bonny plays with his miniature cars and trucks and his Jurassic Park dinosaurs; the admiral checks on his investments and takes his naps; Ruby dusts, cooks, and complains about her shiftless servant; Jayojit observes the neighborhood, thinks about working on a new book, eats his mother's luchis, and gains weight.

Despite its lack of dramatic events, however, *A New World* is anything but dull. Chaudhuri's realistic story is as engrossing as the novels of the Magical Realists dominating Indian fiction on the cusp of the twenty-first century. Not only does he capture the essence of life in upper-class Calcutta society, its nostalgia, and its inherent comedy, but through his protagonist he also reveals what it means to be an exile and, even more fundamentally, what it means to be a human being.

Like many adults shaken by personal crises, Jayojit arrives at his parents' home expecting to recapture the sense of security he knew as a child. However, because his father insisted on spending his retirement years in a place where he had never been based, Calcutta was never Jayojit's home, and therefore it has few associations for him. Moreover, Jayojit himself has had too many new experiences to be able to return to the past. He is indeed a different person from the child he was once was. For example, though his mother takes great pains to cook food he once liked, Jayojit has been so strongly influenced by American notions about diet and health that he cannot enjoy his meals. When he realizes that he is gaining weight, he begs his mother to stop tempting him, but she will not listen. Eventually Jayojit comes to understand that it is not just food that divides him from his parents. Even if he could somehow describe the United States to them (the wide roads, the produce sections of the supermarkets), his mother and father would never be able to envision the life he now leads. He has become cut off not only from his past life but also from his own family.

However, if Jayojit feels isolated from his parents, he is no more so than they are from each other. Even when they get up each morning, they do not speak to each other. Even their daily walk together takes place in silence. If their relationship seems harmonious, it is because their routines are so well established and their communication with each other so limited that there is no possibility of conflict. If Jayojit once believed that marriage would put an end to his loneliness, what he sees in his parents' home, along with his own experience, suggests to him that perhaps isolation is simply the human condition.

Another of Jayojit's discoveries during his months in India involves the inescapable presence of the past. Jayojit sees photographs everywhere of himself as a child, himself with his brother, and Bonny at every stage of his development; although pictures of her are noticeably absent, Amala is, in a sense, a ghost always hovering about the Chatterjees. When his mother fusses about keeping Bonny out of the sun, Jayojit finds himself capitulating; even though her name is never mentioned, Amala is present, silently voicing her fears. She is even more troublesome when Jayojit is alone with his thoughts. Moments from their past together keep intruding into the present, sending him again on his search for the answer to an unanswerable question: How could a marriage of two people from similar backgrounds, sharing so many of the same interests, go so wrong? Another ghost who haunts his thoughts is Arundhati, the young woman his parents found for him after his marriage to Amala failed. Again, Jayojit cannot find the answer to his question: After at first seeming so interested, why did Arundhati refuse him?

It may seem odd that though this novel is entitled *A New World*, the action takes place in the old world rather than in the United States. However, the title is consistent with a major theme in the novel—that of mutability. Since nothing remains the same, it can be argued, every place is always in the process of becoming, and therefore even a country as old as India can be called "new." Moreover, as Jayojit discovers, though the past is always present, one cannot step back into it. Too much has changed; too much is still changing.

The frequent observations about the weather and the seasons in *A New World* serve as constant reminders of the inevitability of change and also of its unpredictability. For example, shortly after his arrival, Jayojit says that during the spring, one cannot tell in the morning just how hot it will be later in the day. It can only be assumed that as the day proceeds, the temperature will almost certainly rise. The characters in the novel also talk at length about the seasons. As spring becomes summer, they comment, each day will be different from the one that preceded it—generally hotter, but it is uncertain just how hot. Everyone knows, too, that every year the rains will come, but no one can predict exactly when. The only certainty, then, is that the weather will change; even the longtime residents cannot predict exactly how or precisely when.

Given the fact that weather is always uncertain, it is not unusual for someone to be caught without an umbrella in the first sudden shower of the rainy season. However, when it is Jayojit who has to take refuge from the rain, he thinks to himself that this year even the monsoons are behaving differently, almost as if they, too, had targeted him for misfortune. He does not seem to notice that others, too, are being rained upon. In this instance and in many others, the author is obviously satirizing his protagonist's preoccupation with himself and his own bad luck. Though Chaudhuri means for Jayojit to be seen sympathetically, he does not look at him as a modern-day Job but instead as a character too obsessed with himself to see anything humorous either in his own situation or in the social comedy around him.

Thus it is through the author's eyes that readers note how easily the American-reared Bonny adapts to India, while his father, though a native, remains ill at ease throughout the summer simply because he has not come to terms with his own problems. Jayojit finds no humor in his parents' eccentricities, but the author draws the elder Chatterjees as an interesting pair whose peculiarities are rather endearing. Ruby's culinary mediocrity and her inability to deal with servants, for instance, are even funnier because she is married to a man who is obsessed with details. The admiral is a man so inflexible that he considers a former drinking partner's failure to move to Calcutta a real betrayal; Ruby is so disorganized that she can barely see to the laundry. If ever a woman needed an automatic washer, Ruby does; however, her husband has so intense a distrust of modern conveniences that he will not even consider buying one. Chaudhuri's view of life as more often comic than tragic is also evident in his hilarious account of the apartment residents' meeting during which a number of colorful characters state their grievances and then disperse, all feeling much better, even though nothing has been resolved. Even after Jayojit begins to accept the inevitability of change, he does not see how funny it is, for example, that Mrs. Gupta has coped with the death of her husband by transferring her affection to a Pomeranian, whom she now walks daily just as she used to walk her ailing spouse.

A New World, then, is a more complex novel than a first reading might indicate. On one level, it is the account of a young man's discovery of some difficult truths about the world and the human condition—among them, that one can neither understand the past nor get rid of it and that the only certainty in this world is change. However, Chaudhuri's novel is also a comedy in which the author gently satirizes both upper-class Indian society and those who, like his protagonist, may have seen a good deal of the world but have not yet learned to laugh at themselves.

Rosemary M. Canfield Reisman

Sources for Further Study

Booklist 97 (October 1, 2000): 320.
The Economist 354 (March 18, 2000): 13.
The New York Times Book Review 105 (October 22, 2000): 7.
Publishers Weekly 247 (October 2, 2000): 60.
The Times Literary Supplement, June 30, 2000, p. 22.

A NEWER WORLD
Kit Carson, John C. Frémont, and the
Claiming of the American West

Author: David Roberts (1943-   )
Publisher: Simon & Schuster (New York). Illustrated.
 320 pp. $25.00
Type of work: History and biography
Time: 1842-1864
Locale: The American West

~

An exploration of the lives of explorer Frémont and mountain man Carson and how they contributed to, and were shaped by, the founding of the American West

~

Principal personages:
> JOHN C. FRÉMONT, United States Army explorer and Civil War general
> KIT CARSON, trapper, frontier scout, and Indian fighter
> JESSIE BENTON FRÉMONT, John Frémont's wife
> THOMAS HART BENTON, United States senator from Missouri and father of Jessie
> JOSEFA JARAMILLO, Carson's third wife
> WILLIAM SHERLEY "OLD BILL" WILLIAMS, legendary mountain man who led Frémont's fourth expedition
> ALEXIS GODEY, mountain man and Indian fighter who participated in Frémont's third and fourth expeditions
> CHARLES PREUSS, German emigrant cartographer who assisted Frémont on his expeditions

For most of U.S. history, the exploration, conquering, and settling of the West has been extolled as a triumph of American strength and ideals. The heroic determination of trailblazers such as Meriwether Lewis and William Clark, the bloody battles with Indians and Mexicans, and the stoic hard work of pioneers and forty-niners are legendary—quintessential elements of an expanding nation locked on the course of manifest destiny. The particular facts of this period and the stories of its denizens long ago merged into a mythic Old West, depicted in Western novels, films, and television shows, and celebrated for the benefit of tourists in towns from Sacramento and Coloma to Santa Fe and San Antonio. Only slightly less romantic have been textbook portrayals of these times, depicting as they do a story of heroic triumph over adversity.

Increasingly, however, revisionist historians and politically sensitive government agencies have attempted to expose the warts of this period. History books, commemorative markers, films, and museum displays now take breaks in their narratives to

David Roberts has published eleven books, including Once They Moved the Wind: Cochise, Geronimo, and the Apache Wars. *He has also written numerous articles on the outdoors and adventure travel for* Men's Journal, Outside, National Geographic, *and* Smithsonian.

point out the environmental damage wrought by gold miners, the decimation of native cultures at the hands of white settlers, the corruption and greed of the railroads, and the sexism, racism, hypocrisy, and other turpitudes that tainted the society being established in the Wild West.

Whereas a more complete view of the West's founding is desirable and even necessary, some of the revisionist efforts have committed the same sin as those they seek to revise, downplaying context and culture and painting the era, and particularly its heretofore heroes, as more corrupt and villainous than they were. It is exceedingly difficult to challenge fairly and convincingly an ensconced myth, particularly since myths, by their nature, rely so heavily on normative considerations. One would hope that a writer shedding new light on a historical subject would resist the temptation to substitute new biases for old ones, and rather offer new interpretations and insights based on new or neglected factual sources. Such is the accomplishment of David Roberts in his portrayal of two of the most significant heroes of their era in the settling of the West.

Roberts, a well-established author with a number of popular works on exploration to his credit, takes as his subjects John C. Frémont and Kit Carson, who in their day were among the country's most famous figures. That fame, to be sure, was founded in part on somewhat dubious sources: Frémont's achievements as an explorer were lionized in somewhat self-congratulatory government reports that he dictated to his wife, who in turn likely embellished them stylistically. His trusted friend Carson, who helped to lead some of Frémont's most important expeditions, was illiterate, and aside from some taciturn memoirs, was depicted in highly fictional dime novels fighting Indians and rescuing frontier women. Subsequent generations examined the men's lives and sought to separate fact from fiction. Roberts, however, makes a unique contribution by examining the relationship between the two men, as well as their individual accomplishments. Throughout, Roberts performs this task with diligence and flair.

The book has three somewhat ambitious purposes. First, it is a biography of Frémont and Carson. Roberts examines their family histories, their early lives, and, most thoroughly, their years together. He attempts to include psychological dimensions in his portraits and makes lengthy discourses speculating on such matters as Carson's attitudes toward Native Americans and Frémont's preoccupation with his place in history.

The biographical facet of the book is complicated by Roberts's desire to capture the relationship between the two men. Although Roberts asserts that his book is not intended as a "dual biography" but rather as an examination of "four campaigns that epitomize the two explorers' triumphs and failures," Roberts nevertheless devotes considerable effort to creating detailed portraits of the two men as individuals. In a sense, *A Newer World* contains three biographies: Frémont's, Carson's, and the team's. In depicting the duo, Roberts makes much of the contrasts between the two men: Frémont the vain, somewhat pompous military man given to garrulity; Carson the plainspoken, taciturn mountain man. As with other great odd couples in history, Frémont and Carson are portrayed as complementing each other's strengths and mitigating each other's weaknesses.

The biographical aspect of the book is also the most scholarly, supported with a careful reading of primary sources and Roberts's own discoveries. Roberts personally visited "virtually every step" of Frémont and Carson's treks, thus lending an authenticity to his conjuring of landscapes and settings. The book also makes frequent references to others' evaluations of the men's lives and is peppered with critiques and conclusions about these previous assessments. It is here that Roberts most consciously attempts to distinguish the myths and revisionist excesses from the actual men. The portraits that emerge are rather sympathetic. While confirming, for instance, that Carson was indeed responsible for untold numbers of Native American deaths, it places Carson's actions in the context of the times, when there were in fact hostile Native American tribes (such as the Blackfoot and Apache) who raided white settlements and killed settlers. It was a time of war, not just between whites and Native Americans but also among different Native American tribes. There was an almost Hobbesian anarchy that imposed its own logic and values.

Battles with Native Americans in the nineteenth century West were hardly evidence of a uniquely genocidal bent of Western settlers. The "great powers" of Europe were almost constantly at war, as were aboriginal tribes on the various continents. Imperialism and colonialism were accepted and expected aspects of international relations. In fact, Roberts notes that, given the prevailing cultural and societal mores, Frémont and Carson possessed views that were notably ahead of the times. Frémont, for example, is revealed to be a fervent abolitionist, notwithstanding his upbringing in antebellum Tennessee and South Carolina. Similarly, readers learn that Carson did not allow the hostilities with certain tribes on the frontier to dictate his views about Native Americans as a whole. Indeed, Roberts traces Carson's gradual development toward becoming a committed champion of Native American rights.

The second function of the book is as a treatise on the founding of the American West. Here, too, Roberts takes the opportunity not only to help strip away the myths connected with manifest destiny, but also to temper the overzealous revisionism of recent years. Frémont's expeditions, while perhaps not crucial to the settling of the West, did advance that purpose. His published reports were highly popular and helped to strengthen the public's interest in and support for Western expansion.

Roberts does not attempt to write anything approaching a complete or even coherent account of all the major events of mid-nineteenth century Western settlement. Instead, he seeks to illuminate some of the motives and philosophy that underlay that mission, as well as expose some of the costs it imposed on others, particularly the Native Americans. In his preface Roberts somewhat sanctimoniously notes that "too few" historians look at Western history from the Native Americans' point of view. To remedy this, he takes long digressions in his narrative to describe the culture and lifeways of various Native American tribes to reflect on the disruption and even tragedy Western expansion caused for those peoples, and to point out where Native American oral accounts of certain events conflict with written white accounts. While these discussions at times can seem out of place (as though they were awkwardly grafted onto the narrative to soothe a nagging conscience), Roberts remains a credible reporter of fact, avoiding, for the most part, the preachy tones that characterize more partisan work.

Happily, Roberts employs a formula for addressing some of the more painful and shameful aspects of U.S. history without encouraging hand-wringing or provoking partisan conflict. He seeks to present neglected facts and identify questionable "truths" promulgated by hagiographers. At the same time, he is slow to second-guess the actions and policies of his nineteenth century ancestors. While acknowledging that many of the values and beliefs of those times would be vilified today, he does not use this fact to vilify the people that held them. In fact, in case the reader fails to note it during the text, in the epilogue Roberts explicitly reveals his disdain for the "militants" who launch "sanctimonious and ahistorical screeds" against past heroes.

Finally, the third purpose of the book is to provide a rollicking story from the Old West—in Roberts's words, "a stirring, seldom-told adventure tale." Here Roberts has mixed success. His avoidance of footnotes and dry scholarly prose is welcome, making many of the vignettes riveting. Such poignant tales as his depiction of Frémont's disastrous fourth expedition (which resorted to cannibalism), as well as his description of harrowing battles with native Americans and raucous annual celebrations among trappers, make for exciting reading.

Unfortunately, what makes *A Newer World* work so well as a biography and critique of manifest destiny serves as an obstacle to its success as a story. Rather than flowing as a cohesive narrative, the book jumps about in time as it tracks the two men at various parts of their lives. It becomes sidetracked in primers on such topics as trapping and Native American rituals. It interrupts itself with reviews of scholarly literature.

Still, Roberts's writing is thoroughly entertaining. His words charge forward with energy and verve, tempered a bit by a wry and understated wit. He demonstrates a powerful command of the language, employing a colorful embellished style that manages to stop (barely) short of florid.

For all this, Roberts's book is a qualified success. In an accessible and entertaining form, he manages to resurrect two largely forgotten heroes of the Old West, to measure their achievements (noting that they both had their faults, "but pure heroes or villains do not exist outside the pages of bad literature"), and along the way to help readers better understand the founding of the West. Roberts writes with authority and evident probity. Yet while his interpretations and arguments are balanced and compelling, the final portrait does not strike one as definitive. The narrative is a bit too breezy and glib—characteristics that work to make the book highly readable, but which detract from its ability to confront the myths and revisionist excesses that have marshaled evidence to their causes. *A Newer World* is an entertaining and illuminating look at the mid-nineteenth century West and its explorers, and while one hopes it will restore some balance to the general public's understanding of those times, it is unlikely to significantly temper scholarship on the topic.

Steve D. Boilard

Sources for Further Study

Library Journal 124 (November 1, 1999): 109.
The New York Times Book Review 105 (February 27, 2000): 20.
Publishers Weekly 246 (December 6, 1999): 65.
The Wall Street Journal, January 11, 2000, p. A24.

NEWJACK
Guarding Sing Sing

Author: Ted Conover (1958-   )
Publisher: Random House (New York). 321 pp. $24.95
Type of work: Sociology
Time: 1997
Locale: New York state, thirty miles north of New York
City

∼

An account by a journalist of his experiences as a cor-rections officer at Sing Sing maximum-security prison in New York

∼

The United States prison system is in a crisis. In 2000, the U.S. inmate population reached a record two million, which means that one person in one hundred forty in the United States was incarcerated. Over the last quarter of the twentieth century, the number of inmates tripled, and the United States locked up more people per capita than almost any other country, running neck and neck with Russia for this dubious distinction. Incarceration rates are six times those of Britain and seventeen times those of Japan. The rising numbers have made prisons a growth industry; California builds a new prison every year to keep up with the demand. The burden of imprison-ment falls disproportionately on racial minorities. In California, for example, a young black man is five times as likely to go to prison as to a state university.

All this takes place in a society in which crime is steadily falling. In the years fol-lowing 1991, for example, violent crime fell roughly 20 percent. The huge increase in rates of imprisonment is accounted for in part by mandatory prison terms for drug of-fenders—a solution that failed to reduce drug abuse. Yet the problem of skyrocketing inmate populations and a failed drug policy passed unmentioned in the 2000 presiden-tial campaign. Politicians always seem ready to take credit for falling crime rates but seem to have no interest in researching the extent to which, if at all, falling crime is re-lated to harsher sentencing laws.

Many of these facts are mentioned by journalist Ted Conover in his engrossing ac-count of the year he spent as a correctional officer (correctional officers, or COs, as they are known, dislike the term "guard") at the notorious maximum-security Sing Sing Prison in New York. Conover, always fascinated by prisons and curious about what the life of a guard was really like, approached the New York Department of Correctional Services with a request to write a profile of the experiences of a new recruit, but he was turned down. So he decided that his only option was to become a CO himself.

Keeping his journalistic intention secret, Conover enrolled in a seven-week train-ing program at the Albany Training Academy. This turned out to resemble a military-style boot camp, and his account of indignities endured, including mandatory exposure to tear gas, seems likely to deter anyone else from following in his footsteps. It strikes Conover that much of what the trainees are put through is similar to what inmates must endure every day.

On completion of the training program, Conover and his fellow graduates were all assigned to Sing Sing, which is considered the least desirable prison in the state as far as being a CO is concerned. "It's a rough place," one of the instructors had said, and Conover recalls how a CO he had become acquainted with told him that his time at Sing Sing was the worst nine months of his life, Vietnam included.

Ted Conover spent a year working as a prison guard at Sing Sing to research Newjack. *His previous books,* Whiteout *and* Coyotes, *were named Notable Books of the Year by* The New York Times. *He has written for* The New Yorker *and is now a contributing writer to* The New York Times Magazine.

Conover soon finds this out for himself, and the reader is left with no doubts that being a CO at Sing Sing is a difficult, stressful, unpleasant, and dangerous job. In 1997, the prison housed 1,813 inmates in maximum security and 556 in medium security. Of that total, over 1,700 had been convicted of violent offenses, including robbery, rape, assault, kidnapping, burglary, and arson. A total of 672 inmates were convicted of murder or manslaughter. Within the prison, disturbances were frequent. "Lots of cuttings lately," says the first deputy superintendent for security, ominously.

Conover starts with four weeks of on-the-job training (OJT). On his first day in the prison, where he assists a regular officer, he feels inadequately prepared, as if he has been certified as a lion tamer before he has ever been left alone with a lion. When he gets to his assigned floor, R-and-W, everything appears chaotic to him: Inmates are walking about all over the place, and the officer in charge is besieged by inmates wanting to make phone calls or be granted other special requests. Conover muddles through, not really sure of what he is doing, and has his first confrontations with inmates. After just a few hours he wonders how he is going to make it to the end of his shift. Trainee officers, like substitute teachers, command little respect.

Conover goes through a rapid learning curve. Although his four weeks of OJT are, in general, dispiriting, he does find one CO whose mastery of the job Conover admires. The key to Officer Smith's competence is that he treats the inmates as human beings, maintains a sense of humor, and is firm yet flexible in carrying out his duties. He regards being a CO as an art, and he has highly developed interpersonal skills. As Conover observes wryly, being a CO is, in a macho kind of way, a "people-skills" profession; so much depends on how the CO interacts with the inmates.

The inmates are a tough bunch. Nevertheless, Conover, like Officer Smith, often succeeds in finding the humanity in them. He seems to grasp quickly that if men are put in situations where they feel powerless, it is inevitable that they will try by any number of tricks and subterfuges to win small victories against the system that emasculates them. It is the COs who must try to ensure that they do not—that the rules are enforced—although Conover recognizes that a good CO, just like a good cop or a good schoolteacher, knows intuitively when to come down hard on an infraction and when to look the other way. As he gets more practice on the job, he generally tries to steer a middle course, not going out of his way to make the inmates like him, but not getting stuck in a rigid "us versus them" mentality, as some of the COs appear to do.

Conover walks the reader through some of his typical days. Part of the job is to be on the lookout for contraband, which includes not only drugs, alcohol, and weapons but a host of other things as well. Inmates are not allowed to possess cassette players with a record function, sneakers worth more than fifty dollars, or more than fourteen newspapers. (Why fourteen? one wonders.) Possessing contraband is one of the ways in which inmates bend the rules, and when Conover discovers a contraband item, a battle of wills often ensues. Will strict enforcement of the rule create widespread resentment, and thus danger, among men who have little to lose anyway? Or will being lax mean that the CO loses authority and the inmates end up running the prison?

One of Conover's less unpleasant assignments is to supervise the gym, which he says sometimes resembles a bazaar, with up to four hundred inmates lifting weights, playing basketball, watching television, playing Scrabble, checkers, or chess, trading or selling various items, and generally milling about. Sometimes Conover is the only officer present, and although this environment seems less threatening than many others in the prison, he is still glad to get through his shift with nothing awful happening. In this prison, the threat of physical violence—either inmate against inmate or inmate against guard—is always in the back of a CO's mind, and during Conover's one-year stint, there were several incidents in which officers and inmates were hurt.

Conover also does duty in the most unsavory place in the whole of Sing Sing, the special housing unit, or SHU, which officers refer to simply as "the box." This is the place of solitary confinement, in which inmates barely leave their cells. Half of the inmates in the box are there for protective custody—there is a risk that they will be attacked by other inmates—and half are there for assaulting guards.

Not surprisingly, the COs who work in the box are several notches more macho than those in the rest of the prison. Perhaps this is just as well. As Conover puts it, "the environment of the Box produced stunning acts of insanity and barbarism." One example was an inmate the officers named Mr. Slurpee, who would "project a spray of urine and feces at officers—from his *mouth*." Behavior of this kind seems not uncommon.

While Conover is on duty in the box, the officers conduct a search for contraband, which involves a "strip-frisk." One inmate refuses and is subjected to what is called a "cell extraction." In other words, he is forcibly removed from his cell and forced to endure the search elsewhere. At first, Conover wonders why anyone would refuse to comply with a strip-frisk, knowing that it is going to happen anyway. Surely it was in the inmates' best interest to comply? Later, in one of the thoughtful reflections that make *Newjack* a rewarding (not just a shocking) book, Conover realizes that

> [S]elf-respect had required him to refuse. His stupidity began to look principled. He was renouncing his imprisonment, our authority, the entire system that had placed him there. If enough people did that together, the corrections system would come tumbling down.

This willingness to look at men as individuals, not merely as inmates to be controlled and subdued, is apparent in another incident. A gang member named Toussaint who has been involved in an altercation is interrogated by a group of COs. Conover notes the idealism inherent in the man's concept of what being a member of a gang means, and his sympathies are more on the side of the charismatic young criminal:

> These gangs of ghetto kids preyed on the weak, but you had to admit that there was a political element to some of them, a mission of self-help and a drive to maintain pride and focus. Toussaint was not unlike an ambassador from a small, fierce, and backward land.

Similarly, a stint in charge of the "visit room" causes Conover to reflect: "It was all about absence, wasn't it—the absence of imprisoned men from the lives of the people who loved them; the absence of love in prison." He does not, however, forget the actions that put the men in prison, which have resulted in an absence of a different kind:

> [T]he absence in the hearts of decent people, the holes that criminals punched in their lives, the absence of the things they took: money, peace of mind, health, and entire lives, because they were selfish or sick or scared or just couldn't wait.

The comment about sickness is relevant. After only a short while on the job it is clear to Conover that many of the inmates are mentally ill, some of them severely so. These are the prisoners who do not know where they are, who set fire to their own cells, or who try to commit suicide. Some are psychotic; others have various personality disorders such as paranoia and bipolar disorder. In CO slang, such inmates are referred to as "bugs." On duty in the psychiatric satellite unit (psych-unit), where he encounters more bizarre and distressing behavior, Conover sits in on some interviews between bugs and prison psychiatric committees. The aim of the drug treatment is to enable the mentally disturbed inmate to return to the general population. COs refer to the medicine as "bug juice."

Conover's humane attitudes seem to survive even his exposure to the worst criminals that society has to offer. He is clearly disturbed by the rapidly rising levels of incarceration, and as far as life in prison is concerned, he regrets that more attention is not paid to "the hope that prisons might do some good for the people in them, that human lives can be fixed instead of thrown away, that there's more to be done than locking doors and knocking heads."

Conservatives who emphasize law and order as well as severe punishment may reject such notions as so much liberal talk, but Conover is a man whose point of view should not be dismissed so glibly: He has been there, in maximum-security Sing Sing, and he knows what he is talking about.

Bryan Aubrey

Sources for Further Study

Booklist 96 (May 15, 2000): 1706.
Choice 38 (November, 2000): 616.
Corrections Today 62 (December, 2000): 11.
Entertainment Weekly, May 26, 2000, p. 68.
Library Journal 125 (June 1, 2000): 160.
Los Angeles Times Book Review, July 9, 2000, p. 8.
Publishers Weekly 247 (April 24, 2000): 79.

NEWTON'S GIFT
How Sir Isaac Newton Unlocked the System of the World

Author: David Berlinski (1942-   )
Publisher: The Free Press (New York). 217 pp. $24.00
Type of work: Biography and science
Time: 1642-1727
Locale: England

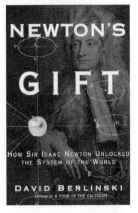

∽

Both a brief overview of the life and character of the man and a nontechnical account of the development of Newtonian mechanics

∽

No student of Western science, or indeed, Western culture, would challenge the assertion that Sir Isaac Newton was one of the most important figures in the development of Western science. David Berlinski makes a somewhat more expansive, although quite defensible and unoriginal claim. For him, Newton "is the largest figure in the history of western science" and "Newtonian mechanics is not only the first, but the greatest, of scientific theories." By intermixing an overview of Newton's life—emphasizing oddity of character over events—with a nontechnical analysis of portions of Newton's masterpiece, the *Philosophiae Naturalis Principia Mathematica* (1687; *The Mathematical Principles of Natural Philosophy*, 1729), Berlinski hopes to persuade readers of the power, impact, and ultimate influence of the English scientist's insights. He argues that Newton's vision of the world—a mechanical world governed by simple mathematical laws—has set the research agenda in the physical sciences for three centuries and continues to do so even today.

To understand Newton is not easy. There are a number of hurdles. First, his mathematics is difficult. After all, Newton was the codiscoverer of calculus, and he used it freely in his *Principia*. Even if the reader is comfortable with college calculus (and not many are conversant with differential equations), the terminology and notation used by Newton has been archaic for over two centuries. Therefore, both a simplification and a translation (of both the mathematics and the Latin of the *Principia*) is necessary if Berlinski is to reach a modern, nonspecialist audience. Berlinski is up to the challenge and rewrites Newton's insights in modern but simplified notation. He offers three different modes of explanation to the reader so as to render Newton's mathematics more understandable: words, symbols, and diagrams. Supplementing the explanations in the body of the book is an appendix supplying equations, definitions, and derivations requiring no mathematics beyond algebra. The result is a volume a bright high school student could understand.

Newton's Gift does not fit neatly into any single category of nonfiction. There are no new insights, either scientific or historical. Berlinski explicitly and accurately de-

David Berlinski has taught philosophy and logic at Stanford, Rutgers, and the University of Puget Sound and mathematics at Columbia and the University of Paris, and he has held a postdoctoral fellowship in molecular biology at Columbia. Since 1982 he has been a full-time writer, and he currently lives in Paris.

nies that he has written either a biography or a full exposition of Newton's contributions to physics. Perhaps half the book is concerned with the life of Newton, but the coverage is sketchy and spotty, emphasizing Newton's quirkiness. The other half of the book is a discussion of Newton's mechanics, explicitly ignoring, except in passing, Newton's experimental work in optics. The dust jacket describes the book as "an appreciation of Newton's greatest accomplishment." This is perhaps the most accurate description possible. By carefully picking and choosing amongst Newton's multifaceted scientific work and the details of Newton's life, Berlinski has constructed his personal vision of Newton. The contrast between the eccentric, very seventeenth century man and the timeless mathematical explanations serves to highlight the rational, mathematical side of Newton. Berlinski appreciates Newton's contributions and wants everyone else to do the same.

As a nontechnical explanation of Newton's mechanics, the work is very successful. Berlinski had proven in such earlier books as *A Tour of the Calculus* (1995) and *The Advent of the Algorithm: The Idea That Rules the World* (2000) that he can explain esoteric mathematics in a manner that is understandable by the mathematically challenged, or at least those who were not students of calculus. In *Newton's Gift*, four chapters comprising some forty pages form the core of the popular exposition of scientific thought. These chapters show Berlinski at his best. He reviews Newton's three laws of motion and the two laws of time and space, translates Newton's geometrical explanations into simplified vector notation, analyzes Newton's concept of gravity, and summarizes and explains the seven propositions which form the basis of the Newtonian system of the world. By focusing on Newton the theoretical or mathematical physicist rather than Newton the experimental physicist, Berlinski plays to his own strengths. The words that Berlinski uses to describe Newton's justification for his proposition of the theory of gravity will serve just as well as descriptors for Berlinski's account: "measured" and "lucid."

As a study of the man, *Newton's Gift* has great limitations and is much less successful than it is as a nontechnical exposition of mathematical physics and celestial mechanics. Biography, to be successful, must understand the subject in the context in which he or she lived. Berlinski was either unwilling or unable to undertake the struggle fully to understand Newton the complex human being in the context of the late seventeenth and early eighteenth centuries or to understand Newton's world. From the first page of the book, where Berlinski dismisses the efforts of two of the leading physicians of early eighteenth century England with the judgment of "masterly incompetence," presumably because their medical knowledge was not up to modern standards, Berlinski takes what a historian would consider the easier road. He filters the events and personalities of the seventeenth and eighteenth centuries through the values of the twenty-first century. Berlinski appreciates that from the perspective of the twentieth century, which witnessed in scientific circles a decrease in religious belief and a disinclination for scientists to pursue philosophical studies, there were two Newtons: the scientist who offered the laws of motion and the student of theology and alchemy who sought fundamental knowledge in other spheres. The ever-present challenge to a biographer of Newton, especially the biographer in the more "rational" late nineteenth and twentieth centuries, has always been to explain how these apparently diverse intellectual activities could come from the same mind. Berlinski simply throws up his hands. If he fully comprehends Isaac Newton, he does not know how to convey that understanding to the reader.

Similarly, the biographer must struggle to recapture, to the best of his or her ability, the life as it was lived, in spite of the loss of evidence and the differences in perspective between the subject of the biography, the biographer, and the readers of the biography. For important historical figures such as Newton, who were figures of almost mythical proportions in their own time and who subsequently have been the subject of interpretation and reinterpretation for generations, the struggle to understand the subject's life is even more difficult. Again, Berlinski recognizes the problem but opts not to engage in the struggle. He admits that "there is always an odd and terrible disassociation between a life as it is lived and a life as has been recorded." In Newton's case, he acknowledges that perhaps alchemy and theology were the true intellectual passions of his life, and mathematical physics a peripheral activity. Berlinski has chosen to "read backward into his life" and view Newton from the perspective of the twenty-first century, not the eighteenth. To be fair, Berlinski is open and explicit about his approach, unlike some biographers who hide their agendas or biases. Nonetheless, the picture being drawn has been edited and filtered.

As is often the case with books targeted at general audiences, there is no scholarly apparatus in *Newton's Gift*. Berlinski supplies no sources for the Newton quotations scattered about the book. He does not even present a list of further readings, let alone a formal bibliography. The only mention of any other publication, Richard Westfall's biography of Newton, *Never at Rest* (1980), acknowledged as the standard study of Newton's life, is marred by Berlinski's misspelling of Westfall's name. This lack of any scholarly apparatus is unfortunate in a number of ways. First, it leaves unanswerable without great work on the reader's part the question of where Berlinski obtained his information about Newton. For example, how did he know that prior to lecturing, Newton sighed "the inward and contained sigh that all teachers sigh"? How broad was Berlinski's gathering of facts? Is he repeating the statements or misstatements of others, or engaging in original interpretations or research? Second, it leaves the reader who seeks more detailed or more sophisticated information about Newton's life or work without guidance. Presumably, Berlinski has thoroughly read the secondary literature on Newton. Why not share his thoughts about that literature? All it would have taken would have been a few paragraphs. Finally, a bibliography, especially a critical bibliography, enables a reader to understand more fully what is new or controversial in *Newton's Gift*. There are other interpretations of Newton's work and other views of his life. Some of these present pictures quite different in detail from those drawn by Berlinski. His particular interpretation would have more weight if he had at least admitted to their existence. All too often, popular expositions of the history of science fail to place themselves in the context of the professional historian.

This book may turn out to be controversial, in part because its author is controversial. Trained as a mathematician and philosopher, Berlinski has gained some notoriety as a critic of evolutionary theories in essays targeted at readers who are nonscientific members of the intellectual community. He has questioned both Charles Darwin's theory of biological evolution and the evolutionary cosmology known as the big bang theory in articles published in *Commentary*, a neoconservative general opinion magazine better known for discussions of contentious social or political issues. As a result, he has been embraced by some creationists, although he has denied that he is a creationist, and attacked by scientists who claim he has ventured into arenas for which he lacks training, understanding, and expertise.

There is no evidence in *Newton's Gift* that Berlinski is a creationist. In it, he writes that "we are largely unable to recapture the intensity of conviction that for all of western history has been associated with theological belief," a conclusion with which no Christian creationist is likely to agree. Moreover, the picture he presents of Newton is not one that would be expected of someone in sympathy with religious fundamentalism. For Berlinski, the Newton seeking the truth hidden in theological writings "has passed beyond the grasp of sympathy," while the Newton of rational mechanics and the calculus "is our contemporary." For the creationists, the opposite would be true. The Newton deep in theological studies would appear familiar, while the mathematical Newton would appear less so.

Historians of science may have feelings similar to those of evolutionary biologists and cosmologists after reading *Newton's Gift*. Berlinski has trod on their turf without a proper understanding of what he was about. Perhaps he should have restricted his book to an exposition of Newton's science and left the man alone.

Marc Rothenberg

Sources for Further Study

Booklist 97 (September 15, 2000): 196.
Library Journal 125 (September 1, 2000): 244.
Publishers Weekly 247 (August 21, 2000): 57.

NICCOLÒ'S SMILE
A Biography of Machiavelli

Author: Maurizio Viroli
*First published: Il sorriso di Niccolò: Storia di Machia-
velli*, 1998, in Italy
Translated from the Italian by Antony Shugaar
Publisher: Farrar, Straus and Giroux (New York). 271
pp. $25.00
Type of work: Biography
Time: 1469-1527
Locale: Primarily northern Italy, particularly Florence

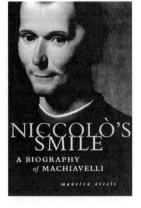

~

*A brief general-interest biography of Machiavelli fo-
cusing primarily on his career as a diplomat, secretary in
the Republic of Florence, and writer*

~

Principal personages:
> NICCOLÒ MACHIAVELLI (1469-1527), author of *Il principe*, 1532 (*The
> Prince*, 1640)
> CESARE BORGIA (c. 1475-1507), duke of Valentino and natural son of
> Pope Alexander VI, Machiavelli's archetypal "Prince"
> BIAGIO BUONACCORSI, Machiavelli's assistant
> POPE CLEMENT VII (1478-1534), born Guilio de' Medici, bastard son of
> Guiliano de' Medici
> FRANCESCO GUICCIARDINI (1483-1540), Florentine historian and states-
> man allied with the Medicis
> POPE LEO X (1475-1521), born Giovanni de' Medici, son of Lorenzo the
> Magnificent
> PIER SODERINI, gonfalonier and opponent of the Medicis, head of the
> Republic of Florence
> FRANCESCO VETTORI, Florentine statesman and Machiavelli's benefactor

Maurizio Viroli was born in Forli, Italy, and received a degree in philosophy from
the University of Bologna and a Ph.D. in social and political sciences at the European
University Institute in Florence. He is the author of numerous works on political theory including *Machiavelli* (1998). He taught at the New School for Social Research,
Georgetown University, and the Scuola Normale Superiore in Pisa before becoming a
professor of politics at Princeton University.

In his famous essay "The Originality of Machiavelli," the late Isaiah Berlin re-
marked that there is something surprising about the variety of interpretations of
Niccolò Machiavelli's political opinions; for example, his *Il principe* (1532; *The
Prince*, 1640) has been called a satire, a cautionary tale, a period piece, anti-Christian,

Maurizio Viroli is a professor of politics at Princeton University. He has published numerous works in political theory, including a study of Machiavelli's political philosophy.

amoral, immoral, humanist, patriotic, realistic, a manual for statecraft, antiutopian, politically pragmatic, idealist, venal, even aesthetic. For hundreds of years, the writings of Machiavelli have disturbed generations of political commentators. For Berlin, his major achievement, and the one which has caused so much concern down through the ages, is that he uncovered, especially in his most famous (or infamous) work, *The Prince*, an insoluble dilemma—namely, that political ends equally ultimate, equally sacred, may contradict each other without any possibility of reconciliation, and thereby Machiavelli undermined one of the fundamental assumptions of Western thought. This insight has bedeviled political thinkers ever since and accounts for his continuing importance.

Machiavelli was born on May 3, 1469, in Florence into an old family from the Oltrarno, south of the river. His father, Bernardo, was from an undistinguished branch of the family, and Niccolò was for all of his life denied access to the upper reaches of Florentine society. He had two sisters, Margherita and Primavera, and a brother, Totto. Of his early years when he was growing up, studying at school and at home, little is known. What is known is that during those years he saw a number of extraordinary political and social changes in his native city. The death of Lorenzo "the Magnificent" de' Medici in 1492 and the rise of the charismatic preacher Girolamo Savonarola hastened the downfall of the Medicis, resulting in the expulsion of the family from Florence in 1494 and a return to republican rule. In 1498, Machiavelli was appointed head of the second chancery of the Florentine Republic and was also made secretary to the Ten of War, and he would serve the republic in various capacities, both diplomatic and administrative, for the next fourteen years. Around August, 1501, Machiavelli married Marietta Corsini, who came from roughly the same social background as her husband. They had four children—a daughter, Bartolomea, and three sons, Bernardo, Guido, and Lodovico. Of his adult personal life little is known except for the brief glimpses of it that appear in his correspondence. The return of the Medicis in 1512 and the overthrow of the republic cost Machiavelli his sinecure, and for the rest of his life Machiavelli would only occasionally undertake official duties, most of the time living in the country as a private citizen and author, writing the books for which he is remembered. Machiavelli died on June 21, 1527, and was buried in the church of Santa Croce in Florence where his monument resides beside those of Michelangelo, Galileo, and Leonardo Bruni.

As Viroli points out, how and why the Council of Eighty and the Great Council of the Republic of Florence chose such a little-known, relatively young man from an impoverished, if not old, family to be a chancellor remains largely a mystery. Machiavelli had no political experience, nor was he a notary or doctor of laws, and as yet he had shown no literary distinction. One of the reasons for his appointment may have been his lack of support for Savonarola who was opposed by both the council and Signoria. Viroli also places some importance for his rapid rise to prominence on Machiavelli's reputation as a wit and well-respected man-about-town and a member of the chancery inner circle. Throughout his biography, Viroli emphasizes the importance of Machiavelli's personality in both his position in the government and his ability to negotiate for it, but surely there had to be other reasons for his rapid climb to fame, among which must have been his ability as a writer, evident first in the authorship of official dispatches and later as a political thinker with both firsthand experience and also wide humanist learning.

With the rapid turnover of the politicians in the Signoria and the ten, secretaries such as Machiavelli, with their long-term appointments, provided the continuity in the government. So his place in the second chancery was an extremely important one. His first diplomatic mission in 1499 to the lord of Piombino was quickly followed by another even more delicate one to the court of Caterina Sforza at Forli, which largely was a failure. As a neophyte diplomat, however, Machiavelli learned quickly the wiles and deceptions needed for negotiations on behalf of the republic and soon became one its most trusted emissaries, increasingly spending his time on the road, a life he seemed to relish so much so that when he was out of power after 1512, he frequently complained in his letters about the inactivity he was forced to endure.

During his years as an official of the republic he came into contact with many of the most powerful and ruthless personalities then engaged in the incessant internecine warfare which plagued Tuscany and northern Italy during the early years of the sixteenth century: Cesare Borgia, Louis XII of France, Ludovico Sforza, Pope Julius II. He also came to know many of the intellectuals of his time both in Florence and throughout the region.

The Great Council allowed the Medicis to return in 1512 as private citizens, but the fractional strife between them and the gonfalonier Pier Soderini, head of the republic, the growing power of the Medici family in the church, and the sacking of the nearby town of Prato by Spanish troops finally collapsed the republic, and on November 7, Machiavelli was removed from his post as secretary. As a staunch supporter of Soderini, he was not welcome in the new regime. His troubles were compounded when a plot against the Medicis was discovered, and Machiavelli was suspected of being one of the organizers (although he was not). He was imprisoned and tortured, and very well might have been executed except that Pope Julius II died and his successor was Giovanni Cardinal de' Medici (Leo X), and the Medicis, now secure in their power, pardoned most of those sentenced for participation in the conspiracy. In early March, 1513, Machiavelli was released from prison. During the rest of his life he tried to obtain government employment but never again regained his former position or prestige.

Machiavelli retired to a house in the country in Sant'Andrea in Percussina left to him by his father. There he lived in rustic isolation, infrequently interrupted by minor official duties; it was also at Sant'Andrea that he wrote the books that would gain him lasting fame. Although he corresponded with his friends about the frustrations of country living, he also found the solitude increased his reading—the reading that would inform his writings. His most famous book, *The Prince* (although more literally translated as *Of Principalities*), was completed by early December, 1513, apparently written rather quickly in the midst of his work on a longer study, the *Discorsi sopra la prima deca di Tito Livio* (1531; *Discourses on the First Ten Books of Titus Livius*, 1636). The treatise was not actually published until 1532, five years after his death. Machiavelli dedicated *The Prince* to Lorenzo de' Medici, grandson of Lorenzo the Magnificent, after its original dedicatee, Giuliano de' Medici, died. The dedication was just one attempt among many to get back into the good graces of the Medici family and regain his former official employment; none of these attempts did much good.

Between 1517 and 1519, Machiavelli composed two comedies. *Andria*, or *Woman of Andros*, was an adapted translation of the play *Andria* (166 B.C.E.; English translation, 1598) by the Roman poet Terence. The second was a satire, *La Mandragola* (pr. c. 1519; *The Mandrake*, 1911), which enjoyed many successful performances during the author's lifetime. Machiavelli had written an earlier play in 1504 called *The Masks*, based on Aristophanes' *Nephelai* (423 B.C.E.; *The Clouds*, 1708), but the only manuscript was destroyed by the author's grandson. Another play inspired by *Casina* (English translation, 1774) by Plautus was performed in 1525. Machiavelli's comic dramas provided an outlet for his wit and humor, which is in more evidence in his correspondence than in his other works.

Perhaps the most ambitious of Machiavelli's literary projects is *Discourses*, the study he apparently set aside in 1513 to write *The Prince*, returning to it in 1515. Machiavelli worked on the project until 1517, but it was never put into final form by the author. It was first published in 1531 (like *The Prince*, after his death). Although a more elaborate account of his political thinking, *Discourses* apparently began from Machiavelli's reading of Livy's *Ab urbe condita libri* (c. 26 B.C.E.-15 C.E.; *The History of Rome*, 1600). Unlike his earlier political work, *Discourses* presents a more rounded examination of the republican form of government, which Machiavelli preferred over princely autocracy. Reading *Discourses* alters somewhat the unfavorable political reputation Machiavelli received through the intervening years.

Finally, among his other major works is *Dell' arte della guerra* (1521; *The Art of War*, 1560), fashioned in the form of a dialogue, a characteristic literary device of the Renaissance. Machiavelli's service to Florence involved him in actively organizing a state militia—which unfortunately did not accord itself very well when actually engaged in battle—and in other military matters throughout his tenure as the second secretary. Although he was never a soldier, he was intimately involved in all manner of ways in the military affairs of Florence. In an age of almost constant warfare, it is little wonder that waging war figures prominently in Machiavelli's political works or that he retained a faith in military solutions to political issues and the art of statecraft. Machiavelli based his text on classical models, including the writings of Cornelius Tacitus and Livy, which often distorted some of his own observations that he gathered through experiences observing such contemporary military leaders as Cesare Borgia and Giovanni delle Bande Nere. Nevertheless, after publication of the book in 1521, it was widely translated and exerted a considerable influence on other treaties on warfare by, among others, Frederick the Great, Napoleon I, and Carl von Clausewitz.

In the final years of his life, Machiavelli wrote two other works. The Medicis commissioned *The Life of Castruccio Castracani*, a short biography of a prominent citizen and *condottiere* (mercenary soldier) from the neighboring town of Lucca. The second commission (from the university the Studio fiorentino), was for *Istorie fiorentine* (*The Florentine History*, 1595), which he completed in 1525. By writing his history, Machiavelli joined the ranks of other distinguished Renaissance historians who at one time or another were associated with the Florentine chancery and whose work Machiavelli drew upon for his own. The history traced the events of his native city from its origins through the year 1492. Unlike other historians, Machiavelli focused on the city's internal affairs, civil discord, and conspiracies. In many ways it is a casebook study for the more theoretical political writings of *The Prince* and *Discourses*.

Machiavelli's life and career epitomized what is thought of as the characteristics of the Renaissance man: He was a diplomat, government functionary, author of dramas and poetry, historian, classical scholar, and political theorist. He was a man of both action and thought. Through his official dispatches, his personal letters, and his longer treatises on politics, warfare, and civic government, written in his graceful and insightful prose, Machiavelli gave to posterity not only a reasoned and colorful description of sixteenth century Italy but also works of enduring value which still can be read for pleasure and instruction.

Charles L. P. Silet

Sources for Further Study

Booklist 97 (October 1, 2000): 320.
Library Journal 125 (October 15, 2000): 80.
The New York Times Book Review 105 (December 3, 2000): 90.
Publishers Weekly 247 (September 11, 2000): 76.

NONZERO
The Logic of Human Destiny

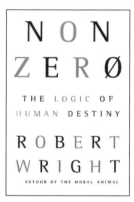

Author: Robert Wright (1957-   )
Publisher: Pantheon Books (New York). 435 pp. $27.50
Type of work: Anthropology, history, natural history, philosophy, and science

~

A theory of the direction of human cultural evolution that uses the idea of the non-zero-sum game to interpret human history and organic evolution

~

Robert Wright is an award-winning essayist and journalist. His 1994 book, *The Moral Animal*, argued that genetic evolution created human morality. Although this earlier work is an interesting presentation of the evolutionary view of human beings, it is essentially a popularization of views held by many evolutionary psychologists and sociobiologists. In *Nonzero*, Wright again takes up the subject of the evolution of human society, but this time he develops an original and farsighted theory.

Many contemporary social and physical scientists reject the view that evolution implies progress. The prevailing view in biology is that species differ because they develop different means of adapting to different environments; thus, the human brain and the bird's wing are specialized adaptations, not properties of "higher" and "lower" animals. In cultural anthropology and sociology, a similar perspective presents the hunting and gathering culture and the modern urban culture as two different but equal strategies for organizing human social life. Scholars and researchers frequently reject the idea that life is somehow moving onward and upward as a remnant of nineteenth century progressivism—an ideology with imperialistic attitudes toward nonhuman creatures and non-European cultures. The ideas of priest, paleontologist, and philosopher Pierre Teilhard de Chardin (1881-1955), who argued that evolution is teleological, or directed toward a goal, tend to be written off as fuzzy mysticism by most scientists.

Wright maintains that there is indeed progress in both organic and cultural evolution. His theory, unlike that of Teilhard de Chardin, is based on purely physical principles, and it is entirely consistent with mainstream Darwinian concepts. Wright draws on game theory to explain progress in human and natural history. Game theorists have long argued that games can be either zero-sum or non-zero-sum in character. The first are those in which one player or set of players benefit at the expense of another player or set of players. Non-zero-sum games, on the other hand, are those in which all participants benefit from their interaction.

Societies, like organisms, take shape as adaptations to environments. A society is a cooperative enterprise. It exists because human beings rely on one another for survival. The more elaborately cooperative a society is, the more efficiently it can meet the demands posed by its environment. There is, then, a push toward what Wright calls "non-zero-sumness" built into the dynamics of social life. Further, human groups compete for resources with other human groups as well as other animals. More highly organized and cooperative groups generally have the competitive advantage over others, so that a form of natural selection favors non-zero-sum characteristics in societies. In addition, human beings learn from others, even from their rivals, so that hostile as well as friendly interaction between sets of people promotes social progress.

Robert Wright is the author of Three Scientists and Their Gods *and* The Moral Animal, *which was named by* The New York Times Book Review *as one of the year's best books. He has received the National Magazine Award for Essay and Criticism and has published in* The Atlantic, The New Yorker, The New York Times Magazine, Time, *and* Slate.

Part 1 of *Nonzero*, which makes up about two-thirds of the book, is dedicated to interpreting human history as the product of cultural evolution, driven by the adaptive advantages of non-zero-sum activities. Wright cites the Shoshone of North America as one of the least complex human societies, since their cooperative social units only rarely extended beyond single families. Still, even the Shoshone came together in larger and more complicated groups when they needed to in order to hunt jackrabbits. The relative simplicity of Shoshone social life was not due to any genetic characteristics of the Shoshone but to the fact that they lived in a sparsely populated environment that offered only small game for hunting and did not demand complex organization.

When an environment or a competition with others pushes a group toward greater cooperation than the occasional hunts of the Shoshone, the result is a "Big Man" culture. The big man is an individual who has achieved special prestige and power and can coordinate the tasks of others and the distribution of resources. War functions as a zero-sum activity, a competition between groups, that has non-zero-sum consequences, since wars tend to unite people and promote the authority of big men. War, the desire of big men to acquire wives and property, and the struggle to overcome scarcity all promote agriculture as a means of acquiring a surplus of resources. The resulting increase in social complexity turns the big man culture into a "chiefdom," a society containing more than one village and organized around a leader with sacred authority. Larger and more interconnected political forms require increasingly efficient means of communication, leading to the development of writing and money.

The trend of history, Wright argues, has moved steadily toward greater geographic integration and global exchange and coordination. Although he cannot predict the form of future world organization, he does believe that the coming "New World Order" is neither a meaningless cliché nor a paranoid right-wing fantasy. Wright admits that much of the movement of history has been brutal, involving wars, slavery, and other horrors, but he claims that the course of history in the long run is toward greater freedom and abundance.

The second part of the book turns from human history to the history of organic life.

Cultural evolution, Wright argues, is a part of biological evolution that has its own built-in tendency toward non-zero-sumness. All multicelled organisms, he points out, can actually be seen as colonies of single-celled creatures that became interdependent. Even the cells themselves, consisting of nuclei and organelles, are made up of formerly independent parts that merged under evolutionary pressures.

The organic basis of cultural evolution leads Wright to intriguing speculations. Some biologists have maintained that an ant colony should be considered a single organism, since ants show such a high degree of cooperation and elaborate division of labor, similar to the division of labor of the organs of an animal's body. In the human brain, interdependence and an intricate system of communication among the specialized cells known as neurons even gives rise to the consciousness that defines the individual self. Similarly, as people become more interconnected, it is at least possible to suggest that they are moving toward the state of a single global organism. As communications technologies take on greater sophistication, it may be possible to imagine the emergence of consciousness from the wiring, as consciousness has emerged from the neural wiring of the brain. Teilhard de Chardin's idea of a "noosphere," a unified envelope of thought around the earth, may actually be a future reality for the human race. Wright's speculations even lead him into theology, a field rarely considered compatible with evolutionary biology. The direction in evolution may suggest a purposive force behind natural selection, a force consistent with some concepts of God.

Nonzero is a fascinating book, written in a comfortable, good-humored style that makes it appealing to a wide audience. Wright makes a good case for reviving the view that human history and evolution itself are progressive in character. His criticisms of Stephen Jay Gould's arguments against progress in evolution make a valuable contribution to the debate over the evolutionary process. Wright exhibits considerable skill and erudition in bringing together evidence from anthropology, history, philosophy, and biology. Still, some readers may feel that Wright's talents as a journalist have enabled him to gloss over some of the weaknesses in his argument and to present his argument in a form that is somewhat more grandiose than the facts warrant.

The subtitle's claim that *Nonzero* describes "the logic of human destiny" is not well supported throughout most of the book. It is true that in the second part, Wright does speak in prophetic terms consistent with the word "destiny." This prophetic part of the book is explicitly offered as speculation, though, and Wright does not claim to have insight into the endpoint toward which humans are moving. In most of the book, he satisfies himself with the more modest achievement of demonstrating that the dynamics of cultural and organic evolution make human and natural history progressive in character. This is not a destiny—it is a tendency. It does not show that life is moving toward any particular goal. Instead, it suggests that the mechanics of life push it in certain ill-defined directions. Wright's leap of faith from direction to purpose, similarly, is more a matter of intellectual gymnastics than sound reasoning. A ball dropped from the roof of a house has direction. This does not provide one with any evidence for or against a purpose behind the force of gravity.

Although Wright is convincing in his claims that increasing interdependence through non-zero-sumness lies behind the movement of history, he is vague about the precise nature of the progress. He seems to be arguing that organisms and human societies move toward ever-greater complexity. As he admits in an appendix, though, there is no agreed-upon definition of social complexity and no way to measure it. The civilization of the contemporary United States is technologically more sophisticated than that of ancient Rome, but it is hard to say which is the more complex system. Since Wright is not arguing simply that human beings have developed better tools in the course of their stay on Earth, the difficulty with identifying and measuring complexity is troubling for his argument.

The optimism of *Nonzero* is encouraging, but readers may be justified in wondering if progress really does make things ultimately better every day in every way. For example, according to Wright, population size is one of the main elements in the non-zero-sum development of societies: The more people there are in an area, the greater the cooperation and exchange of information. Thus, population growth contributes to cultural evolution. At the same time, though, human population growth has arguably become one of the greatest threats to life on Earth. Most scientists would agree that biodiversity on the planet has decreased as humans have multiplied. Wright maintains that too much attention has been given to the negative consequences of population growth and that people have overlooked its positive consequences. Even these positive consequences can have undesirable side effects, though. Greater interdependence and technological sophistication also result in intensified ecological pressures. People can produce more food and, for some, higher standards of living than ever before, but forests disappear daily and waters become polluted with fertilizers precisely because of the diversion of natural energies to human use.

Debates over globalization may also provoke the question of whether a new world order is leading to a brighter future for all. While it is probably true that nations around the world gained from the intensification of world trade, progress perhaps did not bestow its benefits on all in those nations. Unemployment, crowding in cities, and homeless children sleeping on the streets perhaps increased in many developing countries in those years, and many economists argue that these unfortunate developments are direct consequences of global trade and international specialization. It may be that the standard of living in all of these countries will eventually improve (assuming the survival of the race) as a result of non-zero-sumness, but few starving people will be comforted much by the thought that their descendants might be fat and happy.

Some skepticism may be in order, then, as one ponders Wright's efforts at describing the direction of human history. Nevertheless, he has written an important book. In the 1980's and 1990's, the works of authors such as Stephen Jay Gould, Richard Dawkins, E. O. Wilson, Matt Ridley, Steven Pinker, and Daniel Dennett began to make Darwinian evolution once again a hot topic and to show the relevance of evolution to a wide variety of areas of thought. Wright offers a comprehensive, original, and stimulating contribution to this topic.

Carl L. Bankston III

Sources for Further Study

Booklist 96 (January 1, 2000): 843.
The Christian Century 117 (May 24, 2000): 602.
Library Journal 125 (February 15, 2000): 186.
National Review 52 (March 6, 2000): 50.
The New York Times Book Review 105 (January 30, 2000): 6.
Publishers Weekly 247 (January 24, 2000): 303.
The Washington Monthly 22 (April, 2000): 50.
The Wilson Quarterly 24 (Winter, 2000): 103.

NORWEGIAN WOOD

Author: Haruki Murakami (1949-   )
First published: Noruwei no mori, 1987, in Japan
Translated from the Japanese by Jay Rubin
Publisher: Vintage International (New York). 296 pp.
$13.00
Type of work: Novel
Time: 1968-1970
Locale: Tokyo and a sanatorium in the mountains north
of Kyoto

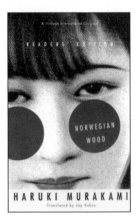

A young man is emotionally torn between two women:
the psychologically troubled girlfriend of his best friend,
who committed suicide, and an unconventional classmate

Principal characters:

> TORU WATANABE, a college student
> KIZUKI, his best friend in high school, who committed suicide at seventeen
> NAOKO, Kizuki's girlfriend, who had known him since they were three
> MIDORI, a classmate of Watanabe
> REIKO, Naoko's roommate at the sanatorium

Haruki Murakami established his reputation, in both Japanese and English, as a writer of surreal, fantastic tales of a world gone slightly awry, where a man can be spiritually possessed by a sheep (*Hitsuji o meguru boken,* 1982; *A Wild Sheep Chase,* 1989) and a hotel can contain an alternate universe (*Dansu dansu dansu,* 1988; *Dance Dance Dance,* 1994), where a man can gain access to an alternate universe by sitting at the bottom of a well (*Nejimaki-dori kuronikuru,* 1994; *The Wind-up Bird Chronicle,* 1997), or where a hero who inhabits alternate universes approaches himself in alternate chapters (*Sekai no owari to hado-boirudo wandarando,* 1985; *Hardboiled Wonderland and the End of the World,* 1991). What is clear is that Haruki Murakami's universes are always alternatives; even the mundane world is inhabited by characters who push against the conformist grain of Japanese society. Murakami is a fan of Raymond Chandler, indeed has translated him into Japanese, and Murakami's protagonists all bear some degree of resemblance to Chandler's hard-boiled, loner detective, Philip Marlowe—his cynicism, his sense of morality, and his propensity to rescue damsels in distress.

In 1968, Toru Watanabe leaves his home town of Kobe to attend university in Tokyo. He lives in a private dormitory, where students from many universities board. He is a loner, spending his time reading American novelists such as F. Scott Fitzgerald and John Updike.

One reason for Watanabe's solitary existence is that when he was in high school, his best friend, Kizuki, committed suicide. Kizuki was smart, charismatic, and popular, seeming to have everything in the world to live for. Watanabe spent most of his time with Kizuki and Kizuki's girlfriend, Naoko. He seems to be reluctant to open up to anyone after this inexplicable loss.

> Until that time, I had understood death as something entirely separate from and independent of life. The hand of death is bound to take us, I had felt, but until the day it reaches out for us, it leaves us alone. This had seemed to me the simple, logical truth. Life is here, death is over there. I am here, not over there.

> The night Kizuki died, however, I lost the ability to see death (and life) in such simple terms. Death was not the opposite of life. It was already here, within my being, it had always been here, and no struggle would permit me to forget that. When it took seventeen-year-old Kizuki that night in May, death took me as well.

One Sunday, two years after Kizuki's suicide, Watanabe runs into Naoko in Tokyo, and they begin to spend their Sundays together walking around the city. It is an ambiguous relationship, not that of boyfriend and girlfriend, but of a deeper emotional connection than a typical college friendship. They never speak of the past, but the fact of Kizuki's death is always there between them. Slowly, Watanabe falls in love with Naoko. On the night of her twentieth birthday, he brings a cake to her apartment to celebrate. After dinner, when Watanabe tries to leave, she begins to cry:

> One big tear spilled from her eye, ran down her cheek, and spattered on a record jacket. Once that first tear broke free, the rest followed in an unbroken stream. Naoko bent forward where she sat on the floor and pressing her palms to the mat, she began to cry with the force of a person vomiting on all fours. . . . Supporting her weight with my left arm, I used my right hand to caress her soft straight hair. And I waited. In that position, I waited for Naoko to stop crying. And I went on waiting. But Naoko's crying never stopped.
> I slept with Naoko that night.

After Watanabe leaves the next morning, Naoko disappears. She moves out of her apartment with no forwarding address. A letter he mails to her parents' address in Kobe is not answered. Finally, after three months, he receives a letter from a sanatorium outside Kyoto. Naoko explains that she is recovering from a nervous breakdown, but cannot explain anything more.

Time goes by. One day, in a small student café, a girl from his History of Drama class approaches him. Her name is Midori, and despite his insistence that he is just "an ordinary guy," she persists in seeing him as unique and iconoclastic. Soon the two of them are spending time together, although she has a boyfriend and he is still emotionally bound to Naoko. Midori is a working-class girl—her father owns a small bookstore in a rundown neighborhood—who was sent to an upper-class high school because of her academic skills. The chip on her shoulder is evident, as are her eccentricities. She relishes, for instance, relating to Watanabe her fantasies, both sexual and interpersonal. These fantasies invariably revolve around her ability to control other people, to subject them to her whims and caprices.

Meanwhile, Naoko sporadically writes letters from her sanatorium. Watanabe goes to visit her, and meets her roommate, Reiko. The sanatorium is a very open, unconventional place, where people work on the land, share group therapy, and attempt to rebalance themselves. Reiko is in her late thirties, a pianist with a history of mental breakdowns. The event that drove her to the sanatorium was a lesbian seduction launched at her by one of

Haruki Murakami is the author of five novels and a collection of short stories that have been translated into English and fifteen other languages, as well as a nonfiction book about the survivors of the Aum Shinrikyo poison gas attack on the Tokyo subway. He was born in Kyoto, Japan, in 1949.

her students, a sociopathic, manipulative thirteen-year-old. She spends much of her time playing music, and whenever Naoko requests that she play the Beatles song "Norwegian Wood," she has to put some money in a jar, because she requests it so often.

Naoko begins to be able to talk to Watanabe about her own past, in particular her relationships with Kizuki and her older sister, another "perfect" teenager who committed suicide. The only flaw in her perfection was that she had a habit of periodically shutting herself up in her room for a day or two; after her suicide, her parents recalled another relative who had shut himself up in his house for four years, then threw himself in front of a train. Naoko was the one who discovered her sister's body, and she retreated to her bedroom for three days afterward, unable to talk. She seems to regard this withdrawal as evidence that she is tainted with the same "flaws" that drove her sister to suicide. These suicides are unexplained to the extent that there is no note explaining why, but it seems that these perfect children choose death over imperfection. The strain is too great for them, and they crack under the pressure.

On his return to Tokyo, Midori takes Watanabe to visit her father, who is in a hospital recovering from surgery for a brain tumor. This is the illness that killed Midori's mother just a few years before. It becomes increasingly clear that Midori's fantasies of bossing other people around are a compensation for the years she has spent tending to ungrateful ailing relatives—her father's reaction to her mother's death was to tell his daughters that one of them should have died instead. Watanabe offers to sit with her father while she goes out and relaxes, and although the man cannot speak (a situation that Murakami indicates by placing his voiceless words within angle brackets) and is almost out of touch with reality, Watanabe talks to him about the small things going on in his life, going to classes, doing laundry, the concept of *deus ex machina*. He persuades Midori's father to eat a cucumber, cut into small pieces, wrapped in *nori*, and dipped in soy sauce:

> "How was that? Good, huh?"
> <Good,> he said.
> "It's good when food tastes good," I said. "It's kind of like proof you're alive."

Nonetheless, the next week Midori's father dies. Midori does her own disappearing act after that, leaving Watanabe torn between his growing love for Midori and his feeling of responsibility to Naoko. He makes another visit to the sanatorium; he attends classes. Midori sells the bookstore and moves into an apartment with her sister; Watanabe moves out of the dormitory into a little house far from the university and tries to persuade Naoko that she should leave the sanatorium and come live with him. Unfortunately, he neglects to tell Midori about his move, and she cuts off communication with him in a fit of pique. At the same time, communication from Naoko dries up as well. Eventually Reiko writes him that Naoko has gotten worse. She is hearing voices. "I had assumed that the only problem was whether she could regain the courage to return to the real world, and that if she managed to do so, the two of us could join forces and make a go of it. Reiko's letter smashed the illusory castle that I had built on that fragile hypothesis, leaving only a flattened surface devoid of feeling." Naoko leaves the sanatorium to get treatment at a more conventional mental hospital. Now he is stuck in limbo, between one girl who cannot speak to him and another who refuses.

Finally Midori breaks her silence and tells him straight out that she has broken up with her boyfriend and is in love with him. He confesses that he loves her, but is still bound to Naoko, even though she does not love him. The problem of choice, however, becomes moot, for soon afterward Naoko commits suicide, hanging herself just as her sister had done.

Watanabe takes off on an aimless journey, wandering from town to town, sleeping on beaches or in flophouses, trying to come to terms with all the death around him. "I had learned one thing from Kizuki's death . . . : 'Death is not the opposite of life but an innate part of life.' By living our lives, we nurture death. True as this might be, it was only one of the truths we had to learn. What I learned from Naoko's death was this: no truth can cure the sorrow we feel from losing a loved one."

When he returns to Toyko, he receives a letter from Reiko; as a result of Naoko's death, she has decided that it is time to leave the sanatorium herself. She is on the way to take up a job teaching music in Hokkaido, and she wants to see him on the way. When she arrives, they talk about Naoko and where their lives may go from here. Finally, they make love. After seeing Reiko off on the train, Watanabe calls Midori.

Norwegian Wood was a sensation when it was published in Japan in 1987. Superficially it is a completely realistic novel, lacking Murakami's usual infusion of Magical Realism. However, in both theme and tone it is unmistakably Murakami in its portrayal of a young man torn between commitments to a melancholy, withdrawn, psychologically troubled woman who does not love him and to one who is unconventional, aggressive, very much of the here and now. "I'm a real, live girl," Midori says, "with real, live blood gushing through my veins. You're holding me in your arms and I'm telling you that I love you." Naoko slips into the Otherworld of death as mysteriously as Kiki dissolves into the Sheep Man's alternate Dolphin Hotel in *Dance Dance Dance*, she is as imprisoned as Kumiko in *The Wind-up Bird Chronicle*. Naoko and Kizuki choose death, where stillness will keep them perfect. Watanabe and Midori choose life because they know they are imperfect, and so is life.

Leslie Ellen Jones

Sources for Further Study

Booklist 96 (June 1, 2000): 1798.
Library Journal 125 (November 1, 2000): 136.
Los Angeles Times Book Review, September 3, 2000, p. 3.
The New York Times Book Review 105 (September 24, 2000): 7.
Publishers Weekly 247 (July 3, 2000): 45.
The Times Literary Supplement, June 2, 2000, p. 24.
The Village Voice 45 (October 3, 2000): 205.

NOTHING LIKE IT IN THE WORLD
The Men Who Built the Transcontinental Railroad, 1863-1869

Author: Stephen E. Ambrose (1936-   )
Publisher: Simon & Schuster (New York). 431 pp.
    $28.00
Type of work: History
Time: 1830 to 1869
Locale: Illinois, Iowa, Nebraska, Colorado territory, Wyoming territory, Utah territory, Nevada, California

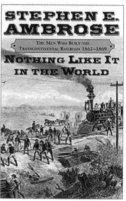

~

The story of the financiers, politicians, engineers, and surveyors; the Irish, Chinese, and other immigrants; the former Union and Confederate soldiers; the Mormons; and other determined men who performed the "impossible" feat of building a transcontinental railroad from Omaha, Nebraska, to Sacramento, California

~

Principal personages:

ABRAHAM LINCOLN (1809-1865), a politician and railroad lawyer, later the sixteenth U.S. president, highly influential in backing the transcontinental railroad to strengthen the union by joining east and west

THEODORE D. JUDAH (1826-1863), the founder of the Central Pacific Railroad, who did not live to see his dream project begun

GENERAL GRENVILLE M. DODGE (1831-1916), the chief engineer of the Union Pacific Railroad and the man who persuaded President Lincoln to support the project

LELAND STANFORD (1824-1893), one of the Big Four of the Central Pacific (CP), largely involved with the political machinations of creating the railroad

COLLIS P. HUNTINGTON (1821-1900), another of the Big Four of the CP, mainly involved with lobbying Congress and borrowing money for the railroad

CHARLES CROCKER (1822-1888), another of the CP's Big Four, an aggressive leader of men, in charge of actual railroad construction

MARK HOPKINS (1814-1878), another of the CP's Big Four, an intellectual who handled bookkeeping and related matters

GENERAL WILLIAM TECUMSEH SHERMAN (1820-1891), the fiery Civil War hero who was largely responsible for protecting railroad workers from hostile Indians

BRIGHAM YOUNG (1801-1877), the Mormon leader whose followers helped lay the tracks through Utah

Nothing Like It in the World hit the top of the *New York Times* nonfiction best-seller list right after publication and was still riding high on the list at the end of 2000. The book is an attractive, state-of-the-art production illustrated with thirty-two pages of black-and-white photographs of men, machinery, and rugged, desolate landscapes. It is a saga of man against nature. It is full of the nuts-and-bolts details of railroad building and does not contain a single female character of any importance. The only women mentioned are those who provide short-term companionship for the rough

Stephen Ambrose is the author of numerous books on American history, including Band of Brothers *and* Citizen Soldiers, *both on World War II,* Eisenhower, Crazy Horse *and* Custer, *and* Undaunted Courage: Meriwether Lewis, Thomas Jefferson, and the Opening of the American West.

men "who work like horses during the day and spend their money like asses" at night in the "Hell on Wheels" towns that fold their tents and follow the track as it snakes across the deserted continent.

The photographs help clarify Ambrose's descriptions of the obstacles the builders met and overcame with cuts, fills, trestles, bridges, tunnels, snowsheds, grades, and switchbacks, all designed to provide a comfortable ride for passengers and a roadbed that would allow a locomotive to pull a string of cars expeditiously over the highest summits. The book is sprinkled with many maps showing the progress of the Union Pacific westward across the plains to Utah and the progress of the Central Pacific over the Sierra Nevada and eastward to where it eventually joined the Union Pacific at Promontory Summit, just north of the Great Salt Lake. The duplicate maps inside the front and back covers show the entire two-thousand-mile-long route from Sacramento across Nevada, Utah territory, Wyoming territory, Colorado territory, and Nebraska. The original grade of the transcontinental railroad is closely followed by present-day Interstate Highway 80, evidencing the skill and perspicacity of the nineteenth century surveyors.

Reviewers inevitably compared Ambrose's book with David Haward Bain's much longer *Empire Express: Building the First Transcontinental Railroad* (1999). Bain is more scholarly, but Ambrose is more interesting. A reviewer for *Time* magazine said that Ambrose "writes with a wide-open throttle." He knows how to turn dry historical and statistical data into dramatic narrative, even though, characteristically, he has read extensively on his subject and provides reliable facts and figures. *Nothing Like It in the World* is generously documented with endnotes, a bibliography, and an index.

In dramatizing his material, Ambrose employs some of the techniques of the New Journalism. He uses poetic descriptions of landscape and weather, invents some dialogue, sprinkles his own informal prose with earthy quotations from books, magazines, and old newspapers, and especially focuses on the biggest dramatic feature of the great building project, the competition between the Union Pacific and the Central Pacific. Most of the chapters alternate between the Union Pacific surveyors and workers moving relentlessly westward and their rivals just as relentlessly moving toward the east. On both sides the emphasis was on speed rather than quality or safety. According to Ambrose, the general principle was: "Nail it down! Get the thing built! We can fix it up later." The actual builders, the men who did the hands-on work, performed herculean feats. In one instance they laid ten miles of track in a single day, something that had never been done, or even dreamed of, before. As many as fifteen thousand workers were employed on each line. Newspapers of the day compared them to the armies of the Civil War.

The overseers and the foremen were extemporizing a new form of production that would inspire men such as Henry Ford to revolutionize manufacturing with assembly-line production. Each individual or team performed a single function. One pair, for example, would do nothing but lay down the ties; a man would come along behind, setting spikes in place but not hammering them down. He would be followed by men who could drive a spike into a tie with exactly three blows of a sledgehammer. They were not overly generous with their use of spikes, either. The early trains provided a rickety ride for nervous dignitaries, sometimes crossing spindly wooden trestles and sometimes clinging precariously to cliff sides above sickening chasms. All the materials had to be shipped a great distance from point of manufacture, and the intention was to add more spikes at some later date.

Throughout his book Ambrose conveys the sense of urgency that drove everyone to lay track as track had never been laid before. The railroad was being followed by poles and wires for the recently invented telegraph, so that the two coasts of the United States would eventually be joined by rapid transportation as well as by even faster transcontinental communication. In the final chapter, titled "Done," the two crews meet in Utah for one of the most eagerly awaited and highly publicized media events in American history. A solid gold spike is ceremoniously driven into a predrilled hole—and quickly extracted to be preserved for posterity. It is now displayed at Stanford University in Palo Alto, California, the institution founded by Central Pacific tycoon Leland Stanford in memory of his son Leland, Jr., who died in 1884 at the age of sixteen.

The Central Pacific's biggest challenge was getting from Sacramento over the Sierra Nevada and down into Reno, Nevada. They were plagued by desertions because laborers were tempted by the chances of striking it rich, or at least earning higher wages, by digging for gold in California or for silver in Nevada. By contrast, after starting from Omaha the Union Pacific had endless miles of flat prairie over which they had little to do except lay down the ties, drop the iron rails, and hammer in the spikes. Their biggest problem for years was the roving bands of Plains Indians, especially the Sioux, the Cheyenne, and the Arapaho, who employed guerrilla tactics that frustrated the U.S. Army soldiers of General Sherman. The Indians' behavior did nothing to endear them to the invaders of their hunting grounds. Some immigrants, though, were courageous enough—or foolhardy enough—to homestead isolated farms out in the middle of the lone prairie, without a neighbor for hundreds of miles in any direction. The so-called red devils tortured, murdered, and scalped men, women, and children. The marauders were motivated by rage and frustration; they had no idea that their murderous raids would bring about the reaction that would destroy them. In one instance quoted by Ambrose, a war party caught a railroad worker alone out on the prairie and skinned him alive. The workers had to carry rifles and revolvers as well as picks and shovels. General Sherman's attitude toward Indians was not unlike his draconian attitude toward the rebellious South during the Civil War. He told the Indians:

> This railroad will be built, and if you are damaged [by it] we must pay you in full, and if your young men will interfere the Great Father, who, out of love for you, withheld his soldiers, will let loose his young men, and you will be swept away. . . . We will build iron roads, and you cannot stop the locomotive any more than you can stop the sun or the moon, and you must submit, and do the best you can.

Ambrose's sympathies are entirely with the railroad builders and the forces of progress. He is quite obviously politically conservative, patriotic, and procapitalist in sympathies. His long list of publication credits includes seven books about Dwight D. Eisenhower and three about Richard M. Nixon, both Republican presidents with conservative views. He approves of the way the U.S. Congress pitted the Central Pacific against the Union Pacific, even though it cost many lives and wasted millions of dollars. He acknowledges that there was graft and outright thievery involved, but does not dwell on the subject. Most of his discussion of the scandal that erupted when the public began to realize how much public money had been siphoned into private pockets is confined to a brief epilogue after the Golden Spike has been driven and the climax of his dramatic narrative has been reached. He emphasizes accomplishment rather than cost:

> It is possible to imagine all kinds of different routes across the continent, or a better way for the government to help private industry, or maybe to have the government build and own it. But those things didn't happen, and what did take place is grand. So we admire those who did it—even if they were far from perfect—for what they were and what they accomplished and how much each of us owes them.

At first it looked as if the Union Pacific would conquer far more territory (and with it acquire far more government subsidy bonds and free government land) than their western competitor. When the Civil War ended in 1865, the Union Pacific had an abundance of cheap labor from well-disciplined young Union and Confederate veterans looking for jobs, adventure, and opportunity. The Central Pacific's first and biggest problem was conquering the seemingly impregnable Sierra Nevada, covered for many months each year by the deepest snows on the continent. The job required blasting many long tunnels through solid rock at the rate of six inches on a bad day and twelve inches on a good one. Much of the arduous and dangerous labor was provided by Chinese immigrants, without whom the Central Pacific might never have reached its goal. The men who performed the labor on both railroads are, as Ambrose acknowledges, the true heroes of the struggle to bridge the continent.

The collection of illustrations contains the famous photograph by A. J. Russell in which the workers and their old-fashioned locomotives meet face to face on May 10, 1869. Because of the telegraph line, the news was conveyed all over the nation in a matter of seconds. There were great celebrations north, south, east, and west, with parades, speech making, and firing of cannons. It was the greatest engineering feat achieved anywhere on earth up to that time. Whereas it had once taken as long as six months to travel from New York to San Francisco, a train passenger could now make the journey in relative comfort and safety in only seven days. People of the day considered this a miracle comparable to landing on the moon. An affluent passenger could travel from coast to coast in a Pullman sleeper car for only $150, and an immigrant could make the journey in third class for only $65. "Together, the transcontinental railroad and the telegraph made modern America possible." In *Nothing Like It in the World*, a combination of scholarship and creative imagination, Ambrose does an excellent job of bringing the past back to life.

Bill Delaney

Sources for Further Study

Booklist 96 (July, 2000): 1970.
Library Journal 125 (August, 2000): 123.
The New York Times Book Review 105 (September 17, 2000): 8.
Publishers Weekly 247 (July 3, 2000): 55.
Time 156 (October 2, 2000): 95.
Trains 60 (December, 2000): 92.
The Wall Street Journal, August 25, 2000, p. W10.

NOWHERE MAN
The Final Days of John Lennon

Author: Robert Rosen (1952-   )
Publisher: Soft Skull Press (New York). 221 pp. $22.50
Type of work: Biography
Time: 1976-1980
Locale: New York City

~

*Rosen's haunting account of the last five years of the
rock idol and former Beatle reveals a reclusive, tormented
genius who falls apart mentally and physically as his marriage crumbles and his creative powers decline*

~

Principal personages:
JOHN LENNON, musician and ex-Beatle
YOKO ONO, artist, his wife
SEAN LENNON, their son

"All I want is truth. Just gimme some truth," John Lennon sang on his 1971 hit album *Imagine.* Years after the former Beatle's assassination on December 8, 1980, biographers, music critics, and fans are still searching for the truth about this enigmatic,
complicated man. When Lennon enjoyed worldwide fame as a member of the Beatles
(the pioneering British rock group popular in the mid- to late 1960's) and later as a solo
artist, his life was scrutinized—and at times, roundly criticized—by the media. He and
his wife, artist Yoko Ono, grabbed their share of headlines when they appeared nude on
the cover of their *Two Virgins* album released in 1968. They also caused a stir in the
spring of 1969 when they conducted a series of "bed-ins" protesting the United States'
involvement in the Vietnam War. Their high-profile activism and escapades came to an
end in 1976, however, when Lennon slipped into seclusion behind the walls of his home
in the Dakota, the posh New York City apartment building where he, his family, and a
retinue of servants lived. He claimed that he wanted to devote his time to his wife and
their new son, Sean. For the next five years, Lennon maintained his low profile, rarely
performing or recording. Lennon and Ono, both masters at manipulating their public
personas, crafted an image of Lennon as a happy househusband who padded around
their apartment baking bread and raising Sean while Ono ran the Lennon empire.

This myth of domestic bliss is called into question by Robert Rosen's controversial
biography. Rosen characterizes Lennon as a prisoner of his own fame, struggling with
drug addiction, bulimia, his resentment against his former partner Paul McCartney,
his tumultuous marriage, and his lack of spiritual and emotional discipline. It is a sad
portrait of an artist who has lost his creative drive and, as a result, his direction in life.

Robert Rosen has written articles for Mother Jones, Soho News, The Villager, Swank, The New York Times, *and speeches for the secretary of the Air Force. In 1996, he won a Hugo Boss poetry award. He is currently automotive correspondent for "The Looseleaf Report," a Los Angeles-based cable television show.*

Rosen claims that his portrayal of Lennon's last years is in part based on the musician's own diaries, which came into Rosen's possession under bizarre circumstances. Shortly after Lennon's death, Fred Seaman, Ono's personal assistant and Rosen's friend, approached the author about writing an unauthorized biography of Lennon. Seaman leaked confidential information to Rosen, which the author carefully recorded in his notes. In May of 1981, Seaman stole Lennon's original journals from the Dakota apartment and gave them to Rosen. Rosen says he worked for months transcribing every detail. Needing a break from his exhausting work, he left on a vacation to Jamaica. When he returned, his apartment had been ransacked and the diaries and his notes were gone. It was later determined that Seaman had stolen the journals back from Rosen after Ono had fired him. Rosen then began the arduous process of reconstructing the lost material entirely from memory.

That reconstruction forms the nucleus of *Nowhere Man*—a book Rosen describes in his introduction as a "work of both investigative journalism and imagination." He further states, "I have used my memory of Lennon's diaries as a roadmap to the truth. But I have used no material from the diaries." His disclaimer no doubt is meant to deflect any legal action on the part of the Lennon estate. The diaries were returned to Ono, and she has said that she will not allow them to be released to the public until the principal players are deceased.

Rosen mentions that his sources include interviews with people who were close to Lennon; the former Beatle's music and published books; information gleaned by traveling to places Lennon lived or vacationed; and books, magazines, and newspaper articles—all legitimate sources for any biographer. However, his warning that imagination played an important role in his portrait of Lennon prepares the reader for the interweaving of fact and fiction that is to come. Thus, his book is not a true biography, but an interpretive re-creation of Lennon's life.

The imaginative aspect of Rosen's book will disappoint readers who desire a more factual treatment of one of the most influential rock and roll musicians of the twentieth century. One creative device Rosen uses is to begin and end the book with "fantasies," an apparent pun on the title of Lennon's *Double Fantasy* album released in 1980. These inventions are seemingly meant to reveal the true nature of Lennon's psyche. The first represents Lennon as a contemporary imitator of Christ, walking the streets of modern-day Jerusalem; the second finds him alive a month after his supposed assassination, reflecting on what his life would have been like had the Beatles never attained celebrity. The messianic implications of these brief chapters call to mind Lennon's notorious comment made in 1966 that the Beatles were "more popular than Jesus" and also reflect Lennon's later, brief conversion to fundamentalist Christianity. Neither fantasy, however, offers fresh insight into Lennon's personality. Instead, both seem superfluous to the story sandwiched between them.

In another misguided attempt to convey what "it was like to be John Lennon," Rosen devotes an entire chapter to Lennon's dream life. Lennon believed in and tried to cultivate what is known as lucid dreaming, the ability to control and program one's dreams. Rosen records that at one point Lennon spent as much as sixteen hours a day asleep. He also speculates on the content of Lennon's dreams, which he asserts were often sexual in nature. Rosen comments in his introduction:

> In rare instances vital information, such as the details of Lennon's dreams, could be neither extrapolated from the public record nor found in an independent source. In those cases, I've used my imagination as best I could to recreate [*sic*] the texture and flavor of Lennon's life.

Although this caveat speaks for itself, it also serves to make the reader suspicious of any factual information Rosen includes in the chapter. How far does he let his imagination take him? Is the material he worked from so thin that he feels it necessary to flesh it out with conjecture?

The previous questions are crucial to judging the quality of Rosen's work. Most chapters are brief, some only half a page long. Yet they often contain more filler than fact. A primary example is the chapter entitled "The Book of Numbers." Ono was deeply involved in the occult, and under her influence Lennon also became a believer. They ran their lives by the mercury retrograde charts, daily consulted their own personal tarot card reader, and practiced magic. Lennon also became interested in numerology. Beginning with the number nine, Rosen details Lennon's obsession with numbers and demonstrates how certain numbers figured into his life. Rosen notes that the Lennons "would not so much as dial a telephone number without first consulting their bible, *Cheiro's Book of Numbers*" and, starting with John's October 9 birth date, goes on to calculate the various numerical values attached to letters that make up John's nicknames and the names of those closest to him. Rosen's analysis succeeds in showing how Lennon's enslavement to numerology revealed his deep insecurity and his intense desire to gain self-knowledge. However, Rosen's meticulous calculations become tedious after the first few pages, and by chapter's end it is difficult to ferret out any further insights from the maze of numbers and letters one has just traveled through.

Although hard information is sparse, Rosen's creative interpretation successfully conveys the sadness, pain, and confusion that permeated Lennon's last years. In one poignant passage, Rosen makes Lennon's love for Sean tangible when he describes a nocturnal visit he made to his son's bedroom:

> John poked his head into Sean's room and stood in the doorway watching him sleep. Sometimes tears welled in his eyes. Sean looked so peaceful. Even after four years, John still couldn't believe he really had a son like Sean. As long as Sean was okay, it didn't matter what else happened. Every day was a miracle.

Lennon's relationship with Ono was more complicated, characterized by a deep longing and pain-filled love. Lennon had come from a broken home, was raised by his mother's sister, and was reconciled with his mother a few years before she died in a car accident. Her passing devastated him. In Ono, he found not only a wife and lover, but also a substitute for the parent he had lost. "Mother," his nickname for his wife, was an emotionally loaded word for Lennon. It represented both the nurturing and controlling aspects of a woman's character. Ono possessed both these traits but tended to be more controlling than nurturing. Her calculating ways caused Lennon to leave her for eighteen months and live with May Pang, Ono's former secretary. Yet Lennon could not forget Ono, and after he returned to her, she became pregnant with their son. By 1980, their marriage was again on a downward spiral. Lennon and Sean went to Bermuda on a vacation, and as Rosen observes, Lennon realized he "was missing Mother very badly." He called her and asked her to come to them. At first she refused, ostensibly because the stars and planets were not right for the trip. Then she relented, but left shortly after she arrived. Later it was discovered Ono was having an affair with another man. Rosen captures Lennon's confusion and pain when he notes:

> Cut off from Mother, he felt adrift, frightened, insecure. Everything was going wrong. Why did Yoko first flatly refuse to come to Bermuda, then stay for less than two days? Why was she now unwilling to speak to him on the telephone? Was she again punishing him for his sins with May Pang? Or for other sins he did not even know about?

The love story that began in the late 1960's and endured so many ups and downs was now finally falling apart. Lennon expressed his anguish in "Losing You," a song that ultimately appeared on *Double Fantasy*.

Uncovering the truth is the main objective of biographers, but there are many facets of truth. Other writers have offered their own perspectives on John Lennon's life, including Albert Goldman in *The Lives of John Lennon* (1988), John Green in *Dakota Days* (1983), and, ironically, Rosen's old friend Fred Seaman in *The Last Days of John Lennon* (1991). A competing biography, *Lennon in America*, published in the same year as Rosen's book by Beatle expert Geoffrey Giuliano, is also purported to be based on Lennon's lost diaries. While Robert Rosen has contributed another tile in the mosaic representing Lennon's life and legacy, his biography is far from definitive. The information he presents is not new and can be found in some of the books mentioned above. His imaginative approach to the material, however, is original and may offer some fresh insight into Lennon's eccentric, erratic life. If readers want a fuller, more accurate portrait of John Lennon, however, they would do well to check out other resources in addition to Rosen's book.

Pegge Bochynski

Sources for Further Study

Booklist 96 (April 15, 2000): 1513.
Christianity Today 44 (June 12, 2000): 86.
Library Journal 125 (May 1, 2000): 116.
Publishers Weekly 247 (May 1, 2000): 58.

ON A DARK NIGHT I LEFT MY SILENT HOUSE

Author: Peter Handke (1942-   )
First published: In einer dunklen Nacht ging ich aus
   meinem stillen Haus, 1997, in Germany
Translated from the German by Krishna Winston
Publisher: Farrar, Straus and Giroux (New York). 186
   pp. $23.00
Type of work: Novel
Time: The present
Locale: Austria, Germany, Switzerland, Italy, France,
   and Spain

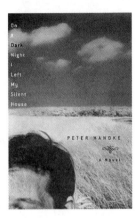

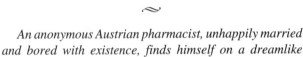

An anonymous Austrian pharmacist, unhappily married
and bored with existence, finds himself on a dreamlike
quest for happiness and a new identity in a surrealistic
grand tour of modern Europe

Principal characters:
   A PHARMACIST who is suffering a midlife crisis
   A POET who no longer writes poetry
   A SUPERANNUATED OLYMPIC CHAMPION ATHLETE

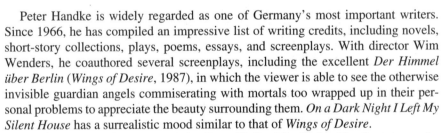

Peter Handke is widely regarded as one of Germany's most important writers. Since 1966, he has compiled an impressive list of writing credits, including novels, short-story collections, plays, poems, essays, and screenplays. With director Wim Wenders, he coauthored several screenplays, including the excellent *Der Himmel über Berlin* (*Wings of Desire*, 1987), in which the viewer is able to see the otherwise invisible guardian angels commiserating with mortals too wrapped up in their personal problems to appreciate the beauty surrounding them. *On a Dark Night I Left My Silent House* has a surrealistic mood similar to that of *Wings of Desire.*

Handke has often been compared to Franz Kafka. Like Kafka, Handke seems to be describing a reality invisible to the naked eye but all too real to the unconscious mind. As in many of Kafka's prose works, the principal character in *On a Dark Night*—a small-town middle-aged pharmacist—seems to be caught up in a dream. He seems to be trying to get somewhere but has only a vague notion of where he is or where he is going. As in many dreams, the dominant mood is one of bewilderment and frustration. Although nothing very dramatic ever happens during this dream journey, the pharmacist—who reminds the novel's narrator of such celebrities as Gary Cooper, Pedro Armendariz, Stan Laurel, Jerry Lewis, Buster Keaton, Edward G. Robinson, Ernest Borgnine, and even some of the "silent unapproachable" female stars—feels entirely changed by the end. Like Samuel Taylor Coleridge's ancient mariner, the

〜

*Peter Handke was born in Austria.
His works include* Absence, The
Jukebox and Other Essays on
Storytelling, *and* My Year in the
No-Man's-Bay.

〜

pharmacist insists on recounting his adventure to the narrator, who tries to structure and make sense of it; so this is a story within a story, or what one reviewer calls a *Rahmenerzählung*.

The setting of the novel has the same haunted look and feel of *Wings of Desire*. A defeated and demoralized nation is reemerging from its ruins, but people are confused about their national identity. The international-style architecture rising from the rubble of the past is cold and forbidding, purely functional and commercially motivated; it expresses nothing about the people it confines and overshadows. The town of Taxham, near Salzburg, where the pharmacist has lived and worked all his life, is becoming cut off from the world by a Gordian knot of freeways, an enormous airport, and new housing developments where streets twist and turn and end up leading into cul de sacs or back to where they started. Outsiders rarely visit Taxham anymore because it is so hard to get to, and townspeople rarely leave the town anymore because it is so hard to find the way out.

Handke seems more interested in describing architecture and landscapes than in describing people. Backgrounds and settings are more important than the characters. This is understandable, since the characters are superfluous and lack empowerment. As in *Wings of Desire*, the characters in Handke's novel are lonely, anonymous little people, so insignificant in their dehumanized environment they might almost be invisible. The pharmacist often sees people who look familiar, even like celebrities, but is never able to pin the correct names on them. In a significant passage (which applies to many of his works) Handke writes:

> I don't know why I've always had this reluctance to describe people—their faces, their bodies, especially particular features—and why I read such descriptions, no matter how skillfully done, with distaste, as if they were unseemly.

The fact that characters are not given names emphasizes their insignificance. The hero, a pharmacist of the old school, still insists on filling prescriptions by combining the various ingredients himself rather than merely counting pills out of bottles. He is married but totally estranged from his wife. They live together but occupy opposite ends of the house and avoid each other.

The pharmacist is so old-fashioned that he takes a medieval interest in the medicinal properties of wild plants, which grow in profusion because there are so many open spaces left over from the havoc of World War II. He is particularly interested in mushrooms. He eats them at home and even brings them along to be cooked for his dinner when he eats in restaurants. Throughout his travels he gathers and samples the various kinds of mushrooms to be found in different parts of Europe. There are more edible types than anyone but an expert would suspect existed; in fact, an expert might deny the existence of such a wide variety. The reader could easily get the impression that the pharmacist's goal is not to find himself or to find love or happiness but to collect mushrooms, the way Vladimir Nabokov collected butterflies. The pharmacist, whose wants are few, enjoys mushrooms for their taste and aroma but also for the psychedelic effects some produce. He will eat dark, malodorous, misshapen fungi no one else would dare sample.

On a Dark Night is also strangely reminiscent of Lewis Carroll's *Alice's Adventures in Wonderland* (1865). Like Alice, the pharmacist is lost in a land where everything seems unreal. Like Alice, he needs to get someplace but is not exactly sure where he wants to go or how to get there. The people he encounters on his surrealistic grand tour of Europe give him no more help than Carroll's Cheshire cat gave little Alice. The fact that the pharmacist is often under the psychedelic influence of strange foreign mushrooms only adds to the disorienting effect of the novel. The reader keeps hoping, like Alice, to wake up, to become reoriented, to return to dull, comfortable normality; thus, it is the reader's motivation more than that of any of the characters that drives the story.

Early in his travels the pharmacist picks up two men who are as footloose as him. One of these eccentric vagabonds is a poet who had once been famous but has since been consigned to limbo. The other was a winter sports champion, but his days of glory ended nearly thirty years earlier. The poet and the athlete are like the people most experience only in dreams. They are Kafkaesque people, strangers who seem to know the reader and who take it for granted that the reader knows them. Characteristically, the pharmacist thinks he has heard of the poet and thinks he remembers the athlete's achievements but cannot be sure of anything. The three travelers stay overnight in a house in the Alps. For some inexplicable reason, their widowed landlady enters the pharmacist's room at night and attacks him without provocation and without warning.

The very next moment she throws herself on him and begins to pound him. She beats him violently, left, right, with both fists, and she has big hands, which she clenches into fists like a man's.

This violent woman, who behaves as unpredictably as the queen of hearts in *Alice in Wonderland*, will reappear later in a different country and attack the hapless pharmacist again. She loves and hates him simultaneously. Her violence represents a combination of repulsion and sexual attraction. Later on, the poet seems to be explaining the woman's bizarre behavior in what is certainly the most interesting and thought-provoking passage in Handke's entire novel. It is only in this passage that reality seems to be trying to break through the dreamlike mood that Handke has been at such pains to establish.

> Lately mutual hostility has been planted between woman and man. These days men and women are furious at each other, without exception. . . . It's not only that we're not loved anymore; they're fighting us. And if love enters the picture, all it does is unleash war. Sooner or later the woman who loves you will be disappointed, in one way or another, and you won't even know why. She's seen through you, she'll explain, but without telling you in what respect. . . . There's not a single couple, whether touchingly young or old and dignified, that couldn't suddenly experience an outbreak of dissension in some situation or other, . . . dissension for which the potential existed between woman and man from the beginning, at least in our own era. . . . And why don't modern men and women leave one another in peace—at least for a while?

Like most tourists, the pharmacist and his two companions are attracted to special events. They attend festivals that are not unlike some of the joyless, commercialized holidays in the United States. These events seem merely obligatory, traditional; they are hollow and meaningless. They are like the exhibitions staged for documentary filmmakers, in which local boys and girls dress up in old-fashioned costumes and self-consciously perform folk dances to the accompaniment of wheezy accordions.

At long last, the poet and the former athlete drive off in the pharmacist's car, leaving him to wander alone for weeks across an emptiness he calls the steppe. Now he is totally lost, and his feeling of disorientation is enhanced by the fact that he must survive almost exclusively on the strange mushrooms that grow there abundantly.

> The many cliffs, as well as the crevasses, and gorges (with rivers and brooks) created unusual echo conditions throughout the town. These conditions didn't merely amplify sounds. They also confused your sense of direction, even where up and down were concerned. Near and far also often became indistinguishable.

The pharmacist's return to Taxham seems almost like a miracle, considering that he could have been as far away as central Russia. Throughout most of the story he has been unable to speak because of a mysterious blow to the head he received. Upon returning to Taxham, he finds he has not only recovered his voice but is now able to sing a strange song of his own composition as well. He insists on telling the narrator the whole story of his summertime adventure and insists on having it written down. The result is the book called *On a Dark Night I Left My Silent House*, whose atmosphere of confusion is further exacerbated by lapses in the pharmacist's memory and the inevitable miscommunications and misunderstandings that occur in conversations. The thesis of Handke's novel might be best expressed by one of Charles Baudelaire's most poignant lines: *Amer savoir, celui qu'on tire du voyage!*—What bitter knowledge one derives from traveling! Taxham is indeed a terrible place to live, and the rest of the world is no better.

Something of the poetic quality of Handke's prose is lost in translation, although the translator, Krishna Winston, is an expert. She is a professor of German studies at Wesleyan University with many published many translations, including works by Johann Wolfgang von Goethe, Christoph Hein, and Günter Grass. Professor Erich Skwara, who reviewed the German language version of *On a Dark Night* for *World Literature Today*, has nothing but enthusiastic praise for all of Handke's works. Skwara writes:

> Every book of his illuminates our growing confusion and makes me think of stained-glass windows in Gothic cathedrals: just as simple and yet complex are these stories, as readily available and healing to anyone stepping inside.

On the other hand, the *Economist* reviewer who read Handke's novel in German and thought it displayed the author's "growing preciousness" made the following generalization about the unpopularity of English translations of recent German fiction:

If you ask German publishers why, their stock answer is simple: While foreign writers from, say, America, Britain or Scandinavia can turn out well-written works with interesting story-lines and even arresting thoughts, modern German novelists have tended to disdain writing readable, entertaining books altogether.

A liking for Handke's metafiction is an acquired taste. One may not realize until after finishing *On A Dark Night* how much one enjoyed it and how well one understood it after all.

Bill Delaney

Sources for Further Study

Booklist 97 (October 1, 2000): 322.
The Economist Review 345 (October 18, 1997): 14.
Los Angeles Times Book Review, November 19, 2000, p. 1.
Publishers Weekly 247 (October 30, 2000): 45.
World Literature Today 72 (Winter, 1998): 123.

ON THE REZ

Author: Ian Frazier (1951-   )
Publisher: Farrar, Straus and Giroux (New York). Illustrated. 311 pp. $25.00
Type of work: Current affairs
Time: About 1850 to the present
Locale: New York City and the Pine Ridge Reservation, South Dakota

～

Frazier describes life on the Pine Ridge Reservation, the history of how the Oglala Sioux came to this condition, and the triumphs and tragedies of Native Americans on and off "the rez"

～

Principal personages:

IAN FRAZIER, the writer, a resident of New York City and then Montana, who describes his encounters with contemporary Native American life

LE WAR LANCE, an Oglala Sioux, friend of Frazier, and the source of many of the stories and incidents in the book

SUANNE BIG CROW, a legendary Pine Ridge High School basketball player killed in a car crash in 1992

LEATRICE "CHICK" BIG CROW, SuAnne's mother and the person who is helping to keep SuAnne's memory alive on the Pine Ridge Reservation

On the Rez is really two books that are yoked together only at the end, but which are compelling for the portraits both paint of Native American life in the United States at the end of the twentieth century. In the first two hundred pages, Ian Frazier describes his many encounters with Native American life and history. Although the focus is on the Plains Indians, and particularly the Oglala Sioux on the Pine Ridge Reservation in South Dakota, their life becomes representative of the fate of Native Americans on and off the reservation and across the United States. Two-thirds of the way through the book, however, Frazier takes up the story of SuAnne Big Crow, and the last third of the book—a vivid description of her life and a moving tribute to the talent and pride she stood for—implies the potential of Native American life everywhere.

Frazier lives in Manhattan when *On the Rez* opens. He meets and befriends Le War Lance, an Oglala Sioux residing in Washington Heights. When Frazier and his family resettle in Missoula, Montana, Frazier drives the eight hundred miles to the Pine Ridge Reservation in South Dakota where Le now lives, and over the course of the next four years visits Pine Ridge a number of times and meets other Oglala Sioux and learns their history, their few successes, and their many sufferings.

Frazier writes that in 1900, there were fewer than a quarter million Native Americans in the United States. At the beginning of the twenty-first century, the population totaled two million or more, making Native Americans the fastest-growing ethnic group in the country. Part of this growth must be attributed to the American Indian Movement (AIM), which began at Pine Ridge and, through a series of public protests, raised awareness of the plight of Native Americans and at the same time spurred hundreds of thousands of Americans to acknowledge their American Indian heritage. The most famous AIM incident occurred in 1973 at Wounded Knee, fifteen miles from the village of Pine Ridge, and marked the slaughter of Indians at that site in 1890. "AIM changed the way people regarded Indians in this country, and the way Indians regarded themselves; in an assimilationist America, they showed that a powerful Indian identity remained."

Ian Frazier is the author of Great Plains *and* Family. *He is probably best known for his humorous pieces from* The New Yorker *and* The Atlantic Monthly, *collected in* Dating Your Mom, *and* Coyote v. Acme, *which was awarded the inaugural Thurber Prize for American Humor.*

Certainly, that identity was necessary because the "saddening statistics" for Native Americans only multiply in Frazier's account:

> Ninety thousand or more Indian families are homeless, living on the street or sharing housing with relatives. Forty percent of Indian households are overcrowded or have inadequate dwellings, compared to about 6 percent for the population at large. Indians are about twice as likely as non-Indians to be murdered. Their death rate from alcoholism is four times the national average, and the rate of fetal alcohol syndrome among their children is thirty-three times higher than for whites.

Actually, as Frazier shows, Native Americans represent a kind of contradiction in American life. On one hand, there is the high incidence of adolescent suicide and alcohol-related car accidents. In addition, "30.9 percent of Indians have incomes below the national poverty line, more than any other race or ethnic group, so the neighborhoods where they live tend to be run-down." On the other hand, Native American tribes now own high-priced real estate in Las Vegas and Palm Springs, and several operate gambling casinos that gross one hundred million dollars or more a year.

Frazier parcels out this information as background to his story of life on Pine Ridge, and that reservation becomes a microcosm of the problems and potential of Indian life at the end of the twentieth century. His history covers Native American life from the Wampanoag who met the Pilgrims at Plymouth Rock through the Cherokee's removal from Georgia in 1839 that became known as the Trail of Tears, to more recent Indian heroes such as Ira Hamilton Hayes in World War II and Olympic runner Billy Mills. The Oglala Sioux are among the best-known tribes in American history, in part because of Wounded Knee, but also for other incidents in their history, such as their loss of the mineral-rich Black Hills and their spiritual autobiography narrated by the Holy Man in *Black Elk Speaks* (1932). Their poverty is emblematic of native Americans living everywhere in the United States.

Shannon County—the county in South Dakota that includes Pine Ridge village and much of the reservation—has the largest percentage of people living in poverty of any county in the nation: 63.1 percent of Shannon County residents have annual incomes that fall below the national poverty line. Of the ten poorest counties in the United States in 1990, four were on Indian reservations in South Dakota.

While the alcoholism rate among adults on Pine Ridge is above 65 percent, there is as yet no alcohol treatment center on the reservation. In some parts of Pine Ridge, housing developments have sprung up, while other areas are marked only by neglect and decay. "Only about three people in ten on Pine Ridge have jobs, and those are mostly with the Bureau of Indian Affairs, the Indian Health Service, or the Oglala tribe." Out of curiosity, Frazier seeks out the richest counties of the United States and finds five of the top ten are in suburban Washington, D.C. "Like the poorest place in the country," Frazier concludes, "the richest places get their money mainly from the federal government."

Frazier's account of Pine Ridge is realistic but not completely negative. He meets and befriends a number of interesting people on the reservation and hears accounts of kindness and heroism among them. He attends the annual powwow and observes traditional dance competitions. His history is full of fascinating figures such as Crazy Horse, the heroic Oglala Sioux leader of the nineteenth century, the Reverend Eugene Buechel, S.J., who compiled the invaluable *Dictionary of the Teton Dakota Sioux Language* (1970) in the twentieth, and AIM leaders Dennis Banks and Russell Means. The last third of Frazier's work takes off, however, when he begins to recount the life and legend of SuAnne Big Crow, a high school basketball star who in the late 1980's set state records and galvanized Lakota Sioux life. Frazier is fascinated by SuAnne because of her many talents and athletic accomplishments and because of an incident in the fall of 1988 when she faced a hostile white crowd at an away game in Lead, South Dakota. Instead of leading her team on the normal introductory lap around the gym, SuAnne

> suddenly stopped when she got to center court. . . . Then she stepped into the jump-ball circle at center court [and] in front of the Lead fans. . . . SuAnne began to sing in Lakota, swaying back and forth in the jump-ball circle, doing the shawl dance, using her warm-up jacket for a shawl. The crowd went completely silent . . . [and then] fans began to cheer and applaud.

When she is killed in an automobile accident, the reservation is devastated. "As SuAnne had predicted just a week or two before, the line of cars in her funeral procession stretched for miles." As her coach recounts, when she arrived at Pine Ridge High School for the memorial assembly, "what stays in my mind is the sound I heard as I walked in—the sound of all those kids in the gym crying."

After SuAnne's death, her legend only grew, especially when her mother helped to build the SuAnne Crow Health and Recreation Center on the reservation, and Frazier uses her life and death to focus the reader's attention on the good things about Indian life on Pine Ridge and its potential everywhere in the United States. "So much is so wrong on Pine Ridge. There's suffering and poverty and violence and alcoholism, and the aura of unstoppability that repeated misfortunes acquire." At the center, however, Frazier finds something else:

> A life of bravery and generosity and victory and heroism was the founding inspiration here, and if SuAnne's death was a terrible sorrow, it also had the effect of holding the good she represented fixed and unchanged. SuAnne Big Crow, though gone forever, is unmistakably still around. The good of her life sustains this place with a power as intangible as gravity, and as real.

Frazier discovers much that is still wrong with Native American lives in the United States. Among other things, "I know that the hopeful, big-sky feeling with which we often invest Western landscapes is at odds with the reality of life on Pine Ridge." In the story of SuAnne Crow—her exploits on the basketball court, the spirit that lived on after her death, her natural abilities, and her Indian pride—Frazier finds hopeful signs for the future. Like the model of the AIM movement, SuAnne's life shows what is possible for Native Americans. Like the increasing number of casinos opening on Native American lands, the chances of rising from poverty greatly increased for some Native Americans since her death.

The main problem with Frazier's book is that it splits into two. The first two-thirds wanders among New York City and Montana and South Dakota, only loosely focused on Frazier's relationship with his friend Le, the rest filled with stories and statistics of Native American life and the failures or blunders of federal Indian policy since at least the middle of the nineteenth century. When Frazier begins his story of SuAnne Crow, however, *On the Rez* kicks into a higher gear, and the last third of the book has a drama and an energy missing from the first two-thirds. Only at the end, in fact, are the two parts of the book pulled together.

Frazier, who early on became fascinated with Native American life, in fact first wrote about it in his 1989 *Great Plains*. He particularly became fascinated about the life of the famous Oglala Sioux leader Crazy Horse, one of his lifelong heroes. He became attracted to Native American life because it represented to him the idea of freedom: "As surely as Indians gave the world corn and tobacco and potatoes, they gave it a revolutionary new idea of what a human being could be." Frazier is a non-Indian trying to get to know Indian life and history and what it is like to live as an Indian, on and off the reservation, at the end of the twentieth century. In his eloquent, sometimes emotional prose, Frazier renders that life as few white writers have in the past, and in this sense *On the Rez* fulfills its purpose.

David Peck

Sources for Further Study

Booklist 96 (November 15, 1999): 578.
Library Journal 124 (November 15, 1999): 87.
The New York Review of Books 47 (February 10, 2000): 26.

The New York Times Book Review 105 (January 16, 2000): 6.
The New Yorker 75 (January 31, 2000): 92.
Publishers Weekly 246 (December 20, 1999): 67.
Time 155 (January 24, 2000): 74.

ON WRITING
A Memoir of the Craft

Author: Stephen King (1947-   )
Publisher: Charles Scribner's Sons (New York). 288 pp.
$25.00
Type of work: Autobiography and literary theory
Time: The 1940's to 2000

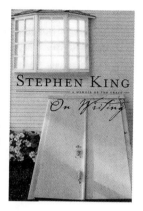

≈

King gives his reader three books in one: an autobiography, a how-to manual for writers, and an account of the 1999 automobile accident that almost killed him

≈

Principal personages:
STEPHEN KING, author
TABITHA KING, his wife
NELLIE RUTH PILLSBURY KING, his mother
DAVID KING, his brother
JOHN GOULD, editor of the Lisbon *Weekly Enterprise*
BRYAN SMITH, the man who involved King in an automobile accident

Stephen King is among the world's best-selling authors. He turned out one or two novels a year for over twenty-five years, bringing his grand total of novels, short stories, screenplays, and even comic books to over forty. His previous books include *Bag of Bones* (1998), *Hearts in Atlantis* (1999), and *Storm of the Century* (1999).

Ever since he published his first book, *Carrie* (1974), King has been asked how he writes on a regular basis. He hints around in interviews and in the forewords to his books, but only now does he finally tell the reader the truth in *On Writing: A Memoir of the Craft*. King has divided *On Writing* into three main parts: autobiography, how to write, and an account of the 1999 automobile accident with Bryan Smith that almost ended his life. Unlike other writing books, King writes *On Writing* as he would write anything else, with the honesty and middle-class crudeness that his fans would expect of him. Instead of being a turn-off, this "middle-of-the-road" style is to King's advantage. Everybody knows he is like McDonald's rather than the Brown Derby, so he tries to write that way, as well.

In the first part, "C.V.," King tells the reader his life story. Unlike other biographies where the author tells everything from beginning to end, King honestly says that he cannot remember everything. Instead, he offers the reader little vignettes from his life, skipping years here and there as need be. By the end of it, though, King has told his readers how he became a writer and what inspired him (his horror influences, though, are more clearly presented in 1981's *Danse Macabre*). Here King is perhaps more "honest" than in the section about writing itself. The reader sees over and over

~

Stephen King has written over fifty novels of horror and suspense, many of which have been made into movies. Among his classics are Carrie, Christine, The Shining, The Dead Zone, The Green Mile, *and* Misery.

~

again how King escaped poverty by writing. He and his brother David started their own newspaper, *Dave's Rag*, and he was submitting fiction to magazines before he was sixteen years old.

The fact that King was writing about the films he saw or anything else that crossed his mind did not really matter. He was writing, and just that by itself was an accomplishment. Writing was hard work, but King loved it. His best example of this is when he was a sports writer for the Lisbon *Weekly Enterprise*, his local newspaper. John Gould, the editor, showed him what to leave in and what to take out. It was simple, and King says Gould showed him in ten minutes the things that he still uses today. The rest of the autobiography tells how King met his wife, Tabitha, started a family, and how *Carrie* almost did not happen.

King also deals with, for the first time in print, his battles with alcohol and drugs in great detail. He started drinking during a high school senior trip to Washington, D.C., and by 1974 King was an alcoholic who gave his dead mother's eulogy while drunk. By 1985, he had added cocaine to his problems. He says that many books he wrote during this time he cannot remember very well, and his novel *Cujo* (1981) he barely remembers writing at all. He finally gave up his addictions after his wife took his wastebasket full of cigarettes, cocaine, beer cans, and other paraphernalia out of his office and told him to choose between them and their marriage. King was writing *Misery* (1987) at this time, a tale about a writer held hostage and forced to take drugs, and he was wondering if the fictional writer and King himself were one and the same. King chose to save his marriage. Amazingly, in spite of the effects of his drug abuse, King continued to write and publish at least one or two best-selling novels each year during the late 1970's and early 1980's.

The second part of the book is called "On Writing." Here King tells the reader how to write through specific, nuts-and-bolts examples. He talks about active and passive verbs, explains why a writer should never use adverbs, and provides examples of good and bad writing. King uses this section to put down on paper what he does and does not do; he says these rules will work for any writer, but they are really either for beginning writers or just those who are curious to know how Stephen King writes. To critics of King's style of writing, his advice sounds like it came from a workaholic: Write every day, seven days a week, no matter what. The advice King gives is honest, but it is also difficult to take. King makes writing sound like work, and though King says he loves writing, he also says point-blank that it is work, even for him.

King offers very precise examples of how to write a novel. He says the first draft should be written with the door closed. If the writer has to think of a word to use, then probably it was not the right word to use in the first place. A beginning writer should write 1,000 words a day, seven days a week; King himself writes 2,000 words a day or 180,000 words in three months. He says that any serious writer should stick to this plan as closely as possible, and wonders what Harper Lee, Thomas Harris, and several other writers who have published significantly fewer books than King are doing with their time instead of writing.

What perhaps is most startling to his fans is this simple fact: King seldom works out plots for his stories in advance. He might have an idea, such as "one kid lost in the woods," and out of that evolves *The Girl Who Loved Tom Gordon* (1999) about a little girl lost in the woods who keeps sane by listening to pitcher Tom Gordon on the radio. King plots once in a great while, but tries to avoid it as much as possible. Considering how long King's books are—six hundred pages on average—this is very surprising. Plot and story are two different things in King's mind, with story being very important and plot being used as a last resort. Everything is secondary to the story itself, something King has hinted at on more than one occasion. He started *Different Seasons* (1982) with the motto, "It is the tale, not he who tells it," and then proceeded to give an example of this very motto with his story "The Breathing Method."

"On Living: A Postscript," the final section of the book, gives readers a blow-by-blow account of how King almost died in June of 1999, and it is as current as King could get prior to printing. It recounts how he was walking along Route 5 in western Maine when he was hit by a van driven by Bryan Smith. Smith was distracted by his rottweiler, Bullet, who was jumping in the back seat and trying to open his Igloo full of meat. Smith turned around to grab the dog and in that split second hit King. The irony of all this is not lost on King; King says that his being hit by the van is very similar to something that might happen in one of his own books.

King recounts sadly that Smith told him he never had an accident before, and marveled that the first time he did, he hit the world-famous author Stephen King. Actually, Smith had been involved in many car accidents similar to this one stretching back to before he was eighteen years old (Smith was forty-two when he hit King). As he was sitting beside King, Smith's voice sounded like what happened to King did not really matter, as if Smith were watching television and having a snack. This strange story goes on even after *On Writing:* Smith killed himself on September 21, 2000, King's birthday. (In interviews, King said that he did not hate Smith and that he wished Smith's life had turned out better.)

King tells all of this with some humor, but at the time there was no humor involved. King's right leg was broken in nine places, his spine was chipped in eight places, his right knee was almost gone, his right lung was collapsed, and four ribs were broken—not to mention the cuts and scrapes all over his body that would require stitches. It would take five surgeries to get King somewhat back to normal, and he still had a long way to go, physically; five weeks after the accident, though, he was back to writing.

That, perhaps, is fitting. The one thing King knows is writing—it is the one thing besides his wife and family that does not let him down. King closes *On Writing* back where he first started—writing in a little room like a laundry room where he wrote *Carrie*—ending his personal journey where he began it. The book he was working on just before the accident was *On Writing*, and *On Writing* is the book to which he returned. That is not all, though. As *On Writing* was going to the printer, word had it that in early 2001 King would release either another long novel, *Dreamcatcher*, or the novel *From a Buick Eight* (the latter had been pushed back because it depicts an automobile accident very similar to the one King himself suffered). As these two books show, the stories of King's retirement from writing are, for now, far from the truth.

While King's personal story is as absorbing as much of his fiction, *On Writing* presents problems for some critics. If this book is a manual for writers, why does King spend almost half of it on his autobiography? If this book is an autobiography, why call it *On Writing*? King chose not to write a "standard" work of either instruction or biography, but to incorporate both in a book that showed how the two are related while providing an entertaining read for anyone. *On Writing* is considerably shorter than his other books, and King says this is deliberate. He does not tell the reader everything about his life, but he says this up front. He does not tell the reader everything about writing, either, but after a while King can only go so far. Then it is the writer's turn to tell the tale.

Kelly Rothenberg

Sources for Further Study

Booklist 96 (July, 2000): 1971.
Daily Telegraph, October 7, 2000, p. 3.
The Guardian, October 7, 2000, p. 10.
Kansas City Star, October 1, 2000, p. 18.
Library Journal 125 (July, 2000): 92.
The New York Times, October 5, 2000, p. B10.
The New York Times Book Review 105 (October 8, 2000): 11.
Publishers Weekly 247 (July 31, 2000): 79.

ONE GOOD TURN
A Natural History of the Screwdriver and the Screw

Author: Witold Rybczynski (1943-   )
Publisher: Charles Scribner's Sons (New York). 173 pp.
   $22.00
Type of work: Essays

~

*A historian of culture and architecture offers an informal
personal quest for the origin of the screwdriver and the screw*

~

Witold Rybczynski is fascinated with tools. In *Home: A Short History of an Idea* (1987), he described how he built a house with only hand tools. He combined his love for architecture and history in *A Clearing in the Distance* (1999), a biography of the nineteenth century American architect Frederick Law Olmstead. *One Good Turn* is the natural product of these earlier books. In his quest for evidence of screwdrivers and screws, Rybczynski moves back in time from the year 2000 to the Greek inventor Archimedes (c. 287-212 B.C.E.).

The text is accompanied by Rybczynski's own drawings of tools and illustrations derived from his wide-reaching research. These illustrations include Italian military engineer Agostino Ramelli's bookwheel and portable flour mill of 1588 and a detail from Meister Francke's altarpiece *Bearing the Cross* (c. 1424) in which a medieval craftsman carries a basket of tools. A page from Denis Diderot and Jean le Rond d'Alembert's *Encyclopédie: Ou, Dictionnaire raisonné des sciences, des arts, et des métiers* (1751-1772; *Encyclopedia*, 1965) depicts drawings of several early screwdrivers. A page of screwdrivers is reproduced from a tool catalog published in 1870 by William Marples & Sons of Sheffield, England. In an appended glossary of tools, Rybczynski draws not just screwdrivers but also braces, augers, adzes, saws, squares, bevels, and levels.

The idea for this book springs from an end-of-millennium fascination with landmarks and Rybczynski's essay on the best tool of the millennium in "The Best of the Millennium," a special issue of the *The New York Times* Sunday magazine. Rybczynski's first candidates for this tool were instruments such as paper clips, fountain pens, and eyeglasses, but his editor preferred a handworking tool. So Rybczynski looked in his own carpenter's toolbox, which gave its name to the first chapter of *One Good Turn*. Rybczynski's squares, bevels, and plumbs could all be traced back to Roman and Egyptian measuring tools, and were thus too early to be the best tools of the second millennium of the present era. So, too, were cutting and shaping tools such as saws, planes, and chisels, as well as various hammering tools. Among his drilling tools, Rybczynski's auger was an ancient invention, and his carpenter's brace was probably medieval in origin. Rybczynski argued that the brace, while important, had

~
Witold Rybczynski is Martin and
Margy Meyer Professor of
Urbanism at the University of
Pennsylvania. He is the author of
Home: A Short History of an Idea,
The Most Beautiful House in the
World, City Life: Urban
Expectations in a New World, *and*
A Clearing in the Distance:
Frederick Law Olmsted and
America in the Nineteenth Century.
~

developed little and did not quite meet the criteria for the tool of a millennium marked by sophisticated technological advancements. In the end, Rybczynski thought of the apparently simple screwdriver, which was unknown to the Romans and seemingly younger than even the medieval brace.

In "Turnscrews," the second chapter of *One Good Turn*, Rybczynski begins his search for the first screwdriver in the *Oxford English Dictionary*, where the earliest entry for the word "screwdriver" was attributed to the Scotsman Peter Nicholson in 1812. Suspecting that the screwdriver was older still, Rybczynski uncovered a labeled illustration of a screwdriver in the third edition of the *Encyclopædia Britannica* (1797). The tenth edition of the *Merriam-Webster's Collegiate Dictionary* included a reference to the tool in a 1779 Virginia will. Raphael A. Salaman's *Dictionary of Tools Used in the Woodworking and Allied Trades* (1975) provided Rybczynski with a critical clue in his quest for the "screwdriver"—a common British word for the tool used to be "turnscrew." Since "turnscrew" is a literal English translation of the French *tournevis*, Rybczynski turned his attention to the French *Encyclopédie*, with three entries on *tournevis* and evidence that the word existed in French as early as 1723. With this material, Rybczynski wrote "One Good Turn," the essay commissioned for the millennial issue of *The New York Times Magazine* of April 18, 1999.

Wondering if the screwdriver was a medieval invention, Rybczynski turned, in chapter three, "Lock, Stock, and Barrel," to the sixteenth century artist Albrecht Dürer, who depicted many tools, but no screwdriver. In a 1588 work on ingenious machines by Ramelli, Rybczynski found no screwdrivers, but he did find some screws on a hand-cranked flour mill. Even earlier were depictions of screws on leg irons and manacles in the *Medieval Housebook*, an anonymous manuscript written c. 1475-1490.

The use of screws in metalwork led Rybczynski to the history of weaponry and to the arquebus, the first shoulder-fired gun, which appeared in Europe in the mid-1400's. Soon, a spring-released arm called a matchlock was invented to control the firing mechanism. In the armory of the Metropolitan Museum of Art in New York, Rybczynski saw matchlocks attached with screws to the stock of a sixteenth century arquebus. In a standard reference book on firearms, Rybczynski found screw-attached matchlocks depicted in illustrations dating to 1475.

Rybczynski then looked more closely at medieval armor. While rivets, pins, and leather straps were first used to attach metal sections of armor, some late sixteenth century renntartsches, which protected the face and neck, were attached to the breastplate with screws with slotted heads. In Charles Ffoulkes's 1912 book on *The Armourer and His Craft*, Rybczynski learned that screws were used to attach helmets to breastplates as early as 1480. He even found here an illustration of a sixteenth century multipurpose tool used for hammering, cutting wire, drawing nails, and turning screws.

In chapter four, "The Biggest Little Invention," Rybczynski moves from the history of the screwdriver to a reflection on the various virtues and uses of nails and screws, which armorers, gun makers, and clock makers used as early as 1550. More widespread use of screws was slowed by the difficulty and expense of making them. Rybczynski describes the growth of the industry, especially in the Midlands region of England in the eighteenth century. Originally a cottage industry in which each screw was meticulously made by hand, screw making was mechanized by the brothers Job and William Wyatt of Staffordshire in 1760. The key to their patented method was the use of a pin to guide the cutting of the thread on a screw attached to a spindle. As a result, Wyatt machine-made screws were more accurate than handmade ones. The introduction of steam power in the nineteenth century made the manufacturing process less expensive, and screws became economical alternatives for a wide variety of wood- and metal-working projects.

Rybczynski also traces the history of screw heads. Square, octagonal, or slotted heads were all used on screws as early as the fifteenth century. Slotted screw heads had the advantage of countersinking, necessary for applications such as the development of door hinges. However, the slot was easily stripped while being tightened and required the use of two hands, one to hold the screw and one to hold the driver. Rybczynski follows a series of American inventions to improve the screw head to avoid stripping and allow for one-handed use. The most successful of such inventions were the socket-headed screw patented in 1907 by the Canadian Peter L. Robertson and the cross-slitted screw head patented in 1936 by Henry M. Phillips of Portland, Oregon. Unlike Phillips, who sold licenses to his patent, Robertson set up his own company to manufacture his screw, and many Ford Model T's were built in Canada with Robertson screws. Although the Robertson screw is tighter fitting, less likely to cam out, and easier to use than the Phillips-head screw, Robertson's unwillingness to sell licenses for the manufacture of his screw was in part responsible for the choice of the inferior Phillips-head screw by United States automobile manufacturers and the establishment of the Phillips-head screw as the international standard.

In chapter five, "Delicate Adjustments," Rybczynski turns from the screw to the screw-cutting lathe. Because the earliest grinders were hand-turned and difficult to wield, only strong and skilled craftsmen could produce them. The Wyatt brothers' invention of a screw-making machine was revolutionary. It allowed the manufacture of precision screws by machines rather than by skilled craftsmen. Observing that the pole lathe was good for woodworking but not for metalworking, Rybczynski suggests that screw manufacturing itself led to the refinement of the lathe for precision metalworking. The *Medieval Housebook* contains an illustration of a vertical table lathe rather than a horizontal pole lathe. On this wooden lathe a hand-cranked lead screw turns a metal blank through a cutter in order to make a screw. On the workbench is a tool which Rybczynski originally mistook for a chisel. When he realized that it fit the head of the lathe cutter on the lathe, Rybczynski knew he had found a German screwdriver even older than the one in the French *Encyclopédie*.

A screw-cutting machine was designed (but not necessarily built) by Leonardo da Vinci c. 1500, and an actual screw-cutting machine was built by Jacques Besson in 1579. Although Besson used pulls and counterweighted cords rather than a crank to turn the lathe, a screw remained the central gear. Besson's machine was used as a hobby for aristocrats and monarchs such as Louis XVI of France—not for manufacture. At the same time, the use of lathes for precision metalworking also became a serious occupation, especially in England. In the second half of the eighteenth century, Jesse Ramsden created a succession of lathes that produced increasingly more accurate screws.

The screw making of the Wyatt brothers and Ramsden's lathe making led to the career of toolmaker Henry Maudslay. With his precision lathe (c. 1797) based upon a regulating screw with a high degree of accuracy, Maudslay produced machines for printing, minting, hole punching in boilerplates, and other purposes. Even more important than his lathe, Rybczynski suggests, was Maudslay's personal devotion to accuracy and precision, to standardization of screws and measurement.

In chapter six Rybczynski celebrates Maudslay's pupils for their "Mechanical Bent" (the title of this chapter). These men include: Joseph Whitworth, who made a micrometer accurate to one-millionth of an inch; Joseph Clement, who built for Charles Babbage a difference engine as a calculating precursor of the modern computer; Richard Roberts, the inventor of a metal-planing machine; and James Nasmyth, inventor of the steam hammer and pile driver. Rybczynski suggests that the creation of such tools is as imaginative and poetic as the creation of a poem or a painting; the screw itself is a poem, a work of art in spiraling metal comparable to the beauty of the helix in seashells and DNA.

As he did with "screwdriver," Rybczynski tracks "screw" in the *Oxford English Dictionary*, where the earliest citation for the word dates to 1404. While the most significant use of the screw was in fifteenth century printing presses, Rybczynski sees this machine as a direct descendant of medieval paper presses and, ultimately, of Roman linen, olive, and wine presses in which vertical screws were used to flatten, squeeze, and press. The invention of such ancient direct-screw presses is attributed to the first century C.E. Greek inventor Hero of Alexandria. Hero also used the screw to design a worm gear, or endless screw, which he used in a hodometer (road measurer) and a dioptra, an ancient theodolite used in surveying. In order to invent the screw press, Hero had to discover the combination of male screw and female nut, and invent a screw tap to make the female nut. As Rybczynski notes, it took about fourteen hundred years for an ingenious person to recognize the potential of the screw as a fastener instead of a gear.

Rybczynski begins his last chapter, "Father of the Screw," with the story of the so-called Antikytheria Mechanism, a set of gearworks from a first century C.E. shipwreck discovered in 1900. Only in 1971 was this mechanism identified as a complex astronomical clock. Rybczynski finds reference in the writings of Cicero to a similar celestial globe built by Archimedes, the father of the screw. Rybczynski tells the traditional stories of Archimedes, including his discovery of the theory of water displacement and the principal of mass, his use of mirrors to set fire to enemy ships, and the effectiveness of his steam cannon. Referring to Archimedes' famous boast, "Just give me somewhere to stand and I shall move the earth," Rybczynski accepts the possibility that Archimedes learned to use a compound pulley to move a beached ship. He also suggests that the Greek invented the endless screw, in part because he gave his name to the water screw used to pump water uphill. *One Good Turn* is thus more than an ode to the humble screwdriver and its precursor, Archimedes' screw. It is a celebration of mechanical invention created not through technological development or evolution, but by the serendipitous nature of human imagination and inspiration.

Thomas J. Sienkewicz

Sources for Further Study

Booklist 96 (July, 2000): 1971.
Daily Telegraph, October 7, 2000, p. 3.
The Guardian, October 7, 2000, p. 10.
Kansas City Star, October 1, 2000, p. 18.
Library Journal 125, (July, 2000): 92.
The New York Times, October 5, 2000, p. B10.
The New York Times Book Review 105 (October 8, 2000): 11.
Publishers Weekly 247 (July 31, 2000): 79.

OPEN CLOSED OPEN
Poems

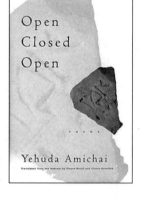

Author: Yehuda Amichai (1924-2000)
First published: Patuach Sagur Patuach, 1998, in Israel
Translated from the Hebrew by Chana Bloch and Chana
  Kronfeld
Publisher: Harcourt (New York). 184 pp. $25.00
Type of work: Poetry
Time: The present, with recollections of the past
Locale: Israel and Europe

~

*Amichai treats a variety of themes, including reflections
on life and death, the Holocaust, Israel's recent past, love,
and his own life experiences*

~

One of Israel's greatest modern poets, Yehuda Amichai, who died in September, 2000, at the age of seventy-six, has written a series of poems in *Open Closed Open* that are among his best accomplishments in verse. They are written in free verse with very strong rhythms and striking metaphors and similes. The title of the collection derives from a rabbinic tale describing the fetus in its mother's womb, when its mouth is closed and its navel is open, but at birth the reverse is true. In one of the first poems in the collection, "I Wasn't One of the Six Million: And What Is My Life Span? Open Closed Open," Amichai writes:

> . . . Before we are born, everything is open
> in the universe without us. For as long as we live, everything is closed
> within us. And when we die, everything is open again.
> Open closed open. That's all we are.

In the rest of the poem and in the poems that follow, Amichai tries to open himself and his world to readers, and he very largely succeeds. Despite a few cryptic utterances, his poetry is lucid and powerful, studded with arresting imagery and allusions that help the reader visualize and understand what he is driving at. He is also a master of irony, as the title of his next poem, "I Foretell the Days of Yore," suggests. In this poem he proclaims that he is "a prophet of what has already been." He goes on to describe the future:

> . . . As when a man sees a woman with a beautiful body
> walking before him in the street
> and looks after her with desire, but she doesn't turn
> to look back, just smooths her skirt a little,
> pulls her blouse tight, fixes the back of her hair, then

> without turning toward the man's gaze
> quickens her step. That's
> what the future is like.

It is attractive, but elusive and mysterious. Only the past can be known. Life is "a series of rehearsals/ for the real show." Extending the metaphor, Amichai says that a rehearsal still allows for changes up until "the real show." Then there is no changing, and "The show closes right after opening night."

Though not conventionally religious in an orthodox sense, Amichai nevertheless is well versed in the Bible and in Jewish tradition. For example, in "The Bible and You, the Bible and You, and Other Midrashim" (Midrashim are commentaries on the Bible and stories), he writes about Gideon choosing his army at the Spring of Harod, Moses, Abraham and his sons, King Saul, Ruth, and others. His account of Abraham and his sons is especially interesting, since Amichai says Abraham had three sons, not two: Yishma-El [Ishmael], "God will hear"; Yitzhak [Isaac], "he will laugh"; and Yivkeh, "he will cry." The youngest is the son no one has ever heard of. He was the one Abraham loved best, and the one Abraham sacrificed; he was the ram. At the end of this section of the poem, Amichai writes: "Yishma-El never heard from God again,/ Yitzhak never laughed again,/ Sarah laughed only once, then laughed no more."

God is very much a presence in these poems, as in "Gods Change, Prayers Are Here to Stay." Here Amichai describes the kind of god he wants and the kind he finds:

> I want a god who is like a door that opens out, not in,
> but God is like a revolving door, which turns, turns on its hinges
> in and out, whirling and turning
> without a beginning, without an end.

In Amichai's view, prayer preceded God, created God, and paradoxically only then God created human beings, who create prayers. God is now absent, but when he "packed up and left the country, He left the Torah/ with the Jews. They have been looking for Him ever since." Jews read the Torah every week aloud to God, "like Scheherazade who told stories to save her life." By the time Simchat Torah rolls around (the end of the cycle of reading Torah, the last of the High Holy Days), "God forgets and they can begin again." God's love for the Jewish people, His people, is "an upside-down love": first "crude and physical," creating miracles, plagues, and commandments; then "more emotion, more soul/ but no body, an unrequited ever-longing love/ for an invisible god in the high heavens. A hopeless love."

In this poem Amichai recalls his own religious upbringing, attending synagogue services, remembering what it felt like to draw out his tallith (prayer shawl) from its velvet bag, putting it on with its striped decoration ("Stripes come from infinity and to infinity they go,/ like airport runways where angels land and take off"), beating his

Yehuda Amichai was born in 1924 in Germany and emigrated to Palestine in 1936. His work has been translated into thirty-four languages. He is perhaps the best-known poet in Israel today.

chest on Rosh Hashanah during the days of penitence, remembering the women behind the lace curtain that separates them from the men, singing the welcome to the Sabbath Bride on Friday nights, the procession of the Torah scroll on Saturday mornings. Amichai juxtaposes against these memories the recollection of Auschwitz, and compares the smoke rising from the crematoria to the smoke rising from the Sistine Chapel when a new pope is elected. For him, after Auschwitz there is no theology, or rather a new theology:

> the Jews who died in the Shoah
> have now come to be like their God,
> who has no likeness of a body and has no body.
> They have no likeness of a body and they have no body.

Amichai's parents emigrated from Germany to Israel in 1936, when Yehuda was twelve years old; hence, they escaped the Holocaust and died in Israel. In "My Parents' Lodging Place," Amichai describes passing their resting place in a cemetery in Jerusalem where he now lives. He remembers how they brought him up—their warnings and exhortations, yelling and screaming, but also their love and care. His mother, he says, was a prophet, but his father was "God and didn't know it." He taught him the commandments and added two to the ten: "Thou shalt not change," and "Thou shalt change." In a poem later in the collection, "My Son Was Drafted," Amichai writes about how he feels toward his own son and echoes the words of his father. He gives him advice, as from an old soldier (Amichai was a veteran of Israel's wars), about drinking a lot of water on a hot day, and on night patrol filling his canteen to the brim so that it does not make sloshing sounds and give him away to the enemy. He follows up by saying that is also how his soul should be in his body, "large and full and silent," though when he makes love he can make all the noise he wants. His daughter is also drafted. When they are both asleep at home in the house near the wall of the Old City of Jerusalem, Amichai considers that "a father is an illusion, just like the wall./ Neither one can protect. Can only love, and worry."

Love looms large in Amichai's poetry, love of all kinds. In "The Language of Love and Tea with Roasted Almonds," he writes that one has to say "I love you" seven times, just as religious Jews say "The Lord is God" seven times at the end of the Yom Kippur service. Lovers "leave fingerprints on each other," "surrender to each other," know each other intimately, gain a sense of the infinite. He not only describes his own feelings of love but also writes about the way women love. He compares the faces of women in love to the face of the Virgin Mary in the pietà, women who remember what has not happened yet, "pain and joy yoked together." He also compares women in love to "our mother Sarah" as she was in Egypt when Abraham had to call her his sister, and to Rachel and Leah making love, and to Rebecca, Isaac's wife. He ends with a wry comment:

> And every loving woman is like Rebecca at the well, saying
> "Drink, and thy camels also." But in our day Rebecca says:
> "The towels are on the top shelf in the white closet
> across from the front door."

Some of the most moving poetry in this collection are Amichai's verses about himself as he grows old and remembers the past, as in "In My Life, on My Life." He thinks of the days of his life as chess pieces (all his life he has played chess, he says): "good and bad, good and bad—I and me,/ I and he, war and love, hope and despair,/ black pieces and white." Now all the pieces are jumbled together and the chessboard has no squares. The game is calm and has no end and no winners or losers. He is calm and listens to the "hollow rules/ clang in the wind." He recalls praying as a child, the aunts who used to tickle him as a child, his return visits to the sands of Ashdod where he once fought for Israel. He compares himself to "a man who holds his wrist up/ to catch a glimpse of Time, even when he isn't wearing a watch." He longs for peace— not in death but in this life. He does not want to fulfill his parents' prophecy that "life is war." He says: "I, may I rest in peace (I, who am still living, say/ May I have peace in the rest of my life./ I want peace right now while I'm still alive." It is a prayer or a wish that many Israelis share.

In "Jerusalem, Jerusalem, Why Jerusalem?" Amichai writes about the place where he lived many years. As anyone who has visited that city knows, it is a place of fascination, and Amichai conveys its myriad aspects. For him, Jerusalem is "like an Atlantis that sank into the sea," from whose bottom people "dredge up ruined walls/ and fragments of faiths, like rust-covered vessels from sunken/ prophecy ships." Along with ancient memories are young ones, too, "a love-memory from last night, see-through memories/ quick as glamor fish caught in a net, thrashing and splashing." His use of metaphor and simile are often like Walt Whitman's—his verse rhythms and cadences, too, as in these lines from section 20:

> I saw the faces of bride and groom under the wedding canopy and almost
> rejoiced. When David lay with Bathsheba I was the voyeur,
> I happened to be there on the roof fixing the pipes, taking down a flag.
> With my own eyes I saw the Chanukah miracle in the Temple,
> I saw General Allenby entering Jaffa Gate,
> I saw God.

The lines, like many of Whitman's, also convey the sense of a universal "I" observing, witnessing all that has happened in this city of many happenings.

One of the last poems in *Open Closed Open*, "Autumn, Love, Commercials," returns to the theme of love, and in its last section expresses much of what Amichai has been saying throughout his collection:

> For love must be spoken, not whispered, that it may be
> seen and heard. It must be without camouflage,
> conspicuous, noisy, like a raucous laugh.
> It must be a kitschy commercial for "Be fruitful and multiply"

Amichai's poems are like the love he proclaims, though hardly "kitschy" and only sometimes "noisy," they are "without camouflage," and they must be seen and heard.

Jay L. Halio

Sources for Further Study

Booklist 96 (March 15, 2000): 1313.
The New Republic 223 (July 3, 2000): 29.
The New York Review of Books 47 (November 2, 2000): 53.
Publishers Weekly 247 (March 27, 2000): 27.
The Virginia Quarterly Review 76 (Summer, 2000): 109.

THE OTHER AMERICAN
The Life of Michael Harrington

Author: Maurice Isserman (1951-   )
Publisher: PublicAffairs (New York). Illustrated. 449 pp.
   $28.50
Type of work: Biography and history
Time: 1920's to 1980's
Locale: The United States

~

*An intellectual biography of Harrington, prominent so-
cialist writer, theorist, and activist for the democratic left
and a founder of Democratic Socialists of America*

~

Principal personage:
   MICHAEL HARRINGTON (1928-1989), author and socialist activist

Intellectual biography, at its best, constructs a narrative of one person's life and thought within the historical crosscurrents of that person's time. The portrait that emerges is thus one of "the thinker" in relation to history, one person in conversation with many others, one life set in the broader context of an era. Maurice Isserman's biography of Democratic Socialist writer and activist Michael Harrington succeeds in the difficult project of biography-based intellectual history. *The Other American: The Life of Michael Harrington* offers readers a meticulously documented look at the American socialist left from the 1920's to the late 1980's, as well as an insight into important philosophical and political issues exemplified throughout Harrington's life. Isserman also uses Harrington's life story to issue his own call to reinvigorate the Democratic Socialist left as a more viable presence in American political life. In this sense, *The Other American* moves from biography to intellectual history to implicit political theory.

Isserman opens his chapter on Harrington's birth and childhood in St. Louis, Missouri, by placing Harrington's life on a comparative time line with other important figures in American political history. Setting Harrington's family in the context of St. Louis's Catholic and labor communities, Isserman foreshadows the important role that the Catholic Worker movement and activist Dorothy Day would play in Harrington's early adult life. Isserman also points to Harrington's later Democratic socialism by invoking reference to Socialist Party leader Norman Thomas and civil rights activist Martin Luther King, Jr. Isserman signals early, and clearly, that *The Other American* will explore Harrington's personal experience in relation to key issues of his time: poverty, labor activism, socialist theory, civil rights, and the relationship between religion and politics. He also introduces readers to Harrington's lifelong mode

Maurice Isserman is William J. Kenen, Jr., Professor of History at Hamilton College and is acknowledged as one of the most important historians of the Left. His books include If I Had a Hammer, The Death of the Old Left and the Birth of the New Left, *and* America Divided: The Civil War of the 1960's, *coauthored with Michael Kazin.*

as an introspective writer and scholar preoccupied with the rigors of intellectual life yet also known for his gregarious public persona.

Key to understanding Michael Harrington's longstanding preoccupation with moral and political issues is his early experience, beginning in the 1950's, with the Catholic Worker movement in New York City, and more particularly, his relationship to well-known Catholic social activist Dorothy Day. Harrington lived and worked at St. Joseph's House, a Catholic residence and social service center for the poor on Manhattan's lower East Side. In this section of the biography, Isserman explores a tension central in Harrington's life generally: the challenge and difficulty of balancing intellectual work (reading, writing, public speaking) with the demands of "hands on" service to people in need. *The Other American,* to its credit, does not romanticize Harrington in this regard and illustrates the many moments in which "theory and practice" failed to fuse in his daily experience at St. Joseph's. Isserman also introduces, through his interesting analysis of Dorothy Day's politics of strategic accommodationism within the Catholic Church hierarchy and Harrington's similar tactic as a journalist for the *Catholic Worker* newspaper, the later collaborative strategies used by Michael Harrington in his work on behalf of the American Left, especially in relation to the Democratic Party.

Isserman thoughtfully recounts Harrington's eventual trouble reconciling his own emerging radical politics and thoroughly "modernist" theology with Catholic dogmatic teaching, a trouble that would eventually lead him to leave the Catholic Worker movement and the Church and shift to a secularized socialist political philosophy. Harrington remained interested throughout his life in the complex questions related to religion, politics, and history: He later explored them in his excellent book *The Politics at God's Funeral* (1983).

In the central chapters of *The Other American,* Isserman shifts to full-fledged intellectual and political history, offering readers a detailed and fascinating interpretive account of Harrington's longstanding involvement with American Socialism. Harrington's intellectual work as a writer and theorist is shown as it evolves within left sectarian political frays from the 1950's to the 1980's. In addition to a thorough analysis of Harrington's thought at each stage along the way, Isserman introduces, in conceptual detail, key intellectual issues and the activists of mid-twentieth century American Socialism: Norman Thomas, David McReynolds, Max Shachtman, Bogdan Denitch, Irving Howe, Bayard Rustin, and many others. Isserman pays close analytical attention to the tensions and "breaks" within the so-called Old Left, where socialists debated anticommunist leftists and also clashed theoretically with "hard-line" Communists as well as apostate former radicals who were advocating forms of neoconservatism. A clear claim emerging in *The Other American* is that the toll of such internecine conflict was enormous, crippling the progress of American Democratic socialism. Here again, Isserman does not romanticize Michael Harrington, showing that despite his reputation as a relatively congenial collaborator with people holding different views than his own, Harrington could mix it up in sectarian political disputes with the best of them, with sometimes destructive political results. Here, the scope of *The Other American* extends far beyond the life of Michael Harrington. Isserman's book is a valuable contribution to the intellectual history of the American Left in general. The extensive interviews he conducted with a wide range of activists and writers are themselves valuable historical sources, and his careful detailing of the eventual emergence of the Democratic Socialists of America is very useful for readers seeking to understand this strand of American Socialism.

Outside the democratic left, Michael Harrington is perhaps best known in the United States as the author of *The Other America* (1962), a detailed analysis of American poverty and a blistering critique of the United States' neglect of the poor. Harrington was a prolific writer, authoring many books and hundreds of articles over his career, but *The Other America*, often referred to as the cornerstone text sparking the 1960's War on Poverty, introduced him to a relatively wide readership. Interestingly, Isserman positions *The Other America* and Harrington's work at this time within the context of Harrington's own version of political pragmatism. Early in the biography, Isserman cites Harrington's preoccupation with this central question:

> How was one to live "in and of the world" while also providing a radical challenge to the "here-and-now, give-and-take political world"? What did socialists have to offer to potential followers beyond "a large, over-all theoretical analysis" that proved difficult to apply in a meaningful way in daily life?

Isserman goes on to show the political contradictions which emerged here in relation to both Harrington's work advising liberal reform projects for the government, such as the War on Poverty, and his sometimes bumpy efforts to collaborate with younger activists of the American New Left. As a socialist, Harrington was criticized by other socialists for his advocacy of "lesser evil" politics within the Democratic Party and for his attempts to work with what other Old Left activists regarded as a naïvely "pro-communist, pro-Soviet" antiwar youth movement. His ongoing interest in, and tendency to speak to, the American middle class also earned him criticism from leftists more committed to traditional Marxist theory. In his treatment of these complex aspects of Harrington's collaborative work, Isserman introduces readers to a range of interpretations of events, people, and ideas, framing them within his own analysis of key issues. In effect, Isserman suggests that Michael Harrington's "tragic" failure as a socialist activist and theorist was that he could not negotiate these tensions more effectively, thus opening better possibilities for true coalition-building in the democratic left. Obviously, Isserman does not hold Harrington single-handedly responsible for the eclipse of left politics from American life, but instead offers Harrington as an illustrative example of the perils facing democratic leftists trying to work within the realities of American politics.

Some readers will, no doubt, take issue with Isserman's analysis of Harrington's life and his interpretations of American socialist history. Isserman is clearly sympathetic to the Democratic Socialist left, and his construction of events involving other activists and viewpoints will invite counterinterpretations. This is not, however, a weakness of the book: In fact, it reflects the impressive degree to which Isserman has engaged broader political and philosophical questions. The success of *The Other American* as intellectual history can be measured, to an important degree, by the extent to which it sparks debate, argument, and further constructive political analysis.

For readers not familiar with Michael Harrington as a writer, or with socialism as a political stance, or with American Left history in general, the book will serve as an energetic introduction to key people, organizations, and political issues. For example, Isserman sets Harrington's many books in the context of intellectual history, especially those works of social analysis such as *The Accidental Century* (1965), *Toward a Democratic Left* (1968), *Socialism* (1972), *The Twilight of Capitalism* (1976), *The New American Poverty* (1984), and *Socialism: Past and Future* (1989). Isserman's account of Harrington's extensive political journalism introduces readers to important liberal and left publications such as *Partisan Review*, *Commonweal*, and especially *Dissent*, an important journal of the democratic left founded in 1954 by Irving Howe and others.

It is only in occasional outbreaks of highly speculative psychobiography that Isserman's credibility as an analyst wobbles a bit, especially in the section where he suggests that Harrington's efforts to be a "good son" to a succession of mentors (Thomas, Day, Shachtman) contributed to a period of nervous exhaustion and debilitating anxiety. The evidence is not there to support the analysis, and Isserman's foray into retrospective psychoanalysis thus seems tangential and unconvincing.

The real strength in *The Other American* is that Isserman uses the life of Michael Harrington to confront bluntly the failures of the United States' twentieth century democratic left while simultaneously gesturing toward the possibility of its regeneration. Even readers not highly sympathetic to Democratic Socialism will find interesting this effort to reinvigorate an important and longstanding movement in American political life. Michael Harrington insisted, up until his death from cancer in 1989, upon the importance of maintaining a socialist vision even against the reality that its implementation might prove impossible in the foreseeable future. Isserman writes:

> Socialism for Michael had become a kind of Kantian categorical imperative, as well as the core of his political and personal identity. To satisfy the demands of conscience, "one acts 'as if' God were there," one acts *as if* socialism were a real possibility. Socialism was also a compelling narrative, just like the biblical account of the teachings and actions of the Judeo-Christian God.

In this quote, the idealism and prophetic stance embodied in the life of Michael Harrington takes center stage. Isserman concludes *The Other American: The Life of Michael Harrington* with the suggestion that no prophet has emerged since Harrington's death to carry the American Democratic Socialist tradition forward. By the end of the book, it will be clear to readers that Isserman means this as an invitation rather than a resignation.

Sharon Carson

Sources for Further Study

The Atlantic Monthly 286 (August, 2000): 92.
Booklist 96 (April 15, 2000): 1505.
Commentary 109 (April, 2000): 65.
Library Journal 125 (May 1, 2000): 126.
The Nation 270 (June 12, 2000): 46.
National Review 52 (May 1, 2000): 57.
The New Republic 222 (April 3, 2000): 34.
Publishers Weekly 247 (March 27, 2000): 62.

PASSIONATE MINDS
Women Rewriting the World

Author: Claudia Roth Pierpont (1952-)
Publisher: Alfred A. Knopf (New York) 298 pp. $26.95.
Type of work: Literary biography and literary criticism

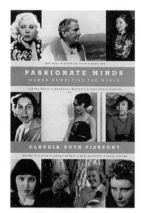

$\sim$

Evocative, interpretive essays on the life paths and works of twelve women, connecting the circumstances of their lives with the shapes, styles, subjects, and situations of their art

$\sim$

Principal personages:
OLIVE SCHREINER, South African "agnostic" novelist whose work sought a reconciliation between Darwinian science and spiritual possibility
GERTRUDE STEIN, pioneering modernist language twister and avatar of an independent feminist pattern of living
ANAÏS NIN, self-mythologizing fabulist creator of a legendary life
MAE WEST, writer, performer, social activist, and, ultimately, cultural icon
MARGARET MITCHELL, author of the book that fixed the image of the American South permanently in the American mind
ZORA NEALE HURSTON, African American writer who revealed an entire social organization previously invisible to most Americans
EUDORA WELTY, revered and celebrated writer who struggled with the contrasts between the expectations and realities of her home ground
MARINA TSVETAYEVA, Russian romantic poet whose life was a paradigm of artistic efforts to survive the persecution of a tyrannical regime
AYN RAND, projector of a radical philosophic position that drew a very sizeable response from mid-twentieth century Americans
DORIS LESSING, visionary feminist artist, committed political activist, and unabashed outspoken advocate for individual freedom
HANNAH ARENDT and MARY MCCARTHY, from radically different backgrounds, who forged a friendship dependent on shared moral values and mutual admiration

It is a natural human impulse to want to know more about an artist one admires, both in order to understand the work in a more profound fashion and out of a fundamental curiosity about the life that led to that work. In spite of the dearth of information available about William Shakespeare's life, endless speculation and invention has surrounded him since his era. An early biographer, John Aubrey (1626-1697), assumed that he could illuminate the writing of people such as Thomas Hobbes (1588-

1679) by recording gossip, snatches of conversation, impressions, and factual information that he mingled with some references to written work, and his *Brief Lives*—gathered by an editor and eventually published in 1898—was a forerunner of the kind of informed commentary that has grown in volume since the seventeenth century. Samuel Johnson, who wrote *Prefaces, Biographical and Critical, to the Works of the English Poets*, 1779-1781 (10 vols.; also known as *The Lives of the Poets*) partly as a promotional task for a consortium of booksellers, com-

∼

Claudia Roth Pierpont has been a contributor to The New Yorker *since 1990, and the essays in* Passionate Minds *were originally published there. She has received a Whiting Writer's Award and a Guggenheim Fellowship, and holds a Ph.D. in Italian Renaissance art history from New York University.*

∼

mented, "The biographical part of literature is what I love most." A kind of countertrend among academics holds that it is a deception and a reduction to assume that there is a direct connection between the work and the life, a position developed with considerable force by the New Critics of the 1930's, a casual confederation of southern writers (notably Allen Tate, John Crowe Ransom, and Robert Penn Warren among them), who stressed the importance of focusing on the work itself. Their useful corrective to the popular notion that the writer is the work was taken much further by the theory-drenched discourse of the late twentieth century which posited that a sort of self-generating text comes into being beyond the efforts of any individual writer.

The tension between the extremes of opposing perspectives on literary creation has occasionally been reconciled in the work of such deft, incisive writers as the poet Donald Hall, whose *Remembering Poets: Reminiscences and Opinions* (1978) combined Hall's personal contacts with Dylan Thomas, Robert Frost, T. S. Eliot, and Ezra Pound with subtle, informative readings of their poetry. However suspicious literary theorists may be concerning the personal component of a literary work, the compelling power of Walt Whitman's declaration, "Who touches this book touches a man" retains an appeal which no professoriat will be able to overcome.

Claudia Roth Pierpont, in a series of essays originally commissioned by and published in *The New Yorker*, has brought Whitman's heartfelt proclamation to the remaining segment of the human species that, prior to the twentieth century, was often ignored or suppressed as artists. The essays, which she has expanded and gathered under the popularizing title *Passionate Minds*, are a demonstration of just how fascinating and illuminating an exploration of the events of a person's life might be when joined with perceptive analysis of his or her work in a supple, lucid presentation that assumes a literate, interested audience ready and eager to learn more about the creator.

The occasion for several of the essays was the issuance of the Library of America editions of their work (Gertrude Stein, Zora Neale Hurston, Eudora Welty), and there is a clear thread of a developing feminist philosophy in the essays. In seeing the possibilities of a collection which would contain several themes that recur throughout the volume—issues of sexual freedom, matters of racial resentment, the constraints of political reality—Pierpont has moved beyond what she calls "women of literary influence" to consider "literary women of influence," including Mae West, Margaret Mitchell, and Ayn Rand in a cohort that might be characterized by mutual distaste. As Pierpont observes, "[T]here is hardly a woman here who would not be scandalized to find herself in company with most of the others." The jaunty, semiconfidential tone of her pronouncement is one of the keys to the exceptional readability of these essays, the fashioning of a narrative voice that is clear, direct, witty, and energetic without underestimating the capacity of the reader to appreciate solid scholarship, original insight, and a seriousness of mind that is worthy of the lives of the women she discusses.

Pierpont studied Italian Renaissance art history at New York University, completing her Ph.D. before joining the staff of *The New Yorker* in 1990. There is a multidisciplinary strategy informing the composition of these essays; Pierpont's strategy involves first a careful reading of her subjects' work, then the gathering of critical and biographical material about them, followed by the composition of a concise account of the ways that the dominant factors in the artist's life were significant features of her work. Pierpont's easy mastery of both the primary work and the extant scholarship, as well as an impressive grasp of the cultural context suffusing the life, provides a foundation for the particular tonal texture that she uses to give each woman's life a singular sense of individuality in spite of some significant shared experiences. While she exhibits a sympathetic understanding of the separate situations each artist faced, the essays on the South African writer Olive Schreiner, the Russian romantic/erotic poet Marina Tsvetayeva, and the Rhodesian English writer Doris Lessing are a bit more distanced than the ones examining American writers, since one of Pierpont's real strengths is her grasp of the social and cultural milieu that she suggests was crucial in determining the direction of each woman's writing life.

Although there is no sense of uncertainty in the discussions of non-American writers, they lack the easy familiarity that occurs in the other essays where Pierpont's knowledge of American society in the twentieth century permits frequent observations that extend her insights. When she describes how Eudora Welty wrote a story, "Where Is the Voice Coming From?", a dramatic monologue set in the mind of Medgar Evers's murderer, in one sitting after hearing of Evers's death, the information is deepened by her observation that when the story was published in *The New Yorker*, "[d]etails had to be altered for legal reasons, because some of the author's inventions were so close to facts discovered in the few days after the killer was caught." Left unsaid, but probably familiar to most American readers, is the fact that the man was not convicted of the crime until decades after the event. Similarly, when she quotes the critic Alfred Kazin on Mary McCarthy, "Her presence on the West Side was like Lear's on the Heath," an entire constellation consisting of fractious New York-based writers hovers around the quote to intrigue and inform readers with some knowledge of the literary world Pierpont is evoking.

Her considerations of Gertrude Stein and Eudora Welty are a blend of concise summary of important moments in their lives, and the ways in which these led to the creation of both an authorial persona and the work, that seems almost inevitable after Pierpont has established the internal and external factors controlling its production. She is especially acute about the psychological aspects of Stein's choices, and the restrictions imposed by a strict, ordered social matrix on Welty's work. The essay on Anaïs Nin manages to combine a tone of almost caustic disparagement with a degree of empathy for Nin's unconventional choices, and when Pierpont brings Nin's relationship with Henry Miller into the picture, she is impressively perceptive about Miller's needs and wishes.

Her manner of dealing with the men who were far from ideally supportive or even minimally decent with respect to the women in *Passionate Minds* is free of dogma and polemic, a considerable and welcome advance over the invective directed against men by some feminist writers. Since Pierpont is handling relationships in which male behavior sometimes calls for condemnation—which she provides—the maturity and perception that she brings to the task makes her criticism especially effective.

Two of the more interesting essays are devoted to Margaret Mitchell and Zora Neale Hurston, one famous in her time and now easily dismissed, the other a shadowy figure during her life, now revered and extolled. Pierpont is not making a case for Mitchell as a really major talent, but she is able to show how she handled material that had an enormous appeal to many Americans in the middle decades of the twentieth century.

Instead of relegating Mitchell to the realm of "unnameable checkout-counter Harlequins," Pierpont traces a tradition reaching back at least to Samuel Richardson's *Clarissa: Or, The History of a Young Lady* (1747-1748) and shows how Mitchell had a canny sense of how to manipulate the subgenre. A series of quotes from Mitchell's letters reveals a sharper intellect and a more fully formed self-awareness than might be expected. This is the element that Lorrie Moore identified as "an intelligent way with gossip," and it is characteristic of Pierpont's eye for apt detail. On a Hollywood version of *Gone with the Wind* (1936), Mitchell wrote to her publisher, "I don't see how it could possibly be made into a movie . . . unless the entire book was scrapped and Shirley Temple cast as 'Bonnie,' Mae West as 'Belle,' and Stepin' Fetchit as 'Uncle Peter.'" When asked by *Vogue* to discuss Scarlett O'Hara's "modernity," she remarked in a letter, "Good God, . . . do they think hard-headed women only came to life in the 1930's? Why don't they read the Old Testament?" In recalling her youth, she described "one of those short-haired, short-skirted, hard-boiled young women who preachers said would go to hell or be hanged before they were thirty."

Hurston's life was marked by extraordinary shifts in mood and in her means of survival as a woman and a writer. "She had never fit happily within any political group," Pierpont observes, "[a]nd she still doesn't." This makes her "the unlikeliest possible candidate for canonization by the black and women's studies departments of our own era," and Pierpont takes this paradox as the central focus of her portrait. In an essay that has no extraneous material, Pierpont conveys the core of Hurston's achievement with trenchant commentary and illuminating insights, highlighted by some of her most forceful writing:

> Without doubt, Hurston was a woman of strong character, and she went through life mostly alone. She burned sorrow and fear like fuel, to keep herself going. She made a point of not needing what she could not have: whites who avoided her company suffered their own loss; . . .

The lyric power of this character analysis is matched by passages such as her description of Hurston's delineation of Tea Cake from *Their Eyes Were Watching God* (1937). Pierpont calls it:

> [A] sermon from the woman's church of Eros. And like the sermons in which Hurston was schooled—like her entire book, as it winds in and out of this realization of sexual grace—her message lives in its music . . . seamlessly, with beauties of invention often indistinguishable from beauties of discovery.

Passionate Minds is a book which Moore praises as "one of the most ceaselessly interesting books I've read in some time," and while there will be some judgments and assertions that every reader will want to question or challenge, the clarity and grace of Pierpont's prose makes her a superb guide to, as she puts it, women who "told stories that changed the way people thought and lived." Continuing her work with a writer whose life has fascinated people as much as his work, Pierpont published an essay on F. Scott Fitzgerald's early version of *The Great Gatsby* (1925) in *The New Yorker*, perhaps the initial installment of a volume which will consider men who also "told stories" with the power to "rewrite the world." On the evidence of the Fitzgerald essay, it too will be a book which, as Morris Dickstein wrote about *Passionate Minds*, "makes most of today's literary scholarship seem lame and ponderous."

Leon Lewis

Sources for Further Study

Booklist 96 (January 1, 2000): 861.
Library Journal 125 (February 11, 2000): 86.
The New York Review of Books 47 (April 13, 2000): 73.
The New York Times Book Review 105 (March 5, 2000): 36.
Publishers Weekly 247 (January 31, 2000): 89.

PASTORAL

Author: Carl Phillips (1959-   )
Publisher: Graywolf Press (St. Paul, Minn.), 74 pp.
    $14.00
Type of work: Poetry

*A complex collection of poems about nature, desire and
the passing of love into the confines of memory and history*

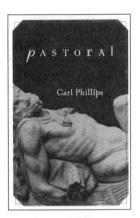

Pastoral is the fourth book of poetry by the distinguished contemporary poet Carl Phillips. The poems are
very complex and make heavy demands upon the reader's
perception and critical abilities. However, the poems reward such a commitment, as
well as the reader's close and sustained attention. The poems are written in free verse
with short, run-on lines that weave their way through a number of complex arguments
and difficult poetic structures. In nearly every poem, the links between the various
sections are not logical but associative, and, at times, not even that. They do, finally,
work their way through contradictions and associative links to some limited affirma-
tions, questions and assertions.

The title of the collection requires comment. Phillips evokes the ancient pastoral
poetic form which portrays an idyllic world of nature and shepherds who have nothing to do but sing of love or nature. Nature is portrayed in most of these poems, but it
is limited to a few images such as the bird, stag, and light; these are precisely observed, but they function as symbols more than as real entities. For example, in one
poem, Phillips describes a natural landscape as "a kind of meadow," since it cannot be
precisely defined. This contrasts with the long pastoral tradition of describing and celebrating the conventionally beautiful aspects of nature. In another poem, he sees the
scene as being "unbeautiful," an obvious variation from the poetic norm and the pastoral tradition.

Phillips is clearly a postmodern poet who rejects the earlier conventions and genres found in traditional poetry, as well as those of modernist poetry. There are, however, a number of repeated themes and images that unify the collection. One of the
most important of these does belong to the pastoral tradition: love. However, Phillips
sees love in terms of the body, an image that appears in nearly every poem; it is not the
idyllic and romantic love of the pastoral tradition, but it is, instead, desire and flesh.
He also constantly describes what a place or perception is "not," rather than confidently describing it. Longing and absence are common feelings in these poems.
Nearly every poem is filled with such negations, which weave their way to a qualified
affirmation or a question.

The first poem in the collection is "A Kind of Meadow." The meadow is first seen

*Carl Phillips, who teaches at
Washington University in St. Louis,
has published three books of poetry:*
From the Devotions, Cortège, *and*
In the Blood. *He has received prizes
and fellowships from the
Guggenheim Foundation and the
Library of Congress and has been a
finalist for the National Book Award
and the National Book Critics
Circle Award.*

as an assemblage of discrete parts that "*stands
for./* A kind of meadow . . . ." It is suffused with
"late light and the already underway/ darkness,"
out of which one expects an antlered stag to
emerge, an image that is found in a number of
poems. This vision of nature is revealed as de-
ceptive, however, since it occurs only "*in poems.*" In addition, it is unattainable in that context and turns into an image of desire and "flesh
at once/ lit and lightless, a way/ out . . . [and]
back". The meadow is clearly not a specific object to be observed, as in the usual nature poetry,
but something that triggers associations and
meditations that affirm the presence, and absence, of flesh and memory.

"Clay" begins by speaking of shape and direction, which are quickly related to the body
and the hands that have touched it. The body and
desire are found in nearly every poem in the collection; they provide the central theme and focus
of *Pastoral*. Shape and direction are turned into
"narrative,/ history our story." The poem ends
with a question: "When did I choose/ The Flesh, Wanting?" Memory and history are
ways of speaking about desire in all of its stages and evanescence. The poet seems to
be uncertain about the choice of "Wanting," and it is something he is left to ponder on
the choice of desire; that is all that can be said at this point.

"Abundance" is a different poem, and a clearer affirmation than is found in most of
the other poems in the book. It begins with the body, only to see other elements as necessary. One of those is the bird, whose "small life/ . . . is home," although "irretriev-
able." History and memory are evoked once more but cannot be captured. The buck
then appears as a beneficent image; it is a return of the stag in "A Kind of Meadow."
His antlers are "branching like hands or/ like trees." They are "Full of blooms . . . that
you must call . . . Prayers; these willed disclosures." The disclosures are presumably
between lovers and are seen as sacred connections, although they remain through the
body.

"Clap of Thunder" uses a number of the same images and themes, but it comes to a
very different resolution. It begins with a stranger calling the poet; he follows and
"*There/ 'tis done with.*" Desire leads to the past, and history, and memory once more.
He returns to an ordinary life, one of "unextraodinary motions/ that define the life . . ."
The poet feels he has failed his art. He then turns to a nameless "You" and calls his attention to a wind-picked tree that has some "lingering fruit" remaining. This is a positive revelation of what remains after all seems to recede to the past. At this moment: "I
begin writing." The act of writing is an antidote to the loss that is experienced in memory and history.

In "Black Box," the body is compared to a

> ... length of
> beach into which the two
> horses, beating
> past us, struck their washaway
> signs in that last light.

It is a scene of turmoil and turbulent sound, and it is, once again, in the past. The soul in contrast can be seen only in terms of waiting. It moves to a "Here/ where the skin has/ reddened" and "the cottonwood's/ leavings cloud the water's/ bank." The poem ends with two questions: "And if the faun did not follow?/ And if the doe . . . disappears?" The anxiety that the beloved will depart or that a part of the value in the world will be irrevocably gone is common in these poems. In this poem it is presented as a question about absence, while other poems turn once beautiful and sustaining experiences into an unrecoverable past.

"Against Him Leaving the Torn Field" is one of the more interesting and sexually explicit poems in the book. It begins with a sexual union that leads to a transformation: "believ[ing] I would not/ breathe the same, it would not be/ my life . . . again . . ." However, there is a contrasting image of a bird who has been shorn and is continually "raveling." This is contrasted to a natural scene that is seen as *Paradise*. The contrasting images are momentarily resolved by a description of "Somewhere else" where the lights are dimmed; however, that is only "Rustle of what no longer is required, being shed." The bird's "shearing," therefore, seems to be getting down to essence rather than being stripped of what it needs. The poem ends with the return of the bird: "There *was* one./ As there will be: yes, another." However, this is followed by a quote from a thirteenth century guide for nuns that is strongly antiflesh. It describes a bird flying better with "little flesh,/ and many feathers" and states: "Though the flesh is/ our enemy, we/ are commanded to support it." Phillips contrasts this with an assertion that the first garlands were woven for the "triumphant" flesh, supported by a quote from the *Iliad* describing the placing of the shield before Achilles. He is, apparently, the embodiment of that flesh and his arming is clearly triumphant. The last two images overcome the objections to the body by Christianity and triumphantly affirm the value of the flesh.

The third section of the book is devoted to four poems about the Greek god Pan. The first speaks of the "Fitful Memories" of Pan, and then the sequence moves to his "Dappled Shroud." The gods have departed, but something of them remains in the world that Phillips evokes. "Dappled Shroud" begins by speaking of how the man, although not the god, stays. The poet then touches him to find that he is not flesh, "but something else/ . . . that/ shimmers" with light. Light is a common image in these poems, and it is nearly always seen in a positive fashion. His shroud is there as a sign of his departure, but a trembling produced by him is "like any song," and that remains. The last line—"The music:"—calls attention to its presence. Music is something that is not lost but remains a part of the god that continues into the world.

"Afterword" is a dream poem in which the gods return. They hold together while "our bodies" do not; they "fall away." The hands of the gods, however, call one back to "a great ease/ like death, poetry . . . " The poet awakes to a scattering of birds, but there is also a more ordinary squirrel. He speaks about waiting and "being afraid it wouldn't come" even though he is "already writing the next poem. . . . " The ending is paradoxical: "somewhere you're still/ with me, you're not with me—" The paradox may refer to memory, in which the beloved can be possessed, although not physically present.

"A Fountain" is a very powerful poem that begins with the familiar negation: The fountain is not the "ocean's/ordinary enough wave . . . but like it." The fountain means "to live—/to flash, even—by self-/ crippling." He goes back in memory to a time of love when he "fell," as the fountain continually falls. Memory leads to a recovery of that love: "We're here, again./ We're/ at the beach." The beloved leaves the water and the water leaves him, a metaphorical connection with the fountain. The poem ends with a powerful image of light joined with the body: "The body—*gleams*."

The last poem in the book is "The Kill." It begins by evoking a memory when "I gave my body up,/ to you." The flesh is both "plenty" and "no/ little sorrow." We "cleave most entirely/ to what most we fear/ losing." This sums up the many descriptions throughout the book of the pains and the joys of love riddled by history and memory. The poem ends by describing the hunt in which "taking/ aim is everything. . . . " The stag image occurs again, and the poem ends with the fullest and most powerful assertion in the book: "and love would/ out all suffering."

Pastoral is an impressive reformulation of the pastoral tradition; it makes essential links between nature and love, although love is seen in terms of the body and flesh. The major themes of the book are the body, nature, memory, and history. These appear, in various forms, in nearly every poem in the collection. Phillips also uses images of light, the stag, and the bird. They are, perhaps, the closest thing to the pastoral tradition in the book. They seem to function as positive images, even though they often appear only to fade away. The structures of the poems are very hard to follow, but with a little patience and some close attention, the reader can experience some compelling poems that make powerful assertions on desire and flesh, even if they are only fleeting memories and are now to be found in the fixed past of history.

James Sullivan

Sources for Further Study

Lambda Book Report 8 (April, 2000): 16.
Publishers Weekly 246 (December 6, 1999): 71.
The Washington Post Book World, May 14, 2000, p. 6.
The Yale Review 88 (April, 2000): 164.
World Literature Today 74 (Summer, 2000): 600.

PASTORALIA

Author: George Saunders (1959-   )
Publisher: Riverhead Books (New York). 188 pp.
    $22.95
Type of work: Short fiction
Time: The present and near future
Locale: Urban United States

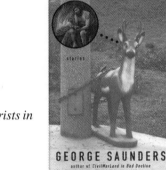

~

*Six stories by one of the most promising new satirists in
American fiction*

~

When George Saunders's first collection of stories, *CivilWarLand in Bad Decline*, appeared in 1996, it received rave reviews, with well-known writers such as Garrison Keillor and Thomas Pynchon calling Saunders a "brilliant new satirist" with a voice "astoundingly tuned." Based on that one book, Saunders was a finalist for the 1996 PEN/Hemingway Award, and *The New Yorker* named him one of the twenty best American fiction writers under forty. In fact, that prominent periodical was so impressed by Saunders that it originally published all six of the stories in his new collection, *Pastoralia*. If that were not encouragement enough, three stories in *Pastoralia* won O. Henry Awards prizes: "The Falls" in 1997 (which won second prize), "Winky" in 1998, and "Sea Oak" in 1999.

The reviewers of Saunders's two collections have called him variously "a cool satirist," "a savage satirist," and a "searing satirist." Typical of the satirist's need for an object of attack, Saunders says he always starts off earnestly toward a target; however, he self-deprecatingly notes, "like the hunting dog who trots out to get the pheasant," he usually comes back with "the lower half of a Barbie doll." Comparing Saunders to Kurt Vonnegut, Thomas Pynchon, and T. Coraghessan Boyle, critics praised his demented black comic view of modern culture.

A primary way Saunders creates this view is to zero in on American pop culture entertainments. Whereas the focus of the title story of Saunders's first collection is a virtual reality theme park that simulates the United States during the Civil War era, the locale of the title story of the new collection is a museum in which two people pretend to be a caveman and woman for the entertainment and edification of the public. The protagonist caveman is paired up with a woman who does not perform her job with sufficient commitment; she often speaks English instead of inarticulate grunts, and she quarrels with her son who visits her on the job. Although the protagonist, who must fax reports to management about his fellow worker, tries to protect her, he is soon discovered and she is forced to leave. A new woman assigned to the cave is more scrupulous than he; the story ends with the reader suspicious that it will not be long before she has him replaced.

George Saunders teaches creative writing at Syracuse University. His book CivilWarLand in Bad Decline *was a finalist for the 1996 PEN/ Hemingway Award and a* New York Times *Notable Book.* The New Yorker *has named him one of the twenty best American fiction writers under forty.*

When asked in an interview why theme parks are often featured in his stories, Saunders said that they create a sort of cartoon-like mood that keeps him from becoming too earnest and serious, reminding him that he is not writing realist fiction and giving him permission to "goof off." However, Saunders is not just "fooling around" in the story; as usual, he has a target, in this case the world of modern work in which bosses are distant anonymous entities with whom workers communicate by fax machines and who insist that they perform in accordance with the boss's view of artificial reality. The couple in Saunders's story, controlled by sophisticated technology, must make their living by pretending to be dumb and inarticulate—a metaphor, Saunders suggests, of how most Americans consider the role they play in the world of work.

However, the central image in *Pastoralia* is not the theme park, as it was in Saunders's first collection; rather, the obsessive image here is the American male "loser" who cannot succeed in the real world and who must create a fantasy compensatory reality. The American loser's creation of his own reality begins in childhood, suggests Saunders, with the shortest, and in many ways, the most heartrending story in the collection, "The End of FIRPO in the World," in which a young overweight and disliked boy named Cody takes imaginative revenge on classmates and neighbors who torment him by putting boogers in their thermoses and plugging their water hoses to make them explode. FIRPO is the word Cody's mother and her boyfriend use to refer to anything he does that they think is bad or dorky. During a bike ride, Cody imagines that his ultimate revenge will occur when he is famous for his splendid ideas, such as plugging up water hoses. The story ends with irony and pathos when he is hit by a car and the only person who has ever told him that he is "beautiful and loved" is the man who has hit him. The story succeeds by initially making the reader scorn Cody for the mean-spirited, vengeful acts he commits and the childish compensation fantasies he entertains, only to make the reader feel sorry for the boy when, with resignation, he accepts that he is the FIRPO his mother and her boyfriend say he is, even as the man who hit him futilely insists that God loves him and that he is beautiful in His sight.

In "The Barber's Unhappiness" and "The Falls," the Cody character has grown up; still fat and ineffective, he is also bald and single and lives with his mother—all sure Saunders signs of being a loser. The barber begins a fantasy sexual life with a pretty girl he sees at traffic school, creating a complete story about her, hoping she is a strict religious virgin who, once married to him, will let it all hang out. When he sees that she is a "big girl," he is put off but soon is able, in his imagination, to "correct" her appearance. He dreams she slims down, developing a body like that of Daisy Mae in the Li'l Abner cartoon, kissing him in the way he has been waiting for his whole life.

The story sympathetically explores the fact that love is always a fantasy projection rather than a realistic evaluation of the other. As the barber walks to meet the girl for their first date, she looks the biggest he has ever seen her. However, he quickly corrects this assessment by imagining that if they were married, she would slim down with his help. He imagines an evening when she asks him to put away the report on how much his international chain of barbershops has earned and to join her in the bedroom so she can show him how grateful she is; she would stand there with her perfect face and Daisy Mae body, smiling at him with unconditional love. This ultimately tender story suggests that many people deal with their unhappiness by re-creating reality to their liking in their imagination; the injunction "be realistic" has no place in the world of George Saunders.

"The Falls" is perhaps the most ambiguous of the three *Pastoralia* stories in which loser-fantasists spend their time imagining an opportunity when they can prove their true worth. The story is a sort of duet of two men walking toward the falls of a river, the apex of the story's narrative tension. Aldo Cummings is a writer who dreams of a time when T-shirts with his picture on them will be available at all the five-and-dime stores; Morse is a family man who feels that his childhood dreams were so bright that he cannot believe he is a nobody. The two men converge at the river in time to witness two young girls in a sinking canoe about to go over the falls. While Cummings stumbles away looking for help, Morse stands at the edge thinking the girls are already dead and that nobody could blame him for not diving in after them. However, even as he thinks this and makes a low sound of despair in his throat, he kicks off his loafers and throws "his long ugly body out across the water." What Saunders establishes in all three of these stories about losers is the paradoxical fact that in reality, life is primarily fantasy. The reader accepts the fact that Morse's dive into the water at the end is the ultimate quixotic act—foolish, hopeless, and brave—that both destroys and redeems him at once.

"Winky" is probably the most cogent example in the collection of Saunders's combination of smart social satire and sometimes sentimental humanity. In this story of Neil Yaniky, a loser who resents caring for his handicapped sister, Saunders nails the modern world of self-help and creative selfishness seminars dead to rights. The inspirational speaker of the seminar Neil attends tells his eager listeners how to get rid of all the people who are ruining their lives by "crapping in their oatmeal." Group members wear colored hats to identify in which stage they are—"Beginning to Begin" or "Moving Ahead in Beginning"—and are taught there is a "Time for Me to Win." However, even as Yaniky is building himself up to throw his sister Winky out, the story shifts to her, preparing cookies, dressing to please, and thinking of him as the "all-time sweetie-pie," insisting that girls are crazy to ignore him just because he is small and bald.

Counterpoint to this childlike inner monologue, Yaniky stalks home in a frenzy, arguing to himself that the world will not crap in his oatmeal and that his sister is a "real energy sink" who drags him down. The two counterpointed sections converge when he opens the door and Winky, acting as crazy as ever, meets him and bumps her head on the storm window. Yaniky sees the years stretch ahead of him bleak and joyless, and he wants to insult her, but he only goes to his room, "calling her terrible names under his breath." The story suggests that to sacrifice the self for another does not have to be done with Christlike humility to be truly unselfish.

The most problematical story here—so absurdly pop-culture gothic it is not surprising that one of the judges who picked it for the 1999 *O. Henry Award Prize Stories* was Stephen King—is "Sea Oak." The story focuses on a man who works at a male strip club called Joysticks and who lives with his Aunt Bernie, sister, and cousin in a subsidized apartment complex called Sea Oak, where there is no sea and no oak, only a rear view of Federal Express. Saunders evokes some funny bits here: the Board of Health that visits the club to make sure the men's penises will not show, a television program of computer simulations of tragedies that never actually occurred but theoretically could. However, the story becomes most absurd when Bernie dies and returns from the grave as a zombie who urges the narrator to show his penis so he can make more money.

The ostensible satiric point of the story is Bernie's expression of the unfulfilled longings of all the losers who die unheralded. However, what the reader most remembers is the grotesque image of Bernie's ears, nose, arms, and legs decaying and falling off. If there is a central thematic line in the story, it occurs when the narrator puts what is left of Bernie's body in a Hefty bag, thinking maybe there are angry dead people everywhere, hiding in rooms and bossing around their scared relatives. The story ends with Bernie's voice in the narrator's dreams crying the anthem of perhaps every pathetic, and somehow sympathetic, loser in Saunders's collection—"Some People get everything and I got nothing. Why? Why did that happen?"

Charles E. May

Sources for Further Study

Booklist 96 (April 15, 2000): 1525.
The Boston Globe, May 14, 2000, p. M1.
Denver Post, May 28, 2000, p. F-04.
Kansas City Star, May 7, 2000, p. J1.
The New York Review of Books 47 (June 29, 2000): 38.
Publishers Weekly 247 (March 13, 2000): 62.
San Francisco Chronicle, May 11, 2000, p. B1.

PATRICK O'BRIAN
A Life Revealed

Author: Dean King
Publisher: Henry Holt (New York). 397 pp. $27.50
Type of work: Literary biography
Time: 1914-1996
Locale: England and France

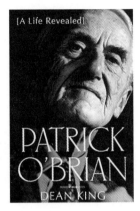

∽

King sheds light on the life of O'Brian, the reclusive author of the immensely popular Aubrey-Maturin novels about seafaring during the Napoleonic era, to help readers understand the source and nature of his literary accomplishment

∽

Literary biography is risky to read. Apart from the damage a biographer may do to the writer's reputation because of partial or mistaken information, the frank truth can disappoint and even disaffect fans, particularly so if they regard the writer with a cultish devotion. Such devotion frequently is the case for fans of Patrick O'Brian (1914-2000), novelist and translator, best known for the twenty novels about Jack Aubrey and Stephen Maturin, Royal Navy officers during England's war with Napoleon. Dean King's *Patrick O'Brian: A Life Revealed* may well prove troublesome for O'Brian fans. Nonetheless, the author insists that only by knowing the truth about O'Brian's life can one fully understand his literary achievement.

Despite King's sympathetic and studiously evenhanded treatment, the book does not present an attractive portrait of O'Brian. Moreover, it raises a nettling side issue concerning literary biography: privacy. As King admits, O'Brian, who intensely disliked discussing his past, refused to cooperate in the project and instructed some of his friends not to help either. O'Brian wanted to be known solely through his writing. As well as complicating King's research, this reticence forced him to rely on documents and literary evidence, second-hand accounts, and, for observations about O'Brian's character, acquaintances and family, some of whom were bitter about his treatment of them. Little came directly from O'Brian, and that mostly through a few letters.

Perhaps because of this difficulty, the book conveys the impression that King undertook the project out of affection for O'Brian's novels (an act of devotion and high hopes), but that he was dismayed by the facts his research unearthed. Even before he began, King was already as expert on the secretive O'Brian as anyone: He compiled a helpful lexicon to the prolific, recondite nautical vocabulary in O'Brian's sea tales and in another book explained the geography of the stories. Moreover, the biography shows King to be a deeply perceptive reader of O'Brian's fiction, a body of work which could come only from an author of immense learning, supple and expressive

~

Dean King is the author of A Sea of Words: A Lexicon and Companion to Patrick O'Brian's Seafaring Tales, Harbors and High Seas, *and* Every Man Will Do His Duty. *His journalism has appeared in publications such as* The New York Times, Outside, Esquire, *and* Travel & Leisure.

~

prose style, humane understanding of human relationships, and profound ability to bring to life a historical period for modern readers of widely different backgrounds. O'Brian was a fresh intellect, a literary genius. Despite King's efforts to be evenhanded and his warning at the outset that the biography does not directly present O'Brian's side of things, what King found as he researched the biography often tarnishes this image of O'Brian. He appears to have been cruelly cold to his family, prickly, curmudgeonly, and egotistical. In addition, he perpetrated a fraud on his fans: Contrary to his claims, he was not born Patrick O'Brian, he was not Irish, and he had never been to sea in a sailing ship.

Patrick O'Brian was born Richard Patrick Russ in rural Buckinghamshire County, England, in 1914. His parents were both English, although his father, a physician and inventor, was the grandson of a German immigrant. The next-to-youngest of nine children, young Patrick was asthmatic and lonely. His mother died when he was four, his father was distant to the children, and although he eventually acquired an attentive stepmother, he was often left to his own devices. He developed a lasting interest in nature; he also turned to reading and, later, to writing stories of his own. These were not puerile efforts, even though the main characters were animals; he began selling short stories to magazines in his early teens and published a book at fifteen. King frequently points out aspects of O'Brian's childhood that turn up in his mature fiction and especially likes to describe places where the boy lived that are featured in the Aubrey-Maturin novels. In fact, the biography often treats O'Brian's life as if it existed solely to prepare him for the nautical novels.

King was unable to verify O'Brian's claims that he attended Oxford, and it seems that he accumulated his extensive knowledge largely through self-directed reading. He continued to write and publish into his twenties, but not without at least one failed foray away from literature: He washed out of Royal Air Force flight school. As O'Brian's publication list lengthens, so do King's plot summaries. He convincingly demonstrates that O'Brian's interest in the theme of friendship between men sharing adventures began early. King identifies several precursors to Aubrey and Maturin.

One of O'Brian's early books fooled reviewers into believing that O'Brian had been trained by Arab storytellers, and this facility for imitation turns up later in his skill at altering his own identity. The reason for the change reads like a romantic adventure itself, but O'Brian clearly was out to find a way to devote himself to writing without the distractions that had burdened him as a young man—namely, his family. He married young (at twenty-one) and in short order had a son, as well as a daughter who died in childhood of a lingering disease. The baby girl's death was traumatic for him, but the marriage was already in trouble, and as World War II began he abandoned his wife and son to be an ambulance driver in London. There he met Mary Tolstoy, a married woman (and countess) who would become O'Brian's second wife.

Their marriage, described by all sources as very close and mutually supportive, lasted the rest of their lives. During the war both served as agents for an English intelligence organization that aided the French Resistance. At war's end, he and Mary divorced their spouses, he changed his name officially to O'Brian, and, following their wedding, they moved to Wales. O'Brian thereafter disowned the stories and two adventure novels published under the "Russ" moniker and concentrated on serious fiction. The result was *Testimonies* (1952), a critical success. Subsequent short-story collections and novels earned him respect in England and the United States but little money—even the first two sea tales, *The Golden Ocean* (1956) and *The Unknown Shore* (1959), were not financial successes.

The O'Brians, however, were content with a life of genteel poverty. They moved to the Mediterranean coast of southern France, built a small house, maintained a garden, and made wine from their own small vineyard. During this time O'Brian's relationship with his family steadily deteriorated. He and his son parted company, never to speak again. He shunned all of his siblings except one brother, who nevertheless complained that O'Brian acted as if they were not in fact related. To supplement his income, O'Brian translated French authors, becoming the principal translator for Simone de Beauvoir. During the mid-seventies he wrote a biography of Pablo Picasso, whom he knew slightly. (He later wrote a biography of Joseph Banks, longtime president of the Royal Society in the eighteenth century.) He enjoyed respect among critics for his own writing and his translations, but he was not widely known, even though he translated *Banco* (1973), the sequel to Henri Charrière's best-selling *Papillon* (1969).

His reputation began to expand after an American editor, a fan of *The Golden Ocean*, asked O'Brian to write a similar sea tale for the publisher J. B. Lippincott Company, possibly to be the first of a series. The result was *Master and Commander* (1969), in which Jack Aubrey meets Stephen Maturin and their long series of adventures begins in a tiny warship cruising the western Mediterranean, the very locale of the O'Brians' home. It was published concurrently by Collins in London. Critics generally liked the books, although some were condescending because they thought historical fiction to be an inferior genre. Sales of the first book and its sequels were modest, so much so that Lippincott and then a second American publisher dropped the series. In England, however, a core of fervent and often illustrious fans (for instance, Iris Murdoch), spread the word about the novels. Even in the United States, the number of readers increased during the 1980's.

In 1990, a venturous editor at W. W. Norton revived the series under an American imprint. Not long afterward, Richard Snow, editor of *American Heritage*, wrote a glowing review of the Aubrey-Maturin novels for *The New York Times Book Review*. In it, Snow discounted the comparisons of O'Brian's sea tales to the Horatio Hornblower novels by C. S. Forester (always a source of irritation to O'Brian) and claimed for O'Brian a greater stature, likening him to Jane Austen for his skill at portraying social behavior. The review set the tone for the publishing phenomenon that followed. O'Brian became one of the best-selling authors of the decade, extolled by historians and writers and in great demand as a speaker. During engagements in England and the

United States, he charmed audiences and displayed a nimbleness of mind that often left his interviewers bewildered. He seemed the epitome of the gentlemanly Irish author, both erudite and witty, in spite of his vagueness about his past.

King relates this accelerating passage to fame with judicious delicacy and concludes the biography with the event that marked the high point of O'Brian's career. It was a dinner honoring him in Greenwich, England, on October 11, 1996. Nearly four hundred ambassadors, politicians, senior military officers, and literati ate an eighteenth century-style naval dinner and toasted him for enriching their lives with his fiction. Given the truth about O'Brian that King uncovered, however, there is an unsettling feeling of put-on about the event. King was well aware of it, writing:

> Throughout life, O'Brian had been a consummate outsider: an intellect who had not gone to Eton or Oxford; an elite who was not from the upper classes; a citizen of the twentieth century who was more at home in the eighteenth. O'Brian was an Irishman who was not Irish; an Englishman who lived in France; a brilliant author in a spurned genre.

In a brief epilogue, King touches upon the final two novels in the Aubrey-Maturin series, Mary O'Brian's death, the grandchildren O'Brian never met, and the revelation, first published in England's *Daily Telegraph* exposé, about O'Brian's real background. It is a sour note on which to end.

Plot summaries (and quotations from book reviewers) sometimes encumber *Patrick O'Brian: A Life Revealed*. This occurs because King is forced to find insight into O'Brian's life by drawing inferences from his fiction, just as he tries to find insight about the fiction by finding parallels to the sparse details available about O'Brian's life. In any case, the book reads well, offers biographically centered discussions of several central O'Brian themes—the nature of male friendship, for example, or a man's inability to love—and tells the astonishing story of an innovative author who did not receive his due until the end of his life, when it came overwhelmingly. Nevertheless, King leaves the reader wondering why O'Brian maintained a pretense about his background and why, in fact, it should matter at all, other than that it left some fans feeling curiously betrayed.

Roger Smith

Sources for Further Study

Booklist 96 (January 1, 2000): 832.
Library Journal 125 (February 15, 2000): 162.
New Leader 83 (March, 2000): 33.
The New York Review of Books 47 (March 9, 2000): 11.
The New York Times Book Review 105 (March 5, 2000): 39.
Publishers Weekly 247 (March 20, 2000): 79.

PLOWING THE DARK

Author: Richard Powers (1957-   )
Published: Farrar, Straus and Giroux (New York). 415
   pp. $25.00
Type of work: Novel
Time: Approximately 1987 to 1990
Locale: Seattle; Beirut and its environs; Lebanon, Ohio;
   Damascus; and Istanbul

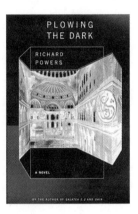

∽

Two stories intertwine, one about the creation of a com-
puter-generated virtual world and the people who create
it, the other about an American held hostage in and around
Beirut by Muslim fundamentalists

∽

Principal characters:
   ADIE KLARPOL, fortyish, a commercial artist
   TED ZIMMERMAN, Adie's former husband, a composer
   STEVIE SPIEGEL, Adie and Ted's long-term friend and former housemate
     in Mahler House at the University of Wisconsin
   TAIMUR MARTIN, born in 1954, an English teacher in Beirut
   GWEN DEVINS, Taimur's lover, mother of his daughter
   SPIDER LIM, JACK "JACKDAW" ACQUERELLI, SUE LOGUE, ARI
     KALADJIAN, KARL EBESEN, RONAN O'REILLY, MICHAEL
     VULGAMOTT, and JONATHAN FREESE, members of the TeraSys virtual
     reality team

Repeat readers of Richard Powers's novels know that they are in for some serious mental gymnastics when they read his work. Powers continually increases the height of the intellectual hurdles over which his readers are expected to catapult as they attempt to position themselves in the fictional worlds he creates.

Plowing the Dark, although perhaps not so intellectually demanding as the author's earlier tour de force, *The Gold Bug Variations* (1991), demands that readers suspend a great deal of their disbelief and enter into a Lewis-Carroll-like world that is on the other side of the looking glass or down the rabbit hole. In this novel, Powers transports his readers to a room belonging to TeraSys in which a computer crew, assisted by artist Adie Klarpol, works in quite undirected ways to create virtually real worlds.

Adie does not quite know why she has been encouraged to quit her job as a commercial artist in Manhattan and come to Seattle to do whatever it is she ends up doing. She has no job description to guide her. No one forces her to punch a time clock, although she and her colleagues in the Realization Lab (RL) work ungodly hours (of

Richard Powers is the author of seven novels, including The Gold Bug Variations, Galatea 2.2, *and* Gain, *which won the James Fenimore Cooper Prize for Historical Fiction.*

their own volition), often existing for days on end eating only Doritos and pizzas delivered to the lab's door. These people appear to have no lives outside the workplace. They routinely log hundred-hour weeks.

Adie is brought here by Stevie Spiegel, who once shared college quarters with her and Ted Zimmerman, whom Adie eventually married. In Mahler House, where they all lived, they had created a space resembling virtual reality in the large attic that topped the run-down dwelling.

Shortly after college, Stevie entered the cyberworld in an all-consuming way. Now, more than twenty years later, he reestablishes contact with Adie and convinces her to come to Seattle to work on the TeraSys project, which creates vast virtual worlds in one small, white room into which people come and, through the use of tracking "stereospectacles," experience worlds distant in time and space.

Some of the RL people—Jackdaw Acquerelli, Sue Logue, Spider Lim, Michael Vulgamott, Ari Kaladjian, Karl Ebesen—create economics rooms or food rooms or weather rooms. Adie, ever interested in art history, creates rooms related to it, including Vincent van Gogh's room in the asylum at Arles. She has the luxury of filling her virtual rooms with artifacts from the whole span of history and can even intermix periods and places if it tweaks her fancy. She, like any advanced programmer, is a virtual god in the virtual world.

Plowing the Dark is structurally reminiscent of Powers's *Galatea 2.2* (1995), in which a cadre of computer experts works feverishly to create a computer capable of passing the master's comprehensive examination in English literature; intertwined with that story is the highly biographical parallel story of a protagonist named, not surprisingly, Richard Powers. *Plowing the Dark* intertwines another story with Powers's tale of how Adie and her colleagues develop virtual worlds in the RL. This second story is about Taimur Martin, a thirty-three-year-old English teacher, who impregnates his girlfriend, Gwen Devins, shortly before heading to the Middle East for a teaching post in Beirut.

Barely settled into his digs, Taimur is abducted from a busy Beirut street by Muslim fundamentalists and whisked off to a dank, dark room where he lies chained to a radiator, permitted only twenty minutes a day (and eventually only five or ten minutes) out of his chains while he attends to such personal matters as defecating and bathing. He is held in absolute isolation in this prison for well over two years before being moved to another location from which, after several more months, he is ultimately released, concluding some three grisly years of incarceration.

In this novel, Powers deals fundamentally with the Platonic question of what constitutes reality. Taimur is much like Plato's figures in the "Allegory of the Cave," chained in such a way that they can see only the wall before them. The shadows they observe on that wall constitute their perceptions of reality. Taimur must construct his own reality from the faint clues he can garner: sounds, smells, reminiscences, a brief, camera-eye's view of the outside when a bullet penetrates the steel sheeting of his cell's window.

As his confinement drags on, Taimur continually loses hope and comes close to mental meltdown. He is sustained, however, by dredging from his subconscious many of the small details of his past life. He gains strength by reconstructing stories his Iranian mother told him and his brother Kamran as they sat at her feet during childhood.

The two narrative strands interspersed in this novel are related largely by their mutual involvement in creating virtual realities—Taimur's desperate imaginings that keep him from totally disintegrating and the RL staff's visualizations. Powers points to this commonality in several places, summing up much of what he needs to convey:

> After ten thousand years of false starts, civilization was at last about to assemble the thing all history conspired toward: a place wide enough to house human restlessness. A device to defeat matter and turn dreams real. This is what those crowds of awakened students demanded: a room where people might finally live. Every displaced peasant would become a painter of the first rank. Every crippled life a restored landscape.

The RL will achieve these ends in mechanistic ways, just as the Air Force achieves virtual reality, as Powers relates, in the simulators it uses to train pilots. This is the first hint of what the RL is really about, a fact that comes home to Adie in the last pages of the book when she realizes that virtual reality is simply an aspect of sophisticated war strategy that the government is enhancing in a variety of clandestine ways.

Jackdaw experienced virtual reality at an early age when he existed in a world of the imagination. Powers writes, "Scientific visualization was born in the first wave of Space Invaders." Readers are told that Jackdaw spent his adolescence alone, "sealed in his bedroom," a kind of foretaste of what lay ahead for him in the RL.

The composition of this novel is astoundingly intricate. Powers drops small crumbs as Hansel and Gretel did in the forest so that would-be rescuers could follow their trail. Powers's trails are more convoluted than those in Engelbert Humperdinck's opera *Hänsel und Gretel* (1893). For example, at one point Adie and Stevie are distracted when a northern flicker smashes into the RL's plate glass and falls lifeless on the ground. It appears dead, but in a short time, it comes to life again, makes some tentative wing flaps, and then flies off.

The bird's resurrection ties in with Taimur's act of self-destruction toward the end of his confinement. He has about abandoned any hope of rescue. His pain, mental and physical, is exceeding bearable limits. In an act of desperation, he bashes his head into the wall of his cell and falls in a heap on the floor. Like the flicker, however, he revives, living on, perhaps stronger for knowing that his body resisted his attempts at self-destruction.

At one point, Powers writes, "VR reinvents the terms of existence. It redefines what it means to be human. All those old dead-end ontological undergrad conundrums? They've now become questions of engineering." Certainly the RL is redefining what it means to be human and the ways in which people will live their lives, but Taimur's confinement is doing virtually the same thing for him, although engineering has nothing to do with his transformation.

The parallelism of the two situations Powers deals with is striking. In essence, VR is nothing new. It has been a human pursuit for as long as humans have inhabited the earth. What Adie and her compatriots are attempting to do in the RL is track their lineage to such artifacts as the petroglyphs in Lascaux Cave in southern France.

Adie, long divorced from Ted, her libidinous college housemate, learns that he has been stricken with multiple sclerosis. His condition deteriorating, he has returned to Lebanon, Ohio, a Shaker community where he grew up. As his days play out, his mind is clear. He still attempts to fulfill commissions to write complex musical compositions. Adie and Stevie fly to Lebanon to spend a final long weekend with Ted, whose situation is not unlike Taimur's.

Ted is imprisoned in his own body, bound by physical restraints to his bed, for his own protection. Like Taimur, his only life is a life of recollection, a fantasy life that helps him to rise above the hopeless state of his desiccated body. It is not coincidental that he, too, is in Lebanon, although his Lebanon is in Ohio.

Ever the master of language, Powers in this book performs admirable feats with words. In all his earlier books, he included some Joycean punning. In this novel, he writes of Stevie's arriving at a girl's apartment to read something he has written, "nerves shattered by caffeine, folding and unfolding a spayed scrap of mongrel doggerel that was probably prosecutable under even the most generous interpretation of the Intellectual Property Protection Act." He also employs catalogs most effectively in several parts of the novel, evoking comparisons with such earlier writers as Walt Whitman, John Dos Passos, and Thomas Wolfe.

As the novel ends, Adie has deduced the task she must complete. Spurred on by William Butler Yeats's poem about Byzantium, she re-creates in VR the Hagia Sophia, that great cathedral/mosque in Istanbul that has suffered a changing of the guard from the Christian to the Muslim faith for a millennium and a half, but that has endured as an overwhelming physical reality of heart-stopping beauty. Karl points to a photograph of the building, reminding Adie that it was "for close to a thousand years, the greatest church in Christendom. And for another five hundred years after that, the greatest mosque in Islam."

At the end of the novel, Adie's life crosses Taimur's with the Hagia Sophia as catalyst. Adie is disenchanted to learn the implications of the work that she and all the others in the RL have been doing. Taimur is now free, but is he free? Gwen awaits, bringing her daughter to Wiesbaden, Germany, to meet him when he is brought there for debriefing. Taimur seems morally bound to marry Gwen, although that is far from what he wants.

The staff of the RL disperses as the novel closes, all going their separate ways, some to marry and settle down, others to find new cyberspace excitements to entice them.

R. Baird Shuman

Sources for Further Study

The Atlantic Monthly 286 (July, 2000): 95.
Booklist 96 (May 1, 2000): 1653.
Knight-Ridder/Tribune News Service, June 7, 2000, p. K-6466.
Library Journal 125 (April 1, 2000): 132.
The New York Times, April 22, 2000, p. A15.
The New York Times Book Review 105 (June 18, 2000): 12.
The New Yorker 76 (July 3, 2000): 83.
Publishers Weekly 247 (April 7, 2000): 48.

POSTVILLE
A Clash of Cultures in Heartland America

Author: Stephen G. Bloom
Publisher: Harcourt (New York) 338 pp. $25.00
Type of work: Current affairs
Time: 1987-2000
Locale: United States

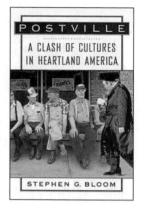

∼

Transplanted from California to Iowa, Bloom unexpect-edly discovers Postville, where cultural conflict between traditional Midwesterners and Hasidic Jews provides microcosmic glimpses of cultural clashes that will likely affect twenty-first century America

∼

The United States Census Bureau reports that the American population topped 281 million in the year 2000, a ten-year gain of about 13 percent in a country that is more pluralistic—ethnically, culturally, religiously—than ever before. A tiny fraction of those people inhabit Postville, Iowa. Its less than 1,500 rural residents live in the northeastern part of the state, not far from the Mississippi River and the state's Wisconsin-Minnesota line, where 90 percent of the people have Lutheran roots. Iowa's population of 2.8 million gets its largest income from manufacturing, but this Midwestern heartland remains best known for agriculture. In pork, corn, and soybean production, 97,000 farms put Iowa first in the nation. Meanwhile, although the latest census found that 28.3 million—about 10 percent—of the U.S. population is foreign-born, Iowa added relatively little to those figures. Its people are more homogeneous and white (96 percent) than the country as a whole. Largely for that reason, the journalist Stephen Bloom found that an obscure Iowa hamlet contained an unexpected story, which the author tells with sensitivity and skill. *Postville*, a cautionary tale, deserves attention. Its fascinating description and thoughtful appraisal of a cultural clash in small-town America provides instructive preparation, personal and public, for a twenty-first century life that keeps the nation coping with tensions between unity and diversity.

In 1993, Bloom became a professor of journalism at the University of Iowa. Climbing into a packed 1979 Volvo, leaving behind his fast-paced career as a writer in San Francisco, one of the most culturally varied cities in the United States, Bloom and his family headed east, scarcely imagining how dissimilar their Iowa City surroundings would be. Houses with big yards and large front porches, a culture that takes hunting seriously, extremes of climate, and a basic honesty that still keeps homes unlocked and gas pumped before paying—these were examples that only began to illustrate how Iowa's sameness made it different. As Stephen and Iris Bloom watched Mikey, their young son, becoming "less and less an urban kid," they missed San Francisco from time to time, but on the whole they liked Iowa. Loneliness, however, created an exception to that rule, and it would be a factor in Bloom's discovery of Postville.

In Iowa, Bloom found, being lonely and being Jewish went together. About 4.5 million of the world's estimated 14 million Jews live in the United States. The Blooms were among the

∽

Stephen G. Bloom has won awards for his journalism for the Los Angeles Times, The San Jose Mercury News, *and other major newspapers. He now teaches journalism at the University of Iowa in Iowa City.*

∽

handful in Iowa, where culture, if not commitment, was steeped so thoroughly in the traditions of Christianity as to make it commonplace that the Easter edition of the Cedar Rapids *Gazette* would feature a banner headline announcing, "HE HAS RISEN." Such a culture, Bloom observed, could lead people to say, "We know, we've been praying for you," when a co-worker responded to their "Merry Christmas" by saying, "Thanks for the good wishes, but you know I'm Jewish." Blatant anti-Semitism was not what Bloom confronted, but the question was how best to "nurture our Jewish souls" in a culture where being Jewish kept one "outside" and without many options for support, especially if one's Jewish identity, like Bloom's, ran deep but not in the conventional channels of organized religion and Jewish agencies.

One morning, feeling "landlocked, stranded in this vast middleland, surrounded by people whose multitudinous farm families went back for generations," Bloom happened to read a magazine that introduced Postville to him. He learned about the ultra-orthodox Lubavitcher Jews who had moved there from Brooklyn, where the Crown Heights section is headquarters for the movement's world population of 200,000, about 25,000 of whom live in that New York area. Contemporary American Lubavitchers trace their roots to Eastern Europe's eighteenth-century Jewish villages (*shtetlach*) and the passionate expression of Jewish faith known as Hasidism that sprang from those places. Led by charismatic rabbis (*rebbes*), these people developed a spirituality informed by belief in the Messiah's coming, a rich heritage of Yiddish storytelling, strict observance of religious and cultural traditions, and hard work.

By 1987 only three Lubavitcher families had arrived in Postville, but the community soon grew to 150, including three dozen rabbis, which gave the Iowa town more rabbis per capita than any other place in America. The answer to Bloom's question— Why had they come?—was largely answered by economics and religion, two factors that historically motivated immigrants to pull up their eastern stakes, within America as well as abroad, and head west for better times and places.

The Lubavitchers had taken over a run-down slaughterhouse on Postville's unincorporated outskirts. They had revived its fortunes by converting the old facility into a profitable business called Agriprocessors. It handled beef, lamb, chicken, and turkey—1.85 million pounds a week—according to the criteria of *glatt* kosher, the most rigorous food preparation standards for Orthodox Jews. With their prized kosher meat packed into refrigerated trucks bound for the large American Jewish communities in New York and Los Angeles, Miami and Chicago—or even jetted to Tel Aviv and Jerusalem—the Lubavitcher entrepreneurs had created jobs and rejuvenated Postville. In a small town of close-knit Iowa families that had lived in the area for generations, the Lubavitchers' business dominance gave them unanticipated influence and power. Those developments created mistrust and dislike.

His curiosity piqued by the journalist's instinct for a good story, a sense of long-lost kinship with those Lubavitcher Jews (no matter how different from him they turned out to be) and the desire to understand what their presence might portend for Postville, Iowa, and symbolize for the United States, Bloom made frequent and pro-longed visits to the town and its kosher meat-packing economy. As a story-seeking stranger, he had no easy access to the town's dynamics, for the Lubavitcher minority and the predominantly Lutheran majority both kept to their clannish ways, which meant eying him with suspicion. Nevertheless, Bloom gradually earned enough trust from all sides so that he understood more clearly why the Lubavitchers' success and Postville's revival did not mean that all was well.

Making his home at the Lysol-scented Pines, a 1950s motel that had seen better days but was still the town's finest, Bloom found Postville reflecting everything he "had grown to expect from rural Iowa towns." Nevertheless, this place also was fundamentally unlike them. Fifty miles distant from the nearest freeway, lacking even a traffic light, Postville might be thirty miles away from the closest McDonald's, but right at hand were close-quartered intersections that raised again the question of how vastly different Americans would get along together.

Postville's gentiles were not all of one mind about the Lubavitchers. There were at least three more or less cohesive factions, with their attitudes influenced by the degree of economic benefit derived from the Lubavitchers. One group tended to welcome them, another inclined toward resentment, and a third, consisting of recent non-Jewish immigrants who had found their way to Postville, cared relatively little about changes in a community that was not much theirs anyway. For most of Postville's mainstream population, however, the Lubavitchers were so different as to be, perhaps, too different. In religion, style of dress, socializing, and business habits (bargaining was foreign in Postville's stores and loyalty meant that buying local was important, even if the prices were higher than at Wal-Mart or in discount catalogs), the presence of these Hasidic Jews could be more problematic than oil that would not mix with water. Many citizens—though by no means all—felt that the Lubavitchers went out of their way to separate themselves and to antagonize the town's non-Jews. Further tainting the Lubavitchers' reputation, two of their number had committed crimes that by northeastern Iowa's standards, says Bloom, "were the equivalent of 'wild-ing.'" As for Postville's Jews, whose success had given them disproportionate leverage and inconsiderateness to match, their position about the town's *goyim* was summed up by Sholom Rubashkin, whose father, Aaron, a Brooklyn butcher, had started the kosher meat-packing operation in 1987. Now the *macher* (leader) of Postville's Lubavitcher community, Sholom told Bloom, "We live by our own rules here, and they've got to understand that!" One group wanted the others to understand them. In Postville, however, reciprocal understanding was scarce all around, and the ways of life that hard experience taught were unlikely to create the give-and-take needed to make more of it. From Bloom's perspective, moreover, Postville's problems were not the town's alone. Turmoil in an Iowa town, suggests Bloom, reflected an increasingly commonplace mind-set in America that "affiliation with your own people" trumped "being part of a larger, world-wide community of humanity."

The showdown took place on Tuesday, August 5, 1997, when Postville went to the polls. Annexation was the issue. If the voters approved, 703 acres would be incorporated, bringing $8 million in newly taxable property under the jurisdiction of a town whose existing property tax base was $23 million. Nobody's life or business would change dramatically if annexation took place—with one important exception. Postville's town council would have greater control of future building and development. Realizing that their autonomy could be curtailed and their public accountability increased, the Lubavitchers opposed annexation. They backed their disapproval by threatening to pack up and leave, a decision that might well reduce Postville to "a dying prairie town." Some locals thought the Lubavitchers were bluffing, but many of Postville's antagonized citizens said "Fine!" They intended their vote for annexation, as Bloom pointedly puts it, to "tell the ultra-orthodox Jews who had taken over Postville to get out. Leave us alone. Don't ever come back." With a large turnout expected from the town's 1,220 eligible voters, what would the outcome be? Like everyone else, Bloom had to wait for the results, but he tells his readers that "I wanted the locals to win, hands down."

When Bill Roe, Jr., the county auditor, tallied the votes, he found that the voter turnout was 57 percent. Bloom thought it was not very large, but Roe corrected him: For a summertime election, anything close to 60 percent was outstanding, and the locals had won, too, although it was not clear that they had done so "hands down." That qualification went beyond the actual election results, which favored annexation 328 (55 percent) to 277 (45 percent), for what happened after the vote showed that Postville's multicultural history, like that of the United States, is still in the making.

The Lubavitchers did not pack up and leave. They took Postville's annexation to court, but to no avail. Meanwhile, Agriprocessors continued to thrive, and Postville kept changing. It could not be said that harmony, let alone love, prevailed, or even that reciprocal understanding advanced more than incrementally. At the municipal pool, the town established the special swimming hours that the Lubavitchers requested. Increasing numbers of non-Jews found employment at Agriprocessors. Postville was not becoming a small-town American "melting pot," but there were signs that the negotiation of differences was being handled better.

On the day of the annexation vote in 1997, Bloom spent some time with Lazar Kamzoil, one of the Lubavitchers with whom he had grown friendly. Jewish though both were, their differences were large and intractable. Bloom says that the moments when they could acknowledge those differences, perhaps even accept them, were "comforting, almost sublime." That is a modest version of the American Dream, which emphasizes *E Pluribus Unum* (One from Many), but the conclusion Bloom drew from Postville seems to be that fulfillment of a modest dream is better than none at all, especially if the acknowledgment and acceptance of differences can expand into the respect and enjoyment of them that Bloom, his family, and many Iowans "bring to the table we now share." As *Postville* implies, the more that happens, the more all kinds of Americans, everywhere, can truly pronounce their positive variations on Bloom's theme: "Iowa has become our home."

John K. Roth

Sources for Further Study

Library Journal 125 (September 1, 2000): 234.
The New York Times, November 3, 2000, p. B45.
The Wall Street Journal, November 3, 2000, p. W13.
The Washington Post Book World, October 15, 2000, p. 13.

QUARREL AND QUANDARY

Author: Cynthia Ozick (1928-   )
Publisher: Alfred A. Knopf (New York). 247 pp. $25.00
Type of work: Essays

∽

A collection of nineteen essays on a variety of topics, many of them about writers and their works, set in the context of moral and intellectual concerns

∽

Cynthia Ozick is a distinguished and respected writer who has excelled in a wide variety of genres, including novels, novellas, short stories, essays, reviews, and literary criticism. Her work has attracted the attention of readers and critics ever since her first book, the novel *Trust* (1966). Of all her fiction, best known is the widely anthologized Holocaust story "The Shawl" (1980), set in Germany in World War II. The short story was republished in *The Shawl* (1989) along with the novella *Rosa*, which depicts the mother years after the events in "The Shawl." The powerful emotional impact of the short story and its sharp imagistic style resonates as a cry for humanity and justice. In her nonfiction, too, Ozick is a meticulous stylist and a voice of conscience. Her essays often start with a specific incident or situation and then sweep forward to illuminate enduring moral and intellectual issues.

Quarrel and Quandary is Ozick's fifth collection of essays, following *Art and Ardor* (1983), *Metaphor and Memory* (1989), *What Henry James Knew and Other Essays on Writers* (1993), and *Fame and Folly* (1996). The essays, or versions of them, originally appeared in such publications as *American Scholar, The New York Times, The New Yorker*, and *The Yale Review*. The nineteen essays cover a wide range of topics, from "A Swedish Novel" (on Göran Tunström's *The Christmas Oratorio*, which Ozick ultimately finds overly poetic); to "The Ladle," (in praise of the dipper, as in to dip soup from a pot); from "Lovesickness" (a personal experience of irrational infatuation) to "Public Intellectuals" (on the responsibility of writers and public thinkers in promoting social values). Whatever her topic, Ozick's writing style itself commands attention.

Several of the essays, in one way or another, take up the question of art and its relation to politics, broadly defined. The first essay in the collection is "Dostoyevsky's Unabomber." Here Ozick compares Raskolnikov in Fyodor Dostoevski's novel *Prestupleniye i nakazaniye* (1866; *Crime and Punishment*, 1886) to the late-twentieth century convicted terrorist Theodore Kaczynski, known as the Unabomber. The analogy seems rather strained, and indeed to a large extent Ozick abandons the comparison to focus only on Dostoevski. Yet this opening essay demonstrates Ozick's ability to juxtapose events from literature with current events, often in thought-provoking

~

Cynthia Ozick is the author of eight works of fiction, including The Puttermesser Papers *and* The Shawl, *and three other collections of essays,* Art and Ardor, Metaphor and Memory, *and* Fame and Folly.

~

ways. As a reviewer in *The New York Times* notes about this collection of essays, "Even when you disagree with her, she electrifies your mind."

In "Who Owns Anne Frank?" Ozick emphasizes her view that Anne Frank, despite her young age, was first and foremost a writer. While hiding from the Nazis in an attic with her family and others in Amsterdam during World War II, Anne kept her diary not only for it to be her "friend," but with the goal of documenting the horrors and eventually publishing it and continuing to be a writer. The betrayal that led Nazis to their hiding place meant her family's extinction in a concentration camp, with only her father Otto Frank surviving. He heavily edited Anne's manuscript, the first of many changes to come. Ozick argues that the way the publication was promoted, and especially the emendations in the subsequent popular stage play and film, thoroughly distort Anne Frank's story because the end is missing, the ending of her life in a concentration camp. What was Anne Frank's diary of fear has been "bowdlerized, distorted, transmuted, traduced, reduced. . . . A deeply truthtelling work has been turned into an instrument of partial truth, surrogate truth, or antitruth." The innumerable editions and stage/film versions have minimized Jewish victimization, minimized German Nazi culpability, sweetened and infantilized Anne to the point that a young actress in 1997 said of the play and her lead role as Anne Frank: "it's funny, it's hopeful, and she's a happy person." Ozick traces in detail the evolution of the false myth of Anne Frank over half a century: this floating over the truth of evil has done justice neither to Anne Frank nor to the cause of social justice.

The theme of writers or filmmakers distorting realities shows up in "The Rights of History and the Rights of Imagination." Ozick cites, for example, William Styron in his novel *Sophie's Choice* (1976) portraying his Auschwitz concentration camp victim not as Jewish but merely as Polish. Creating such a characterization without any commentary blurs the historical realities. In "The Selfishness of Art" Ozick suggests that the novelist Henry James, long an admirable and interesting figure to her, was so wrapped up in his vision of himself as an artist that he was often callous to the suffering of people he knew. Another essay, "Cinematic James," begins by recounting Henry James's love of dramatic form and dialogue which soured for him when his ventures into the theatre world failed, particularly the humiliating failure of his play *Guy Domville* (pb. 1894, pr. 1895). James then proclaimed the novel form far superior to the theatrical. There is some irony, then, in the films that have been based on his novels. In Jane Campion's film version of *The Portrait of a Lady* (1996), the plot of the novel is generally followed, but the conception of the protagonist Isabel Archer (played by Nicole Kidman) is far more Campion's creation than James's. What James created as a tragedy of the defeat of freedom becomes, in the film, "little more than a beautifully embroidered anecdote of a bad marriage."

More laudatory commentaries on writers and the art of writing appear in other essays. In "The Impossibility of Being Kafka," Ozick discusses at length the problems of translation, difficulties certainly in the literal sense of translating accurately from one language to another, but also in understanding the writer's times and realities. Kafka's stories of totalitarianism and alienation grew out of his own experience. Jews were sharply discriminated against in Czechoslovakia. Kafka's native language was German, which made him further outcast in Prague but no less stigmatized by the neighboring anti-Jewish Germans. Although Kafka died of tuberculosis in 1924, his three sisters who survived him perished at Auschwitz and Lodz between 1941 and 1943. Translations, especially of literary works, vary with the cultural outlooks of each succeeding generation, and issues are not necessarily rightly decided on the ground of textual faithfulness. Given the numerous theories of translation, including lyrical, academic, and philological, some critics despair and conclude it should not be done, or done only in the spirit that the translation should be seen as merely as an indication of the original. But, Ozick points out, there is also the impossibility of *not* translating the works of as great and important a writer as Kafka. What would be the impact on the literate world of not having access to the voice and vision of such a writer? Or, at least, of not having had access to the voice and vision of the translator? Kafka's literary works, fortunately, endure, even if the various translations are transient.

Ozick also writes of the innovation and influence of writer Gertrude Stein ("A Prophet of Modernism") and, in a paean to the art of poetry ("What is Poetry About?") Ozick's own striking eloquence calls out: from the common pool of language the poet can "reconfigure, startle, and restart" words; "poetry has the magisterial will and the intimate attentiveness" to decode the norms of life. "Imaginary People," similarly, is a brief but powerful statement on the importance of the "make-believe" of fiction. These essays leave no doubt about Ozick's continuing devotion to literature and to its vital significance in the world.

One of the most intriguing essays of the collection is Ozick's analysis of an ancient text, the Book of Job in the Old Testament of the Bible, written some twenty-five hundred years ago yet always current and always the subject of endless questions about its message. Why would God accept Satan's taunt to test Job to prove Job's faith? Job suffers horrifying and horrifyingly gratuitous afflictions. He painfully loses his family, his wealth, his happiness, honor, and health. The primary question, which re-echoes through the eons, is, why does God allow injustice in the world? In the biblical scripture, God's only "answer" rolls out of the whirlwind, "Where were you, when I laid the foundation of the earth?" The God of the story restores Job to prosperity and replaces his dead wife and children with new ones (even twice the number of sons, and daughters exceedingly comely); but surely this is an unsatisfactory consolation, almost calculated to create indifference and loss of sympathy for the suffering of others. If the central point is that a transcendent God is unknowable, inevitably beyond human understanding, that likewise implies the inevitability of philosophical doubt. That may be the real message.

At the end of the collection is a satisfying set of more relaxed autobiographical essays. Ozick is as deft at writing about her childhood or an early summer job as about universal quarrels and quandaries. "How I Got Fired from My Summer Job," to list one, is as poignant and comic as the title suggests. Here Ozick is twenty-two, just out of graduate school, where she had finished "a fat M.A. thesis on the later novels of Henry James," and looking for a summer job. Thoroughly steeped in literary New Criticism, she carries her "Wellek-and-Warren" *Theory of Literature* book with her. Attracted by its location near Bryant Park and the Forty-second Street Library, where she imagines leisurely lunch hours reading indoors or out, she accepts a job with a firm of accountants. Her interviewer asks her what her Master's is in. She responds "English." He asks her if she can type. She is to fill in rows of numerical digits. The only means of correcting is by using a stiff round typewriter eraser with its miniature whiskbroom at one end and erasing each carbon copy separately. The botched pages—that is every one of them the first day—go directly into the wastepaper basket. By the second day her boss is suggesting she stay in the office for lunch—more time to try typing those forms and also to chat with him about books, which for him consists of two dog-eared self-help books. You'll never get ahead with a book like that, he says after asking her what her book is about. By Friday morning of the first week, she has managed to complete one page for every three or four starts. It is too late. The accountants have decided the book she carries around with her is not compatible with the office or with the errands one of them expects her to do for his daughter who is just her same age. They tell her she can take Friday afternoon off and not to come back on Monday morning. It comes as no surprise; she too knows they are not compatible.

The literary essay is as demanding as other genres, and Ozick is one of only a handful of writers of her time who consistently create works that seem to have the enduring timelessness that differentiates genuine essays from mere articles. In this strong collection, Ozick takes up the subject of "the essay" itself in "She: Portrait of the Essay as a Warm Body." "An essay is a thing of the imagination," she says. "A genuine essay is made out of language and character and mood and temperament and pluck and chance." However fluid and various in its topics, it always has a power, the capacity to "take us in" to the living voice of the writer.

Lois A. Marchino

Sources for Further Study

Booklist 97 (September 15, 2000): 204.
Kirkus Reviews 68 (July 15, 2000): 1019.
Library Journal 125 (September 1, 2000): 209.
The New York Times, September 20, 2000, p. B8.
The New York Times Book Review 105 (October 8, 2000): 6.
Publishers Weekly 247 (August 14, 2000): 336.

THE QUESTION OF BRUNO

Author: Aleksandar Hemon (1964-   )
Publisher: Nan A. Talese/Doubleday (New York). 230
   pp. $22.95
Type of work: Short fiction

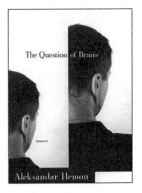

∼

*A collection of linked stories and a novella by a writer
from Bosnia*

∼

Principal characters:
   THE NARRATOR, a voice similar to but not
      identical with Aleksandar Hemon
   THE NARRATOR'S FATHER, who may or may not be a spy
   UNCLE JULIUS, who lives on an island off the coast of Yugoslavia
   JOSEF PRONEK, a Bosnian writer and blues musician
   ANDREA, an American friend of Josef
   ANDREA'S FATHER AND MOTHER
   NANA, Andrea's grandmother

   Born in Sarajevo in 1964, Aleksandar Hemon "moved to Chicago in 1992 with
only a basic command of English," the dust jacket relates. "He began writing in English in 1995." *The Question of Bruno*, his first book, has received considerable ac-
claim. Stuart Dybek compares Hemon to Joseph Conrad, Vladimir Nabokov, and
Jerzy Kosinski, who, "compelled by circumstance to emigrate from their native
tongues, . . . exerted a transformational effect on literature in English. *The Question of
Bruno* promises no less." Parts of the book appeared in *The New Yorker* and *Tri-
Quarterly*, among other journals, and one story, "Islands," was selected for *Best
American Short Stories, 1999.*
   What the dust jacket does not mention is that Hemon took a degree in comparative
literature at the University of Sarajevo. (See Hemon's essay, "The Book of My Life,"
in the December 25, 2000-January 1, 2001 issue of *The New Yorker*, about his profes-
sor and mentor Nikola Koljevic, who became a high-ranking figure in the Serbian
Democratic Party, led by the notorious Radovan Karadzic, "he who was to become
the most wanted war criminal in the world.") Perhaps that was deemed too literary for
the dust jacket copy, adding an unwelcome degree of complexity to a pleasing story.
Yet if any two words sum up Hemon, they are "literary" and "complex."
   The Question of Bruno is indeed an interesting book, though the hyperbole piled
on by Dybek and others does neither the reader nor the author any favors. To put it another way, rather than see this as a book that will exert "a transformational effect on
literature in English"—an embarrassingly grandiose claim—it can be read as a work
that highlights certain trends in contemporary writing: extreme self-consciousness, a

Aleksandar Hemon was born in
Sarajevo and moved to Chicago in
1992 with only a basic command of
English. He began writing in
English in 1995 and has since
published fiction in The New
Yorker, Granta, Tin House, *and*
Best American Short Stories 1999
and 2000.

strong sense of belatedness, a jokey tone, and a taste for pastiche. These qualities and others in the same vein are particularly evident in the work of writers such as David Foster Wallace and Dave Eggers (and in *McSweeney's*, the influential journal edited by Eggers); in less defined form they are pervasive.

The tone is set by the front cover of the dust jacket of *The Question of Bruno*, which shows the same black-and-white photograph twice at different scales: It is a cropped photo of the back of a man's head. The reader who compares this cover photo with the small photo of Aleksandar Hemon on the back flap, accompanying the author biography, will come to the conclusion that it is Hemon himself who appears on the cover, incognito as it were.

Then there is the title of the book. The convention for collections of short fiction is to take the title of one of the pieces and give it to the collection as well. In this case, though, the title of the collection is taken from the novella *Blind Jozef Pronek and Dead Souls*, which comes late in the book. This novella is divided into a number of subsections, each of which has its own title, and one of these is called "The Question of Bruno." So one might say that Hemon plays a little game with the reader, arousing curiosity as to the meaning of the title of the book, then deflating it when the discovery of the source of the title leads merely to a dead end.

From the outset, then, Hemon establishes an air of jokey mystification, one result of which is an ironic distance between the writer and his material. That material is, first and foremost, the war in Bosnia, the governing context of the book even when it is not explicitly mentioned; second, the larger history of twentieth century wars and atrocities; and third, a latter-day version of the immigrant experience. So while on one hand Hemon's most immediate selling point as a writer is his "Bosnian experience," and while he uses that specific, highly charged experience to argue a certain point of view on what it means to be human, period, he wants at the same time to avoid any straightforward notion of a "literature of witness." That would be naïve. Thus, also, while Hemon draws heavily on his family experience in the book, and even refers to his family by name, as one might expect from a memoir rather than a work of fiction, he nevertheless at the same time employs various distancing devices, so that, for example, what happens to his father in one story is different from what happens to his father in another story.

These links between "biographies" of characters—links that often seem imperfect, or arbitrary—reinforce the effect of the dust jacket photo, the title of the collection, and other elements of the book: They suggest a web of meaning that is ultimately pointless or that emphasizes the arbitrary power of the storyteller-as-God. Perhaps they are intended to suggest both the unquenchable human desire to make connections—to "make meaning"—and the futility of that desire.

In the first story, "Islands," the narrator recalls a trip he took as a boy with his family to an island off the coast of Yugoslavia. The Hemons, readers later learn, migrated to Bosnia from Ukraine, and a member of the Ukrainian branch of the family, Uncle Julius, is there on the island. He tells stories about the period during which he was in the gulag under Stalin.

What is most distinctive about the story is its language, which is overloaded with striking similes and odd but effective word choices. "We got up at dawn, ignored the yolky sun," it begins. There is "the thin stocking of smoke on the horizon-thread, then the ship itself, getting bigger, slightly slanted sideways, like a child's drawing." Also striking is the rhythm of the sentences, giving the story terrific momentum and somehow feeling just right for the child's point of view. There are a few lapses, but for the most part it is an enormously assured and impressive performance.

Thematically, "Islands" sets up the whole book. Uncle Julius's stories of cruelties under Stalin rhyme with other human cruelties in the stories that follow, and rhyme, too, with the brutal natural order—or disorder—on the island, where mongooses, imported to control the snakes that were once everywhere on the island, have now themselves multiplied and grown menacing. It is a bleak outlook, seasoned with irony—an irony found also in a later story, "A Coin," with a comparison between Sarajevo, where snipers toy with their hapless victims, and the narrator's apartment, where he must hunt the not-so-hapless cockroaches.

"Islands" also introduces Hemon's lexicon, the writer's equivalent to a painter's palette. On the first page of the story, a German tourist vomits, and several lines are devoted to that; many more people will vomit or almost vomit in the the course of the book. "Vomit" is an indispensable entry in the Hemon lexicon, and other recurring words form a cluster with it: "reeking," for instance.

In one important respect, however, "Islands" does not at all set the agenda for what follows. Given the distinctive style of this story—an achievement that a writer might well seek to exploit—one expects more of the same, but in fact Hemon immediately discards it like a suit of clothes for something radically different. (Later, in the novella, he returns to some of the devices of "Islands," but the total effect is quite different.) The stories that immediately follow "Islands" are not only radically different stylistically from that opening but also quite different from each other. "The Life and Work of Alphonse Kauders" is a Dada-style recitation of political horrors and absurdities, the weakest piece in the book. According to the credits on the copyright page, this story was published, in Serbo-Croatian, in *Best Yugoslav Stories 1990*, but that may be another of Hemon's little jokes.

The next story, "The Sorge Spy Ring," reads like a second, more substantial take on the same material. It recounts the now adolescent narrator's fascination with spying and his suspicion that his father may be a spy, in counterpoint with the story of Richard Sorge, a historical figure (a Soviet spy posted as a press attache in the German embassy in Tokyo), whose exploits Hemon retells and loads with apocryphal detail, in long footnotes that constitute a parallel text to the main narrative. It is a tour de force. In keeping with the jokey tone that pervades Hemon's writing, spying becomes a motif in the collection, and in the acknowledgments at the end of the book, Hemon thanks those who have made "Operation Bruno" possible, acknowledges "operatives" in Chicago and Sarajevo as well as the "New York network," and so on.

The overall treatment of political and historical material in the book is both absurdist and reductive, suggesting that brutal, meaningless scenarios play out at different times in different places with the same remorseless logic (or illogic). Hitler, Stalin, the assassination of Archduke Ferdinand (by a Serb patriot) that started World War I, the atrocities of "ethnic cleansing" in Bosnia: all run together, with the complicity of parties that consider themselves virtuous, as Hemon sketches Churchill and Roosevelt's meeting with Stalin at Yalta in a way that blurs moral distinctions among the victors.

That material, the main theme of the collection, comes together with the most important secondary theme—a disenchanted immigrant's tale—in the longest piece in the volume, the novella *Blind Josef Pronek and Dead Souls*. Pronek is the protagonist (with a biography similar to Hemon's) but not the narrator of this piece, which is delivered in a rather archly omniscient manner, replete with asides to the reader and other devices that deliberately destroy what John Gardner called the "vivid continuous dream" of a fictional narrative. The title of the novella, readers learn, derives from the name of Pronek's blues band, "well known and liked in Sarajevo." Perhaps the allusion to Gogol's novel *Dead Souls* is a hint as to the genre of the novella. There is a good deal of Gogolian grotesquerie in Hemon's tale, but his work is much cruder than Gogol's, largely though not entirely reducible to heavy-handed satire. Still, it is a reminder that if the characters in this novella are caricatures, that is by intention: To claim that Hemon's portrait of America and Americans is not "realistic" is presumably to miss the point.

The novella begins and ends in aiports. Like Hemon, Pronek, a Bosnian writer, arrives in the United States in 1992, apparently via some sort of U.S. government cultural program. After meetings with assorted artistic types—including a a visit with screenwriter and director John Milius in Hollywood—Pronek hooks up with Andrea, a young woman in Chicago whom he met in Europe, and settles in, first in her apartment (shared with an idiotic American boyfriend), then in a drab apartment of his own and on his own, working at a typical assortment of immigrant jobs. When readers last glimpse Pronek, several years later, he is in the Vienna airport, trying to persuade an Austrian official that it is perfectly safe—despite his Bosnian passport—to allow him a brief visit to the city, since he is "an alien resident of the United States" and hence not a potential illegal immigrant to Austria. "At that moment," the narrator informs us, "Pronek understood that he was an oxymoron."

From his initial encounters with Americans in Washington, D.C., right through to the end of the tale, Pronek meets a gallery of fools. Some are well-meaning—many of them are, in fact—but they are fools nonetheless, and whether well-meaning or not, they speak entirely in clichés. The satire, if that is what it is intended to be, is boring, flaccid. The reader begins to wait wearily for the next puppet to appear, to say something about working hard and getting ahead, or to display invincible ignorance about Bosnia. Not that Pronek himself is painted as particularly admirable—just different from the Americans. He is European, after all.

One such encounter occurs in the subsection that gives the book its title, "The Question of Bruno." Readers might think that, at last, they will find out what the title of the book refers to. In this section, Pronek goes with Andrea to the apartment of her parents, near the University of Chicago. Also there is the senile mother (or so one presumes) of Andrea's mother or father (it is not clear which), whom they call "Nana." Andrea's parents try to show themselves as welcoming, culturally enlightened people. They are portrayed, needless to say, as pretentious fools. "We like Kundera," says Andrea's mother. "He's from Czechoslovakia too." This is odd, since a page earlier, correcting Nana, who confused Bosnia with Boston, Andrea's mother has said "Bosnia, Nana, Bosnia. In Yugoslavia, near Czechoslovakia." Apparently Americans forget the little they know from one page to the next.

Yet what is the question of Bruno? It is raised by Nana:

> "Where is Bruno? Is Bruno there in the kitchen?" Nana hollered all of a sudden.
>
> "Calm down, Nana. That's not Bruno. Bruno's gone," Andrea's mother said.
>
> "Come here, Bruno!" Nana yelled toward the kitchen. "Eat with us! We have everything now!"
>
> "Calm down, Nana. Or you'll have to go to your room," Andrea's father said. . . . Andrea's mother was scraping off the remnants of food, little piles of mush, onto a big plate.
>
> "What you [sic] will do with it?" asked Nana. "Don't throw it away, Bruno is hungry. Bruno!"
>
> "We're not going to throw it away," Andrea's mother said. "We'll save it for Bruno."

A few moments later, as Pronek and Andrea are preparing to leave, Nana asks, "Are you going to see Bruno?" Pronek says no, sorry, they are not.

So who is Bruno, and what is his significance? Perhaps another reader will be able to answer. "Bruno" sounds like it could be an Eastern European name—the epigraph for the novella is taken from the Polish writer Bruno Schulz. When Nana talks about Bruno, she sometimes sounds as if she were talking about a dog, but at other times she seems to be talking about—or calling out to—a person. Is Bruno the Eastern European in the subconscious of the West, a not-quite-human figure? When Nana first calls out for Bruno, she interrupts a conversation about the war in Bosnia, in which Andrea's parents express incomprehension. "I tried to understand it, but I simply can't," says Andrea's father. "Thousands of years of hatred, I guess." Is "the question of Bruno" the question repeated by countless commentators in America concerning "those crazy Balkans," a question that betrays criminal naïveté and complacence? If so, Hemon's book may be read as an oblique answer.

John Wilson

Sources for Further Study

Booklist 96 (May 1, 2000): 1651.
Library Journal 125 (July, 2000): 144.
Publishers Weekly 247 (May 15, 2000): 87.
The Yale Review 88 (July, 2000): 159.

RAVELSTEIN

Author: Saul Bellow (1915-   )
Publisher: Viking Press (New York). 233 pp. $24.95
Type of work: Novel
Time: The late 1980's through the late 1990's
Locale: Paris; American Midwest; New Hampshire; St. Martin, West Indies; and Boston

∼

A writer is asked by his dying friend, a flamboyant philosophy professor made rich by a best-selling book, to tell his story, warts and all

∼

Principal characters:
> ABE RAVELSTEIN, a professor of political philosophy at a Midwest university
> CHICK, a writer and friend
> VELA, a beautiful and aristocratic physicist, one of Chick's former wives
> ROSAMUND, Chick's present wife
> NIKKI, Ravelstein's young male companion

In his eulogy for Allan Bloom (1930-1992), the controversial author of the surprise best-seller *The Closing of the American Mind: How Higher Education Has Failed Democracy and Impoverished the Souls of Today's Students* (1987), Saul Bellow said of his friend:

> When he was paralyzed by Guillain-Barré syndrome and sent down to the intensive care unit, he was not expected to survive. I was in his hospital room when he was brought upstairs and returned to his bed. He was no sooner in it than the phone rang—a saleswoman from Loeber Motors was calling. He indicated that he wanted to talk to her and held the phone in his strongly trembling hand. He then began to discuss the upholstery of the Mercedes he had ordered.

The same scene is repeated in *Ravelstein*; in the novel the Mercedes becomes a BMW, Bloom's friend Michael Wu becomes Nikki, and Bellow himself is transmogrified into Chick, a writer "happy with middling returns." Bellow has employed real-life models before, most notably the late lyric poet Delmore Schwartz in *Humboldt's Gift* (1975). However, *Ravelstein* is a *roman à clef* with a vengeance, and critics chimed in with identifications. Professor Felix Davarr in the novel is Bloom's mentor, the philosopher Leo Strauss. Morris Herbst is Bloom's friend Werner Dannhauser; the mythologist Radu Grielescu, who takes great pains to cover over his fascist past, was said to be Mircea Eliade, the philosopher of comparative religion. Even if such one-to-one correspondences are accurate, though,

Saul Bellow won the Nobel Prize in Literature in 1976 and in 1990 was presented with the National Book Foundation Medal for distinguished contribution to American letters. He is the only novelist to have received three National Book Awards, for The Adventures of Augie March, Herzog, *and* Mr. Sammler's Planet.

Ravelstein is not a parlor game but a captivating meditation on the meaning of Eros.

Bellow presents Abe Ravelstein in a series of vignettes, beginning with breakfast in a penthouse room in Paris at the Hôtel Crillon. Ravelstein is immensely charmed when he encounters singer Michael Jackson and his entourage at the same hotel. Ravelstein's publishing success had erased his debts forever, and he was free to indulge his deeply materialistic tastes. He was not only rich, but famous. British prime minister Margaret Thatcher and U.S. president Ronald Reagan had welcomed him as a guest. He had lectured the French about Jean-Jacques Rousseau and was mentored by the writings of Plato (427-347 B.C.E.), most notably *Politeia* (*Republic*, 1701) and *Symposion* (*Symposium*, 1701).

The *Symposium* had taught Ravelstein about Eros. Even though Chick takes pains to say, repeatedly, that his friend "clearly didn't want me to write about his ideas," Chick can hardly refrain from discussing love.

He thought—no, he *saw*—that every soul was looking for its peculiar other, longing for its complement. I'm not going to describe Eros, et cetera, as he saw it. I've done too much of that already: but there is a certain irreducible splendor about it without which we would not be quite human. Love is the highest function of the our species—its vocation. This simply can't be set aside in considering Ravelstein. He never forgot this conviction. It figures in all his judgments.

In the novel, Chick notes that he had encouraged Ravelstein to put his ideas into a book. Though the published title is never mentioned, its original title is. "Souls Without Longing" is what Ravelstein wanted to call it. Chuck writes,

Without its longings your soul was a used inner tube maybe good for one summer at the beach, nothing more. Spirited men and women, the young above all, were devoted to the pursuit of love. By contrast the bourgeois was dominated by fears of violent death. There, in the briefest form possible, you have a sketch of Ravelstein's most important preoccupations.

Ravelstein was no prig. "On the contrary," Chick says, "he saw love as possibly the highest blessing of mankind. A human soul devoid of longing was a soul deformed, deprived of its highest good, sick unto death."

Ravelstein's story is intertwined with talk of love, of Eros. Allan Bloom, in the posthumously published *Love and Friendship* (1993), wrote that

Man is essentially an incomplete being, and full awareness of this incompleteness is essential to his humanity and ground for the specifically human quest for completeness or wholeness. . . . Eros, in its overwhelming and immoderate demands, is the clearest and most powerful inclination toward lost wholeness.

Such a view of Eros forms the backdrop of Bloom's *The Closing of the American Mind*, to which Bellow contributed the foreword. One reviewer, Robert Paul Wolff, suggested that the entire book was a Bellow novel, a satire on the University of Chicago Great Books movement. *Ravelstein* is the novel, but it is no satire, though it is sometimes difficult to unravel truth from fiction.

Throughout the book Chick reminds the reader that Ravelstein had asked him to write a memoir, to become Boswell to his Johnson. However, Chick was not to deal with his philosophical arguments. He writes,

He had expounded those fully himself and they're available in his theoretical books. I make myself responsible for the person, therefore, and since I can't depict him without a certain amount of self-involvement my presence on the margins will have to be tolerated.

Ravelstein, nearly six-and-a-half feet tall, with a large bald head, had a weakness for the classics and for old vaudeville routines, for insider news (some of his students had gone on to high places in government and regularly reported to him), and for celebrity gossip. He reveled in the lives of his best students, sometimes playing matchmaker, but had little patience for those who did not measure up to his intellectual standards. To be one of his disciples, Chick notes, one had to learn Plato in the original Greek. Some students were not cut out for the academic rigors, and Ravelstein simply told them to leave.

At the same time, though, the man was generous with his time and energy, at least to those students he favored. He was not kind, really, and his remarks could wound, but he responded to the high energy of his students and praised their eccentricities. His goal was to help them realize the longings of their souls, whatever those longings turned out to be.

Chick wonders

how to deal with his freaks, quiddities, oddities, his eating, drinking, shaving, dressing, and playfully savaging his students. But that isn't much more than his natural history. Others saw him as bizarre, perverse—grinning, smoking, lecturing, overbearing, impatient, but to me he was brilliant and charming. Out to undermine the social sciences or other university specialties. He was doomed to die because of his irregular sexual ways. About these he was entirely frank with me, with all his close friends. He was considered, to use a term from the past, an invert. Not a "gay." He despised campy homosexuality and took a very low view of "gay pride."

Ravelstein's book about souls made him rich, a millionaire many times over. Chick notes that his friend had always had expensive tastes, but the success of his book meant debt-free living and no need for his friends to bail him out. The novelist's eye takes stock of Ravelstein's apartment:

The living-room sofa of black leather was deep, wide, low. The glass top of the coffee table in front of it was about four inches thick. On it, Ravelstein sometimes spread his effects—the solid-gold Mont Blanc fountain pen, his $20,000 wrist watch, the golden gadget that cut his smuggled Havanas, the extra-large cigarette box filled with Marlboros, his Dunhill lighters, the heavy square glass ashtrays—the long butts neurotically puffed at once or twice and then broken. A great amount of ashes. Near the wall on a stand, sloping, an elaborate many-keyed piece of telephone apparatus—Abe's command post, expertly operated by himself. It saw heavy use. Paris and London called almost as often as Washington. Some of his very close friends in Paris phoned to talk about intimate matters—sex scandals.

Sex, apparently, is Ravelstein's undoing.

He was HIV-positive, he was dying of complications from it. Weakened, he became the host of an endless list of infections. Still he insisted on telling me over and over again what love was—the neediness, the awareness of incompleteness, the longing for wholeness, and how the pains of Eros were joined to the most ecstatic pleasures.

In his last days, Ravelstein turned his attention to his own Jewishness. "Ravelstein went for classical antiquity," Chick had said earlier. "He preferred Athens but he respected Jerusalem greatly." Now his attention was on the collective hatred that sanctioned wholesale slaughter of Jews. He concluded "that it is impossible to get rid of one's origins, it is impossible not to remain a Jew." One must not forsake Jewish history. Ravelstein talks of the coming high holidays and tells Chick to take Rosamund to a synagogue.

Ravelstein succumbed, but Chick reports no memorial service. He is alone with his thoughts. Ravelstein had awakened something in him, and, almost like the philosopher in Plato's allegory of the cave who emerged to see the sun, the illumination of all the images, Chick was seeing something "original."

Chick describes himself as "a serial marrier." In the earlier days of their friendship, Ravelstein would often chide Chick about Vela, a beautiful physicist who, Ravelstein's sources revealed, was having a number of affairs. The news came as a blow to Chick, and near the center of his book he remembers his friend's teaching:

People are beaten at last with their solitary longings and intolerable isolation. They need *the* right, *the* missing portion to complete themselves, and since they can't realistically hope to find that they must accept a companionable substitute. Recognizing that they can't win, they settle. The marriage of true minds seldom occurs. . . . Ravelstein taught that in the modern condition we are in a weak state. The strong state—and this was what he learned from Socrates—comes to us through nature. At the core of the soul is Eros. Eros is overwhelmingly attracted to the sun.

Chick's marriage to Vela fails, but another marriage is imminent. Rosamund, Chick's assistant and a former graduate student of Ravelstein, has fallen in love with him. Chick is in his seventies when he and his new wife are invited to dine with Ravelstein in that Paris hotel, where Ravelstein presses Chick to write his biography.

With Ravelstein dead, the last quarter of the novel focuses on Chick and Rosamund, and their vacation in the Caribbean. Chick eats tainted fish at a restaurant on St. Martin, and Rosamund realizes how ill he is. At her insistence, Chick is rushed to a hospital in Boston and given oxygen. He sees visions for a time and is incoherent, but eventually he recovers. He realizes Eros has not been far:

> Rosamund kept me from dying. I can't represent this without taking it on frontally and I can't take it on frontally while my interests remain centered on Ravelstein. Rosamund had studied love—Rousseauan romantic love and the Platonic Eros as well, with Ravelstein—but she knew far more about it than either her teacher or her husband.

Six years passed after Ravelstein's death before Chick, with Rosamund's encouragement, could write his biography. It turned out to be not only a remembrance of a friend, but also a celebration of the eroticism of philosophy.

Dan Barnett

Sources for Further Study

Booklist 96 (February 15, 2000): 1051.
Esquire 133 (April, 2000): 70.
Library Journal 125 (April 15, 2000): 121.
The Nation 270 (May 15, 2000): 9.
The New York Review of Books 47 (May 25, 2000: 17.
Publishers Weekly 247 (February 28, 2000): 57.

RIMBAUD

Author: Graham Robb (1958-   )
Publisher: W. W. Norton (New York). 551pp. $35.00
Type of work: Literary biography
Time: 1854-1891
Locale: France, Aden, and North Africa

~

*A detailed and compelling biography of one of France's
most remarkable and notorious nineteenth century poets*

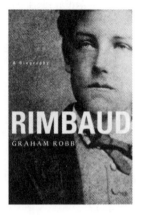

~

Principal personages:
    ARTHUR RIMBAUD, French poet, merchant,
      and explorer
    FRÉDÉRIC RIMBAUD, his father, a captain in the French army who de-
      serted the family
    VITALIE CUIF RIMBAUD, his religious and stern mother
    ISABELLE RIMBAUD, his younger sister
    ERNEST DELAHAYE, a childhood friend and confidant
    GEORGES IZAMBARD, a teacher and friend
    PAUL VERLAINE, an influential poet with whom Rimbaud had a violent
      and passionate affair

Since his death in 1891, there have been numerous biographies written about Rimbaud that have attempted to skew, invent, or cloud altogether who Arthur Rimbaud was. In 1897, Rimbaud's brother-in-law, Paterne Berrichon, published a biography that attempted to sanitize Arthur's life. In this biography, Rimbaud is supposedly sorry for all of his "youthful indiscretions," and he is looked upon as a saint in the eyes of the African natives. Through the efforts of Isabelle and her husband, all the rough edges were removed from Rimbaud. *La Vie de Jean-Arthur Rimbaud* was no more than a "devotional" biography and muddied the waters of Rimbaud scholarship for many years to come. Whatever truth there was in the Berrichon biography became suspect to all serious critics. As Graham Robb points out in the "Epilogue" of *Rimbaud*, the legend of Rimbaud became either all black or all white. There seemed to be no room left for any shades of gray. In 1938, French scholar Enid Starkie published *Arthur Rimbaud*. This remarkable biography quickly became the standard chronicle of Rimbaud's life. The author revised her extraordinary work in 1947 and again in 1961. While Starkie died in 1970, her biography has remained the benchmark by which all other literary biographies of Rimbaud are measured. Starkie devoted much of her life to the study of Rimbaud, and the many readers of her biography have felt that they know Rimbaud intimately because of Starkie's portrait. Graham Robb, therefore, comes to his own project with the understanding of the multitude of myths that surround Arthur Rimbaud.

Acclaimed for his biographies *Balzac: A Life* (1994) and *Victor Hugo* (1997), Robb has taken on the daunting task of attempting to poke holes in the mythology that has grown up around the great nineteenth century French poet. There seems to be an entire cottage industry devoted to publishing something about him every year. As a visionary, a poet, an explorer, a revolutionary, and more, Rimbaud has become many things to a vast number of devoted scholars, artists, and the

Graham Robb is the author of biographies of Victor Hugo and Honoré de Balzac, both of which were named New York Times Notable Books, *as well as a book on Stéphane Mallarmé. He lived in Oxford, England.*

reading public. Having created a scandal seemingly at every turn, Rimbaud is both a biographer's dream and biographer's nightmare. Robb has read what all of the previous scholars have written. He understands that there are adherents of certain points of view who do not wish to have their version of the myth shredded, picked apart, or even questioned. With this as his challenge, Robb has taken some giant steps forward in sifting through the chronology of Rimbaud's short life, while still realizing that there are gaps and puzzles in his life that an honest biographer cannot truly decipher. Robb goes about matter-of-factly detailing how extraordinarily cruel this model student could be, how his whole being—not merely his hypnotic poetry—was a rebellious act against all French civilized conventions. While previous biographers may have skirted around the more horrendous offenses against propriety that Rimbaud committed, Robb seems to relish in their telling.

Born in provincial France in 1854, Jean-Nicholas-Arthur Rimbaud grew up in the town of Charleville, near the Belgian border. He was the second son of Frédéric Rimbaud and Vitalie Cuif Rimbaud. His father was an army officer who spent a good deal of time away from home. His mother was devoutly religious and was very stern with her children. In 1860, Captain Rimbaud left the family home in Charleville for good. Robb appropriately takes the time to detail how Captain Rimbaud was fond of writing commentaries on army affairs as well as reports on Africa. He put together a "compendium of Arab jokes" and produced a "parallel-text translation of the Koran." Although these works were never published, Rimbaud's father exhibited diligence and an ability to make keen observations. His wife saw no value in literary endeavors. Madame Rimbaud was a difficult person to please and her husband decided that the struggle was no longer worth the effort. It is curious to speculate what influence his father's travels and writings had on young Rimbaud, even though he would never see his father after he left the family. It cannot be stressed too much how important it was for Robb to flesh out a more complete portrait of Rimbaud's father. The Rimbaud children would now be at the mercy of their bitter mother. In 1861, both Rimbaud brothers were sent to the Institut Rossat. While his older brother, Frédéric, was not a quick learner, little Arthur proved himself to be a fast study in almost every subject taught at school. He won many prizes at the Institut. In 1865, Madame Rimbaud transferred her sons to the Collège de Charleville. As Rimbaud grew older, his precociousness made it impossible to tolerate his stifling surroundings. He had an insatiable thirst for knowledge and diverse experiences. While he was considered a model student, the internal itch to break away from this provincial and ordinary world in which he found himself soon had to be scratched.

At the Collège de Charleville, young Rimbaud came into contact with a teacher by the name of Georges Izambard. Rimbaud enthusiastically shared the poems and stories that he wrote with Izambard. He became adept at writing Latin verse and won several prizes at regional competitions. In time, he grew to have contempt for the educational system that he had mastered. In July, 1870, the outbreak of the Franco-Prussian War forced the Collège de Charleville to close. This brought an end to Rimbaud's formal education. With the school closed, Izambard moved away from Charleville. Frustrated by what was happening around him, Rimbaud ran away to Paris on August 29, 1870. Having traveled without a ticket, he was imprisoned in Paris. This would be only the first of many escapes away from Charleville that Rimbaud would make. In February, 1871, a French National Assembly was elected. This new assembly had the authority to negotiate an end to the Franco-Prussian War. On March 26 of the same year, the citizens of Paris elected their own revolutionary government, which was known as the Commune. Previous biographers have doubted that Rimbaud was in Paris during the time of the Commune. Robb presents a credible scenario that Rimbaud was in Paris during the Commune. It would only be pure speculation, though, that he actually witnessed the National Assembly troops brutally put an end to the Commune during the week of May 22 to May 28, 1871. According to Robb, this week "was the bloodiest week in French history." The author also gives credence to the suggestion that Rimbaud was raped by a mob of soldiers while he was attempting to escape from the city before the slaughter began. During the chaotic month of May, he wrote "Letter du voyant" ("Seer Letter") in which he speaks of what constitutes the ideal visionary poet.

Encouraged to send some of his poems to the poet Paul Verlaine, Rimbaud sent him a handful of his most outrageous creations in September, 1871. Verlaine was ten years older, married, and an already established poet, but he was so impressed with the vitality of Rimbaud's verse that he raised the money for Rimbaud to come visit him in Paris. Before traveling to Paris, he composed one of his most brilliant poems, "Le Bateau ivre" ("The Drunken Boat"). He took a copy of this masterpiece with him. Both Verlaine and the Parisian literary crowd were impressed by this seventeen-year-old poet's compositions. Unfortunately, Verlaine's friends, wife, and her family became put off by Rimbaud's scandalous behavior. The two poets began a passionate and, at times, violent love affair. During their affair, they spent time in Brussels and London. Their quarrels have become infamous, and on July 10, 1873, Verlaine shot at Rimbaud, hitting him in the left wrist. Verlaine would spend eighteen months in a Belgian prison for this indiscretion. While 1871 to 1873 were very tumultuous years for Rimbaud, he composed most of his major poems during this period, including *Les Illuminations* (1886; *Illuminations*, 1932) and *Une Saison en enfer* (1873; *A Season in Hell*, 1932).

By 1875, Rimbaud had given up writing poetry and began traveling. Robb states that "the process that led him to abandon poetry altogether lasted several years." His poetry inevitably pointed Rimbaud toward the life of a merchant in search of a vast fortune. This can be looked at as a revisionist approach to Rimbaud's life, but Robb boldly lays out the evidence that the two halves of his life are more connected than previously thought. Robb believes that "the seer had turned into a sightseer." Over the next five years, he would go to Stuttgart, Germany, cross the Alps on foot, visit Milan and Siena, Italy, join a Scandinavian circus, and enlist in the Dutch colonial army. Upon arrival in Java, Rimbaud deserted from the army and headed back to Europe. He was adept at learning new languages. In 1880, Rimbaud traveled to Harar, Abyssinia (modern day Ethiopia) and Aden (modern day Yemen). He traded in such commodities as tobacco, incense, ivory, spears, coffee, and guns. Robb makes the point that Rimbaud was helpful to Menelik II, King of Choa and—after 1889—Emperor of Ethiopia, in his fight against Italy. By selling guns to Menelik, he helped an African army for the first time to defeat a European power. While it is part of the Rimbaud legend that he was not a successful merchant, Robb is emphatic that Rimbaud was an excellent merchant and that he made a small fortune. Although he continued diligently to correspond with his mother and sister, he took extra care to keep his money well hidden in order that his mother not get her hands on it. He did such a good job of keeping his fortune away from her in various bank accounts that it is surmised that most of it still remains hidden in 2001. Rimbaud learned many local languages and was respected by those with whom he came in contact for his reliability, courage, and patience. He died on November 10, 1891, in Marseille, France. Doctors had tried to save his life by amputating his right leg, but, in the end, the cancer that afflicted him could not be stopped. His sister, Isabelle, claimed that he converted to Catholicism on his deathbed, but this is very unlikely.

During his short literary career, Rimbaud set out to be truly modern. After having mastered all the accepted poetic forms of his day, he went about shattering them all. He experimented with free verse, and he is considered one of the first poets successfully to exploit the form. Rimbaud also delved into the unconscious and irrational for poetic images. For this reason, many of his most famous poems are open to differing interpretations. He did all of this in a four-year burst of creativity. This precocious teenage monster made himself into a "seer." Robb also details how, in addition to composing revolutionary poetry, Rimbaud abused alcohol and drugs, was uninhibited sexually, was a true anarchist, was unkempt to a fault, and was a cruel practical joker. The author relishes in the telling of the many gruesome jokes Rimbaud played on friend and enemy alike, including pouring sulphuric acid into a drinking companion's drink. He had no respect for the niceties of nineteenth century French society. What he saw were all of its hypocrisies, all of its suffocating impediments to human fulfillment. Out of this rebellion, out of the burst of creativity, Rimbaud grew up to be more like his father than anyone would have expected.

Robb is a compelling biographer who leaves no stone unturned. The author also makes use of many secondary sources—including both Starkie's biography and Charles Nicholl's wonderful *Somebody Else: Arthur Rimbaud in Africa, 1880-91* (1997)—in order to flesh out as complete a portrait of Rimbaud as is humanly possible. While readers should not avoid referring to Starkie's *Arthur Rimbaud* just yet, Robb has written an admirable biography that goes a long way toward bringing Rimbaud's entire life into greater focus.

Jeffry Jensen

Sources for Further Study

Booklist 97 (October 15, 2000): 410.
The Economist 356 (September 23, 2000): 101.
Library Journal 125 (October 1, 2000): 95.
Los Angeles Times Book Review, December 17, 2000, p. 6.
The Nation 271 (December 11, 2000): 32.
New Statesman 129 (September 25, 2000): 72.
The New York Times Book Review 105 (November 19, 2000): 15.
The Spectator 285 (October 7, 2000): 54.
The Times Literary Supplement, October 20, 2000, p. 3.
The Village Voice 45 (October 31, 2000): 144.
The Washington Post Book World, November 26, 2000, p. T9.

THE ROMANTICS

Author: Pankaj Mishra (1969-   )
Publisher: Random House (New York). 265 pp. $23.95
Type of work: Novel
Time: 1989-1996
Locale: Benares, Pondicherry, and Dharamshala, India

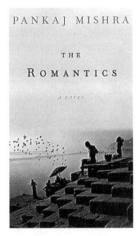

∾

*A young man discovers that though the world appears
to be filled with possibilities, in reality it holds only disap-
pointment*

∾

Principal characters:
> SAMAR, the narrator, a twenty-year-old
> Brahmin
> DIANA WEST ("Miss West"), a middle-aged Englishwoman
> CATHERINE, a beautiful, rich young Frenchwoman with whom Samar
> falls in love
> ANAND, a sitar player, Catherine's future husband
> RAJESH, a mysterious Brahmin, Samar's friend
> MARK, an American living in Benares
> DEBBIE, his scatterbrained lover, also an American

Although *The Romantics* is Pankaj Mishra's first novel, it establishes him as one of India's literary leaders. His nonfiction and criticism are highly regarded, and he is also admired for having discovered such outstanding young novelists as Arundhati Roy, who was awarded the Booker Prize for *The God of Small Things* (1997), and Raj Kamal Jha, whose book *The Blue Bedspread* (1999) has been acclaimed by critics.

The Romantics is patterned on another coming-of-age novel, *L'Éducation senti-mentale* (1869; *Sentimental Education*, 1898), by the French author Gustave Flau-bert. There are many likenesses between the two works. The protagonist of each work is a young man who, having completed his general education, is expected to prepare for a profession. At eighteen, Flaubert's Frédéric Moreau is in Paris to read law; at twenty, Mishra's Samar is in Benares to prepare for his civil service examinations. However, both of them become involved in the world around them, where everyone is interesting and anything seems possible. Like Frédéric, Samar becomes obsessed with a woman he cannot have, and though unlike Frédéric he ultimately attains a de-gree of serenity, Samar, too, settles for a diminished life.

In the latter half of *The Romantics*, Samar mentions *L'Éducation sentimentale* as a book that he has only recently come to appreciate, thanks in part to his discovery of an illuminating essay by Edmund Wilson on Flaubert's politics, in part to his own expe-riences among people unlike any he has known before. In Frédéric, Samar can see

~
Pankaj Mishra is a regular contributor to The New York Review of Books, *the* New Statesman, *and the* Times Literary Supplement, *as well as several Indian publications.* The Romantics *is his first novel.*
~

himself. Moreover, like Flaubert and the Hindu fatalists, Samar comes to believe that life has no meaning and that people have no control over their destinies.

Flaubert's novel and Edmund Wilson's criticism also have a profound influence on Samar's friend Rajesh. He, too, admits that he can identify with Frédéric; moreover, when he realizes how similar his own corrupt society is to that depicted by Flaubert, Rajesh loses hope and abandons his efforts at reform. At their first meeting, Rajesh lectures Samar about a Brahmin's duty; seven years later, Samar learns that the once idealistic Rajesh has become a contract killer.

However, there are several major differences between the two novels. Flaubert writes as an omniscient author, while Mishra limits himself to a single perspective, that of Samar, his first- person narrator. Moreover, *L'Éducation sentimentale* takes place over a period of twenty-seven years, and *The Romantics* just seven.

The fact that Mishra's title is plural indicates an even more important dissimilarity. Though Samar is the central figure in the novel, he is not the only character who has what Mishra calls a romantic view of life, that is, who assumes that anything one dreams, hopes, or imagines can become a reality. By this definition, almost everyone Samar meets through his fellow lodger Diana West is a romantic. Catherine, a young, wealthy Frenchwoman, has drawn her naïve Indian lover Anand into her dream. They are both convinced that when she takes him to France, his skill as a sitar player will bring him fame and fortune, while his status as her husband will gain him acceptance by her family and admission to the highest levels of French society. Another friend of Samar's "Miss West" is an American, Mark, who has persuaded himself and a succession of girlfriends that he is a person of extreme sensitivity and admirable depth, despite the fact that he drifts regularly from job and job and from place to place. Among the other romantics in Miss West's circle are Sarah, a young German woman who, like many Westerners, believes that she has found the truth in an Eastern religion, in her case Buddhism, and Mark's current lover, Debbie, who likes to dabble in ideas but is not bright enough to form a coherent thought, much less a philosophy of life.

Perhaps it is only natural to be a romantic when one is young, but it is unusual to find a middle-aged person who has not come to terms with reality. It is even more surprising when that individual is someone such as Miss West, who is clear-sighted enough to assess Debbie accurately and to predict the problems Catherine, Anand, and Samar do indeed encounter when they refuse to face the truth. However, for all her insights into the other characters, Miss West cannot see her own life for the waste that it is. For twenty years she has been the mistress of a British corporate executive who will never divorce his wife, using as an excuse the possibility that he may go into politics. It was his idea that Miss West should live in Benares, where he feels there is less chance of their liaison being discovered, as it might be if she went home to England, where she would much prefer to live. Though the chances of her marrying and having a family are dwindling with each year that passes, Miss West will not break off with her lover but lives for her memories, always hoping that he will summon her to another of their infrequent meetings.

It is to Mishra's credit that even though there are a number of "romantics" in his cast of characters, rather than just one, the novel is no less unified and no less coherent. One way the author unifies his work is by using a single narrator, whose purpose in telling his story is to make some sense out of a critical period in his own life. However, Mishra has Samar report so fully on the other characters that a reader can arrive at insights into their motivations that do not occur to the narrator even seven years later.

While *The Romantics* is hardly a simple book, it is so well structured that it is admirably coherent. The events are presented in chronological order, with occasional digressions providing information about Samar's past history and his family background. Moreover, each of the three sections into which the book is divided has a specific geographical setting and moves toward a climax and some sort of revelation.

The novel begins with Samar's arrival in Benares, which is not only much larger than anywhere he has ever lived but is also a holy city, believed by the Hindus to offer the possibility of release from the perpetual cycle of death and rebirth. To Samar, however, Benares is merely a place where he can study for the examinations that will assure him of a civil service post; the people he meets there, he believes, will never be more than chance acquaintances who can make his life a bit more pleasant. He obtains lodging with the elderly Panditji, a kindly soul and a fellow Brahmin, and begins taking some meals with Mrs. Pandey, Panditji's wife; he is befriended by Miss West and through her meets a number of other young people, including the fascinating Frenchwoman Catherine; and he looks up another Brahmin, Rajesh, who promises him protection should he ever need it and subsequently takes Samar in after he is caught in a riot at Benares Hindu University. Samar does not see a connection between what Rajesh says about Panditji's son Arjun—that he tried to pay his gambling debts by mortgaging his father's property—and Arjun's being badly beaten. To Samar, Benares is still a magical city, the place where dreams come true. Not until he ventures forth from Benares in the second part of the novel does Samar begin to realize that it holds only the promise of happiness.

Since by now Samar is in love with Catherine, he is delighted when Miss West invites Samar and Catherine to spend a few days with her in Mussoorie; and, after their hostess has to cancel out, leaving the two alone, it seems as if his dreams are coming true. At the end of their stay, Catherine and Samar make a romantic side trip into a remote area, and that night Catherine welcomes Samar into her bed. Back in Benares, however, Catherine goes back to Anand. Though his ailing father has sent for him, Samar remains in Benares, hoping against hope to reconnect with Catherine, but his rereading of *L'Éducation sentimentale* convinces him that, like every other lover, he has been living in a fool's paradise. Samar packs up and moves to Pondicherry, where he confesses to his father that his plans for a civil service career have come to nothing. The section ends with a letter from Catherine expressing profound regret about what happened in Mussoorie and asking Samar never to contact her again. If Benares was the city where Samar thought his dreams would come true, Pondicherry is the place where they are exposed for the illusions that they are.

In the final section of the book, Samar takes a position as a teacher in Dharamshala. After seven years, it is obvious that he will never move on. However, in time Samar discovers that the other romantics of Benares have also surrendered their dreams. Mark turns up in Dharamshala with a forceful new girlfriend who plans to marry him and make him settle down in California. Samar learns from Mark that Miss West has finally broken off her affair, and from another former acquaintance Samar hears the sad truth about his old friend Prakash, who later writes Samar what is in essence a farewell letter. When Samar revisits Benares, he no longer feels at home there. The city is now a vulgar and dangerous place, run by criminals. Arjun is in possession of the lodging house, his parents having died conveniently, and their devoted servant is kept in a dark, cagelike room, where he continually mumbles his old mantra about the destructive power of greed. Miss West seems much older; though she can now return to England, she is no longer enthusiastic about the future, but merely resigned to what fate may bring. Samar learns from Miss West that Anand returned to Benares after it became clear that he would never be accepted in France and that Catherine now seeks only security, which means a conventional marriage to someone of her own kind.

At the end of *L'Éducation sentimentale*, Frédéric does not have any more insight into the world or into himself than he did at the beginning of the novel. By contrast, Samar has come to an understanding of what life can offer. If his quiet life in Dharamshala represents an abandonment of his romantic dreams, it does enable him to fulfill what he now knows is his most profound need: not love or success, not bitter resignation, but simple serenity. At the end of the novel, Samar arrives, cold and wet, at the comfortable new hotel where he is staying while he is in Benares, only to find the power out, the roof leaking, and "hectic men with pails and mops" trying to clean up the mess. Samar cannot even go to his room. However, he does not complain. Indeed, he says, "I was feeling oddly calm." Of all the romantics in Mishra's novel, Samar alone has found how to be contented in a world where dreams do not come true.

Rosemary M. Canfield Reisman

Sources for Further Study

Booklist 96 (February 1, 2000): 1008.
The Economist 354 (March 18, 2000): 13.
Library Journal 125 (January, 2000): 161.
The Nation 270 (April 24, 2000): 36.
New Statesman 129 (February 14, 2000): 55.
The New York Review of Books 47 (February 24, 2000): 8.
The New York Times, March 21, 2000, p. B7.
The New York Times Book Review 105 (February 27, 2000): 12.
Publishers Weekly 247 (January 3, 2000): 57.
The Times Literary Supplement, February 4, 2000, p. 21.

THE ROYAL FAMILY

Author: William T. Vollmann (1959-   )
Publisher: Viking Press (New York). 780 pp. $40.00
Type of work: Novel
Time: The mid- to late 1990's
Locale: Mostly San Francisco, with excursions to Sacramento, Las Vegas, and elsewhere

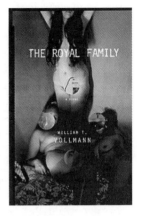

∼

A sad-sack protagonist searches for meaning as he moves from work as a private detective to involvement with a group of prostitutes to life as a hobo, along the way dealing with other sad sacks, death, drugs, degradation, and despair

∼

> *Principal characters:*
> HENRY TYLER, a down-and-out private investigator
> JONAS BRADY, one of Henry's clients, an entrepreneur
> JOHN TYLER, Henry's brother, a corporate lawyer
> IRENE TYLER, John's wife and Henry's beloved, a suicide
> DAN SMOOTH, Henry's friend, a sex pervert
> QUEEN OF THE WHORES (a.k.a. Maj, Africa Johnston), leader of a prostitution ring
> THE TALL MAN (a.k.a. Justin Soames), the queen's associate and enforcer
> DOMINO, STRAWBERRY, YELLOW BIRD, BEATRICE. BERNADETTE, LILY, CHOCOLATE, SUNFLOWER, and KITTY, prostitutes involved with the ring
> CELIA CARO, John's girlfriend and second wife

William T. Vollmann's *The Royal Family* begins like any other hard-boiled detective story. The protagonist, Henry Tyler, is a private investigator who has trouble paying his bills and who occupies a sleazy middle ground somewhere between the police department and the underworld. He has contacts in both areas, knows San Francisco like the palm of his hand (his favorite activity is cruising the mean streets), and has computer skills (which he uses to track information without ever leaving home). The novel begins with Henry in the employ of moneyman Jonas Brady, and they are on a mysterious quest to find the Queen of the Whores (if, in fact, such a person exists). Naturally the quest requires a lot of cruising through the Tenderloin district and a lot of patronizing and questioning of prostitutes, with tough dialogue along the lines of: "—We're not cops, said Brady brightly, but the fat lady only said: Uh huh, and you really love me and you won't come in my mouth and the check is in the mail."

Perhaps this all sounds entertaining in a conventional detective-story way, but

~

William T. Vollmann is the author of five novels, including Butterfly Stories, Whores for Gloria, *and* You Bright and Risen Angels. *His collection of interlinked stories,* The Atlas, *won the PEN Center USA West Award for Fiction. In 1999,* The New Yorker *named him one of the twenty best American writers under the age of forty.*

~

readers should take warning from such dialogue. Eventually, not finding the Queen of the Whores, Brady fires Henry, but by this time Henry has become so fascinated by the quest that he cannot abandon it. Unbelievable as it is, he continues to search on his own, without pay. Supposedly his continuing quest is motivated by a void in his soul (which is believable) and by the recent suicide of his sister-in-law, Irene, whom he loved. In any case, Henry finally does find the Queen, is initiated into her circle, and becomes her lover and devotee—though not without paying a terrible price. Apparently he has to reject the conventional world and experience the self-abasement of the prostitute, including some mortifications of the flesh best not mentioned here.

As one might surmise, *The Royal Family* is loaded with sex, from the straight to the kinky to the perverse. The activities of the prostitutes are described in detail, from their street vigils to their flaccid customers to their crack addiction. One of the main characters, Dan Smooth, is a pedophile. The language of the novel is likewise filled with the slangy lexicon of sex. Yet somehow the novel does not seem pornographic; rather than making sex attractive, it has just the opposite effect. Sex as depicted here tends to be disgusting and degrading. The prostitutes stink, are abscessed and diseased, and are aged before their times. Dan Smooth is a slimy creature, and other characters are hardly more attractive. Overall, the sex trade as depicted in *The Royal Family* seems like a circle out of Dante's Hell.

The novel's depiction of the sex business reaches a kind of climax in a satirical section on the Feminine Circus, a Las Vegas sex emporium opened by Jonas Brady. The emporium's opening is like Oscar night in Hollywood, covered by the media, attended by celebrities and politicians, and protested by the unions. Monstrous crowds of eager customers swarm in, served by "customer support specialists" and "virtualettes" (business lingo for pimps and prostitutes). The prostitutes are supposedly creations of virtual reality, triumphs of modern technology: "And since they're not real, nobody's getting exploited, and there's no disease to worry about. . . . Come to Feminine Circus and indulge your fantasies in a safe, healthy and *tasteful* manner." In actuality, however, the virtualettes are retarded girls or lobotomized prostitutes who are rounded up, caged, and shipped in. The hidden inner workings of the emporium include a Lobotomy Factory and a disposal room (for virtualettes whose customers' fantasies go too far).

Vollmann's brief satire here is worthy of Jonathan Swift or Evelyn Waugh: He savagely pinpoints how the media, business, technology, and politics pander to and exploit a willing American public ("They all stuck together like dogs fornicating in epoxy"). What is harder to swallow is the novel's implication that the old-fashioned, organic kind of prostitution is morally superior to these new, processed forms. Symbolically the Feminine Circus stands in opposition to the Queen of the Whores' circle, which Brady's Boys try to eradicate or capture. While one can allow that the Queen watches over and cares for her girls like an old-fashioned madam, and that she is some sort of voodoo priestess, it is harder to believe in her supposedly supernatural powers or her Jesus-like religious aura that is constantly hinted about (she finally disappears without a trace, record, or social security number). It is likewise hard to believe, in some Dostoevskian logic, that the prostitutes retain or attain a certain beatitude when, in actuality, they are merely spaced out on crack. Henry might fall for this hokum, but surely not readers.

Another reason one cannot accept the high seriousness of these ladies is their weak characterization. They come across as caricatures, like their names, rather than as people the reader can relate to. It is hard to care about them as individuals when their individuality is not much developed beyond stock characterizations. Even the awesome Queen seems more like one of those nice little old black ladies who come out of their house and snag a man passing on the street to open their jar of jam or pickles. What sex appeal Henry sees in her is hard to say, but again Henry is a desperate sort of fellow. The weak characterization of the prostitutes also extends to other characters— for example, Henry's sibling rival John, an obnoxious corporate attorney. In one of many authorial commentaries, Vollmann reports that an editor for the magazines *Grand Street* and *The New Yorker* "asserted that John was a mere caricature." Vollmann playfully defends his characterization not only of the Queen ("mouthpiece of my pompous symbology") and the other prostitutes ("grimy cardboard props dripping with the semen of the vulgar") but also of John; however, Vollmann should have listened to the editor.

Vollmann should also have listened to the Viking Press editor, mentioned in the acknowledgments, who thought the book ought to be cut "by one-third." At 780 pages, *The Royal Family* is far too long, rambling, and postmodern, thereby losing the buildup and intensity of a conventionally plotted novel. Instead of holding together, *The Royal Family* is broken into thirty-six books and 593 chapters (actually snippets ranging from a few pages to one sentence). Some of these books and chapters interrupt the main narrative to describe streets in San Francisco or to deliver authorial comment. One particularly long interruption is "Book X: An Essay on Bail," which unfortunately stands out as one of the best things in the book. Much of the rest of the novel drags, especially the repetitive narration of the lives of the prostitutes and hobos. Meanwhile, some loose ends are not tied up: Readers never learn why Irene committed suicide, except to torment Henry and to show how rotten John was. Worst of all, with Henry at the end still on the skids and searching, the novel just peters out as impotently as one of the prostitutes' drunken old customers. In a plot devoted to an extended search for meaning, one hopes to find some. The only approach toward a climax or epiphany is a brief hallucination or dream segment wherein Irene returns from the dead to tell Henry that the answer "has to do with love."

With all that said, Vollmann remains a talented, learned, and ambitious author who just needs more discipline and craft. He has an extensive vocabulary and the ability to strike out with a memorable phrase, simile, or bit of dialogue. His forte is description, such as the following early sample:

Then she took her dress off, presenting to his secret-loving eyes belly-wrinkles like sandbars, and she took her bra off to let him see her round breasts bulging with silicone, and for him she took off her panties to give to his view her crusty blackish-reddish crotch.

One can also take, for example, the following, somewhat more poetic passage:

It was a fresh cold winter's eve of shiny raincoats and headlights of stalled traffic like luminous pairs of dinner plates stood on their edges; the pavement had become an ebony liquid which reflected upside down the people walking on it, stuck by the soles of their shoes to their inverted selves.

As the latter passage shows, Vollmann has a love of place, notably San Francisco, that is well served by his descriptive powers. To some extent, these stylistic strengths carry the reader along.

Vollmann also brings wide reading and research to bear on his subjects. His learned background is apparent from the epigraphs (heavy on religion) that grace each of the novel's thirty-six books. Vollmann's weighty learning is not just from reading; he also researches the technical details of his subjects and does some field investigation. For example, Henry's work introduces readers to various police report forms, databases, and investigative techniques; Vollmann acquired such technical details by consulting the public defenders, bail bondsmen, and private investigators listed in his acknowledgments. The stomach-turning autopsy on Dan Smooth's corpse, while the coroner sips his cup of coffee, is another example of technically informed writing. In researching the novel Vollmann also rode freight trains, strolled the Tenderloin district, frequented bars, and consulted prostitutes: "Most of all, I would like to thank the San Francisco and Sacramento street prostitutes whom I have gotten to know over the years. Without them I never could have imagined 'the life.'"

How well Vollmann succeeds in imagining "the life" is a matter of opinion, but there is no doubt that he calls attention to it. His novel raises awareness of a soft underbelly of American society that leaders and perhaps everyone else—except for those who donate to and work for shelters—had rather not think too much about: a world of prostitution, drug addiction, homelessness, and hobo jungles. Yet this is a world that confronts anyone who walks America's streets and that "gated communities" such as the one described in *The Royal Family* attempt to wall off. It is no coincidence that the homeless (in the novel and in life) wheel around shopping carts—symbols of the consumer society that they are not part of, except as victims. Such "losers" (one of the terms Henry's brother John applies to him) are often blamed for creating their own fates, but Vollmann's novel also indicts families, institutions, and society for being so uncaring that "losers" can find community only among themselves.

In *The Royal Family*, despite all of the novel's imperfections, Vollmann looks at the big picture—at society as a whole, with the Tyler family a microcosm that recalls the biblical first family. Henry is said to bear the mark of Cain and to be one of the Canaanites, but in this novel the biblical story is somewhat reversed, reflecting the reversal of values in America. Overall, the pervading religious references in *The Royal*

Family give the novel an alarming prophetic tone, an impending sense of biblical wrath. The religious references go right along with Vollmann's depiction of America as a modern-day Sodom and Gomorrah.

Harold Branam

Sources for Further Study

Library Journal 125 (July, 2000): 144.
The Nation 271 (September 18, 2000): 31.
The New York Times Book Review 105 (August 20, 2000): 5.
Publishers Weekly 247 (June 5, 2000): 69.
The Wall Street Journal, August 11, 2000, p. W9.

RUDYARD KIPLING
A Life

Author: Harry Ricketts (1950-   )
Publisher: Carroll & Graf (New York). Illustrated. 434
    pp. $28.00
Type of work: Literary biography
Time: 1865-1936
Locale: India and various locations in England

～

*In a detailed and lively account of Kipling's life,
Ricketts also analyzes the literary works that emerged from
that popular but controversial career*

～

Principal personages:
> RUDYARD KIPLING, the poet and short-story writer who came, in his life-
>   time, to represent the British Empire
> CAROLINE (CARRIE) KIPLING, his devoted and protective wife
> JOSEPHINE KIPLING, their daughter, who died at the age of six
> JOHN KIPLING, their son, killed in France at the beginning of World War I
> ELSIE KIPLING, their only surviving child
> LOCKWOOD KIPLING, Rudyard's father, and an important influence on
>   his life and career
> ALICE KIPLING, Rudyard's mother

Rudyard Kipling was, as Harry Ricketts shows, as diverse as his literary works. The author of such classic children's stories as "Rikki-Tikki-Tavi" (1895) and "Wee Willie Winkie" (1888), *The Jungle Book* (1894), and *Just So Stories* (1902) and the composer of some of the most famous poetry in the English-speaking world, such as "If" (1910) and "Recessional" (1899), Kipling also came to represent the British Empire in some of its most imperialistic moments at the end of the nineteenth and beginning of the twentieth centuries. Ricketts' evenhanded biography captures "Kipling's chameleon nature, the ability he celebrated in characters such as Mowgli and Kim to cross boundaries and switch identities," reveals Kipling's troubled childhood as the main source for his several personalities, but also uncovers the deep, often mythic literary elements in Kipling's works which continue to draw readers, and especially younger readers, to him.

Kipling was the only child of British parents who followed a career in India. After early years with his family, Kipling and his younger sister Alice (Trix) were sent to live at Lorne Lodge, Southsea, near Portsmouth on the south coast of England. They would not see their parents again for five years and, while their surrogate family in Southsea provided for their creature comforts, the children were clearly deprived of love and affection. This "House of Desolation," as Kipling later called Lorne Lodge, would come to haunt his life and many of his writings, not only in the twin themes of family and orphanhood that underlie his work, but in the hatred that fueled much of his fiction. "Hatred, and its consequences," Ricketts argues, "formed the core of some of his greatest

~

Harry Ricketts is a poet and the author of Nothing to Declare: Selected Writings, 1977-1997.

~

stories, and it was a subject that he explored with an insight and an honesty few others have matched." Part of Kipling's success would come from the successful ways that he transmuted "the Southsea legacy into imaginative gain." For almost his entire career, in short, Kipling was tapping sources in his own painful childhood.

Kipling returned to India at the age of sixteen and was soon working as a reporter and editor for a series of Anglo-Indian papers. His poetry and fiction began appearing almost at once, and by the age of nineteen Kipling had published his first collection of poems and stories, *Quartette* (1885). Thus was established his pattern of serial and then book publication, and in the next few years, through collections such as *Departmental Ditties* (1886) and *Plain Tales from the Hills* (1888), and stories such as "The Man Who Would Be King" (1889) Rudyard Kipling became a recognizable literary personality. At the very same time, however, he was outgrowing his provincial Anglo-Indian audience, and in 1889, at the age of twenty-three, he left India for London.

Kipling was anxious about his literary future in his native country, but it did not take him long to establish himself in a number of newspapers and journals, to make lasting friends and contacts, and to start to publish works (such as *The Light That Failed* in 1890 and *Barrack-Room Ballads* in 1892) and build a reputation in England that, within a decade, would make him one of the most famous writers in the English-speaking world. In fact, the 1890's would probably be the happiest and most productive period in Kipling's life. As he came to be compared with older writers such as Mark Twain and Robert Louis Stevenson, he also found personal happiness when he met and married the American Caroline Balestier. Three children would be born to the couple, although only one would survive into adulthood.

In one of the ironies of Anglo-American literary history, Kipling very nearly became an American writer. Rudyard and Carrie Balestier Kipling settled in 1893 in Brattleboro, Vermont, to be near his wife's family, and in a few years built a house there, "Naulakha," named after an adventure novel that Kipling wrote with his brother-in-law, Wolcott Balestier, in 1892. Kipling was putting down other American roots, reading and meeting American writers such as Henry Adams and William Dean Howells, and befriending political figures such as Theodore Roosevelt. Meanwhile, he continued to publish works which only expanded his reputation: *The Jungle Book* in 1894, *The Second Jungle Book* the following year, and *Captains Courageous* (the only novel of his to use exclusively American materials) in 1897. He was then thirty-two years old.

This idyllic period in Kipling's life began to come unravelled when another brother-in-law and neighbor, Beatty Balestier, in what can only be understood as jealous rage, brought legal action against Kipling. The suit went against Beatty, but soon after that judgment Kipling and his family fled the conflict and animosity to return to England. Kipling's American adventure had ended.

The England the Kiplings returned to at the end of the 1890's had changed dramatically. Not only had Britain entered into the Boer War (1899-1902), but the lively literary scene was now dominated by what was to become known as the Decadence Movement, through writers such as Oscar Wilde. Kipling would side with England in the first war and against the writers of the second, and increasingly in the remaining decades of his life he would come to be seen by critics as a racist and imperialist writer out of touch with the literature of his own country. In defending the "Empire" from its enemies, Kipling's voice became shrill and jingoistic. He wrote of "the White Man's Burden" and, in the famous poem, "Recessional," of the manifest British destiny in the world. All of this made him more popular with many readers, but it kept him from the critical praise he truly desired.

The public Kipling continued as one of the most popular writers in the world at the turn of the century, winning the Nobel Prize in Literature in 1907. However, the private Kipling knew more and more tragedy. The Kiplings lost their daughter Josephine in 1899 at age six, and their only son, John, fifteen years later at the outset of World War I. The tragic personal losses, Ricketts shows, only calcified Kipling's political attitudes: "Acute personal stress followed by a hardening of the political stance: the by now familiar pattern." He was, as Ricketts puts it in the title of one chapter, "A Sadder and a Harder Man," and those hardened attitudes would be reflected in his growing anti-Semitism and misogyny (e.g., "The female of the species is more deadly than the male.") One of his "most famous panegyrics of raw masculine courage on the borders of Empire," "The Ballad of East and West" (1899) opens with the famous line, "Oh, East is East, and West is West, and never the twain shall meet," which Ricketts describes as a "dogmatic assertion of an unbridgeable racial gulf between peoples." The older Kipling saw only gulfs.

The popular works would continue to flow: the novel *Kim* in 1901, *Just So Stories* a year later, poems such as "If"—still probably the most famous poem in English, Ricketts believes—a few years later. Yet Kipling seemed increasingly out of touch with both literature and history. Ricketts argues that Kipling influenced the literary Modernism that would flourish in the Anglo-American literary world from the 1920's on, and he is probably right, but early Modernist writers (such as T. S. Eliot) recognized Kipling's limitations and the ways he was stuck in a nineteenth century Victorian world. As Henry James wrote about Kipling in a letter to another friend in 1894,

He sends me too his jungle book which I have read with extreme admiration. But *how* it closes his doors & sets his limit! The rise to 'higher types' that one hoped for—I mean the care for life in a finer way—is the rise to the mongoose & the care for the wolf. The *violence* of it all, the almost exclusive preoccupation with fighting & killing, is also singularly characteristic.

The pattern would hardly change. During World War I, Kipling devoted his energies to bolstering troop morale and, after the death of his son, he set himself to write the history of the Irish Guards, the regiment in which John had served and died. By the time of his own death in 1936, Kipling was already a relic of the past; in the title of an essay written by the American literary critic Edmund Wilson after his death (and an essay that Ricketts wisely uses), he was already "The Kipling that Nobody Read." As Ricketts notes, when Thomas Hardy died in 1928, Kipling was one of six of the most celebrated writers of the day who helped to carry the casket. When Kipling died a few years later, not a single writer appeared as pallbearer. Kipling, the literary figure, had died some decades before. What remained, as Wilson noted, were poems in college literature textbooks and stories in children's books.

Ricketts' account of Kipling's life is clear and straightforward. Unlike many modern biographers, he does not try to psychoanalyze Kipling or discover hidden motivation. The life and the works are at the forefront here. While there is little on Kipling's inner emotional life, there is much more analysis of the literature, and Ricketts uncovers layers of meanings in the poems, stories, and novels. He is best at showing the influence that Kipling's early, unhappy years had on his life and work, not only in the ways that he treasured family, but in the peculiar vision through which Kipling came to see the British Empire as his own extended family. Similarly, the literature is loaded with stories of abandonment and orphanhood, but the treatment of these themes often creates a child-like intimacy for the reader. "His stories derive much of their power from his ability to charm the reader into feeling like a co-conspirator, even a co-author, sharing fascinating secrets, swapping privileged information." In many ways Kipling resembles an American writer thirty years his senior whom he interviewed on his first trip to the United States: Mark Twain. Both writers were immensely popular and travelled widely in their careers, both adored their families and created literary classics based on their own childhoods, and both were unique at capturing dialect and native idiom at a time when most popular literature was romantic and unrealistic in language. The crucial difference is that as Twain aged and underwent the same personal tragedies that Kipling knew, his bitterness was translated into literature such as "The War Prayer" (1905) and "The Man That Corrupted Hadleyburg" (1900) works aimed at challenging the glib popular assumptions of church and state. Kipling's deepening morbidity turned him into an even more conservative writer and British subject. The photographs that illustrate this biography witness Kipling's transformation into that reactionary Victorian.

David Peck

Sources for Further Study

The Atlantic Monthly 285 (April, 2000): 132.
Booklist 96 (March 1, 2000): 1189.
Choice 37 (July/August, 2000): 1983.
Library Journal 125 (February 15, 2000): 162.
New Statesman 128 (February 19, 1999): 45.
The New York Times Book Review 105 (April 30, 2000): 16.
Publishers Weekly 247 (February 14, 2000): 180.
The Wall Street Journal, March 30, 2000, p. A28.

SAVING THE HEART
The Battle to Conquer Coronary Disease

Author: Stephen Klaidman (1938-   )
Publisher: Oxford University Press (New York). 272 pp. $27.50
Type of work: Ethics, history of science, and medicine
Time: The twentieth century
Locale: The United States

~

Surveying the history of cardiology, Klaidman also scrutinizes the modern scientific, ethical, and business issues affecting the treatments for heart disease

~

Principal personages:
> JAMES HERRICK, physician who first linked coronary artery disease and heart attacks
> JOHN H. GIBBONS, inventor of the heart-lung machine
> MASON SONES, radiologist who developed angiography
> RENÉ FAVALORO, surgeon who perfected coronary bypass surgery
> ANDREAS GRÜNTZIG, cardiologist who pioneered angioplasty

Stephen Klaidman's *Saving the Heart* is about equal parts history and science journalism. It is readable, contains insightfully presented historical and technical information, includes a few clarifying photographs and illustrations, offers judicious recommendations, and is blessedly clear in describing the treatments for coronary artery disease (CAD), a leading cause of death in the United States. It is also polemical, sometimes misleading, and strangely resentful of the science and medical system it describes. Fans of the history of science, but even more those who suffer from heart disease, should welcome this book, because there is no equivalent up-to-date survey of cardiology and cardiac surgery available. Readers, however, should be aware that the book is more than reportage. Klaidman has an eye for controversy and murky ethics, and he shapes his style accordingly.

That style belongs to modern investigative journalism. It can have a salutary effect on public issues, but it is primarily a persuasive form of rhetoric and often appeals to the reader's predilections and fears as much as it presents a faithful accounting of the subject. So there is the danger of misapplied emphasis, overselectivity, and coloring of information. In Klaidman's case, the principal stylistic techniques are anecdotes, capsule biographies, hyperbole, and rhetorical questions. The first two appear more often. In fact, Klaidman relies on dramatic stories of operations and scientific or business innovations to relate the development of cardiac care technology. Brief biographies of the innovators accompany their introduction into the narrative. In both cases this is natural and dramatic, but it all depends upon which details are chosen, and therein lies the danger. Klaidman writes to emphasize conflict, and to do so he sometimes includes biographical details unconnected to the medical subject at hand.

Even without the emotional appeals, it is easy to agree with Klaidman that medicine in the United States suffers from serious problems. He

∽

Stephen Klaidman is a senior research fellow at the Kennedy Institute of Ethics at Georgetown University. His other books include Health in the Headlines *and* The Virtuous Journalist.

∽

is a senior research fellow at the Kennedy Institute of Ethics of Georgetown University and clearly knows an ethical conflict when he sees one. He sees several: between innovation and established practice; between the need for experimental procedures and patient safety; among the triad of researcher, clinician, and medical entrepreneur; between bureaucratic ethics reviews and the pressure to try out new treatments; and between the financial interest of physicians and optimal care for their patients. Who can be surprised that such conflicts exist? Where there is innovation and competition, there will be uncertainty, and where uncertainty exists there are bound to be ethical concerns. The problem is that Klaidman frequently communicates his own frustration and outrage about such matters to readers, even to the point of name-calling, as when he denounces the use of placebos as a sham and refers to scoffing among conservative doctors without providing much in the way of evidence of the scoffing.

Let the reader be on guard. Given that, trenchant, timely value awaits readers in *Saving the Heart*. Klaidman provides a reasonable review of ethical issues and beautifully clear set-piece explanations of technical matters, such as the process of atherosclerosis and the techniques of bypass surgery. An appendix tells readers what sorts of questions they should ask their cardiologists and surgeons and the kinds of answers to look for. One chapter offers penetrating, sometimes grimly funny insights into how surgeons view themselves. (For instance, in a list of characteristics surgeons find most necessary, decisiveness and aggressiveness come before manual dexterity and intellect.) Another chapter follows the case of a nearly ideal cardiac patient—well informed, well insured, and patient. In fact, this is a crucial chapter because it involves the responsibilities of patients in their own treatment and recovery. Otherwise, Klaidman spends so much time covering the medical establishment and its supporting research and development industry that the patient's role looks wholly passive and dependent, which is not the case.

The book also contains a wealth of historical information concerning the rise of modern knowledge about heart disease and its treatments, from the first definition of angina pectoris in 1768 to the development of robot surgery in the late 1990's. Along the way, readers learn the virtues and drawbacks of angioplasty (use of a balloon on a catheter to clear clogged arteries), bypass surgeries of various kinds, stenting (placing a tiny mesh tube in arteries to keep them open), and drug treatments to dissolve clots or keep them from forming. The drama of the anecdotes and mini-biographies that forms the core of most chapters makes stirring reading.

Klaidman's overall reaction to his subject is ambivalent; the book conveys this clearly. He clearly admires many of the people he interviewed and judiciously appreciates the benefits of modern medicine. Like everyone, he wants a system that minimizes mistakes of judgment and the influence of private and corporate greed, while continuing to produce advances extending and improving life. Yet it is not clear that he believes medicine as conducted in the United States can manage it. His tone is often ominous, particularly when recounting the behavior of medical technology companies, and his critique of the science of medicine is often disapproving.

Klaidman dismisses the value of clinical studies cavalierly, referring to them as "so-called evidence-based medicine." He says that the data from even the best medical studies is as useful for choosing treatments as reading a book about basketball star Michael Jordan is useful for learning to play the game. A ridiculous hyperbole, but it reveals his distaste. True, his basic complaint has substance. Medical studies are often difficult to interpret and yield ambiguous data that can be manipulated to support biased conclusions. They frequently continue rather than settle medical controversies. What, however, does he expect? Studies and experiments are not done when the choice of a treatment or the solution to a problem is obvious, only when it is in doubt. Even imperfect studies give physicians more to go on in making a difficult treatment choice than no studies at all. Ideally, yes, all medical research should produce definite, clear, unslanted results, but research, and especially clinical trials, is usually complex, expensive, and restricted by ethical concerns. Although he mentions these obstacles, Klaidman expresses little sympathy for them. Nor does he mention that all disciplines relying on the scientific method, medicine included, progress by a give-and-take of data and ideas and by repeat studies to ensure their results are reliable.

Instead, the book champions the maverick doctor who discovers a new physiological fact or develops a drug, procedure, or device despite the "scoffing conservatism" of the medical establishment. It is the central conflict that his narrative thrives on. To buttress the approach, Klaidman applies the theory of philosopher Thomas Kuhn. Studying the history of astronomy and physics, Kuhn found that science advances by means of periodic revolutions, which alter the accepted paradigm for the relation of theory to fact. Using Kuhn's ideas is unfortunate; even his admirers came to hold that the theory is untenable without modification. Still, Klaidman supplies plenty of innovative mavericks: James Herrick, the researcher who, in 1912, first linked coronary artery disease and heart attacks (a discovery greeted largely by silence); John H. Gibbons, inventor of the heart-lung machine who really wanted to be a poet; Mason Sones, the irascible, combative radiologist who developed angiography; René Favaloro, the Argentine surgeon who came to the United States so he could perfect coronary bypass surgery; Andreas Grüntzig, the German cardiologist who pioneered angioplasty even though others thought it dangerous and unworkable; and others.

They all encountered skepticism. What exactly, however, does Klaidman mean by "medical conservatism"? If he means wariness about sloppiness, wishful thinking, error, and outright fraud—and there are many, many examples of harmful mavericks in the history of medicine—then conservatism is a good thing, even if scoffing is involved. Patients may well find it to their advantage that their physicians want some sort of proof, not just promise. Let the mavericks prove themselves.

One aspect of choosing a treatment for CAD that troubles Klaidman, and rightly so, is money. Angioplasty and stenting are cheaper than bypass surgery, for example, and both are more expensive than management with diet and drugs. So which is chosen may depend upon the payoff to the doctor involved. Invasive cardiologists (those who use catheters for diagnosis and treatment) may insist upon angioplasty because it is, in Klaidman's terms, their cash cow. For surgeons, it is the bypass operation. Moreover, noninvasive cardiologists are likely to resent that they earn much less for their care than do their technology-wielding colleagues. In other words, Klaidman finds doctors can be greedy, even to the point of performing unnecessary procedures to earn more. It is a real problem, although hardly unique to doctors. Americans are remarkably permissive about greed, and in any case, many honest, talented people are attracted to medicine because they can work very hard and become wealthy, rather than work very hard and not become wealthy.

In this light, Klaidman makes some reasonable recommendations, but whether they are practicable is another matter. Following diagnosis of CAD, he suggests, the choice among treatments should be left to a review panel composed of a cardiac surgeon, invasive cardiologist, and noninvasive cardiologist. Thereby, even the appearance of financial conflict of interest would be removed. Klaidman also calls for a new subdiscipline of internal medicine in which physicians would be specially trained to diagnose and manage cardiac patients and make referrals for invasive treatments. There are problems with both recommendations. Doctors may resist the panel idea, and not so much because it could cut their earnings but because it would take up yet more of their time and delay treatment. As for the subdiscipline idea, many internists already manage CAD and make referrals and are likely to resent a new layer of specialty that removes patients from their care.

Another problem Klaidman discusses is the relation of the medical technology industry and doctors. There are huge profits to be made with devices used in vascular and cardiac procedures, and companies aggressively compete for doctors' acceptance. They are not above designing trials expressly to ballyhoo the benefits of inventions or offering doctors financial incentives—all to serve the bottom line rather than patients. Some doctors even own stock in the companies that make the devices they use. Whether effective marketing and doctor-business relationships produce risky or inappropriate health care is a signal question for modern medicine. Even more important, the explosion of medical technology has changed the focus from bedside observation and disease management to use of technology, Klaidman points out. This means, he continues, that doctors are encouraged to replace clinical judgment with technology—in other words, to use expensive equipment to answer a question rather than think carefully about it.

There is, indeed, much to worry about in connection with modern treatments for cardiac disease—and by extension all medicine dependent upon technology—and Klaidman helps readers to worry. Where so much scientific talent, business acumen, and money exist in the absence of a national policy and regulation there is likely to be confusion and trouble, even egregious abuses of the precious doctor-patient trust. *Saving the Heart* is an in-depth, although not always balanced, review of the influences on the doctor and business sides of that trust. Unfortunately, Klaidman does not discuss the patient side so thoroughly or critically, but he does offer educated readers who have CAD a monitory preview of the world they are entering when they go to their cardiologist for help.

Roger Smith

Sources for Further Study

American Scientist, July/August, 2000, p. 372.
Booklist 96 (December 15, 1999): 745.
Choice 37 (June, 2000): 1848.
The Lancet 356 (September 30, 2000): 1202.
Library Journal 124 (December, 1999): 172.
New England Journal of Medicine 317 (March 9, 2000): 746.
Publishers Weekly 246 (November 15, 1999): 47.

SCANDALMONGER

Author: William Safire (1929-   )
Publisher: Simon & Schuster (New York). 496 pp.
  $27.00
Type of work: Novel
Time: 1792-1803
Locale: Northeastern United States and Virginia

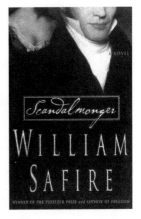

~

Safire re-creates the scandal-filled period of American history during the presidencies of George Washington, John Adams, and Thomas Jefferson, revealing how the growth of the newspaper industry affected politics in the newly formed United States

~

Principal characters:
> JAMES THOMSON CALLENDER, political journalist and newspaper publisher
> ALEXANDER HAMILTON, prominent Federalist politician
> THOMAS JEFFERSON, leader of the Republicans in national politics
> JAMES MADISON, Jefferson's protégé and leader in the Republican faction
> JAMES MONROE, another of Jefferson's protégés and prominent Republican politician
> WILLIAM COBBETT, political writer and Callender's chief rival
> JOHN BECKLEY, ally of the Jefferson faction and political appointee
> MARIA REYNOLDS CLEMENT, subject of a number of scandals in the late eighteenth century

The debate over the proper relationship between history and fiction in revealing or recasting the past has occupied both historians and literary critics since Sir Walter Scott published *Waverley: Or, 'Tis Sixty Years Since* in 1814. However, while the question of what constitutes a "historical novel" has long been the subject of discussion among critics, readers have shown consistent affinity for fictional works that re-create the past in order to entertain and educate. Most historical novels follow a simple formula: A series of fictional characters form the main interest in a work set in a particular period of history, and the lives of these fictional characters often intersect with, or are heavily influenced by, the actions of historical personages, often of notable significance. When the fictional characters are given too much credit for influencing history—as they are, for example, in Herman Wouk's *The Winds of War* (1971) and *War and Remembrance* (1978)—the work is often called "historical romance," indicating the implausibility of the tale. While that has not stopped millions of readers

759

William Safire is a senior columnist for The New York Times *and a winner of the Pulitzer Prize for distinguished commentary. He has written twenty-four books, including* On Language, Lend Me Your Ears, *and the novels* Full Disclosure, Freedom, *and* Sleeper Spy.

from buying and enjoying such novels, literary purists have insisted that proper historical fiction should stick close to the documentary record of the past.

If one uses this approach in judging the quality of historical fiction, William Safire's *Scandalmonger* will easily rise near the top of any ranked listing. In this tour de force, the Pulitzer Prize-winning political journalist uses only historical persons to weave an intriguing tale of political backbiting, innuendo, half-truths, and scandals set in the first decades of the new American republic. What many readers will find most surprising is that, like the characters in the novels, all of the stories about them are in some sense true. Each of the scandals Safire reports through his characters is part of a historical record that belies the idyllic vision many Americans have grown to accept as factual. In *Scandalmonger*, Safire informs readers that he is "trying to use a dramatic form to simulate past events and to bring long-ago lives to life." His use of fictional techniques is aimed at presenting "a close look at what I conjecture was actually going on among those real people."

At the center of this story is the Scottish immigrant James Thomson Callender, a journalist with a flair for gathering private information and using it to discredit the opponents of whatever political faction happened to be providing him support. The novel opens in the waning years of George Washington's administration. The Republicans in Congress, seeking to gain political advantage over the Federalists led by Washington, discover that the secretary of the treasury, Alexander Hamilton, may be engaging in financial speculation using inside information. They turn to Callender for assistance, with surprising results; though he cannot prove the charges of financial misconduct, he uncovers an affair between Hamilton and Maria Reynolds, estranged wife of a political functionary. Hamilton's hopes of succeeding Washington are dealt a fatal blow.

Buoyed by the notoriety he receives in uncovering the scandal, Callender goes on to produce scurrilous accounts about others. He is equally harsh on John Adams, whose uncomfortable term as the nation's leader was a period of particularly vicious behind-the-scenes political maneuvering in both political parties. Callender is not even above publishing jibes about Washington, whose imperial demeanor makes him repugnant to many of the Jeffersonian Republicans.

For a time, Callender enjoys the favor of the Republicans, as they use him to discredit one after another of the Federalists who might challenge Jefferson for the presidency. Aided by John Beckley, clerk of the House of Representatives, and Maria

Reynolds, Callender weaves stories of immoral behavior and political chicanery that lead ultimately to Jefferson's election. The tide of fortune turns when the Republicans are in office, however, as Jefferson tries to distance himself from the scandalmonger. Hurt by the rejection, Callender then strikes out at his former patron, bringing to light a number of personal foibles that discredit the new president in the eyes of foe and friend alike.

As a result, Callender becomes a man hated by both Republicans and Federalists, shunned from proper society. Ironically, he is befriended only by Maria Reynolds, a woman whose reputation he had ruined in writing about her affair with Hamilton. hey become friends, then lovers, shoring up each other's spirits as the opposition to Callender becomes more oppressive. Callender himself becomes the object of a scandal-mongering journalist who turns his own sons against him by claiming Callender had conspired to murder his wife nearly a decade earlier. In the midst of a heated war of words aimed simultaneously at destroying Jefferson and restoring his own reputation, Callender dies by drowning in a shallow bog, under very suspicious circumstances. Jefferson, finally rid of this nuisance, turns his attention to the pressing matters of state, namely, the acquisition from Napoleon Bonaparte of the tract of land known as the Louisiana Purchase.

Safire tells Callender's story with great wit and a strong sense of plotting and suspense. Among the most notable achievements of this novel are the portraits of several great men in American history, some quite at odds with the generally held view of their rectitude and selfless dedication to the new United States. Perhaps the best among these re-creations is that of the idealistic Thomas Jefferson. Safire's Jefferson is a far cry from the idealistic young radical responsible for drafting the Declaration of Independence. He is hardly even likable. Rather, he is portrayed as particularly smug and calculating, aloof from the fray but always directing action from behind the scenes, never close enough to be tainted personally by any of the scandals that plague his political rivals. This all changes, however, when Callender moves to Richmond to escape harassment by the Federalist supporters. There, close to sources that know of Jefferson's past and present dealings with women, Callender is able to use his vitriolic prose to smear the reputation of the man who had been held in esteem second only to Washington in the eyes of his countrymen.

Portraits of other historical figures are equally well drawn, with similar results. Both James Madison and James Monroe appear as political henchmen to the great Jefferson, motivated as much by the promise of political advancement as they are by their commitment to the ideals of republican government. Other figures such as John Marshall, Samuel Chase, Aaron Burr, Henry "Lighthorse" Lee, and Dr. Benjamin Rush receive less extended treatment, brought in for important cameo appearances to show their parts in shaping the political scene in these decades that were so crucial for the new country trying to establish itself as an independent nation. Safire also presents a well-rounded portrait of one of the most famous journalists of the day, William Cobbett, whose work in the United States and England has led to his being regarded by succeeding generations as "the first media giant." It is in Cobbett's voice that Safire expresses one of the crucial themes of the novel. Acknowledging to his wife that the aging George Washington was without doubt the principal reason people in the newly created nation had quickly developed "a sense of national self-confidence," the journalist goes on to wonder to himself: "As the primary rebel passed from the scene, could the nation created around 'the greatest leader of the age' survive the division threatened by the disorganizing faction led by Jefferson?" *Scandalmonger* displays vividly just how much of a threat that divisiveness really was.

For readers interested in knowing how much of the work is drawn from the historical record and how much is the product of the author's imagination, Safire provides copious notes in a section he titles "The Underbook," indicating whether the words of the characters are drawn directly from records, diaries, speeches, or newspaper accounts, or whether he has taken the liberty of creating dialogue and scene to supplement the historical record. Using these real-life men and women who were heavily involved in incidents surrounding the vilification of public officials, Safire also traces the development of the federal and state laws governing libel and sedition.

His careful mining of his sources allows Safire to present views expressed by some of the country's icons that are not well known, or in some cases contradictory to received opinion regarding their positions on key issues concerning government. One of the most striking examples of this technique is his inclusion of Jefferson's own words to describe his attitude toward the press. Many readers will be familiar with Jefferson's oft-quoted pronouncement that, given a choice between a strong government and a free press, he would opt for the latter. Safire chooses to have his fictional Thomas Jefferson instead recite words he expressed privately in an 1807 letter to John Norville: "Nothing can now be believed which is seen in a newspaper. Truth itself becomes suspicious by being put into that polluted vehicle." Given the attacks to which he was subjected by newsmen eager to tarnish his reputation, the remark is wholly understandable.

Virtually every event described in the novel has a firm basis in history, with one notable exception. The love affair between the demoralized and outcast Callender and the ostracized Maria Reynolds is purely fictional. As Safire tells readers in his notes, "Maria Reynolds and James Callender never met." Somehow, after reading Safire's moving account of their mutual affection, one wishes they had.

Although he is careful to keep his narrative focus on the historical period about which he writes, Safire manages to construct a tale that offers a lesson for readers separated by centuries from these events. Astute readers will become aware of the subtle parallels between the late eighteenth century and the late twentieth. The administrations of Washington, Adams, and Jefferson bear some eerie similarities to the last presidencies of the twentieth century—those of Ronald Reagan, George Bush, and Bill Clinton. The first of each triumvirate achieved a certain level of veneration in his two terms in office; the second served only one term, never able to emerge from the long shadow cast by his predecessor; the third, from a different party, charted a new direction for the country, but was plagued in his own day by scandals that tarred his image and perhaps limited his effectiveness in office. Additionally, as Safire demonstrates brilliantly in *Scandalmonger*, the ever-vigilant press in the eighteenth century was as quick to expose the foibles of the Founding Fathers as the present-day media have been to probe for scandals in successive Republican and Democratic administrations. In some ways, Safire suggests, America has not really changed much at all.

Laurence W. Mazzeno

Sources for Further Study

Booklist 96 (December 15, 1999): 739.
Columbia Journalism Review 33 (January/February, 2000): 77.
GQ 70 (February, 2000): 110.
Insight on the News 106 (March 20, 2000): 27.
Library Journal 125 (January, 2000): 162.
The New York Review of Books 47 (April 13, 2000): 67.
The New York Times Book Review 105 (February 6, 2000): 10.
Publishers Weekly 246 (December 20, 1999): 53.
Time 155 (February 21, 2000): 128.

SEEING MARY PLAIN
A Life of Mary McCarthy

Author: Frances Kiernan
Publisher: W. W. Norton (New York). 845 pp. $35.00
Type of work: Literary biography
Time: 1912-1989
Locale: Minneapolis; Seattle; Poughkeepsie, New York;
New York City; Newport, Rhode Island; The Cape
(Massachusetts); Paris; and Castine, Maine

~

A comprehensive biography full of vivid details and an-
ecdotes but marred by a lack of focus on certain essential
aspects of McCarthy's life and work

~

Principal personages:
MARY MCCARTHY, the famous American writer
KEVIN MCCARTHY, Mary's brother
PRESTON MCCARTHY, Mary's brother
HAROLD JOHNSRUD, Mary's first husband
EDMUND WILSON, Mary's second husband
BOWDEN BROADWATER, Mary's third husband
JAMES WEST, Mary's fourth husband
REUEL WILSON, Mary's only son
HANNAH ARENDT, Mary's close friend and an important writer
PHILIP RAHV, Mary's lover and editor of *Partisan Review*
DWIGHT MACDONALD, important critic and Mary's close friend

This is the fourth biography of Mary McCarthy. Doris Grumbach's *The Company She Kept* (1967) is an incomplete but still valuable book because the biographer was able to interview her subject extensively—even though McCarthy had repudiated Grumbach's work by the time it was published. Carol Gelderman, for *Mary McCarthy: A Life* (1988), had her subject's complete cooperation and retained her confidence. Carol Brightman, for *Writing Dangerously: Mary McCarthy and Her World* (1992), enjoyed access to McCarthy and was able to supply much new information in her biography. It would seem that Brightman's work completed a cycle. A long book and well written, it surely obviated any need for yet another biography. After all, although McCarthy is an important figure in American literary history, it is not clear that any of her books will enter the literary canon. Indeed, McCarthy herself expressed doubts about the lasting value of her work.

In certain respects Frances Kiernan surmounts these reservations about whether yet another book on Mary McCarthy is needed. Kiernan meets the fundamental requirement for a new biography, which Matthew Bruccoli put succinctly when asked why he had written a new biography of F. Scott Fitzgerald: "more facts." Kiernan has diligently interviewed new and old sources and provides a welter of new data and interpretation. In addition, she has chosen a subject who is colorful by definition; that is, people just love to talk and to speculate about Mary McCarthy because she was so outspoken and provocative. Moreover, to write about Mary McCarthy is to write about many of the most important writers of her time. Not only did McCarthy know so many of the important New

Frances Kiernan was fiction editor for The New Yorker *for twenty-one years.*

York intellectuals, such as Alfred Kazin, William Phillips, Philip Rahv, and the other writers who clustered around the influential *Partisan Review*; she was also married to America's most important critic, Edmund Wilson, and she involved herself in the major controversies of her time, especially anticommunism and the Vietnam War. What is more, her fiction constantly draws on her life, with many of her characters only thinly disguised versions of Edmund Wilson, Philip Rahv, and many other notable literary personalities. Further thinking about Mary McCarthy is therefore, as Carol Brightman suggests in the subtitle of her biography, inextricably connected to thinking about the world she inhabited and shaped, a world that will continue to shape the future, which means that in the future her world will undoubtedly be assessed again and again. Mary McCarthy, in other words, is likely to remain a perennial temptation to the biographer.

Aside from new facts and interpretations, how does the form and style of Kiernan's biography differ from its predecessors? Her most striking innovation is to include many excerpts from her interviews. Perhaps half the book is a record of her interviews, which she weaves together with her narrative. The advantage of this method is that the voices of history come vividly alive without mediation from the biographer. The disadvantage is that Kiernan sometimes allows the voices to deal with difficult issues around which there is no consensus. Perhaps it is honest for the biographer to simply present conflicting evidence without trying to reconcile contradictions; on the other hand, such a method employed too often seems like an abnegation of the biographer's responsibility. Should not a biographer steeped in the evidence provide an interpretation—even if that interpretation has to be tentative or qualified?

A case in point is Mary McCarthy's marriage to Edmund Wilson. Some of the documents Kiernan cites, and some of her interviewees, strongly suggest that Wilson beat his wife savagely. Certainly McCarthy herself claimed that he did. On the other hand, Wilson's daughter Rosalind strongly objects to this portrait of her father, and Kiernan cites other documents that are ambiguous enough to leave room for doubt. Kiernan's handling of this explosive issue might seem fair, except that she does not cite, let alone deal with, important sources. It is astonishing, for example, that her Notes section does not even refer to Jeffrey Meyers's major biography of Edmund Wilson.

Meyers is not even listed in her bibliography. This seems especially strange since Kiernan does generously acknowledge the work of earlier McCarthy biographers. However, they did not have the kind of access to Wilson's papers that Meyers did.

A similar problem occurs when Kiernan deals with the lawsuit Lillian Hellman brought against McCarthy, who had called Hellman a liar on *The Dick Cavett Show*. Kiernan lists only Joan Mellen's book on Hellman in her bibliography, ignoring the biographies by William Wright and Carl Rollyson. Again, Kiernan was not obligated to deal with the work of other biographers except insofar as their work had a direct bearing on her own conclusions. She blunders, however, when she speculates on whether or not Hellman's lawyer, Ephraim London, charged her a fee. She cites McCarthy's attorney, Benjamin O'Sullivan, as speculating that London worked for free. However, this is not a matter for speculation. Biographer Carl Rollyson asked London if he charged Hellman a fee, and London said he did not. It is dismaying that Kiernan has not bothered to nail down elementary facts established by earlier books. In this case it is important to know that Hellman's resources were unlimited, whereas McCarthy feared bankruptcy.

Sometimes Kiernan is so busy recording the testimony of her witnesses that she does not ponder its significance. Thus she reports McCarthy acknowledging Rebecca West as one of her early role models. Kiernan describes West as "known for her wit, her striking looks, her socialist politics, and her glamorous circle of male friends." This inadequate description completely misses the point: West was a contrarian; she stirred the pot even when it meant she lost friends and took unpopular positions. Again and again, this is what McCarthy does—adopt daring, contentious positions— but Kiernan only skims the surface of West's influence and the deep need McCarthy had to re-create this British writer's style in an American setting.

This tendency toward the superficial, of not quite thinking through the parallels and comparisons of McCarthy to other women writers, surfaces again in Kiernan's handling of McCarthy and Susan Sontag. Kiernan observes that both women tended to identify and sometimes to seek the protection and patronage of powerful males. The trouble is that Kiernan thinks the powerful male in Sontag's case is her husband, Philip Rieff. Rieff, though, was never a particularly powerful figure, and Sontag divorced him before she became a published writer. The powerful male in Sontag's life is her publisher, Roger Straus, who made certain that no book of hers ever went out of print and tirelessly worked to get her translated into twenty-three foreign languages. To the extent that there is a parallel between McCarthy and Sontag, it is in their choice of publishers. Like Sontag, McCarthy found her true consort in power with William Jovanovich, her publisher, who shrewdly laid the groundwork for McCarthy's huge best-seller, *The Group* (1963).

Nevertheless, Kiernan's biography is indispensable. She has sought out other biographers—such as Michael Wrezin—who generously gave her copies of his interview tapes with Dwight Macdonald. To hear Macdonald's own words as told to another biographer is itself a way of corroborating Kiernan's own view of Macdonald as a warm yet still critical friend of McCarthy. McCarthy critics—such as Lionel Abel and Alfred Kazin—are given ample room to express their views, yet Kiernan's biography never loses sympathy for its subject. Others such as Susan Sontag speak for the first time on the record about McCarthy. Indeed, Sontag has one of the great lines in the biography: "Mary came into the room like an aircraft carrier."

Kiernan's biography is an excellent introduction to the period and personalities McCarthy confronted. There are indelible portraits of a rather thuggish Philip Rahv tutoring McCarthy, his lover, in the intricacies of anti-Stalinism; of an aging, impatient, and alcoholic Edmund Wilson almost browbeating McCarthy into trying her luck as a writer of fiction and then championing her early fiction at a time when most of his colleagues saw her only as a critic and doubted her promise as a novelist; of the rather fey Bowden Broadwater, who became McCarthy's impresario and water boy even as his own hope of a writing career vanished; of James West, American diplomat, smitten with McCarthy, leaving his young wife and children in order to serve her—but also to steady her by refusing to be intimidated by her waspish intellect; of Hannah Arendt, who treated McCarthy gently, acting as the mother McCarthy never had, the mother McCarthy lost in the World War I influenza epidemic. Similarly, many of the males in McCarthy's life had a fatherly relationship with her, although as she grew older McCarthy seemed to have less of a need for that kind of paternal guidance. Indeed, her final, long marriage to James West seems to have been a relationship founded on mutual respect, not dependence.

Kiernan was fortunate to secure the testimony of McCarthy's brothers, Kevin and Preston. They clearly admired their sister, although Preston saw little of her until late in her life. Kevin was close to her, but he seems to have had enough perspective to describe his sister objectively, calmly pointing out that his recollections of their childhood as orphans were not as dire as his sister's.

Kiernan's biography has a nice arc to it. Whereas McCarthy made terrible choices in men in her early life—her first husband seems like a temporary port in the storm of her conflicting feelings about a career—her later involvements were more self-knowing, even if she did sometimes choose unstable men such as critic John Davenport, a notorious drunk. She seemed ready to settle down with a James West who supported her career to the hilt even when he lost patience with her fits of carping criticism—which she quickly ended in his presence. Near the end of her life McCarthy became a dedicated teacher at Bard College. Unlike most literary figures, she was quite willing to sacrifice time she could have spent on writing to cater to her students. She knew she was teaching at some cost to her own creative efforts, yet she believed strongly in conveying her knowledge to another generation—perhaps because Miss Sandison, one of her favorite teachers at Vassar, did as much for McCarthy. Finally, the biography and McCarthy's life come full circle when Kiernan describes how her subject made her peace with Vassar after the 1963 publication of *The Group* (her critical novel about Vassar life had created an uproar there). All of McCarthy's papers are now housed at her alma mater, where they will undoubtedly be consulted by generations of biographers and scholars of culture.

Carl Rollyson

Sources for Further Study

Booklist 96 (February 1, 2000): 1004.
Commentary 109 (March, 2000): 53.
Library Journal 125 (January, 2000): 106.
The Nation 270 (June 12, 2000): 20.
The New York Times Book Review 105 (March 26, 2000): 8.
Publishers Weekly 247 (February 7, 2000): 73.
St. Louis Post-Dispatch, March 12, 2000, p. F10.
Time 155 (March 27, 2000): 97.
The Washington Times, April 2, 2000, p. B8.

SHAKESPEARE'S LANGUAGE

Author: Frank Kermode (1919-   )
Publisher: Farrar, Straus and Giroux (New York). 324
    pp. $30.00
Type of work: Literary criticism
Time: 1594-1608
Locale: England

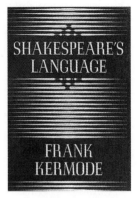

∾

Between 1594 and 1608, Kermode argues, the language
of Shakespeare's plays was transformed, acquiring a new
complexity that arose out of the playwright's increasingly
successful attempts to represent dramatically the excite-
ment and confusion of thought under stress

∾

In the highly politicized, hyperspecialized, and careerist world of Anglo-American literary criticism, those critics who manage to command near universal respect
and attention are few indeed. Sir Frank Kermode is one of them. Over the course of a
long and productive literary life, Kermode has established himself as that rarest of
creatures—a brilliant generalist. He has produced works of criticism in such diverse
areas as Renaissance literature, Romanticism, the theory of fiction, the novel, and narrative theory—to name a few. Among his best known books are *The Sense of an Ending* (1967), *The Genesis of Secrecy: On the Interpretation of Narrative* (1979), and
Forms of Attention (1985). Kermode has written on Shakespeare on a number of occasions, and edited the 1958 Arden edition of *The Tempest.*

In *Shakespeare's Language* Kermode is working against the grain of current criticism. Focusing unfashionably upon the poetics of Shakespeare's plays, he has no particular political agenda to promote. Indeed, *Shakespeare's Language* seems to exist in
a world serenely indifferent to the political turf wars of the academy, perhaps in part
because Kermode has written this book, as he states in the preface, primarily for a
"non-professional audience." The work is divided into two parts. Part One, some
sixty pages long, surveys Shakespeare's early and middle periods; Part Two consists
of fifteen brief and highly readable chapters, one for each of the plays written after
1600. Footnotes and references to the massive body of Shakespeare criticism are used
sparingly.

Between 1594 and 1608, Kermode argues, Shakespearean drama underwent a
transformation that may be described as a movement from the drama of rhetorical
gesture to a drama of "personation," a term that itself dates back to the Elizabethan
period and that refers to a "fuller representation of character." While this transformation is apparent to some degree in the works of other playwrights of the time, it is
Shakespeare, especially in his great tragedies, who pioneered the change. More pre-

∼

*Frank Kermode has taught at
University College, London, and
Cambridge University, and has
been a visiting professor at
Columbia, Harvard, Yale, and
several other American colleges.
His books include his memoir,* Not
Entitled, *as well as* Forms of
Attention, The Genesis of Secrecy,
and The Sense of an Ending.

∼

cisely, Kermode defines the drama of personation as "the representation of excited, anxious
thought; the weighing of confused possibilities
and dubious motives . . . as in the meditation of a
person under stress to whom all that he is considering can be a prelude to vital choices, emotional
and political."

English drama before Shakespeare, and even
much of Shakespeare's own early work, is essentially nondramatic, claims Kermode; which is to
say that the earlier dramaturgy was a matter of
following the rules of poetic composition, rules
derived from the classical rhetoric learned in the
schools. Stichomythia (dialogue in alternate lines), anaphora, epistrophe, epanalepsis
(all forms of repetition), such rhetorical figures and hundreds of others were stock-
piled for convenient use in such manuals of classical style as Puttenham's *The Art of
English Poesie* (1589). Shakespeare's English history plays, most of them composed
in the mid-1590's, are heavily dependent upon the use of such figures, albeit a more
refined use than one ordinarily finds in other plays of the period. Even in *Richard II*
(pr. c. 1595-1596), still one of Shakespeare's most celebrated and studied dramas, one
finds the speeches dominated by ornamentation of classical origin.

On the other hand, *Richard II* may also be seen as a transitional play, one in which
certain speeches display a clear indication of the development of Shakespeare's language toward a fuller, more engaged sense of character. Thus when Richard's favorite, Bushy, addresses the Queen in act 2, his language is less than transparent; it bears
the traces of the struggle of thought to find expression in speech commensurate to the
emotion of the moment, but falling somewhat short. Bushy seeks to console the
Queen by reminding her that the "substance of a grief" is a thing distinct from the
many "shadows" of grief—the images projected by sorrow that play upon the mind's
eye like so many "perspectives, which rightly gaz'd upon/ Show nothing but confusion." Thus the Queen, "looking awry" upon Richard's departure, "Find[s] shapes of
grief, more than himself, to wail,/ Which, look'd on as it is, is nought but shadows."
Bushy concludes his advice as follows: "More than your lord's departure weep not—
more is not seen,/ Or if it be, 'tis with false sorrow's eye,/ Which for things true weeps
things imaginary."

As Kermode demonstrates, the word "perspectives" is the key to this passage and
suggests that Bushy is drawing an analogy to the tricks of perspective employed in
certain well-known sixteenth century paintings, such as Hans Holbein the Younger's
The Ambassadors (1533), in which the image appears differently when viewed from
the side ("awry") rather than from front and center. In fact, such paintings, to be
viewed correctly, must be viewed "awry," which is why Bushy's analogy ends up,
says Kermode, in "something of a muddle." For by the logic of his analogy, he really
ought to be advising the Queen to look not "rightly" upon her grief, but "awry."
Kermode further notes that this somewhat convoluted analogy departed from the

usual rhetorical rules for consolatory speeches. While Kermode does not claim here that Bushy's confusion was deliberately intended by the playwright, he does feel that the passage demonstrates a fresh departure:

> The exciting thing about Bushy's speech is that in it we find Shakespeare struggling with a sentiment rendered stubborn by the circumstances that the speaker appears to be thinking, is doing his intellectual best to get his consolation across, and is getting slightly muddled in the process, the slight muddle being a by-product of the effort to represent intellection, or rather to do it.

Kermode demonstrates that by 1600 Shakespeare had mastered the representation of intellection, and nowhere is this perfected skill more apparent than in *Hamlet* (pr. c. 1600-1601). One of the best examples occurs in act 3, just after the well-known "Mousetrap" scene in which Hamlet attempts to "catch the conscience" of the king, his uncle Claudius. Most readers will readily recall the circumstances. After the rigged performance of the play-within-a-play designed to provoke Claudius to reveal his guilt for the murder of the elder Hamlet, the stricken king unburdens himself in soliloquy:

> May one be pardon'd and retain th' offence?
> In the corrupted currents of this world
> Offense's gilded hand may shove by justice,
> And oft 'tis seen the wicked prize itself
> Buys out the law, but 'tis not so above:
> There is no shuffling, there the action lies
> In his true nature, and we ourselves compell'd
> Even to the teeth and forehead of our faults,
> To give in evidence.

To paraphrase this powerfully compacted (in more than one sense) passage is almost itself criminal. Yet Claudius is saying something to this effect: Is it possible to seek forgiveness for a crime, and yet keep the benefit of that same crime? In this world below, the law can be bought and the criminal may escape punishment. In Heaven, though, no double-dealing prevails; there the crime is seen for what it is, and the criminal forced to incriminate himself. While theatergoers, if they wish to stay abreast of the play's unfolding action, will hardly have the leisure to paraphrase such a speech, they will at least understand that here Claudius is desperately seeking some relief from his conscience, yet still clinging to the office (the kingship) that he has stolen. The phrase, "retain the offense" is, as Kermode notes, somewhat elliptical, precisely in the way that anguished thought can be. Given the leisure to examine the passage closely, one can see that the ellipsis sets up the, at first glance, almost invisible allegory to follow. In the third line, "Offense's gilded hand" functions as the personification of the criminal act itself. One is meant to see, as though in a kind of verbal dumbshow, Offense proffering a bribe ("gilded hand") to the law. The allegory remains unobtrusively alive in lines 5 and 6 in the use of the pronoun "his," then converges with the plural "we" and "our" when Claudius indirectly applies the allegory to his own case.

This deft and oblique proliferation of legal terms culminating in an allegorical courtroom scene is all the more powerful for being merely suggested, and is for that reason a clear departure from the older rhetorical mode. It is the final three lines of Claudius's speech that clinch the matter. To be compelled to give evidence "Even to the teeth and forehead of our faults" is to be forced to incriminate ourselves; that much should be apparent at first reading. Yet even the Elizabethans, far more tolerant of mixed metaphor than people today, must have found this an unsettling instance of forced language. A playwright of lesser courage might simply have written, "Even to the forehead of our fault," thus salvaging the personification of Offense without venturing to the very edge of the grotesque. Most interpreters have understood the coupling of "forehead" and "teeth" to imply a violent confrontation between accuser and accused. Kermode is surely right to say that the posture of the accused is one of total penitence, "so that the face, teeth, and brows will be ashamed, not defiant." The violence of the language is an example of the kind of risk that Shakespeare takes again and again in the plays of this period as he strives to "work out violent emotion in . . . language subjected to the pressure and slippage of bold, even anguished metaphor."

For the most part Kermode's claim that Shakespeare's language undergoes a radical and original transformation between 1594 and 1608 (and beyond) is convincingly argued and abundantly, even obsessively illustrated. Aside from the chapter on *Hamlet*, probably the best in the book, the chapters on *King Lear* (pr. c. 1605-1606) and *The Tempest* (pr. 1611) are also splendid. However, as intent as he is upon providing fresh proofs of Shakespeare's originality, Kermode never engages in bardolatry. He routinely draws his readers' attention to Shakespeare's not infrequent lapses of poetic judgment. The playwright's habitual use of doubling devices such as hendiadys—the deliberate pairing of words to express a single idea—is often productive of striking effects. When Laertes, advising his sister Ophelia how to regard the young Hamlet's amorous attentions, insists that "the trifling of his favor" is but "a fashion and toy in blood," it is impossible to pry apart "fashion" and "toy" without doing damage to the figure. However, at times Shakespeare's fondness for doublets yields little of value, as when Lady Macbeth greets Duncan in act one of *Macbeth* (pr. 1606): "All our service/ In every point twice done, and then done double,/ Were poor and single business to contend/ Against those honors deep and broad wherewith/ Your Majesty loads our house." Here doubling amounts to little more than redundancy, and Kermode humorously comments that in this instance the great Lady Macbeth sounds like nothing so much as an accountant.

Shakespeare's Language is not without weaknesses. The chapters on *Othello* (pr. 1604, rev. 1623) and *Julius Caesar* (pr. c. 1599-1600) are almost lethargic. While praising both plays, Kermode appears at a loss to say anything memorable about them. Occasionally, too, he makes sweeping claims that cry out for more justification than the author is willing to provide. After a masterful treatment of the first half of *Measure for Measure* (pr. 1604), Kermode abruptly ends the chapter on a dismissive note. "Much has been written in defense of the second half of *Measure for Measure*, but it is surely a muddle. There are some fine things in it, of course . . . but it tends to be prosy and incredible." Kermode is not the first to have registered this complaint about this play, but some critics of real distinction have in recent years found a good deal more there than muddle. Kermode leaves the reader wishing that he had devoted more than a mere paragraph in support of the claim.

Kermode's stated purpose of addressing not primarily an academic but a "non-professional audience" is no doubt a commendable aim, and one must agree that it is not an aim "well served by modern critics, who on the whole seem to have little time for [Shakespeare's] language [and] tend to talk past it in technicalities or down to it in arcanely expressed platitudes." Kermode has certainly avoided arcane platitudes (if not platitudes altogether), and for the most part kept the technicalities to a minimum. While accessible by comparison to the kind of specialized criticism that Kermode deplores, this is nonetheless a demanding book. It is in no sense an introduction to Shakespeare's work. In fact, there is hardly a paragraph that does not assume a reader already intimate with the plays and their complex web of plot and characterization. Given that *caveat*, *Shakespeare's Language* well serves those readers who, having read the plays with some understanding, and having seen at least some of them performed, wish to enhance their knowledge of the plays' intricacy of language and structure. To that end Kermode is the most reliable of guides.

Jack Trotter

Sources for Further Study

American Scholar 69 (Summer, 2000): 146.
Choice 38 (October, 2000): 330.
The Economist 355 (April 29, 2000): 82.
Library Journal 125 (April 15, 2000): 90.
The New Republic 222 (June 26, 2000): 27.
The New York Review of Books 47 (August 10, 2000): 35.
Publishers Weekly 247 (May 1, 2000): 56.
The Wall Street Journal, July 6, 2000, p. A24.
Wilson Quarterly 24 (Autumn, 2000): 131.

THE SIKHS

Author: Patwant Singh (1925-   )
Publisher: Alfred A. Knopf (New York). 276 pp. $27.50
Type of work: History and current affairs
Time: 1469 to the present
Locale: India

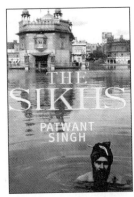

≈

*A lively but hagiographic history of the Sikhs, which
also illuminates political tensions in India today*

≈

Principal personages:
GURU NANAK DEV (1469-1539), the
    founder of the Sikh faith
GURU GOBIND SINGH (1666-1708), the tenth and last guru in the line es-
    tablished by Guru Nanak Dev
RANJIT SINGH (1780-1839), the nineteenth-century leader who expanded
    Sikh rule to its greatest extent

By any measure, the story of the Sikhs is a remarkable one. From humble beginnings in the late fifteenth century, they have grown to number more than 16 million.
Largely concentrated in the Punjab region of India, they have also spread their faith
around the world in a diaspora exceeding one million. Indeed, Sikhs who came to California as farmers at the beginning of the twentieth century were among the very first
Indian immigrants to the United States.

Wherever they go, the Sikhs are distinctive, especially for the turbans worn by
most Sikh men. Moreover, wherever they go, they are a living contradiction to the
secularization theories that reigned unchallenged in social science from its founding
in the nineteenth century through the 1960s, after which the stubborn persistence of
religion became too obtrusive to ignore or explain away. According to the prophets of
secularization, modernity and religious traditions were fundamentally contradictory,
and the gradual triumph of the former spelled the decline and eventual disappearance
of the latter. Yet something funny happened on the way to the secular city, as a photograph in Patwant Singh's *The Sikhs* wonderfully illustrates: A Sikh pilot, in his Indian
Air Force uniform and his turban, stands next to his Mirage 2000 jet fighter.

Mention of the persistence of religion in the modern—or is it the postmodern?—
world brings to mind another facet of the Sikh story: the way that religious and ethnic
identity (the two often conflated) can fuel conflict. Ask the average American what
comes to mind in association with "Sikh" and, if there is not a total blank, the answer
will probably include political violence—especially among Americans old enough to
remember clearly the assassination of Indian prime minister Indira Gandhi on October 31, 1984, by two of her Sikh bodyguards. The assassination occurred less than

five months after Gandhi had ordered an armored assault to flush out an allegedly dangerous Sikh leader and his closest followers, an assault that destroyed the Sikhs' most sacred site, the Golden Temple complex, and left more than five thousand Sikhs dead. Many more Sikhs—at least three thousand—were killed in revenge by Hindu mobs in the immediate aftermath of the assassination.

Patwant Singh has published books and articles on India, international affairs, the environment, and the arts. He has been a frequent television and radio commentator, and has traveled and lectured all over the world. From 1957 to 1988, he was editor and publisher of the international magazine Design.

For readers who want to move beyond such fragmentary images to a deeper understanding and appreciation of Sikh history and culture, Patwant Singh has written a sprightly history, a fast-moving narrative in which the author does not hesitate to offer his opinions. This is no work of academic history—though Singh, the editor and publisher from 1957 to 1988 of the international magazine, *Design*, has written widely on his people—nor does it pretend to be. It is not enough, however, to say that Patwant Singh has not taken up the mantle of the professedly "objective" historian, for this is a frankly apologetic work, a hagiographic tribute to the Sikh people—which does not prevent the author from criticizing certain of his fellow Sikhs on occasion—and, by the same token, a sharply observed, all-out attack on the Brahmins who have dominated India for millennia and who continue to dominate Indian society today. It is highly unusual for such a book to appear under the imprint of a publisher such as Alfred A. Knopf, and it would be very interesting to know how that came about. Nonetheless, taken with a grain of salt, the book offers a engaging, if sometimes exasperating, overview of Sikh history.

The word "Sikh" derives from a Sanskrit word, *shishya*, meaning "disciple" or "devoted follower." It was applied to followers of the founder of Sikhism, Guru Nanak Dev, who was born to a Hindu family in a village near Lahore in 1469. Nanak's followers were attracted by his remarkable religious vision, articulated in teachings that were later committed to writing and became the foundation of the *Adi Granth* (also called the *Granth Sahib* and the *Guru Granth Sahib*), the Sikh scriptures. Nanak's teachings—pithy, poetic, and profound—differed both from the Hinduism that was the majority religion in his time and from Islam, the faith of the invaders who ruled Hindustan at that time. "There is no Hindu/ There is no Mussulman [i.e., Muslim]," Nanak provocatively declared. He meant that the truth, proceeding from the one God, did not lie in the rituals and observances of Hindus or Muslims or other religious believers, but rather in following an inner path. Indeed, in its early form, Sikhism was strongly inner-directed. In a passage reminiscent of the New Testament, Nanak taught:

> If you believe in pollution at birth, there is pollution everywhere.
> There are creatures in cow-dung and in wood.
> There is life in each grain of corn.
> Water is the source of life of life, sap for all things.
> Then how can one escape pollution? Pollution pollutes only the ignorant.

The pollution of the mind is greed, the pollution of the tongue lying. . . .
The pollution in which people commonly believe is all superstition.
Birth and death are by divine will, by divine will men come and go.
What is given to us to eat and drink is pure.
They who have arrived at the truth remain untouched by pollution.

Nanak was particularly critical of the caste system that perpetuated inequality from generation to generation, and still does so in India today. No wonder many were attracted to his message.

Before his death in 1539, Nanak named a successor. A line of teachers or gurus followed, culminating with the tenth, Guru Gobind Singh, whose father, Guru Tegh Bahadur, had been beheaded in 1675 after torture by Muslim captors; he refused to renounce his faith and convert to Islam. One of Tegh Bahadur's followers recovered his head and brought it to the nine-year-old Gobind for cremation. This is but one salient instance of a powerful tradition of martyrdom that persists in Sikhism, along with a fiercely combative spirit nurtured by centuries of conflict.

Although his life was short—he was killed at the age of 42—Guru Gobind Singh was destined to become one of the greatest of the Sikh leaders, and it was he who, according to Sikh tradition, instituted the Khalsa, the religious order to which most Sikhs belong, and the so-called "Five K's," five items (each beginning with the letter "k") that every male Sikh in the Khalsa is required to wear: *kesh* (long hair), *kanga* (a comb), *kara* (a steel wristband), *kachh* (short breeches), and *kirpan* (a short sword). He also ordained that male Sikhs in the Khalsa should have the surname *Singh* ("lion"), while females should add the name *Kaur* ("lioness" or "princess") to their given name—hence the predominance of the family name "Singh" among Sikhs.

Gobind took a shaping role in Sikhism in another decisive way. According to Sikh tradition, before he died from the wound that killed him, Gobind announced that he was the last of the personal gurus, and that henceforth the *Granth Sahib* (the Sikh scriptures) and the Khalsa would together be the source of authority in the Sikh community. Today, centuries after Gobind's death, Sikhs revere and are guided by the *Adi Granth* much as Christians regard the Bible.

Here as elsewhere, it should be noted, Patwant Singh hews strictly to Sikh tradition without taking into account scholarship both inside and outside the Sikh community that offers different perspectives. For example, there is considerable evidence that the "Five K's" were not institutionalized until the late nineteenth century, under the impetus of the Singh Sabha movement, a reform movement within Sikhism, rather than at the end of the seventeenth century under Guru Gobind Singh. Readers interested in such perspectives might turn to *Sikhism* (1997), by Hew McLeod, the dean of Western scholars of Sikhism, and *The Construction of Religious Boundaries: Culture, Identity, and Diversity in the Sikh Tradition* (1994), a prize-winning revisionist history by Harjot Oberoi, a Sikh scholar.

In political terms, the Sikhs enjoyed their greatest success under the rule of Ranjit Singh in the early nineteenth century. Like many leaders in that period of nationalist fervor, Ranjit Singh, though small in stature, was a larger-than-life figure, a man whose energies and ambitions and appetites were king-sized. He occupies a somewhat ambiguous place in Sikh memory, where he is honored for carving out a large territory for his people and admired for his derring-do, but seen by some as having compromised too much in the quest for power. Hence, after his death in 1839 and the collapse of Sikh power after two wars with the British, a variety of reform movements began to stir within Sikhism.

In the ferment of those movements in the late nineteenth and early twentieth centuries, some Sikhs actively resisted the British Raj, while the majority sought to make a life as best as they could. (Many Sikhs served in the British army, with great distinction and uncommon valor.) Still others chose to emigrate to Great Britain, the United States, and elsewhere. The Partition of 1947, with the withdrawal of the British and India's division into a majority Hindu state (India) and a majority Muslim state (Pakistan), brought terrible suffering and loss of both land and life to the Sikhs. Thousands who lived on what became the Muslim side of the line died at the time of Partition.

Nor did the Sikhs fare well in political terms in the early decades of independent India. A building sense of discriminatory treatment fueled radicalism and calls for an independent Sikh state, Khalistan ("Land of the Pure"). It is not clear how deep such feeling runs in the Sikh community, which has prospered nonetheless. Still, like other minorities in India, Sikhs cannot help but be conscious of their vulnerability. "In the Hindi heartland of India," Patwant Singh warns, "currents of intolerance and a tendency toward violence are making a mockery of mannerly politics." Yet he concludes on an optimistic note, noting the resilience that has served his people well over the centuries. One may also hope that the spirit of tolerance embodied by Nanak, the Sikh founder, will be sustained in the twenty-first century not only by his followers but by all religious believers.

John Wilson

Sources for Further Study

Booklist 96 (April 1, 2000): 1431.
The Economist 355 (May 13, 2000): 9.
Library Journal 125 (February 15, 2000): 183.
Los Angeles Times, April 29, 2000, p. B2.
Publishers Weekly 247 (March 13, 2000): 72.

SO I AM GLAD

Author: A. L. Kennedy (1966-   )
Publisher: Alfred A. Knopf (New York). 276 pp. $23.00
Type of work: Novel
Time: Late 1990's
Locale: Glasgow, Scotland, and Paris, France

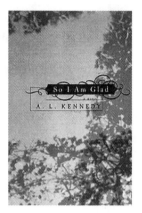

~

*An emotionally neutral young woman discovers a
strange young man who claims to have appeared in a room
in her shared house and has no memory of his identity*

~

Principal characters:

> JENNIFER WILSON, a young woman who works as a radio announcer and
> denies that she has ever felt any emotions
> SAVINIEN DE CYRANO DE BERGERAC, called Martin until he remembers
> his own name, who believes he has come spontaneously into
> Jennifer's time and house following a timeless period after his death

A. L. Kennedy is a Scottish novelist from Glasgow. *So I Am Glad* is her first full-length novel to be published in the United States. Told in first-person point of view by Jennifer Wilson, the protagonist, the story immediately thrusts the reader into the sexually active yet emotionally devoid and depressing life of the narrator. Kennedy has taken quite a chance here in choosing a main character who not only is emotionally aloof and self-contained, but also proves to be a temporarily repentant sadist. Many readers might be tempted to abandon this novel from the beginning, but sticking with the story through the end yields an incredible reward, a bittersweet ending wherein both Jennifer and Cyrano/Martin irrevocably change. When so many other novels flounder at the end, this is a rare exception.

Jennifer introduces herself in the first chapter, explaining her active sex life forthrightly and unashamedly, taking the practical view that sex is good for filling time. She goes on to remark upon discovering her own lack of emotion, her failure to build any human relationships with her lovers, and credits her inability to experience emotions as responsible. While others might see her as remote, a "cold fish," she simply sees herself as calm. She fantasizes that other people are filled with emotions like rioting "moles" that they learn to keep more or less to themselves after early childhood, but she has none of these secret tunneling mammals inside her. She claims to have learned over her life to mimic emotional responses appropriately, and she states that nothing bad has ever happened to her to make her the way she is. In that statement, she is self-deceiving. Little by little, readers learn of the odd and abusive childhood that made her what she is as the novel begins.

In the next chapter, Jennifer meets Martin, a young man who has appeared magically in an empty bedroom in the house she shares with three other young people. One of the housemates is away, and those remaining are expecting someone named Martin to replace Peter while he is gone. When this strange man wanders down into the common parts of the house, Jennifer mistakes him for the new roommate Martin and ad-

A. L. Kennedy's first novel was Original Bliss. She is a frequent columnist for the Guardian. *So I Am Glad has won three prizes in her native Scotland.*

dresses him as such. Having at first no memory of who he is, where he is, or why, he accepts this christening as fact, but can offer nothing more about himself. Martin's demeanor, however, quickly leads to Jennifer's realization that something is wrong with him, and she also notices that he seems to have a faint shine in the dark, not only when he opens his mouth, but also a silvery gleam that covers his body. Jennifer decides it has something to do with his tears, sweat, and saliva.

Jennifer and Martin begin the long process of sorting through what he knows and does not know, but Jennifer decides to keep her knowledge that this man is not the Martin they are expecting to herself. She seems to enjoy having this secret, mysterious person who assures her that he is no danger to her, even though he does not know who he is. Her Martin is philosophical and poetic, weaving a tale of his experience before waking up in the upstairs room that he believes was his afterlife.

The other roommates accept Martin, although they begin to wonder why he is not forthcoming with his share of the rent. To cover for him and to keep him in the house, Jennifer begins to pay his rent. Martin both appreciates this, because he seems helpless in the modern world, and agonizes over causing her such trouble. Jennifer is fascinated with his unfolding personality and memories.

The day comes when Martin remembers his name, an occasion that fills him with joy. After describing a scene from his life as a soldier, kneeling to pray before battle, he says, "I was Savinien de Cyrano de Bergerac and I was true." By true he means to God; God enters into Savinien's conversation often as he tries to understand why he has come to life again centuries following his death.

The real danger here is that Kennedy delivers this information and then steps back without giving any hints about its truth or fiction. Immediately following Savinien's declaration, readers follow Jennifer to the radio station and learn more about the work she does, and about her former lover Steve, who used her recommendation to gain employment and now records the words she reads. Readers share Jennifer's memories of the sadistic and masochistic relationship they had, the game they played where she was Captain Bligh, punishing a wayward sailor, played by Steve. She admits to having enjoyed the game somewhat; it somehow compensated for the empty areas of her life.

The chapter that follows reveals the experiences of Jennifer's early life at the hands of her parents. Interestingly, Jennifer begins this chapter by saying that it is not about her, when it seems to be at the heart of her emotional life. She cautions readers that they will not like what they hear and even encourages them to skip the chapter altogether. Although her parents were intelligent, educated people, they made their young child sit on their bed and watch them while they had sex. Jennifer also blames herself for not being careful not to let this happen, although she admits that it probably was not her fault, and dismisses it by saying that all families have things that happen in them.

Next Jennifer goes through the difficult transition to accepting Martin as Savinien, though she is certain he is not really the famous character. He is pleased that she knows his name. She leaps forward here and talks of a visit they later make to Paris, which Savinien seems to remember from his life long ago, and she shares his talk of love and devotion. When Jennifer's voice returns to the present in the next chapter, it is to relate the details of her sadistic/masochistic relationship with Steve, all to set the scene for her darkest tale yet.

Here is where the reader will be most challenged. By alternating Jennifer's growing relationship with Savinien with tales of her past, Kennedy slowly builds sympathy for this difficult character. It is almost not sufficient, however. Savinien talks of his life, and of a duel wherein he had to kill a young man full of life, and regretted the necessity of doing so. Jennifer relates how her parents died while engaging in sex in a speeding vehicle, and how relieved she was that they were gone from her life at last. Jennifer relates Savinien's tale of how he schooled himself in killing and how that skill is worthless here, and the mistake she made in reminding this proud man that he was totally dependent on her. Savinien leaves a note thanking her and disappears.

While Savinien is gone, Jennifer answers Steve's invitation to engage in a sadistic/masochistic episode. Jennifer finds savage release in this, going further than she ever has. Unfortunately, Steve is injured so badly by her that he misses four days of work and must depend on her to care for him, until he finally asks her never to return. That is when Jennifer reminds readers chillingly, "Well, I only told you I was calm. I never even suggested that I was nice."

Savinien is eventually found, under the influence of and in the possession of some kind of drug. At this point he seems either to be someone mentally deranged or, at the least, to be using his grandiose claim to sponge off Jennifer. This is the closest Kennedy takes the reader to disbelief in Savinien, to questioning all that has gone before, all the details of his life in France, all the poetry and philosophy, as nothing more than a hustle.

When he has recovered, Savinien tells Jennifer that he did terrible things while he was gone, although he does not think that he killed anyone. He sets about building a garden to repay her kindness, and finally they become lovers. After all this time, Jennifer cares about someone; she loves, and it changes everything. No longer able to read the news dispassionately, she is all too aware of the troubled earth where her loved one must live, of poisoned air and political ineptitude.

The garden is completed, but one morning someone has destroyed it, and that someone keeps returning to break it up again. When the neighborhood helps them rebuild in a day-long block party, Savinien identifies the dangerous man and sets out to solve the problem. Jennifer follows Savinien to a nearby park and witnesses his battle with the man, where she sees that Savinien does possess superior fighting skills. Her cry interrupts the savage battle, and Savinien does not kill his enemy as a result. At first Jennifer rejects Savinien. However, his insistence that this is the man he has always been, and his explanation of why he had to act as he did, finally satisfies her, and she returns to him, physically and emotionally.

Following this episode, somehow their lives and love begin to seem more fragile. They both dream of lying under trees, looking up at a blue sky. Jennifer is afraid of this dream and what it might mean about Savinien. He thinks it means something about death. Savinien decides that he must go home to Paris, and, despite her fears that he is leaving her, Jennifer learns that he fully expects her to accompany him on this journey.

Their trip together is filled with love and wonder, but also sadness for Savinien. Although he is filled with joy to be once more in the sunlight of France, breathing its air and walking the streets of Paris, so much has changed. He knows the twists and turns of streets, but finds the houses he knew gone, replaced by more modern buildings. At a used bookstore they find reference to the published works of Cyrano de Bergerac, and Savinien is pleased to know that an old friend has published his writings. However, when they go to the library and actually view the works, Savinien's anger at the changes that his friend made to his words sour the experience for him. The next day, however, Savinien forgives his friend, taking comfort that his original manuscripts still exist.

Jennifer wishes they had never come to France, and yet feels that they had no choice. They make love, and Savinien tells her that he is afraid. He says that they must go on, to the place where he died. The town itself, when they arrive, seems quiet, peaceful. Savinien laughs when he finds that apartment blocks have replaced the house where he died, thinking somehow that they are safe. At the heels of his relief, he feels ill again, and then they both see the narrow trees and the burning blue sky of their dreams.

Savinien stumbles toward it, while Jennifer tries to hold him back, helping him along as he begins to lose his strength and the power of his senses. She releases him only when she realizes that he is heading back toward his death and that she does not want to die with him. He has strength and breath left only to thank her, to say goodbye. At this point, readers know beyond doubt that the author meant this man to be Savinien de Cyrano de Bergerac, and one feels Jennifer's tragic loss as she sees him fall and disappear into the brick path as though the earth were a sea that took him beneath its waves. Jennifer has changed, has lost her calm and found her emotions.

Patricia Masserman

Sources for Further Study

Booklist 96 (November 1, 1999): 509.
The Economist 343 (April, 1999): 83.
Library Journal 125 (January, 2000): 160.
The New York Times Book Review 105 (February 27, 2000): 18.
Publishers Weekly 246 (November 1, 1999): 74.
The Wall Street Journal, January 14, 2000, p. WK10.

SONGLINES IN MICHAELTREE
New and Collected Poems

Author: Michael S. Harper (1938-   )
Publisher: University of Illinois Press (Urbana). 389 pp.
   $34.95
Type of work: Poetry

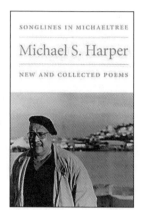

~

Selections from eight previous volumes by Harper, with additional new poems by a writer with one of the most distinctively singular voices in contemporary American literature

~

Michael Harper, in the poetry and essays he has written since his first book, *Dear John, Dear Coltrane*, was published in 1970, has assumed as his artistic responsibility one of the most ancient and esteemed offices available to a writer. Locating himself in a tradition that can be traced back to Homer and beyond, Harper has accepted the obligations inherent in working to establish and proclaim a record of a community's history, and to celebrate the accomplishments of those outstanding figures of that community whose achievements stand for the values and spiritual qualities of a cultural realm. Framing the volume, Harper has placed at the start and close of the book a poem of six stanzas, each line repeated three times, beginning with the triad, "*When there is no history*," and followed by an image of "*a blind nation in storm*" that is "*belted in these ruins.*" This is an emphatic declaration of a poetic credo, an insistence on the reclamation from silence and suppression of the three-centuries epoch of African Americans in the United States. In accordance with the more personal perspective of the postmodern poet in the late twentieth century, Harper has balanced his exploration of significant figures in his community with a deeply felt, intensely evocative expression of the members of his own close family, tender and touching poems that illuminate the origins of the "songlines" in the "Michaeltree" that stands as an emblem of the poet's life.

Harper has carefully arranged the book to recall the poems he regards as particularly important from previous volumes and to provide additional material to assist the reader in understanding a life committed to teaching and writing. There is an explanatory section of "Notes to the Poems" which contains contextual information that enables even those readers familiar with Harper's themes and concerns more fully to understand and appreciate the specific details of many works. For instance, while people who have followed Harper's progress as a poet will immediately recognize the name of the great musician John Coltrane who is central to Harper's sensibility, the note to "Here Where Coltrane Is" points out that the poem "shares a title with a recording of a live concert" but adds, "The poem is meant to suggest the real and imaginary losses and gains of the sixties." This kind of candor enhances a prior perception and is very helpful when Harper is probing historical data that may elude all but those who share his expertise. The note to "Deathwatch," for instance, acknowledges "two resonant debts," including "W. E. B. Du Bois's correspondence when 'experts' on race relations asked him, 'Are Negroes unable to cry?'" These extensions of the poems are akin to the conversational introductions that might occur at one of Harper's public readings and function as a teaching text complementing the poem's other qualities.

Michael S. Harper is a professor of English at Brown University. His books of poetry include Honorable Amendments, Images of Kin, *and* History Is Your Own Heartbeat. *He has received many awards, among them the Melville Cane Award of the Poetry Society of America, the Black Academy of Arts and Letters Award, and the Robert Hayden Poetry Award.*

Along with the "Notes," there is an invitation directed "To the Reader" in which Harper takes the reader through a journey that describes the evolution of his creative consciousness. The essay is conceived as an acknowledgment of crucial asistance, gratitude for the encouragement of mentors such as the "pioneering writers: Robert Hayden, Sterling A. Brown and Ralph Ellison" mingled with illuminating personal items such as the fact that "My godson, Rafael Stepto, gave me the moniker *Michaeltree*. He was four years old, in 1979, and the riff caught and held," or the anecdote which describes Harper reading on the University of Zululand campus where a listener asked for a copy of *Southern Road* (1929) by Sterling Brown, and then "proceeded to copy the poems, in ink on both arms, writing with either hand." Like much of Harper's prose, this essay assumes that the reader will be ready to accept the intellectual challenge of thinking through a statement like the use of the "pietà motif" in the painter/sculptor Oliver Jackson's work, "'an improvisation in the classical mode, by rigorous attention to the line, figurative wholeness, shadow and light, and his own signature in fraternal rendering with full implications of brotherhood, sacrifice, and the mysterious dimensionality of race." The third of these pieces, "Notes on Form and Fictions," is presented as a classical *ars poetica*, in which a serious examination of poetic technique is interlaced with an individual artist's own accommodation to and innovations with the materials of his craft. As the heart of this essay is Harper's essential proclamation of purpose: "I began to write poems because I could not see those elements of my life that I considered sacred reflected in my courses of study: scientific, literary, and linguistic." This leads directly to the most characteristic features of his work, perhaps most striking among them the primary position of African American music as a source for the shape, language, rhythms, and near-mythic hero-figures of his poetry.

In Harper's first book, with a title that could be seen as an address and homage to John Coltrane, the title poem itself is like an invocation to the Muses, pledging the poet's fealty to the spirit of total commitment that made Coltrane's music so stirring and requesting access to the mysterious, cosmic forces which enable a man to reach the level of consciousness exemplified by the chorus of one of Coltrane's signature pieces, "A Love Supreme." Throughout the *Collected Poems*, there are numerous references to fabled members of Coltrane's groups, particularly the drummer Elvin Jones ("Elvin's Blues"), the bassist Paul Chambers ("Mr. P. C."), the pianist McCoy Tyner ("My Book on Trane" cycle), as if each man had taken part in a quest that marked the most gratifying moments of their lives. This mode is expanded as Harper apotheosizes other black people whose struggles and achievements stand as highlights in history: Charlie Parker ("*'Bird Lives':* Charlie Parker in St. Louis"), Alice Walker ("Alice"), Jackie Robinson ("Blackjack"), Gwendolyn Brooks ("Madimba: Gwendolyn Brooks," and a five-poem cycle including "Wizardry: The Poetic Saga in Song of Gwendolyn Brooks"), as well as less publicly acclaimed but equally influential people such as the painter Romare Bearden, the poet Paul Dunbar, the writer James Weldon Johnson, and the educator John Hope Franklin. Then, as if linking an entire nation in a chain of human endeavor, Harper writes with similar fervor and insight about his own family, reaching back toward earlier generations in "Thimble," which refers to Henrietta Bowers, "the first black undertaker in the United States . . . and a conductor on the underground railroad" who was "the maternal ancestor of the poet's mother," and writing amidst the pain of loss about the death of his son in "We Assume: On the Death of Our Son, Reuben Masai Harper." One of the strongest aspects of Harper's work is his ability to find appropriate language to convey the salient points of the lives of each of these people and to make each poem a unique occasion. In this, he is also working in the spirit of Coltrane, whose compositions or thematic albums were separate productions, but whose style was always recognizable and distinct.

At the root of this capability is an absolute faith in the materials of his art. As an epigraph to his first book, Harper writes tersely in the poem "Alone": "A friend told me/ He'd risen above jazz./ I leave him there." This suggests the isolation of a person who rejects his heritage, and more significantly, the poet's insistence on following the truth of his being regardless of transitory trends or the chimera of critical approval. Throughout the volume, similarly succinct statements reaffirm this fundamental belief, sometimes as parts of a poem, as in the concluding stanza from "Brother John:"

> I'm a black man; I am;
> black; I am; I'm a black
> man; I am; I am;
> I'm a black man;
> I'm a black man;
> I am; I'm a black man;
> I am:

which operates as a call-and-response solo; sometimes as a semi-haiku, as in "Black Cryptogram:"

> When God
> created
> the black child
> He was
> showing off

which is a modulated demonstration of communal pride; or sometimes as an unexpected appreciation of a kindred spirit from another realm, as in "Sinatra (1915-98)",
where Harper notes the "scant frame/ at the edge of conquistadorial defeat" of another
outsider whose mega-popularity never entirely removed the pugnacious mettle of a
man how knew "how to win when up against the wall, always."

For Harper, Coltrane's life stands as the epitome of valiant struggles against pain
and loss. At moments of deepest involvement, Harper is ready to risk hitting a wrong
note by adopting the literal voice of Coltrane's mind. In "Dear John, Dear Coltrane,"
"It is Coltrane, himself, who is singing," Harper notes. It is a song that arises in the
poet's heart as well:

> *Why you so black?*
> *cause I am*
> *Why you so funky?*
> *cause I am*
> *Why you so black?*
> *cause I am*
> *why you so sweet?*
> *cause I am*
> *why you so black?*
> *cause I am*
> *a love supreme, a love supreme:*

an echo and variation of the last stanza of "Brother John" and a reiteration of the dominant motif of Harper's writing life. Similarly, the three poems that conclude *My Book
on Trane* seem to meld and fuse the poet's soul/spirit with that of the musician, his secret sharer or surrogate brother, close kin whose life and music was dedicated to "my
playing for my ancestors:" And "how could I do otherwise,/ passing so quickly in this
galaxy," where life's ultimate quest was for "A LOVE SUPREME," as Harper states
in the final measures of "Peace on Earth."

The force of these poems resonates throughout the volume, yet there is actually a
great deal more to Harper's work, one of the reasons that the book is so rich and why it
requires and will reward repeated readings. As university professor and professor of
English at Brown University for many years, Harper has developed an impressive intellectual grasp of literature and literary scholarship, permitting an engagement with
cultural, political, and aesthetic issues that informs poems suich as his "Frederick
Douglas Cycle," a group of eight poems that serves as an excellent introduction to and
evocation of Douglas's life. The towering presence of Ralph Ellison is apparent in
"The Body Politic," "The Pen," and "Goin' to the Territory," while the allusions and
references in "Queries to Alice Elizabeth: An Obituary, Palm Sunday, 1998," indicate
an exhilarating ease with a range of diverse cultural strains. While Harper has often
been praised for his mastery of "the oral traditions of jazz and the blues," there are few
contemporary poets who are as innovative and successful in utilizing forms that fit
their subject. In his later books, following some of the circumstances of perception
that he recounts in "Rhythmic Arrangements (On Prosody)," Harper has renewed

older forms such as the couplet and employed them so effectively and with such invention that the entire field of poetic possibility seems to have been enlarged.

In *Other Traditions* (2000), a collection of lectures wherein the well-known poet John Ashbery discusses six people whose work he likes, Ashbery mentions that he turns to them for a "poetic jump-start" at moments of creative emptiness. While this strategy is understandable—in some ways akin to Harper's responses to the music of blues and jazz giants—on the abundant evidence of *Songlines in Michaeltree*, it is unlikely that Harper is ever without the energizing fire of what could fairly be labeled his calling. As he puts it in the last paragraph of his "Notes on Form and Fictions": "In the best of times, when I was fully awake, the act of composition in the making of images was the only point at which I was fully alive."

Leon Lewis

Sources for Further Study

Publishers Weekly 247 (August 28, 2000): 79.
The Washington Post Book World, September 24, 2000, p. 12.

SOUL BY SOUL
Life Inside the Antebellum Slave Market

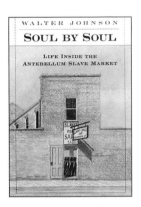

Author: Walter Johnson (1967-   )
Publisher: Harvard University Press (Cambridge, Mass.).
   Illustrated. 283 pp. $26.00
Type of work: History
Time: c. 1808-1865
Locale: Southern United States, especially the New Or-
   leans slave markets

~

*Centering on the New Orleans slave markets, this exten-
sively researched book documents, analyzes, and interprets the everyday business of the slave trade from the perspectives of slaves, traders, and buyers*

~

Soul by Soul is an impressive work of scholarship, winner of Harvard University Press's Thomas J. Wilson Prize, awarded to the best first book accepted by the press each year. Even though it is his first book, it is surprising to see that Walter Johnson, an assistant professor of history at New York University, wrote it while in only his early thirties. His research for the work is so voluminous and authoritative that one might imagine him as a senior scholar at the top of his field, but obviously he has many years as a leading scholar ahead of him.

Soul by Soul is not a chronological history full of big-name personalities; rather, it is an analytical history of everyday life in the slave trade, featuring nameless people, people with only one name, or people who have full names only because they were listed in court records or left written documents. Basing his work on extensive reading of nineteenth century slave narratives, Louisiana Supreme Court records, letters of slaveholders, and sales papers ("notarized Acts of Sale" and "traders' slave record books, price lists, and advertisements"), Johnson documents and interprets the domestic slave trade that reached its peak in the first half of the nineteenth century. The slave trade was spurred by two circumstances: The United States Constitution (1789) ended the importing of slaves after 1808, and the tobacco-growing areas around Chesapeake Bay declined while the cotton-growing areas of the Southwest (Alabama, Mississippi, Louisiana) prospered. By shuffling coffles, oceangoing vessels, and Mississippi River craft, hundreds of thousands of slaves moved from the older and upper parts of the South to the Southwest territory, served most prominently by the slave markets of New Orleans. These are the markets upon which Soul by Soul focuses.

Through the New Orleans markets, Johnson takes a close look at the commercial side of slave trading. For those in it, trading slaves was only a business, a capitalist

Walter Johnson is an assistant professor of history at New York University. Soul by Soul *has been awarded the Thomas J. Wilson Prize of Harvard University Press.*

venture, just another way to make a dollar. Nor was it exactly an easy way: There were many risks and problems, with the merchandise getting sick, dying, running away, or in general not co-operating. For both sellers and buyers, the merchandise was considered chattel. After a long overland drive, the slaves were "fed up" and allowed to heal so they would look like prime stock. At the market they were kept in "pens" and given the run of the "yard" for exercise. They were graded and priced according to such qualities as age, sex, size, and skin color. The blackest were considered the strongest for work in the fields, while lighter-skinned slaves were thought more suited for house duty. Slaves with special skills, such as cooking or carpentry, brought premium prices, and some women were sold as "breeders." Men were sometimes dressed in suits and top hats and women in calico dresses, and until 1852 in New Orleans it was legal to display them on the street outside the market. However, buyers were allowed to question and feel the merchandise, and there were undressing rooms where the product could be examined more intimately. In Louisiana there were also redhibition laws (lemon laws) that allowed returns for up to a year, and sometimes slaves were sold on a trial basis.

Even so, the rule of the slave market was "Buyer beware!" As Johnson points out, slick merchandising came into play: By and large, the traders were selling fantasies, and the buyers were shopping for fantasies. Besides feeding and dressing up the slaves, the traders sometimes doctored them up (with the help of physicians), invented nice-sounding life stories for them, and prompted the slaves to play the roles. Sometimes the slaves were made to dance and act happy, but warned not to say they had serious medical problems or had ever run away. Since the buyers were usually ignorant of the slaves' backgrounds, they were easily duped, so they might take along an experienced friend to help them make a purchase. However, they also contributed to their own fleecing by harboring fantasies of wealth, power, sex, and importance. The idea of ruling over their own little world of slavery was too much for some men to resist.

Johnson tells the story of one such man, John Knight, who dreamed of establishing a plantation utopia. Perhaps seeing himself as another Thomas Jefferson, he bought a Louisiana plantation and sent a shopping list for about sixty slaves to his father-in-law in Maryland. He also announced his plans to provide model housing, give the slaves a siesta during the hot part of the day, and hire a benevolent overseer. However, nothing turned out as he had planned. Upon inspection, the shipment of slaves from Maryland included one free man, two with phony names, and others who were sick; they could not stand the working conditions in humid, mosquito-infested Louisiana; and the overseer drove them unmercifully. Soon the slaves were dying in the fields or running away. Within a year, Knight's dream had turned into a nightmare, and he was desperately trying to cut his losses by selling the plantation and remaining slaves.

Still, spectacular failures such as Knight's did little to shake the overall social order of the antebellum South, where, as Johnson points out, slaves made (or unmade) the man. If a man had money to invest, slaves were the way to go. Besides anchoring the economy, slaves were status symbols, and the more one owned, the more status one had in the society. A man with many slaves could cut a fine paternalistic figure (after all, he took care of them all). However, acquiring even one slave made a man more imposing, and acquiring one for his wife made her a lady. Meanwhile, the poor man who had no slaves, who did the same work that slaves did, was hardly better than a slave himself. For these and other reasons, white Southerners wrapped their fantasies up in slaveholding and treated slaves as a form of property that one could do with almost as one pleased (including whipping and such bizarre gestures as giving a slave for a Christmas present).

In the final analysis, though, white Southerners could not deny the slaves' humanity without denying their own, and this impasse led to other rationalizations and contradictions at the heart of Southern slaveholding existence. A prime example is the slave market itself, which was not a respectable place. White people walking by were subject to offensive remarks by slaves on display outside (until the 1852 law put a stop to sidewalk vending). Word got around about white men seen in the slave market shopping for female flesh. Like other places of sin, the slave market was a man's world that no white woman would enter (although some white women bought and even trafficked in slaves by using their husbands as fronts), and it was walled off from sight in a neighborhood that would permit it, hiding the South's dirty little secret. Slave traders were stigmatized as lowlife shylocks: No good person would associate with such despicable riffraff. As for slavery itself, white Southerners rationalized it by developing theories of racism and paternalism that saw blacks as inferior creatures who needed a caring master. These theories had hard going, however, in the face of reality.

Reality included a third party to any slave deal: the slave. One might associate slavery with abject powerlessness, but Johnson shows convincingly that such was far from the case. There was always the possibility of a slave rebellion, especially when slaves were being transported on ships or in overland coffles and vastly outnumbered their captors. For example, Johnson tells about an 1841 rebellion aboard the *Creole* in which the slaves took over, imprisoned their captors, and sailed to freedom in Nassau—where their released former masters met them in the streets and begged them to reconsider! Johnson also cites examples of individual rebellion: Solomon Northup, a free man kidnapped into slavery who flogged his cruel master with a whip; and an unnamed woman with such a sharp tongue that her master and mistress returned her to the dealer. Sometimes rebellion took the form of self-mutilation (such as cutting off a finger or two) or suicide, but most often it consisted of running away. Many slaves ran away when driven to desperation by harsh working conditions or separation from spouse and family. For others, running away was a temporary expedient: Johnson tells about a woman who took her children and hid in the woods every time a slave trader appeared in the vicinity, and about a man for sale who hid in the woods until his master agreed to sell him to a neighbor.

These and other examples that Johnson gives show that the slaves sometimes had working interpersonal relationships with their masters and formed intricate networks of communication among themselves. His examples also show that slaves had the ability to influence, to some extent, their own sale. When families were being broken up for sale, they would cry heart-rendingly and occasionally affect the hearts of their masters or mistresses. In the slave markets the slaves would size up the buyers much as they were being sized up and behave accordingly (occasionally they even had intelligence from outside about certain buyers, especially those with a reputation for cruelty). The slaves had the advantage of being in control of information about themselves while sellers and buyers remained relatively ignorant: Although they had to be careful to avoid a whipping, the slaves could put on an act or conceal, reveal, and manufacture information about themselves at will. After the sale, if their buyer proved unworthy, they could also do things to bring about their return to the seller.

Johnson's constant awareness of slaves, sellers, and buyers interacting as people is possibly the strongest feature of *Soul by Soul*. However, nothing Johnson says lessens the inhumanity of slavery; on the contrary, his extensive documentation and sometimes lurid details bring home slavery's enormity. He thereby helps prevent slavery from becoming a mere historical abstraction, a forgotten American holocaust. In Johnson's hands slavery becomes part of living history whose influence continues into the present and even defines some national characteristics. Readers might consider him revisionist, a spawn of political correctness—a tendency seen in his language, which mixes diction from current commerce and performance theory with terms from slavery days. However, such language, aside from being used with literary subtlety, puts his subject into context and perspective: The greatest difficulty in reading *Soul by Soul* is imagining people as chattel, yet at one time this assumption was commonplace. Perhaps the shift in thinking is a measure of how far humans have come, yet one wonders what unexamined assumptions of today are likewise waiting to explode. In any event, Johnson is an excellent writer at the same time that he is a careful researcher. His fifty pages of documentation conveniently come as endnotes. The endnotes also contain a few choice items of information, but mostly they provide a rich bibliography for anyone investigating the "peculiar institution" of slavery.

Harold Branam

Sources for Further Study

Booklist 96 (February 15, 2000): 1077.
Library Journal 124 (November 15, 1999): 80.
The New Yorker 76 (March 13, 2000): 93.
Publishers Weekly 246 (December 20, 1999): 64.

THE SOUND OF ONE HAND CLAPPING

Author: Richard Flanagan (1961-   )
First published: 1997, in Australia
Publisher: Atlantic Monthly Press (New York). 432 pp.
    $24.00
Type of work: Novel
Time: The 1950's and 1990
Locale: Small work villages on Tasmania; Sydney, Australia

~

Bojan Buloh and his wife, Maria, and daughter, Sonja,
are refugees from Eastern Europe who settle in Tasmania
and struggle with a legacy of pain and trauma

~

    Principal characters:
        BOJAN BULOH, a Slovenian refugee who flees to Australia
        MARIA BULOH, his wife
        SONJA BULOH, their daughter

The novel opens ominously with a woman named Maria Buloh surreptitiously leaving her home to trudge off in the snow for an unspecified destination. As she prepares, her three-year-old daughter, Sonja, awakens and calls for her mother. Through a succession of eighty-six short chapters, the narrative shuffles between events in the 1950's and the thirty-eight-year-old Sonja's pregnancy in 1990.

Sonja and her father, Bojan, are refugees from Nazi-occupied Slovenia and have relocated to Tasmania in the hope of obtaining Australian citizenship and a better life. Like other refugees from Eastern Europe, Buloh can find only arduous work in the hydroelectric camps as the government undertakes a project of building dams and harnessing the region's abundant water. Buloh cannot adequately care for his daughter, so she is shipped off to a succession of foster homes where she is ignored, reprimanded, or sexually abused. Her fondest hope is reunion with her father, which eventually occurs, but not with the results she anticipates.

Her father is an emotionally blasted creature, a "wog," as the local vernacular has it, who breaks his back at work and his spirit at night at the local bar. Frequently, in fits of rage and self-disgust, he lashes out at Sonja, beating her so ferociously that her blood spatters the walls, and so fiercely on one occasion that she loses her sense of smell. There are intermittent moments of tenderness—when the two build furniture, when he sews a dress, and when they visit the apple farm of Jean Direen. However, Sonja's experiences emotionally deaden her, and she departs at sixteen, drifting through a succession of jobs in Sydney and from one loveless encounter to another.

After learning of her pregnancy, Sonja returns to Tasmania to inform her father

*Richard Flanagan won the 1995
Victorian Premier's Literary Award
for First Fiction and the South
Australian Premier's Literary
Award for Fiction for his first novel,
Death of a River Guide. He has
directed a film based on* The Sound
of One Hand Clapping, *which has
been released in Australia and
Germany.*

and lay her past to rest, but once again she encounters anger and disapproval. After another acrimonious quarrel, Sonja visits a friend of her mother who persuades her to stay on the island. Eventually Sonja quits her job and finds a dismal house to rent. Bojan gradually undergoes a change of heart and achieves a rapprochement with his daughter after she gives birth to a girl.

On the surface, the novel seems to be a sentimental potboiler, and indeed it is flawed throughout with melodrama and saccharine sentimentality; however, Flanagan does manage to plumb some serious themes. The first of these is the searing legacy of despair and self-destructiveness. Both Bojan and his wife are emotional *mutiles de guerre*, having witnessed unforgettable atrocities when the Nazis invaded Slovenia. Maria was raped at twelve and forced to watch her father's murder, and one of her cherished keepsakes is a grim photo of him lying in his coffin, a memento that Sonja inherits. Maria, however, is a thinly developed character, and thus the full weight of psychological trauma is evinced through the lives of Bojan and Sonya.

A young Bojan sees more in a few months than most do in a lifetime, and one of his most searing memories is of Slovenian partisans captured and executed by the Nazis, with the exception of one who is forced to dig a mass grave. When the digging goes slowly in the rocky soil, the Nazis

> made the partisan squat in his shallow hole and they filled the hole back in, leaving only the partisan's head exposed.
> Then they kicked that head back and forth like some weird fixed football until the partisan was dead. They left in a lighthearted mood, as if after a fine day's hunting. Bojan, fearful of being discovered, remained high up in the pine tree all the rest of the morning and all the afternoon, and only came down with the sun's descent. And all that long time he was in the pine tree Bojan sobbed silently, staring down at that head erupting from the earth at a broken angle, like a snapped flower stem.

Shortly after his wife's disappearance, Bojan and a crew are being transported to a work site when their truck halts in the woods and they view Maria's lifeless body hanging in a tree. Once again the memory is penetrating in its grim particularities:

> [They gazed] past the battered burgundy shoes to the small, delicate icicles already growing from the coat's frayed ends, and higher, higher yet, up that snow-rimed scarlet coat and though now giddy with horror still their gaze continued to rise; from the ice-stiffened old grey hemp rope that collared her garrotted neck like a snake-coil of steel; to the white face above it, with lolling tongue and milky, dead eyes.

The result is a life lived hard with a determination not to be touched emotionally. Late in the novel Bojan looks back on his past and views it as a "nightmarish hallucination." "Life had revealed itself to Bojan Buloh as the triumph of evil," and now he wages a silent war with that evil, never giving in but believing in its tenacity, until he opens himself to his daughter's and granddaughter's love and cautiously admits, "You know the world can only take so much happiness. So much happiness is good, but too much is a very bad thing."

Sonja inherits the family disposition to sadness, and it would seem that this is a legacy that will steamroll its way through the generations. Like her father, she builds up elaborate psychic armor, and others in the work camp notice how unlike other children she is, a child "who was not like a child at all, but whose face was a mask containing God knows what queer thoughts." She prides herself on her stoicism during her father's beatings and realizes that "the idea of love struck her once more as faintly comical, strongly treacherous, and forever elusive."

Like so many abused children, she sees adults as adversaries and wonders why they are always inexplicably angry at her. Their abuse is gradually transformed into self-loathing and a sense of diminishment. "For she felt guilt in her waking life, felt that all things, most particularly her own self, were her fault, and the fault was one of character, of a person who was ultimately incapable of good." She feels she is punished simply because she deserves it and that she lacks any essence. "Something had consumed everything Sonja was. . . . She felt as if there was nothing encased within her but ash." Her only comfort is her determination not to show emotion. "'You never cry,' said Sonja. 'No matter how bad you feel, you never cry.'"

A theme related to this legacy of anguish is that of history—global and personal. Both father and daughter often meditate on the past; it haunts them in dreams and reasserts itself everywhere. Both have their individual strategies for evasion, but like the water imagery that rains down and drenches everything (many, many scenes are set against torrential downpours), the past is invasive and engulfing. Bojan is obsessed with the war and the memory of his wife's disappearance, while Sonja wrestles with one recollection after another of domestic strife, and her preference is to become "a stranger to her past." For her, the nexus of public and private history arrives when she is driving home from work and learns that the Berlin Wall has fallen.

> It meant nothing to her, this news, that history, and she sat there enveloped in smoke, both part of and beyond history, forgotten by history, irrelevant to history, yet shaped entirely by it . . . in the end history—like the Berlin Wall—shaped her, but would not in the end determine her, because in the end it cannot account for the great irrational—the great *human*—forces: the destructive power of evil, the redeeming power of love.

From this emerges her desire to return home and come to terms with her history.

The chapters are arranged in kaleidoscopic fashion, oscillating between different points of view and dramatic temporal shifts. Through these, Flanagan is able to develop Bojan and his daughter as highly distinct, individual creations, and the fractured sequence mirrors the sense of fragmentation and disruption that blights their lives. However, the technique is overused, and many of the chapters read like set pieces, the work of a miniaturist who cannot find a more coherent structure for his narrative. This restricted scope may be due in part to the fact that the novel was written from the screenplay and film of the same name that Flanagan wrote and directed. Nevertheless, the technique in his hands is distracting, and many scenes are simply duplicative and deserving of trimming or even exclusion.

Flanagan is at his best when creating sharply defined images and motifs. One of the most telling of these is the tiny tea set that Sonja plays with as a child. The day after her mother's disappearance, some of the neighbor women attempt to distract the child by arranging the set on a box for an imaginary party. The impassive child methodically drops each piece until all are broken, symbols of the fractured lives she and Bojan will live. Those pieces remain with Sonja as an adult, tucked away in her purse and occasionally removed in futile attempts to reassemble them. The suggestion is that once broken, lives may never be repaired. However, the theme of redemption finds expression in these shards when Bojan, during Sonja's convalescence after giving birth, painstakingly repairs them. "Finally together in one piece, once more complete. She saw that his work was, as ever, true and careful, the few fractures that remained apparent only as hairlines." Not coincidentally, the tea set is restored at the same time Bojan determines to remain with his daughter and renounce his old life.

Another of these defining images is the edelweiss, flower of love, from Bojan's homeland. He recalls climbing the mountains to pick these flowers for Maria, and one in particular that he presented to her before their flight to Australia. Their star-shaped petals he likens to points on a compass that mark their direction away from their past and all that has scarred their lives. The night that Maria trudges off in the snow, she packs the odds and ends that define her meager existence, and at the top of her suitcase she places a dried edelweiss. The symbol is now of a dried-up love, and the compass leads only to deeper despair.

A third important image is the Tasmanian dam where Bojan finds work. The project is an ambitious government undertaking, which an official at Bojan's naturalization ceremony describes in decidedly inflated terms:

> "The path to the new Australia is lit not only by the electricity that will come forth
> from your labours here at Butlers Gorge, but by your conviction that the new world can
> be better than the old."

For all the seeming progress, though, the dam is an aging, decaying structure, and on a fateful journey to visit his daughter, Bojan narrowly escapes its collapse in a deluge. The parallel with the Bulohs and other refugees is unmistakable—for all their seeming solidity, they are fragile creations, easily broken and not so easily repaired.

The Sound of One Hand Clapping was awarded the Australian Booksellers Book of the Year award in 1997 and is Flanagan's second novel. It is a work of undeniable strengths, but one that is also flawed in serious ways. Flanagan's strength is the depth of his psychological insight, a depth of vision that could be strengthened if the novel were not so overwritten and in places emotionally overwrought.

David W. Madden

Sources for Further Study

Booklist 96 (December 15, 1999): 757.
The Economist 348 (July 11, 1998): S17.
Library Journal 125 (January, 2000): 158.
Los Angeles Times Book Review, March 12, 2000, p. 8.
The New York Times Book Review 105 (April 2, 2000): 22.
Publishers Weekly 247 (January 3, 2000): 55.
San Francisco Chronicle Book Review, May 21, 2000, p. 7.
The Times Literary Supplement, March 13, 1998, p. 22.
The Washington Post Book World, March, 26, 2000, p. 2.
World and I 15 (August, 2000): 246.

SQUARES AND COURTYARDS

Author: Marilyn Hacker (1942-   )
Publisher: W. W. Norton (New York). 107 pp. $21.00
Type of work: Poetry

≈

*Formalist poet Hacker's newest collection combines el-
egy and joy in these poems of friendship, love, and loss*

≈

Squares and Courtyards, Marilyn Hacker's ninth collection of poetry, is a moving and satisfying book of grace-
fully crafted poems. Although her topics center on loss,
disease, and death, the poems work through levels of sadness and obstacle to celebrate hard-won glimpses of possibility.

Hacker is one of the best known of contemporary poets, and her work has been recognized with numerous prizes and awards. Her collection *Winter Numbers* (1994)
won the Lenore Marshall Poetry Prize and a Lambda Literary Award; she received
other honors including the National Book Award, the Bernard F. Connors Prize, and
fellowships from the Guggenheim Foundation and the Ingram Merrill Foundation.
Editor of *The Kenyon Review* from 1990 until 1994, she also edited *Thirteenth Moon*,
a feminist literary journal, *The Little Magazine*, *Quark*, and a special issue of *Ploughshares*. Her editing has been characterized by a fruitful effort to open up journals to
subjects and ideologies not thought of as mainstream. Raised in the Bronx, Hacker
was soon aware of the prejudices and exclusions prevalent in the United States in the
1950's: Her parents were the first in their families to go to college, but were barred
from many professional jobs in New York because they were Jews. In her poetry
Hacker attacks and exposes prejudice and the many obvious and subtle forms it takes.

Hacker's experiences as a resident of two very different urban centers—New York
(where she served as director of the creative writing program at the City College of New
York) and Paris—are overwhelmingly present in her work, providing the "squares and
courtyards" where lives take shape, flourish, and end in her poems. The title poem links
Paris and New York and other cities of Hacker's life in a shifting narrative that traces
the relationship between self and history. These are intriguing poems of place, and yet
they are not travel poems or regional poems—they are more like tapestries that weave
person and place and history and the present into a single seamless fabric.

Although she is an outspoken political activist, Hacker writes poetry that is nevertheless poetry first. She uses received and invented forms to communicate thoughts and
impressions both universal and particular. The politics of her poetry are effective because they are organic to the poems; the poetry of the work is not garnish for politics.
Often the forms seem more flexible than they actually turn out to be, if the reader traces
them attentively, because they do not draw attention to themselves. Some forms are

more obvious, such as the haiku sequence and the
crowns of sonnets, but even there the form seems
gently directive rather than controlling.

    Squares and Courtyards uses a variety of
forms including the haiku, sonnet sequences,
sapphic verse, and less commonly known patterns, some of recent invention, to celebrate and
mourn memorable and memoir-worthy individuals. The poems seem to surge within the forms
like the sea in its tides, the emotion within the
poem unobtrusively contained. What makes these poems appealing to those who are
ordinarily not readers of formal poetry is their apparent ease and lack of strain, which
is complemented by precision of language and image.

Marilyn Hacker teaches English at Hofstra University. She is the author of eight other books of poems, including Winter Numbers, Selected Poems: 1965-1990, *and* Love, Death, and the Changing of Seasons.

    These poems have a lot of pain in them, particularly but not exclusively women's
pain. Breast cancer looms large, and the poems on this subject speak of and to the increasing number of women who undergo treatment, are returned to their lives, and
find their world transformed by the experience itself and by the realization that they
cannot know for sure that the cancer will not recur. Most live but some do not, and this
awareness underscores daily experiences and reconfigures relationships. The reader
is made aware of breast cancer not with an icon, but with an irony-tinged epigram instead in "A Colleague":

> Head in my office, one foot in the hall,
> she poised her briefcase—briefly—on a shelf.
> "We're all just waiting for the axe to fall.
> I ought to have a mammogram myself."

    Yet one of the most memorable poems here is about the death of a man, a street
person. In "Street Scenes: Sunday Evening," Monsieur Guy has died of cold, and in
the church his friends stand out in sharp contrast to the comfortable bourgeois churchgoers. The opening lines set the scene directly and unsentimentally:

> Flowers at the plinth, curbside, said he wouldn't be back—
> a bucket of red tulips, with a sign:
> he died the night of February 9th
> of cold—hand-scrawled, but worded like a plaque
> for an assassinated partisan
> "shot here in '42 by the SS."
> His friends (it said) are invited to Mass
> at the Eglise St-Paul, rue St-Antoine.

The tightly formal narrative evokes the pathos of the street death and the community
of outcasts it brings together briefly, in the shadow of those dressed in "Mink/ coats,
camels' hair" who occupy the center pews. Haves and have-nots are together briefly
on the neutral ground of the church, where the regular mass is being conducted for the
usual parishioners. Then the "young street musicians"

> struck up unfunereal Vivaldi
> as recessional music Monsieur Guy
> (and I) had heard on numberless Sundays.
> We went to our respective fasts and dinners.

The scene brings into sharp relief the Parisian consciousness of class. The street people are social and have their own community not far from that of the comfortable churchgoers who ignore them.

The formal distance of this piece, however, is unusual; most of the book is charged with pain and light, seemingly directly experienced in the form of deaths of friends, encounters with death, contrasts between a past and a present which are both problematic and grief-dimmed. The joy comes from glimmers of beauty that slip into the scenes and from the happiness of friendship and love, even when these things are threatened—perhaps because of the threat. How death is perceived and reacted to by the young, the middle-aged, and the old is described in telling detail, as the subjects range from the speaker's daughter, who has lost her best friend in a senseless accident, to her old friend Zenka, dying in London at eighty-four.

"Paragraphs from a Daybook" is a sequence of fifteen-line rhymed poems that are mostly elegiac in tone although slivers of pleasure and joy shine through here and there. The form was invented by Hayden Carruth, who makes a cameo appearance in the poem; it is a rhymed poem he gave the quirky name of "the paragraph" and a rhyme scheme of *ababaaccdedefef*. The paragraph has a variety of line lengths: lines 3 and 10 are 3-stressed, lines 7, 8, and 12 are 4-stressed, and the remainder of the lines are iambic pentameter. The effect is similar to that of a flexible iambic pentameter, although it is a more complicated (and much more demanding) form. The poems reflect on details of Hacker's childhood and the interconnection between her life and her friends' lives and her life and the elements of history that she has directly and indirectly experienced. Growing up Jewish in the United States, connected, though not within the nuclear family, to the Holocaust, learning what death is and finding it more and more a shadow over life—these experiences are detailed and their connections traced. The section beginning with an address to Hayden takes on a tone of longing and regret that sounds a little like Wallace Stevens:

> Death is the scandal we wake up to, Hayden:
> that flash in childhood, then every blue day.
> Once conscious of desire, we're laden
> with its accountability.
> Death and the singer; death and the maiden:
> duets you've taken both voices, and played in-
> to measured words, their numbers cast-
> out lines which lured a shape out past
> the lovely bodies which it mimed and praised.

The segment and much of the poem asks what the poet can make of death—the deaths of those nearest and her own. Part of the answer seems to be to let the fruits of earth, real and metaphorical, be tasted.

> Cherry-ripe: dark sweet *burlats*, scarlet *reverchons*
> firm-fleshed and tart in the mouth,
> *bigarreaux*, peach-and-white *napoléons*
> as the harvest moves north
> from Provence to the banks of the Yonne

The pleasure of the fruit is also the pleasure of words—the sweet delights of language, one of the stays against death. Then there is the whole delicious scene of the cherry sellers and the happy desire of the taster, the buyer. The French words themselves, identifying the different kinds of cherries, taste good to the reader. Does the dark randomness of accident, of deadly illness, cancel out the happiness of the cycle of desire and its satisfaction? Stevens asks a similar question in "Sunday Morning":

> Shall she not find in comforts of the sun,
> In pungent fruit and bright, green wings, or else
> In any balm or beauty of the earth,
> Things to be cherished like the thought of heaven?

Stevens's answer is a yes and a no, a combination of joy and elegy, in which language is a large portion of the verve of living. Hacker's answer may be similar, although in her work friendship and love loom larger in her book of delights, and her poetry expresses throughout a sense of social obligation. It is not sufficient or responsible to withdraw into a meditation or a world of words in Hacker's view; these are not poems that make the reader want to go out and sit under a tree and listen to grass grow; rather, they imbue the sense that things need to be done. Since death cannot be stopped, care and comfort for the dying and support for the bereaved should be provided. Words and experiences are indeed a delight, but not a solitary one. These messages are not expressed but telegraphed through the actions and reflections of the poems' speakers. There is a pleasure in community, in being not just a single self but a part of the life that flows through city streets, as she indicates in the wonderful series of haiku that constitutes "Letter to Munnsville N.Y. from the Rue de Turenne":

> Robust old women
> and men going to market
> pull their wheeled caddies
>
> along the pavement
> Sunday morning, as nuns go
> to break bread and pray.
>
> Sometimes I'd like to
> fade into the market crowd:
> shawled, sack of soup greens.
>
> Get rid of the "I"?
> One more woman gets on line
> at the bakery.

The poems of *Squares and Courtyards* are uncompromising, and they do not provide solutions for the loss and grief they explore. Indeed, the book ends on one of the harshest of the disasters narrated: the death of the speaker's grandmother in a street accident, when the speaker, as a child, was too small to have a sense of what had happened. The full story of the first death, which the speaker unknowingly played a part in causing, follows the others, suggesting an origin for the wound of loss that reverberates throughout the collection. The tough-mindedness of *Squares and Courtyards* is appropriate for a poet who has always avoided easy answers.

Janet McCann

Sources for Further Study

American Book Review 21 (September/October, 2000): 18.
Booklist 96 (January 1, 2000): 864.
Publishers Weekly 246 (December 6, 1999): 72.
The Virginia Quarterly Review 76 (Summer, 2000): 107.
The Yale Review 88 (July, 2000): 171.

STERN MEN

Author: Elizabeth Gilbert (1969-   )
Publisher: Houghton Mifflin (Boston). 289 pp. $24.00
Type of work: Novel
Time: The 1950's through the 1980's
Locale: Two islands off the Maine coast; Concord, New
  Hampshire

~

*The story of a resourceful young woman who manages
to bring peace to two warring islands and prosperity to the
lobstermen who live there*

~

Principal characters:
  RUTH THOMAS, a young woman from Fort Niles Island
  STANLEY THOMAS, her father, a successful lobsterman
  MARY SMITH-ELLIS THOMAS, her mother, now Vera Ellis's unpaid companion
  RICKY THOMAS, Ruth's retarded younger brother
  LANFORD ELLIS, a wealthy, elderly man, the only surviving son of Dr.
    Jules Ellis
  VERA ELLIS, his spoiled, selfish sister
  TOBY WISHNELL, a minister from Courne Haven Island
  OWNEY WISHNELL, his handsome nephew, a would-be lobsterman

The title story of Elizabeth Gilbert's short-story collection *Pilgrims* (1997) is about a city girl's abortive romance with a Wyoming ranch hand; in "Elks," another story from the same collection, relatives from the city visit a woman who has made her home in the rural West and who now seems as foreign to them as they do to her. *Stern Men*, too, is about people, place, and commitment. It is also about how a determined, intelligent woman can transform an entire community.

When he first sees her shortly after her birth in 1958, the aging bachelor Senator Simon Addams is sure that Ruth Thomas will be someone special. However, to the other residents of Fort Niles Island, she is just another lobsterman's child, though admittedly her father Stanley Thomas is better off than most. When she married Stanley, Mary Smith-Ellis Thomas left both Concord, New Hampshire, and the rich, selfish Vera Ellis, who considered Mary her personal handmaiden, on duty twenty-four hours a day. Mary and Stanley are happy together, and with the birth of a bright little daughter, their lives seem complete. Then, when Ruth is nine, the Thomases have a son, Ricky, who proves to be severely retarded. Shocked and grieved, Stanley points out that his family has never produced a child like Ricky and charges Mary with having unknowingly carried a genetic flaw. Mary knows very little about her antecedents.

Elizabeth Gilbert is writer-at-large for GQ *and has published fiction in many magazines. Her short-story collection* Pilgrims *was a finalist for the 1998 PEN/Hemingway Award, a* New York Times *Notable Book, and the winner of Best First Fiction awards from the* Paris Review, *the* Southern Review, *and* Ploughshares.

Her mother, Jane Smith-Ellis, was a foundling adopted by Dr. Jules Ellis, Vera's father, because his little Vera had asked for a playmate. Jane later produced an illegitimate child, and she would never identify the father of the baby, except to say that he was an immigrant, presumably one of the Italians who worked at the Ellis Marble Company, the source of the Ellis family fortune. Deeply hurt by Stanley's attitude and increasingly aware of the fact that her husband and she do not have the resources they will need if they are to keep their baby, Mary sees no alternative but to accept Lanford's proposition and return to Vera, who is only too willing to provide a home for Ricky and some assistance for his mother if Mary will come back into her service.

At the time, Ruth is too happy being mothered by an exuberant neighbor, Rhonda Pommeroy, to feel the loss of her own mother. Even after she goes back home, she still gets more than her share of attention from her father, Rhonda, Senator Simon Addams, and the rest of the islanders. Though she sometimes visits her mother in Concord, Ruth can never be as close to her as she once was. Vera has complete control over the household, including Mary; and whatever energy Mary has left after she has attended to all of Vera's needs she expends on her son.

However, if Mary has only a minimal influence over her daughter, Lanford and Vera Ellis are rich and powerful enough to make decisions on Mary's behalf, and they do not intend to have their niece's daughter be anything less than a credit to the Ellis family. After she has completed all the schooling the island offers, the Ellises send Ruth to boarding school in Delaware, and as soon as she graduates, they start discussing college. However, Ruth does not mean to remain on Fort Niles just for a summer. She does not intend to leave the island for college or any other project the Ellises may devise. To herself, Ruth has to admit that she may regret her obstinacy, for even though she misses Fort Niles when she is away from it, once she is back home she soon finds herself at loose ends. She would be happy working with her father on his boat, but he is adamant that lobstering is strictly for men. There are no longer any other jobs on Fort Niles, no new businesses unless one counts the hair-styling enterprise Rhonda started up after her husband was drowned. Ruth cannot even become a wife and mother unless she marries one of Rhonda Pommeroy's rowdy boys, and Webster, the only intelligent one of Rhonda's seven, has no interest in anything except digging for artifacts.

Like the Westerners in Gilbert's short stories, Ruth knows where she belongs. Even though Fort Niles does not seem to offer her much of a future, she will spend her life there. At this point, a third of the way through the novel, the author seems to have left only one question to be resolved by the end of the book: Will her heroine's obsession with place result in the waste of her considerable talents or will she find a way to make a life for herself without leaving her island? However, Gilbert does not settle for so simple-minded a plot. By the end of the novel, she has fitted every character, every incident, every seemingly casual observation into a marvelously complex story which, though often funny, has a very serious theme.

One example of this movement from what seems a simple situation to something much more complex involves Ruth's relationship with the Ellises. It is obvious that one reason Ruth clings so fiercely to her island is that by doing so, she sees herself as standing up to the Ellises. Ruth knows what happens when one gives in to them. Ruth's grandmother evidently committed suicide because she could no longer endure her life with Vera, and it may well be that if it were not for her devotion to her helpless son, Ruth's mother might have been driven to the same means of escape. Ruth is so conscious of the fact that Mary's connection with the Ellises cost her a husband, a daughter, and her very identity that she herself has a healthy fear of them. For that reason, she tries to avoid any contact not only with Vera but with Lanford Ellis as well. Although he is much more likeable than his dictatorial sister, Ruth suspects that he is just as dangerous. Moreover, she recognizes in him an intelligence at least as sharp as her own and, despite his age, a will as strong as hers. Every time she is with Lanford, Ruth feels that he is scheming to deprive her of her very identity. Moreover, to the islanders, the Ellis family represents wealth, power, and big business, and Ruth is committed to the lobstermen, who, like her, value their independence above all.

If the novel were simply a matter of Ruth's fate, it would be hard to justify the author's beginning her book with an eleven-page prologue, filled with what purports to be historical background, though readers know the islands to be fictional creations. In the eighteenth century, readers are told, one brother killed another brother, murdered his children, and took his wife, who was more fruitful than the woman he had married. The author then proceeds to an account of the twentieth century lobster wars between the people of Fort Niles Island and those who lived on Courne Haven, people so closely related that they all look alike, attend the same churches, hold the same political views, and share both a passion for independence and a distrust of outsiders. There was no antagonism between the two islands until lobster became a delicacy instead of a nuisance and, just as in the earlier incident, covetousness took over. Ever since the islanders became lobstermen, there has been intermittent violence, and the people of the two islands have hated one another.

Only Stanley's late father, Ebbett, had the good sense to pull out his traps while the lobstermen were fighting, thereby avoiding the financial losses they all suffered and winning the respect of Dr. Jules Ellis, who could appreciate sound business decisions. The significance of this account does not become evident until much later in the book, when the author begins to tie the various threads of her plot together. Similarly, one might not even notice the author's paragraph about how how much better the islanders would have done if they had cooperated with each other, rather than attempting to destroy each other. However, later it becomes evident that, in the prologue, Gilbert has not only prepared for a happy ending as far as Ruth is concerned, but also has indicated that her novel is about war and reconciliation, hatred and redemptive forgiveness.

When Ruth first approaches Lanford, she thinks of him as the embodiment of evil. Even when he offers her some concession, as when he agrees to give Senator Simons his natural history museum, Ruth continues to suspect Lanford of Machiavellian machinations, though she does see something of herself in his quick wit and strong will. As time goes on, however, they gradually learn to trust each other, and by the end of *Stern Men* they have become friends.

Though she had no intention of doing so, Ruth also plays an important role in putting an end to the hostility between Fort Niles Island and Courne Haven Island. Ruth and the minister's nephew, Owney Wishnell, fall so violently in love that even the inter-island feud cannot keep them apart. However, though they do get married, it is not their romance but Ruth's business sense that brings the two families and the two islands together. It is Ruth who brings together her father and the best businessman from Courne Haven and persuades them to consider how cooperative buying and selling would increase their profits. They are so successful that the rest of the islanders soon decide they can no longer afford hostility. The book ends with an epilogue set six years after Ruth's permanent return to Fort Niles Island. Whereas the prologue focused on conflicts, the epilogue emphasizes good feeling. The two islands have become one prosperous community. Ruth has a husband she loves, a growing family, a business she enjoys, and the house she has always wanted.

If the conflicts in *Stern Men* are perhaps resolved too easily, the author must be forgiven for erring on the side of hope instead of despair. Moreover, even if one does not believe that love will bring hostile families together, Gilbert is very persuasive as to the power of profit. *Stern Men* is a fine first novel, with an interesting setting, believable characters, and dialogue that always rings true. Elizabeth Gilbert's most impressive achievements, however, are her flawless plotting and her intricate interweaving of plot and theme. Like a magician, she points out one element, then another, and then still another, until, with a final flourish, she reveals the truth, that everything in her book is part of a marvelous whole.

Rosemary M. Canfield Reisman

Sources for Further Study

Booklist 96 (April 1, 2000): 1434.
Entertainment Weekly, May 19, 2000, p. 68.
Fortune 142 (July 10, 2000): 314.
Library Journal 125 (April 1, 2000): 129.
The New York Times Book Review 105 (June 4, 2000): 18.
Publishers Weekly 247 (March 20, 2000): 71.

SUSAN SONTAG
The Making of an Icon

Authors: Carl E. Rollyson and Lisa O. Paddock
Publisher: W. W. Norton (New York). 370 pp. $29.95
Type of work: Literary biography
Time: 1933-1999
Locale: New York, California, Chicago, Boston, Paris,
  Vietnam, Korea, Poland, and Sarajevo

≈

*The first, and unauthorized, biography of the American
leftist intellectual essayist, fiction writer, and political activist Sontag, a book which diminishes rather than en-
larges its subject*

≈

Principal personages:
> SUSAN SONTAG, leftist intellectual, essayist, and fiction writer
> DAVID RIEFF, her son, literary editor and independent journalist
> ALFRED CHESTER, fiction writer and Sontag's onetime intimate
> MARIA IRENE FORNÉS, painter, playwright, and Sontag's first serious
>   lover
> ROGER STRAUS, Sontag's longtime advocate and publisher
> CAMILLE PAGLIA, cultural critic and longtime Sontag adversary
> EDMUND WHITE, fiction writer, essayist, and Sontag's onetime intimate
> ANNIE LEIBOVITZ, celebrity photographer and Sontag's longtime com-
>   panion

The fact that Carl Rollyson has previously written unauthorized biographies of
Marilyn Monroe (*Marilyn Monroe: A Life of the Actress*, 1986), Lillian Hellman
(*Lillian Hellman: Her Legend and her Legacy*, 1988), and Rebecca West (*Rebecca
West: A Life*, 1996) tells something about his fascination with women who blur the
lines between art and celebrity. In stark contrast to the romantic image of the great artist as one who works best in a state of solitary confinement under a series of depriva-
tions, Rollyson's biographical subjects are figures who revel in pleasure, thrive in the
spotlight, vigorously court public opinion, and who are as obsessed with their image
as they are with being consummate artisans in their respective fields. Their strong
physical presence and overt erotic character complicate their relationships with their
contemporaries, their critics, and their devoted "fans."

Rollyson, an English professor at Baruch College, and his wife Lisa Paddock, a
lawyer and freelance writer, make it clear when they write that "Sontag's striking
looks seem inseparable from her intellectual appeal," that they are drawn to writing
the life of Susan Sontag precisely because of what they perceive to be her iconic ce-

~

Carl Rollyson is a professor of English at Baruch College. He has published biographies of Marilyn Monroe, Lillian Hellman, Martha Gellhorn, Norman Mailer, and Rebecca West, as well as Biography: An Annotated Bibliography.

~

Lisa Paddock is a former English professor and lawyer. She now works as a freelance writer and is the author of many essays, articles, reviews, and books, including Facts About the Supreme Court, Contrapuntal in Integration: A Study of Three Faulkner Short Story Volumes, Herman Melville A to Z, *and* The Brontës A to Z.

~

lebrity status in American letters and culture. In one moment of exuberant hyperbole, they even compare her to the goddess Athena. Somewhat under the sway of Sontag's physical attractiveness and amazon-like public persona, both drawn toward and repelled by what they term their "magnetic" subject, they are ultimately less interested in understanding the life through the work than they are in dissecting Sontag as "a dream of Susan Sontag." Viewing Sontag as a sensual and visual object as much as an author, book jacket photographs of Sontag receive almost as much attention as the content of Sontag's writings. Their book, therefore, more properly belongs in the genre of gossipy celebrity biography than critical or literary biography, with Sontag herself as the unwilling subject. Sontag's rich and varied career is somewhat glossed over in favor of more deeply analyzing the machinations and cultural effects of her self-promotion, glamour, and fame.

For Rollyson and Paddock, the evolution of Sontag the celebrity icon involved an "act of will" extending over decades, and their book takes apart the life and career of Sontag as if it were an image-projecting machine that bears not only the marks of Sontag becoming Sontag, but also of the times in which she lived and worked. The close and often incestuous intellectual and artistic circles of writers, critics, and publishers who lived and worked in Paris and New York City from the 1960's through the 1980's come under special scrutiny. Of more interest than the value of the content of Sontag's writings are the ways in which those writings were packaged and marketed, and their critical reception managed and controlled by Sontag and her longtime publisher, Roger Straus. Sontag's political activism is also described as a series of staged and managed "events," rather than pure gestures of a radically leftist political sensibility. Rollyson and Paddock do not themselves level the accusatory finger at Sontag so much as they allow her contemporaries and critical observers to demystify and derail what is often described in their book as her lofty, haughty, and moral persona. While negative assessments of her drive for power and fame predominate throughout the book, the authors also include positive assessments of her writings, activism, and personal and professional behavior that occasionally reveal Sontag's warmer and more generous side. Nonetheless, it is only when detailing Sontag's initial bout with cancer in 1975, and her subsequent writing of *Illness as Metaphor* (1978), that the authors of this biography seem to be in outright sympathy with their subject; for the most part, Sontag comes off as a smart yet self-important and icily stupefying gorgon.

Sontag herself has always been reticent regarding details from her childhood, portraying herself as solitary and bored by her surroundings and sharing anecdotes that highlight her intellectual precociousness, and for the most part the biography echoes this viewpoint. Sontag was born on January 16, 1933, in Manhattan to Mildred and Jack Rosenblatt, who spent much of their time in China, where Sontag's father had a fur trading business, while Sontag lived with her grandparents. When Sontag was five, her father died of tuberculosis, and her mother moved Susan and her younger sister, Judith, first to Miami and then to Tucson, where they eventually lived in an extremely modest bungalow on a dirt road, quite a few steps down from their former life. It was in the backyard of this house that the ten-year-old Susan dug a six-by-six-foot hole because she wanted "a place to sit in." The authors return to this hole several times throughout the biography. They see it as a metaphor for Sontag's introspective nature and dark sensibility, as well as for her lifelong desire to be in the "world elsewhere," which usually means Europe, a place she is drawn to again and again in her life and work. In 1945, Sontag's mother married Captain Nathan Sontag, and in 1946 the family moved to California, where Sontag attended North Hollywood High. For the most part, Sontag is depicted in her early years as having been a voracious reader and intellectual prodigy who emulated Marie Curie at the age of ten, shared André Gide's dedication to the cult of art at age thirteen, visited Thomas Mann as a high school student, and enrolled at the University of Chicago at the tender age of sixteen after one semester at Berkeley. Sontag was drawn to the university's legacy of student activism, its demanding Great Books approach, and its European ambience.

At Chicago, Sontag immediately placed into graduate courses, where she studied with such scholarly greats as Leo Strauss and Kenneth Burke, who once described her as "a genius in the making." She finished her degree in less than two years. Perhaps the most decisive event of Sontag's time at Chicago was her first encounter in 1950 with Philip Rieff, an instructor of sociology. Sontag turned up as an auditor in Rieff's class, Social Science II, in December of her second year and they were married ten days later. He was twenty-eight; she was seventeen. One of the most often-repeated anecdotes regarding this match is that when Sontag was eighteen and she was reading George Eliot's *Middlemarch* (1871-1872), she burst into tears because, in her words, she "realized not only that *I* was Dorothea but that, a few months earlier, I had married Mr. Casaubon." Despite these early misgivings about marriage to "a reactionary pedant," Sontag and Rieff moved to Boston, and on September 28, 1952, Sontag gave birth to their son, David. In 1954 Sontag enrolled at Harvard, where she received her master's degree in philosophy. At the same time Sontag was helping her husband with the book that would establish Rieff's reputation, *Freud: The Mind of the Moralist* (1959). Despite all this activity, Sontag was feeling restless and perhaps constrained by marriage and motherhood, and after receiving a fellowship from the American Association of University Women that would help her to prepare a doctoral dissertation on ethics at St. Anne's College, Oxford, she left for England in the fall of 1957. Rieff went to Stanford at the same time to take up a fellowship, and David was left with Philip's family.

Sontag never finished her doctoral thesis; finally giving in to the urge to live in the exotic "world elsewhere," she moved to Paris. Supposedly she was going to continue her studies at the Sorbonne after her first semester at Oxford, where she had been disenchanted by England's "sadly arrogant provincialism." Paris provided Sontag with her true contemporary education, and it is at the moment Sontag arrives there in the winter of 1958 that the authors finally begin to hone their true subject: the "making" of a cultural icon. From this point forward, the book charts Sontag's supposedly continual pursuit and seduction of the artistic, beautiful, connected people through whom she will ascend into the orbit of literary stardom. Her first important connection was to Alfred Chester, a young fiction writer from Brooklyn who was edging himself into notoriety after his first three books, and whom Sontag met through an old friend from Berkeley. Chester was able to introduce Sontag to writers who published in *Commentary*, *Partisan Review*, and *The Paris Review*. It is in Paris that Sontag pursued a more sensual life, nurturing the "new sensibility" for the avant-garde and the artist *engagé*, while also aspiring to the status of the elite artists she met there. Her marriage to the provincial Rieff suffered in the implied comparison. Upon arriving back in the United States in 1959, she told Rieff that she wanted a divorce, and at the age of twenty-six she reclaimed David from Rieff's parents and moved to New York, where she was clearly intent, according to the authors, on "making it."

For Rollyson and Paddock, the decisive event of Sontag's new and ambitious life in New York was the taking up of her career by Roger Straus, of the eminent publishing house of Farrar, Straus (soon to be Farrar, Straus and Giroux), who "encouraged her to regard herself as a special case." The authors would seem to imply that Sontag's first novel, *The Benefactor* (1963), which Chester called "her very boring first novel," was not a particularly strong or easily accessible work, but because Straus was so smitten with "the idea of Susan Sontag," he became her literary impresario, championing her work and engineering every last detail of her career, thereby ensuring her future success and stature. Although reviews of *The Benefactor* were mixed and its sales weak, the brilliant success of Sontag's essay "Notes on Camp," in *Partisan Review*'s fall 1964 issue, catapulted her into a position as one of the hottest properties in the cultural spotlight, and the publication of her first collection of essays, *Against Interpretation*, in 1966 ensured her future as one of the literary lions in Farrar, Straus and Giroux's den.

Much of the rest of the book is taken up with tracing Sontag's supposedly carefully orchestrated career, in which she avoids teaching and lecturing whenever possible in order to spend all her time writing, switching back and forth between fiction and cultural criticism, with occasional forays into film and stage directing, finally resolving to be, with *The Volcano Lover* (1992) and *In America* (2000), a traditional and even best-selling novelist. When she does venture out to teach or lecture on the book circuit, she is often depicted as overly demanding and ungracious. Also charted are Sontag's adventures as a political activist, first in North Vietnam in 1968, in Israel in 1973, in North Korea in 1988, and finally in Sarajevo in the early 1990's. In each instance, Sontag's activism is seen as a blend of aggrandizing self-promotion and misguided good intentions. Sontag is also portrayed as an apostate who rejects once-promulgated leftist viewpoints and even publicly castigates the leftist intelligentsia when it serves her self-promoting purposes. Although mainly characterizing her rule as president of the American PEN Center from 1987 to 1989 as contentious and commissar-like, the authors provide a lot of testimony to Sontag's courage for being one of the first writers to speak out against the death sentence pronounced on the British novelist Salman Rushdie by the Iranian government in 1989.

Rather than analyzing her various works with an eye toward revealing Sontag's inner life, those works are breezily summarized, with the authors' attention mainly focused upon Sontag's personal and professional behavior, and the voices of those with old axes to grind predominate. The authors even comment, in their concluding chapter, in what is a sweeping dismissal of the possible longevity of Sontag's work, that "[i]t is probable that she will be renowned for her style and form long after the specific content of her work falls into desuetude." In every chapter there is at least one disquisition, if not several, upon Sontag's "look." Much attention is paid to her various hairstyles, outfits, and book jacket photographs, which are seen as having been carefully staged by Sontag to ensure her iconic status as a sensual, alluring, and powerful intellectual figure who defines the hippest contemporary moment. Perhaps the most sensationalist aspect of the biography is the "outing" of Sontag's various lesbian love affairs, apparently never a secret to the New York and Parisian literary worlds. Sontag is taken to task by various writers, including her onetime friend and openly gay novelist Edmund White, for not being more open about her sexuality and for not foregrounding it in her work, especially in *AIDS and Its Metaphors* (1989). Even Sontag's close relationship with her son, David, comes under criticism for being unseemly and unnatural in its intimacy, and for the fierce way the two protect and defend each other's work.

Because Rollyson and Paddock's biography relies so heavily for its testimony upon those who are many steps removed from Sontag's closest circle of acquaintances and family, and because those who know her best would not speak to the authors, the biography has a tendency to read like a tabloid version of a life. Furthermore, because the authors eschew footnotes and citations keyed to exact page numbers, and instead provide chapter-by-chapter summaries of sources at the end of the book, one cannot be altogether certain of the accuracy or objectivity of the events described in the book. Additionally, much testimony within the biography itself is quoted and paraphrased out of context. However, Rollyson and Paddock are not far off the mark when they contend, as they do throughout their book, that Sontag is an elusive, purposely self-mystifying figure who sees herself as a "dream of self-creation, of self-fulfillment, of standing alone." In the last pages of Sontag's novel *The Volcano Lover*, the poet and radical newspaper publisher Eleonora de Fonesca Pimentel, seen by many critics as a sly self-portrait of Sontag herself, tells the reader, after her own violent death during the Neapolitan Revolution of 1799, that "I was independent. . . . I did not think of myself as a woman first of all. . . . I wanted to be pure flame." It seems fitting somehow to let Sontag have the last word here.

Eileen A. Joy

Sources for Further Study

Booklist 96 (June 1, 2000): 1795.
Choice 38 (December, 2000): 709.
The Economist 357 (October 21, 2000): 100.
Library Journal 125 (August, 2000): 104.
The New York Times Book Review 105 (October 29, 2000): 16.
Publishers Weekly 247 (June 12, 2000): 61.
The Village Voice 45 (July 18, 2000): 61.

TALKING DIRTY TO THE GODS

Author: Yusef Komunyakaa (1947-   )
Publisher: Farrar, Straus and Giroux (New York). 134
   pp. $23.00
Type of work: Poetry

~

*Award-winning poet Komunyakaa offers 132 new po-
ems, each one composed of four quatrains, juxtaposing
mythology, jazz riffs, and contemporary culture in an un-
ashamed examination of life in all its forms*

~

Born in Bogalusa, Louisiana, in 1947, Yusef Komunyakaa has traveled far in his
poetic journey. His awards range from the Bronze Star he won while serving in the
Army during the Vietnam War to the 1994 Pulitzer Prize for his collection *Neon Vernacular: New and Selected Poems* (1993). This volume also won the Kingsley Tufts
Award, and the William Faulkner Award. His collection *Thieves of Paradise* (1998)
was a 1999 National Book Critics Circle Award finalist, and he continues to accumulate critical praise for his work. A prolific writer, in 2000, the same year he published
Talking Dirty to the Gods, he also published a collection of essays and criticism, *Blue
Notes: Essays, Interviews, and Commentaries.* Yet another collection of poetry, *Pleasure Dome: New and Collected Poems 1975-1999*, appeared in spring of 2001.
Komunyakaa, a professor in the Council of Humanities and Creative Writing program at Princeton, has published nine collections of poetry, two anthologies, and a
number of recordings, including collaborative efforts with musicians.

Critics and scholars have tried to describe Komunyakaa as a Southern writer, or a
black writer, or a Vietnam War poet, or a jazz poet. In truth, all of these descriptions
fit. In works such as *Dien Cai Dao* (1988), for example, Komunyakaa demonstrates
his ability to translate lived trauma into poetry of witness. Yet none of these
descriptors do justice to the range of Komunyakaa's talent. It would be better, perhaps, to cease trying to slip him into some easy category and instead to examine
Komunyakaa as a poet of the first degree, a writer whose impact will continue to exert
influence on writers for years to come.

There may be no better place to start than with Komunyakaa's 2000 volume of poetry *Talking Dirty to the Gods*. In this work, Komunyakaa turns away from the free-
form verse and short lines that have characterized a good deal of his poetry and
toward a formal, highly structured, highly polished series of four-line, four-stanza
poems. Always the innovator, Komunyakaa challenges himself to create a complete
book of lyric meditations controlled by the four-line, four-stanza form. In the hands of
a less talented poet, such an experiment could have turned tedious at best and disastrous at worst. Komunyakaa's language and subject matter, however, are so inven-

∼

*Yusef Komunyakaa teaches at
Princeton University. He has
written eleven books of poems,
including* Thieves of Paradise, *a
finalist for the National Book
Critics Circle Award, and* Neon
Vernacular, *for which he received
the Pulitzer Prize.*

∼

tive, so quirky, and so well integrated that the form does not detract. Indeed, the form, so well established and evident on the printed page, becomes fluid and flexible in the reading, as if the poems need the human voice to provide the variety and rhythm that the rigidity of the form might seem to preclude. There is something almost Zen-like in the practice, in the way that Komunyakaa's poems become meditations on life on Earth within the boundaries of his chosen form.

Talking Dirty to the Gods takes as its subject all forms of life, from slime molds, wasps, and Greek gods, to absent lovers, contemporary artists, and dead poets. In these poems, Komunyakaa's language can be jazzy, serious, allusive (and elusive), satiric, or all of the above, sometimes in the same poem. The poems, then, are connected by their attention to the traditions of the past as well as by the inventiveness of the language.

Komunyakaa's desire to make internal connections among these poems is evident in several ways, including his use of titles. The first poem is called "Hearsay," while the last is "Heresy." Within the volume are poems titled by each of the seven deadly sins, forming yet another internal link. There are also poems that seem to carry on an internal dialogue with each other, most notably "The Goddess of Quotas," "The God of Variables," "The Goddess of Quotas Laments," and "The God of Variables Laments." Further, he links an additional two poems by their gender opposition, "Incubus" and "Succubus."

Komunyakaa includes a number of poems titled by months and arranged chronologically. Beginning with his poem "Janus," Komunyakaa introduces the notion of passing time: "The new year/ Gazes back to Lot's wife/ Lost in a dream of summer/ While the season's first snow falls." At nearly the end of the book, Komunyakaa returns to this theme in "November's Nocturne": "A rainstorm slants into an icy/ Wedge. Windows & doors whine/ A jam session of bedsprings/ In love's deep twilight. . . . " The passage from winter, through spring and summer, and back to winter again provides a subtle frame for the collection, a frame that reflects the mutability and melancholy of conscious life.

Many of the poems in the volume draw on Komunyakaa's extensive knowledge of mythologies of the world, including Judeo-Christian beliefs, as well as on his connections to jazz and his intense interest in the natural world. Indeed, a reader with little knowledge of classical allusions may be daunted by the dazzling variety of mythological characters who people his poems. In "Infidelity," for example, Komunyakaa uses the Greek god Zeus, known for his amorous affairs, as his subject: "Zeus always introduces himself/ As one who needs stitching/ Back together with kisses." In the lovely "Pyramus and Thisbe," Komunyakaa uses the classical story of doomed lovers to relate something of his own life: "At nine,// I didn t know delicious words/ To say to a girl."

Komunyakaa does not limit himself to classical allusions, however. Sometimes musicians figure in his poems, as in "Speed Ball," a meditation on Chet Baker; sometimes his gaze includes eastern allusion, as in "Ukiyo-e." Sometimes he chooses to juxtapose unlikely allusions from different sources. In each case, however, his use of allusion is both deft and accurate. The result can be a wry humor; readers do not expect, for example, to find Pan "raising Cain." More often, the allusions serve to connect Komunyakaa's reflections to the very oldest and truest stories humans know.

Some of these stories include the troubled love between father and son. In the poem "Isaac," the narrator is Abraham's son. In the biblical story, God instructs Abraham to kill Isaac, only to stay his hand at the last possible moment. Komunyakaa gives Isaac these words: "I bear a knife scar,/ But still love him as a son/ Should. I am his terror./ Sometimes I sleep with one eye/ Open. He's made promises/ Anyone with good sense knows/ He can't keep. . . . " The edgy danger between father and son, between parent and offspring seems both troubling and true in Komunyakaa's lines. In a number of other poems, Komunyakaa alludes to the tools of his father's trade and to his father himself. "Meditation on a File" seems to do both. "You belong/ To a dead man, made to fit/ A keyhole of metal to search/ For light, to rasp burrs off/ In slivers thin as hair . . . "

Some of the stories are about love (and lust) between men and women. In "April's Fool," for example, the narrator recalls a young girl whose name he carved in an oak desk and who is killed by a car while riding her bicycle. He connects lust with words in the poem "Lust," conjuring the feel of a name on lips, "Words, juicy as passion fruit/ On her tongue." He also comments on the transitory, momentary nature of love and lust in his poem "May," a meditation that at first seems to be about mayflies, whose life span is a single day, a day of sex and death. Komunyakaa even refers to the fatal love between a man and woman in his poem "A Famous Ghost." In this poem, the narrator is the dead poet, Sylvia Plath, who committed suicide by putting her head in a gas oven. Her husband, Ted Hughes, found the rest of his poetic career tainted by the speculations surrounding Plath's death. Most telling, perhaps, is the line from the poem "My last breath// stole from his. . . . " marking Komunyakaa's recognition that death steals from life just as life steals from death.

Komunyakaa also includes many poems that take as their subjects the natural world. He writes of slime molds, polecats, raccoons, hyenas, and wasps, among others. Many of these poems concern the cycle of life, the way that life feeds off itself. In "Ode to the Raccoon," for example, Komunyakaa describes both the living raccoon and the raccoon on the plate, surrounded by sweet potatoes and red peppers. In this poem, he juxtaposes religious images such as that of the raccoon washing his "paws at the altar" with images of the raccoon hunt. The blessings that the raccoon ironically receives in the last line are those said across a table.

It is in poems such as "Bedazzled" where Komunyakaa's virtuosity seems most evident. "A jeweled wasp stuns/ A cockroach & plants an egg/ Inside. . . . " the poem opens. Again, the poet reflects on the way that life grows out of death; the young wasp larva uses the cockroach's living body as its sustenance, taking the roach's life force and making it his own. Although this event is from the natural world, there is nonetheless the sense of evil in this poem. The image of the "premature stinger" waiting "like a bad idea, almost// Hidden . . . " tightens the tension in the middle of the poem. There is a murderous quality to the wasp, a sense of the predatory made that much worse by its lack of consciousness and lack of conscience. In the last line, Komunyakaa tells the reader that the newly hatched wasp is as "Bright as Satan's lost tiepin."

The longer one spends with the collection as a whole, the more the poems seem to move in the same direction. Although each of the poems is individually powerful, and although the poems take on different subjects, the collection itself seems poised to say something important about the cycles of time, of space, of nature, of life. Komunyakaa builds the poems in opposition to each other in order to present the full picture; for each reference to a point in time, such as October, there is another reference to the conjoining of past and present, such as the comparison of Zeus to a rock singer. Nature, while portrayed in stunning images, is also brutal in these poems. Life is both sweet and melancholy, fertile and sterile.

Just as ritual connects people with their mytho-historic pasts, these little poetic rituals allow readers to observe the comic and tragic dimensions of all life, not just human. Through his heart-breaking facility with language and myth, Komunyakaa demonstrates a profound understanding of the ways that life feeds on death and death on life. This is a collection of poetry worth reading again and again, its subtle nuances unfolding slowly with each approach.

Diane Andrews Henningfeld

Sources for Further Study

Booklist 96 (August, 2000): 210.
Library Journal 125 (August, 2000): 110.
The New York Times Book Review 105 (December 10, 2000): 36.
Publishers Weekly 247 (July 24, 2000): 82.

THEREMIN
Ether Music and Espionage

Author: Albert Glinsky
Foreword by Robert Moog
Publisher: University of Illinois Press (Urbana). Illustrated. 403 pp. $34.95
Type of work: Biography, history, history of science, music, and technology
Time: 1896-1993
Locale: St. Petersburg (Leningrad), Russia; Berlin and Frankfurt, Germany; Paris, France; London, England; New York City, New York, United States; Kolyma, Siberia, Union of Soviet Socialist Republics; and Moscow, Union of Soviet Socialist Republics

~

The first English-language biography of a versatile inventor whose long career carried him from the worlds of science, technology, and music to those of political repression and intrigue

~

Principal personages:
> LEON THEREMIN (LEV SERGEYEVICH TERMEN), scientist and designer of musical instruments
> EKATERINA (KATIA) CONSTANTINOVA, Theremin's first wife
> ABRAM FEDOROVICH IOFFE, Theremin's scientific mentor
> JOSEPH SCHILLINGER, avant-garde composer
> LUCIE BIGELOW ROSEN, socialite and patron of the arts
> CLARA REISENBERG (later ROCKMORE), prominent thereminist
> LAVINIA WILLIAMS, Theremin's second wife

Even though few listeners are likely to recognize its name, almost everyone has at one time or another heard an electronic musical instrument known to the cognoscenti as the theremin (pronounced "THAIR-uh-min" in the English-speaking world). The Beach Boys' 1966 hit song "Good Vibrations" utilized the instrument to happy, loopy effect. Two decades earlier Miklos Rozsa's soundtrack to the Alfred Hitchcock film *Spellbound* (1945) had featured the theremin to suggest an undercurrent of paranoia. Since then countless B-grade movies have relied on the theremin's unearthly sound to establish an atmosphere of alien or supernatural menace.

The theremin takes its name from Russian inventor Leon Theremin (who preferred the Russian pronunciation of his name, "tair-MEN"). Theremin's genius led him to design and perfect a number of inventions, musical and otherwise, but it would also place him—as a citizen of what became the Union of Soviet Socialist Republics in

∼

Albert Glinsky is a composer and associate professor of music at Mercyhurst College, with degrees from The Juilliard School and a Ph.D. from New York University. His work has been honored by the National Endowment for the Arts and the American Academy of Arts and Letters.

∼

1917—in an extraordinarily precarious position. The twists and turns of Theremin's long life mirror the history of the twentieth century, and the details of that life are explored for the first time by composer and music professor Albert Glinsky.

Leon Theremin (or Lev Sergeyevich Termen, as he was known in his mother country) was born in St. Petersburg, Russia, in 1896. Young Leon was precocious, reading the encyclopedia at the age of three and repairing watches at seven. He began playing the piano at age five and the cello four years later, realizing even then that "there was a gap between music itself and its mechanical production." At a slightly older age Theremin began experimenting with magnetism and electricity.

Theremin's gifts marked him out in school, and as a result he was allowed to attend the lectures mounted by rising physics star Abram Fedorovich Ioffe in defense of his thesis and dissertation. Ioffe was so impressed with Theremin that he took him on as a protégé, a move that probably saved the student's life. When Theremin was drafted a few years later to fight in the First World War for the Tsar, his status and knowledge kept him out of the front lines, and he was instead assigned to an engineering school.

The first stages of Theremin's scientific and technical career found him in the forefront of radio and television ("distance vision") design. One of the most telling sections of Glinsky's biography describes how Theremin's inventions were pressed into the service of the new Soviet state for official communication and surveillance, while in the West such developments were marketed to the very proletariat that the Soviets ostensibly championed. For his efforts Theremin was hailed as "the Russian Edison," but he would eventually pay a high price for the bargain he had made with his masters.

Theremin's most important invention, and the one for which he is remembered, was the musical instrument eventually named after him. The theremin, which is the only musical instrument played without being touched, operates thanks to several principles of electronics. The first of these is heterodyning, which dictates that any two frequencies will combine to produce a third, lower, frequency equal to the difference between the original two. In the case of the theremin, one oscillator (or radio-frequency generator) produces a set frequency. Another oscillator, attached to an antenna, produces a frequency that varies as the player moves his or her hand in relation to the antenna—in technical terms, adding capacity or capacitance to the oscillator. The two original frequencies being generated lie in the radio spectrum, far beyond the range of human hearing, yet the resulting pitch is audible. A second antenna, mounted to a right angle to the first, allows the player to alter the volume—as conveyed by a loudspeaker—with his or her other hand.

Theremin initially called his invention the "etherphone," a reference to the medium—ether—that some scientists still believed filled space and conducted electromagnetic waves.

Theremin demonstrated his new invention to Abram Ioffe in October, 1920, and held a small recital of familiar classical tunes in November. Sensing a propaganda tool of enormous potential, the Soviet government pressed Theremin into touring with his impressive instrument, first within the Soviet Union and then, beginning in 1927, abroad. Following him at something of a distance was his wife, Katia, whom he had married in 1924. The toast of several European capitals, Theremin entered the United States in late 1927. Here he would license his invention with RCA, which built and marketed the theremin as a simple instrument that could be mastered in a matter of hours. At the same time, Theremin helped relay critical American technological information back to the Soviet Union under cover of an entity known as the American Trading Organization, or Amtorg. Katia followed Theremin to the United States in 1928, but she and Theremin ended up living apart and eventually divorced in 1934.

As Glinsky makes clear, Theremin was not the only electronic musical instrument designer of his time. The ideas that the Russian inventor employed were in the air, if not necessarily the ether. One Jörg Mager had developed what he called an "Electrophon" about 1921; subsequently refining and renaming it the "Sphärophon," he demonstrated it in public in 1926. Even earlier, in 1918, French inventor Armand Givelet had developed something he called the "Clavier à Lampe," demonstrating it in public for the first time in 1927. The following year another Frenchman, Maurice Martenot, introduced a highly sophisticated instrument that would eventually be known as the ondes martenot.

The greatest threat to the theremin came from American Lee De Forest, the self-styled "father of radio." De Forest was the inventor of the triode (or three-element vacuum tube) that had replaced the two-element tube in radio receivers. He had also, he would later claim, experimented with the heterodyne method of producing sounds in 1915. In any case De Forest's company successfully sued RCA in 1931 for patent infringement, and production of the theremin ceased.

At this point Theremin was aided by composer and fellow Soviet expatriate Joseph Schillinger and socialite Lucie Bigelow Rosen. The former wrote several compositions for the theremin, championed the inventor, and commissioned him to design several other instruments. The latter provided him with a well-equipped studio when his source of income from RCA dried up. During this time Theremin also met a young woman named Clara Reisenberg, destined (under the name Clara Rockmore) to become the most talented performer the instrument would ever enjoy. Yet the inventor found himself increasingly thwarted. His visionary schemes—which today one would recognize as very early versions of virtual reality and the Internet—far outstripped the existing level of technology necessary to support them. His financial affairs grew ever more complicated, eventually resulting in rifts with friends and supporters. Clara Reisenberg turned down his proposal of marriage. When, in 1938, Theremin instead married Lavinia Williams, a young art student whose ancestry was Irish, Native American and African American, yet more friends deserted him.

Theremin surreptitiously arranged to leave the United States in 1938 aboard a Soviet freighter. Although he was assured that Lavinia would be allowed to follow him shortly, it is hard to know whether he believed the promise. In any case, Theremin told

Lavinia nothing of his plans, and to her it appeared that he had been abducted. As it turned out, he might as well have been, for much of his subsequent life in the Soviet Union was bleak. Soon after his return, Theremin was caught up in the mass arrests sweeping the Soviet Union, spending nine months in Siberia. He was rescued in order to work on a series of state projects—first, warplanes, about which he knew nothing; and next, eavesdropping devices, about which, it turned out, he quickly learned quite a bit. For his efforts in successfully bugging the American, British, and French embassies in Moscow, Theremin was awarded—in secrecy—the prestigious Stalin Prize.

In 1991 American filmmaker Steven M. Martin tracked down Theremin in Moscow and brought him back to the United State for the first time in more than half a century. The documentary that Martin directed—*Theremin, An Electric Odyssey* (1993)—has played to enthusiastic audiences around the world and reintroduced Theremin to yet more generations. The day after the documentary premiered on British television, Theremin died.

Albert Glinsky worked thirteen years on Leon Theremin's biography, yet frustratingly enough, the life that he chronicles was one of missed opportunities. Many were due to the machinations of the Soviet state, while others were due to Theremin's own naïveté and occasional duplicity. Others still were simply bad luck. So overwhelming are the events that Theremin was involved in—his chaotic business ventures, the fury of Stalin's mad purges, the German invasion of the Soviet Union—that he sometimes vanishes from view. At one point Glinsky describes Theremin as being "weary of the whole corporate tangle," a sentiment that Glinsky's readers will share.

Perhaps the ultimate irony is that Theremin had little effect on the so-called "serious" or art music that he grew up playing and loving. Most of the original compositions featuring the theremin are forgotten; some were rewritten to incorporate more sophisticated instruments that minimized the troubling glissando, or "slide" between notes, that characterized the theremin. Instead, Theremin became a prime if unintentional force in popular music and other forms of entertainment. The theme of the radio serial *The Green Hornet* (1936-1952) was a theremin rendition of Nikolay Rimsky-Korsakov's "Flight of the Bumblebee"—a harbinger of things to come.

Theremin's ultimate importance lies in his influence on younger generations of inventors and musicians. Although Lee De Forest's 1931 suit destroyed the theremin commercially, countless electronic hobbyists later built their own versions of the instrument—a relatively simple project—to amaze their friends and neighbors. As Robert Moog explains in his foreword to Glinsky's biography, he put together his first theremin in 1949 and regards the Russian inventor as his "hero and virtual mentor." (Moog went on to design and build the musical synthesizers associated with his name today.) When Moog describes meeting the aged Clara Rockmore and helping restore her theremin—which she feared had deteriorated beyond repair—readers will grasp something of the love and enthusiasm that this neglected figure has aroused among his admirers.

Grove Koger

Sources for Further Study

Booklist 97 (October 1, 2000): 310.
Library Journal 125 (October 1, 2000): 100.
Publishers Weekly 247 (September 18, 2000): 99.
The Washington Post Book World, December 17, 2000, p. 6.

THOMAS KUHN
A Philosophical History for Our Times

Author: Steve Fuller (1959-   )
Publisher: University of Chicago Press (Chicago). 472
  pp. $35.00
Type of work: History of science, philosophy, sociology
Time: 1922-1996
Locale: United States and Western Europe

~

A polemic against Kuhn's The Structure of Scientific
Revolutions, *claiming that the book was sociopolitical in
origin, conventional (not revolutionary) in content, and ru-
inous in its influence on the natural and social sciences*

~

When Thomas S. Kuhn died on July 18, 1996, obituaries appearing in many academic as well as popular publications praised the work of this physicist, historian, and
philosopher as providing the twentieth century's most penetrating analysis of scientific development. His influential book *The Structure of Scientific Revolutions* (1962)
sold, in its English edition, more than a million copies, and its ideas spread via twenty-
five translations to countries around the world. Such Kuhnian terms as "paradigm
shift," which encapsulated his view of scientific revolutions, became inextricably intertwined with how scientists and other scholars analyzed what they did, and the term
became so popular that it appeared in *New Yorker* cartoons and as the name of a rock
group. In short, Kuhn's treatise accomplished what few scholarly books have ever
done—it changed the way specialists thought about their fields and shaped the way
the public understood science.

In *The Structure of Scientific Revolutions*, Kuhn saw history as possessing the
power to transform the image of science as a means of amassing discoveries. Before
Kuhn's work, thinkers about science saw its progress as the accumulation of deep insights by great geniuses, but after Kuhn, the "paradigm" became the central concept
for understanding the evolution of science. A paradigm is a universally recognized
scientific achievement, such as the sun-centered system of the Polish astronomer
Nicolaus Copernicus, that provides a model for how a community of practitioners interprets phenomena and solves problems. During "normal science," the paradigm
provides a scientific community with a context for articulating its ideas and applying
them to new situations. However, scientists sometimes encounter new phenomena
(anomalies) that the paradigm cannot explain. As these anomalies accumulate, some
scientists may start to question the dominant paradigm. If one of these scientists
comes up with a set of ideas that solves both the problems solved by the old paradigm
and its anomalies while also suggesting new problems to be solved, and if this new set

of ideas is accepted by the scientific community, then a scientific revolution (a paradigm shift) has occurred. Kuhn further argued that competing paradigms are incompatible with each other (the earth-centered and sun-centered systems are radically different), so much so that he called their views of the world incommensurable.

Steve Fuller encountered this analysis of science early in his career, and he went on to interview Kuhn, study his works, and analyze the writings of the many scholars who have praised

Steve Fuller is a professor of sociology at the University of Warwick. He is the author of Social Epistemology, Philosophy of Science and Its Discontents, Science, *and* The Governance of Science: Ideology and the Future of the Open Society.

and criticized his accomplishments. Fuller's career as a social epistemologist has well prepared him for his revisionist treatment of Kuhn's life and work in *Thomas Kuhn: A Philosophical History for Our Times*. His American career has included appointments in philosophy, science and technology studies, and the rhetoric of science, while his subsequent British career at the University of Durham and the University of Warwick has centered on sociology and social policy. His previous books include *Philosophy, Rhetoric, and the End of Knowledge: The Coming of Science and Technology Studies* (1993) and *The Governance of Science: Ideology and the Future of the Open Society* (2000). One scholar who is sympathetic to Fuller's views believes that his contributions represent "the most creative addition to the philosophy of science since Kuhn's work on scientific revolutions," but others who deeply admire Kuhn's vision of science have found Fuller's treatment overly critical and mean-spirited. Fuller admits that he is out to dethrone Kuhn, since he feels that *The Structure of Scientific Revolutions* has been overpraised, misunderstood, and detrimental in its influence on science and those who analyze it.

As a self-described "devout social constructivist," Fuller is in favor of a democratized "citizen science" and against the elitist science described in Kuhn's normal science. Some of the aims of Fuller's book are to convince readers who believed that *The Structure of Scientific Revolutions* is both a good and important book that it is bad in its ideas and deleterious in its influence. To accomplish these tasks, Fuller divides his own book into two main sections: chapters 1 through 4 deal with the background to the writing of *The Structure of Scientific Revolutions*, while chapters 5 through 8 are concerned with this book's influence on social scientists, philosophers of science, and sociologists of science.

One of the principal points of Fuller's early analysis is that *The Structure of Scientific Revolutions* is not a book for the ages but a book shaped by the Cold War (when it was conceived, written, and published). During part of this time Kuhn was teaching in James Bryant Conant's General Education Program at Harvard University. Conant, a chemist who became president of Harvard, was what Fuller calls an "action intellectual," someone who wanted to determine the place of science in post-World War II American society and in an increasingly dangerous and competitive world. Fuller implausibly insists that Kuhn's analysis of normal and revolutionary science derived from Conant's Cold-War worldview. Conant certainly wanted to keep science free from unwelcome political influences, but Fuller thinks that Kuhn analogously strove to secure the autonomy of communities of scientists by situating them within paradigms. This sociopolitical account of the origin of Kuhn's ideas contradicts his own story of how he arrived at the basic insight that led to his book. Kuhn was *not* thinking about politics when he had the epiphany that resulted in *The Structure of Scientific Revolutions*; instead, he was studying Aristotle's writings about motion and realized that Aristotle was doing not bad physics but good ancient Greek philosophy. Aristotle was rationally solving intellectual problems within a set of ideas he and his community of scholars accepted.

Besides this Conant-inspired context, Fuller sees Kuhn's work in the tradition of Western intellectual development "from Plato to NATO." This pilgrimage of the Western mind had two paths: The first, extending from Socrates through the Enlightenment to the philosophers Ernst Mach and Karl Popper, is critical, libertarian, and risk-taking, whereas the second, extending from Plato through positivism to the physicists Max Planck and Thomas Kuhn, is foundational, authoritarian, and risk-averse. Fuller, who places himself on the first path, sees his book as essentially a critical account of the second path written from the perspective of the first.

To deepen his analysis of the dichotomous character of the West's intellectual evolution, Fuller discusses the debate at the end of the nineteenth and the beginning of the twentieth century between Ernst Mach and Max Planck. For the realist Planck, science should be the search for important truths about the real world; for the instrumentalist Mach, science should be concerned with the search for ideas that could serve as tools to help fulfill basic human needs. The debate between Mach and Planck was not simply academic, since important social, political, and educational issues were at stake. Mach was a liberal democrat who believed that science and technology were the most reliable ways of adapting the material world to human interests. Planck was a conservative capitalist who believed that science should be the quest by elites for the most comprehensive picture of reality, which would be useful to society only if scientists were isolated from social and political pressures. Some scholars feel that this overly polarized account of the Mach-Planck debate neglects many of the agreements they shared about the nature of science, but Fuller, who sees Mach as the champion of the "citizen science" he espouses, regretfully admits that Planck won the debate. Furthermore, Fuller thinks that Kuhn is clearly the intellectual heir of Planck.

The second half of Fuller's book shows how Kuhn's ideas of paradigms and paradigm shifts have been misunderstood and misapplied by scholars in the humanities and social sciences. Fuller believes that Kuhn's book had such a wide and receptive audience because these captivated academics had a vested interest in his view of science and scientific change. The scheme of *The Structure of Scientific Revolutions* gave humanists and social scientists a way of assuming the prestige of the natural sciences while prescinding from the severely restricted nature of Kuhn's own analysis. Kuhn's model of scientific change was based largely on one science (physics), a restricted time period (1620-1920), and a single region (mainly Europe). In constructing his general model, Kuhn neglected other sciences, times, and cultures. Particularly irksome to Fuller is Kuhn's neglect of the social sciences, but Kuhn felt that the social sciences lacked genuine paradigms. This did not stop social scientists from appropriating Kuhn's scheme, an action Fuller finds disheartening, since he believes that these Kuhn-like applications have corrupted the appliers.

"Paradigmitis" is the name that Fuller gives to the disease affecting scholars who have been taken in by Kuhn's arguments. Paradigmitis leads its sufferers to reason that if a methodological strategy works in one case (physics), it must work in others (the humanities and social sciences). Fuller is particularly critical of the new field of science and technology studies (STS), because STS proponents see *The Structure of Scientific Revolutions* as their founding document, leading to STS theories that, according to Fuller, "rarely escape banality."

Fuller plays the role of Kuhn's critic throughout most of his book, but, turnabout being fair play, the critic himself can be criticized, often by using his own arguments. For example, he understands the rules by which scholars play their intellectual games, but he rarely treats Kuhn, a distinguished academic, with the respect, courtesy, and charity to which his accomplishments entitle him. Fuller describes Kuhn as a dwarf standing on the shoulders of giants, a historical philistine, a methodological naïf, a pop historiographer, and a failure at Harvard because Kuhn failed to be tenured there. He also sees Kuhn as ignorant of the social sciences, "deaf" to biology, and insensitive to his own historicity. He calls Kuhn a "prig historian" because, out of an exaggerated sense of conformity, he uses past historical figures to smugly buttress his own authority. He also compares Kuhn to Chance, the character played by Peter Sellers in the film *Being There* (1979). Like the childlike Chance, whose naïve utterances are taken as brilliant aperçus by the powerful and knowledgeable, Kuhn's enigmatic sayings lead to a similar "comedy of errors" when they are misinterpreted by various academics. Even those who are critical of Kuhn's views will find Fuller's depiction of him as a simpleton untrue and offensive.

Besides his excessively harsh attacks on "Saint Thomas Kuhn" (perhaps an ironic characterization), Fuller can also be faulted for his exaggerated distortion of Kuhn's influence. Fuller attaches entirely too much blame on *The Structure of Scientific Revolutions* for various problems in the social sciences. He claims that scholars in several fields have distorted their disciplines in order to imitate Kuhn's normal science, but the responsibility for this distortion rests with the social scientists, not Kuhn. Scholars habitually shape knowledge to their interests, but an overly passionate devotion to these interests can distort their perception of reality. Fuller acknowledges that he favors scholars who display an awareness of the sociohistorical setting in which they stake their claim to knowledge, and since Kuhn fails to do this, he suffers severely in Fuller's estimation. On the other hand, some scholars have found deep flaws in Fuller's own thesis that the validity of scientific claims is relative to the social conditions of their circulation. Fuller wants a democratic policy of science, where ordinary people rather than elites shape its development, but this is neither desirable nor possible in a culture permeated by a professionalized science.

Fuller's book raises an extreme question: Did Kuhn really waste his life by developing a worthless, even harmful theory of science? A Fuller critic might well respond with another question: Has Fuller wasted his time by elaborating a worthless, even harmful critique of Kuhn? According to many scholars, *The Structure of Scientific Revolutions*, though seriously flawed in many ways, has done great good. It stimulated many talented people to become scientists and historians of science. It expanded and deepened the debate about the nature of science and how science evolves. It clarified how research communities create new knowledge, and it also fostered critical techniques for scrutinizing these communities and the types of knowledge they produce. Kuhn's book is also much more clearly written than Fuller's, whose arguments often become mired in picayune squabbles among specialists. Kuhn also realized how an adeptly chosen concrete example can illuminate a highly abstract discussion, a technique that Fuller could have profitably employed. In the epiphany that led to his most famous book, Kuhn learned not to disparage Aristotle's arguments but to understand them in a historical context. Was Kuhn's view of the past as faulty as Fuller makes it out to be? Is not Kuhn to be admired for what he has done, just as Aristotle was? Fuller states that his book will have achieved its purpose if it helps raise questions about how Kuhn's book has been legitimated. Fuller's book itself raises troubling questions. However, impertinent questions have a way of leading to pertinent answers.

Robert J. Paradowski

Sources for Further Study

Booklist 96 (May 15, 2000): 1712.
Choice 38 (November, 2000): 553.
The Chronicle of Higher Education 47 (September 15, 2000): A18.
Library Journal 125 (August, 2000): 148.
Scientific American 283 (September, 2000): 104.
Technology Review 103 (September, 2000): 126.

TIEPOLO'S HOUND

Author: Derek Walcott (1930-   )
Publisher: Farrar, Straus and Giroux (New York). 164 pp. $30.00
Type of work: Poetry and fine arts
Time: 1830-1903, 1930-1990's, sixteenth century, eighteenth century
Locale: St. Thomas, St. Lucia, and Trinidad, West Indies; New York, N.Y.; Paris and Pontoise, France; London, England; Venice, Italy; and Spain

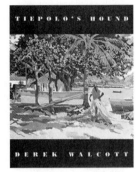

A poetic meditation on the life and work of the Caribbean-born French Impressionist painter Camille Pissarro, the author's search for a Venetian painting he saw as a young man, and the complex and sometimes vexing relations between art and cultural identity

Principal personages:
CAMILLE PISSARRO, French Impressionist painter
PAULO VERONESE and GIOVANNI BATTISTA TIEPOLO, Venetian painters
DEREK WALCOTT, West Indian poet and painter

Tiepolo's Hound is the third book-length poem of Derek Walcott's four decades of work as a poet and dramatist. Walcott is a writer whose stature as a major figure of West Indian and postcolonial world literature was recognized with the Nobel Prize for Literature in 1992. Following his autobiographical *Another Life* (1973) and *Omeros* (1990), in which Walcott transformed Homeric materials into an epic of Caribbean life, *Tiepolo's Hound* in part returns to the lyric poet's autobiographical mode. It also becomes biography, however, as Walcott interweaves an account of the life and art of the French Impressionist painter Camille Pissarro (1830-1903) with the story of his own belated search for a detail in a Venetian painting that he had seen in an astonishing visionary moment as a young man on his first visit to the Metropolitan Museum of Art in New York City. The book also incorporates reproductions of Walcott's watercolors and oil paintings, predominantly Caribbean scenes but also portraits, including a self-portrait and two representations of the painter Paul Gauguin (1848-1903), and several European scenes.

At times these materials seem bizarrely unrelated, or connected only by the facts that Pissarro and Walcott are both artists and that Walcott's quest in pursuit of the hound in the remembered Venetian painting is a search for a work of art. The parallels between Pissarro's experiences and Walcott's own life are clear. Pissarro was born on the Caribbean island of St. Thomas in 1830, and Walcott was born on the Caribbean

∼

Derek Walcott received the Nobel Prize in Literature in 1992. His works include Collected Poems: 1948-1984, Omeros, *and* The Bounty.

∼

island of St. Lucia in 1930. Pissarro's family were Sephardic Jews who had emigrated to a Danish-ruled but largely French-speaking island that still employed slave labor, while Walcott grew up on a British-ruled but largely French- and patois-speaking island, as the descendant of both English colonists and slaves brought from Africa. To be a painter, Pissarro felt compelled to move to France and become a leading figure of the Impressionist movement, his West Indian origins largely forgotten, while Walcott, though he has spent considerable time teaching and living in the United States, was able to develop an identity as an internationally recognized writer who has played a major role in the formation of a modern West Indian literary culture.

These parallels and differences, along with Walcott's lifelong interest in painting, would seem to offer plenty of scope for a long poem, and indeed the sections of *Tiepolo's Hound* that concern Pissarro tend to be so compellingly written and for long stretches so dominate the book that the title seems oddly chosen and the poet's quest for the hound a diversion from the poem's central interest. The reader may also wonder why the poet is determined to journey to Venice to look for a painting he saw in New York, a question Walcott never answers. Finally, adding to the reader's puzzlement about the poem's title, Walcott sometimes says the original painting was by Paolo Veronese (1528-1588), sometimes says it was by Giovanni Battista Tiepolo (1696-1770), and in the end decides that he will never be able to decide which it was and does not want to know anyway, asserting that in a sense the hound was painted by both. One is left to feel that *Tiepolo's Hound* was chosen as the title simply because it is more euphonious than *Veronese's Hound* would have been.

Underlying the poem's shifts in direction and focus, though, and justifying its uncertainties, is the poem's autobiographical core: Walcott's wrestling with his own problems of cultural identity, which gives a tension both to his meditations on Pissarro and the quest driven by the intensity of his memory of the brush stroke representing the hound's thigh. What does it mean to him, and what did it mean to Pissarro, that Pissarro left St. Thomas for France? Did Pissarro betray his native place? Was not France "his" too ("His name, Pissarro, hidden in the word Paris")? What did it mean to Pissarro that as a child and young man he heard the voices of "Mission slaves// chanting deliverance from all their sins/ in tidal couplets of lament and answer"? Can their voices be heard in the melancholy rustling of the poplars in the landscapes Pissarro painted in Pontoise? One of the poem's most frequently recurring images is that of a black dog, a "mongrel," West Indian; versions of it both haunt Walcott and follow Pissarro. Why is Walcott also so haunted by "Tiepolo's" *white* hound: Must the color have a racial significance? In Veronese's *Feast at the House of Levi*, close to the original of the painting of Walcott's vision, not only is the hound a subordinate detail in a richly represented Venetian (and also Jewish) feast, but a Moor, or Moors, stand to the side, marginal, observing. Walcott must probe at his own identification with the Moor, the figure whose relation to European culture is that of the marginal, the colonized, or even the enslaved.

In a densely tangled passage late in the poem, the original vision of the hound, its revelation "so exact in its lucency" of art's power, is the event that has led Walcott in his own development as an artist and has brought him to a point where he is both a Theseus searching through labyrinths for the minotaur beast which is "history," and the beast itself, "a beast// that was my fear, my self, my craft,/ not the white elegant wolfhound at the feast." He continues:

> If recognition was the grace I needed
> to elevate my race from its foul lair
>
> by prayer, by poetry, by couplets repeated
> over its carcase, I was both slain and slayer.

"History" has long been a vexing subject for Walcott. In his 1974 essay "The Muse of History" he rejected both what he called the literature of recrimination, tied to colonialism, and the literature of nostalgia for a Europe of ruins, Europe as a "nourishing museum." His own project, he said, was to celebrate the Caribbean as a world renewed, another Eden. Yet he could not evade the bitterness of historical reality, even as he wanted to celebrate the wonder of the "gift" of the new world out of the "groaning and soldering" of the two old ones. Both recrimination and nostalgia threaten to surface in *Tiepolo's Hound* as he describes his journey to Venice—the museum Europe to which he had been introduced in childhood by his father's art books—to look for Veronese and Tiepolo, and struggles to reconcile his deep admiration for Pissarro with the feeling that Pissarro somehow betrayed his origins.

What resolves this emotional tangle and makes the book finally a moving whole of which "Tiepolo's hound" can be the triumphant concluding image is the combination of Walcott's homage to Pissarro's persistence as an artist in France through experiences of alienation and recurrent self-doubt, and Walcott's own poetic and painterly love of the Caribbean landscape which, in childhood, they shared. Of Pissarro, Walcott asks, "What would have been his future had he stayed?/ He was Art's subject as much as any empire's"—and readers know that the future as West Indian artist given the young Walcott by his generation's new access to higher education in the West Indies and by the Rockefeller Foundation's support of Walcott's West Indian theater project had no equivalent for Pissarro a century earlier. Walcott imagines Pissarro's discovery that the monumental works of European tradition that he finds in the Louvre are not where he can find himself, and imagines his discovery of his own vision outside the museum, in the streets of Paris and the modern, secular, myth-erasing art of the nineteenth century, with its new understanding of light. Walcott's account of Pissarro dwells especially on the years Pissarro spent in Pontoise, painting its landscapes and buildings again and again in changing lights and weathers, never getting it "right," suffering poverty and repeated rejection by the Academy, and always trying again. Walcott touches on Pissarro's 1870 flight to London with Monet, when the Franco-Prussian War brought pillaging soldiers to his village, and on the

Jewish Pissarro's experience of the anti-Semitism of the Dreyfus affair in the 1890's.
The real point of it all, though, is Pissarro's wonderful paintings of "the ordinary."
Walcott says,

> The Salon's choice
> omitted him repeatedly. Who would want
> 300 versions of visions of Pontoise
> when Claude would need just one to get it right?
> Rejection intensified defiance,
> stubborn as Cézanne's stones in the stone light
> of L'Estaque, its blue morne in the distance.
> So his own canvases stayed as they were,
> without narrative pathos, they would insist
> on the raw vehemence of real weather,
> snow-spattered mud, grey gardens in grey mist.

Paul Cézanne worked intensively with Pissarro, whose painting he hugely admired; Tiepolo learned from Veronese's work; Walcott, near the end of *Tiepolo's
Hound*, feels that he and Pissarro are doubles. His own paintings, though a pleasing
part of a beautifully produced book, are minor accomplishments, but the loose yet
carefully structured poetic form he uses here is a satisfying medium for a meditative
art that in some respects is an equivalent of Pissarro's. Like Pissarro, he circles, comes
back again and again to the same subjects, the same problems, the same images,
though always with a difference. He divides *Tiepolo's Hound* into four books that are
in turn divided into shorter poems. His loose narrative of Pissarro's life dominates the
first two books and parts of the third and fourth; Walcott's own developing relation
with art is a subject from the beginning, and the quest for the hound occupies much of
the fourth book. His fundamental verse form here is couplets, arranged so that the end
sounds of one couplet rhyme, sometimes very loosely, with the end sounds of the
next, a malleable *ab, ab* form which lends itself to a discourse that makes distinctions,
draws boundaries, only to let them blur again (as, for instance, with the similarities
and differences between himself and Pissarro). The rhymes allow sharply pointed effects, linking "St. Thomas" and "Pontoise," for example, and "Pissarro" and "sorrow," but are usually less obtrusive. Walcott likens his couplets to Pissarro's brush
strokes; he also gets a flowing and sliding effect with syntactical slips and with words
whose meanings point in two directions (Pissarro, newly in Pontoise, is "an immi-
grant/ prodigal with confirmations," both the prodigal runaway from his native place
and the artist prodigal with talent and discovery).

Loose forms and long, circling poems that evade tight narrative structure are liable
to overinclusiveness, to long passages that lose poetic intensity, and *Tiepolo's Hound*
does not avoid these failings. The intensity of the moment, the moment of artistic revelation, however, is the center of the poem and the justification, paradoxically, of its
meanderings:

> . . . in the tints of Tiepolo's sky,
> in the yellowing linen of a still life by Chardin,

> in that stroke of light that catches a hound's thigh,
> the paint is all that counts, no guilt, no pardon,
> no history, but the sense of narrative time
> annihilated in the devotion of the acolyte,
> as undeniable as instinct, the brushstroke's rhyme
> and page and canvas know one empire only: light.

Light dominates Walcott's Caribbean landscapes, and Tiepolo's hound, metaphorically the inspiration for Walcott's fiction of Pissarro, finally points him back to the black Caribbean hound that is "the mongrel's heir," an abandoned puppy: "we set it down in the village to survive/ like all my ancestry. The hound was here." Coming near the end of the poem, this passage makes sense of the inconclusiveness of Walcott's search for the Venetian painting that has haunted his memory; his pilgrimage has a conclusion after all in his return home and the voyage into self that the poem has created. In its last lines, the poet looks to the constellations, reformed by his book: "the round// of the charted stars, the Archer, aiming his bow,/ the Bear, and the studded collar of Tiepolo's hound."

Anne Howells

Sources for Further Study

Booklist 96 (February 15, 2000): 1075.
The New York Review of Books 47 (May 11, 2000): 27.
Publishers Weekly 247 (February 7, 2000): 69.
Time 155 (April 3, 2000): 81.
The Virginia Quarterly Review 76 (Autumn, 2000): 144.

TIME TO BE IN EARNEST
A Fragment of Autobiography

Author: P. D. James (1920-   )
Publisher: Alfred A. Knopf (New York). Illustrated. 269
   pp. $25.00
Type of work: Autobiography and diaries
Time: 1920-1998
Locale: England and the United States

≈

A memoir in the form of a diary by a major crime fiction writer, this is an engagingly informative book in which James not only deals with daily experiences, but also reflects upon the past and discusses her craft

≈

Principal personage:
   P. D. JAMES, English crime fiction novelist

Unlike many authors, British novelist P. D. James has been neither a diarist nor an inveterate letter writer, and she regularly discourages potential biographers, but on August 3, 1997, her seventy-seventh birthday, this doyenne of modern mystery writers started keeping a record of the ensuing year. She was inspired by Samuel Johnson's dictum that "at seventy-seven it is time to be in earnest" as well as her desire to preserve "just one year that otherwise might be lost, not only to children and grandchildren who might have an interest but, with the advance of age and perhaps the onset of the dreaded Alzheimer's, lost also to me." The published book deals with only about 100 days of the year's 365, and James admits it is "incomplete, with more omitted than has been recorded." For example, she deliberately skips events "painful to dwell upon" and "other matters over which memory has exercised its self-defensive censorship." Authorial disclaimers notwithstanding, *Time to Be in Earnest* is more than a mere "fragment of autobiography"; rather, it is an expansive memoir in the guise of a diary that progresses chronologically, but James often becomes retrospective as present experiences recall the past. Because her daily routine usually includes speeches, organization meetings, and sessions of the House of Lords (she became Baroness James of Holland Park, a life peer, in 1991), the book abounds with her ideas about such matters as detective fiction, authors classic and contemporary, discrimination against women in the workplace, and suggestions for reforming the British Broadcasting Corporation (BBC), House of Lords, and Church of England. About the last, she says that from childhood she has

> inherited a love of and devotion to the Church of England which is still strong, although . . .
> much of its former dignity, scholarly tolerance, beauty and order, have been not so much
> lost as wantonly thrown away, together with its incomparable liturgy.

A keen sense of belonging to a community of professionals has led her to involvement and leadership positions not only with the board of governors of the BBC, but also with the British Council, Society of Authors (of which she was president), Whitbread Literary Awards, and Booker Prize committee (whose panel of judges she chaired in 1987). Among her public activities in her seventy-seventh year, she twice appeared as a panelist on a BBC quiz show; taped a master class about novel writing for Meridian Television; spoke to the Southwold Archaeological and Natural History Society, Scottish Medico-Legal Society, Essex Autistic Society, Jane Austen Society, and Dorset Victim Support; and also lectured at the Cheltenham Literary Festival, St. German's Cathedral on the Isle of Man, and Trinity and Lincoln Colleges, Oxford. Because her fourteenth novel, *A Certain Justice*, was published in this year of record (1997), she also had many obligatory receptions, signings, and tours, including a fortnight in the United States, brief trips to France and Norway, and a planned Australian tour for which she gave previsit interviews.

P. D. James is the author of fifteen books. She spent thirty years working in the British Civil Service, including the Police and Criminal Law Divisions of the Home Office, and has served as a magistrate and as a governor of the BBC. In 1991, she was created Baroness James of Holland Park.

With seemingly boundless energy, James makes her rounds primarily by public transportation—buses, trains, London's underground—rather than by taxis or chauffeured cars, and visits with children, grandchildren, and friends are interspersed with the public and official activities that fill her daily calendar. Presumably on days not included in the diary she was planning or writing her next novel, book review, or speech.

Aside from describing her hectic schedule, commenting about people she meets and meals they share, and summarizing lectures, James does not write much about less immediate matters. She manages, however, to give pithy revelations of her childhood: a peripatetic lifestyle because her father frequently changed jobs; a loving father and mentally ill mother, who stayed together largely due to a Victorian obligation to marriage vows; supportive and nurturing grandparents; sound traditional schooling; and a freedom from fear and want that fostered an overall security. Consistent with a stated reluctance to deal with the unpleasant, James does not write much about her husband Connor or her marriage, a union that was marred by his mental illness, periods of institutionalization, and early death. About her husband she makes just two extended statements:

> I have never found, or indeed looked for, anyone else with whom I have wanted to spend the rest of my life. I think of Connor with love and with grief for all he has missed: the grandchildren in whom he would have taken such joy, my success, which would have made the burden of mental illness easier to bear—as money always does—the journeys, the laughter, the small triumphs and the day-to-day living we haven't shared.

Later, on his birthday:

> I still miss him daily, which means that no day goes by in which he doesn't enter into my mind: a sight which he would have relished, a joke which he would have enjoyed, something seen or read which could be shared with him, the reiteration of familiar gossip, opinions, prejudices, which are part of a marriage.

From these comments she segues into extended commentaries about mental illness and its treatment. Nor does James have much to say about her children and grandchildren, whom she sees regularly for brief visits and on formal occasions. A closeness is apparent, however, especially with the younger generation, as one anecdote suggests:

> I returned to find a call on the answerphone from granddaughter Beatrice. She is due here with her bridge partner, Rachel, and Rachel's boyfriend to play bridge in the English squad. Bea said that there were two more friends, whom she ironically described as clean-living boys, who had no bed for the night, so she has told them that they could turn up with their sleeping bags and sleep at my house. Last year there was only one clean-living lad. Next year, no doubt, there will be three or four clean-living boys trooping in with their sleeping bags. However, there is plenty of room and I like civilized, lively and intelligent young people.

Except for her parents, James does not provide last names for her family members, neither husband, in-laws, married daughters, nor grandchildren. When she sent the manuscript of her first novel to an agent or publisher, she recalls,

> I wrote down Phyllis James, Phyllis D. James, P. D. James, and decided that the last and shortest was enigmatic and would look best on the book spine. It never occurred to me to write other than under my maiden name.

Separating private from public, personal from professional, is common among mystery fiction writers, many of whom hide behind pseudonyms, and even when writing autobiographically James parts the curtain only slightly, discussing in greater detail and devoting more space to her cat, Polly-Hodge, than to any family member. As a result, this wife, mother, and grandmother who does not reveal her married name remains somewhat elusive, so this diary/autobiography is largely about P. D. James and Baroness James, honored writer and public figure. Unsurprisingly, when she focuses upon teachers and authors who influenced her, sources of the Christian morality that pervades her novels, her analysis of problems facing the British Broadcasting Corporation, and her suggestions for reforming the House of Lords, she is most forthcoming.

Indeed, such an emphasis should satisfy most readers of *Time to Be in Earnest*, who probably are interested mainly in James the writer, who since her 1962 debut novel has received consistent critical praise and has enjoyed sustained popularity with readers around the world. Touted almost from the beginning as successor to such genre grande dames as Agatha Christie, Ngaio Marsh, Margery Allingham, and Dorothy L. Sayers, James has moved beyond their predictable plot patterns and stereotypical characters, regularly challenging and extending the boundaries of the genre while writing in the general tradition of her predecessors (to whom she makes respectful acknowledgments). According to many critics, in fact, she is the first modern mystery writer to have scaled the barrier into mainstream fiction: Her plotting and characterization are more complex than is the norm for the genre, she invariably develops a pervasive thematic underpinning to her plots, and her varied settings are organic parts of the whole rather than mere backdrops. Perhaps most important, she experiments. *Innocent Blood* (1980), for instance, is a crime story without a detective that has an Oedipal quest theme and is the only James book inspired by an actual murder as well as, she notes, an act of Parliament. *The Skull Beneath the Skin* (1982) is a parody of the whodunit genre, a sly nod to an Agatha Christie classic, *Ten Little Indians* (1939). *The Children of Men* (1992), which almost defies classification, is a kind of dystopian novel that also is a Christian fable or morality tale and her only book with a linear plot structure—and, she recalls, "the only one of my novels which has not earned its advance, a depressing and somewhat demeaning thought."

Murder that is bloody and gruesome, quite different from the genteel manner in which most of her Golden Age predecessors display their victims, is a recurring presence in James's books, a reflection of her credo as a whodunit writer:

> The detective story is, after all, one way in which we can cope with violent death, fictionalize it, give it a recognizable shape and, at the end of the book, show that even the most intractable mystery is capable of solution, not by supernatural means or by good fortune, but by human intelligence, human perseverance, and human courage.

About her practice of "describing the dead victim realistically, and indeed vividly," she calls the discovery of the body a moment "of horror and high drama, and the reader should experience both." Further, "the scene is often most effective when [the discoverer] is herself or himself innocent." She also believes that crime writers of the new century, unlike their predecessors who were held to lower standards of realism, must be knowledgeable about forensic medicine, police procedures, and scientific methods of criminal investigation. Further, unlike mystery fiction of the past, the genre today is "less assured in its affirmation of official law and order" and is "moving ever closer to the sensibilities and moral ambiguities of the so-called 'straight' novel." How does she react to the hard-boiled mystery fiction that has emerged from the Raymond Chandler-Dashiell Hammett-Gregory Macdonald tradition?

> Too many male crime writers, obsessed with violence and with the search for what they, a uniquely privileged generation, see as the gritty reality which they have never personally experienced, are portraying a world as nihilistic as it is bloody. Perhaps it is to the women we must look for psychological subtlety and the exploration of moral choice, which for me are at the heart of even the most grittily realistic of crime fiction.

Amidst the change she observes and advocates, a rare constant is what James thinks is the most credible motive for murder, "the one for which the reader can feel some sympathy." It is "the murderer's wish to advantage, protect or avenge someone he or she greatly loves." Although the reader should not sympathize with a murderer, whatever the circumstances, James says, "I think there should be empathy and understanding." Setting also is important, even central, to her novels, nearly all of which have originated with her reactions to places. As an example she describes the origin of *Devices and Desires* (1989), one of many James novels set in East Anglia. While exploring Suffolk, she stood alone on a deserted beach, observing "the cold and dangerous North Sea" and listening to the receding waves and hissing wind. Looking south, she

> saw the silent and stark outline of Sizewell nuclear power station dominating the coastline. I thought of all the lives that have been lived on this shore . . . and the concrete pillboxes, part of the defences against the expected German invasion on this coast. And immediately I knew with an almost physical surge of excitement that I had a novel. The next book would be set on a lonely stretch of East Anglian coast under the shadow of a nuclear power station.

Like the tower in *The Black Tower* (1975), the power station in *Devices and Desires* has a symbolic importance.

Given the experimentation that has been a hallmark of her mystery writing, it is not at all surprising that when James in her eighth decade decided to write about herself, she should do so in a hybrid autobiographical form that serves her purposes eminently well, revealing only as much as she wants to share about the past, her career, her family, and her beliefs. The result is a determinedly upbeat account that is an informative, enjoyable, sometimes provocative, occasionally witty read that concludes with James encouragingly asserting her intent to continue writing mysteries as long as she can do so. She offers no clues to what may be forthcoming.

Gerald H. Strauss

Sources for Further Study

Booklist 96 (March 1, 2000): 1146.
Library Journal 125 (May 15, 2000): 94.
Publishers Weekly 247 (March 27, 2000): 61.

THE TIPPING POINT
How Little Things Can Make a Big Difference

Author: Malcolm Gladwell (1963-   )
Publisher: Little, Brown (Boston). 288 pp. $24.95
Type of work: Sociology and psychology
Locale: Mostly the United States

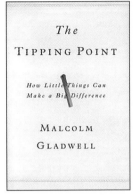

~

The rapid spread of a medical epidemic starting from a few infected individuals is an analogy for the sudden rise in popularity of a new social trend that is triggered off by a small event

~

Malcolm Gladwell was a journalist for *The Washington Post* and later became a staff writer for *The New Yorker*. In December of 1996 he published an article on the idea of a "tipping point," the moment when a social trend crosses a threshold and starts to spread like wildfire. The original article was expanded into this book, with many additional examples.

How does a style of clothing become trendy? What causes a sudden drop in the crime rate of a major city? Under what circumstances can a political cause explode into a revolutionary mass movement? Why do some advertisements stick in people's minds while others are ignored? How does a book become a best-seller? These are the kind of questions for which Gladwell tries to find a common denominator. Just as a single match can start a large wildfire under the right conditions, or one sick individual in a crowd can bring about a flu epidemic, Gladwell argues that little things can make a big difference in social dynamics. He selects examples from a wide variety of social situations to illustrate how an idea or trend can become contagious, spreading quickly from a small beginning to a mass audience.

For example, Hush Puppy shoes, with lightweight crepe soles and suede uppers, were a popular brand in the 1970's, but by the early 1990's sales had dropped to about 30,000 pairs per year and executives at the Wolverine Shoe Company were thinking about phasing them out. In 1995, however, Hush Puppies became a local fad among a group of young people in Manhattan. Subsequently, several nationally known fashion designers decided to incorporate the shoes in their fall showings. By the end of the year, over 400,000 pairs were sold. In 1996, sales increased to more than one million pairs, and the next year to almost two million. All this happened basically by word of mouth, without an advertising campaign by the manufacturer.

In a very different type of case, the New York City crime rate from 1975 to 1992 was very high, totaling over 600,000 felonies per year, including about 2,000 murders. In 1993, a tipping point was reached and the crime rate decreased dramatically. Within five years, serious crimes dropped to one-half and murders to one-third. What

∼

Malcolm Gladwell has been a
business and science writer at The
Washington Post *and is currently a*
staff writer for The New Yorker.

∼

caused this huge decline? Some long-term trends such as less drug use, aging of the population, and improvement in the economy might explain a gradual decrease, but not the sudden drop that actually occurred.

Gladwell argues that the sudden decrease in crime can be attributed to two other factors. One of these was cleaning up graffiti in the subway system. Instead of assigning police resources to stop violent crimes, funds were allocated to remove graffiti by repainting. If a car was vandalized, it was repainted the next day. It took almost five years to clean up thousands of cars. Subway director David Gunn justified the subway cleanup project as follows: "The graffiti was symbolic of the collapse of the system. When you looked at the process of rebuilding the organization and morale, you had to win the battle against graffiti. Without winning that battle, all the management reforms and physical changes just weren't going to happen." The project put into practice the so-called Broken Windows theory of criminal behavior, developed by criminologists George Kelling and James Q. Wilson.

> If a window is broken and left unrepaired, people walking by will conclude that no one cares and no one is in charge. Soon, more windows will be broken, and the sense of anarchy will spread from the building to the street on which it faces, sending a signal that anything goes. In a city, relatively minor problems like graffiti, public disorder, and aggressive panhandling, they write, are all the equivalent of broken windows, invitations to more serious crimes.

In trying to restore orderliness for the subway system, another seemingly minor offense had to be addressed. People had gotten into the habit of climbing over or around the turnstiles to avoid paying their fare. The problem became so widespread that as many as 170,000 people per day rode the subways without paying. The loss of revenue was not as important as the loss of respect for law and order. Transit police in plain clothes were assigned to arrest fare-beaters. They were handcuffed and left standing on the platform for a while as a public signal that such behavior was no longer tolerated. The remarkable result of this new policy was not only that people paid their fares but also that serious crimes such as robbery, rape, and murder dropped more than 50 percent. Taking a firm stand on minor offenses brought the major felonies down as well, so that New York became one of the safest large cities in the world.

In the realm of revolution, the famous midnight ride of Paul Revere is cited by Gladwell as the most dramatic historical example of a word-of-mouth epidemic. It mobilized local militias to confront British troops in open rebellion for the first time. The Battle of Lexington, on April 19, 1775, was the tipping point that marked the start of the American Revolution.

For some time, New England town meetings had been the forum for anti-British speeches objecting to excessive taxation in the colonies. The Boston Tea Party in 1773 was a public act of defiance, but at that time the situation was not yet ripe for a military confrontation. Paul Revere's ride was the trigger that focused anti-British sentiment, assembling a large force of militia at Lexington and at Concord that, although poorly armed, nevertheless won a significant victory over the redcoats, forcing them to retreat to Boston in disarray.

Why was Paul Revere's ride so effective in generating widespread participation? As in his other tipping point examples, Gladwell tries to analyze why a little thing, in this case a solo horseman, can make such a big difference, generating the opening salvo of the War of Independence. He emphasizes the important role of Revere as an initiator, a sociable man with a large network of acquaintances in the countryside around Boston. From past contacts, he already knew the men who were community leaders and on whom he could depend to transmit the message that "The British are coming!"

On the same night as Revere's ride, another horseman named William Dawes carried the same message from Boston to Lexington by a different route. Dawes was not a "connector" of people like Revere, so his message did not spread beyond the few individuals whom he personally warned. From the towns where he had gone, no militia groups came to join the patriots at Lexington and Concord. To stimulate a word-of-mouth epidemic, not only must the timing and the circumstances be right but also the initiator must be a person who knows and is known by a large number of people.

In the world of advertising and marketing, the goal is to generate a message or slogan that will stick in people's minds and, it is hoped, sell their product. Many people still remember the slogan "Winston tastes good like a cigarette should" or Wendy's famous line "Where's the beef?" These advertisements had a unique "stickiness," providing name recognition for the manufacturers.

Gladwell describes a highly successful advertising campaign for Columbia Records in the 1970's. Television viewers were told to hunt for a picture of a gold box in their *TV Guide* or *Parade* magazine. If they found one, they could send it in to obtain a free record of their choice. Searching for the gold box "made the reader/viewer part of an interactive advertising system. Viewers were not just an audience but had become participants." Audience participation was an effective method to increase the "stickiness" of the advertisement. Since people are exposed to an increasing number of commercials in the media, a special gimmick helped to make the message stand out from among the general clutter.

In 1996, a book was published entitled *Divine Secrets of the Ya-Ya Sisterhood*, written by Rebecca Wells. It had modest sales of fifteen thousand copies during the first year. Two years later, a phenomenal surge in popularity occurred. It went through forty-eight printings and sold over two million copies.

In order to understand this epidemic, Gladwell points out that the book first became popular among women's reading groups. The story deals with mother-daughter relationships, providing an opening for women to share personal experiences with other members of their group. Reading the book and then discussing it afterward made it into a meaningful social experience for the participants. The tipping point for book sales came when women went to their bookstores to buy extra copies for friends or family members. The enthusiasm spread from one reading group to another. Gladwell explains, "Women began forming Ya-Ya Sisterhood groups of their own, in imitation of the group described in the book." The lesson of *Divine Secrets of the Ya-Ya Sisterhood* is that "small, close-knit groups have the power to magnify the epidemic potential of a message or idea."

A variety of other examples are cited by Gladwell to illustrate the concept of a tipping point in social epidemics. One is the story of John Wesley, the founder of Methodism, who had remarkable success during the 1780's by forming his converts into religious societies. Another tells about the first episodes of the television program *Sesame Street*, which attracted a large audience of children and their parents. A sociological study of the adoption of hybrid seed corn among initially reluctant Iowa farmers in the 1930's provides another interesting example.

In the last part of his book, Gladwell applies his tipping point analysis to the epidemic of cigarette smoking among high school and college students. While smoking by adults continues to decline, the number of adolescents who smoke increased by more than 30 percent in the 1990's. It is apparent that health warnings, higher prices for cigarettes, and advertising restrictions are not making an impact on this age group. The effect of role models who set teenage fashions and behavior is much stronger than adult warnings about long-term health hazards.

Gladwell is pessimistic about being able to influence the dominant personalities in the youth culture in order to reverse the smoking epidemic. Instead he proposes two alternative strategies. He cites a theory by addiction experts Neal Benowitz and Jack Henningfield that a dose of less than five milligrams of nicotine per day is probably below the threshold to produce addiction. Five milligrams may be the tipping point for making an occasional smoker into an addict. If tobacco companies were required to reduce the total nicotine content in a pack of cigarettes below this threshold, they suggest, it would "prevent or limit the development of addiction in most young people."

Gladwell's second proposal to tip the teenage smoking epidemic downward is based on studies that have shown a strong correlation between smoking and depression. For some people, genetic factors may cause an imbalance in certain chemicals produced by the brain which are important to regulate a person's moods. If smoking is caused by feeling depressed and if depression is due to a chemical imbalance, then drugs that are useful to treat depression may be a good antidote against dependence on nicotine.

In his writing, Gladwell has assembled examples from a great variety of situations which all demonstrate a tipping point. What caused the tipping effect is quite variable, however. There is no single mechanism that works in all situations. For the *Divine Secrets of the Ya-Ya Sisterhood*, small discussion groups were the key factor. For Columbia Records, audience participation tipped the balance. For Paul Revere's ride, his role as a recognized community leader was essential. In the New York subway system, fixing "broken windows" tipped the crime rate downward. If one deliberately tries to create a tipping point in order to produce a socially desirable outcome, the challenge remains to discover what mechanism would be effective in a particular situation.

Hans G. Graetzer

Sources for Further Study

Booklist 96 (February 15, 2000): 1059.
Library Journal 125 (March 1, 2000): 112.
The New York Review of Books 47 (June 15, 2000): 41.
The New York Times Book Review 105 (March 5, 2000): 8.
Publishers Weekly 247 (February 14, 2000): 187.
Time 155 (February 28, 2000): 90.

THE TRANSLINGUAL IMAGINATION

Author: Steven G. Kellman (1947-   )
Publisher: University of Nebraska Press (Lincoln). 160
   pp. $37.50
Type of work: Literary history and literary criticism

~

*A veteran comparatist seeks and finds new perspectives
in the work of writers fluent in more than one language,
who may often be seen as testing the limits of language itself*

~

Beginning with the articles eventually subsumed in *The Self-Begetting Novel*
(1980), Steven G. Kellman has distinguished himself in the field of comparative literature as historian, critic, and scholar of what has often been seen as "experimental"
fiction. In *The Translingual Imagination*, Kellman privileges the experimental nature
of all creative writing, memoir as well as fiction, by focusing upon writers whose expression embraces more than one language, or, at the very least, occurs in an acquired,
as opposed to native, idiom. Revisiting certain works and authors already considered
in *The Self-Begetting Novel*, Kellman both broadens and deepens his inquiry, moving
on to explore the work of authors unpublished (or undiscovered) at the time of the earlier studies.

As Kellman points out from the start, the phenomenon here described as translingualism is as old as writing itself: Relatively few of the authors who rose to prominence under the Roman Empire were native speakers of Latin; for most, it was an idiom acquired in adolescence or maturity, through education and effort. During the
Middle Ages and into the early modern period, writers and thinkers throughout Europe learned and perfected Latin in order to reach a wide audience of their peers; more
recently, writers from northern and eastern Europe likewise chose English, French, or
German to achieve wider dissemination of their work. It was during the twentieth century, however, that translingualism developed in the form that Kellman has chosen as
the object of his study, a phenomenon owing at least in part to developments in history
and politics.

Early in his exposition, Kellman takes care to distinguish between "ambilinguals,"
those who write with equal facility (and eventual literary merit) in more than one language, and "monolingual translinguals" whose written expression is confined to an
acquired idiom. To be sure, Samuel Beckett and Vladimir Nabokov emerge as the
best known and among the most able ambilinguals of their generation (and perhaps of
all time); as Kellman points out, Nabokov would rank as a major Russian writer had
he never written a word in English, and Beckett's literary fortunes have relatively little to do with his mature decision to write originally in his acquired French. Among

the more notable monolingual translinguals cited by Kellman are Eugène Ionesco, whose plays written in French call attention to the strangeness (and frequent uselessness) of all language, and Léopold Sédar Senghor, the Senegalese poet and statesman who chose French as the vehicle of his postcolonial assertions. For each well-known figure cited, however, there are dozens of lesser-known ones whose work Kellman seeks to discover for his readers.

In his third chapter, "Translingual Africa," Kellman explores in breadth and some depth the experience of both white and black authors writing from and about Africa during the twentieth century. Among the former are Karen Blixen, a Danish colonist who reinvented herself as Isak Dinesen to write tales in English, and Fernando Pessoa, a Portuguese reared in South Africa, whose poetry spans both Portuguese and English in a variety of auctorial voices. Among the latter, Kellman foregrounds the case of the Kenyan

Steven G. Kellman is a professor of comparative literature at the University of Texas, San Antonio. His books include The Self-Begetting Novel *and* Loving Reading: Erotics of the Text. *He is a film reviewer and a director of the National Book Critics Circle.*

Ngugi wa Thiong'o who, after completing a distinguished body of work in English as James Ngugi, returned to his native Gikuyu in order to write plays that would reach an audience whose members might or might not be able to read. Kellman's subsequent chapter deals with the career of J. M. Coetzee, born in South Africa in 1940 to an Afrikaner and his British wife. Although his family spoke Afrikaans in the home and his English was learned mainly in school, Coetzee chose English for his professional writing, both creative and expository, and in time pursued the Ph.D. at the University of Texas, Austin, completing it with a dissertation on the fiction of Samuel Beckett. For Kellman, Coetzee's affinity for Beckett was no accident. "Translinguals are not only a large and important category of authors. As acutely conscious of their links to others as to the problematics of language, they constitute a tradition, not an arbitrary assemblage."

As Kellman points out, Coetzee's early creative writing responds to Beckett, "reading" Beckett in the very act of writing, and for at least a decade after completing his Ph.D., the South African continued to publish articles and essays on Beckett's work. The critic has also published on Nabokov's *Pale Fire* (1962), a novel that figures prominently in Steven Kellman's *The Self-Begetting Novel*, together with Beckett's trilogy originally written in French: *Malloy* (1951; English translation, 1955), *Malone muert* (1951; *Malone Dies*, 1956), and *L'Innommable* (1953; *The Unnamable*, 1958).

In the fifth chapter of *The Translingual Imagination*, Kellman returns to *Pale Fire* as an "object lesson" in the possibilities of translingualism, specifically as an extension of the imagination. "The novel's self-consciousness about its own meaning," explains Kellman, "is compounded exponentially by means of an imaginary language, Zemblan." As Kellman points out, the invention of Zemblan was not Nabokov's first attempt to invent an imaginary language, but rather his most successful, all the more so in that the idiom itself is presented as a (possible) symptom of mental illness on the part of the character Kinbote/Botkin. Nabokov, who spoke freely and often of his translingualism and its difficulties, maintained throughout his life that thought occurs outside language, clearly envisioned *Pale Fire* as a superlingual *tour de force*, and in that effort he quite probably succeeded.

Like *The Self-Begetting Novel* some twenty years earlier, *The Translingual Imagination* collects and reworks material previously published over several years in a variety of periodicals. A certain unevenness of presentation is therefore no doubt to be expected, and those readers seeking systematic exposition are likely to come away disappointed.

Kellman's close reading of *Pale Fire*, for example, is followed by expository studies of two contemporary writers somewhat less known to the reading public. Both authors, Eva Hoffman and Louis Begley, were born in Poland and now reside in the United States, where they write and publish in English. Hoffman, who like Coetzee pursued the study of English to the doctoral level, was born Ewa Wydra in 1946 and emigrated with her family to Canada in 1959, eventually settling in the United States after study at Rice and Harvard Universities; she is known primarily for her memoirs and essays, which focus upon the problematics of linguistic identity and cultural assimilation. *Lost in Translation: A Life in a New Language* (1989) conveys a pervasive sense of displacement, of not "belonging" anywhere. Like J. M. Coetzee, Eva Hoffman is well acquainted with the translingual tradition, having studied Beckett and Nabokov, among others. In *Lost in Translation*, she responds specifically to *The Promised Land* (1912), a once-famous memoir by Mary Antin (1881-1949) describing the immigrant experience at the end of the nineteenth century. As Kellman points out, Antin and Hoffman were born exactly sixty-five years apart, and both arrived in the New World at the impressionable age of thirteen. During that time, however, political developments on both sides of the Atlantic created a larger gulf than mere chronology might suggest. Antin, born in Tsarist Russia, was reared as a speaker of Yiddish; Ewa Wydra, born in the aftermath of World War II to parents who feared a resurgence of anti-Semitism, learned Polish as her first language, hearing Yiddish only as a secret "code" exchanged between her parents; as a teenager transplanted to the New World, she remained attached to Polish expressions that seemed to have no English equivalent. "Instead of the seamless transition from one language to another," observes Kellman, Hoffman finds herself "suspended, inarticulately, between Polish and English . . . ." As a scholar of modern and/or postmodern literature, however, Hoffman will in time at least be able to articulate her problems. "Polish obtrudes through Hoffman's English," notes Kellman, "reminding her that languages are never exactly commensurate, that each always processes experience in its own unique way." Such, indeed, is the central issue of Kellman's study, the challenge faced—and passed on to the reader—by writers whose thought spans more than a single language.

Louis Begley, like Hoffman a Jewish native of Poland, did not begin publishing fiction until he was in his late fifties, after a successful career in international corporate law.

"For Begley and his characters," notes Kellman, "language is multiple and a mechanism of survival, through cunning adaptation. Born in Poland in 1933," Kellman goes on, "Begley managed to live through the Holocaust—the single greatest challenge to Jewish continuity—in part through a linguistic glibness than enabled him to pass for Aryan." One can only assume, as does Kellman, that Begley's first published novel, *Wartime Lies* (1991), in many ways replicates the author's own experience through the adventures of the nine-year-old protagonist Maciek, a picaresque hero out of sheer necessity. The theme of lying, as of self-deception, continues in Begley's subsequent fiction, which blends into the mainstream of the American novel of manners. With such novels as *As Max Saw It* (1994), *About Schmidt* (1996) and *Mistler's Exit* (1998), the refugee-turned-attorney-turned-novelist excels in the creation and portrayal of unreliable narrators who defy the reader to interpolate between the lines of their deceptions, thus presenting an additional dimension to Begley's deft social and psychological satire. Implied but understated in Kellman's summary of Begley's works and career is the contrast with the life and career of Jerzy Kosinski, likewise born in Poland during 1933 and once hailed as a "literary" survivor of the Holocaust, whose works fell under suspicion of fraud and who died a suicide in 1991, the year of Begley's first publication.

Kellman's final chapter, apart from a brief epilogue, deals with the work of the author and filmmaker John Sayles who, unlike the authors considered earlier, emerges as a translingual by choice, a monolingual who ventures outside the "box" of his own language to follow the reach of his imagination by choosing Spanish as the vehicle of his expression. Beginning with the novel *Los Gusanos* (1991; the worms), written in both English and Spanish, Sayles extended his experiment with the film *Hombres Armados/Men with Guns* (1997), filmed in Mexico but set somewhere further south, in a fictional but all-too-believable Latin American country torn apart by violence. As Kellman observes, "Sayles's working proficiency in the language is testimony to a stubborn determination to portray life as it is lived beyond the syntactical structures of his imperial native tongue." With dialogue not only in Spanish but in various tribal languages, *Hombres Armados* describes the truly quixotic adventures of an aging physician who ventures into the hinterlands to visit former students whom he has trained, only to find that all have vanished or died, victims of the prevailing violence, the men with guns. As Kellman points out, Sayles's native English would indeed have been inadequate to the task of his projected exposition, which succeeds as art even if it failed commercially, as it was no doubt expected to do. What matters for Sayles, as for Kellman, is emergence from the "box" imposed by a single language.

As Kellman implies in his preface to *The Translingual Imagination*, the book itself might well be seen as a preface, a prologue to further, deeper investigation by individual readers intrigued by its basic premise. Both in the body of the text and in an appended list of translingual authors, Kellman prepares the way for future analysis and inquiry: Mentioned only briefly, for example, are such authors as Jeannette Lander, a

New York native reared in Atlanta who has lived in Berlin since the 1960's and whose novels, set in the American South, are written in German "laced with Yiddish and African American dialogue." Intended for the general, if uncommonly committed, reader, Kellman's latest volume extends the discipline of comparative literature out of the classroom and into the marketplace, inviting fresh readings of both the new and the apparently familiar.

David B. Parsell

Sources for Further Study

The Nation 271 (November 27, 2000): 23.
The Times Literary Supplement, November 3, 2000, p. 32.

THE TRIPLE HELIX
Gene, Organism, and Environment

Author: Richard Lewontin (1929-   )
First published: Gene, organismo, e ambiente, 1998, in
  Italy
Publisher: Harvard University Press (Cambridge, Mass.).
  Illustrated. 136 pp. $22.95
Type of work: Science, philosophy, and history of science

∼

*Lewontin takes fellow biologists to task, especially
those involved in genetic research, for excessive specialization and failure to appreciate how the interactions between individual organisms and their environments influence growth and natural selection*

∼

The Triple Helix contains three chapters that originally were lectures delivered by
Richard Lewontin to the Lezioni Italiani in Milan. In them, Lewontin, the Alexander
Agassiz Research Professor at Harvard University's Museum of Comparative Zoology, admonishes researchers in the life sciences for ignoring important ideas and so
overspecializing that their results, especially those concerning genes and inheritance,
are misleading. He proposes that a revolution in the biological sciences is needed to
redirect modern research. Apparently because these lectures were heavily critical, his
editor suggested adding a fourth with recommendations for improvement.

   The central question that unites the four essays is a vexing one: Why are individual
organisms, even those of the same species, both similar and different? The answer has
more than scientific value; it has deep philosophical and social implications, because
it concerns how people should think about nature and view themselves in relation to
it. Lewontin's approach to the answer departs from that of mainstream biology and
the popular accounts derived from it that shape public opinion.

   "Gene and Organism" opens with a warning about metaphors: They are useful in
solving problems but lead scientists astray if taken too literally. A dominant metaphor
in biological theory, says Lewontin, comes from René Descartes's metaphor of nature
as a machine—the clockwork universe. For example, it appears in modern life science
in the description of deoxyribonucleic acid (DNA) as a "blueprint" or the genetic
"program" that determines the development of every organism. The mechanistic metaphor carries the implication that DNA is self-sufficient in replicating itself and manufacturing proteins for metabolism. Lewontin adjudges this view of an organism's relation to its genetic heritage as insufficient, producing bad biology. He sets forth
examples of studies about plants, flies, and human intelligence both to show how the
evidence casts much doubt on the DNA-as-software theory and to warn that, in the

∼

*Richard Lewontin is Alexander
Agassiz Research Professor at the
Museum of Comparative Zoology at
Harvard University. His books
include* Biology and Ideology, Not
in Our Genes, *and* Human
Diversity.

∼

case of intelligence studies, it can have incorrect and invidious social implications.

Its environment is also a necessary part of an organism's growth, Lewontin insists, and, specifically, the order of environmental influences that the organism passes through. However, a third influence is also apparent at the cellular level: random molecular interactions that result in biochemicals' processing at differing rates among cells and in a variety of cell sizes. Genetic inheritance, the sequence of external environments, and random molecular events form a mutually influencing "ontogenetic process." (Presumably, this is the "triple helix" of the book's title. Lewontin does not use the phrase, which may be the publisher's addition.) It is a stunning essay, combining clear, cogent references to Platonic and Cartesian philosophy, Darwinian natural selection theory, and microbiology to argue that modern biologists have indeed neglected environmental influences in order to concentrate on decoding genes. Moreover, Lewontin points out that promised medical benefits from linking human diseases to specific genes—benefits that may be exaggerated—attract the largest share of money for research. Even more important, to him at least, genetic studies fail to explain why individuals in the same species can vary so much in appearance and behavior. If DNA were really like a computer, he quips, it would be a very poor one that computed such a variety of answers to a problem from the same program.

Just as the first essay addresses misconceptions in the gene-organism relation, "Organism and Environment" considers how evolutionary biology became straitjacketed by its prevailing investigative methods. He considers the traditional conceptions of the ecological niche, fitness, and adaptive value, predicated on the view that species are passively adapted to an environment by internal and external evolutionary forces, to be outdated. He criticizes the trend in which researchers identify a specific trait in an organism and then hunt in its environment for an external, physical cause for it, the cause being some feature of the eco-niche that requires the trait for survival. The view that the environment is a priori and causally independent of the organism is, he says, clearly wrong. He calls for a new understanding of the organism-environment relation.

He recommends that instead of the "metaphor of adaptation" biologists model their research on the metaphor of construction. Environmental niches cannot exist without organisms in them. The idea of an empty niche is specious. Therefore, within the constraints of natural physical laws, organisms literally construct their environments. In this refreshing reversal of a traditional biological conception, Lewontin educes five lines of reasoning, drawing on evidence from paleontology, animal behavior, plant development, species succession, the search for life on Mars, and even economics. First, the activities of a species determine which elements of the external world are used and which combinations of them are relevant to its constituent organisms. Second, a species, by its very presence, shapes its environment as it uses up fuel and gives off heat and waste products, because, third, this process constantly alters the resources available and the physical conditions, such as temperature and humidity. Fourth, organisms temper the effects of variations in external conditions to make best use of available resources—by, for instance, storing food for the winter or building shelter. Finally, organisms reprocess signals from the outside world to fit their internal requirements for metabolism and reaction to stimuli, as when photons striking the eye are converted into electrochemical signals that the brain can react to. In all these senses, organisms individually, and a species as a whole, are not passive. They actively mold the environment to support them. Moreover, aside from the infrequent catastrophes that suddenly alter physical conditions, such as asteroid impacts or volcanism, organisms are the leading cause of environmental change.

Environmentalists may find this approach unpalatable when Lewontin points out its political consequences. He calls such slogans as "save the environment" and "stop extinctions" false because environments change and species go extinct constantly from far more than human causes. What environmentalism really aims to do, he contends, is to control environmental change in such a way that it is agreeable to humans: a fight for the status quo against the immense forces of change in nature.

"Parts and Wholes, Causes and Effects" continues the discussion about reductionism and the presumption that nature, like a machine, can be divided into clear chains of cause and effect. Lewontin agrees that analytic scientific methods are enormously successful, and their opposite, radical holism, does not afford practical knowledge of nature's workings. Nevertheless, science's very success led to overreliance on a simplified view about parts and wholes and causes and effects, encouraging scientists to investigate only problems that can be solved readily by dividing the subject into parts and figuring out what each does while ignoring larger interrelations. His major example is the study of DNA coding for proteins. Decoding may reveal which genes produce which proteins but does not define the final form of the protein—because a key process, protein folding, is independent of DNA—and thus its function.

Lewontin believes that the nature-as-machine model, however successful for physics and chemistry, is inadequate for biology in several ways: No clear and unique procedure for dividing an organism into organs or systems exists; organisms are very complex, affected by a large number of weak forces, which makes it difficult to identify specific causes and effects; and, finally, every organism exists in a unique place and time, vastly complicating the discovery of universal laws. He cites the Human Genome Project as a large-scale reductionist effort that is misdirected. Cutting up the genome into genes does indeed yield knowledge but misses much by ignoring other DNA influences (these are unnamed, but perhaps crossover is an example), assuming that every gene has a function, and neglecting to take into account environmental effects on protein synthesis. He finds the usual experimental methods for identifying the function of genes—introducing mutations and then hunting for the effect in an organism's phenotype—to be particularly crude and distorting.

Genes, organisms, and environments must be understood as reciprocally influencing, a process of coevolution, Lewontin writes. The point is intriguing, but the subsequent discussion is more tantalizing and disturbing than enlightening. He distinguishes between causes and agencies in biological studies, a distinction usually overlooked, and comments upon the political effects of the confusion. For instance, much research money is devoted to defeating what are usually considered to be the causes of death, such as heart disease or cancer. To Lewontin, however, these are the mere agencies of death, some of any number of possible ways in which the true causes—poor nutrition and overwork—may manifest themselves. At the end of the chapter he makes the claim, which must dumbfound those with acquired immunodeficiency syndrome (AIDS), that the death rate in Africa depends more on systems of international production and exchange than on medical care, however effective. Certainly, poverty is related to AIDS, but it seems particularly insensitive to imply that simply improving the standard of living would save those already afflicted.

The final essay, "Directions in the Study of Biology," opens with a disarming admission. It is easy to be a critic, Lewontin says, and he promises to make up for the excessively negative tenor of the first three essays with positive suggestions. Readers may be disappointed, though, in the low level of specificity in them. He recommends that research concentrate upon finding the physical and temporal boundaries of major subsystems. Biologists should also pursue general systems of explanation for which biological processes are special cases, but he acknowledges that the multidiscipline theories advanced thus far—catastrophe theory and chaos theory—were not very helpful and the current heuristic star, complexity theory, is primarily speculative.

Then Lewontin appears to retreat. What is needed, he writes, is not so much a revolutionary new approach as simply a lot of hard work on details, keeping in mind, first, that understanding function comes from knowledge about form and shape and, second, that it is perilous to draw general conclusions in biology based upon a small number of readily studied examples. Is this really news to other biologists? No, Lewontin admits. Every biologist is well aware of the deficiencies of research. His closing recommendation, which may strike readers as vapid after the penetrating critiques of the other essays, is that biologists must take into account the heterogeneity of organisms and coevolutionary forces in their research.

The Triple Helix is meant for fellow biologists. General readers coming to it may feel that they have wandered into the middle of an argument. Still, the book offers them three benefits, in addition to its pleasant prose style and the window it opens on the state of modern biology. It clearly makes conceptual distinctions that are often poorly understood, as is the case for the difference between an agency and a cause. It comments, albeit briefly, on misconceptions concerning biotechnology, especially in medicine. Most generally, it surveys the history of the scientific method, taking care to distinguish the special difficulties it presents for the life sciences.

Roger Smith

Sources for Further Study

Booklist 96 (March 15, 2000): 1304.
Library Journal 125 (April 1, 2000): 126.
The New York Times Book Review 105 (April 16, 2000): 24.
Publishers Weekly 247 (April 10, 2000): 81.

ULTIMA THULE

Author: Davis McCombs (1969-   )
Foreword by W. S. Merwin
Publisher: Yale University Press (New Haven, Conn.) 72
  pp. $19.00; paperback $11.00
Type of work: Poetry
Time: The mid-1800's and the 1990's
Locale: Mammoth Cave, Kentucky

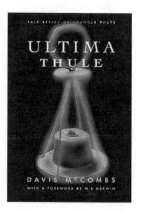

~

A sequence of poems all dealing with the unusual land-
scapes of Kentucky's Mammoth Cave—and the very differ-
ent human psyches that encounter this landscape, from a
nineteenth century slave to a contemporary poet

~

Principal characters:
> STEPHEN BISHOP, a pre-Civil War African American slave and tour
>   guide for Mammoth Cave
> DAVIS MCCOMBS, a park ranger at the cave who conveys his emotional
>   involvement with the landscape through his poetry

   Though the generation of poets to which Davis McCombs belongs has hardly yet
reached maturity, some common denominators can be identified. One of them is an
interest in both history and landscape, concerns that are at the heart of *Ultima Thule*.
McCombs works as a park ranger in Kentucky's Mammoth Cave Natural Park. The
term "ultima Thule" was coined by the ancient Romans to name islands in the far
North Atlantic that their ships could not reach. Ultima Thule has since become a syn-
onym for any area difficult for humans to access. Thus, it is not surprising that the
people who first explored the Mammoth Cave complex in the early nineteenth century gave this name to the least accessible cave of the group.
   Before he begins his first set of poems, McCombs provides the reader with a re-
print of an 1845 map of Mammoth Cave. This shows the reader he is depicting a real
landscape, not just an imaginative one. The poems are not just free-floating artifacts.
They are tied to a concrete topographical image, and the reader can measure the poems against the map through the course of the book. Other poets might scan the geographical specifics of Mammoth Cave in favor of a more interior or subjective vision.
McCombs, however, wants it to be known he is dealing with an actual place that has
accrued centuries of historical meaning.
   The first part of the book, subtitled "Ultima Thule" (just like the title of the overall
book), takes advantage of the map immediately, though in a directly inverse way.
This section is a sequence of sonnets narrated by Stephen Bishop, an African American slave who serves as a tour guide at Mammoth Cave in the decades preceding the

Civil War. In an author's note, McCombs explains that Bishop, a real historical personage, was the slave of Dr. John Croghan, who owned Mammoth Cave and tried to market it as a locale for rest cures as well as a vacation spot. McCombs's poetic version of Bishop starts the first poem in the sequence, "Candlewriting," by recalling his childhood, which he describes as a "mapless country." In addition to the normal confusions of childhood, Bishop, an overworked field hand, is denied any purpose in life and has no control over his situation and no sense of autonomy to give him hope that the situation might

~

Davis McCombs was a Wallace Stegner Fellow at Stanford University from 1996 to 1998. His poetry has appeared in The Best American Poetry 1996, *the* Missouri Review, no roses review, *and the* Columbia Poetry Review. Ultima Thule *is the winner of the Yale Series of Younger Poets competition.*

~

change. His way out ends up being knowing how to read and write—a skill frequently forbidden slaves because slave owners knew that literacy would entail a desire for enfranchisement. Bishop learns to write by the light of a candle. Through this "candlewriting" he encounters a representation of language that will help him master, or "map," his situation. In conjunction with the map a few pages before, the reader realizes that McCombs intends language and mapping to be two parallel modes of representation, both of which can empower those who comprehend them. This point is driven home when the reader realizes that Bishop himself made the map at the front.

Even though Bishop is Croghan's slave, being a tour guide puts him in the rare role (for a black man in the antebellum South) of guiding and directing white people, namely the tourists who visit Mammoth Cave. Bishop knows the territory of the cave in a way they do not. His knowledge becomes symbolic of an awareness of a subjective, interior darkness. The cave has recesses where man can rarely go. It is not like the rest of the landscape, which can be read as a kind of book of nature.

Croghan treats Bishop relatively kindly, and the slave respects the doctor for his scientific knowledge and intellectual agility. The doctor, as a professional man, is so esteemed by society as a kind of expert that he can operate outside the usual Southern codes that stipulate that a master can pass on only the most menial and functional skills to a slave. Bishop becomes genuinely learned in matters of both geology and geography, and much else besides. Yet Bishop feels that, partially due to his status as a slave and partially due to his knowledge of areas of the cave complex Croghan has not experienced, his knowledge is in some areas actually deeper than the doctor's. Bishop knows suffering as well as the exhilaration of knowledge; he is aware of physical ills that can, at least temporarily, be cured, as well as social ills, such as slavery and the divisions it causes, both in the nation as a whole and within an individual's soul.

The "Ultima Thule" sequence reveals little about Bishop's personal life. He seems to be in love with a woman named Charlotte, who offers him a sense of serenity but who is sketched only vaguely and may even be a phantom suggested by the way light moves in the caves. Bishop also suggests that the white women he guides around the cave call out his name at night as if they were still lost—this presumably amounting to some sort of romantic fantasy about him. Yet the reader knows much more about

Bishop's inner life than about his outer experience. He is not overly religious in conventional terms, but sees God as present both in the light and the darkness of the cave. He is proud of his detailed knowledge of the cave's remote nooks and crannies but knows that the cave may hold an absence of meaning as much as a kind of dark plenitude. Bishop, at times, is sympathetic to the caves, and, tour guide though he is, is skeptical of the human ability to explore them fully. McCombs notes that Bishop's death at the relatively young age of thirty-seven is unexplained; perhaps, the poet speculates at the end of the sequence, Bishop simply was lost in the caves when he went too close to the "margins of the map" he himself had designed.

McCombs does not reveal all this information about Bishop in a direct sequence. The reader has to tease it out through hints and gradual revelations. The sonnets in the sequence are not obtrusive as sonnets: It is more by their shape on the page than by their sound that they are recognizable. McCombs uses repetition of word patterns and assonance far more than conventional rhyme to give his poems an understated formality. Another poet might have highlighted the exoticism of the landscapes inside Mammoth Cave and the way they are like nothing else on the surface of the earth. While Bishop's voice gives the reader a sense of the strangeness of the cave's grape-shaped stones and eyeless fish, his musings stress the experiential over the visual. Bishop's voice, though unmistakably a nineteenth century one, is not overly archaic: He speaks in a grave, almost reticent mode of curiosity impelled by witness.

The second section of the volume, "The River and Underneath the River," consists of poems about Mammoth Cave and other Kentucky landscapes, but with no single voice or theme. McCombs displays his identity as a local poet whose love of his own landscape manifests itself in fresh and versatile forms. Floyd Collins, the revered cave explorer who disappeared in 1925, is the other famous name besides Bishop associated with Mammoth Cave. In "Floyd's Last Passage," McCombs gives an account of Collins. The poems in this section are not in sonnet form and are diverse in meter and subject matter. They include the poem "Ponds," about the way earthquakes can make ponds ephemeral features of the landscape; "April Fifth, Nineteen Hundred Eighty-Three," about the juxtaposition of a terrible flood and the onset of teenage romantic awareness; "Kentucky," a surreal collection of sensory images associated with McCombs's home state; and "Watermelons," a dramatic viewpoint from the viewpoint of these large fruits. These poems, less dependent on Mammoth Cave as their subject, exuberantly display McCombs's linguistic brio and density of evocation.

Yet Mammoth Cave is never forgotten. A leitmotif in these poems is the limestone composition of the cave complex. Ancient yet susceptible to change and dissolution, limestone is emblematic of both permanence and transition in geological processes. The reader may harken back to W. H. Auden's poem "In Praise of Limestone," which, though written about English landscapes far from McCombs's Kentucky, is similarly intrigued by the potential for (in geological terms) rapid change in seemingly stable landscapes. The caves are not fixed in place; they are part of the earth's slow movement. If that movement is too gradual for detection, McCombs, in poems such as "Freemartin" and "Flowstone," gives the illusion of tapping into these processes, even going back to the Ice Age when this entire area was under water. In "Salts Cave," a relatively more recent period in the cave's history is considered: the Native American presence in the caves. The Bishop persona also considers Indian remains in "Indian Mummy," but displays less confidence than McCombs's "own" voice about the possibility of fully knowing this level of the past.

The third section of the book, "The Dark Country," returns to the sonnet form, again totally without strict rhyme schemes. This time, though, the poems have a contemporary setting, and the reader hears McCombs's own voice. Many of these poems are clearly inspired by incidents in his career as a park ranger. In "Dismantling the Cave Gate" McCombs's coworkers take down an old fixture and find themselves able to hear the "moan" of the cave produced by the wind whirling through its sinuous crevasses—a sound so eerie it disturbs even a group of fluttering bats. This is not personification on the part of the poet: It is the cave's own natural sound as heard by anyone there.

McCombs records how something one might imagine to be a poet's prerogative—giving animate sound to an inanimate object—in fact can happen through the natural process. In these poems, McCombs takes advantage of the fact that he is not an outsider or interloper on these landscapes. He knows them as well as anybody and thus is not a mere tourist. He does not merely stop by, annex Mammoth Cave and its environs to his poetic experience, and move on. His long, continuing, and sustaining involvement with the area gives the poems not only topographic accuracy but also imaginative empathy.

In "Premonitions," for instance, the landscape reflects the poet's own emotional involvements. In "Comet Hale-Bopp," the poet contrasts the darkness inside the caves with that of the night sky and imagines the Native American inhabitants of the area finding that their ability to explore the depths of the caves compensates for the inscrutability of the celestial mysteries. In "Pushing a Lead" the reader sees the poet as both participant and spectator, working in the cave yet contemplating how its depths dwarf any human effort. Finally, the collection returns to its beginnings. In "Stephen Bishop's Grave," the reader hears the poet's own perspective on the protagonist of *Ultima Thule*'s first section. McCombs has no illusions that Bishop will see the poetry he has written as somehow redeeming his life. McCombs's pale inventions cannot change the fact that Bishop "would prefer the company of rain to [his] own." The poet, however nevertheless tried to vigilantly keep faith with this crucial figure in the history of the cave area he so loves. In "Cave Mummies," the Indian remains are once more evoked: One can excavate the material vestiges of the distant past, McCombs seems to muse, but will they ever reveal the subconscious motivations that shape existence in both past and present? Can these ever be fully brought to the light?

Ultima Thule's intimate sense of its setting of Mammoth Cave is its great asset. By the end of the book, the reader knows this remote corner of Kentucky well and has experienced its rendering vividly and faithfully in poetic terms. The book's strength may also, though, be a partial liability. If McCombs has a greater sense of place than counterpart American poets of former generations, he may lack some of their inspiration—inspiration that may come from seeing beyond mere "place." Nonetheless, *Ultima Thule* is an impressive first book.

Nicholas Birns

Sources for Further Study

Booklist 96 (March 15, 2000): 1317.
The New York Times Book Review 105 (June 11, 2000): 22.
Publishers Weekly 247 (April 24, 2000): 84.
San Francisco Chronicle, April 16, 2000, p. 4.

UNDUE INFLUENCE

Author: Anita Brookner (1928-   )
First published: 1999, in Great Britain
Publisher: Random House (New York). 240 pp. $24.00
Type of work: Novel
Time: The present
Locale: London

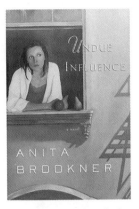

∼

A young woman who prides herself on "making connec-
tions" tries to make sense of life and love

∼

Principal characters:

> CLAIRE PITT, the twenty-nine-year-old unmarried narrator who works in
> the Ex Libris bookstore transcribing articles and notes left by a minor
> writer of the 1950's
> MURIEL COLLIER, eighty-two years old, co-owner of the Ex Libris book-
> store
> HESTER COLLIER, her eighty-seven-year-old sister and co-owner of the
> bookstore
> CAROLINE "WIGGY" WILSON, Claire's closest friend
> MARTIN GIBSON, a former teacher who cares for his invalid wife
> CYNTHIA GIBSON, Martin's beautiful and wealthy wife
> SUE, Cynthia's day nurse

Like a number of Anita Brookner's previous heroines, Claire Pitt is essentially lonely—almost isolated from the world around her. As a single woman living alone since the death of her mother, she has only one close friend, no prospects for marriage, and a job that brings her into contact with very few people. Indeed, her job is as solitary as her personal life, for she has been engaged by the elderly owners of the Ex Libris bookshop to transcribe the nature articles and advice columns that St. John Collier (father of the store's owners) wrote in the 1950's. It is congenial work, in spite of—or perhaps because of—its relative isolation in the basement of a tranquil second-hand bookshop. What Claire particularly likes is contemplating the evidently calm and serene world of the 1950's as depicted by the magazines in which St. John's articles appeared.

Isolation began in Claire's childhood when her widowed mother remarried a structural engineer unused to children and their noise. Consequently, Claire learned to live quietly, mainly in her room, reading. When her stepfather suffered a stroke, incapacity made him dictatorial, peevish, and short-tempered; Claire's mother spent the rest of her married life nursing this man until a second stroke brought his death.

In the opening pages of the novel, Claire as narrator announces her two convictions: one is that "everyone is profoundly eccentric," the other that "everything is con-

Anita Brookner has written nineteen novels, including Falling Slowly, Visitors, *and* Hotel du Lac, *which won the Booker Prize. She is an international authority on eighteenth century painting and the first female Slade Professor at Cambridge University.*

nected." By the latter she means that she can imagine links between events that might seem unrelated. In other words, Claire writes fictions in her head, although she tends to take them not as fictions but as descriptions of reality. Unfortunately, she does not grasp that her two convictions are to some extent contradictory, and hence she is often surprised when the connections she imagines between people and events turn out to be incorrect. To this extent, then, the novel has a metafictional flavor, though rather than use this postmodern term, it might be just as well to use an old-fashioned one: unreliable narrator.

Superficially, *Undue Influence* resembles an old-fashioned love story with an unhappy ending. While working in the bookshop one day, Claire is distracted from her typing by the presence of a handsome, impeccably dressed customer. He turns out to be a Martin Gibson in search of German Romantic poetry. Claire promises to deliver the book he wants if she can locate it, which she does, only to discover that Martin is married to an invalid. There are direct parallels between the Gibsons and Claire's own parents, only in the Gibsons' case it is the wife who ruthlessly exploits her illness to dominate and manipulate her husband. Cynthia Gibson asks Claire to visit again, and this time Claire brings her best friend, Wiggy, but the visit is unsatisfactory as Cynthia wants not visitors but an audience—people to witness her domination of Martin. After their second visit, also a failure, Claire receives a note from Sue, Cynthia's day nurse, indicating that Cynthia has died. Events unfavorable to others seem to be moving in Claire's favor, as Martin's attentions to her suggest romance. Moreover, when Hester Collins falls and breaks her wrist and Claire takes over at the bookshop, everything seems poised for an almost Victorian happy ending: marriage and the management, if not the ownership, of a congenial business.

This is a contemporary novel, however, not a Victorian melodrama. Dinner with Martin at a pretentious restaurant with show-off food is not a success, and Muriel seems not to trust Claire's management of the bookstore. Claire invites Martin to dinner at her flat, and he ends up spending the night, but everything soon crumbles: Martin goes to Italy for a holiday with friends, and Muriel announces that she is selling the shop. Soon, Claire is unemployed, and although Martin again comes to Claire's for dinner, she realizes that there is nothing between them. As Claire prepares to take a holiday, she visits Wiggy and learns that Sue and Martin are engaged. "This was the one connection I had failed to make. It was the greatest failure of my life and no future success could ever obliterate it."

For Claire, future successes seem unlikely. Claire herself is in many ways an attractive person, to whom success in some form seems due. The world around her, however, does not seem conducive to romance or even satisfaction in any other facet of life. The unhappy aspects of Claire's parents' marriage have already been noted, although Claire does come to realize, "Suddenly I was filled with love for them both, and this was new to me. I saw that they had made the best of things, had done their duty, that theirs were tame lives, but lives that they had managed for themselves." The Gibsons' marriage, too, is marred by manipulation. Hester and Muriel Collins never married, because their widowed father virtually demanded that they devote their lives first to him, then afterward to his literary career. As Claire comes to realize, however, St. John's literary efforts were feeble ones, and before the end even he realized he had nothing significant to say.

Nor does the single, independent life promise anything more fulfilling than marriage. Wiggy is almost as lonely as Claire. She derives only small comfort and perhaps some pleasure from her affair with a married man. Wiggy's neighbor, Eileen Bateman, enjoyed her years as a working woman and after retirement took pleasure in bicycle trips and a robust independence. She died alone in her sleep, however; her legacy to Wiggy is a pile of holiday brochures advertising places she never had the courage to visit. Hester and Muriel appeared to have made peace with life, running their father's bookstore and overseeing his literary legacy, until Hester's injury and rapid decline turns their lifelong "marriage" into just another instance of one partner caring for the other.

For all her insight into the predatory, even parasitical, nature of human relationships, Claire has little or nothing to offer in their place. She, too, is greedy for attention. She wants a friend and trust; she wants to figure in someone else's plans. That is why she is so disappointed when Martin is not interested in what is on her mind and when he shows that he is too self-centered and preoccupied even to ask her questions about herself. His emancipation, she theorizes, depends on his ability to ignore others' expectations.

It would be tempting to see this novel as Brookner's statement on the plight of women in contemporary Western society, for most of the characters are female, and certainly women bear the brunt of men's exploitation. Cynthia's manipulation and domination of Martin suggests that Brookner is interested in a larger idea, however—the human tendency to use, manipulate, and dominate—to achieve emancipation by ignoring others' expectations. There is little or no give-and-take in human affairs, she seems to suggest, only giving on one side and taking on the other. That, however, may be the price for lasting human relationships, married or otherwise. Using and being used may be the price one pays for lasting human friendship or love.

At the formal level, this is also a novel about the ability of the imagination to make connections, and here again Brookner demonstrates a certain degree of postmodern skepticism. *Undue Influence* is not as experimental and playful as *Incidents in the Rue Laugier* (1995), but it would be hard to miss the fact that Claire is trying to grasp or create meaning imaginatively. This novel is, in essence, her attempt to make sense of life—to explain to herself why neither her job nor her affair with Martin is more satisfactory. Because of the novel's point of view, however, it is difficult to know whether Claire has succeeded in her endeavor. To the end, she creates fiction about others: Her last attempt is a rather bleak prediction about the life a little girl will live as the center of conflict between her mother and grandmother. Near the end of the novel, she concludes that she has failed with Martin in part because she was too candid with him:

> Those gods of Olympus, with their enviable lack of conscience, are probably the ones to emulate. Their reputation has not noticeably suffered from their unashamed preoccupation with sex and influence. Those who have been taught to love their enemies, sometimes to the detriment of friends, will always be sunk in a morass of self-questioning, timorous restraint taking the place of robust self-interest.

A moment later, however, she admits, "Perhaps for the first time in my life I did not understand myself. Nor did I altogether want to."

It may be, indeed, that Claire's desire to understand herself and to "make connections" in the life around her is interfering with what she most wants to achieve. Her vulgar, elderly neighbor, Mrs. Dilnot, still loves to gamble and get tipsy on wine. She has a memory well stocked with vacations and affairs, and her advice to Claire seems clichéd but sensible: Seize the day. It is shortly after this advice from Mrs. Dilnot that she learns Martin is now with Sue.

Claire is in many ways a typical Brookner protagonist—lonely, cautious, reflective, timid. In her earlier novel *Visitors* (1997), Brookner allowed her female protagonist a glimmer of hope for more active engagement in the world, more openness. Perhaps when Claire returns from her vacation, she too will step out into the world, participate more in it, and reflect less pessimistically on it.

For all its pessimism, however, *Undue Influence* is not a bleak novel. Claire is an engaging character and narrator—intelligent, thoughtful, often shrewd in her insights and projections. If her fictions are intended as a comment on fiction making itself, then the novel suggests that while fiction's powers are limited, they are nonetheless real. On the realistic level, the novel has interesting points to make about the plight of contemporary humanity in its battle against loneliness and alienation. For all her failures, Claire remains hopeful. Having come to realize that it is probably impossible to love or be loved without some form of exploitation, she may indeed find what she is looking for.

Claire's ultimate fate is perhaps less important than the journey she has taken readers on through this narrative. Seeing the world through Claire's alert and perceptive eyes is a rewarding experience, and once again Brookner has offered a novel that, for all its Jamesian traditionalism, casts new light on life on the cusp of the millennium.

Dean Baldwin

Sources for Further Study

Booklist 96 (October 15, 1999): 394.
Library Journal 124 (November 15, 1999): 97.
The New York Times Book Review 105 (January 23, 2000): 34.

AN UNFORTUNATE WOMAN

Author: Richard Brautigan (1935-1984)
Publisher: St. Martin's Press (New York). 110 pp.
  $17.95
Type of work: Novel
Time: Six months in 1982
Locale: Various locations including Hawaii, San Fran-
  cisco, Montana, New York, Illinois, and Canada

～

An anonymous writer with the initials R. B. charts his
travels over a six month period in an attempt to sort out his
life and chart the exact course he is taking after a neigh-
bor's death

～

Principal characters:
    R. B., the author of the diary
    HIS ESTRANGED DAUGHTER

The novel is presented as a diary of daily entries which are soon broken by lost days and months and which the protagonist describes as the "route of a calendar map following one man's existence during a few months period of time." The protagonist is, if nothing else, incurably peripatetic, jumping among cities, states, countries, and a variety of homes and apartments. Beginning in January and extending to June, 1982, he wanders between locations, friends, and a disjointed series of experiences, only to arrive at a seeming still point: watching a sunset and scribbling in his notebook. As he explains at the outset, "We'll go on with this journey that isn't really getting any shorter because it's already taken this long to get here, which is a place where we are almost starting over again."

Howling through this otherwise quiet novel is a palpable sense of isolation, an overwhelming separation in spite of the narrator's apparent devotion to and concern for others. The lives of his family and friends are important to him, but usually only in so far as they produce a mood or feeling, which always leaves the reader centered on the protagonist. For instance, on a visit to a friend in Buffalo where he is to lecture, the narrator's plans are interrupted first by the rape of the friend's neighbor and next by an intruder who terrifies the friend and his wife. After changing their plans and head-ing to Toronto for a few days, the writer concludes, once back in San Francisco, "My trip East had turned out exactly the opposite of what I had intended. I just wanted to have some fun and maybe a few pleasant memories along the way." Pleasant memo-ries, however, are never part of this novel's equation.

Most of the narrator's relationships, especially love relationships, are transitory

∼

Richard Brautigan published eleven novels, a book of short stories, and eight books of poetry before committing suicide in 1984. He is best known for Trout Fishing in America. *An Unfortunate Woman was published posthumously under the supervision of his daughter, Ianthe Brautigan.*

∼

and ultimately unfulfilling. The narrator constantly ponders his next sexual conquest, but no sooner does he attract a woman than he repels her. Lovers are simply means to an erotic end, not partners in any true sense, and when the narrator thinks he is being amusing or avant in his descriptions of sex, he is more often annoying. During one affair, he describes a seduction technique which involves engaging the woman in deep conversation and then suddenly interrupting her with the request that she disrobe. He is proud that she obliges (confiding that women always do) and then imagines the reader posing the following questions, "'Do you take your clothes off?' 'No.' 'Why not? 'Because it's not the effect that I want to produce. '" The double standard and the exploitative nature of these relationships ensure further isolation and despondency.

There is, however, a measure of pathos in this insulation and self-absorption that can be clearly seen in his description of a lonely forty-seventh birthday. Absent are friends, a celebration, any gifts; instead, he describes himself as "very distant, almost in exile from my own sentimentality." Riding across the San Francisco Bay on rapid transit, he wonders what might happen if he were to announce his birthday to the other passengers and spins out a series of amusing scenarios, which end in silence and the terse conclusion: "I just know I won't be 46 again."

The deepest moment of alienation occurs late in the novel when he describes a rift in his relationship with his daughter. After eight months of silence, she phones on Father's Day, and the two can only talk in superficialities, incapable of even agreeing on a date for a future meeting. After abruptly ending the call, he wishes she had never phoned and laments, "I don't know what's going to happen between my daughter and me. I've searched through the possibilities like an archaeologist. These ruins puzzle and haunt me."

Isolation reinforces the novel's central preoccupation with death, and given the close identification of the narrator with Brautigan himself and the widely publicized details of his suicide in 1984, the novel is hauntingly prophetic. A common misconception about Brautigan's works is that they are airy paeans to flower power and the blissful acceptance of all life. On the contrary, all of his major works concern themselves with death, and in *An Unfortunate Woman* the preoccupation is more overt and obvious.

The story begins with three ominous events: a prefatory letter to a female friend who has died of a heart attack after battling cancer, a single woman's shoe lying forlornly in a Maui intersection, and the suicide of a woman living in the narrator's rooming house in Berkeley. While he takes up each of these incidents in different parts of the narrative, it is the third, the suicide, which serves as the leitmotif of the story. He wonders how to explain the death if someone phoned and asked to speak to the departed, or what might have happened had she been momentarily diverted from her grim task by another call, or why he feels compelled to return to the house and take up residence there again. The house itself is ominous, with its dark wood and high ceilings and rooms that defy easy categorization. Most important, though, it is a place that swallows light, so that "the shadows in the house have been here for a long time, shadows to begin with and then decades of shadows added to those shadows, and also gathering, adding to them this day. . . . " Later in the novel an encroaching electrical storm offers a similar shadowing effect, with ponderous gray clouds enveloping the sky and obliterating the sun.

When visiting Hawaii, he shuns beaches and sunshine for a dilapidated Japanese cemetery, which he describes in minute, extended detail. "I've always been fascinated by cemeteries and have probably spent too much time of my limited living time in hundreds of them wherever I've been in this world." The relationship with his estranged daughter is like a visit to another cemetery, in this case a place of the living dead, and like his other relationships, it is most compelling for its sense of a truncated conclusion rather than any quality of duration. The novel begins with a quote from Euripides' *Iphigeneiaē en Aulidi* (405 B.C.E.; *Iphigenia in Aulis*, 1782), with the soon-to-be-sacrificed daughter inquiring about her future, and ends seriocomically with, "Iphigenia, your daddy's home from Troy!" The echoes of a daughter sacrificed and a father slain hang over this story like a grim pall.

One of the marks of Brautigan's enduring popularity is his inventive, no-holds-barred approach to storytelling. He never wrote a conventional novel, and his ex-wife even commented that he had to learn painstakingly how not to write like a poet. This novel abounds in self-conscious, metafictional asides, so that the reader can never entirely enter the story without remembering the presence of a creator who willfully intrudes at unexpected moments. Frequently the protagonist interrupts his narrative to indulge an off-handed impulse or take a new tack. One of the most amusing of these comes after he fails to recall where time has gone and imagines himself in a courtroom with Lewis Carroll's punctual White Rabbit as a juror and a censorious judge who convicts him of "second-degree chronological negligence."

Repeatedly the narrator reminds the reader of the story's artifice by asserting that one of his characters is not like those "in a normal book," labeling himself a "selfish writer" for asserting his will over the story, or remarking that the story could have countless beginnings. When he becomes skeptical of his own methods, he frets that he "should have invented a different and much shorter technique to say what I wanted to say in the very beginning," that he is doing things "in a roundabout way," and that "there are so many loose ends, unfinished possibilities, beginnings endings."

There is an obsessive concern with the reactions of the reader, almost as if the narrative is an enterprise to be negotiated. He often imagines the audience asking pointed questions about aspects of the narrative ("where did I get the hot dog, anyway? Some of you are asking"), which culminates in a page-long interrogation between reader and author investigating myriad details about a broken leg. When he grows weary of the writing and the impression it may be making, he emphasizes the power of the reader's position: "You have read the book. I have not. I of course remember things in it, but I am at a great disadvantage right now. I am literally in the palm of your hand as I finish."

At the heart of all this self-consciousness is the writer's desire for control. His life and world, like his dying friends and estranged daughter, are eluding him; he can only barely keep track of the days, and at one juncture he complains that he has lost track of one hundred of them. Language becomes a refuge, one that he even calls his "home," from a "reality" that is often rendered unreal. Whereas his life is disorganized and full of unwelcome deviations, his prose is a realm of freedom, linguistic play, and unceasing invention. The deaths which surround him are actually portents of a more troubling death, that of his imagination and narrative control: "one of the doomed purposes of this book is an attempt to keep the past and the present functioning simultaneously."

Another hallmark of Brautigan's style is his playful, capricious use of language. His best works are full of whimsical, unexpected figurative tropes, and this novel features a number of these. Thus a sun bather becomes "a suntan lotion postage stamp," tombstones are "signatures of immortality," and drifting cottonwood seeds transform into "late June abstract snow." A favorite technique is enumeration, where the narrator will tick off, *ad seriatum*, features of something that catches his imagination. Consequently, to mark his hundred-day lacuna, the narrator writes the dates of each lost day, and to chart his narrative progress, he counts words on a number of pages. Overwhelmed by events during a visit to a Midwest university, he numerically arranges separate episodes, with meticulous subsets for minor details in a compulsive version of writer's outline.

Brautigan finished *An Unfortunate Woman* in 1983, but his friends, agent, and publisher all discouraged its publication. It did appear in France in 1994 as *Cahier d'un retour de troie*. It is not one of his best fictions—after 1968 and eight more novels, he never equaled the brilliance of his first three, *A Confederate General from Big Sur* (1964), *Trout Fishing in America* (1967), and *In Watermelon Sugar* (1968)—but it is still an oddly fascinating work. Characteristic flourishes continue to appear, at moments it fleetingly reminds one of the writer's earlier works, and many of Brautigan's unique concerns appear once again. Reading the book reminds one that Brautigan was an original talent, a meteor that streaked across the literary heavens and burned itself out, and *An Unfortunate Woman* brings that career to a clearer sense of closure.

David W. Madden

Sources for Further Study

Booklist 96 (June 1, 2000): 1835.
Library Journal 125 (July, 2000): 90.
Los Angeles Times Book Review, June 4, 2000, p. 11.
Publishers Weekly 247 (May 15, 2000): 86.

VACLAV HAVEL
A Political Tragedy in Six Acts

Author: John Keane (1949-   )
First published: 1999, in Great Britain
Publisher: Basic Books (New York). Illustrated. 532 pp.
    $27.50
Type of work: Biography
Time: 1936-1999
Locale: Czechoslovakia and the Czech Republic

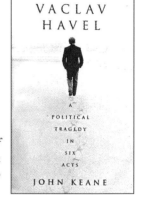

≈

*Unauthorized biography of one of the great leaders of
the twentieth century, who spoke out against Communism
and became a spokesman for morality in politics, only to
prove inept at politics*

≈

Principal personages:

VÁCLAV HAVEL, Czech playwright and politician, one of the key figures
    in the overthrow of Communism
ALEXANDER DUBČEK, Slovak politician who in 1968 attempted to give a
    human face to Communism in Czechoslovakia and was Havel's chief
    rival for power from 1989 to 1990
OLGA HAVELOVA, Václav's intelligent, long-suffering first wife, who di-
    vorced him, partly over disagreements about politics, shortly before
    dying of cancer in 1996
DAGMAR HAVELOVA, an actress who married Havel in January of 1997
    but was unable to fit easily into the role of first lady
VÁCLAV KLAUS, hardheaded economist who oversaw the conversion
    from communism to democracy, from command-economy to free
    market

The title betrays the pessimistic tone of the volume. The customary view of Václav
Havel is that of an unusual man who could have been very ordinary except that he
chose to express ordinary dreams in extraordinary language, suffering imprisonment
and risking death for having done so. Keane's Havel, in contrast, is an unusually
flawed individual who could not have functioned normally in ordinary times in any
society. His Havel is one who sees absurdity and pointlessness in every situation, who
drinks too much, succumbs too easily to women, talks more than he listens, and is
close to incompetent in the complex world of practical politics and economics. His
Havel is a great man who falls short of achieving his potential; hence, the tragedy of
Havel's life at every stage—as student, as playwright, as husband, as political martyr,
and, most of all, as politician.

~

John Keane has written eleven books, including Civil Society: Old Images, New Visions, The Media and Democracy, *and a highly acclaimed biography of Tom Paine. He was also the editor of Havel's* The Power of the Powerless: Citizens Against the State in Central-Eastern Europe.

~

Keane interjects himself into the story more often than is common for biographers. He believes in the current academic conceit that all narratives are reconstructions, hence fictions. Thus, written history is nothing more than a fiction based on fact, or a "faction." He thus justifies elimination of entire episodes of his subject's life and the insertion of philosophical passages more typical of the lecture hall than a book. His concluding chapter, in fact, is an essay on death and its implications for politicians who are aged or ill. His neologisms and judgmental pronouncements may become bothersome, but they are offset by his knowledge of political philosophy and the Czech social, intellectual, and political scene, which he gained through twenty years of experience working in central Europe and five years of writing this book. Awkwardly, although Keane interviewed many of Havel's friends and associates, he never spoke to his subject personally or communicated with him by correspondence.

Havel was born in 1936 to a family well known in Prague's merchant and political circles, with a beloved uncle who was prominent in the motion picture industry. His father withdrew to the country to escape the dangers of the Hitler tyranny and then lost what remained of the family fortune when the Communists took power. "The young prince" was taught by his strong-willed and well-educated mother and a succession of female au pairs, then entered into a good local school. By age ten, Havel was an overweight bookworm who was not good at sports or horseplay. Soon enough, the Communists closed the school and assigned him, along with other "class enemies," to a state school for manual labor training. His parents managed to evade his becoming a proletarian by arranging dancing classes, a comfortable apprenticeship, night school, and private tutoring.

Stalinism held few terrors for the teenaged Havel, who organized a group of friends to discuss forbidden topics. Making himself the head of these "36ers," he displayed evidence of the talent that would eventually make him the leader of the "Charter 77" dissidents.

In a very real sense, Havel did not "drop out" of the new socialist society; instead, like most members of the middle class and almost all ethnic Germans, he was booted out—as a result, he became aware of the idiocy of this system, its hypocritical claims of fairness and justice, its humorlessness, its narrow-minded and unimaginative bureaucracy, and its utter lack of real inspiration or aspiration. Then he was drafted into what is by its very nature the most humorless and bureaucratic aspect of any modern society—the army. There he took his first steps into the theater. The theater of the absurd, naturally.

Havel's genius lay in universalizing the themes of the human situation he observed in his homeland. The individual is trapped not merely in communism, but in the modern world, in the processes of a society that limits choices, in the reality of a human existence that frustrates doing the best with the choices that are made. Stalinism and the Cold War hardly appear in his plays, but they were the reality of the daily lives of those who attended the theater; the audiences saw in his works a description of their situation. International audiences recognized, in addition, the anticommunist implications of his themes, but these faded into the background once the magic of the stage caught them up. Havel's characters were both funny and easily recognized.

European audiences took theater more seriously than did American ones. For them, seeing a play was only the beginning of the experience. The discussions over beer, wine, and coffee that followed were even more important than the acting. The analyses quickly uncovered the political themes beneath the surface of Havel's humor. Thus Havel became well known among the many good Czech writers of this era who used humor and sex to underline the grimness of the puritan communist utopia; but his politics were still too vague for anyone to attack them or even bother to inquire into their details.

The events of 1968 changed Havel's perception of socialist reality into a plan for action. Alexander Dubček's effort to transform communism peacefully was crushed by force, but with insufficient force to quiet the discontent totally. The Communists demoted hundreds of thousands to manual labor, but executed no one. Anyone with the courage to go to jail could still speak out.

Havel was the needle of the Czech moral compass in the years to follow. His essay *The Power of the Powerless* made him the inspiring leader of those intellectuals who signed Charter 77 after less than a decade of repression, and he suffered imprisonment courageously. Unlike many revolutionaries, he did not thrive on the martyrdom of prison life or glory in the prospects that this might open to him. He missed his cigarettes, his women, and the alcohol greatly, but most of all, he hungered for opportunities to talk. He had time only for thinking.

What thoughts he had, though! These would appear in future speeches that thrilled the world and in the plays that sprang to life later. These were the thoughts that would make him a world-renowned spokesman for morality in politics and society.

Havel was released from prison in 1983 on medical grounds, but also as a government concession to international pressure to live up to human rights conventions. His first actions were not to make plans for political action, but to indulge in extramarital affairs and binge drinking and fall into a deep mental depression. *Largo desolato* (pb. 1985; English translation, 1987) reflected both the powerlessness of life in prison and outside. *Pokouœení* (pb. 1986; *Temptation*, 1988) portrays a Faust without power dealing with those in power; *Vyrozumìní* (pr. 1965; *The Memorandum*, 1967) describes the language games of the bureaucracy. Havel, the reluctant revolutionary, was propelled to the front by the Velvet Revolution of November, 1989, because there was no other potential leader than Alexander Dubček, an honorable man, but one who had failed in 1968 and who had no more vision now than before.

Although the Communists abdicated power peacefully, it was a close-run thing; more than a few heads were bloodied by the security police in the early days. Havel was elected president by the Communist parliament (which probably anticipated being able to control him, and in any case had no stomach for the bloodletting that would be necessary to retain power), but only after he had narrowly escaped death by drowning when he fell, dead drunk, into an icy millpond and was rushed apparently lifeless to the hospital. This experience had apparently alerted him to need to apply himself more seriously to his duties; soon thereafter he organized an umbrella party, Civic Forum, and persuaded Dubček to support his candidacy.

Havel was, Keane proposes, the crowned head of a Republic, à la Novalis, in which the monarch's charismatic qualities would inspire his subjects to higher cultural levels. Novalis's king was a poet, a director of the theater, with the citizens as fellow actors. Havel, however, did not get far beyond designing new uniforms for the presidential guard. Surrounded by advisers who were anything but models of republican behavior, Havel became smitten by his international fame and the potential for self-indulgence. Close friends and his wife left him.

Troubles came in droves. First, his government had to remove Communists, who were often impossibly corrupt and incompetent, from important posts; then it had to draw up a new, democratic constitution; then accomplish the "Velvet Divorce" with Slovakia, whose hard-line rulers stood in the way of reforms. Keane is less than happy with Havel's performance here, seeing him as increasingly self-absorbed and manipulative. Keane is even less enamored of Václav Klaus, who had observed how Margaret Thatcher's economic policies had reinvigorated Great Britain, and who insisted on making the conversion to Western practices as quickly as possible. Quickly did not always mean efficiently, or without opportunities to line one's pockets, and soon enough Klaus's hard-line reforms were undermined by colleagues' corruption and opponents' seizing on the widespread hardships that accompanied budgetary realism. Havel understood the need for a swift break with the past, at least intellectually, though his heart favored a Czech Republic with an open beer spigot for those who thirsted, and he often used his international forums to speak to the principle that a civil society should serve the weak and powerless, not merely clear the way for those able to help themselves.

In effect, Havel became an international figure whose soul-searching speeches were applauded abroad and who was admired at home for having raised the prestige of the Czech Republic, but as far as domestic politics were concerned, he was a marginal power. Even when Klaus lost power, other less well-known politicians came to the fore, not Havel. Policies changed, but never did they reflect the high-minded, otherworldly concerns of the president. Fundamentally, this was the fault of a man who had never sought to master the skills of the politicians, but it also reflected Havel's worsening physical condition. Havel had never taken care of himself, and nature now began to take revenge for this neglect. Several times he was near death, and observers began to talk about him as if he had already passed from the scene.

The medical crises that began in late 1996 and became increasingly worse through 1999 were paralleled by an unhealthy family life. Havel's second wife, an actress, was not respected by the public, which made her the butt of many cruel jokes. Havel won reelection to the presidency in late 1997, but it was not clear what he wanted to do with the power the office held. Havel had become a character in one of his own plays—powerless, frustrated, and unhappy; and he had no clear idea how to bring the performance to an end.

William L. Urban

Sources for Further Study

Booklist 96 (July, 2000): 2003.
The Economist 353 (October 16, 1999): 6.
International Affairs 76 (April, 2000): 387.
Publishers Weekly 247 (June 26, 2000): 63.
The Spectator 283 (October 23, 1999): 51.
The Times Literary Supplement, December 10, 1999, p. 3.
Washington Monthly 32 (September, 2000): 48.

VERTIGO

Author: W. G. Sebald (1944-   )
First published: Schwindel. Gefühle, 1990, in Germany
Translated from the German by Michael Hulse
Publisher: New Directions Books (New York). 263 pp.
    $23.95
Type of work: Novel
Time: 1980 and 1987
Locale: Northern Italy and southern Germany

~

An intriguing and confounding mix of memoir, travel-ogue, and literary history that creates a portrait of one very modern European artist along with a profound medi-tation on what it means to be a writer

~

Principal characters:

THE UNNAMED NARRATOR, who shares biographical facts with the au-thor, both being Germans living abroad in England

HENRI BEYLE, soldier in Napoleon I's army, failed lover, and future writer

DR. K., Deputy Secretary of the Prague Workers' Insurance and "failed" writer with great posthumous fame

SEELOS LUKAS, the one person the narrator visits on his return to his hometown of W.

GRANDFATHER, the one family member whom the narrator seems to identify with and admire

MATHILD, Lukas's aunt and the grandfather's one friend, a woman with a mysterious past and uncommon authority with unfathomable influ-ence on the narrator

HANS SCHLAG, a hunter whose ghost haunts each of the book's four sec-tions

ROMANA, who runs the tap room at the inn, captures the young narrator's heart, and runs off with Hans

Almost any review of *Vertigo* (including this one) will start by saying how difficult it is to categorize the fiction of W. G. Sebald. He mixes his genres, ignores writerly conventions, and strews his books, not always very helpfully, with photographs and documents. *Vertigo* consists of two apparently factual meditations on writers and two apparently factual accounts of trips the narrator took, one in 1980 and the other in 1987. All factual, all apparently true, yet undoubtedly fiction. If it is harder to call this book a novel, that is only, perhaps, because readers have not learned how to read Sebald.

The critical consensus is that *Emigrants* (*Die Ausgewanderten*, 1993, translated 1996), the last book Sebald wrote and the first translated, is the author's most successful, but he accomplishes something remarkable in *Vertigo*, which is as ambitious as any work of fiction can ever be. This book is so full of ideas and detail that it induces a kind of vertigo just to contemplate them: love, war, disasters, art, identity, memory, time, place, dislocation, and geography. Instead of an exhaustive, Proustian immersion in these things, Sebald opts for something more associative, as in poetry or dreams, using a deceptively simple technique. The book contains four self-contained, apparently freestanding stories, and in a book that delights in doubles and doubling, Sebald sets them in pairs that work with each other and all together like a loom, the warp and woof creating a design of such intricacy it almost cannot be unraveled. Then Sebald contrives to show the back of the rug as well.

~

W. G. Sebald was born in Germany and has taught in Switzerland and Great Britain. He has won the Berlin Literature Prize, the Literatur Nord Prize, the Mörike Prize, and the Johannes Bobrowski Medal. His novel The Rings of Saturn *won the* Los Angeles Times Book Award for Fiction.

~

The first section, "Beyle, or Love is a Madness Most Discreet," follows the seventeen-year-old Beyle, a young officer in Napoleon I's army of invasion. Almost immediately, Sebald says that Beyle's experiences, not written down till many years later, provide "eloquent proof of the various difficulties entailed in the act of recollection." This is one of the main themes of the book, but it is matched by another, which is the imperative to remember despite (or because) of the impossibility of remembering accurately.

In German, *schwindel* refers to the dizzy disorientation of vertigo and amnesia, but an English speaker can easily identify its other meaning. Obviously Sebald, who has been teaching German literature and translation in East Anglia, England, for thirty years and knows English better than most of his readers, does not mean to suggest that his book, or any art, swindles its audience. Rather, he is suggesting that in all art there is an element of fraud, a trace (or more!) of the bogus, which in no way tarnishes the luster of art. To the contrary: Art is impossible without it. It is like the plaster cast of his love-object's hand which Beyle cherishes the more because of the imperfection of one pinkie.

Beyle, whom Sebald nowhere identifies by his more famous penname, Stendhal (1783-1842), is a notorious failure at love (and at war) not because he is ugly, but because he confuses his inner feelings for facts in the world. He does not just see with his eyes, he creates what he sees. The two-word German title, *Schwindel. Gefühle*, is translated into the single word, *Vertigo*, yet it is significant that *gefühle* means emotion, which reinforces the interior source of the swoon. Beyle fails at love for the same reason he succeeds at writing—because his intense self-absorption allows him to be enraptured only in such a way that he can look, never possess. This seems to be a necessary condition for the artist, who cannot make the world conform to his desires and so replaces the world with his art.

The second section, *"All'estero,"* translated as "abroad," is also a kind of swoon, a dreamlike account of two trips that the narrator (Sebald in everything but name) took to northern Italy (the cradle of modern culture) and to the Tyrol (cradle of modern butchery).

Here the narrator seems to be stumbling along in the footprints of Franz Kafka, Stendhal, and others, having lost his way and identity after a fit of vertigo in Vienna where he sees Dante (1265-1321) walking along the street. This is not the last historical person to pop up and vanish like the White Rabbit. Ludwig II (1845-1886), the Mad King of Bavaria (Sebald's homeland), not only makes several personal appearances, but also shows up in the name of the mad terrorist group *Organizzazione Ludwig*, whose members (two young men) may or may not (most likely not) have been the two men the narrator keeps encountering all around northern Italy. Then there are the twins who look like the young Kafka, photo supplied.

Sebald is not open or clear about anything, and yet he will not allow the accusation of obscurity or obfuscation. That is one purpose of the documents and photographs, which Sebald plunks down with the same urgency as a three-card-monte dealer: it's here, here, here, right here. Only it is never there.

The documentation seems by and large to be authentic, but he never makes any claim except that of juxtaposition. There is a jocular element to some of this; talking about the Altenburg castle, for instance, he provides a photo of what is obviously a garden ornament. When he says a person has done something repeatedly, he may repeat an illustration. He is also prone to using pieces of photos, usually the eyes. The reader may also sometimes find "clues" in the illustrations that are not referred to in the text, like the word written on a calendar page, "Waterloo"—one of the most famous tropes in literature being Stendhal's use of that battle to stand for the impossibility of understanding, much less reconstructing, experience.

The third section, "Dr. K. Takes the Waters at Riva," is about Dr. K.'s attempt to escape his past and his trouble with love by taking the cure at Riva on Lake Garda, where Beyle had already been, one hundred years before, trailing along behind another unreachable love-object. Dr. K. is not identified as Kafka (1883-1924) though the "K" would be a dead giveaway were it not for the slight incongruity of the "doctor" (of law). Sebald is not just playing a game with readers since Kafka himself insisted on the distance implied in that title. Unlike Beyle, Kafka's trouble was not finding love, but keeping it away. Sebald suggests that this, too, is necessary for writers— he has no interest in resolving the contradiction; that can only be done in a tortured, unsatisfactory way by the author's life and work. What is important, then, is the way Kafka's experience at Riva is reconfigured three years later as "The Hunter Gracchus." This is one of Kafka's fables, a story of a great huntsman whose body wanders the lake for countless years because of the careless touch of the oarsman. His "ceaseless journey" is a "penitence for a longing for love," though Sebald wonders "what love could have been sufficient to spare the child [Kafka] the terrors of love?"

The final section, *"Il ritorno in patria"* is the return home, the inevitable contraction after the effort to escape. This is the ebb and tide of life against the tug of art. So it is fitting that this final section does not explain Sebald the man, but Sebald the artist, and for a long stretch, Sebald the child, father to the artist. Everything that comes before is "explained" here; readers see the back of the rug, and because readers have been prepared, it has an unexpected impact.

Though it starts off much like the second section, with the narrator going back to his hometown W. for an unspecified reason and wandering around much like the "tourist" he is everywhere else, things change when he approaches Seelos Lukas. Their talks about the past, which the narrator terms "unlikely," "absurd," and "appalling," and the past for Lukas, which "became blurred as if he was out in a fog," provide nonetheless a gateway into the most lucid and compelling part of the whole book. The reader is transported to the narrator's childhood with an immediacy of experience as nowhere else in the novel. Central to the boy's development is his crush on Romana, the lovely bartender, who is seduced by Hans Schlag the huntsman. The narrator has watched them making love and notices the dull look in her eye as she submits. It is the same look that the child sees in the eye of suicide—the same look that Beyle sees in the dead horses at the one battle that he participated in.

The narrator cannot escape the bestiality of his townsmen—with World War II and the Holocaust little more than another disaster in W.'s long history, one item in a list the narrator's beautiful teacher makes the class write down. It is as if they had no responsibility for it, the final and irredeemable proof of man's brutishness.

To the child narrator only the hunter Schlag stands apart, and when he dies (probably a murder victim), the child becomes deathly ill after seeing his body borne along on its bier, the fourth such apparition in the book. Instead of dying, the child escapes through art. All around the area the paintings and murals of Hengge, the local artist, have a vitality and life that none of the people do. An awareness of the greater world is provided by Mathild, Lukas's aunt and a good friend of the narrator's grandfather. She gave the narrator a glimpse of an outside world in various ways, including an atlas, which may explain his lifelong obsession with geography and maps. She was an oversized figure in his memory. Now, he goes back to her old house with Lukas to investigate the attic he was always forbidden to enter as a child, threatened with a bogey man called "the grey (sic) *chasseur*."

Now, in the decaying remains of her life, he finds that she was a woman both religious and politically radical—an outcast in the town, an inner exile, not unlike the narrator himself. He finds the gray *chasseur*, the gray uniform of an Austrian cavalry officer, who would have led a company of men across the Alps and over into Italy to be killed at Marengo fighting against Napoleon I. The book comes full circle, then, from Beyle marching with Napoleon I down to Marengo.

What a novel! What authority of voice! Sebald belongs to a literary tradition where the interior voice dominates—an interior voice that is an extreme version of the self. Kafka belonged to this tradition, obviously, as does Sebald's near contemporary Thomas Bernhard (1931-1989), whom one is almost tempted to call his fellow countryman. Both share a disgust for their native lands, and both authors detest the absurdity of their times. Both show, also, a certain lack of interest in accommodating the reader. Bernhard is notorious for his refusal to paragraph, and Sebald's paragraphing is unusual, too, but it is the least difficult part of his compelling, if confounding work.

At first glance it might seem arbitrary—the way he mixes narrative and dialogue all together without quotation marks—but it is not confusing once one realizes it is Sebald's interior voice that accounts for the odd mix of genres and styles and the apparent indifference to proper paragraph breaks and quotations. What he hears resonates the same way that what he thinks does. Everything that he experiences is filtered through that interior voice so that it takes on some of its qualities. The tone is so seductive and so authoritative that sometimes readers will have to step back from the writing to realize just how bizarre Sebald's world is.

It is a world where nothing is so real as the inanimate. The reader cannot help but feel that Sebald's real friends are the paintings he visits like relatives and old friends, especially those of Antonio Pisanello (c. 1395-1455) and the angels of Giotto di Bondone (1266-1337); these were artists whose realism did not depend upon the swindle of perspective. This is a writer whose postmodernism has very deep, very old roots.

Philip McDermott

Sources for Further Study

Newsweek 135 (April 25, 2000): 99.
The New York Review of Books 47 (June 15, 2000): 52.
The New York Times, May 22, 2000, p. B8.
The New York Times Book Review 105 (June 11, 2000): 20.
The New Yorker 76 (May 29, 2000): 128.
Publishers Weekly 247 (April 24, 2000): 62.
The Spectator 283 (December 25, 1999): 65.
The Times Literary Supplement, February 25, 2000, p. 3.
The Village Voice 45 (June 6, 2000): 125.
The Wall Street Journal 236 (July 14, 2000): W6.

VIRTUAL TIBET
Searching for Shangri-La from the Himalayas to Hollywood

Author: Orville Schell (1940   )
Publisher: Henry Holt (New York). 340 pp. $26.00.
Type of work: History
Time: The eighth century to the present
Locale: Tibet, Europe, India, Argentina, and Hollywood

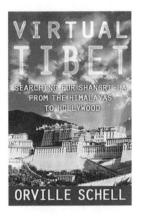

∼

An informative and engaging overview of the history of
the West's fascination with the enigmatic East as embodied
geographically, religiously, and mythically by the territory
and people of Tibet

∼

Principal personages:
>ORVILLE SCHELL, author, and dean of the Graduate School of Journal-
>ism, University of California, Berkeley
>HEINRICH HARRER, Austrian mountain climber and author of *Seven*
>*Years in Tibet*
>THE FOURTEENTH DALAI LAMA, spiritual leader of Tibet
>BRAD PITT, star of Jean-Jacques Annaud's film *Seven Years in Tibet*
>JAMES HILTON, author of the 1933 bestseller *Lost Horizon*

Like the complicated braids worn by Tibetan peasantry, Orville Schell's book *Virtual Tibet* is really several disparate strands of inquiry brought together into a seamless, and seemingly simple, whole. Tibet, it appears, is not just a geographic region the size of Western Europe, hemmed in by the Kunlun Shan, the deserts of Qinghai and Xinjiang Uygur, the Tibetan Plateau, and the Himalayas. No, it is an isolated and inscrutable geographic and psychic territory onto which both individual people and whole countries have projected their deepest spiritual longings, adventurous hopes, and political agendas. Schell traces the quality and tenor of these longings from 779 C.E., when Indian Buddhists brought the teachings of Prince Siddhartha Gautama to Samye, just south of Lhasa, all the way to twentieth century Hollywood, where Tibetan Buddhism, much transformed over the centuries, is so admired by the dream makers and policy shakers of that other great locus of psychic power and myth-making.

Nothing could be more exotic or desirable to the materialistic and acquisitive West, especially in its periods of self-reflection or economic depression, Schell points out, than a Buddhist theocracy nestled in the last uncharted territory on the face of the earth. The four noble truths of Buddhism—that life is full of suffering, that most suffering can be traced directly to attachment and desire, that it is possible to free oneself from such attachment and desire, and that enlightenment can be had for free through

873

~

Orville Schell is the dean of the Graduate School of Journalism at the University of California, Berkeley. He has written Mandate of Heaven, Discos and Democracy, The China Reader, *and twelve other books. His articles have appeared in* The New Yorker, The New York Review of Books, *and* Newsweek, *among others.*

~

meditation, compassion, and right action—have called to Western seekers over the centuries. From Heinrich Harrer, sitting out the ravages of World War II in Lhasa; to conspiratorially inclined, Hollywood director Oliver Stone; to Steven Seagal, who manages to reconcile a career in violent action-adventure films with recognition of his status as a Buddhist *tulku*, the reincarnation of Chungdrag Dorje, a revered seventeenth century custodian of Buddhist texts, Buddhism has had its adherents in the West. From Helena Petrovna Blavatsky, who founded the Theosophical Society in New York in 1875 after claiming a seven-year sojourn in Tibet, to Parisian Alexandra David-Neel (1868-1969) who, camouflaged in Tibetan clothes, was the first white woman ever to enter the sacred city of Lhasa in 1927, Westerners have been powerfully drawn to the mysteries of the East, and nowhere more strongly than to the hidden recesses of Tibet. Tibetan Buddhism is an exacting discipline though, so it is often altered rather alarmingly for Western consumption: For example, ersatz gurus of the 1960's such as Timothy Leary thought it might be possible to just bypass all that wearisome meditation and add instant nirvana to his instant coffee through the use of quicker and stronger stimulants such as LSD. The rich and the famous of Hollywood have hoped to attain enlightenment by simply adding a resident Lama to their roster of personal trainers, gardeners, and bodyguards.

However, as Schell points out, spiritual uplift is not the only kind of uplift that drew pilgrims to Tibet. Harrer, author of the adventure *Seven Years in Tibet* (1953), was, after all, a celebrated Austrian mountain climber with ambiguous but real ties to the Nazis before he escaped a British prisoner-of-war camp and trekked over the peaks to Tibet to become the unlikely tutor to the Fourteenth Dalai Lama.

For some, it is not enlightenment but Everest that is Tibet's greatest allure. Mountaineering came of age as a sport in the nineteenth century, and romantics began to place their spiritual bets on nature rather than religion as the winning means to achieve the sacred. The British Alpine Club was founded in 1857, and all over the world hikers were reporting the transports available at high altitudes. In the United States, John Muir was extolling the beauty of the Sierra Nevada in the same year, 1869, that Elizabeth Sarah "Nina" Mazuchelli became the first Western woman to trek to the base of Mount Everest. Everest, towering at 29,028 feet, the world's highest peak and magnificent beyond words, quickly became the mecca of mountain climbing, making Tibet the number-one destination for adventurers, who sometimes conquered and sometimes lost their lives, but who always projected something of themselves onto the blank whiteness of Everest's forbidding flanks, furthering the mystique of an isolated and fiercely protected Tibet.

It is ironic for Tibet, and "ironic" is a word that comes up frequently in Schell's narrative, that the Tibetans' very quest for privacy and sometimes autonomy often proves to be, in the modern world, their greatest political weakness. It is difficult for Tibetans to understand the West's importunate desire to go where it is uninvited. Sheer curiosity on this scale is unknown in Lhasa, where isolation over the centuries made the Tibetans very naïve about worldwide geopolitical realities. Tibetans would have been very surprised if they knew that the mapping of Tibet, laboriously undertaken by disguised British cartographers and their specially trained Indian helpers, was largely motivated by British paranoia over the Soviet Union's possible interest in annexing the area. They were equally unprepared for China's "liberation" of Tibet in 1950 by Mao Zedong, who was simply operating on the very old Han Chinese idea of manifest destiny, the same idea that drove the reannexation of Hong Kong and Macau. What can a territory, largely operating as an independent state and committed spiritually to nonviolence, do when invaded and occupied by a powerful and militarily developed country such as China? Not very much, unless it is willing to abandon its isolation and accept help from the outside world. Tibet did this in the thirteenth century when it allied itself with the Mongols and their leader, the Great Khan, forming a symbiotic relationship in which the Mongols provided security and the Tibetans provided spiritual solace. Schell's book really probes the question of whether this tactic might work again, only this time Tibet has accepted help and given spiritual solace to an even more unusual ally: Hollywood.

Schell uses the production of Jean Jacques Annaud's 1997 film of Harrer's *Seven Years in Tibet* as a way of probing this paradoxical alliance of extreme Tibetan introversion and extreme Hollywood extroversion. At the nexus of gentility and brashness, selflessness and self-regard, poverty and wealth, powerlessness and power mongering, a country is in peril and a film of its no-longer-existent glory was made in, of all places, Argentina. Before this sixty-five-million-dollar paean to Tibet's past, however, there is a long history of Hollywood's fascination with Tibet and things of the East. One has only to stand on the corner of Hollywood and Vine, the vortex of Hollywood and its influence, to see Sid Grauman's Chinese Theater, opened in 1927, as much a mecca for lovers of theatre and kitsch as Lhasa is for devotees of the Buddha. In addition, there is a string of films, dating back from Frank Capra's 1937 version of James Hilton's *Lost Horizon*, whose ideal Shangri-La was a thinly veiled, plaster-of-paris version of Tibet, all the way up to Joan Chen's *Xiu Xiu: The Sent Down Girl*, released in 1999, which got director Chen banned from ever working in China again. The defining moment, however, of the alliance between Hollywood and Tibet was certainly when actor Richard Gere, longtime Buddhist and Tibetan activist, used his shining moment at the microphone at the 1993 Academy Awards to protest China's occupation of Tibet to a largely unaware and bewildered audience of film lovers. The East had given Gere Tibetan Buddhism, and Gere had given Tibet a place in the world's consciousness.

So Annaud, fascinated by Tibet for all the reasons Westerners always have been, took up the gauntlet and mounted a lavish production of *Seven Years in Tibet*. Tibet's spiritual message, much needed in Beverly Hills and Laurel Canyon; Tibet's magnificent scenery, crying out for a cinematographer to do it justice; and Tibet's inaccessibility (China would not allow filming there) all combined to make Tibet once again irresistible as an idea to Western minds. So Annaud and his crew, accepting hardships no less arduous than the original pursuers of Tibet, rebuilt, Hollywood-style, a complete replica of Lhasa in the Argentine Los Andes. It is here where the ironies, of which Schell is so aware and so fond, begin to mount up.

While Annaud builds a breathtaking pseudo-Lhasa in the Argentine Los Andes, the real Tibetan Lhasa is being brutally occupied by the Chinese, who are filling it with ugly postwar concrete bunker housing. While the real Lhasa is opened by the Chinese to tourists, who can arrive comfortably at the Gongkar International Airport and check into the Lhasa Holiday Inn, Annaud's set is turned into an impregnable fortress of security and seclusion for his Hollywood stars. While the real Lhasa is being repopulated by Han Chinese occupiers, Annaud's film is being cast with real Tibetan exiles from all over the world. While the real Lhasa is bereft of its royal family and the Dalai Lama, Annaud's film has the Dalai Lama's actual sister playing his own mother in one of the most unusual bits of casting in Hollywood history. While the real, and formerly reclusive, Dalai Lama becomes one of the most accessible spiritual leaders on earth, it is impossible for *Virtual Tibet's* author Schell to get an interview with Brad Pitt on the set of *Seven Years in Tibet*. In a peculiar and very sad way, the virtual Tibet of Annaud's film set is an almost perfect reflection of the West's projections on Tibet, and in many ways it is closer to the actual Tibet of the nineteenth century than to the Tibet occupied by China at the beginning of the twenty-first century.

So can Hollywood, like the Mongols before it, galvanize all its money, power, and magic and save any of the Tibets which Schell has explored in his book *Virtual Tibet?* The Tibet of Western dreams, the Tibet of the Dalai Lama's theocracy, the Tibet of spiritual and temporal exclusivity? No, it seems that this ur-fantasy of a Hollywood rescue is just the last in a series of misguided projections of a Western world destined always to just miss the point and fail to gain entrance to the forbidden city of Lhasa.

Cynthia Lee Katona

Sources for Further Study

Booklist 96 (May 15, 2000): 1727.
Harper's Magazine 296 (April, 1998): 39.
Library Journal 125 (April 15, 2000): 115.
The New York Review of Books 47 (June 29, 2000): 12.
The New York Times Book Review 105 (June 25, 2000): 14.
Publishers Weekly 247 (April 24, 2000): 70.

THE VISION OF EMMA BLAU

Author: Ursula Hegi (1946-   )
Publisher: Simon & Schuster (New York). 432 pp.
  $25.00
Type of work: Novel
Time: 1881-1990
Locale: Primarily along the shores of Lake
  Winnipesaukee, New Hampshire, with brief forays into
  Germany along the Rhine River near Düsseldorf

A multigenerational drama of a German American family's rise to prominence in a small New England community and the self-generated curse that dismantles its dream

~

Principal characters:
> STEFAN BLAU, a German-born émigré to the United States
> HELENE BLAU, Stefan's third wife
> GRETA BLAU CREED, Stefan's oldest child by his first wife
> TOBIAS BLAU, Stefan's son by his second wife
> ROBERT BLAU, Stefan and Helene's son
> YVONNE BLAU, Robert's glamorous wife
> EMMA BLAU, Robert's younger child and Stefan's adored granddaughter
> CALEB BLAU, Robert's firstborn
> STEFAN BLAU (MILES), Emma's illegitimate son

The Vision of Emma Blau by Ursula Hegi is a novel with a noteworthy pedigree: not a sequel per se, but a third fictional meditation on the familial destinies and individual moral crises of a cast of interrelated characters spanning more than a century of modern history, introduced by the author in two books published in the preceding decade. *Floating in My Mother's Palm* (1990) and *Stones from the River* (1994), the latter an Oprah's Book Club selection, portrayed life in the fictional German town of Burgdorf between 1915 and 1952. These two works emerged from Hegi's preoccupation with the world of her own childhood in western Germany, where she too negotiated a culture conflicted by unacknowledged guilt for the crimes of the Third Reich. Even as these previous volumes explored a tortured Old World connection to the problem of evil that modern Germans evaded at their own spiritual peril, *The Vision of Emma Blau* allows Hegi to examine evil's reseeding in her adopted country, where ostensibly sunnier human success stories harbor their own soul-crushing betrayals.

  The Vision of Emma Blau refers to people and places from Hegi's previous books, which allows fans some intriguing backstory. Burgdorf quickly recedes into the narrative distance, however, as Hegi's real subject emerges: an elucidation of the truth

Ursula Hegi was born in Germany and moved to the United States at the age of eighteen. Her previous novels include Intrusions, Unearned Pleasures and Other Stories, Floating in My Mother's Palm, Salt Dancers, *and* Stones from the River, *which was nominated for a PEN/ Faulkner award. She is also the author of the nonfiction* Tearing the Silence: On Being German in America.

behind Stefan Blau's fabled teenage flight to America in 1894, where he completes the quintessential immigrant odyssey, reinventing himself through equal parts luck, daring, skill, and tenacity. Far less infatuated by the archetypal dimensions of that transatlantic journey, Helene Montag Blau arrives in the United States many years later, at age thirty-one, having become her childhood friend's third wife; she soon discovers Stefan's far greater interest in her ability to raise his two motherless offspring than in her own desire for the passionate union seemingly promised by their long correspondence.

The true love of Stefan's life is the monument to his American-fed aspiration that he constructs on the shores of Lake Winnipesaukee, New Hampshire: a massive, elegant, European-style apartment house he names the Wasserburg (or "water fortress"). Born of a vision he has while rowing across the lake in the aftermath of a deadly Manhattan restaurant fire, the Wasserburg is the primary motivation behind his opening of an elegant French restaurant in the small New England resort community he has made his new home. Though the sophisticated restaurant initially puzzles the residents, they not only ensure its success with their patronage but yield up to its proprietor in relatively quick succession two of their favorite daughters. It is through the banker father of his first wife, Elizabeth, that Stefan secures the interest-free loan that allows him to begin planning the Wasserburg in earnest, and it is his second wife Sara's indefatigable energy that finally brings the structure to vibrant life. Through the Wasserburg, Hegi dissects the American Dream itself, with its origins in the romantic idealism of the Old World transformed by nineteenth century bourgeois materialism into unprecedented levels of acquisition and consumption in the New World.

Ironically, though, Stefan's very American trajectory from rags to riches is bounded throughout by an ambivalence about giving himself completely to his new context. Even as Stefan self-consciously shapes himself into an American, the Wasserburg exudes a European sensibility that registers as a none-too-subtle critique of American cultural barrenness. In old age, as his building ceases to retain its allure, Stefan retreats into the German language of his childhood, using it to convey to his granddaughter Emma his dream of a Wasserburg immune to time. Through Stefan's cultural identity crisis, Hegi dramatizes the hybrid nature of the immigrant sensibility, a blending of allegiances that precludes one from belonging completely to either the home or the adopted country.

In contrast to the historical sweep of Hegi's previous works, the real dramas in *The Vision of Emma Blau* unfold in the psychological interstices among kin warily negotiating with one another on a private stage. Each of the principals must come to terms with a morally compromising legacy: not only the Wasserburg itself but also the example of its founder, a man who embodied in his life's work the American equation between unimpeded ambition and self-definition. Perhaps it is in this light that the somewhat hackneyed conceit of a family curse dismantling Stefan's dynastic pretensions might best be seen. The origins of this curse lie in Stefan's bad faith with his Flynn in-laws as he fails, decade after decade, to acknowledge, much less repay, the generous loan that made the Wasserburg possible. While the upkeep of his self-generated world is always pressing upon Stefan as the more crucial use for his money, what is actually at work is the familiar pattern of the hoarder. Yet denying the Flynns their money denies it to his oldest daughter, Greta, their only heir, and so what began as Stefan's underprivileging of obligations to nonblood kin actually functions as the first of many fractures of the blood kin bond itself that continue to multiply as the story proceeds. Mrs. Flynn's will turns the loan over to the bank to execute on Greta's behalf. Helene, Stefan's immediate heir, alters her will on the eve of her death to give her son Robert sole claim to the Wasserburg. In an unwitting parody of his father's ethical dereliction, Robert postpones for years any effort to reconfigure ownership of the building to include his alienated half siblings, Greta and Tobias, as equal partners, only to die suddenly as a direct result of his bulimia. Spendthrift Yvonne, Robert's heir, further erodes the financial base needed to repair and remodel the decaying Wasserburg, so maddening her daughter Emma that the young woman convinces her mother to deed the structure exclusively to her. Emma's heretofore doting brother Caleb condemns her acquisitiveness, noticing that Emma seems in no rush either to rectify the earlier disinheritance of her aunt and uncle or to avoid the comparable violation of denying him a share of Robert's estate.

In putting the Wasserburg ahead of everything else in her life, Emma is faithfully practicing the dictum taught her by her grandfather that "Getting what you want . . . has to do with holding it in your mind so strongly that you keep returning to it—without thinking—so that you are always linked to it." In doing so, however, she loses touch with the human responsibilities that supposedly inform her quest for worldly success and material security; keeping the building alive and appealing to new clientele becomes Emma's *raison d'être* and relegates every other pursuit to the margins. In her romantic life, she enters into an affair with an older married doctor who for years shares her life only on Wednesday evenings, even after the birth of their son, revealingly named Stefan. This relationship, like the Wasserburg itself, displaces Emma's engagement with the world as an individual in her own right, until she is brought up short by two striking developments: the discovery that her son has established his own vicarious family by befriending his unwitting half brother Oliver, and the humiliation of hosting a party for the disaffected residents of the Wasserburg to which most of them refuse to come. Emma suddenly realizes how she has given in on several levels to the family compulsion "to only want what wasn't yours." That greediness had once been identified as a German trait by an embittered Jewish tenant; the novel suggests, however, that it is equally present among those infected with the possibilities of the American Dream.

Contemplating the stars whose patterns Stefan had taught her to decipher as a girl, just as his own mother had once taught him, Emma recognizes the need to take her place in the Blau constellation by contributing productively to the living drama of family in the here and now instead of serving a desiccated past. The trajectory of this distinctly American family saga, then, bypasses the wholesale moral ruin that concludes so many tragically inflected European sagas: Emma's repentance secures her the redemptive grace to see things clearly at last, and she finds a reawakened appetite to take to the open road and "live in a place she'd never been to," to remake herself by her own lights, just as Stefan had once done. Tellingly, Stefan himself never sees Emma enact that iconic dance of his vision, for it happens at his own funeral. It has taken Emma half a lifetime to achieve the autonomy signaled by that liberatory gig.

Given such sweeping themes and such complex characters, *The Vision of Emma Blau* offers many pleasures to the thoughtful reader. The world of the Wasserburg is lovingly evoked, and Hegi is adept at conveying the emotional paradoxes of family life. She is clearly dedicated to creating a fuller picture of female sexuality than one traditionally finds in mainstream fiction—she candidly depicts the yearnings and habits of mature women and the sexual compromises of long-lived marriages. One of her most potent themes involves the parent/child nexus, with its myriad opportunities for wreaking psychological devastation. In Hegi's fictional universe, as in the real one, parents bear great responsibility because they are capable of doing such great harm. Yet she is not unsympathetic to the price of such responsibility, particularly upon women, and therefore she joins the ranks of novelists such as Margaret Atwood, Jane Smiley, and Toni Morrison, who have attempted to divest motherhood of its sentimental baggage.

Yet for all these strengths, *The Vision of Emma Blau* is not fully successful in its execution, in great part because too many characters are ascribed too many major subplots for Hegi to manage in any but the most schematic fashion. Because Hegi's characters do compel the reader's interest, it is frustrating to watch the cranking of the narrative machinery that whisks one or the other away for long stretches only to be dropped back in for formulaic clan gatherings such as funerals. Despite its decade-long march to publication, *The Vision of Emma Blau* feels as though it has not yet undergone a full settling and editing process that would have pruned its loose ends and eliminated its episodes of faulty grammar or overwrought sentence construction.

Hegi is fond of a forecasting technique that alerts her reader to the play of the future upon some plot element in the present, using this device to express her belief "that the present, future, and past merge within any given moment." Together Hegi's three Burgdorf-inspired works suggest the mysterious design of each individual life that only God and the fiction writer can see whole. In *The Vision of Emma Blau*, such forecasts are overused and often intrusive, however, too often placed in the service of the mundane instead of the kind of transgenerational linkages that enlarge the meaningfulness of the present. It is just such a fusing of time frames that opens the novel, as the grown Emma struggles to understand how the life she inhabits has become cripplingly entangled in past patterns that it is her responsibility to break. For several hundred pages Hegi plots her way back to this richly suggestive moment in order to release Emma from the story in which she is trapped. The imaginative arch of that effort is laudable and for the most part rewarding, even if the artistic scaffolding beneath it wobbles.

Barbara Kitt Seidman

Sources for Further Study

The Atlantic Monthly 285 (March, 2000): 116.
Booklist 96 (November 15, 1999): 580.
Library Journal 124 (December, 1999): 186.
The New York Times Book Review 105 (February 13, 2000): 17.
The New Yorker 76 (April 17, 2000): 121.
Publishers Weekly 246 (November 29, 1999): 51.

W. E. B. DU BOIS
The Fight for Equality and the American Century, 1919-1963

Author: David Levering Lewis (1936-   )
Publisher: Henry Holt (New York). 715 pp. $35.00
Type of work: Biography
Time: 1919-1963, with regressions to earlier years
Locale: New York City, Chicago, Paris, Brussels, London, Geneva, and Accra, Ghana

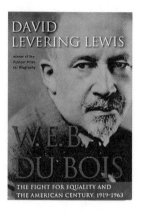

∾

This second volume in Lewis's massive biography of Du Bois focuses on the last forty-four years of Du Bois's life

∾

Principal personages:
WILLIAM EDWARD BURGHARDT DU BOIS,
    black activist and author, founding editor of *The Crisis*
NINA DU BOIS, Du Bois's first wife
YOLANDA DU BOIS, the Du Bois's daughter and only child
SHIRLEY GRAHAM DU BOIS, Du Bois's second wife
MARCUS GARVEY, black activist, leader of the "back to Africa" movement
KWAME NKRUMA, president of Ghana who encouraged Du Bois to resettle there
FRANCIS MARION WHITE, official of the National Association for the Advancement of Colored People (NAACP)

William Edward Burghardt Du Bois was bigger than life. Among the most celebrated intellectuals of his day, he was the founding editor of *The Crisis*, a monthly magazine dealing with black issues and serving as the major mouthpiece of the NAACP. Its monthly circulation in the early 1920's exceeded one hundred thousand copies. Du Bois's articles and editorials in it attracted a wide range of readers, black and white, and were a motivating force in demanding that African Americans be accorded the civil rights guaranteed by the Constitution to all United States citizens.

Given the monumental dimensions of its subject, it is not surprising that David Levering Lewis's two-volume biography of W. E. B. Du Bois is monumental in its dimensions. The first volume, *W. E. B. Du Bois: Biography of a Race, 1868-1919*, appearing in 1993, was awarded the Pulitzer Prize in biography as well as the Bancroft and Parkman prizes. For both its breadth and depth of coverage, Lewis's two-volume biography is in a class with Arthur and Barbara Gelb's *O'Neill* (1962) and David McCullough's *Truman* (1992). His massive research is presented in an elegant, well-considered prose style as impressive as that for which Du Bois himself was renowned.

If volume 1 is, as its subtitle suggests, the biography of a race, volume 2 is equally ambitious. Lewis, after considering the subtitle *The Biography of a Century*, opted for the less encompassing *The Fight for Equality and the American Century*. Besides presenting the biography of a man who was a driving force in the struggle for racial equality through his association with the NAACP, the Pan-African Congress, and *The Crisis*, this volume provides one of the most significant accounts of the complex events that led to the racial turmoil of the 1960's and early 1970's, resulting in civil rights legislation that dramatically changed the standing of African Americans, indeed of all minorities, in the United States.

David Levering Lewis is Martin Luther King, Jr., Professor of History at Rutgers University. He is the author of King: A Biography, When Harlem Was in Vogue, *and* The Race to Fashoda. *The previous volume of his biography,* W. E. B. Du Bois: Biography of a Race, 1868-1919, *won the Pulitzer, Parkman, and Bancroft Prizes.*

Volume 2 begins in the year after World War I. Mainstream America was optimistic about its future now that the "war to end all wars" was behind it and the American continent emerged unscathed. African Americans, particularly in the South, where separate but equal was the rule, were still relegated to second-class citizenship in many states, north and south. Nevertheless, a black intelligentsia was growing. The Harlem Renaissance was about to blossom full-blown in the black community centered in New York's Harlem. Blacks were being encouraged to write. Their books were being published and read widely by both black and white audiences. Black music and dance flourished.

At the same time, a national fear of communism was building and was to culminate in the Red Scares of the 1920's and later in the 1950's, when Joseph McCarthy and others were obsessed with ferreting out communists. This fear launched the career of J. Edgar Hoover as head of the Federal Bureau of Investigation (FBI). His "Radicalism and Sedition among Negroes as Reflected in Their Publications" (1919) brought him to the attention of Attorney General A. Mitchell Palmer, who smoothed the path to Hoover's becoming a force in important investigative wings of the Department of Justice that predated the FBI.

It was in this climate that W. E. B. Du Bois founded *The Crisis*, which quickly became a sounding board for challenging the status quo as it applied to black citizens. Responding to mainstream fears about the threat of communism, Du Bois contended that "the danger facing the nation came not from Communist revolution but from the consequences of its own moral and humanitarian failure." As this sentiment grew in Du Bois, it eventually caused him in the final years of his life to join the Communist Party and relocate in Accra, Ghana, where President Kwame Nkruma offered him sanctuary. On his ninety-fifth birthday, Du Bois, now residing in Ghana, became a citizen of that country after the United States Department of State refused to renew his passport.

Lewis presents a Du Bois who was clearly a genius, gifted, opinionated, and, as he grew older, increasingly intransigent in his views. Du Bois had the strong libido that often is part of the makeup of males who are overly ambitious. His long-suffering first wife, Nina, came eventually to accept her husband's dalliances and even to entertain some of his paramours in her home. Many of Du Bois's female professional associates were involved sexually with him. At times there were fears of scandal in the offices of *The Crisis* as well as in such associations as the NAACP and the Pan-African Association, in which he played prominent roles.

In this regard, Lewis reports that in the late 1920's and early 1930's, when Du Bois's wife and daughter were living in Paris, Du Bois "became sexually ever more exuberant to such a degree that [his sexual activities] resembled the compulsiveness of a Casanova." Lewis explains Du Bois's "serial affairs, several of which were the equivalent of parallel marriages," by saying that they seemed "to imply some deep-seated emotional incompleteness that had probably remained unresolved since the death of his mother." It is to Lewis's credit that he does not dwell on the prurient aspects of Du Bois's life, but brings them in as tastefully as he can only to help readers understand some of his professional choices.

Perhaps the most compelling part of this biography is the author's careful construction of the ongoing political scenarios regarding the status of African Americans from 1919 until Du Bois's death in 1963. Du Bois became for most blacks, and for many white people as well, the embodiment of the NAACP, although as time passed he clashed with Marcus Garvey and Francis Marion White, both of whom became major forces in the organization, and eventually distanced himself from them and from the association.

Du Bois began as an elitist supporter of the Talented Tenth movement, but gradually moved away from it. He was attracted initially by the excitement and promise of the Harlem Renaissance that flourished from the 1920's until the 1940's. In time, however, he viewed this movement less as an artistic groundswell than as a civil rights initiative parading under a false banner.

For many complex reasons, including a quite obvious homophobia that Lewis details, Du Bois drifted away from that movement, convinced that black problems had to be solved not through artistic means but through economic change that would bring equality to black people everywhere. Convinced of this necessity, Du Bois became active in the Pan-African movement and was instrumental in convening several Pan-African Congresses. He also was a strong supporter of Africa for Africans, that is, a demand for developing the continent for the benefit of its native inhabitants rather than for the benefit of Europeans and Americans bent on exploitation. Implicit in this demand is the granting of independence to African countries that had for generations been dominated by European countries.

Lewis traces in considerable and valuable detail Du Bois's increasing Africanism, his sanguine hopes and expectations for the homeland of his ancestors, and his exhilaration in realizing the potential of this vast continent. As time passed, Du Bois became totally convinced that a capitalist economic system had little to offer African Americans and probably even less to offer black people in Africa. He moved increasingly toward communism as a viable solution to the social problems and inequities that had plagued African Americans for their whole history in the United States.

Du Bois's views became increasingly global. He and Shirley Graham, who became his second wife in 1951, were deeply involved with the Peace Information Center, which was considered a communist-affiliated organization. It circulated a peace petition, called the Stockholm Appeal, that received a million and a half signatures, including those of two Nobel laureates, five Protestant bishops, and such other notables as Thomas Mann, George Bernard Shaw, and Madame Sun Yat-sen.

Secretary of State Dean Acheson labeled the Stockholm Appeal "a propaganda trick in the spurious 'peace offensive' of the Soviet Union." It must be remembered that the United States at this time was beset by a public hysteria against communism. Senator Joseph McCarthy was inflaming the masses as he carried out his efforts to find communists wherever he could, even in places where they did not actually exist. Obviously, Du Bois was an important McCarthy target.

When a grand jury handed down indictments for Du Bois and officers of the Peace Information Center, with arraignment scheduled for February 16, 1951, Shirley Graham advanced the date of her marriage to Du Bois from February 27 to February 14, because her marriage to him would preclude the necessity of giving evidence against him under oath.

By the late 1950's, Du Bois had entertained the notion of resettling in Accra, Ghana. President Kwame Nkruma encouraged him during a visit to the United States in 1958 to move to Ghana, offering him a house in Accra's best section as well as government research facilities so that Du Bois could pursue his plans for creating a secretariat for the *Encyclopedia Africana*. Du Bois attended the official ceremonies surrounding the establishment of the Republic of Ghana in July, 1960. On November 16, 1960, when Du Bois attended the inauguration of Nnamdi Azikiwe as the first African governor-general and commander-in-chief of Nigeria, he realized that his dream for a new Africa was moving toward fruition.

On February 15, 1961, Du Bois received word that the Ghana Academy of Learning had accepted and endorsed the *Encyclopedia Africana* project and had voted substantial financial support for it. On October 1, 1961, largely as a protest against America's anticommunism and all that it implied, Du Bois applied for membership in the Communist Party, writing to Gus Hall, chairman of the Communist Party of the United States of America, "Today, I have reached a firm conclusion. Capitalism cannot reform itself; it is doomed to self-destruction." Then, with Shirley, he departed for Ghana, where he spent his last two years. He was ninety-three years old when he made this move. Ghana welcomed Du Bois warmly and enthusiastically.

In 1962 Du Bois was stricken with prostate cancer. He went to Moscow seeking surgery, but when physicians there considered the risk too great, he went to Bucharest, Romania, where the surgery was performed. The operation was not successful, nor was a second operation in London for the removal of the prostate. He returned to Accra, where his ninety-fifth birthday was marked by his taking Ghanian citizenship and by his receiving an honorary doctoral degree from the University of Ghana. Shortly thereafter, he died.

In his final days, Du Bois expressed his gratitude to President Nkruma for enabling him to live out the last years of his life in Ghana. Ever energetic and ambitious, he apologized to Nkruma for not having been able to complete the *Encyclopedia Africana* project that meant so much to him.

R. Baird Shuman

Sources for Further Study

Booklist 96 (August, 2000): 2070.
Library Journal 125 (September 15, 2000): 88.
The New York Times Book Review 105 (November 5, 2000): 15.
Publishers Weekly 247 (September 25, 2000): 103.
Time 156 (October 30, 2000): 86.
The Village Voice 45 (October 31, 2000): 146.

WANDERLUST
A History of Walking

Author: Rebecca Solnit
Publisher: Viking Press (New York). 326 pp. $24.95
Type of work: History, philosophy, and memoirs

≈

An informal, wide-ranging, and anecdotal meditation
on the history of walking as a cultural activity

≈

Did the large brain of *Homo sapiens*, enclosed in its bony case and balanced quite improbably on top of the column of the body, develop before or after the species began to walk erect? What is the relationship between bipedalism—walking on two feet—and the development of human communities? One might expect these questions to be the concern of anthropologists and scientists exploring the nature of evolution, but it is a measure of the scope of Rebecca Solnit's curious and lively survey of the history of walking that the ordinary reader can traverse the distance between the terrain of early hominid study and the streets of modern San Francisco, roaming on the byways of the early romantic poetry and the alleys of nineteenth century Paris along the way, with scarcely any disorientation or strain.

Wanderlust: A History of Walking is described on its dust jacket as "the first general history of walking." This seems an unlikely claim, given the fact that the author herself cites previous works on the subject that seem to fit the description, but it is certainly an elegant, comprehensive, and extremely readable contribution to the genre, however small that may be. Written by an author whose previous published works have been about landscape and public space, *Wanderlust* is a meditation in narrative form on the meaning of a human activity that traverses both yet is so basic that it seldom registers on the conscious mind. Despite its formal title, the book is not a traditional history but rather a leisurely journey along a winding road that occasionally winds back upon itself but reaches, in the end, a destination that has been at times invisible to the traveler but well known to the guide. The reader stops to observe fine vistas, paces a few steps down pathways off to the side that tempt further exploration, twists about a bit in labyrinths set up by the creator for a bit of diverting exercise, and finally arrives at the goal willing to go a bit further and perhaps sorry that the excursion has come to an end.

If the above paragraph seems to depend too much on metaphors of travel, such is the inevitable result of embracing one of the author's central convictions: Walking is so much a part of historical existence that humans describe much of their conscious experience in terms of physical movement through space and time. Life, people say, is a journey; narrative is movement toward a goal. People explore, they follow a

~

*Rebecca Solnit has written about
visual art, public space, landscape,
and environmental issues for a
number of magazines. Her previous
books include* Secret Exhibition,
Savage Dreams, *and* A Book of
Migrations.

~

course, they ramble, they detour, they progress.
Solnit's sensitivity to the hidden and visible
meanings of everyday language—displayed in
her fluent and imaginative prose as well as in her
discussion of the implications of everyday discourse—enriches her approach to the historical
subject and lifts the book into the realm of literary exploration.

The structure of the book carries the reader
from the early eighteenth century—when walking was valorized as a subject of public culture in
Enlightenment Europe—to the end of the twentieth century when walking as a source of pleasure
and means of transport seems to have lost its capacity to inspire thought. Henri Rousseau and
Søren Kirkegaard are the "walking" philosophers who lay the path, linking in their autobiographical writings the exploration of physical
space and the development of ideas as they, respectively, roam the countryside of Switzerland
and stroll the streets of Copenhagen. The connection of body to mind they articulate
allows Solnit, then, to report on the often very funny anthropological debates about
the evolution of human locomotion "If it [walking] once separated us from the rest of
the animals," she concludes, "it now—like sex and birth, like breathing and eating—
connects us to the limits of the biological."

Solnit often begins and ends her chapters with personal experiences. Her discussion of pilgrimage—the walk in search of something, a tradition with ancient roots—
is set within a description of her own trip with friends to the Santuario de Chimayó
pilgrimage in New Mexico. The topic encompasses the history of the Peace Pilgrim,
an unnamed woman who set out in 1953 to march against war and died, still moving;
nearly thirty years later, the Selma-to-Montgomery march during the Civil Rights
years; and the fundraising walkathons of the 1980's and 1990's. A chapter on labyrinths moves from a contemplation of the movement from literal experience to abstraction in the ritualized progress through the stations of the cross in Roman Catholic
tradition to the establishment of the memory palace as a repository of information:

> Memory, like the mind and time, is unimaginable without physical dimensions . . . if
> memory is imagined as a real space—a place, theater, library—then the act of remem-
> bering is imagined as a real act, that is, as a physical act: as walking.

If there is a hero in this book, it is surely William Wordsworth. Although the second
part of the book is entitled "From the Garden to the Wild," the heart of it is the chapter
"The Legs of William Wordsworth." The English poet's sensibility, particularly as
expressed in his diaries and in his vast poem, "The Prelude," forms a touchstone of
Romantic and post-Romantic attitudes toward landscape. The section deals both di-

rectly and obliquely with the connection between, in the author's terms, social liberation and the passion for nature as it was expressed at the beginning of the nineteenth century when the walking of Elizabeth Bennett in Jane Austen's *Pride and Prejudice* (1813), for example, was seen to be inextricable from the essential good sense of her nature, and the more modern concept of walking as a social or political activity. This allows the author to connect mountain climbing—a highly specialized form of walking—to the wilderness clubs of pre- and post-Nazi Germany, and then to the Sierra Club and its mission to protect the environment. Wordsworth's passion for vistas and views, his valuation of the rough and simple as subjects for human contemplation, is replaced in social consciousness first by a compulsion for extreme experience and then, as cities replace forests and farmlands as human spaces, by a need to protect and control what is in danger of being lost.

Some modern cities—New York, London, and Rome, perhaps—offer their own kinds of vista to the determined walker and are given their due, but it is Paris, Solnit argues, with its wide boulevards and great plazas, that has offered the richest urban experience to the pedestrian of the nineteenth and twentieth centuries. The creature who is "a walker in the city," to use the title of Alfred Kazin's 1951 autobiography that is, sadly, not quoted in *Wanderlust*, has at hand experiences quite different from the immersion in natural beauty and the opportunity for solitary contemplation that so moved Wordsworth. The vision is much darker in cities, the landscape human and social. Charles Dickens, Walt Whitman, Virginia Woolf, Frank O'Hara, and Allen Ginsberg may write of the joys of crowds or miseries of the poor, but they all know and relish the territories they have made their own by walking through them and, like many of their fellow poets and novelists, they are firmly rooted in their urban surroundings where the constant encounter with strangers acts as a stimulus to imagination and a spur to the senses.

The archetype here is the flaneur—the detached observer who strolls the alleys and boulevards, merging with the crowds and relishing them. Solnit quotes Walter Benjamin, Charles Baudelaire, and others who see in this mysterious Parisian wanderer the representative modern man, the haunter of arcades and alleys who pursues his life glancing through windows, stopping at cafés, and relishing the streets. Because the only female equivalent to the flaneur is the streetwalker (the prostitute), Solnit is led to a discussion of gender politics where urban streets and gathering places become theaters where the dramas of race, class, and sexual orientation are performed.

The sinking arc of the book's curve marks the end of the Wordsworthian era. Walking loses its associations with pleasure and leisure. In the last decades of the twentieth century, outside some exceptional areas, walking is done for exercise when it is done at all. Suburbs are built without sidewalks. Shopping malls pursue the ideal of store-side parking. Gyms provide treadmills and StairMasters in rooms equipped with television sets so people can waste as little time as possible while they move their feet. There are walking races and race-walk clubs, but walking as a cultural act, the real subject of *Wanderlust*, is on the verge of disappearing. The book ends with Las Vegas, where crowds deprived of real cities mill about on the Strip defying and subverting the casinos' attempts to privatize the sidewalks and control open space.

Like many other works of nonfiction, *Wanderlust: A History of Walking* is part history, part memoir. The author writes in her preface that the subject arose naturally from her work on a catalog for an exhibition about walking and thinking presented in Denmark in 1996. She also wrote at length about her participation in a march in Nevada protesting nuclear armament. Although the history of walking might lend itself equally well to a more conventional treatment, this framework of personal experience allows for an anecdotal approach and thematic structure that may serve to disarm the reader who might otherwise prefer a more direct approach. It also allows for quick changes in chronology that may seem arbitrary or confusing and for a sense that the advantages of the personal approach may be offset in part by the limitations. Are Paris and San Francisco really the best cities for walking, or are they simply the ones that the author has spent the most time in? Nonetheless, Solnit was thorough in her research, and she writes with remarkable fluency and grace.

It would be a mistake to finish any discussion of this quite satisfying excursion without noting that the design of the book, as well as its structure, reinforces the theme. Beneath the text of every page is a path—a footpath of quotations to be exact— that runs from the beginning of the journey to the final page. They are not footnotes (the usual bibliographic apparatus is in place at the end), but quotations that relate to the subjects discussed above that form a running—more accurately, a walking—commentary on the narrative. Drawn from sources that range from Toni Morrison's *Song of Solomon* (1977) to *The New York Times*, the words call attention to the linear nature of the printed line and the way in which the eyes, as well as the mind and the body, follow defined paths.

Jean W. Ashton

Sources for Further Study

Booklist 96 (March 15, 2000): 1312.
Library Journal 125 (February 15, 2000): 186.
Natural History 109 (April, 2000): 90.
The New York Times Book Review 105 (May 21, 2000): 7.
Publishers Weekly 247 (February 28, 2000): 69.

WAY OUT THERE IN THE BLUE
Reagan, Star Wars, and the End of the Cold War

Author: Frances FitzGerald (1940-   )
Publisher: Simon & Schuster (New York). 592 pp.
    $30.00
Type of work: Current affairs and history
Time: 1981-2000
Locale: The United States

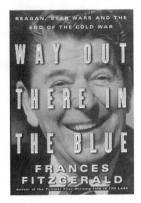

≈

An analytic narrative of the rise of the Strategic Defense Initiative under Ronald Reagan and its impact on American foreign policy and the end of the Cold War

≈

Principal personages:
  RONALD REAGAN, president of the United States, 1981-1989
  CASPAR WEINBERGER, Reagan's secretary of defense
  GEORGE SCHULTZ, Reagan's secretary of state
  JAMES BAKER, Reagan's treasury secretary
  GEORGE BUSH, Reagan's vice president
  MIKHAIL GORBACHEV, leader of the Soviet Union, 1985-1991
  EDWARD TELLER, noted scientist

A Pulitzer-Prize winner for her book on Vietnam, *Fire in the Lake* (1972), and author of other books on critical issues, Frances FitzGerald examines one of the most controversial military programs of the last two decades of the twentieth century, the Strategic Defense Initiative (SDI) that United States president Ronald Reagan announced in March, 1983. Although it remained a concept rather than an actual program, seventeen years later the antimissile defense proposal was an issue between Governor George W. Bush and Vice President Albert Gore, Jr., as part of the 2000 presidential campaign. The Clinton administration was also discussing deployment of a limited system against potential adversaries such as North Korea and Iraq as its time in office wound down in 2000. SDI is both a historical issue of the Reagan years and a modern subject of political debate. FitzGerald's well-documented and detailed narrative is a penetrating and often very funny look at Ronald Reagan's presidency from the perspective of his pet military project.

Although the documentary record of the Reagan years had not yet been opened to researchers to anywhere near completeness at the Ronald Reagan Presidential Library, FitzGerald mined the extensive memoir literature produced by the men and women who worked for Reagan in the White House. She also effectively used the government reports and documents that emerged as the controversies over SDI raged on in the 1980's. Although the primary sources for the Reagan presidency will no

~

Frances FitzGerald has worked as a journalist in the United States, Vietnam, the Middle East, Europe, Central America, and the South Pacific. She is the author of Fire in the Lake, America Revisited, *and* Cities on a Hill. *She has received many awards, including the Pulitzer Prize, the National Book Award, and the Bancroft Prize for history.*

~

doubt modify some of her particular conclusions, her work stands as an impressive example of contemporary history.

FitzGerald shows how SDI arose from Reagan's fascination with science fiction and technology as a way of defending the United States against a Soviet missile attack. The doctrine of nuclear deterrence was something that Reagan disliked as an idea and did not understand as a military policy. It is sobering to read that the president was uncertain about the exact nature of the various elements of the nation's nuclear forces, particularly the role of submarines. FitzGerald traces the ideas of space defense enthusiasts who sold Reagan on the idea that a shield against incoming missiles could be made into a practical reality. Since very few reputable scientists believed that a missile defense could safeguard the American people as a whole, there was a high degree of wishful thinking and hyperbole about how SDI was presented in the mid-1980's. One aide told Reagan, for example, that the concept would surely be popular with the American people because the crowds at professional football games enthusiastically shouted, "Defense, defense."

The portrait of Reagan that emerges from FitzGerald's book is a devastating one. She does not patronize him or take cheap shots at the former president, but tries instead to understand his inscrutable leadership style that so often baffled those closest to him. Aloof and detached, moving through each day like an actor on a sound stage, Reagan treated the presidency as a star turn and dutifully hit the chalk marks that his staff placed on the floor when he spoke. Sometimes he even looked for directorial guidance he had received in Hollywood and did not see himself as the ultimate decision maker for the government he headed.

Her portrait of Reagan is not a negative caricature. She recognizes the president's genuine concern about a nuclear holocaust and his reservations about the strategy of deterrence. He also grasped, earlier than many of his advisers, that a confrontational stance toward the Soviet Union was not a political winner. FitzGerald might have done more to emphasize the role of First Lady Nancy Reagan in making the second Reagan term a period of arms control and better relations between East and West.

Some of the most hilarious episodes in the book occur, however, when Reagan trots out in summit negotiations the anecdotes from popular magazines that he loved so much. At the Washington summit in 1987, Reagan informed Mikhail Gorbachev about an article in *People* magazine regarding "a twelve-hundred-pound man who never left his bedroom." As an incredulous Vice President George Bush and Treasury

Secretary James Baker looked on, a puzzled Gorbachev asked his interpreter: "Is this real fact?" The reader sympathizes with the Soviet leader's bewilderment. In the end, Reagan remains as indecipherable to FitzGerald and the reader as he was to his contemporaries. Even more than Franklin D. Roosevelt and Lyndon Johnson, Reagan comes across as one of the most self-contained and enigmatic presidents in American history. Perhaps the closest comparison might be with Andrew Jackson, who exerted the same kind of fascination on the American people that Reagan did.

Another sobering aspect of the book is the extent to which SDI depended on the willingness of its exponents to rig the evidence or make false promises in the faith that technology would in time bear out their dreams. This book will not enhance the historical reputations of Caspar Weinberger, secretary of defense in the Reagan administration, or noted scientist Edward Teller. If the book has a hero, it is Secretary of State George Shultz, who comes across as a grown-up able to function in the real world of the 1980's. When Reagan and Gorbachev met in Washington in 1987 and Reagan proved ill prepared, Shultz chided him: "Mr. President, that was a disaster. That man is tough. He's prepared. And you can't just sit there telling jokes." The spectacle of bureaucratic infighting, which was characteristic of the Reagan years, casts something of a shadow over the nostalgia that Republican conservatives now profess for the era when the "Great Communicator" was in charge of the nation.

FitzGerald engages two other important historical issues in the book. To what extent did SDI contribute to the collapse of the Soviet Union during the administration of George Bush from 1989 to 1993? In the 1990's, Reagan revisionism asserted that his presidency had scared the Soviets into spending themselves into bankruptcy, and SDI was a significant contributor to that process of economic decay. FitzGerald argues that internal Soviet economic and political weaknesses were larger elements in the decline of the Soviet Union. She cautions against imputing too much influence to American actions. Gorbachev and his reforms unleashed forces within the Soviet Union that accelerated the decline that was already under way. As she indicates, the same people who argued during the late 1970's that the Soviet Union was an implacable adversary bent on world domination whatever the cost contended twenty years later that Reagan had seen the rottenness at the core of that country and exploited it through SDI and his related military buildup.

For the purposes of the debate about the merits of an antimissile system, FitzGerald's tale shows that the practicality of SDI proved an elusive goal that never came close to fruition. Although Reagan talked of putting an invulnerable shield over all the American people, policymakers in the know understood that such a defense was impossible from the start. Cartoon renditions of rockets blowing up all incoming missiles in the fashion of the *Star Wars* films were never attainable through any technology that existed in the 1980's or even the 1990's. It might be possible to defend some key elements of the American nuclear deterrent through an antimissile system, but that program lacked the sales appeal of a shield over the citizens of the United States. Yet even that more modest goal proved elusive. FitzGerald dissects the schemes that rose and fell as practical implementations of the SDI concept. Lasers were going to shoot down the enemy rockets. Satellites in space, thousands in number, were going to seek and destroy Soviet intercontinental ballistic missiles. The ideas came and went—"High Frontier" "smart rocks," and "Brilliant Pebbles"—all designed to provide the technological fix that the proponents of SDI thought was just over the horizon.

In the process, a huge amount of money was spent, more than sixty billion dollars by some estimates. FitzGerald does not delve much into the linkages between defense contractors and the inner workings of the SDI program. Her focus is primarily on the conceptual and policy development of the initiative as it illuminates the internal history of the Reagan administration. That much of these funds was wasted or spent on programs with little or no chance of tangible accomplishment seems indisputable. Future scholars will have to follow the money to see to what extent the SDI endeavor became a perpetual pork barrel for those with access to its riches.

The book is enlightening on a number of other topics relating to the Reagan and Bush years. The summits between Gorbachev and Reagan in the 1980's are rendered vividly with a shrewd sense of human drama as the two leaders met. By humanizing Gorbachev and treating him as an equal, Reagan undermined the rationale for regarding the Soviet Union as "the evil empire" and made the Cold War seem a relic of the past even before the Soviet Union itself collapsed. Ironically, one of the points of tension between the Reagan and Bush administrations was the sense among Bush and his advisers that Reagan had moved too fast toward an accommodation with Moscow.

In the years after Reagan left office, SDI moved away from its initial purpose as the Soviet military threat receded. The new focus became "rogue states" such as Iraq and North Korea that, heedless of the prospect of nuclear annihilation if they attacked the United States, would act so irrationally that they might launch a smaller missile strike out of ideological commitment or religious fanaticism. For Republicans nostalgic for the Reagan years, the prospect of a vulnerable American open to what might be called "rogue rage" proved an alluring political weapon to wield against their Democratic enemies. To counter such tactics, the Clinton administration kept the antimissile system research going, even as tests of the program resulted in embarrassing public failures. Meanwhile, Republican presidential candidate George W. Bush proposed, if elected, to create a more ambitious mechanism. Conciliatory noises from North Korea in the summer of 2000 only shifted the potential danger to China or Iraq. Rogue states became "states of concern," and the story begun under Ronald Reagan unfolded in ongoing complexity. It became apparent that if a threat to justify an antimissile system did not exist, one would have to be invented.

FitzGerald's book provoked strong reactions—pro and con—from those involved in SDI. She is no fan of the program, but neither is she an ideologue creating stereotypes of actual historical actors. Her book contains deft portraits of the major players in this controversy and provides refreshing insights for its readers. Some judicious trimming would have improved the pace of what is a long account of a convoluted topic. The second half of the book lacks the energy and sustained interest of the story of how Star Wars came into being during the Reagan presidential campaign and the early years of the first term. Yet *Way Out There in the Blue* is a superior example of policy-making history that provides important background information for making a judicious appraisal of the direction of missile defenses. It is also a gripping tale that makes defense policy, arms control issues, and presidential policy making in the late twentieth century come alive.

Lewis L. Gould

Sources for Further Study

Booklist 96 (March 1, 2000): 1192.
Business Week, May 1, 2000, p. 29.
Commentary 109 (May, 2000): 75.
Foreign Affairs 79 (March/April, 2000): 136.
Library Journal 125 (March 1, 2000): 109.
The Nation 270 (June 12, 2000): 26.
The New York Review of Books 47 (May 11, 2000): 4.
The New Yorker 76 (May 15, 2000): 92.
Publishers Weekly 247 (February 28, 2000): 71.
Science 289 (July 21, 2000): 397.

WHAT I THINK I DID
A Season of Survival in Two Acts

Author: Larry Woiwode (1941-   )
Publisher: Basic Books (New York). 300 pp. $25.00
Type of work: Memoirs
Time: 1960-1996
Locale: North Dakota, with detours to Illinois and New
   York City

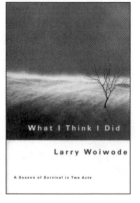

≈

*A respected American novelist tells the story of his
growing up and of his early adventures in the literary
world*

≈

Larry Woiwode's writing has been widely acclaimed, receiving many prizes and positive reviews, but his fiction has never really become part of the literary mainstream. This autobiography, Woiwode's second work of nonfiction following *Silent Passengers*, a book on the biblical Book of Acts published in 1993, may well bring Woiwode a widened readership.

Woiwode relates his memoir from the vantage point of the winter of 1996-1997, whose cold and isolation are a natural spur to retrospection. Woiwode resettled as an adult in his childhood home of North Dakota. He lived as a young child around Sykeston, North Dakota, in the middle of the state measured on both north-south and east-west axes. Woiwode sketches the cultural and ethnic background of the community—founded in the late nineteenth century by an English entrepreneur (one of the many who were so influential in building up the High Plains west of the Mississippi River in this era), then in the twentieth century largely populated by *Volgadeutsch* (Germans who had settled in Russia for an extended period). As an adult, Woiwode moved to a 160-acre farm near Mott, North Dakota, on the Cannonball River in the southwestern corner of the state; his books are sold in the supermarket in Mott. Woiwode's family traced its origin to German-speaking Silesia (now in the Czech Republic), although Woiwode was correctly informed by a love interest in college that the name is not German at all but Slavic. Sometimes spelled Voivode, it is frequently found across the history of Eastern Europe into the twentieth century as a title for a local chieftain. Woiwode's family pronounces their name "y-WOODie," far from what it would be in Eastern Europe, where the pronunciation would be closer to "voi-VODE." Woiwode provides the reader with a sense of the background and temperament of his immediate forebears, including the early and traumatic death of his mother. All this is prelude to the harsh winter of 1996-1997.

Woiwode senses that the upcoming winter will be a hard one and arranges the delivery of a huge wood-burning furnace. In the midst of the furnace's installation,

Woiwode's authorial voice flashes back to memories of his and his wife's initial resettlement in North Dakota and their homeschooling of their four children—Joseph, Newlyn, Ruth, and Laurel. Woiwode provides not only detailed descriptions of his life and his community but also mechanical and engineering details of his new furnace and his electrical connections. These latter details give a sense of completeness to the scene, beyond any merely pastoral rusticity. When he says, "An openness like a field beyond a house, or a *feeling* of a field opening up, is a place I shouldn't go, because a real field isn't there," he gives a glimpse not just of the physical reality but of the phenomenology of a field as well. A field is never totally present to the perceiver as he stands within it; the full reality of the idea of a field exists only when the field is perceived from a distance. Combined with Woiwode's keenly observant descriptions of tools, fences, tractors, and snowdrifts, the book gives both a sense of what it is like on the Great Plains and what it is like to *live*, in a subjective sense, on the plains. Woiwode is grounded in North Dakota; he knows its history, its politics, its religion, its land, and its people.

∽

Larry Woiwode's first novel, What I'm Going to Do, I Think, *received the William Faulkner Foundation Award; his second,* Beyond the Bedroom Wall, *was a finalist for both the National Book Award and the National Book Critics Circle Award. His fiction has appeared in* The Atlantic Monthly, Esquire, Harper's, The New Yorker, *and many other publications.*

∽

The danger represented by the snowstorm sharpens Woiwode's recollective powers as he muses over various areas of his family life and literary career. A consistent structure emerges in which Woiwode reflects on three kinds of relationships. The first kind is outward and nostalgic—his interchanges with his various literary mentors and colleagues. The second is inward and future-oriented—his relationship with his family and his attempts to develop his children in a certain way and mold their character in accordance with certain values. The third is parallel and takes place in the present, relating to his neighbors and fellow North Dakotans, with whom he shares struggles with the land and with life. This is the dimension of one's life that one has the least control over—how the past is remembered and how the future is anticipated is partially up to the mind, but the present is open to fate. In a particularly affecting passage, Woiwode chronicles the death from cancer of his neighbor Valeria, which conjures the specter of his own mother's death. He gives a wrenching description of decaying flowers at a funeral, an image of a cathartic coming-to-terms with death. Woiwode's relationships with his neighbors are among the most interesting in the entire book. The inhabitants of the Cannonball River area are not folk rustics. They are self-aware and often highly educated people who are faithful and fit companions for Woiwode's family during the hard winter. The book conveys a real feeling for both places and people, and landscapes inhabited and experiences shared by a comparative few are rendered present by the writer's skill.

The storm becomes fiercer. Woiwode realizes he has made several pivotal mistakes in preparing for the storm. There is a sense of being at nature's mercies as the same elemental forces that provide beauty and sustenance to these North Dakotans for most of the year now threaten their very lives. In order to feed his wood-burning furnace, Woiwode has to sacrifice a beloved set of the works of Charles Dickens. Some of Woiwode's family are trapped in a town across the South Dakota border, and he wonders if he will ever see them again. At a point like this, in a house potentially about to be buried under snow, it might seem preposterous that the writer ever knew such luminaries as the writers John Cheever or John Updike, ever hobnobbed in the literary circles of the sophisticated East Coast. Although Woiwode does not comment explicitly on the incongruity, the narrative overlay of past and present he provides strongly suggests it. In fact, time serves the author as a structuring device, a way to give order to his material. The author's recollective strategies deploy a grid of before-and-after on material that would otherwise be side-by-side.

There is an "Intermission" in the middle of the book that is somewhat reminiscent of the "Time Passes" section in Virginia Woolf's novel *Between the Acts* (1941). Like Woolf's, Woiwode's intermission is more abstract and difficult than the rest of the book and displays a sort of metaphysical speculation that is only implied in the narrative accounts that come before and after it.

In the second half of the book, its structure becomes clearer, as does the book's place in the structure of Woiwode's overall career. The first half is called "Snow with Tints of Then," meaning that it was largely set in the harsh winter and in occasional flashbacks. The second half is called "Then with Tints of Snow," implying retrospection with tinges of present-day awareness (from an older perspective). A similar echo occurs between the title of this book, *What I Think I Did*, and the title of Woiwode's first novel, *What I'm Going to Do, I Think* (1969). Again, a reflexive relation is set up between present and past. In the present, the writer completes the action with his memoir that in the past he had commenced with his first novel.

Woiwode shifts from wintry contemplation to remembrance of youth. Though he was born in North Dakota, he moves to Illinois with his family at the age of eight. When he goes to college at the University of Illinois a decade later, he becomes interested in acting, spurred by a memorable course on William Shakespeare he takes with a professor named Charles Shattuck. In his early twenties, Woiwode finds himself simultaneously an ordinary college student and an aspiring writer and actor. Even though he attends a large state university in the Midwest, Woiwode begins to find a foothold in the literary world, partially through the assistance and inspiration provided by his teacher George Scouffas. Woiwode's major literary contact becomes the famed writer and *New Yorker* editor William Maxwell, who was also a mentor to John Updike and many writers of Woiwode's generation. Woiwode meets Maxwell when the latter gives a talk at the Urbana campus. Maxwell encourages the young writer to come to New York City and try his luck in the dramatic and literary arenas. Woiwode follows this advice, and his story takes on the contours of the archetypal "young man from the provinces."

Maxwell shepherds a story of Woiwode's to publication in *The New Yorker* and introduces him to writers and staff of that storied magazine. Maxwell also permits Woiwode to use the former's country house for some months provided that Woiwode takes care of the flowers in the garden. Woiwode rifles through his absent host's papers, though he stops short of reading a secret map giving directions to the hideaway of the reclusive writer J. D. Salinger. Woiwode meets famous writers such as the novelist Eudora Welty (who is encountered by chance at a "seedy Longchamps" on lower Fifth Avenue) and the poet Robert Lowell as well as behind-the-scenes figures such as the renowned editors Robert Giroux and Michael di Capua. He also forms a friendship with the then-unknown actor Robert De Niro. Woiwode provides an amusing vignette about an occasion where his wife serves as a model for De Niro's father, a painter. Woiwode gives an ample and evocative portrait of the New York literary world of the 1960's, in some ways like that of four decades later, in other ways as vanished forever as the Silesia of Woiwode's German-speaking ancestors. Throughout, his manner is articulate and frank as he relates the pain and ambition of being a young writer.

It is well known that in the late 1970's Woiwode became a Christian of a particularly Calvinist stripe and later became a member of the Orthodox Presbyterian Church. He is known as a Christian writer, and his primary constituency during the latter part of his career has been Christian readers of literature. Woiwode makes only a few Christian references in this memoir, and the book's retrospective portion ends a decade before his conversion. However, the later Woiwode's Christianity may come into the latter portion of *What I Think I Did* as a kind of implied critique. The book ends with Woiwode's sense that he—that is, his career—has been launched. This success on a national, even a world, stage is a far cry from the author's low-key boyhood in remote North Dakota and midstate Illinois. Woiwode conveys a sense of a justified exhilaration, of pride in his craftsmanship as a writer and awe at the recognition his writing has received. It may, though, be averred that the purpose of writing is not to be successful at it but to convey to a readership deep meanings inside the mind of the author. Success might be a by-product of worthwhile efforts, and one to be neither scanted nor scorned, but it is not the essence of either writing or life. When Woiwode's later Christianity is considered, it might well be hypothesized that Woiwode is deliberately making this point and that the theme of success in the latter part of the book is to be subject to an ironic treatment from a Christian perspective that will always note the limits of merely human success. It is to be hoped that Woiwode will explore this question when he writes the second volume of what is so far an original and compelling autobiography.

Nicholas Birns

Sources for Further Study

America 183 (September 9, 2000): 17.
The New York Times Book Review 105 (June 11, 2000): 25.
The New Yorker 76 (June 12, 2000): 109.
Publishers Weekly 247 (April 17, 2000): 64.

WHEN WE WERE ORPHANS

Author: Kazuo Ishiguro (1954-   )
Publisher: Alfred A. Knopf (New York). 336 pp. $25.00
Type of work: Novel
Time: The early twentieth century
Locale: London and Shanghai

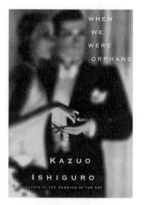

≈

Ishiguro's fifth novel explores the betrayals of memory when an expatriate detective attempts to save his long-lost kidnapped parents in Shanghai

≈

Principal characters:
> CHRISTOPHER BANKS, a criminal detective in search of his past
> JENNIFER, Christopher's adopted daughter
> SIR CECIL MEDHURST, a distinguished aristocrat who sinks into gambling debt in Shanghai
> SARAH HEMMINGS, a social climber who marries Cecil Medhurst
> WANG KU, a Shanghai warlord involved in the opium trade
> UNCLE PHILLIP, a friend of the Banks family who runs a philanthropic organization
> AKIRA YAMASHITA, Christopher's Japanese childhood friend
> DIANA BANKS, Christopher's beautiful mother who agitates against the opium trade in Shanghai
> MR. BANKS, Christopher's father who is presumed kidnapped

Since the popular and critical success of his Booker Prize-winning novel *The Remains of the Day* (1989), Kazuo Ishiguro has experimented with the novel form from the position of his heightened celebrity. Since *When We Were Orphans* draws on his two previous works for its aesthetic plan, some discussion of the former novels provides a useful sense of context. In *The Remains of the Day*, Ishiguro draws on the conventions of nineteenth century British fiction, allowing social forms to bind and control the more unruly human pathos underlying the storyline. It is both a well-oiled traditional novel, well deserving its Merchant-Ivory film production, and a postmodern commentary on how professional identity can undermine humanity. Following the self-denial of his butler's code of ethics, the narrator, Stevens, chooses to ignore his father's death in order to serve drinks to his master's guests. By the end of the novel, he learns that his sense of duty has cost him the one possible love of his life and that he performed that duty for a man who foolishly helped the Nazis before World War II. Ultimately, Stevens has little to show for his life except the futile sense of a job well done.

Since the success of *The Remains of the Day*, Ishiguro has searched for a new fictional form to help explore his characteristic themes of exile, the vagaries of identity, the role of the artist in society, and the distortions of memory. His next work, *The Unconsoled* (1995), switched to a more Kafkaesque narrative mode. This novel concerns a young, accomplished pianist's visit to a European city for a recital. Far more surreal and daring in its construction than anything Ishiguro had written before, this novel shows the risks inherent in imitating Kafka's narrative style. Kafka's novels

∼

Kazuo Ishiguro was born in Japan and moved to Britain at the age of five. He is the author of four previous novels, including the Booker Prize-winning The Remains of the Day. *He has received an Order of the British Empire and was also named a Chevalier dans l'Ordre des Arts et des Lettres.*

∼

manage to blend dream and reality with an allegorical undertow that hints at all kinds of contexts, from totalitarian guilt to existential questions of identity to religious allegory. His hypnogogic stories always hint at more underneath the surface. Writers who try to imitate Kafka have no trouble with the surreal, but the sense of an underlying pattern is much harder to reproduce. Ishiguro's *The Unconsoled* suffers from the comparison. As time and space warp and shift, walls appear out of nowhere, and the narrator finds himself giving impromptu dinner speeches in his bathrobe. Such anxious scenes become repetitiously dull pretty quickly. With mixed reviews and a poor public reception, *The Unconsoled* was a disappointing follow-up.

Ishiguro's *When We Were Orphans* bears traces of both the nineteenth century English novel craft of *Remains* and the surreality of *The Unconsoled*. While still retaining some Kafkaesque moments, *When We Were Orphans* marks a retreat from the radical experimentation of the previous novel. This time following the generic parameters of a detective novel, Ishiguro explores how seemingly casual events and patterns of behavior in one's youth can influence adult identity. Christopher Banks, the novel's narrator, is born in Shanghai and lives there in the International Settlement until first his father and then his mother inexplicably disappear, presumably kidnapped by opium smugglers because of his mother's strong political stand against them. At the age of seven, Christopher abruptly leaves Shanghai to go to school in the country of his parents, England, where he grows up to become a detective who gains some notoriety for his crime-solving. By weaving together unreliable memories with current events of the 1930's, Ishiguro reveals that Christopher wants to return to Shanghai to solve the crime of his parents' kidnapping and thereby free himself from the burden of the past. When he was a child, he would play detective games in which he would save his father from the kidnappers, and as an adult he decides to carry out that very design by returning to Shanghai.

Because of Christopher's remoteness and detachment as a narrator, the novel can seem aloof from its subject matter. Ishiguro never allows the reader to really see Christopher at work except when he is observing something with his magnifying glass or taking notes. In contrast to the more fully realized butler in *The Remains of the Day*, Christopher's detective career seems more an idea than a fully realized occupation. Ishiguro admits in an interview that he writes with a kind of shorthand when it comes to details. Since people live in the image glut of television and films, Ishiguro believes the novelist should suggest images already in the reader's head: "You don't have to describe very much as a novelist. You can just, with a few little key words, evoke certain images. To a certain extent you can muck about with stereotypes and stereotypical images and you juxtapose them in unlikely ways." While this technique lends itself to narrative speed and economy, Ishiguro runs the risk of thinning out his descriptive palette. Without enough quotidian detail, scenes sometimes slide by on convention, leaving the novel insufficiently grounded in a particular time and place.

However, not fitting into one's milieu is part of Ishiguro's point. As a boy he was uprooted, this time from Japan at the age of five, and transplanted in England, where he grew up always viewing England from both outside and inside simultaneously. His works reflect the postmodern writer's increasing concern with the blending and blurring of international boundary lines. What goes for Ishiguro also applies to his lead character. At home neither in England nor in Shanghai, Christopher cultivates an imaginary zone in between where he can combat evil to make up for the loss of his parents. While Banks has his successes in criminal detection, Ishiguro ultimately exposes him as naïve about his roots in the world. He needs to return to Shanghai to see through his delusions of recovering his parents.

As the storyline develops, Ishiguro conveys a straight Proustian concern with the unreliability of memory. Early on, Banks keeps noting how his old friends have radically different memories of his childhood in England. When he remembers himself as fitting in smoothly, they remember him as "withdrawn and moody." A success as a detective investigating other people's crimes, Christopher shows himself inept and solipsistic when it comes to seeing himself. Oddly, Ishiguro allows side characters to play along with Christopher's delusions, perhaps out of deference to his reputation, perhaps as a way to string him along. Thus, when he arrives back in Shanghai during the bombing of the Sino-Japanese war, Guest finds himself planning a ceremony at Jessfield Park to celebrate the freeing of his parents who have been missing for over twenty years. When he was a child, he used to plan the same thing with his friend Akira. The idea of celebrating such a long-term unsolved crime seems like wish-fulfillment. There is no thought of his parents being somewhere else or dead. In effect, Christopher returns to the playacting of his youth as an adult professional. Hardly mindful of the war raging around him, Christopher sets off at the merest of hints to find the house where his parents presumably still reside behind enemy lines. He encounters bombed-out slums, dead bodies, civilians armed with spades, and a passed out Japanese soldier that he is sure is Akira, his old playmate. Wounded and delirious, they crawl through holes in the walls, listening to the screams of the wounded, and all Christopher can think of is his parents. The scenes create a dreamlike confluence of the idealized past and the grotesque present. For Christopher, the mythos of his youth remains far more powerful than the evidence of the devastation around him.

On occasion, Christopher has intimations of escape from both his search and his occupation. Romance could provide one such exit, but Christopher allows his professional obligations to interfere with his dalliance with Sarah Hemmings, who stands out in the novel for her aggressive social climbing. She attempts to use Christopher's social connections to crash an upper crust party honoring Cecil Medhurst, and once she does get in, she goes on to marry Cecil, even though he is clearly too old for her. Later she and Cecil lead Christopher out to Shanghai, and after Cecil becomes corrupted by gambling, Sarah invites Christopher to drop his investigation into his parents' disappearance and run off with her to Macao. When Sarah asks Christopher to leave with her, she expresses a yearning for some stable affection that would replace all of the rootless professional striving of the novel's characters. As she says,

> All I know is that I've wasted all these years looking for something, a sort of trophy I'd get only if I really, really did enough to deserve it. But I don't want it any more, I want something else now, something warm and sheltering, something I can turn to, regardless of what I do, regardless of who I become. Something that will just be *there*, always, like tomorrow's sky.

Even though Christopher feels a great sense of relief when he agrees to her proposal to drop everything and run away, he ironically learns of a "break" in the case concerning his parents just when he is set to leave, and ultimately backs out. As in *The Remains of the Day*, the main character's occupation takes precedence over romance.

Naturally, the evil that Banks seeks to battle proves far more virulent that he had anticipated, and he soon learns that his parents long ago went their separate ways. After he recovers from his fruitless search through the bombed out cityscape, Christopher's Uncle Philip finally fills him in. His father had actually run off with his mistress and died soon after. Meanwhile, in her righteous fury over the opium trade, his mother had physically insulted a Chinese war lord, Wang Ku, who abducted and sexually enslaved her for years in exchange for funding young Christopher's British education. Christopher's illusions are exposed as childish, but the novel remains ambivalent about which perspective is better—the cynical view of the adult or the more heroic view of the child. When Christopher notices that the children suffering war conditions have to "learn so early how ghastly things really are," the Japanese soldier who adopts Akira's role replies: "When we nostalgic, we remember. A world better than this world we discover when we grow. We remember and wish good world would come back again."

Working from an aesthetic borne out of an unease between loyalties to different cultures and different times, Ishiguro searches for moments of Eastern peace amidst the more European quest for identity through achievement. In its graceful and detached way, *When We Were Orphans* illustrates how little control people have over the larger myths that dictate their lives.

Roy C. Flannagan

Sources for Further Study

Booklist 96 (July, 2000): 1974.
The Economist 355 (April 15, 2000): 12.

Library Journal 125 (August, 2000): 157.
Los Angeles Times Book Review, September 24, 2000, p. 2.
The New Leader 83 (September/October, 2000): 42.
The New Republic 223 (October 16, 2000): 43.
The New York Review of Books 47 (October 5, 2000): 4.
The New York Times, September 19, 2000, p. E7.
The New York Times Book Review 105 (September 24, 2000): 12.
Publishers Weekly 247 (July 10, 2000): 41.
Time 156 (September 18, 2000): 86.
The Times Literary Supplement, March 31, 2000, p. 21.

THE WHITE DEATH
A History of Tuberculosis

Author: Thomas Dormandy
Publisher: New York University Press (New York). 433
  pp. $29.95
Type of work: History of science and medicine
Time: Primarily 1700-2000
Locale: Western Europe and the United States

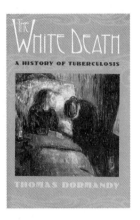

≈

A history of tuberculosis with commentary and fascinat-
ing anecdotes about people who suffered from the disease,
doctors who either helped or hindered medical advances,
and quacks who took advantage of desperate patients

≈

Principal personages:
> ALBERT CALMETTE (1863-1933), developer of a vaccine in 1923 to pro-
> vide immunization against tuberculosis, especially for children
> ROBERT KOCH (1843-1910), discoverer of the bacterium that causes tu-
> berculosis, Nobel Prize recipient in 1905
> RENÉ LAËNNEC (1781-1826), inventor of the stethoscope in 1818, used
> to diagnose lung ailments such as bronchitis, asthma, or tuberculosis
> CLEMENS VON PIRQUET (1874-1929), developer of a skin test in 1907 in
> which a positive allergic reaction indicated tuberculosis
> EDWARD LIVINGSTON TRUDEAU (1845-1915), founder of a renowned
> sanatorium for tubercular patients at Lake Saranac, New York
> WILHELM CONRAD ROENTGEN (1845-1923), inventor of X-ray apparatus
> in 1896, making early diagnosis of lung tuberculosis possible
> SELMAN ABRAHAM WAKSMAN (1888-1973), discoverer of the antibiotic
> drug streptomycin, Nobel Prize recipient in 1952

Thomas Dormandy is an established author in the field of medical history. His writing style is a combination of scholarly research, human interest anecdotes, and occasional wry comments about the medical profession. "White death" was a term given to tuberculosis because patients commonly looked pale and anemic as they lay in bed. Frequently they suffered for several years with severe coughing, loss of weight, low energy, and spitting up of blood from the lungs. By contrast, "Black Death" referred to the plague that devastated Europe in the 1300's, one of its symptoms being blood blisters that turned black under the skin.

Scattered throughout Dormandy's book are the stories of well-known people who suffered and died from tuberculosis. The author provides biographical information about these people and shows how the disease affected their personal lives and their creative work. Many of these individuals lived in the nineteenth and early twentieth centuries, when tuberculosis was very prevalent and had no known cure. It may surprise the reader to recognize quite a few of the famous people on the following list, each of whom died of the disease in midcareer:

> John Keats, English poet, died in 1821, age twenty-five
> Carl Maria von Weber, German composer, died in 1826, age thirty-nine
> Frédéric Chopin, Polish pianist and composer, died in 1849, age thirty-nine
> Emily Brontë, English writer, died in 1848, age thirty
> Charlotte Brontë, English writer, died in 1855, age thirty-nine
> Henry David Thoreau, American writer, died in 1862, age forty-four
> Robert Louis Stevenson, Scottish author, died in 1894, age forty-four
> Anton Chekhov, Russian dramatist, died in 1904, age forty-four
> Amedeo Modigliani, Italian/French painter, died in 1920, age thirty-six
> Katherine Mansfield, English writer, died in 1923, age thirty-four
> David H. Lawrence, English novelist, died in 1930, age forty-four
> Franz Kafka, Austrian writer, died in 1924, age forty
> George Orwell, English writer, died in 1950, age forty-six

Dormandy gives numerous examples of writers, artists, and musicians who incorporated the emotional trauma of extended suffering into their work. *The White Death* has as its cover illustration a famous painting by the Norwegian artist Edvard Munch, a haunting deathbed picture of his sister Sophie, who died of tuberculosis at age sixteen, with her despondent mother sitting by her side. Dormandy gives poignant quotations from the correspondence of Katherine Mansfield with her literary friends, in which she recorded the peaks and valleys of her six-year illness. Giacomo Puccini's opera *La Bohème* (1896) and the Giuseppe Verdi opera *La Traviata* (1853) both have heroines who tragically die of tuberculosis in the last scene. A famous novel by the German writer Thomas Mann, *Der Zauberberg* (1924; *The Magic Mountain*, 1927), takes place at a sanatorium in the Swiss Alps where the life of patients is dominated by their illness. Dormandy quotes from Anton Chekhov's lengthy correspondence with an actress friend during his extended sickness. Betty MacDonald, who became famous for her humorous story about life on a chicken farm in *The Egg and I* (1945), later told about her depressing confinement in a tubercular sanatorium in *The Plague and I* (1948).

As a general principle in the medical profession, if an illness can be diagnosed and treated early, the likelihood of recovery is increased. When a tubercular patient is already spitting up blood, it is usually too late for treatment. Dormandy describes the rather limited techniques for early diagnosis that were available before the discovery of X rays. The simple procedure of tapping the chest can help an experienced physician to identify tubercular cavities or abscesses in the lungs. This technique was first used in the eighteenth century by a Viennese doctor who had seen his father tapping the outsides of wine casks to determine the degree of fermentation. The stethoscope as a listening instrument was not invented until 1818. A skin test for tuberculosis was developed by Clemens von Pirquet in 1907. If the skin became red, von Pirquet called it an allergic reaction, indicating either active tuberculosis or an earlier episode of the

disease that had been healed by the immune system. A follow-up chest X ray would then be
given to show whether the lungs were damaged.

~

Thomas Dormandy is a consultant
pathologist who lives in London. He
has published numerous articles
and books on medical and scientific
topics.

~

Dormandy describes in some detail the life
and work of Robert Koch, who in 1882 discovered the bacterium that causes tuberculosis.
Koch worked with a microscope and various
staining dyes, like the other "microbe hunters" of
the nineteenth century who identified the germs that cause rabies, smallpox, diphthe-
ria, tetanus, and anthrax. Unfortunately, no vaccine against tuberculosis was found
until 1923, and there was no cure until Selman Waksman's discovery of the antibiotic
streptomycin in 1943. This left the field wide open for quacks to peddle their useless
elixirs and potions.

One of the worst charlatans, according to Dormandy, was an Englishman named
Major C. H. Stevens. From South Africa he brought back a concoction called
"Umkaloabo," which was used by witch doctors there. He gave away free samples to
twenty-two tubercular patients, afterward claiming that they all got better. He set up a
company employing fifty people to manufacture and ship Umkaloabo to all parts of
the world. His advertising mailings, featuring enthusiastic testimonials by patients
and articles by alleged medical authorities, helped him to make a small fortune. When
the British Medical Association raised objections to his claims, he challenged them to
"inoculate him . . . with 'the fiercest tuberculosis germs they could find' and then observe him curing himself with Umkaloabo. The offer was declined as unethical, but
his sales soared." This useless patent medicine and dozens of others like it became
popular, according to Dormandy, because they promised "the alleviation or cure in
which the recipient so fervently wished to believe."

For sixty years after Koch's discovery of the tuberculosis bacterium, the search for
a miracle drug to provide a cure was without success. Medical doctors began to ask: If
drugs are not the answer, could lung surgery provide a cure? Starting about 1900, a
surgical technique called "collapse therapy" came into vogue. The idea was to make
an incision in one side of the chest, inject some gas to provide pressure, and force one
of the lungs to collapse. The other lung could maintain sufficient respiration. The collapsed lung would be immobilized for a period of several weeks or months so that le-
sions and tubercular cavities in the lung could heal. The analogy was made that a broken bone had to be immobilized to allow healing to take place. The constant motion of
the lung as it inflates and deflates presumably interfered with the healing process.
Thousands of these lung surgeries were done by well-meaning physicians, but unfortunately the surgery was hazardous and costly, while the benefit was marginal at best.

The concept of a sanatorium to accommodate tubercular patients first became popular in the Black Forest region of Germany in the 1850's. From there it spread to Switzerland, where, it was argued, it was beneficial to live "above sea level: there the reduced atmospheric pressure would ease the pumping action of the heart muscle and
this in turn would improve the body's general metabolism, including its capacity to
overcome diseases." A prescription of fresh air, mild exercise, long rest periods, and

large meals was supposed to let the body heal itself. It was an expensive treatment. Swiss mountain towns such as Davos and Saint Moritz attracted wealthy patrons to their sanatoriums, which were

> . . . in all but name luxury hotels with armies of chambermaids, porters, [and] and a staff-guest ratio of about fifteen to one. . . . Glossy advertisements emphasised the quality and abundance of their tables (with sample menus in full) rather than details of the therapeutic regimes or cure rates.

For the less affluent, "bottled air" from a spa at Bad Ischl in the Alps was sold to people for home use.

In the United States, the sanatorium movement had its start in the 1880's at Lake Saranac in the Adirondack Mountains of New York. The founder was Edward Trudeau, a recent medical school graduate who had been diagnosed with advanced tuberculosis at age twenty-five. Thinking he was close to death, he took a trip to Saranac, near Lake Placid, and made a remarkable recovery there. He became an enthusiastic promoter of its beneficial climate. His doctor colleagues began to send their tubercular patients to him to be treated. Trudeau discovered that he had a talent as a fundraiser, getting wealthy donors to make charitable contributions to build lodging facilities for his patients. Many doctors who were interested in setting up sanatoriums in other parts of the country made a pilgrimage to see his operation. When Trudeau died (of tuberculosis) in 1915 at age 69, Saranac had about 1,500 guest houses and cottages.

A public health measure that helped greatly to reduce the incidence of tuberculosis was pasteurization of milk, along with tubercular testing of cattle. This was widely adopted in the United States, but in England the opposition was fierce. The farm lobby and the veterinarians, whose business depended on the good will of farmers, successfully resisted all compulsory legislation until the late 1940's. Opponents claimed that "pasteurisation significantly diminished the nutritive value of milk [and] induced rapid tooth decay, [and] 'meddling with wholesome natural food' threatened British national strength and fertility."

In the 1970's, with the availability of streptomycin and other powerful drugs, there was great optimism that the conquest of tuberculosis was imminent. The U.S. Centers for Disease Control and Prevention "confidently predicted that . . . the United States would be a tuberculosis-free zone by 2005." However, Dormandy points out that "tuberculosis had a habit of staging unexpected comebacks." From 1985 to 1990, approximately seven million new cases of tuberculosis were diagnosed worldwide, with a high annual rate of increase especially in southern Africa and in inner-city slum areas. Part of the reason seems to be the close association of tuberculosis with human immunodeficiency virus (HIV) and acquired immunodeficiency syndrome (AIDS). When the immune system is deficient in a patient, an infection such as tuberculosis has the opportunity to overwhelm the body's defense mechanism.

Another disturbing development in the last decade of the twentieth century was the emergence of multidrug resistance (MDR). An investigation of an outbreak of tuberculosis in New York City revealed that the bacteria were resistant to all seven of the most effective therapeutic drugs available. An explanation for MDR is not clearly established yet, but Dormandy suggests that mutant "strains may emerge all the time, just as genetic mutants and chromosomal abnormalities emerge in human populations. . . . Once, however, the dominant type has been eliminated by a particular drug, drug-resistant freaks may seize their chance." A 1997 survey of street people in London found that as many as 10 percent of individuals with tuberculosis carried a drug-resistant strain. The fear exists that MDR tuberculosis could spread outside urban ghetto areas and become an epidemic. The hope is that research for new drugs and better governmental policies for general health care will be able to control such an outbreak.

Hans G. Graetzer

Sources for Further Study

Choice 38 (October, 2000): 363.
English Historical Review 115 (April, 2000): 417.
Library Journal 125 (March 1, 2000): 118.
New Statesman 128 (February 19, 1999): 47.
Publishers Weekly 247 (March 6, 2000): 97.
The Times Literary Supplement, August 20, 1999, p. 32.

WHITE TEETH

Author: Zadie Smith (1975-   )
Publisher: Random House (New York). 448 pp. $24.95
Type of work: Novel
Time: The nineteenth and twentieth centuries
Locale: London

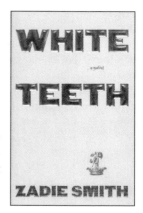

~

*A comic novel about the ways in which the past im-
pinges on the present as first- and second-generation immigrants struggle either to maintain traditions or break
free of them in multiethnic, postcolonial London*

~

Principal characters:
ARCHIE JONES, nondescript, ne'er-do-well Englishman
CLARA BOWDEN, his much younger Jamaican-born wife
IRIE, their daughter
SAMAD IQBAL, Bangladeshi immigrant and waiter
ALSANA, his much younger wife
MAGID MILLAT, their twin sons
MARCUS CHALFEN, a scientist
JULIA CHALFEN, his wife, a horticulturalist

Praise for Zadie Smith's debut novel, *White Teeth*, has been so nearly universal as
to make the harshness of one notice all the more surprising—and sobering:

> This kind of precocity in so young a writer has one half the audience standing to ap-
> plaud and the other half wishing, as with child performers of the past (Shirley Temple,
> Bonnie Langford et al.), she would just stay still and shut up. *White Teeth* is the literary
> equivalent of a hyperactive, ginger-haired, tap-dancing 10-year-old.

Published anonymously in the English magazine *Butterfly*, this scathing notice was in
fact written by Smith herself and is less tongue-in-cheek than one might think and
more in keeping with this conspicuously attractive, immensely talented, and assured
but surprisingly self-deprecating writer's assessment of what quickly became one of
the most talked about novels of the new millennium. As Smith elsewhere pointed out,
"I have great ambitions of writing a very great book. I just don't think this is it." Her
English publisher, Hamish Hamilton, clearly thought differently, at least about the
novel's commercial possibilities, offering a quarter-million-pound advance on the
basis of just the first eighty pages. So did those who made it the favorite to win the
Orange Prize for best fiction in English by a woman. (*White Teeth* lost, however,
although it did win both the *Guardian* and the Whitbread First Novel awards.) More-

over, the British Broadcasting Company made
plans to turn Smith's novel into a television
miniseries.

The overwhelming attention left the twenty-
four-year-old Smith richer but otherwise unfazed
and still living in the multiethnic Willesden area
of north London where she grew up, the daughter of an Englishman and his much younger Jamaican wife. Despite receiving little encouragement from her teachers, Smith was determined to
go not just to college but to Cambridge, where
she majored in English, contributed to student
literary publications, and at age twenty-one began *White Teeth*. The excerpt was published in
the autumn, 1999, issue of *Granta*—significantly
situated immediately following one from postcolonial theorist Edward W. Said's memoir *Out
of Place*. It offered the general public a first, tantalizing taste of Smith's engaging, exuberantly

Zadie Smith wrote White Teeth *in
her senior year at Cambridge
University. The novel was short-
listed for the Orange Prize and has
been widely acclaimed as one of the
most original first novels in
decades.*

excessive style, albeit in a format that could not begin to hint at the wide range and
narrative intricacies of this ambitious and immensely accomplished novel, for which
the qualifier (or epithet) "first" seems not so much unnecessary as improbable.

Divided into four parts, each tied to a major character (or characters) and focusing
on two specific years (1974, 1945; 1984, 1857; 1990, 1907; 1992, 1999), *White Teeth*
explores in seriocomic fashion the ways in which the past impinges on the present as
characters struggle either to maintain traditions or get free of them. The presence of
the past is everywhere in Smith's novel (although not in any way that T. S. Eliot
would recognize or approve). So are teeth: false, buck, and missing, as well as ca-
nines, molars, and root canals. The novel begins (or, given its deepening, dispersed
prehistory, opens) early in the morning of January 1, 1975, with Archie Jones sitting
in his car attempting suicide on the Willesden high street, which "was no kind of
place. It was not a place a man came to die. It was a place a man came to in order to go
other places via the A41"—even a man like Archie, after a dull childhood, a bad marriage, and a dead-end job, a man without aims, hopes, or ambitions, a man "never able
to make a decision, never able to state a position" without first flipping a coin, suicide
included. Archie is "the bloke in the joke" shooed away by a *halal* butcher awaiting a
delivery in the very spot where Archie has parked. Wandering around later that day,
the forty-seven-year-old Archie stumbles upon the aftermath of an "end of the world
party" and meets the stunningly attractive nineteen-year-old Clara Bowden, minus
her upper teeth (knocked out in a recent motor scooter accident) and in flight from her
apocalypse-obsessed mother, a Jehovah's Witness. Six weeks later they marry,
spending much of their wedding day sorting out a parking ticket issued during the ceremony. The bloke in the joke is right.

The novel switches to Samad Miah Iqbal (or "Ick-ball" in the English mispronunciation), whom Archie once saved from suicide when they served together at the very end of World War II, two of the misfits and castoffs in the comically ill-fated "Buggered Battalion." Samad is an Indian during the war, a Pakistani after independence/partition, and a Bangladeshi by the time he immigrates to London in 1973 with his young bride, Alsana (she of fine features, sharp tongue, and enormous feet). Eleven years later, the couple scrapes together enough money from Samad's dead-end job waiting tables at his cousin's West End restaurant and Alsana's sewing for a Soho sex shop to move from Whitechapel in the city's East End to Willesden, just four blocks from Archie and Clara. Unlike the nearly inert, "history-less" Archie, Samad is a man obsessed with the past, particularly his great-grandfather Mangal Pande, a Hindu, who fired the first shot of the Great Mutiny of 1857 (whether motivated by conviction or drink is not as clear as Samad would like to believe). Samad is similarly obsessed with his religion, Islam, and the purity it demands (a purity he guiltily, comically falls well short of). While waiting tables, he awaits his destiny, filling the time by fueling his sense of grievance over his fallen state: a "sad" man who "feels like he has screwed everything up" (which he has), "a faulty, broken, stupid, one-handed waiter of a man who had spent eighteen years in a strange land and had made no more mark than this," his name carved in five-inch-high letters on a bench in Trafalgar Square where he had bled copiously after cutting his hand at work soon after his arrival in England.

Smith's novel is a half-Dickensian, half-Rabelaisian tale of one city but two families (later four) over two (actually six) generations, a song about the way people live (and not just in London). There is another switch in narrative focus to Archie and Clara's daughter, Irie, and Samad and Alsana's twin sons, Magid and Millat. Dismayed by how Western his sons have become, cash-strapped Samad, who comically combines patriarchal arrogance and henpecked fear, manages to send his favorite son back to Bangladesh (without first informing his wife), only to have Magid return seven years later a caricature of Englishness. While Magid is away, "mutinous Millat" experiments with sex, drugs, and antiauthoritarian behavior before this "social chameleon" solves the problem of his "split-level consciousness" by joining a group whose Islamic fundamentalism Samad finds no more appealing than Magid's Anglophilia. Meanwhile, Irie (whose name means peace) has problems of her own. Just as large and unattractive as Clara once was—Irie "looked like the love child of Diana Ross and Englebert Humperdinck"—she tries to make herself more appealing to the handsome Millat by having her hair dyed and straightened. Although her plan goes hilariously awry (as most plans do in Smith's novel), her desire is perfectly understandable; it is the longing not just for Millat but for that "paradise" of pure contingency and choice that Samad fears. "If religion is the opiate of the people, tradition is an even more sinister analgesic, simply because it rarely appears sinister." Nonetheless, the tradition-obsessed Samad is not altogether wrong to hold on as desperately and absurdly as he does, given his and other immigrants' justifiable fears of "dissolution, disappearance," against which nationalist fears "of infection, penetration, miscegenation" seem "peanuts," at least to someone like Samad.

In this way Smith very effectively dramatizes the conflict between the need for freedom and the need to belong. The need is there in the numerous street crews, including the Raggastanis, who speak

> a strange mix of Jamaican patois, Bengali, Gujarati, and English. Their ethos, their manifesto, if it could be called that, [is] equally a hybrid thing: Allah *featured*, but more as a collective big brother than a supreme being, a . . . *geezer* who would fight in their corner if necessary.

So Millat joins the burners of Salman Rushdie's *The Satanic Verses* (1988)—not because he considers the author an infidel or the book offensive (he has not even read it), but because he finds in the crowd's anger something akin to his own. Later he will join Keepers of the Eternal and Victorious Islamic Nation,

> a radical new movement where politics and religion were two sides of the same coin. A group that took freely from Garveyism, the American Civil Rights movement, and the thought of Elijah Muhammad, yet remained within the letter of the Qur'ân.

"That's a wicked name. It's got a wicked kung-fu kick-arse sound to it," says Millat, and an unfortunately comical acronym: KEVIN. There is no lack of collectives to which individual characters turn in order to satisfy their need to belong: FATE (Fighting Animal Torture and Exploitation); Jehovah's Witnesses; O'Connell's, the men-only former poolroom-now-café owned by Iraqi brothers Abdul-Mickey and Abdul-Colin, where Samad and Archie take shelter from the domestic and cultural storms. Then there is Chalfenism, the secular religion, as it were, of the Chalfens, thoroughly assimilated third-generation German-Polish Jews (originally named Chalfenovsky): Marcus, a professor of molecular biology, and Julia, the horticulturalist he married for the wide hips well-suited to giving birth to his genetically superior offspring. Supremely self-confident and reasonably well-to-do, the Chalfens see themselves as heirs of the Enlightenment. The reader sees them rather differently: as pompous North London liberals bearing the torch of social planning and do-goodism of a certain and certainly overbearing kind.

All good things must come to an end, even a novel in which "the end is simply the beginning of an even larger story." For Smith that means bringing the diverse narrative strands and political and cultural groups together on New Year's Eve at the Pennet Institute, where Marcus and his pen pal turned protégé, Magid, unveil Marcus's latest creation, FutureMouse, to an audience of invited guests, interested parties, protesters, saboteurs (FATE, KEVIN), and one would-be assassin (Millat), while outside Clara's mother and some of her fellow believers await (yet again) the end of the world as revelers party in Trafalgar Square. Genetically altered to live twice as long as normal mice, to sprout tumors in predetermined places at preset times, and most ominously and hilariously, to change from brown to albino white, FutureMouse "holds out the tantalizing promise of a new phase in human history, where we are not victims of the random but instead directors and arbitrators of our own fate." In a city in which London Transport cannot get the trains to run as scheduled, however, the promise that FutureMouse offers of better living through bioengineering seems not so much alarming as risible, especially in a novel about the joys of randomness and diversity, accidental hybridity and cultural complementarity.

White Teeth brilliantly and energetically examines differences of all kinds: national, ethnic, political, religious, sexual, racial, class. Its cast of Dickensian caricatures, its diversity of voices, from the neutral tones of Archie to Jamaican patois, Indian-inflected English, and the carefully as well as comically cultivated speech of the Chalfens, suggest that Smith's ear for the linguistic variety of contemporary London is as good as her eye for detail and her adroit manipulation of both for her own comic purposes. More celebratory than satirical, it offers what Smith herself has called a "utopian" view of race relations, of what those relations might, should, "maybe" will be. In it, even burners of *The Satanic Verses* and a French doctor who collaborated with the Nazis get off lightly. Generous to a fault, often implying that "love is all you need," *White Teeth* is (to borrow Rushdie's description of his own *Satanic Verses*) "a love-song to our mongrel selves . . . for change by fusion, change by conjoining." It is also, along with works such as Ayub Khan-Din's 1997 play and 1999 film *East Is East*, a sign of the times, of the browning of London, and of that colonial invention, English literature, begun by Rushdie and Hanif Kureishi. Having mastered the comic sprawl and exuberant irreverence of that wing of the English novel tradition running from Laurence Sterne's *The Life and Opinions of Tristram Shandy, Gent.* (1759-1767) to Rushdie's *Midnight's Children* (1981), not only in a single go but also with such panache and to such acclaim, Smith set her sights, in the new novel she began, on the quiet restraint of the tradition's other wing. That wing extends from Jane Austen to the second-most-talked-about English novel of the new millennium, *Mr. Phillips* (2000), John Lanchester's story of a day in the life of (appropriately enough) a white Londoner recently made redundant.

Robert A. Morace

Sources for Further Study

Booklist 96 (April 1, 2000): 1436.
The Boston Globe, April 30, 2000, p. J1.
Library Journal 125 (April 1, 2000): 132.
The New York Times, April 25, 2000, p. E1.
The New York Times Book Review 105 (April 30, 2000): 7.
The New Yorker 75 (October 18-25, 2000): 182.
Newsweek 135 (May 1, 2000): 73.
Publishers Weekly 247 (March 13, 2000): 60.
USA Today, April 27, 2000, p. 9.
The Wall Street Journal, April 28, 2000, p. W6.
The Washington Post Book World, May 21, 2000, p. 7.

WILD DECEMBERS

Author: Edna O'Brien (1936-   )
First published: 1999, in Great Britain
Publisher: Houghton Mifflin (Boston). 261 pp. $24.00
Type of work: Novel
Time: The twentieth century
Locale: A small community in the Irish mountains

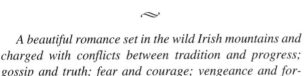

~

A beautiful romance set in the wild Irish mountains and charged with conflicts between tradition and progress; gossip and truth; fear and courage; vengeance and forgiveness; hate and love; and death and life

~

Principal characters:
> MICK "THE SHEPHERD" BUGLER, an Australian who moves to Ireland to work the land he inherited
> JOSEPH BRENNAN, a vengeful neighbor who develops a deep hatred of the Shepherd
> BREEGE, his sister, who falls in love with the Shepherd

An author of more than twenty books, stage plays, teleplays, and screenplays for juveniles and adults, Edna O'Brien is a recipient of the Kingsley Amis Award (1962), the *Los Angeles Times* Book Prize for Fiction (1990), and an honorary membership in the American Academy of Arts and Letters. Born in a small Irish village, educated in a convent, local schools, and a Dublin college, and evaluated by the *Irish Times* "as one of our bravest and best novelists," O'Brien lived in London, raising two sons and writing until 1986, when she moved to New York to teach creative writing at a city college.

The title of the novel is borrowed from Emily Brontë: "[F]ifteen wild Decembers/ From those brown hills have melted into spring—/ Faithful indeed is the spirit that remembers." It is used as a motto. How perfectly guiding it is, one realizes after reading a short, poignant prologue painting the wild and ominous beauty of the Irish mountains, scant in arable land and pasture. That is the home the Irish love with passion, some with a survival instinct and greed beyond tolerance, the collective memory of the potato famine still present in their psyche together with the fear of its return. That fear is, O'Brien shows, their real enemy that

> [c]an come at any hour, . . . because the enemy is always there . . . locked in a tribal hunger that bubbles in the blood . . . waiting to rise again . . . to pit neighbour against neighbour . . . in the crazed and phantom lust for a lip of land.

O'Brien's *Wild Decembers* confirms her already notorious expertise in the themes Irish, human, and universal, as well as her skill in dissecting all stages of love. Like

Edna O'Brien has written eighteen works of fiction, including Down by the River, House of Splendid Isolation, Time and Tides, *and* Lantern Slides, *which won the* Los Angeles Times *Book Prize for Fiction. Born and raised in Ireland, she now lives in London. She is an honorary member of the American Academy of Arts and Letters.*

life itself, her themes are both simple and complex: the basic questions of existence raised by the human mind and literature since the beginning of time. Like William Shakespeare, Herman Melville, and all those who understand the laws of nature and human behavior, O'Brien shows how those eternal questions live in the actions and lives of real people, the characters of her novel.

The bipolarity in nature constantly generates conflicts that people have to resolve within themselves—-and with others. The flaws in human nature may turn a conflict into a tragedy on a personal, micro level or escalate into feuds between families. *Wild Decembers* is about the meaning of life and death, love and hate, war and peace. It is about the strife between the old and new, good and evil, ignorance and enlightenment, courage and fear, and much more. O'Brien's main characters are survivors, but their values and life philosophies vary, and that naturally polarizes them. Some of them will show love and acceptance, readily embracing the new and different. Others will be nourished on hate and prejudice, too narrow-minded to recognize a messiah bringing a better life for all. They opt to see evil when they cannot fathom the content.

The first chapter introduces the major protagonists: Mick Bugler, nicknamed "the Shepherd," a settler from Australia who inherited the mountain land in the small community of Cloontha; Joseph Brennan, a native, who has always lived on this land, just like his predecessors—a staunch bachelor, devoted to alcohol and stories of old family feuds; Breege, his sister, a young, beautiful woman with the purity and freshness of a mountain spring—a nurturer, completely dedicated to her brother. When the Brennans meet the newcomer, he is riding a tractor, the first seen in these God-forgotten quarters. Both the rider and his machine (like any novelty) arouse excitement and bonding. For a while, a friendship between these three neighbors is budding. In Breege, it starts as fascination and steadily grows into love. In Joseph, a small conflict turns into a feud, supported by his narrow vision of reality and his tendency toward fear and hatred. The conflict is further enhanced by the individual vendettas of other neighbors, creating a cumulative effect aimed at a total destruction of the unwanted intruder.

Crock, the community gossip, a villain of Iago's magnitude—maimed by nature at birth, a hater of the world for his own ugliness and vengeful of all lovers for a humiliating memory in his childhood—secretly starts spinning an entangling web of lies. His secret lust for the innocent Breege fixates his revenge on the Shepherd, the handsome object of Breege's affection. Rita and Reena, two local infamous sorceress-seductress-sisters, further fan the flames of hatred. They abuse the Shepherd's trust and fulfill their lust upon his body, boasting of the victory.

In spite of these adversities, the industrious Shepherd enthusiastically continues to develop his land using modern technology. Meanwhile, Joseph—blinded by alcohol and enraged by malicious gossip—blames him for the loss of his ancestral land and savagely beats him in the local bar. Summoned to court, venom and alcohol boiling in his blood, Joseph does more harm to himself than anyone else could. The judge, disgusted and offended, sentences him to jail. Now, Joseph covets revenge more than ever. Then, without explanation, the Shepherd drops the charges. Despite this, Joseph persists in demanding his rights to the land, even after he receives an official report confirming the Shepherd's legal ownership. Again, to restore peace, the Shepherd offers to settle.

Breege's love for the Shepherd gains new depth. Powerfully involved in this love-hate trio, she starts seeing her brother's real self beyond his words. Like a delicate mountain weed, her love grows powerfully deep roots under harsh conditions. She learns the shepherd has a fiancée in Australia from her brother, who readily embraces the distorted image of the Shepherd as immoral and righteously deserving of his wrath. Shy and secret at first, Breege's love now feels shameful and forbidden. In the middle of this threatening world, it must stay a secret. A double secret, one that even the Shepherd may not live to know.

More complications arise to deepen Joseph's hatred and the Shepherd and Breege's growing love. All the tributary conflicts now seem to join into one powerful torrent. Magnetically drawn to each other, the young couple spends a moonlit night together on the local island. Just then, sensing a change in the Shepherd's letters, his foxy fiancée, Rosemary, arrives unexpectedly, afraid that their short sexual liaison may not lead to marriage. Using multiple manipulative seduction techniques, including faked pregnancy, Rosemary tries to force the Shepherd into a speedy marriage. After church, surrounded by a bunch of hypocritical women, she flaunts her power over him. In search of "the woman" to blame for the obvious change, she follows Breege into the toilet, showing the modest ring the Shepherd gave her in Australia, stabbing her with words, "He'll always come back to me. . . . Because I have this."

In this moment of brutal awakening, Breege feels she is having "a stroke." Frantically, she runs off, seeking refuge in the nativity manger in the church. When discovered, she receives harsh, humiliating treatment from the invasively curious ladies of the church. The emotional shock that caused Breege to lose speech makes it impossible to explain what is ailing her. The women believe she must have a shameful secret. There seems to be no one around who can understand Breege's suffering. Always certain in his perception, her brother writes her off as insane and puts her in the hospital. Mute and helpless, unable to communicate, she gets "professionally" diagnosed with hysteria *ad absurdum*. For Breege, it is hardly "the season of peace and good will toward men."

Santa Claus appears at the psychiatric ward bearing gifts, creating an atmosphere of good will. He entreats Breege to help him sing Christmas carols. Not knowing she is mute, he persists. Moved by his enthusiasm, she starts uttering the words of the song the Shepherd gave her. As amazed as the others by this miracle, she freely sings—in a rich, beautiful voice—her own love song, her own hymn to the season of love and good will. Truly, the spirit of Christmas is upon her!

Not knowing any of this, but having heard about Breege's predicament, the Shepherd searches the hospital for her. Not allowed to see her, he leaves a bouquet of heather gathered from the place where they spent the night. His short note offers hope for better times. It ends: "I'll think of you and I hope that you won't think too unkindly of me. Fond love, Mick."

At home, however, Rosemary continues her hysterical jealous rages, screaming, "I don't care if she dies." For the first time, the Shepherd sees her as the woman "whose softest bit . . . is [her] teeth," as he had been warned in Australia. He refuses to succumb to her unfair, cruel demands, and Rosemary storms off, enraged.

Now aware of his true feelings, the Shepherd writes to Joseph: For the sake of Breege, he is willing to give up the mountain. That triggers the worst instincts in Joseph. In a maniacal frenzy of jealousy and revenge equal to Captain Ahab's, he murders the Shepherd. Alarmed by the shot, Breege races to the field and embraces her lover's body. Desperately, she tries to breathe life back into him. The scene echoes the great Greek tragedies, inspiring a powerful catharsis in the reader. Like Romeo and Juliet's, the Shepherd and Breege's love, doomed to drown in the maelstrom of a family feud, now is turning hatred and bloodshed "into an instrument of peace." The perpetrator is in jail. The time of atonement has arrived. The sacrifice of love, like a rainbow, like a bridge over troubled waters, uncovers in people their compassionate selves. There is hope that the Shepherd and Breege's love child will live to see better, more enlightened, and happier times. The message is clear: *Amor vincit omnia.* Love conquers all.

Easily identifying with the characters of this novel for their universal humanity, the reader will breathlessly participate in the emotionally charged and conflict-driven plot with its exciting roller coaster of love-hate, friendship-feuding, forgiveness-retaliation, and the ultimate life-death-resurrection resolution. The entwined triangle of the main characters carries in itself a powerful emotional tension, heightening the overall drama of the novel. O'Brien's masterfully sketched minor characters successfully add a logical cause-and-effect chain of events that, in turn, expresses the characters' true nature and the message.

Long after completing the book, the reader will stay deeply touched not only by the scenes of gentle passion and magic beauty, but also by the equally powerful eruptions of physical violence, orgiastic bacchanalia, and pathetic courtroom scenes.

O'Brien's description of the "locked in" patients provides a sharp contrast to the "sane" people on the "outside" who cause harm and destruction. The patients' natural acceptance of each other is unforgettable in its healing impact on the reader. As a writer, O'Brien does not strive to create angels and devils, but real people whose actions result from their psyche—their individual or collective memories. She does not just blame the "curses" of society, but shows a way out through understanding, love and enlightenment.

The plot, with its complex interdependence between the characters, their actions, thoughts, and emotions, successfully blends into a highly exciting, meaningful, and entertaining story. The stream-of-consciousness technique and the writing style offer a feast of masterfully selected words, sensual details, powerful imagery, revealing metaphors and contrasts, careful foreshadowing, complex symbolism, and so much more. Readers young and old will find *Wild Decembers* an endlessly fresh, nourishing well of intellectual, spiritual, and emotional food.

Mira Mataric

Sources for Further Study

Booklist 96 (February 1, 2000): 996.
Commonweal 127 (May 5, 2000): 19.
The New Yorker 76 (June 5, 2000): 89.
Publishers Weekly 247 (January 31, 2000): 77.
Time 155 (April 17, 2000): 82.
The Virginia Quarterly Review 76 (Autumn, 2000): 136.

WILD LIFE

Author: Molly Gloss (1944-   )
Publisher: Simon & Schuster (New York). 256 pp.
    $24.00
Type of work: Novel
Time: The early 1900's
Locale: Farming and logging communities in southwest-
    ern Washington State

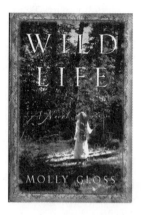

~

*A thirty-five-year-old widow who writes adventure fic-
tion heads off to the wilderness in search of the grandchild
of her housekeeper and meets a tribe of wild creatures*

~

Principal characters:

CHARLOTTE BRIDGER DRUMMOND, a writer whose life is changed after
    five weeks of a primitive existence in the wilderness
MELBA PELTON, Charlotte's housekeeper
HORACE STUBAND, a farmer and neighbor to Charlotte

The novel opens in 1999 when a grandchild of Charlotte Bridger Drummond stumbles across a journal and assorted literary papers and sends them off to her sister for
possible publication. The diary extends from March to June of 1905, when Charlotte
reviews her placid existence and sets off on a life-altering adventure.

Initially, Charlotte's days are spent chasing her five boys around her farm while
she tries to steal a few hours for writing potboilers to earn a meager income. A con-
firmed feminist, Charlotte is often at comical odds with her fifty-two-year-old housekeeper, Melba Pelton, who disapproves of Charlotte's housekeeping and liberated demeanor. When word arrives that Melba's granddaughter has been lost in the woods,
Charlotte sets off into the wilderness, as much out of hubris as out of concern and so-
licitude. When she becomes separated from her search party and disoriented, she
eventually falls in with a tribe of Sasquatch-like creatures and lives with them for a
few weeks. In that time she loses all touch with humanity, her old life, and, she fears,
her sanity. Eventually she is discovered by some conservationists and reunited with
her family.

~

*Molly Gloss has written three
novels.* The Jump-Off Creek *won
the* Northwest Booksellers Award,
and Dazzle of the Day *was a* New
York Times *Notable Book.*

~

In one respect the novel stands as a contemporary example of beautiful local color writing.
The novel in fact begins with a map of southwestern Washington and a prefatory note in
which Gloss announces her fidelity to history
and geography, and Charlotte often refers to
writers such as Willa Cather as inspirations. The

re-creation of the novel's rural communities at the turn of the twentieth century reveals a fragile time when one way of life was rapidly giving way to another. Additionally, the narrative is occasionally interrupted by interchapters that offer portraits of the principal characters in Charlotte's life that remind the reader of daguerreotypes in an old photo album.

However, the strongest indications of local color writing come in the precise evocations of landscape and place:

> The Skamokawa anchorage is both deep and sheltered; log booms lie in the sloughs in bad weather, and there are a few small hand-logging outfits who skid down to the river and hang their booms in the Columbia River, east and west of the town. We are long in years, as Western towns go, and in the self-conscious manner of the logging West, much is made of the "old days" before the donkey engine—the days of ox teams and bull-whackers and monstrous trees so immense as to challenge the imagination. Now the big trees have all been cut for miles around, and there is a packet that stops daily on a westbound trip to Astoria, and another on an eastbound to Kalama, Ridgefield, and Portland, and we get every kind of local river traffic—tugs and trawlers as well as rowboats and barges. We are, if not entirely civilized, entirely modern, and consider ourselves at the center of Western commerce and industry.

At the same time, the novel is a work of literary primitivism, with Charlotte suspicious of civilized pretensions and conventions. The novel plays repeatedly on its title and the implications of "wildness." Charlotte, for instance, relies on wildness as a central principle in child rearing: "It's my argument that a child's happiness and well-being decreases in direct proportion to the degree of his civilization." However, it is the sojourn in the woods that leads to Charlotte's full immersion in the Other; she refers to herself as a "stinking wild creature," learns the rudiments of the tribe's language, and develops a bond with a particular creature "as if we were two women." The identification with these creatures becomes so complete that she is fired upon by a hunter and shuns returning to humankind, feeling she now inhabits "a new world, wild and terrible."

Central to the novel's concerns is the theme of community, which Charlotte contemplates continually and which is hardly surprising for a woman who feels she inhabits the periphery of her town and the publishing world. In Skamokawa she is the resident oddball, refusing to wear shoes around the farm she neglects and leaves uncultivated, dressing in men's pants, smoking a cigar, and writing her stories in a windowless, unheated tool shed. As she writes, "There's not much point in dressing outlandishly if it goes unnoticed." While good, God-fearing people attend Sunday services, she gallivants around on her bicycle, against the accepted wisdom of the era: "As regards women, the intoxication of flying through the streets under one's own power is said to lead to unspecified, doubtless shameful, acts of immorality." Abandoned by her husband after his business fails, Charlotte fiercely cherishes her freedom, though Melba finds her condition scandalous and tries to marry her off to Horace Stuband, a taciturn neighboring farmer.

While she contends that her neighbors are "hardened to my ways," she is still regarded as a lunatic and shunned, and for her part she has little to do with them. Her remove to the forest only accentuates her isolation from communal intercourse, but ironically she finds an all-too-brief sense of belonging with creatures not of her own species. Here she is accepted for exactly who and what she is, and is even invited to participate in one of their most sacred rituals. After a young member of the tribe is killed by a hunter and the tribe recovers the corpse, they consume it:

> It was a sacrament by which this child redeemed the lives of his family. His corporeal body will be found nowhere—he is buried within the bodies of his mother, his father— and thus their lives, their objective existence, undivulged, shall remain a secret closely kept from the brutal world of Men.

Her separation seems complete until she is returned to civilization, an unwelcome reunion because "I am afraid of people, so much so that I fear I shall always go on like this." However, after her rescue she sees the world and others with new eyes. Stuband, whom she had regarded as dull and ill-educated, becomes an unexpected source of comfort and reveals Charlotte's desire for others despite her assertions of flinty individuality.

> Ours is not a relationship of devotion, but Stuband and I are long acquainted and have old knowledge of each other's losses and successes, burdens and fortunate outcomes. I believe we have a dim understanding: like a tough plant that survives drought and flood and snow and sun, our relation to each other must be deep-rooted and stronger than a relation that is tender and looked after.

The source of much of Charlotte's independence is her feminism, which she expresses through numerous reflections, asides, even disquisitions on the place and condition of women in society. She contemplates the effects of burgeoning technology playing a role in female emancipation, the intellectual freedom that education encourages, and the structure that marriage inevitably imposes on women. The persistence and sheer number of these meditations and the stridency with which they are presented become overbearing and predictable. Whenever confronted with adversity, Charlotte can be relied upon to offer another extended comment on female constraint.

However, once she wanders into the woods, Charlotte, like so many writers before her, especially in the twentieth century, literally discovers her own voice. Gone are the rhetorically predictable sermons, replaced with probing, original observations. This may in fact be Gloss's point: In a society where independence—physical as well as intellectual—like Charlotte's appears freakish, such a woman might well feel compelled to defend and justify her existence. Freed of those constraints, she is freed to express her own unique thoughts.

Indeed, among the wild creatures she feels a particular kinship with the female she names Cleo, and that closeness gives rise to a sensation of connectedness and immense communion. She describes this condition in one of the novel's most moving passages:

In silence we two women and the baby watched the sun set and twilight fall. . . . I felt that we had climbed high above thought; here we could sit distracted, holding nothing in our minds but the glory of the sky—the miracle of the cold moon upon the white peak of the mountain. . . . I began to cry, which I have not done for oh so very long—whether for my nameless boys or for my situation or for all the dead and lost children, in truth I cannot say. . . . The mother almost certainly understood its meaning, for she began to join me in mourning, raising her voice in an opening phrase. . . . By such small increments the old lines that set me apart, that defined me, are erased. The sky by then was dark as a bear's mouth, and our keening song, unearthly, wordless as water, rose up into it and was swallowed whole.

Her experience in the wild releases her and reinforces her feminism, but a feminism now on her terms and a feminism that reveals her need for the Other in the figures of the creatures and the once-ignored Stuband.

Wild Life is an intricately constructed fiction that is as much a metafictional examination of the workings of narrative as it is a story of a woman's pilgrimage. The story begins with a letter detailing how the manuscript of this diary has seen the light of day and its distinct anomalies:

It's mostly (apparently) a diary. Some of the diary pages were torn out and stuck in at other places, so the dates are not entirely consecutive; and there's a bunch of other stuff interleafed too. . . . The smaller scraps of paper shoved in between the pages are mostly quotations from various people, newspaper clippings, that kind of thing.

Thus the novel is assembled like the layers of a Chinese box, with numerous narratives and prose fragments nestled within one another. These include Charlotte's other published and unpublished works, newspaper clippings, folk songs, quotes from novels and nonfictional studies, character studies, and the like.

Metafictions are by nature self-conscious examinations of the ways in which consciousness constructs and maintains "reality," and indeed Charlotte is forever contemplating who she is, what her role in the world is, and what relationship her writing has to that sense of identity. Before her trek she is fascinated by stories of "Wild Men of the Woods" that are brought back from the logging camps by the lost girl's father. She even plans a story about them, and once confronted by the creatures she questions the testimony of her eyes:

My mind has been cut loose from its moorings and now follows its usual course, adrift in a wild beast fable: they are the Mountain Giants from the hidden caves of the See-Ah-Tiks, and I am the intrepid Girl Explorer, Helena Reed.

The novel never firmly resolves whether her account is factual or the product of a body long deprived of nourishment and an imagination overtaxed. What is significant, though, is that the act of writing is essential to Charlotte's very being and her salvation: "I think I must be writing for both of us [she and Cleo who has lost her child]—writing as women have always written—to make sense of what the heart cannot take in all at once."

Wild Life is a daring, richly imagined novel that can be read in a host of ways, each of which presents rewards and satisfactions that exceed the ordinary reading experience. Although Gloss has written other well-received novels, this is the work that may very well bring her much-deserved and wider recognition, and it is a rare narrative experience.

David W. Madden

Sources for Further Study

The Atlantic Monthly 286 (July, 2000): 98.
Booklist 96 (June 1, 2000): 1851.
Library Journal 125 (June 1, 2000): 196.
New Statesman 128 (September, 2000): 57.
The New York Times Book Review 105 (September 24, 2000): 30.
Publishers Weekly 247 (May 8, 2000): 204.
The Washington Post Book World, July 23, 2000, p. 4.

WORDS ALONE
The Poet T. S. Eliot

Author: Denis Donoghue (1928-   )
Publisher: Yale University Press (New Haven, Conn.).
   326 pp. $26.95
Type of work: Literary criticism
Time: 1946 to the 1990's
Locale: Northern Ireland, Dublin, and London

*Donoghue, having discovered Eliot's poetry in 1946
when he left his native Warrenpoint to attend University
College in Dublin, writes autobiographically about the experience and offers a close reading of Eliot's major poems
and essays*

≈

Words Alone: The Poet T. S. Eliot is a unique critical work that intermixes literary
biography with intimate autobiographical information about Denis Donoghue, its author, University Professor and Henry James Professor of English and American Letters at New York University. In his close reading of Eliot's major poems and some of
his essays, Donoghue provides insights into Eliot's writing against a backdrop of autobiographical reminiscence reflecting how, as a university student in Dublin in 1946,
he first read Eliot.

   Donoghue's earliest exposure to the poet was through his relatively unsophisti-
cated reading of "The Love Song of J. Alfred Prufrock," a poem that spoke directly
to him as, according to Donoghue, it still speaks directly to young people who read
it. In his earliest reading of the poem, he considered it to be a gloomy self-assess-
ment of someone who had little going for him. He came to see more in the poem in
subsequent readings, finding intimations of spiritual panic, of a confused mind in a
void, and of the spiritual bankruptcy of life in general. Donoghue, as he matured and
read more widely, was exposed to a broad panoply of critical theories regarding the
poem, most of them considerably more sophisticated than his own early impressions of the work.

   Remembering his own initial views of the poem helps Donoghue to understand why
his students, the majority of whom have been exposed to little Eliot beyond "The Love
Song of J. Alfred Prufrock," find in the poem reflections of their personal insecurities
about what they perceive as their own inadequacies. Proceeding from the autobiographical base he establishes early in his study, Donoghue traces significant advances in his
own critical understandings and perceptions. This approach humanizes his criticism
and puts it on a plane that those unacquainted with recent critical theory can understand
and appreciate, although the uninitiated will have to work diligently to keep up with

~

Denis Donoghue is University
Professor and Henry James
Professor of English and American
Letters at New York University. His
book The Practice of Reading
received the Robert Penn Warren/
Cleanth Brooks Award for literary
criticism. He is also the author of
Walter Pater: Lover of Strange
Souls, Warrenpoint, *and many other*
books.

~

Donoghue's often complex arguments that, fortunately, are well articulated.

The study is enhanced by Donoghue's musical background. Shortly after beginning his studies at University College, he became a student of lieder at the Royal Irish Academy of Music. This experience has had a profound effect upon his reading of many of Eliot's poems, which he views as "music become speech." Donoghue states, "If he were a composer, I think he would have gone to school with [Arnold] Schoenberg, [Anton von] Webern, or [Alban] Berg." Donoghue is ever cognizant, in a musical sense, of Eliot's rhythms and even more particularly of his tones and tone shifts.

Donoghue aptly compares and contrasts Eliot to other poets. He devotes an entire twenty-five-page chapter, "Stevens and Eliot," to making extensive comparisons between Wallace Stevens and Eliot, but countless other comparisons occur throughout the book. Donoghue notes similarities between Charles Baudelaire and Eliot, noting that both often exemplify cities in their works, although he denies that there is any hard evidence to suggest that "The Love Song of J. Alfred Prufrock" is a refutation of the pastoral qualities of William Wordsworth, as some critics have suggested.

Donoghue is at his best in his discussions of "The Love Song of J. Alfred Prufrock" and *The Waste Land* (1922). In focusing on "the diversity of languages with which 'The Waste Land' ends," he contends that "Eliot wanted to transcend the limits of any single language so that he could gain for his poem at least an air of universal application. . . . Eliot was remarkably sensitive not only to associations and contrasts but also to transitions from one tone to another." He goes on to say that when Eliot does something that creates a jolt for the reader, as the ending of *The Waste Land* surely does, he employs the technique to transport his audience "from one plane of reality to another."

Of particular interest is Donoghue's comparison of the first drafts of *The Waste Land*, as edited by Valerie Eliot and published in 1971 under the title *The Waste Land: A Facsimile and Transcript of the Original Drafts*, with the final version of the poem published in 1922. This fruitful exploration places Donoghue in opposition to various earlier critics who link the poem to Eliot's supposed conception of the breakdown of Western civilization, as suggested by Oswald Spengler in his pessimistic but influential book *Der Untergang des Abendlandes* (1918-1922; *The Decline of the West*, 1926). Spengler speculates that civilizations move in cycles and that Western civilization at the end of World War I was in a downward cycle, soon to be overtaken by a more vigorous Asian civilization.

Certainly much of Spengler's pessimism coincides with Eliot's as he expresses it in *The Waste Land*. Donoghue, however, in referring to the early drafts of *The Waste Land* that were not available to some previous scholars, points out that lines written before 1915, fully three years before Eliot could have read *The Decline of the West*, expressed the sort of Spenglerian pessimism that misled some earlier Eliot scholars.

Moving away from a Spenglerian interpretation, Donoghue considers whether there might be a relationship between marriage and the poem. Eliot married Vivienne Haigh-Wood on June 26, 1915, quite against the wishes of his American father, who, as a result of Eliot's residing permanently in England and marrying an English-woman, disinherited his son. The very act of marrying Vivienne alienated Eliot from his family, but the marriage was a terribly troubled one that ended with Vivienne in a mental institution, legally separated from the poet, who, supposedly because of religious scruples, did not seek a divorce.

Given this background, Donoghue reads *The Waste Land* not as a poem of universal despair, as it has often been interpreted, but rather as a poem of particular guilt. As the poem's movement of feeling through its words progresses, according to Donoghue, it "corresponds, however obscurely, to the act of penance." Certainly, as Donoghue notes later in the book, penance is a strong theme in much of Eliot's writing, one that is partic-ularly notable, for example, in the depiction of Celia Copplestone in *The Cocktail Party* (pr. 1949).

Eliot's search for answers in religion, most notably in his baptism and confirma-tion in the Anglican Church, followed a period of ill health during which he com-pleted the final draft of *The Waste Land*. This was a period of considerable self-doubt for Eliot. His marriage was going badly. Vivienne's growing neuroticism, along with a semi-invalidism that required Eliot to be her nurse more than her husband, surely had a profound impact upon his outlook as it was reflected in his writing.

At about this time Eliot renounced his United States citizenship. Like Henry James before him, he became a British subject, feeling that the aristocratic tradition of cul-ture had vanished from the United States. Donoghue cites Eliot's comment that James's becoming a British citizen made him not an Englishman so much as a Euro-pean—something that, according to Donoghue, might also be said of Eliot.

Donoghue comments on Eliot's lifelong friendship with Emily Hale, a schoolmis-tress he met in February, 1913. According to Donoghue, Eliot fell in love with Hale. He might have married her had he not married Vivienne two years later. He remained close to Hale, presumably on a platonic basis, for years to come. Donoghue seeks to attribute some of Eliot's discontent and inner turmoil to the unrequited love he felt for Hale.

This explanation is perhaps too facile. It would be productive to examine Eliot from a psychoanalytical standpoint that might reveal a suppressed homosexuality that would explain a great deal about the poet. There is little to suggest that Eliot ever acted out any homosexual feelings he might have had, but there seems an adequate basis for attributing such feelings to him. This would also explain his reluctance to di-vorce Vivienne and gain the freedom that such an act would have given him. It would also help to explain the guilt/penance emphasis in both his poetry and his plays.

In order to understand Eliot and his work, one must also understand his religious conversion and all that it implies. Donoghue does a masterful job of analyzing this conversion and of relating the poet's religious views to many important aspects of his writing, both poetry and drama. Raised a Unitarian and the descendant of a grandfather who was a Unitarian minister, Eliot needed a more rigid religious structure than his ancestral church provided.

Donoghue, while acknowledging that *The Waste Land*, written prior to Eliot's conversion to Anglicanism, is his finest poem, rejects the notion that the poetry of the years following his conversion is inferior to his earlier work. He cites as examples of excellence in Eliot's postconversion poetry "Ash Wednesday," "Marina," and each of the *Four Quartets* (1943) except for "The Dry Salvages." He might also have mentioned the profound effect that Eliot's conversion had upon his dramatic writing, most notably in *Murder in the Cathedral* (pr., pb. 1935) and in *The Cocktail Party*, which Grover Smith, in *T. S. Eliot's Poetry and Plays: A Study in Sources and Meaning* (1956), views as having a "theological underpattern."

Donoghue cites correspondence between Paul Elmer More and Eliot in which Eliot refers to the void that exists in those who lack a religious instinct. Such people are, in Eliot's terms, not aware of that void, but Eliot claims to have been painfully aware of it, claiming that it drove him toward asceticism or sensuality. He contends that Christianity reconciles him to life, which he views as otherwise disgusting.

Eliot was driven, according to Donoghue, by two major religious traditions, the Augustinian, which involved theological exactitudes, and mysticism. He found in Dante's *La divina commedia* (c. 1320; *The Divine Comedy*, 1802) and *La vita nuova* (c. 1292; *Vita Nuova*, 1861) the means of reconciling the theological traditions he most valued. He revealed that "Ash Wednesday" was an attempt to apply the philosophy of the *Vita Nuova* to a contemporary context.

One might question why Eliot, as he moved toward his conversion, opted for Anglicanism rather than Roman Catholicism. Donoghue contends that he reached this decision as a means of paying tribute to seventeenth century England, from which his forebears had departed to begin their new lives in America.

Eliot came to view the main objective of human life as that of glorifying God and enjoying God forever. This emphasis tends to diminish one's attitude toward mere humans. It is this attitude, indeed this deep-seated philosophical conviction, that explains at least in part what Donoghue calls his heartless treatment of those who cared for and about him, notably Emily Hale, Mary Trevelyan, and John Hayward, faithful friends whom Eliot used unconscionably. Donoghue writes, "He felt that much of human life was disgusting. In his Christian years he believed that his best practice, in addition to daily prayer, was to regard human relations as provisional and ancillary to some relation beyond them."

Much influenced by the theological hierarchy contrived by the Roman church and extensively elucidated in *The Divine Comedy*, Eliot fully accepted the concepts of heaven, purgatory, and hell, contending that those who deny a future life are already in a hell of their own creation because their mortal life is one of constant torment. Such a contention reflects the inner struggle that was a constant in Eliot's life and that shaped his view of the human condition, leading him to the conclusion that it was disgusting.

As Donoghue presents him, Eliot is the prototype of the man who is so religious that he dismisses the human race and lives not for his own time but in the hope of some eternal glory to come after his death. Such a view may well be classified as fanaticism, which, despite his gentlemanly outward demeanor, characterizes T. S. Eliot.

R. Baird Shuman

Sources for Further Study

Library Journal 125 (October 15, 2000): 69.
The New York Times Book Review 105 (November 26, 2000): 17.
Publishers Weekly 247 (October 16, 2000): 62.

WORLD ENOUGH AND TIME
The Life of Andrew Marvell

Author: Nicholas Murray
Publisher: St. Martin's Press (New York). Illustrated.
 294 pp. $27.95
Type of work: Literary biography
Time: 1621-1678
Locale: Vicinity of Hull, Cambridge, and London, England, as well as several European countries

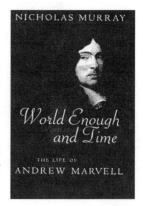

~

*This biography of an outstanding English poet grounds
its subject firmly in the context of the religious and political
tumult of mid-seventeenth century England*

~

Principal personages:
ANDREW MARVELL, poet and member of Parliament
REVEREND ANDREW MARVELL, the poet's father, a Puritan minister
CHARLES II, king of England from 1660 to 1685
OLIVER CROMWELL, English civil war antimonarchical leader and later ruler
THOMAS, LORD FAIRFAX, civil war general, employer of the young Marvell
JOHN MILTON, poet and official of the Cromwellian government
SAMUEL PARKER, Anglican bishop, the most virulent of Marvell's enemies

In 1680 a woman named Mary Palmer who claimed to be the widow of Andrew Marvell, best known at the time as a longtime member of Parliament for Hull, made an attempt to secure Marvell's estate. Her alleged inspection of his London quarters turned up only "a few Books & papers of small value." Among these papers would have been his unpublished poems, including several immortal poems of the English language. Nevertheless, Palmer decided to publish the poems the following year, although for more than two centuries they attracted the attention of only a few connoisseurs. It is unlikely that they will again suffer such neglect. They are the justification for any modern biography of a man earlier admired mainly as a principled champion of Puritanism in an age of religious and political strife.

Before the eighteenth century, singular success at poetry did not suffice to render a man notable. As far as public records go, Geoffrey Chaucer was a customs official and sometime diplomat, Sir Philip Sidney the scion of a noble family and a military hero, William Shakespeare an actor. The bulk of the available facts about Marvell pertain to his early labors as a tutor in the household of Thomas, Lord Fairfax, his un-

930

easy maneuvering through England's midcen-
tury political turmoil, and his services on behalf
of the merchants of Hull, especially as a member
of Parliament for most of his later life. His younger contemporary John Dryden is probably the
first major English poet to make a name for him-
self by means of his verse—primarily because he excelled at religious and political
satire, forms that Marvell too practiced competently but not superlatively.

Nicholas Murray is the author of biographies of Matthew Arnold and Bruce Chatwin.

Marvell's career constitutes a severe challenge to his modern biographer. Whereas
critics of Marvell the poet—a numerous and active group in recent years—can concentrate on a small but fascinating body of lyric poetry, the biographer must try to re-
create not merely the life of a public man who happened to be an accomplished writer
but also a revelation of a significant poet. The critic may, but need not, relate the poetry to the life; the biographer of a poet must do so. How is that to be done, however,
when poems are essentially timeless ones such as "The Garden," "The Definition of
Love," and "To His Coy Mistress," which remained in manuscript until after the
poet's death?

Murray has faced up to this difficult challenge bravely. He was able to take advantage of a few points of reference in Marvell's life, one of them a position that facili-
tated the poet's contribution to a genre that changing taste and changing social conditions have rendered obsolete: the country house poem. Murray regards "Upon
Appleton House, to My Lord Fairfax" as the culmination of a series of such poems
originating with Ben Jonson's tribute to the Sidney family, "To Penshurst." As he
aptly explains this type of poem,

> It was a way of seeing the country house and praising it, not as a rich man's prize, but
> as the hub of a traditional, ordered, ethical way of life. It stressed the social function of
> the house in its community and the relationship of this domestic economy to nature.

Beginning probably in 1650 when he was twenty-nine, Marvell tutored Lord Fairfax's
daughter Mary at Nun Appleton House, once a Cistercian nunnery but later Fairfax's
Yorkshire estate. The poem can be dated between that year and 1652, when Marvell
seems to have moved on. This poem declares him poetically mature, already the master
of the octosyllabic couplet at which Marvell is unsurpassed in English poetry.

It is also clear that he composed "An Horatian Ode upon Cromwell's Return from
Ireland" in 1650. This poem reflects his ambivalent attitude toward a man with whose
stormy career he was to be associated in the decade that followed, while demonstrating rare skill at a form much cultivated by Renaissance classicists. Thus it can be seen
that by his thirtieth year Marvell was capable of his best work. If one assumes that his
service to Fairfax provided him with a reasonable amount of leisure amid congenial
surroundings, it is easy to concur with Murray's speculation that pastoral poems such
as "The Garden," with its bewitching couplets ("How vainly men themselves amaze/
To win the palm, the oak, or bays"; "Annihilating all that's made/ To a green thought
in a green shade"), and the several poems about mowers date from this period in his
life.

"The Garden" is also one of the cluster of poems tantalizingly suggesting facets of Marvell's elusive personal life. For instance, the speaker judges it "two paradises . . . to live in paradise alone." Like most Marvellians, Murray rejects Mary Palmer's claim to be Marvell's widow and accepts the conclusion that Marvell remained a bachelor at his death at the age of fifty-seven. However, did he ever have a mistress, coy or otherwise? The speaker of Marvell's most celebrated work locates himself "by the tide of Humber"; the poet himself was born in Winestead and grew up in nearby Hull along the Humber estuary. Murray wisely refrains from drawing any firm conclusions from such nuggets, but he does feel obliged, as probably any biographer would today, to consider the evidence, in or out of his poetry, that might point to homosexuality in his unmarried subject. His judgment, however, is that such scraps as exist fall short of proving anything. "Marvell's is not a poetry of personality. He does not follow a confessional aesthetic," Murray cautions—though this obvious truth is not likely to discourage readers convinced that self-revelation is inevitable in a body of lyric poetry.

As the son of a not-entirely-conforming clergyman (the Reverend Andrew Marvell was, for instance, disciplined at one point for failure to emphasize the Prayer Book sufficiently in his services), Marvell learned early the difficulties of satisfying both conscience and the expectations of authorities. His success at safely performing this balancing act in an era of intense religious and political conflict is one of his more remarkable achievements. The 1650 ode on Cromwell justifies the initiatives of a man who in the past year had demonstrated complicity in the execution of King Charles I and utter ruthlessness in campaigns against royalist forces in Ireland and Scotland, yet poignantly describes the king who "bowed his comely head" to the executioner's axe and reminds Cromwell that he must subordinate personal ambition to the good of the "Republic." Marvell served as "Cromwell's unofficial laureate" (to use Murray's phrase) in the early years of the Protectorate and later assisted John Milton, Cromwell's Latin secretary. Yet unlike Milton, Marvell spent no time in prison at the Restoration of King Charles II but retained for the rest of his life the Parliamentary seat to which he had first been elected early in 1659 and which, after some months out of office, he resumed a few weeks before the triumphal return of the monarch. The tensions that complicate and enrich his best poems also pervaded his political career.

As Murray points out, none of Marvell's finest poems can confidently be ascribed to the eighteen years of his life after the Restoration, though the possibility cannot be entirely discounted. The poems known to date from this period are religious and political satires, often charged with powerful metaphors but usually defective as unified wholes and lacking the universality of Dryden's and Alexander Pope's best work. Although his skill at deflecting serious threats to life and liberty never failed him, Marvell contracted bitter enemies, of whom Bishop Samuel Parker must be judged the most virulent. In 1672 Marvell issued a prose satire, *The Rehearsal Transpros'd*, attacking Parker as representative of conservative prelates who refused to sanction the king's policy of indulgence toward English nonconformists. Marvell had always championed Protestant (though not Catholic) dissent, but in this effort he alarmed some dissenters, who feared that his efforts on their behalf would open the door to a resurgence of "popery." Not only did Marvell enrage the bishop by heaping personal abuse on him; he actually contrived to trip the man into the gutter when they happened to meet on a London street. Parker, however, succeeded neither in prosecuting Marvell nor in gaining much sympathy when he published a scurrilous counterattack the following year.

Oddly, Marvell got into deeper trouble for administering an apparently accidental blow to a fellow legislator. Rising to defend himself against a charge of disorderliness in the House of Commons, he tripped over the feet of a fellow member whom he regarded as his friend. A number of eyewitnesses insisted that when Marvell reached out to regain his balance he had boxed the ear of the other man, and for this they demanded that Marvell be committed to prison. The context and Marvell's reputation help explain this hostile reaction. Parliament was disputing a bill, prompted by the fear of a return of Catholicism to power in the realm, that would require children of the royal family to be educated in the Protestant religion. Although a fervent anti-Catholic, Marvell refused to be a party to any measure that would further empower English Protestant bishops. In this matter, not just personal animus but also a sincere devotion to religious liberty which he had absorbed from his clergyman father motivated him. However, Marvell's hot temper had more than once alienated even those whose support a more diplomatic politician might have won to his cause.

It is of such matters, and not fine poetry, that Marvell's later life—at least the life now detectable—consisted. The reader of Murray's biography is likely to emerge with the impression that public life killed the poet in Marvell or at least maimed him by encouraging the prostitution of his talent in controversies about which his modern admirer knows little and cares less. It is inescapable that Marvell was no Milton, determined to produce in the fullness of time a magnum opus. Nor does the available evidence suggest that he continued to exercise his lyrical gift, as for instance the busy cleric John Donne surely did earlier in the same century. As a result, Andrew Marvell must be denied the status of "major poet." He was an immensely talented man who composed either as an avocation or, increasingly in later years, as a weapon in the service of a political vocation.

Could Nicholas Murray have done more to illuminate the wellsprings of Marvell's poetry? He might have investigated the extent to which seventeenth century intellectual currents other than specifically religious and political ones fashioned his subject's outlook. Did scientific skepticism lurk behind the arresting reminder to the "coy mistress" that "yonder all before us lie/ Deserts of vast eternity"? What philosophical tradition nourished his preoccupation with fate in "The Definition of Love," among other poems?

In the absence of facts about specific educational influences on the young Marvell and his reading habits, Murray may have decided that to probe such matters would be to plunge into a thicket of speculation little suited to the biographer. In the end he stuck to an essentially modest account of what can be confidently known or plausibly inferred about a poet likely to remain as elusive as he has proven to be to date. Within these limitations Murray has served Marvell and Marvellians well.

Robert P. Ellis

Sources for Further Study

Contemporary Review 277 (August, 2000): 120.
The Economist 355 (June 17, 2000): 13.
Kirkus Reviews 68 (January 15, 2000): 105.
New Criterion 18 (June, 2000): 78.
The New York Times Book Review 105 (July 9, 2000): 31.
Publishers Weekly 247 (March 6, 2000): 96.
The Spectator 283 (December 18, 1999): 69.
The Times Literary Supplement, January 28, 2000, p. 9.

THE YEARS WITH LAURA DÍAZ

Author: Carlos Fuentes (1928-   )
First published: Los años con Laura Díaz, 1999, in
    Mexico
Translated from the Spanish by Alfred Mac Adam
Publisher: Farrar, Straus and Giroux (New York). 516
    pp. $26.00
Type of work: Novel
Time: 1898-2000
Locale: Mexico, Spain, and the United States

*As the new millennium debuts, Fuentes produces an in-
tricate historical drama of Mexican political and personal
struggle through the scrim, or, perhaps more accurately, a
mirror of his heroine, Laura Díaz*

Principal characters:
  LAURA DÍAZ
  SANTIAGO, her brother
  JORGE MAURA and others, her lovers
  JUAN FRANCISCO, her spouse

The Years with Laura Díaz is Carlos Fuentes's most recent venture into a passionate chronicle of the growing pains of his nation and its interaction with other nations.
The book draws on elements from his family history—the dedication speaks of it as a
book of his ancestry—with some of the characters loosely based on offspring from his
family tree and stories from his family's oral tradition. It incorporates the volatile political events and active players of the twentieth century in Mexico, the United States,
and worldwide. The book is accented with the subcultures of art, architecture, and
even fashion that make up the rich but flawed fabric of the time. Laura Díaz, born at
the dawn of the century and gifted with a long and fecund life, is the occasion and cen-
terpiece of the story that he tells.

Readers see the heroine's multifaceted and colorful life through the kaleidoscope
of seventy years of change: personal, cultural, political. Child Laura, born to an abundance of family and funds, is nourished behind the walls of privilege on her grandfather's coffee plantation. The household includes her grandmother, whose courageous
confrontation with a bandit results in the loss of several of her fingers to his machete.
Readers meet a gaggle of aunts. Two of them carry the weight of failed aspirations to
become, respectively, a writer and a celebrated pianist. These shriveling spinsters
seem to epitomize an expiring past that is mother to a barren future. Laura's other
aunt, an illegitimate mulatto rescued from a life of prostitution by her grandmother,

~

Carlos Fuentes has served as
Panama's ambassador to France
and has received many awards for
his accomplishments as a novelist,
essayist, and commentator, among
them the Cervantes Prize in 1987.
He is the author of more than
twenty books, including The Death
of Artemio Cruz *and* A New Time
for Mexico.

~

eventually trades her years of devoted service to family for dancing on painful legs as her life nears its end. Readers meet Laura's mother, given to the tasks of hearth and home, and the grandparents, who offer advice for her future. Laura, hemmed in and defined by the predictable mores of her era and status, seems destined to model her life on the images projected by the women in her family circle. She marries and bears children, but does not find happiness, nor does she find lingering satisfaction in the series of lovers who occupy her bed and her yearnings as her marriage cools.

As the novel unfolds, the speed at which the characters enter and excite its pages increases. Relatives and friends, lovers and children come on stage, struggle through their sometimes convoluted lines, and then are quickly gone—sometimes through violent means—as the kaleidoscope shifts its colored shards. In her search for identity, Laura embraces both the bodies and the political pain of the lovers she takes. Not until she loses her last lover, an American political exile from the Senator Joseph McCarthy witch-hunts of the 1950's, and reaches the wisdom of her sixties does she emerge as an independent thinker and emancipated observer of the times rather than a passive victim of them. Only in her later years does Laura Díaz, too long the accompanying refrain to the songs of others, become a major theme in her own right.

There is a poignant scene early in the novel that perhaps expresses the kernel of the book's message. Laura, still little more than a child, has a conversation with her dying grandmother. Cosima Kelsen reminisces about the dashing bandit who had cut off her fingers with his machete as she, then a young woman, traveled to Mexico City to buy accessories for her home in Veracruz. There is a hint that the old woman now regrets not running away with him to a life of adventure and unorthodoxy. "You should have seen what a handsome man he was, what fire, how bold he was." She admonishes Laura that fear should not keep the younger woman from seizing opportunities as they come, since "you don't get a second chance." Later, at her grandmother's funeral, Laura's attention is diverted from the sobriety of the moment by a marvelous white crow, symbolically a call to escape the blackness of death symbolized in the funeral dress of her mother and aunts. As she views herself in the mirror, though, Laura sees little promise of a dazzling future for herself. However, promises will come true—much later. Not surprisingly, mirror images abound in the book.

Because the scope of the novel is so vast, Fuentes from time to time summarizes the action and character relationships for his readers. This is initially a helpful device, as it is easy to lose track of who has done what with whom during the five hundred pages. By the last time the author provides this aid, however, it has become intrusive. Perhaps the author had difficulty himself keeping track of characters that appear on stage for so brief a time, a blaze of light to be quickly extinguished as the action of the play moves on. Sometimes one feels that there are too many years spent with the heroine, with little happening to warrant such a meticulous journal. On the other hand, Fuentes does bring the story line of each character to some degree of closure. As the book moves to conclusion, Laura is forever running into someone from her past whose story line the author feels must be brought to conclusion—much too self-consciously like a novel.

The book jacket calls this five hundred-page work Fuentes's "most important novel in decades." Perhaps this is true. Certainly the content is critical to understanding the complexity of intersection among the Spanish, Mexican, and American elements that form the syncretic stew of the modern North American continent. Certainly there are moments in the novel when the author reaches brilliance, engulfing the reader in the emotional eddy of his powerful description. His account of Laura's reunion with her most successful former lover, Jorge Maura, now doing penance for the evils of the world in a monastery in Spain, is one of them. The description of this encounter is gripping. Unfortunately, the novel remains uneven in its ability to compel the reader, with arid patches of infertile dialogue deposited among some well-watered flowerings of brilliance.

The rich images and references the author can and does use motivate the reader to explore other works that detail what *The Years with Laura Díaz* treats with illusion. After reading in the introductory chapter the description of the great Diego Rivera mural in Detroit, one is tempted to visit it. Is Laura Díaz really painted there, and what did she look like next to the rendering of Rivera's crippled lover? Fuentes uses subtle allusions that evoke—for those who wish to pursue them—much more than the words on paper. In the final pages of the book he mentions in passing the emigration in 1970 of Laura's grandson from Mexico to the United States, "after another wound named Tlatelolco." Historically, a college established by the Spaniards at Tlatelolco was a failed sixteenth century experiment, an attempt to educate native Mexican Indians from aristocratic families in the culture of the conquerors. The project's failure occurred not because of the lack of ability of the pupils, but because the Indians proved to be such apt learners. They surpassed the talents of the conquerors and, educated, were no longer suited to work as cheap labor in the mines and haciendas of their European masters. Fuentes pulls no punches in exposing the pain and suffering of his people.

The book is not without flaws. While providing the ongoing trajectory of the novel, the character of Laura remains elusive. There is the author's description of her physical features and dress. There is a presentation of her family history, rooted in the courage of her grandmother and the stoicism of her grandfather. The reader rests long enough on the patio of the ancestral home—both at the beginning and toward the close of the work—to see her context. Cameos of events are colored with the brilliant Mexican sun: the fancy balls of her teenage years, the horrific death of her brother Santiago, the steamy descriptions of her attempts to find satisfying and lasting love in the political leanings and loins of a series of men. Still, who is Laura Díaz? Is she a woman who finally manages to transcend her history, who has an abrupt metanoia into an independent photographer whose images bring her fame? Is she a somewhat indulgent but thoroughly modern grandmother, opening her house to young lovers dogged by parental disapproval? Just when the picture begins to focus, the scene changes and the reader is left holding an unsatisfying bag.

There is at first the temptation to conclude that Fuentes is no longer potent in his portrayal of character. His past works seem more successful at presenting his main characters to the audience. Artemio Cruz, from the novel *La muerte de Artemio Cruz* (1962; *The Death of Artemio Cruz*, 1964), is anything but elusive. His unlikable image lingers like yesterday's garlic in the mental pores of the reader. Even the characters who live only in brief chapters in *La frontera de cristal* (1995; *The Crystal Frontier*, 1997) seem more delineated than do any outlined here. One would expect a live and talking character, the Laura of so many years, to be more accessible than one without speech and confined to a wheelchair, as in "The Line of Oblivion." Is it possible that Fuentes has lost his incisive edge in character development? Perhaps there is another answer. Perhaps it is not the character of Laura Díaz that is the real subject of this work. Perhaps Fuentes sees the main character of this vast novel as twentieth century Mexico herself, birthed in the turmoil of the nascent era and struggling to find its identity through the experiences of love and death, through the tasting of political unrest and passionate art, through betrayal and loyalty and intersection with the various tectonic plates of shifting reality and political styles. It is unlikely that mere coincidence explains the congruence of Laura's year of birth (1898) with the Spanish-American War. Fuentes is too knowledgeable about history and purposeful about what he writes to allow this to occur. The end of the novel, set as it is in the ferment of Chicano identity in the City of Angels, likewise conjures up allusions and connections. Early in the novel a priest asks Laura in the confessional whether she looks at herself nude in the mirror. Perhaps Fuentes is asking the same question of his country: Does Laura Díaz, perhaps Mexico herself, find no surprise as she peers into a mirror that Fuentes holds up?

If one reads the novel through this lens, it makes more sense. Perhaps Laura Díaz is the image in the buried mirror of Fuentes's earlier nonfiction work. Perhaps she is the collective memory of Mexico's past and a glint of its hope for the future. If that is the intent, the result is no less brilliant than Fuentes's earlier work. Often fiction reflects more clearly what is real than reality itself. A picture may be worth a thousand words. This mural of history may say more than a photographic recounting of factual text, bringing to bear as it does the passionate expression of the artist himself. One has only to look at the work of such artists as Diego Rivera to see that truth.

Carlos Fuentes's past work has done much to bring understanding to the complex relationship of Mexico with the United States. He writes with a compelling passion and understanding of the intricate history that has resulted in modern Mexico. Narrative has power. The significance of this book is its incarnation of the history of his beloved country in the form of his heroine. She is the perilous journey of people floating their aspirations from the old country to the new, the tale of emergence of independence in the twentieth century. She embodies the terminal groaning that accompanies the birth of what is to be, while not knowing what it will become. The years of Laura Díaz, the hundred years of Mexico, move from war and colonial structures to promise and creativity seeded in the art of her grandson, the fourth Santiago. It is a compelling movement that draws the reader with it.

Dolores L. Christie

Sources for Further Study

Booklist 97 (September 1, 2000): 6.
Library Journal 125 (October 1, 2000): 147.
Los Angeles Times, October 18, 2000, p. E1.
The New York Times Book Review 105 (November 12, 2000): 8.
Publishers Weekly 247 (September 18, 2000): 85.
The Washington Post Book World, October 15, 2000, p. 7.

YELTSIN
A Revolutionary Life

Author: Leon Aron (1954-   )
Publisher: St. Martin's Press (New York). Illustrated.
   934 pp. $35.00
Type of work: Biography and history
Time: 1931-1998
Locale: Russia (formerly the Soviet Union), especially
   Yekaterinburg (formerly Sverdlovsk) and Moscow

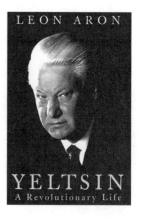

∾

*A political biography that emphasizes the role of Boris
Yeltsin as leader of the revolutionary changes that took
place in Russia after the fall of the Soviet Union*

∾

> *Principal personages:*
> BORIS N. YELTSIN, president of Russia from 1992 to 1999
> MIKHAIL GORBACHEV, president of the Soviet Union and Communist
>   leader, 1985-1991
> EGOR GAIDAR, advocate of free-market reform and critic of the
>   Chechnya War

   Leon Aron is the director of Russian studies at the American Enterprise Institute.
Born and raised in Moscow, he entered the United States at the age of twenty-three as
a political refugee. After receiving his Ph.D. from Columbia University, Aron published numerous scholarly and journalistic articles about Russian affairs and was a
frequent commentator for radio and television news programs. Although specialists
will disagree with many of Aron's interpretations, no one can question his knowledge
of and enthusiasm for the subject of the book.
   Yeltsin: A Revolutionary Life is an interesting and impressive work based on exhaustive research. Although somewhat thin in regard to Yeltsin's personal life, the
book is filled with details about all aspects of Yeltsin's political career. Scholars will
be happy to find more than one hundred pages of documented notes and sixty pages of
bibliography, with an emphasis on sources in the Russian language. In addition to
printed materials, Aron gathers much of his information from interviews with politicians, journalists, and other individuals associated with the events of the book. For the
benefit of readers not familiar with Russian terms, Aron provides a very helpful glossary.
   Aron interprets Yeltsin and his policies in a much more favorable light than do
most Western journalists and historians. Yeltsin emerges as a "man of the people"
who met the challenge of presiding over a revolutionary transformation from a police
state to an open and tolerant society. In a summary of his achievements, Aron writes:

"He made irreversible the collapse of Soviet totalitarian communism, dissolved the Russian empire, ended state ownership of the economy—and held together and rebuilt his country while it coped with new reality and losses." While acknowledging mistakes and a few character flaws, Aron always gives the Russian leader the benefit of every doubt.

Leon Aron was born in Moscow and received his early education there. He received his M.A., M.Phil, and Ph.D. degrees from Columbia University. He is resident scholar and director of Russian Studies at the American Enterprise Institute in Washington, D.C., and is a frequent commentator on current politics and U.S.-Russian relations.

The book went to press about a year before Yeltsin took an early retirement on December 31, 1999. Thus, the work cannot consider Yeltsin's apology for the failures of his economic policies or his selection of Vladimir Putin as a successor. Similarly, the book was written before a number of revelations about possible bribes involving Yeltsin and his daughter, Tatyana Dyachenko. In addition, Aron's book does not analyze the resumption of bitter fighting in Chechnya in 1999.

The first forty-seven pages of the book explore Yeltsin's life before he became a Communist official in 1975. His childhood was basically a struggle for survival, a common experience of Russian children during the period. He probably resented many Stalinist policies. His grandfather perished as an opponent of collectivization, and his father served three years in a labor camp on charges of anti-Soviet agitation. Yeltsin was a good student, but he was also a rebel and a risk-taker. As an example, Aron explains how he blew off two fingers while playing with a live grenade. After completing an engineering degree at the Urals Polytechnic Institute, he worked on large construction projects in Sverdlovsk and the Urals. Often working fifteen hours a day, he acquired a reputation for emphasizing efficiency and as an authoritarian supervisor who was quick to punish subordinates.

When Yeltsin applied for membership in the Communist Party, according to Aron, his major motive was to advance his career. Although he had to pass a test on Marxist-Leninist principles, he apparently had no strong ideological convictions at the time. In 1976, he was appointed first secretary of the Sverdlovsk Regional Party Committee. Although something of a populist, Yeltsin gave no indications of liberalism during this period. Like others in the party's apparatus, he delivered "shameless encomiums" to Leonid Brezhnev, and he did not hesitate to obey orders to destroy the historical Ipatyev house, where the family of Nicholas II had been murdered.

In 1985, Yeltsin's career began to change directions after the new Communist leader, Mikhail Gorbachev, appointed him first secretary of the Moscow Party Committee. Aron observes that the party "needed someone, fast, who could take over and thoroughly clean up the city." Yeltsin was quickly elevated to membership in the Politburo, where he enthusiastically supported Gorbachev's reformist policies of *glasnost* (openness) and *perestroika* (economic restructuring). By 1987, Yeltsin was sharply criticizing the Soviet leadership for its refusal to institute reforms more rapidly. Irritated, Gorbachev removed him from the Politburo and the Moscow City Committee. Although humiliated, Yeltsin was allowed to stay in Moscow in a lesser position. Aron suggests that Gorbachev wanted to use the "firebreathing radical" to encourage conservatives to accept moderate reforms.

With the dramatic revolutions in Eastern Europe in 1989, Aron argues that the combination of economic, political, and nationalistic crises in Russia pushed Yeltsin to accelerate his "political drift." By this time, he had gone far beyond Gorbachev's "new thinking" and had become an avowed "social democrat" advocating a multi-party system, private ownership of the means of production, a transfer of power from the Communist Party to the parliament, a recognition of sovereignty for the Soviet republics, and a new constitution guaranteeing the primacy of law and individual freedoms. Marxist-Leninists were terrified by such ideas. Gorbachev accused Yeltsin of rejecting "democratic socialism" and of advocating a break-up of the Soviet Union. Gorbachev's reforms, however, made it possible for Yeltsin to turn to Russian voters, where his program enjoyed a great deal of popular appeal, especially among young people. On June 12, 1991, in Russia's first democratic presidential election, Yeltsin captured 57 percent of the vote in a contest with four other candidates.

Most historians and journalists of the West agree with Aron's favorable portrayal of how Yeltsin opposed the attempted coup of August, 1991. When the hard-line Communists tried to seize power, they made the mistake of not putting the Russian president in custody. Yeltsin denounced them as "outlaws" and declared himself to be commander-in-chief of Soviet armed forces on Russian soil. With his instinct for the dramatic, he stood atop a Soviet tank to read an appeal to the Russian people. Thousands of Russians came to his support. "By instinct, courage and luck," writes Aron, "Yeltsin again found himself at the centre of the popular revolt against the totalitarian state, and gave it, as he had since 1989, focus and expression." The failure of the coup hastened the demise of the Soviet Union, which was replaced by the Commonwealth of Independent States on December 31, 1991. With Gorbachev's resignation, Yeltsin became head of state over the second most powerful country in the world.

Aron has no doubt but that Russia "changed fundamentally for the better" during the Yeltsin presidency. As far as political institutions are concerned, there is much to be said in favor of Aron's point of view. The constitution of 1993 provided for multi-party elections and guaranteed most of the individual freedoms found in the U.S. Bill of Rights, among them a system of separation of powers, including judicial review. Aron also stresses Yeltsin's rejection of traditional Russian imperialism, his opposition to anti-Semitism, and his consistent support for the independence of the Baltic provinces and other nations outside the Russian Federation. In looking at these revolutionary changes, Aron excessively minimizes the role of Gorbachev's *glasnost*, although he does acknowledge that it was "begun by Gorbachev and consolidated by Yeltsin."

In the economic realm, Aron does not deny that the Russian people experienced a worsening of conditions under Yeltsin's watch, but he expresses hope that the long-term consequences of Yeltsin's policies will be positive. Economists disagree about the reasons why these policies did not work very well. Those of a left-wing leaning blame Yeltsin's early attempt to institute free-market principles in a rapid "shock therapy," following the capitalistic theories of Egor Gaidar. They argue that the rapid end to price controls and the privatization program resulted in hyperinflation and wiped out much of the country's savings. Given the heritage of the Soviet welfare state, most Russians were not prepared to see one-third of the population relegated below the poverty level while a minority became fabulously wealthy. By late 1992, Yeltsin reverted to deficit financing and many Soviet-age regulations under the leadership of Viktor Chernomyrdin. Proponents of the free-market model criticize Yeltsin and Chernomyrdin for not continuing Gadar's policies, and they insist that such policies have succeeded in the Czech Republic, Slovakia, Hungary, and Poland. Regardless of which view is correct, Yeltsin cannot avoid taking responsibility for the consequences of his decisions as president.

Aron classifies Yeltsin as an "authoritarian democrat," and he argues that Yeltsin's willingness to stretch his legal powers was in the tradition of Abraham Lincoln and Charles de Gaulle. Like these two leaders, Yeltsin sometimes went beyond the formal limits of his constitutional authority, as when he dissolved the parliament during the crisis of 1993. Aron argues, nevertheless, that he never "crossed the line" to become a dictator, and that he always yielded to the decisions of the constitutional court. In defending Yeltsin's actions during the 1993 conflict with the parliament, Aron is no doubt correct in observing that his opponents were the first to resort to violence and that their triumph would have diminished the prospects for constitutional democracy. Yeltsin, however, appeared to be looking for a fight when he accused his opponents of conducting an "armed fascist-communist mutiny," and he was excessively quick to order the bombardment and attack on the Russian White House, resulting in at least sixty deaths.

Aron does not try to defend Russia's conduct in the war against the breakaway province of Chechnya, and he even admits that Yeltsin prosecuted the war "incompetently, with appalling brutality, and in complete disregard of his country's public opinion." Perhaps 100,000 people died from the relentless bombing attacks, and hundreds of thousands of civilians became refugees. Although it is important to recognize that Chechnya is a part of the Russian Federation, Yeltsin's behavior in the conflict appeared reminiscent of Russia's imperial past. If Yeltsin was wise to agree to most of the Chechen demands in the peace treaty of 1997, he should have sought a compromise while his position was stronger. Clearly Aron engages in wishful thinking when he praises the peace treaty for resolving the issue of Chechen sovereignty.

Aron often refers to the recurring health problems of the Russian president. It is very difficult to keep up with the times that he was incapacitated and hospitalized because of cardiovascular problems of one kind or another, often accompanied by bouts of serious depression. Also, Aron admits that by 1994 Yeltsin's drinking was becoming "embarrassing" and was interfering with his work. Given the perilous state of Yeltsin's health when the election of 1996 occurred, it is likely that his place in history would shine brighter if he had declined to run for a second term. If he had retired at that time, perhaps the Russian government would have benefited from a healthier and more sober president.

Yeltsin: A Revolutionary Life provides a great deal of information and insight into one of the most significant developments of the end of the twentieth century: the termination of the Soviet Union and the birth of a democratic, capitalistic Russia. Indeed, some readers will find the book more detailed than they would like, especially the portions dealing with Yeltsin's middle years in Sverdlovsk. Nonetheless, it is not only a book that can be read from beginning to end but also a book that is a useful reference tool for looking up specific topics relating to contemporary Russian history.

Thomas T. Lewis

Sources for Further Study

Booklist 96 (February 15, 2000): 1076.
Library Journal 125 (February 15, 2000): 173.
The Nation 270 (March 27, 2000): 25.
The New York Times, December 22, 1999, p. A27.
The New York Times Book Review 105 (March 19, 2000): 4.
Publishers Weekly 247 (March 6, 2000): 93.

MAGILL'S
LITERARY ANNUAL
2001

BIOGRAPHICAL WORKS BY SUBJECT

1977-2001

ABEL, LIONEL
  Intellectual Follies (Abel) (85) 451
ABERNATHY, RALPH DAVID
  And the Walls Came Tumbling Down
    (Abernathy) (90) 39
ACHEBE, CHINUA
  Home and Exile (Achebe) (01) 408
ACHESON, DEAN
  Dean Acheson (McLellan) (77) 197
ADAMS, ABIGAIL
  Descent from Glory (Nagel) (H-84) 121
ADAMS, CHARLES FRANCIS
  Descent from Glory (Nagel) (H-84) 121
ADAMS, HENRY
  Descent from Glory (Nagel) (H-84) 121
  Five of Hearts, The (O'Toole) (91) 295
  Letters of Henry Adams, 1858-1892, The
    (Adams) (84) 441
  Letters of Henry Adams, 1892-1918, The
    (Adams) (90) 516
ADAMS, JOHN
  Descent from Glory (Nagel) (H-84) 121
  Faces of Revolution (Bailyn) (91) 279
  John Adams (Ferling) (93) 413
ADAMS, JOHN G.
  Without Precedent (Adams) (H-84) 497
ADAMS, JOHN QUINCY
  Descent from Glory (Nagel) (H-84) 121
  John Quincy Adams (Nagel) (98) 472
ADAMS, MIRIAM "CLOVER"
  Five of Hearts, The (O'Toole) (91) 295
ADLER, MORTIMER J.
  Philosopher at Large (Adler) (78) 654
AGEE, JAMES
  James Agee (Bergreen) (85) 473
AGEE, JOEL
  Twelve Years (Agee) (82) 854
AIKEN, CONRAD
  Conrad Aiken (Butscher) (89) 207
  Selected Letters of Conrad Aiken (Aiken) (79) 652
AKHMATOVA, ANNA
  Akhmatova Journals, 1938-41, The
    (Chukovskaya) (95) 19
  Anna Akhmatova (Reeder) (95) 38
  Nightingale Fever (Hingley) (82) 555
ALABI, PANTO
  Alabi's World (Price) (91) 10
ALBEE, EDWARD
  Edward Albee (Gussow) (00) 199
ALEXANDER
  Search for Alexander, The (Lane Fox) (81) 712
ALI, MUHAMMAD
  King of the World (Remnick) (99) 453
ALLEN, FRED
  Province of Reason (Warner) (H-85) 368
ALLEN, PAULA GUNN
  I Tell You Now (Swann and Krupat,
    eds.) (88) 413

ALLENDE, SALVADOR
  Overthrow of Allende and the Politics of Chile,
    1964-1976, The (Sigmund) (78) 630
ALS, HILTON
  Women, The (Als) (98) 874
ALSOP, JOSEPH "JOE"
  Taking on the World (Merry) (97) 802
ALSOP, STEWART
  Taking on the World (Merry) (97) 802
AMIS, KINGSLEY
  Kingsley Amis (Jacobs) (99) 457
AMIS, MARTIN
  Experience (Amis) (01) 290
ANDERSON, SHERWOOD
  Sherwood Anderson (Anderson) (85) 820
  Sherwood Anderson (Townsend) (88) 817
ANGELOU, MAYA
  All God's Children Need Traveling Shoes
    (Angelou) (87) 25
  Singin' and Swingin' and Gettin' Merry like
    Christmas (Angelou) (77) 738
ANGERMEYER, JOHANNA
  My Father's Island (Angermeyer) (91) 614
ANTHONY, SUSAN B.
  Elizabeth Cady Stanton, Susan B. Anthony,
    Correspondence, Writings, Speeches (Stanton
    and Anthony) (82) 214
  Not for Ourselves Alone (Ward and
    Burns) (00) 580
ANTIN, MARY
  Province of Reason (Warner) (H-85) 368
ARBUS, DIANE NEMEROV
  Diane Arbus (Bosworth) (96) 174
ARENDT, HANNAH
  Between Friends (Arendt and McCarthy) (96) 73
  Hannah Arendt (Hill, ed.) (80) 395
  Hannah Arendt (Young-Bruehl) (83) 322
  Passionate Minds (Pierpont) (01) 694
ARLETTY
  Six Exceptional Women (Lord) (95) 724
ARNOLD, MATTHEW
  Life of Matthew Arnold, A (Murray) (98) 500
  Matthew Arnold (Honan) (82) 518
ARTAUD, ANTONIN
  Antonin Artaud (Artaud) (77) 52
  Antonin Artaud (Esslin) (78) 68
ASHE, ARTHUR
  Days of Grace (Ashe and Rampersad) (94) 213
ATHENS, LONNIE
  Why They Kill (Rhodes) (00) 843
ATTLEE, CLEMENT
  Attlee (Harris) (H-84) 33
AUDEN, W. H.
  Auden (Davenport-Hines) (97) 79
  Later Auden (Mendelson) (00) 475
  W. H. Auden (Carpenter) (82) 923
  W. H. Auden (Osborne) (80) 860
AUGUSTINE, SAINT
  Saint Augustine (Wills) (00) 665

BIOGRAPHICAL WORKS BY SUBJECT

CATEGORY INDEX

1977-2001

ANTHROPOLOGY. *See* SOCIOLOGY,
ARCHAEOLOGY, and ANTHROPOLOGY

ARCHAEOLOGY. *See* SOCIOLOGY,
ARCHAEOLOGY, and ANTHROPOLOGY

AUTOBIOGRAPHY, MEMOIRS, DIARIES, and
LETTERS
Abba Eban (Eban) (78) 1
Accidental Autobiography, An (Harrison) (97) 1
Adieux (Beauvoir) (85) 1
Aké (Soyinka) (83) 10
Akhmatova Journals, 1938-41, The
(Chukovskaya) (95) 19
Albert Einstein (Einstein) (80) 19
All God's Children Need Traveling Shoes
(Angelou) (87) 25
All Rivers Run to the Sea (Wiesel) (96) 18
Always Straight Ahead (Neuman) (94) 11
Amateur, The (Lesser) (00) 10
Amazing Grace (Norris) (99) 40
America Inside Out (Schoenbrun) (H-85) 22
American Childhood, An (Dillard) (88) 25
American Life, An (Reagan) (91) 24
American Requiem, An (Carroll) (97) 38
And the Sea Is Never Full (Wiesel) (00) 22
And the Walls Came Tumbling Down
(Abernathy) (90) 39
Angela's Ashes (McCourt) (97) 43
Anne Sexton (Sexton) (78) 54
Another World, 1897-1917 (Eden) (78) 59
Answer to History (Mohammad Reza Pahlavi) (81) 47
Antonin Artaud (Artaud) (77) 52
Anything Your Little Heart Desires (Bosworth) (98) 68
Arna Bontemps-Langston Hughes Letters, 1925-1927
(Bontemps and Hughes) (81) 57
Around the Day in Eighty Worlds (Cortázar) (87) 45
Arrivals and Departures (Rovere) (77) 62
As I Saw It (Rusk) (91) 56
Asking for Trouble (Woods) (82) 28
Assault on Mount Helicon (Barnard) (85) 27
Atlantic High (Buckley) (83) 29
Autobiography of a Face (Grealy) (95) 56

Autobiography of Values (Lindbergh) (79) 43
Basil Street Blues (Holroyd) (01) 64
Becoming a Doctor (Konner) (88) 77
Becoming a Man (Monette) (93) 62
Berlin Diaries, 1940-1945 (Vassiltchikov) (88) 95
Bernard Shaw, 1856-1898 (Holroyd) (89) 89
Bernard Shaw, Collected Letters, 1926-1950
(Shaw) (89) 84
Better Class of Person, A (Osborne) (82) 45
Between Friends (Arendt and McCarthy) (96) 73
Beyond the Dragon's Mouth (Naipaul) (86) 56
Blessings in Disguise (Guinness) (87) 71
Blind Ambition (Dean) (77) 96
Bloods (Terry) (H-85) 48
Blooming (Toth) (82) 55
Blue-Eyed Child of Fortune (Duncan, ed.) (93) 91
Born on the Fourth of July (Kovic) (77) 115
Borrowed Time (Monette) (89) 112
Boston Boy (Hentoff) (87) 84
Boswell (Boswell) (78) 140
Boyhood (Coetzee) (98) 134
Breaking Ranks (Podhoretz) (80) 101
Breaking with Moscow (Shevchenko) (86) 81
Broken Cord, The (Dorris) (90) 76
Bronx Primitive (Simon) (83) 80
Brothers and Keepers (Wideman) (85) 57
Burning the Days (Salter) (98) 138
Byron's Letters and Journals, 1822-1823
(Byron) (81) 108
Cassandra (Wolf) (85) 74
Chance Meetings (Saroyan) (79) 92
Charles Darwin's Letters (Darwin) (97) 148
Cherry (Karr) (01) 181
Chief, The (Morrow) (86) 121
Childhood (Sarraute) (85) 89
China Men (Kingston) (81) 137
Chinabound (Fairbank) (H-83) 61
Christopher and His Kind (Isherwood) (77) 158
Circle of Hanh, The (Weigl) (01) 190
Clear Pictures (Price) (90) 104
Clinging to the Wreckage (Mortimer) (83) 127
Cloak of Light, A (Morris) (86) 140
Cloister Walk, The (Norris) (97) 160

CATEGORY INDEX

CATEGORY INDEX

CATEGORY INDEX

CATEGORY INDEX

CATEGORY INDEX

CATEGORY INDEX

CATEGORY INDEX

CATEGORY INDEX

CATEGORY INDEX

999

CATEGORY INDEX

CATEGORY INDEX

CATEGORY INDEX

CATEGORY INDEX

1007

CATEGORY INDEX

CATEGORY INDEX

CATEGORY INDEX

CATEGORY INDEX

CATEGORY INDEX

TITLE INDEX

1977-2001

TITLE INDEX

TITLE INDEX

TITLE INDEX

TITLE INDEX

TITLE INDEX

Island of the Colorblind and Cycad Island, The
  (Sacks) (98) 454
Island of the Day Before, The (Eco) (96) 385
Islands, the Universe, Home (Ehrlich) (92) 364
Israel (Gilbert) (99) 427
Issa Valley, The (Miłosz) (82) 403
It All Adds Up (Bellow) (95) 381
It Seemed Like Nothing Happened (Carroll) (H-83) 220
Italian Days (Harrison) (90) 441
Italian Fascism (De Grand) (H-83) 224
Italian Folktales (Calvino) (81) 450
Itinerary (Paz) (01) 471
I've Known Rivers (Lawrence-Lightfoot) (95) 384
Ivy (Spurling) (85) 461
Ivy Days (Toth) (85) 466

J. Edgar Hoover (Gentry) (92) 369
J. G. Frazer (Ackerman) (89) 418
J. P. Morgan (Jackson) (H-84) 257
Jack (Parmet) (81) 454
Jack (Sinclair) (78) 454
Jack Gance (Just) (90) 445
Jack Maggs (Carey) (99) 432
Jack of Diamonds (Spencer) (89) 405
Jack Tars and Commodores (Fowler) (H-85) 246
Jackie Robinson (Rampersad) (98) 458
Jackson Pollock (Naifeh and Smith) (91) 466
Jacques Lacan (Roudinesco) (98) 463
Jailbird (Vonnegut) (80) 436
James Agee (Bergreen) (85) 473
James Baldwin (Leeming) (95) 388
James Boswell (Brady) (85) 479
James Dickey (Hart) (01) 475
James Gould Cozzens (Bruccoli) (84) 384
James Jones (Garrett) (85) 484
James Joyce (Costello) (94) 418
James Thurber (Kinney) (96) 389
Jameses (Lewis) (92) 374
Jane Austen (Honan) (89) 409
Jane Austen (Nokes) (98) 468
Jane Austen (Tanner) (87) 435
Janus (Koestler) (79) 326
Japan Before Perry (Totman) (82) 408
Japan in War and Peace (Dower) (95) 392
Japanese, The (Reischauer) (78) 459
Jasmine (Mukherjee) (90) 450
Jason the Sailor (Wakoski) (94) 422
Jazz (Morrison) (93) 403
Jean-Jacques (Cranston) (H-84) 237
Jean Rhys (Angier) (92) 379
Jean Stafford (Goodman) (91) 471
Jean Stafford (Roberts) (89) 414
Jean Toomer, Artist (McKay) (85) 489
Jefferson and the Presidency (Johnstone) (79) 331
Jefferson Davis (Eaton) (78) 464
Jerzy Kosinski (Sloan) (97) 470
Jesse (Frady) (97) 474
Jesse (Richardson) (85) 494
Jesus' Son (Johnson) (94) 427
Jesus Through the Centuries (Pelikan) (86) 482
Jew vs. Jew (Freedman) (01) 480
Jewish Self-Hatred (Gilman) (87) 440
Jews (Hertzberg and Hirt-Manheimer) (99) 436
Jews in the Eyes of the Germans (Low) (80) 439
Jews of East Central Europe Between the World Wars,
  The (Mendelsohn) (H-84) 243
JFK (Hamilton) (93) 408
Joan of Arc (Gordon) (01) 485
Joan of Arc (Lucie-Smith) (78) 472
Joe (Brown) (92) 384
Joe Dimaggio (Cramer) (01) 489
Joe Papp (Epstein) (95) 396
Johann Sebastian Bach (Wolff) (01) 494

John Adams (Ferling) (93) 413
John Calvin (Bouwsma) (88) 433
John Cheever (Donaldson) (89) 422
John Cheever (Hunt) (84) 389
John D. (Hawke) (81) 459
John Dewey and American Democracy
  (Westbrook) (92) 388
John Dewey and the High Tide of American Liberalism
  (Ryan) (96) 393
John Dickinson (Flower) (H-84) 248
John Dollar (Wiggins) (90) 454
John Dos Passos (Ludington) (81) 464
John Dryden and His World (Winn) (88) 438
John Foster Dulles (Pruessen) (H-83) 229
John Glenn (Glenn and Taylor) (00) 443
John Henry Newman (Ker) (90) 459
John L. Lewis (Dubofsky and Van Tine) (78) 478
John Maynard Keynes (Hession) (H-85) 250
John Maynard Keynes (Skidelsky) (95) 400
John Quincy Adams (Nagel) (98) 472
John Ruskin, The Early Years (Hilton) (86) 487
John Ruskin, The Later Years (Hilton) (01) 499
John Ruskin (Hilton) (01) 499
John Steinbeck (Parini) (96) 398
John Wayne's America (Wills) (98) 477
Joke, The (Kundera) (83) 363
Jonathan Swift (Glendinning) (00) 448
Jorge Luis Borges (Monegal) (80) 444
Joseph Brodsky and the Creation of Exile
  (Bethea) (95) 404
Joseph Conrad (Karl) (80) 449
Joseph Conrad (Najder) (84) 395
Joseph Conrad (Tennant) (82) 412
Joseph Cornell's Theater of the Mind
  (Cornell) (95) 408
Josephine Herbst (Langer) (85) 499
Journals (Ginsberg) (78) 483
Journals, 1939-1983 (Spender) (87) 446
Journals of Denton Welch, The (Welch) (85) 504
Journals of John Cheever, The (Cheever) (92) 393
Journals of Sylvia Plath, The (Plath) (83) 367
Journals of Thornton Wilder, 1939-1961, The
  (Wilder) (86) 491
Journey for Our Times, A (Salisbury) (H-84) 252
Journey into Space (Murray) (90) 464
Journey to the End of the Millennium, A
  (Yehoshua) (00) 453
Journey to the Sky (Highwater) (79) 335
Journey to the West, Vol. IV, The (Wu Ch'êng-
  ên) (84) 401
Joy Luck Club, The (Tan) (90) 468
Joyce's Book of the Dark (Bishop) (88) 443
Joyce's Dislocutions (Senn) (85) 509
Joyce's Voices (Kenner) (79) 340
Jubal Sackett (L'Amour) (86) 496
Jubilation (Tomlinson) (96) 403
Julip (Harrison) (95) 413
Julius Streicher (Bytwerk) (H-83) 234
July's People (Gordimer) (82) 417
Jump (Gordimer) (92) 398
Juneteenth (Ellison) (00) 457
Just Above My Head (Baldwin) (80) 456
Just as I Thought (Paley) (99) 441
Just Representations (Cozzens) (79) 343
Justice at Nuremberg (Conot) (H-84) 261
Justice Crucified (Feuerlicht) (78) 487
Justice Oliver Wendell Holmes (White) (94) 431

Kaddish (Wieseltier) (99) 445
Kafka (Hayman) (83) 372
Karl Marx (Padover) (79) 349
Karl Marx (Wheen) (01) 504
Kasparov Versus Deep Blue (Newborn) (98) 482

TITLE INDEX

TITLE INDEX

Portage to San Cristóbal of A. H., The
(Steiner) (83) 616
Portraits (Shils) (98) 639
Portraits of the Artist in Exile (Potts, ed.) (80) 675
Possessing the Secret of Joy (Walker) (93) 651
Possession (Byatt) (91) 679
Postscript to *The Name of the Rose* (Eco) (85) 697
Postville (Bloom) (01) 716
Pound/Ford, the Story of a Literary Friendship (Pound
and Ford) (83) 621
Pound/Lewis (Pound and Lewis) (86) 747
Pound/Williams (Pound and Williams) (97) 675
Poverty and Compassion (Himmelfarb) (92) 627
Power and Principle (Brzezinski) (H-84) 351
Power Game, The (Smith) (89) 658
Power on the Left (Lader) (80) 697
Power to Lead, The (Burns) (H-85) 363
Powers That Be, The (Halberstam) (80) 684
Practice of Reading, The (Donoghue) (99) 636
Practicing History (Tuchman) (82) 647
PrairyErth (Heat-Moon) (92) 632
Prayer for Owen Meany, A (Irving) (90) 677
Prayer for the Dying, A (O'Nan) (00) 622
Praying for Sheetrock (Greene) (92) 636
Preacher King, The (Lischer) (96) 601
Prehistoric Avebury (Burl) (80) 688
Preparing for the Twenty-first Century
(Kennedy) (94) 658
Presence of Ford Madox Ford, The (Stang,
ed.) (82) 652
Presidency of Lyndon B. Johnson, The (Bornet) (H-
84) 355
President Kennedy (Reeves) (94) 662
Price of Power, The (Hersh) (H-84) 361
Price Was High, The (Fitzgerald) (80) 693
Prick of Noon, The (De Vries) (86) 752
Pride of Family (Ione) (92) 641
Primacy or World Order (Hoffmann) (79) 551
Primary Colors (Klein) (97) 679
Primary Colors, The (Theroux) (95) 613
Prince of Our Disorder, A (Mack) (77) 637
Principle of Hope, The (Bloch) (87) 670
Printing Technology, Letters, and Samuel Johnson
(Kernan) (88) 710
Prisoner's Dilemma (Powers) (89) 663
Prisoners of Hope (Hughes) (84) 705
Private Demons (Oppenheimer) (89) 668
Private World, The (Unamuno) (85) 701
Prize, The (Yergin) (92) 645
Prize Stories 1978 (Abrahams, ed.) (79) 556
"Probable Cause" *and* "Beyond Reasonable Doubt"
(Shapiro) (93) 75
Problems and Other Stories (Updike) (80) 697
Problems of Dostoevsky's Poetics (Bakhtin) (85) 706
Prodigal Child, A (Storey) (84) 711
Profane Art, The (Oates) (84) 716
Professing Poetry (Wain) (79) 561
Profession of the Playwright, The (Stephens) (93) 655
Professor of Desire, The (Roth) (78) 669
Progress and Privilege (Tucker) (H-83) 352
Progress of Love, The (Munro) (87) 677
Progressive Presidents, The (Blum) (81) 665
Promethean Fire (Lumsden and Wilson) (H-84) 366
Promise of Light, The (Watkins) (94) 667
Promise of Pragmatism, The (Diggins) (95) 617
Promise of Rest, The (Price) (96) 606
Promised Land, The (Lemann) (92) 650
Proper Study of Mankind, The (Berlin) (99) 640
Property and Freedom (Pipes) (00) 626
Prophets of Past Time (Dawson) (89) 674
Protecting Soldiers and Mothers (Skocpol) (94) 671
Proust Screenplay, The (Pinter) (78) 673
Providence (Brookner) (85) 712

Province of Reason (Warner) (H-85) 368
Provinces (Miłosz) (92) 656
Proximity to Death (McFeely) (00) 630
Psychopathic God, The (Waite) (78) 677
Puffball (Weldon) (81) 670
Pugilist at Rest, The (Jones) (94) 676
Puritan Way of Death, The (Stannard) (78) 682
Purple America (Moody) (98) 643
Purple Decades, The (Wolfe) (83) 626
Pursued by Furies (Bowker) (96) 610
Pursuit of Power, The (McNeill) (H-83) 357
Pushcart Prize, III, The (Henderson, ed.) (79) 565
Pushkin (Feinstein) (00) 634
Puttermesser Papers, The (Ozick) (98) 648

Quality of Mercy, The (Shawcross) (H-85) 373
Quantity Theory of Insanity, The (Self) (96) 615
Quantum Philosophy (Omnès) (00) 638
Quarantine (Crace) (99) 645
Quarrel and Quandary (Ozick) (01) 721
Queens, Concubines, and Dowagers (Stafford) (H-
84) 371
Quest for El Cid, The (Fletcher) (91) 684
Question of Bruno, The (Hemon) (01) 725
Question of Character, A (Reeves) (92) 660
Question of Hu, The (Spence) (89) 679
Questioning the Millennium (Gould) (98) 652
Quinn's Book (Kennedy) (89) 683

Rabbi of Lud, The (Elkin) (88) 715
Rabbis and Wives (Grade) (83) 630
Rabbit at Rest (Updike) (91) 688
Rabbit Is Rich (Updike) (82) 656
Rabbiter's Bounty, The (Murray) (93) 660
Race and Slavery in the Middle East (Lewis) (91) 692
Rachel and Her Children (Kozol) (89) 687
Rachel Carson (Lear) (98) 656
Radiant Way, The (Drabble) (88) 720
Radical Son (Horowitz) (98) 661
Radicalism of the American Revolution, The
(Wood) (93) 665
Rage of Edmund Burke, The (Kramnick) (78) 686
Ragman's Son, The (Douglas) (89) 692
Raider, The (Ford) (77) 642
Rainbow Grocery, The (Dickey) (79) 570
Rainbows, Snowflakes, and Quarks (von Baeyer) (H-
85) 379
Ralph Waldo Emerson (McAleer) (85) 717
Rameau's Niece (Schine) (94) 680
Randall Jarrell (Pritchard) (91) 696
Randall Jarrell's Letters (Jarrell) (86) 757
Ranke (Krieger) (78) 690
Ransom of Russian Art, The (McPhee) (95) 622
Rape of the Rose, The (Hughes) (94) 684
Rat Man of Paris (West) (87) 681
Rates of Exchange (Bradbury) (84) 721
Ratner's Star (DeLillo) (77) 647
Ravelstein (Bellow) (01) 731
Ray (Hannah) (81) 674
Raymond Chandler (Hiney) (98) 665
Reaching Judgment at Nuremberg (Smith) (78) 695
Reading *Billy Budd* (Parker) (92) 665
Reading for the Plot (Brooks) (85) 723
Reading Raymond Carver (Runyon) (93) 669
Reagan (Cannon) (H-83) 362
Reagan's America (Wills) (88) 725
Real Life of Alejandro Mayta, The (Vargas
Llosa) (87) 685
Real Losses, Imaginary Gains (Morris) (77) 652
Real Presences (Steiner) (90) 681
Real Shakespeare, The (Sams) (96) 619
Realistic Imagination, The (Levine) (83) 635

1051

TITLE INDEX

TITLE INDEX

TITLE INDEX

U and I (Baker) (92) 844
Ultima Thule (McCombs) (01) 850
Ulverton (Thorpe) (94) 814
Unafraid of the Dark (Bray) (99) 812
Unattainable Earth (Miłosz) (87) 892
Unauthorized Freud (Crews, ed.) (99) 817
Unbearable Heart, The (Hahn) (97) 843
Unbearable Lightness of Being, The
   (Kundera) (85) 958
Unbeliever, The (Parker) (89) 864
Uncertain Greatness (Morris) (78) 869
Uncertain Partners (Goncharov, Lewis, and
   Xue) (95) 809
Uncertainty (Cassidy) (93) 824
Uncivil Liberties (Trillin) (83) 849
Uncle (Markus) (79) 783
Uncle of Europe (Brook-Shepherd) (77) 861
Uncollected Poems (Rilke) (97) 848
Uncollected Stories of William Faulkner
   (Faulkner) (80) 838
Unconsoled, The (Ishiguro) (96) 786
Undaunted Courage (Ambrose) (97) 853
Under Briggflatts (Davie) (91) 833
Under My Skin (Lessing) (95) 814
Under Review (Powell) (95) 819
Under the Banyan Tree (Narayan) (86) 918
Under the 82nd Airborne (Eisenberg) (93) 829
Under the Eye of the Clock (Nolan) (89) 868
Under the Fifth Sun (Shorris) (81) 844
Under the Jaguar Sun (Calvino) (89) 872
Under the Sign of Saturn (Sontag) (81) 848
Under the Vulture-Tree (Bottoms) (88) 919
Under Western Skies (Worster) (93) 833
Underground Empire, The (Mills) (87) 896
Underpainter, The (Urquhart) (98) 782
Undersong (Lorde) (93) 838
Understand This (Tervalon) (95) 823
Understanding Inflation (Case) (82) 866
Undertaking, The (Lynch) (98) 786
Underworld (DeLillo) (98) 791
Undiscovered Mind, The (Horgan) (00) 780
Undue Influence (Brookner) (01) 855
Undying Grass, The (Kemal) (79) 787
Unequal Justice (Auerbach) (77) 866
Unexpected Vista, The (Trefil) (H-84) 462
Unfinished Presidency, The (Brinkley) (99) 822
Unfinished War, The (Capps) (H-83) 440
Unfortunate Woman, An (Brautigan) (01) 859
Union Street (Barker) (84) 895
United States (Vidal) (94) 819
United States and the Berlin Blockade, 1948-1949, The
   (Shlaim) (H-84) 469
United States and the Caribbean, 1900-1970, The
   (Langley) (81) 853
United States in the Middle East, The (Tillman) (H-
   83) 445
Unknown Matisse, The (Spurling) (99) 826
Unlocking the Air (Le Guin) (97) 858
Unlocking the English Language (Burchfield) (92) 849
Unmade Bed, The (Sagan) (79) 791
Unraveling of America, The (Matusow) (H-85) 460
Unreliable Memoirs (James) (82) 870
Unseen Revolution, The (Drucker) (77) 872
Unsettling of America, The (Berry) (79) 795
Unsuitable Attachment, An (Pym) (83) 855
Unsuspected Revolution, The (Llerena) (79) 799
Unto the Sons (Talese) (93) 842
Unto the Soul (Appelfeld) (95) 827
Untouchable, The (Banville) (98) 796
Untying the Knot (Hasan-Rokem and Shulman,
   eds.) (97) 862
Unwanted, The (Marrus) (86) 923
Unwelcome Strangers (Reimers) (99) 830

Up at Oxford (Mehta) (94) 823
Upon This Rock (Freedman) (94) 827
Uses of Enchantment, The (Bettelheim) (77) 876
U.S.S.R. in Crisis (Goldman) (H-84) 472
Utopia Parkway (Solomon) (98) 801
Utopian Pessimist (McLellan) (91) 838
Utz (Chatwin) (90) 835

V Was for Victory (Blum) (77) 880
Vaclav Havel (Keane) (01) 863
Valley of Darkness (Havens) (79) 804
Vanessa Bell (Spalding) (84) 900
Van Gogh (Sweetman) (91) 843
Van Gogh's Room at Arles (Elkin) (94) 831
Vanished (Morris) (89) 877
Vanished Imam, The (Ajami) (87) 901
Van Wyck Brooks (Nelson) (82) 874
Various Antidotes (Scott) (95) 831
Vatican Diplomacy and the Jews During the Holocaust,
   1939-1943 (Morley) (81) 861
Vectors and Smoothable Curves (Bronk) (84) 905
Ved Mehta Reader, A (Mehta) (99) 834
Veil (Woodward) (88) 923
Velázquez (Brown) (87) 907
Venetian Vespers, The (Hecht) (80) 841
Venona (Haynes and Klehr) (00) 784
Ventriloquist, The (Huff) (78) 873
Véra (Mrs. Vladimir Nabokov) (Schiff) (00) 789
Vermont Papers, The (Bryan and
   McClaughry) (90) 839
Vertigo (Sebald) (01) 868
Very Old Bones (Kennedy) (93) 846
Very Private Eye, A (Pym) (85) 964
Viaduct, The (Wheldon) (84) 910
Vice (Ai) (00) 793
Victor Hugo (Robb) (99) 838
Victor Hugo and the Visionary Novel
   (Brombert) (85) 969
Victorian Anthropology (Stocking) (88) 928
Victorian Feminists (Caine) (93) 851
Victory over Japan (Gilchrist) (85) 973
Vietnam 1945 (Marr) (97) 867
View from 80, The (Cowley) (81) 867
View from Highway 1, The (Arlen) (77) 884
View from the UN (Thant) (79) 809
View of Victorian Literature, A (Tillotson) (79) 814
View with a Grain of Sand (Szymborska) (96) 790
Views & Spectacles (Weiss) (80) 846
Vigour of Prophecy, The (Henry) (91) 847
Viking World, The (Graham-Campbell) (81) 873
Village of Longing, The, and Dancehall Days
   (O'Brien) (91) 851
Villages (Critchfield) (82) 879
Vindication (Sherwood) (94) 835
Vindication of Tradition, The (Pelikan) (H-85) 467
Vineland (Pynchon) (90) 844
Viper Jazz (Tate) (77) 888
Virginia Woolf (Gordon) (86) 927
Virginia Woolf (King) (96) 794
Virginia Woolf (Lee) (98) 805
Virtual Light (Gibson) (94) 839
Virtual Tibet (Schell) (01) 873
Vision of Emma Blau, The (Hegi) (01) 877
Visions from San Francisco Bay (Miłosz) (83) 860
Visions of Harmony (Taylor) (88) 932
Visions of Kerouac (Duberman) (78) 878
Visitors (Brookner) (99) 842
Vita (Glendinning) (84) 916
Vita Nova (Glück) (00) 797
Vladimir Nabokov, The American Years
   (Boyd) (92) 854
Vladimir Nabokov, The Russian Years (Boyd) (91) 856

1059

TITLE INDEX

AUTHOR INDEX

1977-2001

AUTHOR INDEX

AUTHOR INDEX

AUTHOR INDEX

BLUM, D. STEVEN
Walter Lippmann (H-85) 470
BLUM, JEROME
End of the Old Order in Rural Europe,
The (79) 188
BLUM, JOHN MORTON
Progressive Presidents, The (81) 665
V Was for Victory (77) 880
BLUM, ROBERT M.
Drawing the Line (H-83) 104
BLY, CAROL
Letters from the Country (82) 444
BLY, ROBERT
American Poetry (91) 29
Man in the Black Coat Turns, The (83) 439
BODE, CARL, editor
New Mencken Letters, The (78) 603
BOK, SISSELA
Mayhem (99) 534
BOLAND, EAVAN
In a Time of Violence (95) 343
BÖLL, HEINRICH
And Never Said a Word (79) 29
Bread of Those Early Years, The (77) 119
Missing Persons and Other Essays (78) 577
Stories of Heinrich Böll, The (87) 827
What's to Become of the Boy? (85) 1018
BOMBAL, MARÍA LUISA
New Islands and Other Stories (83) 523
BONKOVSKY, FREDERICK O.
International Norms and National Policy (81) 445
BONNER, RAYMOND
Waltzing with a Dictator (88) 949
BONNIFIELD, PAUL
Dust Bowl, The (80) 251
BONTEMPS, ARNA, and LANGSTON HUGHES
Arna Bontemps-Langston Hughes Letters, 1925-
1927 (81) 57
BOORSTIN, DANIEL J.
Discoverers, The (H-84) 130
Seekers, The (99) 697
BOOTH, PHILIP
Before Sleep (81) 71
Relations (87) 703
Selves (91) 731
BOOTH, WAYNE C.
Company We Keep, The (89) 202
For the Love of It (00) 273
Vocation of a Teacher, The (90) 854
BORGES, JORGE LUIS
Book of Sand, The (78) 131
Borges, a Reader (82) 63
Selected Non-Fictions (00) 683
Selected Poems (00) 688
BORGES, JORGE LUIS, and ADOLFO BIOY-
CASARES
Six Problems for Don Isidro Parodi (82) 771
BORJAS, GEORGE J.
Heaven's Door (00) 367
BORK, ROBERT H.
Tempting of America, The (90) 787
BORNET, VAUGHN DAVIS
Presidency of Lyndon B. Johnson, The (H-84) 355
BOSWELL, JAMES
Boswell (78) 140

BOSWELL, JOHN
Kindness of Strangers, The (90) 486
Same-Sex Unions in Premodern Europe (95) 687
BOSWELL, ROBERT
American Owned Love (98) 41
BOSWORTH, PATRICIA
Anything Your Little Heart Desires (98) 68
Diane Arbus (96) 174
Montgomery Clift (79) 457
BOSWORTH, SHEILA
Almost Innocent (85) 7
BOTTOMS, DAVID
Under the Vulture-Tree (88) 919
BOURJAILY, VANCE
Game Men Play, A (81) 364
Now Playing at Canterbury (77) 575
BOURNE, KENNETH
Palmerston (H-83) 329
BOUWSMA, WILLIAM J.
John Calvin (88) 433
BOWDEN, MARK
Black Hawk Down (00) 70
BOWEN, ELIZABETH
Collected Stories of Elizabeth Bowen,
The (81) 173
BOWERS, EDGAR
Collected Poems (98) 177
BOWKER, GORDON
Pursued by Furies (96) 610
BOWLBY, JOHN
Charles Darwin (92) 83
BOWLES, JANE
Out in the World (86) 723
BOWLES, PAUL
In Touch (95) 372
Collected Stories, 1939-1976 (80) 151
BOYD, BRIAN
Vladimir Nabokov, The American Years (92) 854
Vladimir Nabokov, The Russian Years (91) 856
BOYD, WILLIAM
Ice-Cream War, An (84) 363
BOYERS, ROBERT
Atrocity and Amnesia (86) 43
BOYLAN, CLARE
Holy Pictures (84) 347
BOYLE, KAY
Fifty Stories (81) 325
Words That Must Somehow Be Said (86) 966
BOYLE, NICHOLAS
Goethe, 1749-1790 (92) 247
Goethe, 1790-1803 (01) 356
BOYLE, T. CORAGHESSAN
East Is East (91) 240
Friend of the Earth, A (01) 310
Greasy Lake and Other Stories (86) 372
If the River Was Whiskey (90) 406
Road to Wellville, The (94) 709
T. C. Boyle Stories (99) 742
Tortilla Curtain, The (96) 764
Without a Hero (95) 880
World's End (88) 988
BRADBURY, MALCOLM
Rates of Exchange (84) 721
BRADBURY, RAY
Death Is a Lonely Business (86) 222
Stories of Ray Bradbury, The (81) 769

1069

AUTHOR INDEX

AUTHOR INDEX

AUTHOR INDEX

AUTHOR INDEX

DOTY, MARK
  Atlantis (96) 55
  Heaven's Coast (97) 368
  My Alexandria (94) 547
DOUGLAS, ANN
  Terrible Honesty (96) 736
DOUGLAS, ELLEN
  Rock Cried Out, The (80) 722
DOUGLAS, KIRK
  Ragman's Son, The (89) 692
DOUGLAS, MARY
  Risk and Blame (93) 687
DOVE, RITA
  Grace Notes (90) 324
  Mother Love (96) 486
  Through the Ivory Gate (93) 792
DOVLATOV, SERGEI
  Zone, The (86) 985
DOWART, JEFFREY M.
  Conflict of Duty (H-84) 96
DOWER, JOHN W.
  Japan in War and Peace (95) 392
  War Without Mercy (87) 947
DOYLE, RODDY
  Paddy Clarke Ha Ha Ha (94) 603
  Star Called Henry, A (00) 729
  Woman Who Walked into Doors, The (97) 895
DRABBLE, MARGARET
  Angus Wilson (97) 48
  Ice Age, The (78) 431
  Middle Ground, The (81) 564
  Radiant Way, The (88) 720
  Witch of Exmoor, The (98) 858
DRAKE, WILLIAM
  Sara Teasdale (80) 741
DRAPER, THEODORE
  Struggle for Power, A (97) 787
DREYFUSS, JOEL, and CHARLES LAWRENCE III
  Bakke Case, The (80) 45
DRUCKER, PETER F.
  Unseen Revolution, The (77) 872
DRURY, ALLEN
  God Against the Gods, A (77) 332
  Return to Thebes (78) 708
DRURY, TOM
  End of Vandalism, The (95) 204
  Hunts in Dreams (01) 437
D'SOUZA, DINESH
  End of Racism, The (96) 227
DUBERMAN, MARTIN BAUML
  Paul Robeson (90) 652
  Visions of Kerouac (78) 878
DUBIE, NORMAN
  Groom Falconer (90) 338
  Selected and New Poems (84) 761
  Springhouse, The (87) 818
DUBNER, STEPHEN
  Turbulent Souls (99) 803
DUBOFSKY, MELVIN, and WARREN VAN TINE
  John L. Lewis (78) 478
DU BOIS, W. E. B.
  Writings (88) 993
DUBUS, ANDRE
  Dancing After Hours (97) 196
  Meditations from a Movable Chair (99) 538
  Times Are Never So Bad, The (84) 873

DUBY, GEORGES, editor
  History of Private Life, Revelations of the
    Medieval World, A (89) 349
DUFFY, EAMON
  Saints and Sinners (98) 683
DUGGER, RONNIE
  Politician, The (H-83) 348
DUIKER, WILLIAM J.
  Ho Chi Minh (01) 403
DUNBAR-NELSON, ALICE
  Give Us Each Day (86) 349
DUNCAN, ROBERT
  Ground Work (85) 329
  Selected Prose, A (96) 690
DUNCAN, RUSSELL, editor
  Blue-Eyed Child of Fortune (93) 91
DUNCAN-JONES, KATHERINE
  Sir Philip Sidney (92) 761
DUNEIER, MITCHELL
  Slim's Table (93) 744
DUNLOP, JOHN B., RICHARD S. HAUGH, and
  MICHAEL NICHOLSON, editors
  Solzhenitsyn in Exile (86) 843
DUNLOP, RICHARD
  Donovan (H-83) 99
DUNNE, GERALD T.
  Hugo Black and the Judicial Revolution
    (78) 418
DUNNE, JOHN GREGORY
  Dutch Shea, Jr. (83) 216
  Harp (90) 364
DUONG THU HUONG
  Paradise of the Blind (94) 607
DUPUY, T. N.
  Genius for War, A (78) 332
DURANT, WILL, and ARIEL DURANT
  Age of Napoleon, The (77) 33
  Dual Autobiography, A (78) 280
DURAS, MARGUERITE
  Lover, The (86) 547
  War, The (87) 941
DURRELL, LAWRENCE
  Sicilian Carousel (78) 771
DYBEK, STUART
  Coast of Chicago, The (91) 142
DYSON, FREEMAN J.
  Infinite in All Directions (89) 381
DYSON, MICHAEL ERIC
  I May Not Get There with You (01) 442

EAGLETON, TERRY
  Literary Theory (84) 464
EARLY, GERALD
  One Nation Under a Groove (96) 537
EATON, CLEMENT
  Jefferson Davis (78) 464
EBAN, ABBA
  Abba Eban (78) 1
  New Diplomacy, The (H-84) 317
EBERHART, RICHARD
  Of Poetry and Poets (80) 610
EBERSTADT, FERNANDA
  Isaac and His Devils (92) 359
  Low Tide (86) 551
  When the Sons of Heaven Meet the Daughters of
    the Earth (98) 836

AUTHOR INDEX

AUTHOR INDEX

AUTHOR INDEX

HANDLIN, OSCAR, and LILIAN HANDLIN
Restless People, A (H-83) 366

HANKLA, CATHRYN
Phenomena (84) 686

HANNAH, BARRY
Airships (79) 5
Hey Jack! (88) 382
Ray (81) 674

HANSEN, BROOKS
Chess Garden, The (96) 98

HANSEN, RON
Assassination of Jesse James by the Coward Robert
Ford, The (84) 54
Hitler's Niece (00) 391

HARDWICK, ELIZABETH
Bartleby in Manhattan (84) 82
Sleepless Nights (80) 768

HARDY, BARBARA
Advantage of Lyric, The (78) 11

HARJO, JOY
Woman Who Fell from the Sky, The (96) 822

HARPER, MICHAEL S.
Songlines in Michaeltree (01) 782

HARR, JONATHAN
Civil Action, A (96) 116

HARRINGTON, ANNE
Medicine, Mind, and the Double Brain (88) 539

HARRINGTON, MICHAEL
Twilight of Capitalism, The (77) 857

HARRIS, ALEX, editor
World Unsuspected, A (88) 984

HARRIS, KENNETH
Attlee (H-84) 33

HARRIS, MACDONALD
Hemingway's Suitcase (91) 390
Yukiko (78) 942

HARRIS, MARVIN
Cultural Materialism (80) 170

HARRIS, RICHARD
Freedom Spent (77) 304

HARRISON, BARBARA GRIZZUTI
Accidental Autobiography, An (97) 1
Italian Days (90) 441

HARRISON, DAVID
White Tribe of Africa, The (H-83) 459

HARRISON, EDWARD
Darkness at Night (88) 233

HARRISON, GILBERT A.
Enthusiast, The (84) 272

HARRISON, GORDON
Mosquitoes, Malaria and Man (79) 466

HARRISON, JIM
Dalva (89) 212
Julip (95) 413
Legends of the Fall (80) 462
Selected & New Poems (83) 718

HARRISON, TONY
Selected Poems (88) 812

HART, HENRY
James Dickey (01) 475

HART, JOHN MASON
Revolutionary Mexico (89) 717

HARTRICH, EDWIN
Fourth and Richest Reich, The (81) 353

HARUF, KENT
Plainsong (00) 614

HARVEY, NANCY LENZ
Thomas Cardinal Wolsey (81) 800

HARWIT, MARTIN
Cosmic Discovery (82) 135

HASAN-ROKEM, GALIT, and DAVID SHULMAN,
editors
Untying the Knot (97) 862

HASLIP, JOAN
Catherine the Great (78) 155

HASS, ROBERT
Twentieth Century Pleasures (85) 941

HASSLER, JON
Love Hunter, The (82) 499

HASTINGS, MAX
Korean War, The (88) 447
Overlord (H-85) 349

HASTINGS, MAX, and SIMON JENKINS
Battle for the Falklands, The (H-84) 43

HASTINGS, SELINA
Evelyn Waugh (96) 237

HATCH, JAMES V.
Sorrow Is the Only Faithful One (94) 755

HATTAWAY, HERMAN, RICHARD E. BERINGER,
ARCHER JONES, and WILLIAM N. STILL, JR.
Why the South Lost the Civil War (87) 980

HAUGH, RICHARD S., MICHAEL NICHOLSON, and
JOHN B. DUNLOP
Solzhenitsyn in Exile (86) 843

HAVEL, VÁCLAV
Disturbing the Peace (91) 216
Letters to Olga (89) 492

HAVELOCK, ERIC A.
Muse Learns to Write, The (87) 590

HAVENS, THOMAS R. H.
Valley of Darkness (79) 804

HAWKE, DAVID FREEMAN
John D. (81) 459

HAWKES, JOHN
Passion Artist, The (80) 644
Travesty (77) 837

HAWKING, STEPHEN W.
Black Holes and Baby Universes and Other
Essays (94) 94
Brief History of Time, A (89) 121

HAYDEN, ROBERT
Angle of Ascent (77) 48
Collected Poems (86) 152

HAYMAN, RONALD
Brecht (84) 118
Kafka (83) 372

HAYNES, JOHN EARL, and HARVEY KLEHR
Venona (00) 784

HAYNES, JOHN EARL, HARVEY KLEHR, and
FRIDRIKH IGOREVICH FIRSOV, editors
Secret World of American Communism,
The (96) 685

HAYSLIP, LE LY, with JAY WURTS
When Heaven and Earth Changed Places (90) 879

HAYWARD, MAX
Writers in Russia (84) 977

HAZZARD, SHIRLEY
Transit of Venus, The (81) 822

H. D.
End to Torment (80) 290
Gift, The (83) 278
HERmione (82) 349

1089

1093

AUTHOR INDEX

AUTHOR INDEX

AUTHOR INDEX

MOERS, ELLEN
  Literary Women (77) 439
MOHAMMAD REZA PAHLAVI
  Answer to History (81) 47
MOJTABAI, A. G.
  Autumn (83) 39
  Stopping Place, A (80) 785
MOLESWORTH, CHARLES
  Marianne Moore (91) 562
MOMADAY, N. SCOTT
  Man Made of Words, The (98) 534
  Names, The (78) 594
MONEGAL, EMIR RODRIGUEZ
  Jorge Luis Borges (80) 444
MONETTE, PAUL
  Becoming a Man (93) 62
  Borrowed Time (89) 112
MONK, RAY
  Bertrand Russell (97) 105
MONTAGUE, JOHN
  Dead Kingdom, The (85) 167
  Mount Eagle (90) 591
MONTALE, EUGENIO
  New Poems (77) 553
  Second Life of Art, The (83) 705
MONTGOMERY, DAVID
  Fall of the House of Labor, The (88) 308
MOODY, RICK
  Purple America (98) 643
MOONEY, MICHAEL MACDONALD
  Evelyn Nesbit and Stanford White (77) 260
MOORE, BRIAN
  Black Robe (86) 61
  Doctor's Wife, The (77) 226
  Lies of Silence (91) 527
  Magician's Wife, The (99) 506
  No Other Life (94) 563
  Statement, The (97) 782
MOORE, HAROLD G., and JOSEPH L. GALLOWAY
  We Were Soldiers Once . . . and Young (93) 868
MOORE, JAMES, and ADRIAN DESMOND
  Darwin (93) 196
MOORE, LORRIE
  Birds of America (99) 105
MOORE, MARIANNE
  Complete Poems of Marianne Moore, The (82) 126
  Complete Prose of Marianne Moore, The (87) 165
  Selected Letters of Marianne Moore, The (98) 702
MOORE, SUSANNA
  Whiteness of Bones, The (90) 884
MOOREHEAD, CAROLINE
  Bertrand Russell (94) 85
MORACE, ROBERT A.
  Dialogic Novels of Malcolm Bradbury and David
    Lodge, The (90) 173
MORAN, MARSHA, PATRICK MORAN, and
  NORAH K. BARR, eds.
  M. F. K. Fisher (99) 501
MORAVEC, HANS
  Robot (99) 670
MORAVIA, ALBERTO
  1934 (84) 613
  Time of Desecration (81) 809

MORELL, THEODOR GILBERT, and DAVID
  IRVING
  Secret Diaries of Hitler's Doctor, The
    (H-84) 398
MORGAN, JOHN S.
  Robert Fulton (78) 726
MORGAN, ROBERT
  Groundwork (80) 390
MORGAN, TED
  Churchill (H-83) 65
  FDR (86) 269
  Maugham (81) 559
MORGENTHAU, HENRY, III
  Mostly Morgenthaus (92) 529
MORLEY, JOHN F.
  Vatican Diplomacy and the Jews During the
    Holocaust, 1939-1943 (81) 861
MORRIS, CHARLES R.
  American Catholic (98) 36
MORRIS, EDMUND
  Dutch (00) 185
  Rise of Theodore Roosevelt, The (80) 717
MORRIS, HERBERT
  Little Voices of the Pears, The (90) 535
MORRIS, JAN
  Fifty Years of Europe (98) 308
MORRIS, MARY MCGARRY
  Dangerous Woman, A (92) 138
  Vanished (89) 877
MORRIS, RICHARD B.
  Witnesses at the Creation (86) 959
MORRIS, ROGER
  Richard Milhous Nixon (90) 694
  Uncertain Greatness (78) 869
MORRIS, WRIGHT
  Cloak of Light, A (86) 140
  Collected Stories (87) 160
  Earthly Delights, Unearthly Adornments
    (79) 175
  Fork River Space Project, The (78) 319
  Plains Song (81) 655
  Real Losses, Imaginary Gains (77) 652
  Solo (84) 803
  Time Pieces (90) 805
  Will's Boy (82) 950
MORRISON, TONI
  Beloved (88) 85
  Jazz (93) 403
  Paradise (99) 615
  Song of Solomon (78) 789
  Tar Baby (82) 828
MORRISON, WILBUR H.
  Fortress Without a Roof (H-83) 150
MORROW, LANCE
  Chief, The (86) 121
MORSON, GARY SAUL
  Narrative and Freedom (95) 523
MORSON, GARY SAUL, and CARYL EMERSON
  Mikhail Bakhtin (92) 500
MORTIMER, JOHN
  Clinging to the Wreckage (83) 127
  Paradise Postponed (87) 640
MOSCATI, SABATINO, editor
  Phoenicians, The (90) 665

1107

AUTHOR INDEX

PAVIĆ, MILORAD
Dictionary of the Khazars (89) 245
PAWEL, ERNST
Labyrinth of Exile, The (90) 495
Nightmare of Reason, The (85) 645
PAYNE, STANLEY G.
Fascism (81) 314
PAZ, OCTAVIO
Collected Poems of Octavio Paz, The (88) 169
Itinerary (01) 471
One Earth, Four or Five Worlds (86) 701
Selected Poems (85) 802
Sor Juana (89) 808
PEARS, IAIN
Instance of the Fingerpost, An (99) 418
PEARSALL, DEREK
Life of Geoffrey Chaucer, The (93) 459
PEARSON, JOHN
Sitwells, The (80) 763
PEARSON, T. R.
Off for the Sweet Hereafter (87) 611
PEERY, JANET
River Beyond the World, The (97) 701
PELEVIN, VICTOR
Buddha's Little Finger (01) 153
PELIKAN, JAROSLAV
Jesus Through the Centuries (86) 482
Vindication of Tradition, The (H-85) 467
PENROSE, ROGER
Emperor's New Mind, The (90) 207
Shadows of the Mind (95) 705
PERCY, WALKER
Lancelot (78) 501
Lost in the Cosmos (84) 482
Second Coming, The (81) 717
Signposts in a Strange Land (92) 747
Thanatos Syndrome, The (88) 883
PEREC, GEORGES
Void, A (96) 799
PERELMAN, S. J.
Last Laugh, The (82) 433
PERL, JEFFREY M.
Skepticism and Modern Enmity (91) 746
Tradition of Return, The (85) 917
PERRETT, GEOFFREY
America in the Twenties (H-83) 33
Dream of Greatness, A (80) 226
PERROT, MICHELLE, editor
History of Private Life, From the Fires of
Revolution to the Great War, A (91) 404
PERRY, BRUCE
Malcolm (92) 474
PERRY, RICHARD
Montgomery's Children (85) 629
No Other Tale to Tell (95) 559
PERSICO, JOSEPH E.
Imperial Rockefeller, The (H-83) 206
PERSICO, JOSEPH E., with COLIN L. POWELL
My American Journey (96) 494
PETER, JOHN
Vladimir's Carrot (88) 937
PETERS, CATHERINE
King of Inventors, The (94) 440
PETERS, JOAN
From Time Immemorial (H-85) 156

PETERS, MARGOT
May Sarton (98) 551
PETERS, WILLIAM
More Perfect Union, A (88) 589
PETERSON, MERRILL D.
Great Triumvirate, The (88) 363
Lincoln in American Memory (95) 435
PETESCH, NATALIE L. M.
Duncan's Colony (83) 210
PETITFILS, PIERRE
Rimbaud (88) 765
PETROSKI, HENRY
Pencil, The (91) 656
PFAFF, WILLIAM
Wrath of Nations, The (94) 864
PHELPS, TIMOTHY M., and HELEN WINTERNITZ
Capitol Games (93) 128
PHILBRICK, NATHANIEL
In the Heart of the Sea (01) 457
PHILLIPS, CARL
Pastoral (01) 699
PHILLIPS, JAYNE ANNE
Machine Dreams (85) 589
Shelter (95) 709
PHILLIPS, JOHN A.
Eve (H-85) 130
PHILLIPS, KEVIN
Cousins' Wars, The (00) 146
Politics of Rich and Poor, The (91) 674
PHILLIPS, WILLIAM
Parisan View, A (85) 677
PIAGET, JEAN
Grasp of Consciousness, The (77) 341
PICHOIS, CLAUDE
Baudelaire (91) 70
PICKOVER, CLIFFORD A.
Time (99) 760
PIERCY, MARGE
Available Light (89) 63
Braided Lives (83) 75
Circles on the Water (83) 119
Gone to Soldiers (88) 358
Longings of Women, The (95) 446
PIERPONT, CLAUDIA ROTH
Passionate Minds (01) 694
PINCHERLE, ALBERTO. See MORAVIA, ALBERTO
PINCKNEY, DARRYL
High Cotton (93) 335
PINKARD, TERRY
Hegel (01) 393
PINKER, STEVEN
How the Mind Works (98) 401
Language Instinct, The (95) 431
Words and Rules (00) 863
PINSKY, ROBERT
Explanation of America, An (81) 293
Figured Wheel, The (97) 278
History of My Heart (85) 399
Sounds of Poetry, The (99) 724
Want Bone, The (91) 866
PINSKY, ROBERT, translator
Inferno of Dante, The (96) 376
PINTER, HAROLD
Proust Screenplay, The (78) 673
PIPES, RICHARD
Property and Freedom (00) 626

AUTHOR INDEX

AUTHOR INDEX

ROTH, PHILIP
  American Pastoral (98) 45
  Anatomy Lesson, The (84) 26
  Counterlife, The (88) 204
  Deception (91) 188
  Facts, The (89) 288
  Ghost Writer, The (80) 354
  Human Stain, The (01) 427
  I Married a Communist (99) 406
  Operation Shylock (94) 581
  Patrimony (92) 615
  Professor of Desire, The (78) 669
  Sabbath's Theater (96) 672
  Zuckerman Unbound (82) 981

ROTHENBERG, GUNTHER E.
  Art of Warfare in the Age of Napoleon,
    The (79) 38

ROTHMAN, ELLEN K.
  Hands and Hearts (H-85) 195

ROUDINESCO, ELIZABETH
  Jacques Lacan (98) 463

ROVERE, RICHARD H.
  Arrivals and Departures (77) 62
  Final Reports (H-85) 141

ROWAN, CARL T.
  Dream Makers, Dream Breakers (94) 252

ROWSE, A. L.
  Eminent Elizabethans (H-84) 147

ROY, ARUNDHATI
  God of Small Things, The (98) 357

RUBENFELD, FLORENCE
  Clement Greenberg (99) 181

RUBIN, LOUIS D., JR., editor
  History of Southern Literature, The (86) 426

RUDDICK, SARA, and PAMELA DANIELS, editors
  Working It Out (78) 937

RUDMAN, MARK
  Millennium Hotel, The (97) 586

RUÍZ, RAMÓN EDUARDO
  Great Rebellion, The (81) 396

RUKEYSER, MURIEL
  Collected Poems, The (80) 148

RUNYON, RANDOLPH PAUL
  Reading Raymond Carver (93) 669

RUSH, NORMAN
  Mating (92) 490

RUSHDIE, SALMAN
  Ground Beneath Her Feet, The (00) 341
  Haroun and the Sea of Stories (91) 376
  Imaginary Homelands (92) 324
  Moor's Last Sigh, The (96) 478
  Satanic Verses, The (90) 711
  Shame (84) 788

RUSK, DEAN
  As I Saw It (91) 56

RUSKIN, JOHN, and THOMAS CARLYLE
  Correspondence of Thomas Carlyle and John
    Ruskin, The (83) 153

RUSS, JOANNA
  How to Suppress Women's Writing (84) 353

RUSSELL, JEFFREY BURTON
  History of Heaven, A (98) 387
  Lucifer (H-85) 272
  Mephistopheles (87) 553

RUSSO, JOHN PAUL
  I. A. Richards (90) 401
  Straight Man (98) 745

RYAN, ALAN
  John Dewey and the High Tide of American
    Liberalism (96) 393

RYAN, PAUL B., and THOMAS A. BAILEY
  Hitler vs. Roosevelt (80) 404

RYBCZYNSKI, WITOLD
  Clearing in the Distance, A (00) 126
  Home (87) 402
  Most Beautiful House in the World, The (90) 582
  One Good Turn (01) 679

RYMER, RUSS
  Genie (94) 345

SÁBATO, ERNESTO
  On Heroes and Tombs (82) 585

SACHAR, HOWARD M.
  Diaspora (86) 226
  History of the Jews in America, A (93) 340

SACKS, OLIVER
  Anthropologist on Mars, An (96) 47
  Island of the Colorblind and Cycad Island,
    The (98) 454
  Man Who Mistook His Wife for a Hat,
    The (87) 516
  Seeing Voices (90) 720

SAFIRE, WILLIAM
  Scandalmonger (01) 759

SAFRANSKI, RÜDIGER
  Martin Heidegger (99) 529
  Schopenhauer and the Wild Years of
    Philosophy (91) 711

SAGAN, CARL
  Broca's Brain (80) 116

SAGAN, FRANÇOISE
  Silken Eyes (78) 776
  Unmade Bed, The (79) 791

SAHLINS, MARSHALL
  How "Natives" Think (96) 338

SAHLINS, MARSHALL, and PATRICK V. KIRCH
  Anahulu (93) 20

SAID, EDWARD W.
  Culture and Imperialism (94) 181
  Out of Place (00) 597
  World, the Text, and the Critic, The (84) 971

ST. AUBYN, GILES
  Edward VII (80) 264

ST. JOHN, DAVID
  Study for the World's Body (95) 777

SAKHAROV, ANDREI
  Memoirs (91) 582

SALISBURY, HARRISON E.
  Journey for Our Times, A (H-84) 252
  Long March, The (86) 537
  New Emperors, The (93) 554
  Russia in Revolution, 1900-1930 (79) 622

SALTER, JAMES
  Burning the Days (98) 138
  Dusk and Other Stories (89) 254

SALTER, MARY JO
  Henry Purcell in Japan (86) 411

SALWAK, DALE, editor
  Life and Work of Barbara Pym, The (88) 471

SALYER, LUCY E.
  Laws Harsh as Tigers (96) 418

SAMPSON, ANTHONY
  Mandela (00) 506

1117

AUTHOR INDEX

AUTHOR INDEX

AUTHOR INDEX

AUTHOR INDEX